We Fought at GETTYSBURG

We Fought at GETTYSBURG

Firsthand Accounts by the Survivors of the

17TH CONNECTICUT VOLUNTEER INFANTRY

Carolyn Ivanoff

GETTYSBURG
PUBLISHING

Published by Gettysburg Publishing, LLC
www.gettysburgpublishing.com

Library of Congress Cataloging-in-Publication Data

Names: Ivanoff, Carolyn, author. | Noble, Wiliam H. (William Henry), 1813-1894. History of the Seventeenth C.V. regiment.
Title: We fought at Gettysburg : firsthand accounts by the survivors of the 17th Connecticut Volunteer Infantry / Carolyn Ivanoff.
Description: First edition. | [Trumbull, Connecticut] : Gettysburg Publishing, [2023] | Includes bibliographical references and index.
Identifiers: LCCN 2023002240 | ISBN 9780999304945 (Hardbackback) | ISBN 9781734627664 (eBook)
Subjects: LCSH: United States. Army. Connecticut Infantry Regiment, 17th (1862-1865) | Gettysburg, Battle of, Gettysburg, Pa., 1863. | United States--History--Civil War, 1861-1865--Regimental histories.
Classification: LCC E475.53 .I93 2023 | DDC 973.7/3490922746--dc23/eng/20230120
LC record available at https://lccn.loc.gov/2023002240

Printed and bound in the United States of America

First Edition

To the men of the 17th Connecticut
who gave their lives at Gettysburg.

"We show the effects of war although we are but young soldiers. Many have laid their bodies down to bleach upon the soil of this state . . . We go forth with our life in one hand and the weapons of war in the other. We know not when we may have to surrender our life. If sooner or later I hope I may be prepared at all times."

–Captain Wilson French, Co. G, 17th Connecticut

Letter to his wife written from Virginia
on the march to Gettysburg, June 1863

Roll Call of the Honored DEAD

Lt. Col. Douglas Fowler
Sergt. Samuel Comstock
Priv. Elephalet Mead
Priv. William S. Gregory
Corpl. Henry Burns
Priv. Michael Fox
Priv. William W. Westlake
Priv. Calvin Nobles
Capt. James E. Moore
Sergt. William O. Dauchy
Sergt. August E. Bronson
Sergt. Bethel S. Barnum
Priv. Frank J. Benson
Priv. Theodore Blackman
Priv. Smith Delevan
Priv. Daniel H. Purdy
Priv. Richard B. Taylor
Priv. Rufus Warren
Priv. Joseph S. Whitlock
Corpl. Alvah E. Wilcox
Priv. William F. Bradley
Priv. John R. Booth
Priv. Stephen C. Crofut
Priv. Wilbur B. Morgan
Priv. John W. Metcalf
Sergt. Edwin D. Pickett
Priv. John A. Black
Priv. Lawrence Carney
Priv. Crassius M. Crabbe
Corpl. James Gordon
Priv. Francis C. Foote
Priv. James Flynn
Priv. George H. Gurnsey
Priv. Francis Nash
Priv John Welsh

Missing from the Monument

Priv. Sylvester Britto
Priv. James W. Cable
Priv. John Cavanagh
Priv. James Lavery

Contents

Preface

This volume follows the 17th Connecticut Infantry Regiment during the Gettysburg Campaign and beyond in June and July 1863. In writing this volume I have relied on an extensive bibliography, but more importantly, I have relied on the words of the soldiers themselves. I have worked with Private William Warren's remarkable, unpublished, multivolume manuscript on and off over the years. This manuscript and its precious firsthand accounts form the core of this book. Private Warren, a member of the regiment's Company C, compiled a voluminous record of the unit's experiences in hopes of writing a regimental history. He drew from his own diary and the diaries his comrades lent him. He also relied on correspondence with veterans who wrote to him about their service in the regiment. The challenge for this volume was in building a sequential narrative frame around these first-hand accounts collected by Warren from the regiment's survivors. The narratives depict a range of personal experiences from the survivors, the wounded, the prisoners—men who witnessed the deaths of their comrades, who nursed their wounded friends in hospitals, and who soldiered on after the battle.

Warren's history of the 17th Connecticut never came to fruition. He devoted himself to compiling and collecting accounts of the regiment's service and experiences until his death in 1918, but he could never bring himself to complete the history or effectively edit it. The tragedy of the material is that it was never completed or published as a regimental history. Warren compiled these memories into a thirteen-volume manuscript that is housed in the Bridgeport History Center. Through these accounts we come as close as possible to seeing what the soldiers themselves saw, thought, and felt on the battlefield. These priceless accounts preserve a precious legacy from those soldiers to us. The memories of old soldiers are often criticized as the memories of old men, distorted by time and other factors, but these are the words of those who survived the trauma of battle and lived. This is as close as we in the twenty-first century can come to seeing the battle through their eyes, to understand what they experienced. Above all this is their story, their legacy, in the words they left behind. I wish to honor them and their sacrifices with this volume and share their experiences and insights. All honor belongs to these men who fought for their lives, who lost friends, and who suffered on this great battlefield.

Warren's manuscript is massive, rambling, and challenging. Warren's lifework was left unfinished, but history remains alive in its sprawling volumes. The volumes are compelling and fascinating, but are easy to lose one's way in. A defined scope and sequence are nonexistent in most of the volumes. Even the volumes Warren marks for specific time periods (e.g., Chancellorsville, Gettysburg) digress. Portions of the same volume jump randomly to other times and places.

In editing and annotating accounts for this book I had to confine myself to the most relevant material in the manuscript on the Gettysburg Campaign. In doing so I selectively combed Volume III, which Warren labeled as 250 pages of history and introduced with a preface dedicated to the battle. I also used parts of Warren's handwritten volume titled "Gleanings" for additional Gettysburg content, along with the handwritten and annotated index that accompanied approximately two hundred photographs Warren reproduced and bound into another volume. Warren's annotated photographic index of the members of the regiment appears as an appendix to this volume, published for the first time. Information from other Warren volumes was included where relevant, along with loose papers and notes from four manuscript boxes in the Bridgeport History Center. To present this material in a unified manner it was necessary to discriminately ignore parts of the manuscript and Warren's writings lest I disappear down the proverbial rabbit hole and not surface with any form of a cohesive book on Gettysburg. It was necessary to selectively pare the material and organize it into a manageable narrative and an understandable sequence.

My goal in writing this book was to distill, define, and illuminate for the reader the experiences of the 17th Connecticut in the Battle of Gettysburg and beyond. It is my fervent hope that this volume presents these men and their words in a respectful, readable, and compelling manner that honors their service, sacrifice, and memory.

Carolyn Ivanoff
Seymour, Connecticut

CHAPTER 1

The Fairfield County Regiment

Connecticut is a small state with a long history of support for the nation. During the American Revolution Connecticut was known as the Provision State for its loyal support and provisioning for the Continental Army. By the eve of the Civil War, however, economic considerations had strained those loyalties. Little Connecticut had become a manufacturing powerhouse, one with many ties to lucrative Southern markets, and the state's businesses were loath to cut those ties. Even after South Carolina seceded from the Union on December 20, 1860, the Hazard Powder Company of Hazardville continued to sell powder to Southern agents until as late as April 7, 1861. The following week, on April 12, Confederate artillery used a good amount of high-quality Connecticut powder to batter the walls of Fort Sumter.[1]

The state's conflicting economic motivations were reflected in a tumultuous political climate, one in which Connecticut exhibited a marked sympathy for pro-Southern Democratic candidates. This tendency was of special concern to loyal unionists ahead of the 1860 elections.[2] At the time Connecticut's governor was elected annually, with state elections held the first Monday of April, and the spring gubernatorial election was often a bellwether for other elections around the nation, similar to the modern Iowa caucus and New Hampshire primary. This was especially true in 1860, when Connecticut's gubernatorial race was closely watched as a possible predictor of the November presidential election.[3] Despite the state's deep political divisions, Republican William Buckingham was able to win reelection. Buckingham, who was first elected to the office in 1858, would serve as governor throughout the Civil War, winning election each year by narrow margins. He would remain loyal to President Abraham Lincoln and the Union.

Despite Buckingham's victory, deep divisions were evident throughout the state during the early months of the war. Connecticut's "Peace Democrats" opposed the war and supported a peaceful resolution to the conflict, and to this end peace rallies were held throughout the state in the spring and summer of 1861. One such rally was organized by William S. Pomeroy and Nathaniel Morse, the editors of Bridgeport's anti-Lincoln, pro-Democratic newspaper *The Weekly Farmer*, who wrote several editorials critical of the president and took a pro-Southern stance after the Union defeat at the First Battle of Bull Run in July 1861. On August 24, 1861, Pomeroy and Morse convened more than one thousand armed "peace men" in Stepney, Fairfield County, with the crowd gathering to raise a flag bearing the word "Peace" in large letters and declare their opposition to the war. Families came from surrounding towns to see the flag raised and to implore the government to "stop the unrighteous war." The crowd gathered around the flag to cheers and swore to defend it against all comers. The speakers' platform was packed with well-connected antiwar orators.[4]

Governor William Alfred Buckingham, c. 1865.
(Author's Collection)

The Stepney rally corresponded with the mustering out of Connecticut men who had served at First Bull Run and had fulfilled their initial ninety-day enlistments. These soldiers were in no mood to tolerate what they considered traitors in their midst. From the speakers' platform, the preacher Charles Smith was asking for the blessings of God upon the peace movement when he saw Bridgeport omnibuses coming over the hill. These large, horse-drawn passenger wagons, the equivalent of public transportation in the 1800s, were decked out in all manner of pro-Union banners and loaded with armed former soldiers, vocal pro-Union men, and several Bridgeport celebrities including P. T. Barnum and Elias Howe Jr. The horse-drawn buses plowed over the hill and into the crowd, heading straight for the pole flying the peace flag. This created a panic on the speakers' platform, sending the orators running to take refuge in a cornfield.[5]

Some of the "peace men" rallied and drew their weapons as the flag was cut to the ground. A musket and revolver were taken from them by soldiers; another man fired a revolver and was chased into the fields. The soldiers disarmed several men with loaded muskets and seized other weapons from a nearby shed. As the Stars and Stripes was run up the pole to wild cheers, Barnum was carried on the shoulders of the soldiers to the speakers' platform, where he made a rousing patriotic speech in support of the Union. The "Star-Spangled Banner" was sung and a series of resolutions in support of the Union and the war effort were passed. When Howe followed with a speech, the peace crowd threatened to shoot the Unionist speakers. Howe shouted, "If they fire a gun, boys, burn the whole town and I'll pay for it." The soldiers then threatened to return to Bridgeport and raid the offices of the *Weekly Farmer*, which had published what they considered traitorous articles and editorials in the wake of Bull Run; their leaders appealed to them against such action and the crowd relented. As the patriotic crowd returned to Bridgeport they were met with approval and much cheering.[6]

Upon their return to Bridgeport, the Union men remained agitated. A crowd of belligerent Unionists gathered downtown at a meeting that featured speeches, patriotic songs, and bonfires. A riot ensued at the corner of Wall and Water Streets where the offices of the *Weekly Farmer* stood. Rioters attacked the newspaper offices and ransacked the building, threw papers and desks from the windows, and smashed the presses. Nathaniel Morse made a narrow escape, reportedly running along the roof of an adjoining building to escape the rioters. The paper would not operate again for several years. The second-oldest photograph of Bridgeport, a glass ambrotype, portrays the corner of Water and Wall Streets shortly after the riot. It captures a view of the street littered with papers and includes some of the rioters.[7]

Despite the deep divisions within the state exemplified by the Bridgeport riot, Connecticut under Buckingham's administration would become an arsenal for the Union. Manufacturers such as Hazard, Hotchkiss, Colt, Whitney, Winchester, Sharps, Henry, Collins, Savage, Spencer, and many more would produce arms for the Union cause.[8] The Nutmeg State also supplied manpower: from an 1860 population of 460,188,

An 1861 glass ambrotype portrays the corner of Wall and Water Streets in Bridgeport and the offices of the *Weekly Farmer* newspaper in the aftermath of the pro-Union riot that destroyed the paper's presses. (Bridgeport History Center)

Connecticut would provide 39,395 troops to the Union effort, filling twenty-nine infantry regiments, two heavy artillery regiments, three light batteries, and one cavalry regiment.[9] In the summer of 1862, in answer to Lincoln's call for 300,000 men, Buckingham issued a ringing appeal: "Close your manufactories and workshops, turn aside from your farms and your business, leave for a while your families and your homes, meet face to face the enemies of your liberties! Haste, and you will rescue many noble men now struggling against superior numbers, and speedily secure the blessings of peace and good government."[10] Recruiting drives were held across that state that summer in order to fulfill the state's quota of 7,145 men, or six regiments, as imposed by the Federal government.[11] A $50 bounty was approved by the state for each volunteer; individual towns awarded bounties as well, ranging from $50 to $200 per man.[12]

The 17th Connecticut Infantry Regiment would be formed that summer. The 17th was unofficially referred to as the Fairfield County Regiment because all its companies were recruited from within that county, which comprises the southwestern corner of the state bordering New York, with a panhandle jutting into that neighboring state; this makeup was unlike the other Connecticut regiments, which were recruited from throughout the state. The unit's organization reflected a typical Union regiment of one thousand men, led by a colonel. Each regiment carried a state numerical designation (the 17th Connecticut Regiment was also referred to as the 17th Connecticut Volunteer Infantry or 17th CVI) and was divided into ten companies of one hundred men, with each company led by a captain. Each company was designated by a letter, *A* through *K*; the letter *J* was skipped as it was difficult to distinguish between lowercase letters *i* and *j*. The 17th Connecticut was a three-year regiment, with enlisted men taking an oath to serve for such a term. After the First Battle of Bull Run and Lincoln's calls for more volunteers from the loyal states to put down the rebellion, Connecticut recruited several nine-month regiments, but like the 17th, the bulk of the regiments of 1862, the best Connecticut would offer the Union, were three-year units.

The captains of the 17th helped recruit the men of their companies. Several of these captains had served in the three-month regiments that the state recruited after Fort Sumter in anticipation of a short summer war. The situation was the same elsewhere in the state, and army recruiters were busy. Like those of the 17th, many of these recruiters sought to raise companies in which they would become officers. These future officers attended patriotic rallies, held meetings, and in some cases paid home visits to men eligible for military service to induce them to enlist. With the threat of a draft hanging over towns that failed to supply their quota of manpower, and the state and federal bounties for enlistment being offered, many men became amenable to joining regiments of their choice. The age of enlistment without requiring parental permission was eighteen, and thousands of young men joined with friends and relatives to enlist.

Among the recruits was William H. Warren, a twenty-year-old Danbury railroad hand. He never forgot the recruiter who came to his home to try obtaining his enlistment in the summer of 1862. Warren would record the incident in his memoirs, alongside a photograph of Captain Samuel Bailey, the unsuccessful recruiting officer: "Samuel G. Bailey, Captain of Company K, 23rd Connecticut Regiment, who came to my home,

William H. Warren as he appeared before his enlistment in August 1862. (Courtesy of the William H. Warren Family)

Captain Samuel G. Bailey, Company K, 23rd Connecticut. (Bridgeport History Center)

William H. Warren immediately after his enlistment, photographed holding a kepi. (Courtesy of the William H. Warren Family)

while recruiting the above company, with a squad of men, calling me out into the front yard, and gathering around me, tried their best to influence me to enlist. My mother mistrusting what was going on, also came out, and in strong language informed them that I could not go, so that settled it, and they went away. A few days later I enlisted in another company."[13]

In 1862, the hand that rocked the cradle was a powerful influence that even an army recruiter would not challenge. Warren's mother had the last word that day, but her only son would soon join the boys in blue and be off to war. That August, William Warren enlisted as a private in Company C, composed of Danbury men, in the Fairfield County Regiment.

William H. Noble, prominent Bridgeport businessman and occasional P. T. Barnum partner, was commissioned the regiment's colonel; Charles Walter was named lieutenant colonel. Recruiting was active throughout July in Fairfield County and the regiment was full by the middle of August with over one thousand men.[14] The regiment was stationed at Bridgeport's Camp Aiken, in what is now Seaside Park, during the muster-in period before it departed for the front. Many prominent businessmen funded the regiment: Company F, the Lockwood Guards, was raised in three days through an offer of $1,000 by LeGrand Lockwood.[15] Elias Howe Jr., the sewing machine magnate who was the wealthiest man in Connecticut—with an annual income of $250,000—enlisted as a private in Company D. In 1862 the monthly salary for a Union private soldier was $13 a month, so Howe wasn't enlisting for the money, although many men did sign up for that reason; bounties could be substantial for an ordinary working man and were crucial in supporting families left behind. Company D was nicknamed the Howe Rifles in appreciation for Howe's support. When the regiment left for the front on September 3, Howe was among its ranks, "his long hair cut tight to his head and a musket on his shoulder."[16] Howe would serve as the regiment's postmaster, though his poor health meant he was often absent from the regiment and he had a tent to himself when he was present.[17]

Although Howe's health was precarious and he was in his forties, he was a patriot who wanted to support the Union cause with more than just his money Despite his ill health and frequent absences from the regiment, Howe remained ever supportive of the men of the 17th. During the autumn of 1862 Howe ensured that the regiment would receive its mail by personally making trips between the camp and Baltimore. During December 1862, "The regiment suffered considerable discomfort in snow-clad 'shelters' and in long marches through Virginia mud." Not having been paid, the men needed money. Private Elias Howe took it upon himself to personally advance the $13,000 due them,[18] and then he stood in line with the regiment to receive his private's pay of $28.00 of his own money. Howe died shortly after the war in 1867 in Brooklyn, New York, at the age of forty-eight. The men of the 17th Connecticut never forgot Howe's generosity or patriotism: When the men returned home after the war and formed the Grand Army of the Republic (GAR) Union veterans' organization, the men from Bridgeport named their post in honor of Private Elias Howe Jr.

Elias Howe Jr., the inventor of the sewing machine, was the wealthiest man in Connecticut when he enlisted as a private in Company D. (Author's Collection)

On September 3, 1862, the 17th Connecticut departed Bridgeport for the front. Thousands of well-wishers from all over the state came to cheer their departure. Governor Buckingham reviewed the regiment; during a cannon salute at South Norwalk a premature discharge of the cannon shattered the arm of one Joseph Hawkins, who later died from the effects of the amputation.[19] After a stop in New York, the regiment proceeded by rail to Baltimore where it arrived late in the evening, tired and hungry. Finding no transportation available to Washington, the men spent the night in the open street.[20]

Carte de visite of Col. William H. Noble. (Author's Collection)

The defenses of Baltimore were under the command of Major General John E. Wool. When the 17th arrived in the city, Baltimore was under threat from Confederate cavalry. General Wool detained the regiment at Fort Marshall, an earthwork fort with barracks, overlooking the city's harbor. Colonel Noble sought a transfer from the War Department so the 17th could continue to its original assignment in the Eleventh Corps under Major General Franz Sigel. General Wool was so incensed by Noble's request to leave that the general ordered the 17th to be outside the city limits before noon the next day or "face the consequences." The next night the regiment arrived at Washington, DC, and two weeks later was ordered to report to General Sigel in Virginia. On November 5, the 17th Connecticut was placed in the First Division, Second Brigade, of the Eleventh Corps.[21]

The 17th Connecticut was one of the five regiments of the Second Brigade. Four Ohio Regiments—the 25th, 55th, 75th, and 107th—composed the rest, and these regiments, except for the 55th Ohio, would serve together in the Second Brigade for the rest of the war in Virginia, South Carolina, and Florida.[22] On December 6 the regiment began a difficult seven-day march though slush and snow toward Fredericksburg, Virginia.[23] The 17th was held in reserve during the disastrous slaughter at the Battle of Fredericksburg on December 13. After the battle, the regiment established its winter camp at Brooke Station, Virginia. The men erected winter huts of logs and mud and endured the boredom and privations of military life, spending the months performing drill, parade, and picket duty.[24]

At the end of April 1863, as the terrible weather receded into spring and the deep Virginia mud dried, the roads became passable and the campaign season began. After two years of war in the Eastern Theater with little to show for it, the Army of the Potomac began its latest campaign with high hopes.[25]

CHAPTER 2

Disaster at Chancellorsville

The war was entering its third year in the spring of 1863. It was not going well for the Army of the Potomac. After the Fredericksburg defeat and the ensuing "Mud March" debacle, President Lincoln replaced Ambrose Burnside with Joseph Hooker as the army's commander. Hooker was known as "Fighting Joe" after a newspaper's punctuation error left the dash out of the phrase "Fighting—Joe Hooker," and the nickname stuck. Hooker disliked the sobriquet because he felt it made him sound rash.[1] The nickname aside, Hooker's appointment was popular with his men, who were confident in his leadership.

Upon his appointment, Hooker worked to reorganize, reequip, and to ensure that his men were supplied over the winter months with good food. He also made it his mission to raise morale. Hooker assigned each army corps a unique badge designed to increase morale and esprit de corps. The badges were immediately accepted by the troops, who received a symbol made of felt to be attached to their caps. Each army corps had its own symbol: a circle for the First Corps, trefoil for the Second, crescent moon for the Eleventh, and so forth. Within each corps, the symbols were red for the First Division, white for the Second Division, and blue for the Third Division. The badges created a quick way for a commander to identify his men, and the men were proud to wear them.

The 17th Connecticut wore the red crescent moon as part of the Second Brigade in the First Division of the Eleventh Corps. The Eleventh Corps included many German-speaking regiments and immigrants referred to collectively as the "Dutch." In the spring of 1863, the "newly reorganized" Eleventh Corps was a diverse and disparate melding of the 1861 Germanic units, early-war Ohio units, summer of 1862 Yankee regiments, and summer of 1862 Germanic regiments. One regiment, the 82nd Illinois, was multiethnic German, Swiss, Scandinavian, Irish, and Jewish from Chicago and St. Clair County.[2]

Maj. Gen. Joseph Hooker. (Library of Congress)

Oliver Otis Howard, commander of the Eleventh Corps. (Library of Congress)

The 107th Ohio, brigaded with the 17th Connecticut, was considered an ethnic German regiment. The 17th Connecticut was considered a Yankee regiment but had its share of immigrants. These Connecticut men were thoroughly integrated into their communities and committed to the Union cause. Among them was the regiment's lieutenant colonel, Charles Walter, a thirty-one-year-old stonecutter born in Denmark.[3] He had fought at Bull Run with the 1st Connecticut, been captured there, and spent a year in rebel prisons.[4] German-born brothers William and Charles Wurtz, along with their cousin Frederick Lindheim, had enlisted in the 17th Connecticut with four other men from the Bridgeport saddlery shop where they worked.[5] The well-liked and highly regarded Lieutenant Henry Quien, from Danbury, was born in Germany, the third of six brothers. Quien had fought at Bull Run as a private under Captain James Moore in the 3rd Connecticut, and both were now part of the 17th. Quien was commissioned a lieutenant in Captain Moore's Company C.[6]

Major General Oliver Otis Howard had taken command of the Eleventh Corps on April 2, 1863, replacing Sigel. Howard was a Maine man who earned a degree from Bowdoin University at age nineteen and graduated from West Point in 1854, later teaching mathematics there. Before the war Howard served with the frontier army. He was personally brave and had lost an arm at the Battle of Fair Oaks in 1862, but his leadership was considered uninspiring. He was known as "The Christian General," "Old Prayer Book," or, more insultingly, as a "Christ Kisser." His religious fervor was grating to his soldiers even in a nineteenth-century America that was deeply devout. He was a committed abolitionist. After the war he would head the Freedmen's Bureau and Howard University would be named for him. He was also a teetotaler who frowned on the beer drinking of his German soldiers. He was stiff and ill at ease among the Eleventh Corps, and his men did not warm to him.[7] Major General Carl Schurz, commanding the Third Division of the Eleventh Corps, would remember, "They looked at him with dubious curiosity. Not a cheer would be started when he rode along the front."[8]

A pencil drawing by Edwin Forbes, May 1, 1863, of the sleepy little crossroads of Chancellorsville. The Chancellor House would be burned during the battle. (Library of Congress)

The Chancellorsville Campaign began on April 27, 1863. The army was in fine spirits and fine form as it began its march. Hooker's plan was to leave a portion of his army in place as a decoy and march the bulk of his force of 130,000 men around and behind the unsuspecting Confederates still in winter camp across the Rappahannock River. Hooker planned to trap the outnumbered Confederates against the river or force them to retreat toward Richmond, giving Confederate commander Robert E. Lee no choice but to engage in battle.[9] Hooker's plan was a solid one and he was enamored of it. "My plans are perfect," he declared, "and when I carry them out, may God have mercy on General Lee, for I will have none." The plan began successfully with the Union troops covering some forty miles in three days. Hooker then divided his army into three columns. On April 30, Hooker took over a former country inn known as the Chancellor House as his headquarters. It was part of Chancellorsville, a small country crossroads on the edge of a forested tract in northern Virginia known as the Wilderness.[10]

Selah Blakeman, Company D, 17th Connecticut. (Stratford Historical Society)

The weather was extremely warm and the road to Chancellorsville was strewn with surplus belongings discarded by the marching army. The Eleventh Corps crossed the Rappahannock River at Kelly's Ford by pontoons and the Rapidan River at Germanna Ford by temporary bridge and by wading the river.[11] A week after the battle Private Selah Blakeman, a member of Company D of the 17th Connecticut, would write home to his brother in Stratford: "It was one week ago today the other side of the Rappahanock and I don't think that I shall ever forget the day if I should live to be an old man . . . We crost the Rappahanock Tuesday night at 1 oclock, Wed night we crost the Rapidan about 2, it was very dark and rainy. It is a bad river to cross it runs very quick and it is steep and rocky on each side. Thurs night we got to our place where we were to wait for the Rebs."[12]

As the Army of the Potomac formed its battle lines, the Eleventh Corps was placed on the extreme right. The 17th Connecticut was in place near a small farmhouse that was rented by a tenant, John Hatch, a native of Farmington, Connecticut.[13] Referred to as the Hatch Farm in Connecticut accounts, this small farm is better known as the Talley Farm.[14] On May 2 the 17th Connecticut found its right wing deployed in the farm's garden.[15] The farm was the headquarters of First Division commander Charles Devens, who did not imbue his division with confidence. He detested many of his subordinates and the men of German descent; Devens's disrespect and dismissal of the worth of his men probably contributed to his disregard of their reports of enemy troop movements around the Union line on the battle's second day. Devens may have also been further impaired by more than bigotry: His horse had run his leg into a tree early on May 1 and Devens may have been coping with pain through the bottle. Some sources claim he was inebriated at the time of Stonewall Jackson's assault on May 2.[16]

The battle opened on May 1. To that point Hooker's plan had unfolded very well. His 130,000-man army was in position to successfully challenge Lee's greatly outnumbered Army of Northern Virginia, which mustered approximately 60,000 troops.[17] Despite the knowledge he was woefully outnumbered, Lee aggressively and unconventionally divided his forces in the face of a superior enemy. Lee left about 10,000 men with General Jubal Early to serve as a decoy along the Rappahannock. He then turned away from the river with 50,000 men to attack Hooker's main body. Lee planned to use surprise and the treacherous Wilderness to entangle Hooker's army and diminish its numerical advantage.[18]

Fighting was raging in the undergrowth when Hooker issued orders for Union troops to be withdrawn toward Chancellorsville. This sudden and inexplicable order flabbergasted his generals. Darius Couch, commander of the Second Corps, would write after the war, "The position thus abandoned was high ground, more or less open in front, over which an army might move and artillery be used advantageously . . . left in the hands of the enemy, his batteries, established on its crests and slopes, would command the position at Chancellorsville."[19] With Hooker's order for withdrawal, this is exactly what happened, setting the stage for the Union army's greatest defeat and Lee's greatest victory. Back at the Chancellor House, Hooker told Couch, "It is all right, I have got Lee just where I want him; he must fight me on my own ground." Couch would write, "The advantages gained by the successful marches of his lieutenants were to culminate in fighting a defensive battle in that nest of thickets . . . I retired from his presence with the belief that my commanding general was a whipped man."[20]

On the night of May 1, Lee and Stonewall Jackson, seated on hardtack boxes abandoned by the Union withdrawal earlier in the day, would meet to formulate their strategy. Having discovered that Hooker's right flank was "in the air" and vulnerable,

Jackson proposed that he march his entire corps, some 26,000 men, twelve miles around the Union army along narrow dirt roads and dense forest and attack the Union right flank. Lee, left with only 14,000 men, would have to hold Hooker's much larger army in place from the front. Both generals understood the huge risks, and both knew the huge rewards if the plan was successful.[21]

At about 7 a.m. Jackson got his columns moving. As they passed Lee's headquarters, Jackson and Lee spoke briefly in a last meeting as Jackson left to accompany his men. Jackson hoped the circuitous route would hide his march from the Federals. His orders were "Permit no straggling. See that the column is kept closed. Press on, press on!" When Hooker received news that the Confederates were on the march he correctly, at first, concluded that Lee would try to flank him. However, he did nothing to address the issue, nor did he order any harassment of Jackson's column. Federal artillery did fire on the column, but the continued reports that the Confederates were heading west convinced Hooker that they were retreating.[22]

All throughout the day of May 2 Generals Hooker, Howard, and Devens insisted that the enemy was in retreat. These general officers paid no heed to what their men on the front lines were telling them. Colonel Noble, his 17th Connecticut stationed on the line's extreme right, remembered, "The warnings came in all throughout the day. Horseman after horseman rode into my post and was sent to headquarters with the information that the enemy was heavily marching along our front and proceeding to our right; and last of all an officer reported the rebels massing for attack." Howard discounted these reports as either the imagination, or the fears, of the reporters.[23]

Late in the afternoon of May 2, Companies G and I of the 17th Connecticut were on picket duty on the line's flank. Many of the men in the Eleventh Corps, including the rest of the 17th Connecticut, gathered around their campfires relaxing and cooking their suppers, napping, or writing home. Many of the men had stacked their arms. With Hooker announcing the Confederates were retreating and Howard discarding any reports of an attack, few if any regiments in the Eleventh Corps were in position to repel the Confederate onslaught.[24] Among the first indications that the Confederates were forming and advancing in an unseen battle line straddling the Orange Turnpike were the animals—first the chipmunks, squirrels, and foxes, and then the larger deer—being flushed out of the woods and running through the Federal camps. Shortly after 5 p.m., Jackson ordered the assault forward.[25] The Confederates startled the Union pickets, the attackers screaming their bloodcurdling rebel yell as they crashed through the dense underbrush; the assault smashed into the Federal camps, catching the Eleventh Corps off guard. A handful of Union troops tried to form ranks and get off a few rounds. Some fled without firing a shot. The attack soon became a general retreat and ultimately a complete rout of the entire Eleventh Corps.[26] The chaos of close combat, combined with the thick, acrid smoke, gunfire, screaming attackers, and maimed and wounded men, produced pandemonium.

Although the two companies of 17th Connecticut pickets had been quickly overwhelmed, most of the men returned to their regiment. Colonel Noble organized the regiment facing west and the men of the 17th Connecticut were able to fire several

Artist Alfred Waud's sketch of the Eleventh Corps fleeing the Confederate onslaught.
(Library of Congress)

volleys into the Confederate horde rushing toward them before they fled toward Chancellorsville. The regiment did not stop until reaching the rifle pits near Devens's headquarters, gasping for breath. The 17th Connecticut's brief stand was costly: Colonel Noble was badly wounded, Lieutenant Colonel Walter was killed, and the unit sustained more than one hundred casualties. The regiment's short-lived stand, however, gave Adolphus Buschbeck's brigade on the left crucial time to change front and check the Confederate juggernaut while Howard and Hooker patched together a temporary defensive line.[27]

Wilson French, Company G, in his lieutenant's uniform.
(Bridgeport History Center)

Companies G and I of the 17th Connecticut were among the first Union troops to be hit by the Confederate assault. First Lieutenant Wilson French was commanding Company G when the attack struck; he would be promoted to captain following the battle. French wrote his wife, Martha, an account of the battle on May 8. The letter is missing both the first and last pages, but French's vivid description of his first combat has survived.

> *at ten minutes to six my picket posted right, and was thinking about getting something to eat, the indication I had of their coming was two splendid deer came running through our lines. I ordered my men to fire, then they poured a volley of musketry and shell into us. I got up on a log about 3 feet high to see them and my men for we was in thick woods. It was Jackson's force 40 thousand* [sic] *strong that attacked us. I made my men fire and fall back to another tree, then load and fire until the rebels got so close to us. We could hear them sing out to us, "halt you damn sons of B—" then I ordered my men out I believe everyone got out of the woods safe, then I ran for dear life. . . . I have heard of Iron rain and leaden hail but I never saw it before, the shots dropped all around and shells burst over my head. I could dodge the shell, but the shot I could not see only as they struck by me. I could hear them buzz around my head. God only knows how I came out of it without being hit. . . . We poured volley after volley into them until we was ordered to leave. The right wing of the 17th Regt was the last to leave the ground they done good credit to the state. When I got back to our regiment, I found them at their post laying flat on their bellies loading and firing. I took my place with them . . . Col. Walters was shot close by me. I fear he is dead. Lt. Hubbell of Co E. was struck with a piece of spent shell at my side. ____ was shot in the head at my left. Abner Bennett of my company had a ball pass through his coat. Williams of my company shot in the foot. The right wing of the 17th Regt was the last to leave the ground. We retreated expecting to fall back of the 12th Corps and form a line of battle but when we got there they was running. I stopped with the colors and Maj. Brady and Capt. McCarty, and Lacy and tried to rally the regiment, but could not, we moved on half mile farther then halted every man we could, with pistol and sword in hand, we rallied them then moved off to form the Brigade . . .*
>
> *Genl Howard and Genl Devens of our corps did not show much generalship when the attack was made. Genl Devens compliments me and my company for our bravery on picket. I have been reproved by different ones for exposing myself so much under fire. Some thought I was rash. I had rather it would be so than be called a coward as some officers in our Brigade. . . . I have four wounded in my company that I know of . . . Col Noble was wounded on Saturday. He showed great courage. He is well spoken of by all.*[28]

The Eleventh Corps brigades of Buschbeck and Nathaniel McLean were briefly able to hold their ground but were ultimately compelled to fall back.[29] At the rifle pits near Devens's headquarters at the Talley Farm, the 17th was ordered to lie down. It was here that Lieutenant Colonel Walter rose to assess the situation and was seen to drop, shot through the head and killed. The officers of the 17th Connecticut valiantly tried to maintain order during the disorganized retreat. The regiment succumbed to

Lt. Col. Charles Walter, killed at Chancellorsville.
(Bridgeport History Center)

the Confederates converging on all sides and was subjected to withering fire. In the thick of it, Colonel Noble gallantly rallied his men to return fire. Upon seeing him, General McLean cried out, "He is by God the bravest man of us all!"[30] Noble was soon shot in the arm, severing an artery. He remained on the field until loss of blood disabled him and he could no longer control his horse. The horse had also been wounded and died soon after. Noble was taken to the rear. After their stand at the rifle pits near headquarters, the regiment remained there throughout the night in support of a battery.[31]

On May 9 Justus Silliman, Company H, wrote a long and detailed letter home to his mother in New Canaan. He told her of the losses of the regiment and wrote frankly about the lack of generalship that led up to the disaster: "It is reported that Col Lee [55th Ohio] before the fight sent out scouts who returned and reported the enemy on our flank making preparations to attack us, that he reported this to Howard and desired permission to change front, at which the Gen replied that if he was afraid to remain at his post he could be relieved. I believe Lee has since resigned. . . . There was certainly a want of generalship somewhere or we would not have been surprised and flanked as we were."[32]

Selah Blakeman wrote about his experiences in the battle to his brother Anson in Stratford:

> *Thursday night we got to our place where we were to wait for the Rebs. Friday we were on picket. We came into the Regt Saturday morning. We lay in line of battle all day. We were close by Division headquarters, the right wing of the Regt was lying in the garden to the house. We were supporting a battery. About 5oclock in the afternoon the fight began . . . it come like a clap of thunder. They came in right length ways of the rifle pits where we were. There was some troops outside of us. We were ordered to lye down which we did but sudden for the way the shell and bulletts came in there was curious. I never saw a garden plowed and planted so quick before in my life but we never run until we had orders . . . a man don't know what he can stand until he has to stand it. I lost everything only what I had on my back, only* [had] *my belts and gun. There is 83 men gone from the Regt. Col. Wounded., Leuit. Col. Killed, 6 commission officers missing, our 1st Lieut. is wounded, 2 sergeants, 1 corporal and 10 privates are gone from Co. D. But I hate the Rebs worse now than ever. I have got to settle with them for what they got of me.*[33]

After Chancellorsville, the falsehood of cowardice against the Eleventh Corps erupted. The corps' reputation was forever destroyed, despite it suffering more than 2,400 casualties. The entire corps was mocked as "the Flying Dutchmen," "Howard's Cowards," and the "Flying Crescent." The corps became more divided than ever. The Yankees in the corps took great pains to disassociate their units from the "Cowardly Dutch," or the ethnic German regiments of the corps. Many men in the Eleventh Corps took pains to point out their own good service. In an article in the *Connecticut War Record*, the writer from the 17th Connecticut stated,

> *As a part of the Eleventh Corps we had to bear our share of the unjust censure passed upon it by those who knew nothing of the situation in which it had been placed, still we had the glory of being in the brigade that received the just praise of standing the longest, even as long as duty demanded. It is true as it is noteworthy that the 17th Connecticut, for the first time brought under fire, did not retreat until ordered to, and then in good order, though under circumstances the most trying even to the veteran soldiers . . . At that time to have stood was to be butchered or taken prisoner; to retreat a duty, and this they did in obedience to orders.*[34]

For so many of the men of the 17th Connecticut, and the Eleventh Corps, Chancellorsville was a bitter defeat for which they felt betrayed by their leadership and unjustly blamed.

The regiment spent May 3 and 4 in the rear guarding the road to the United States Ford on the Rappahannock River. The 17th Connecticut suffered 222 casualties (killed, wounded, captured, missing) in the battle, most of them on May 2.[35] After the withdrawal of troops from the battlefield, the regiment and its corps were sent back to their old bivouac at Brooke Station until the Army of the Potomac began following Lee's advance into Pennsylvania and the Gettysburg Campaign began.[36]

The skulls and bones of unburied soldiers on the south side of the Plank Road in Chancellorsville are hauntingly visible in this 1865 stereoview of the battlefield. (Library of Congress)

CHAPTER 3

The Hard Road to Gettysburg

Immediately following the shocking defeat at Chancellorsville, the Union high command began its maneuvering to deflect the blame for the fiasco. Most of the rank and file believed that the defeat was a failure of leadership. The men maintained that they were good soldiers and believed they had been badly led. Captain Sanford Chaffee, of the 20th Connecticut, overheard one private sum up the attitude of the common soldiers after the battle: "It was only the officers that got licked, we wasn't."[1] Many of the officers and men believed the defeat at Chancellorsville resulted from a failure of generalship in particular. Those in the Eleventh Corps remembered how General Howard had ignored warnings of Confederate activity on their part of the line. Private Justus Silliman, Company H, 17th Connecticut, would write home to his brother on June 7, "I have no doubt that Gen Howard is an earnest patriot, a Christian and a gentleman but he lacks keen foresight and strategy. . . . It is true the A.P. [Army of the Potomac] accomplished but little since its organization though I think it is composed of better drilled and as good fighting men as can be found. The reasons for its failure I think are as follows. The incompetency and treachery of some of its commanding generals; the continual interference of politicians at W[ashington]."[2] Silliman's assessment of the leadership was shared by many of the enlisted men. People throughout the nation, as well as many in the Army, found Hooker's excuses for the defeat appalling. The commander tried to shift the blame in multiple directions: "The Cavalry have failed in executing their orders"; "General [John] Sedgwick [the Sixth Corps commander] failed in the execution of his orders." Putting the best face on the defeat, Hooker claimed his forces had "inflicted heavier blows than we have received." Few were fooled. The nation was shocked and angered by the terrible defeat. President Lincoln was in agony, asking "My God! My God! What will the Country say?" General Couch refused to serve under

Hooker any longer and asked to be relieved. John Reynolds, commander of the First Corps, urged that Hooker be removed.[3]

The search for scapegoats for the Chancellorsville fiasco went from the highest to lowest ranks in the army, but the greatest blame would fall on the Eleventh Corps, also known as the "German Corps" or the "Dutch Corps." It would be unjustly condemned for the defeat at Chancellorsville and mocked as the "Flying Dutchmen," and the "Damn Dutch." The men of the Eleventh Corps carried this heavy and unfair burden with them to Gettysburg.[4]

During the war years, "German" and "Dutch" were used as labels of contempt toward immigrants who had arrived in the 1840s, 50s, and 60s and who supplanted the Irish as the new "foreigners" in America. "German," or the popular slang "Dutch," became an unsavory label. Prejudice ran deep in the American psyche. The Know-Nothing Party and other American nativists targeted Germans and called for limits and exclusions on immigration. Nineteenth-century nativists feared the waves of non-English-speaking Germans, believing that they brought with them Catholic and Jewish influences and freethinking ideas that would damage the fabric of Puritan and Protestant America. The German love of beer was viewed as especially damaging, believed to lead to indiscriminate alcoholism. Beer drinking was particularly frowned upon by American Protestants on the Sabbath as well as on other solemn occasions.[5] Well into the twentieth century, Yankee Puritan stock thought drinking was not apropos to various occasions where it was believed to pollute the importance and solemnity of events, or create an atmosphere for lowbrow and unethical behavior. In the early years of the twentieth century, former 17th Connecticut private J. Henry Blakeman of Stratford, a veteran of Company D, would be elected to serve four terms in the Connecticut State Legislature. He was proud to sponsor a bill that required saloons to remain closed on Memorial Day.[6] Shortly after Blakeman's legislation passed the Connecticut Legislature, the Eighteenth Amendment made the entire nation dry.

J. Henry Blakeman, Connecticut legislator, in 1917. Photograph from *History of Bridgeport and Vicinity*, George Curtis Waldo Jr.
(Author's Collection)

The issue of slavery was another source of division. Many German immigrants and German political leaders opposed slavery and spoke out forcefully against the institution.[7] The abolitionist stance of German Eleventh Corps leadership, such as General Carl Schurz, and that of some regiments, caused friction among the ranks in a Union army still divided on the slavery issue, and it added to ethnic prejudices. Many native-born Union officers and soldiers disdained the idea, and would dispute that they were fighting to free the slaves; they fought to preserve the Union. Native-born American racial prejudice, as well as anti-German ethnic prejudice, was often made evident through actions and letters home. Discrimination, anti-immigrant sentiments, scapegoating, and Yankee superiority all created tensions within the Eleventh Corps in particular and in the Army of the Potomac in general. All these elements made for a restless, difficult atmosphere surrounding the Eleventh Corps, including the 17th Connecticut, as the Gettysburg Campaign began.

Along with the command and ethnic stressors after the Battle of Chancellorsville, the Eleventh Corps was challenged by another potential weakness: its manpower. The corps would remain the smallest in the Army of the Potomac despite efforts in 1862 to bulk up its numbers with new regiments after Lincoln's call for 300,000 men. Instead of the normal three brigades in a division, the Eleventh Corps had only two, affecting its battlefield strength.[8]

After Chancellorsville, the 17th Connecticut remained in the First Division of the Eleventh Corps. The regiment would see many changes due to casualties and resignations. Colonel Noble had been seriously wounded in the right arm and his horse killed. Lieutenant Colonel Charles Walter was killed, shot through the head while fighting beside Captain Wilson French. French would write home to his wife that when Walter's body was found the rebels had stripped him down to his underwear, and Confederates had even stripped the shoes off the dead horses.[9] Elsewhere, Captain Lacy, Company D, was listed as slightly wounded, and he resigned on May 9, 1863.[10] Contemporary regimental correspondence home indicated he was not missed by his men and included some veiled accusations of cowardice.[11] In Company G, Captain James E. Dunham during the winter of 1863 was promoted to be provost-marshal on the staff of Gen. Devens. After Chancellorsville, the politically connected Dunham resigned to accept the position of provost-marshal of the Fourth District of Connecticut. First Lieutenant Wilson French was promoted to captain of Company G, much to the relief of his men who recognized his bravery at Chancellorsville. French had been the company's de facto captain while Dunham was posted to headquarters and during his frequent absences from the regiment.[12]

Captain Wilson French, Company G. (Captain Wilson French Collection)

After the death of Lieutenant Colonel Walter at Chancellorsville, Major Allen Brady, an experienced officer and a strong leader, expected to be promoted to lieutenant colonel. Born in 1822 in Middlesex County, Massachusetts, Brady was listed in the 1860 census as a thirty-seven-year-old shirt manufacturer living in Torrington, Connecticut, with his wife, Lucinda, and children William, age seven, and Mary, age four.[13] Brady had served in the 3rd Connecticut, a three-month regiment, as lieutenant colonel. When the colonel of the 3rd proved ineffective and resigned, Brady expected Governor Buckingham to appoint him to the post. However, Buckingham passed him over and promoted Lieutenant Colonel John L. Chatfield. An infuriated

Brady refused to recognize Chatfield as his superior and was deprived of his sword—essentially being put under arrest for blatant insubordination—but when the 3rd was mustered out in August 1861 Brady was released and mustered out as well.[14] In August 1862, Brady was commissioned as captain of Company B in the three-year 17th Connecticut and was quickly promoted to major. After the death of Walter, Brady felt he deserved the promotion to lieutenant colonel, but he was again passed over. The promotion went to Norwalk resident Douglas Fowler, captain of Company A. Fowler was also a veteran of the 3rd Connecticut, in which he was a company commander. Both officers gained combat experience at First Bull Run and both men could be fractious with superiors. Brady was frustrated when Fowler was promoted over him, but he remained major of the regiment. Never a popular officer among the men, it would be Brady's steadfast leadership that would salvage the regiment as a fighting entity after its retreat on July 1 at Gettysburg.[15] Brady would rally the survivors to fight valiantly again on the second day of the battle.

Maj. Allen G. Brady.
(Dale Call Collection)

Lt. Col. Douglas Fowler.
(Captain Wilson French Collection)

Douglas Fowler was born in Guilford, Connecticut, in 1826. He was a locksmith by trade. In 1853 he married Melissa Jane Nash, who passed away after the death of the couple's infant daughter in 1855. At the war's outbreak in 1861, the thirty-five-year-old widower was living in Norwalk.[16] He served as captain of Company G in the 3rd Connecticut and fought at First Bull Run. When his three-month enlistment expired Fowler enlisted in the 8th Connecticut in September 1861 as captain of Company H. Fowler would resign his commission in the 8th Connecticut in January 1862. Private Oliver Cromwell Case, 8th Connecticut, would write to his sister Abbie that "Capt. Fowler got into a fuss with the Lieut. Col. at Annapolis and sent in his resignation."[17] The "fuss" was regimental politics and differences of opinion over promotion. Fowler, apparently disgusted, resigned. He didn't stay home for long. By August 1862 he had recruited Company A out of Norwalk for the 17th Connecticut and was again a captain, this time in a three-year regiment. After Walter was killed and Colonel Noble badly wounded at Chancellorsville, Fowler would lead the 17th into battle at Gettysburg.

On June 5, 1863, Private William Warren remembered the reading of the promotion order:

> *An order was issued making the following promotions. Generally, orders read to the regiment on parade were not of any interest unless they pertained to a move, but this order was particularly listened to. It read as follows: First Lieutenant McQuhae of Company A, is promoted to be Captain of that company. Second Lieutenant Craw is promoted to First Lieutenant; Sergeant Ells is promoted to be Second Lieutenant; Lieutenant French is promoted to be Captain of Company G; Second Lieutenant Dennis to be first Lieutenant, and First Sergeant D. Bartram to be Second Lieutenant; Adjutant Hubbell is promoted to be Captain of Company D, Sergeant Major Chatfield to be Adjutant, and Corporal Betts, of Company A, to be Sergeant-Major.*[18]

General Howard remained the commander of the Eleventh Corps. He never acknowledged his own limitations at Chancellorsville, but he was keenly aware of the depression and demoralization, sharp criticism, negative press, and blame inflicted on his corps. Yet Howard's "awareness" never brought him to the point of vigorously defending his men against the slander and scapegoating.[19] After Chancellorsville, Howard chose to look outside the Eleventh Corps to replace Generals Devens and McLean and fill other vacancies. This exacerbated the continuing distrust and resentment between Howard and his officers, especially his German leadership, particularly since Howard made no secret that he wanted proven fighters to help him whip the Eleventh Corps into shape.[20] On June 8, 1863, on the eve of departure for Gettysburg, Captain French would write to his wife, Martha Bouton French, "My Dear Wife: We have a West Point Man named Ames for Brigadier General." This was West Pointer, strict disciplinarian, and military martinet Adelbert Ames. Ames would become the brigade commander under twenty-eight-year-old General Francis Channing Barlow, who would command the division under Howard. Captain French would also write Martha that Ames was arresting officers who displeased him, saying "We have to toe the mark pretty well now, to keep from being arrested. Some one or more of the officers in the Brigade are arrested most every day."[21]

Brigadier General Adelbert Ames was born in Rockland, Maine. He had gone to sea as a teenager and graduated from West Point in 1861. He earned the Medal of Honor at Bull Run. He was the first colonel of the 20th Maine. That unit's lieutenant colonel at the time, Joshua Lawrence Chamberlain, admired him; Joshua's brother, Tom Chamberlain, did not. Tom wrote to their sister, "I tell you he is about as savage a man you ever saw. . . I swear the men will shoot him the first battle we are in."[22]

Whatever the men of the 20th Maine thought about their colonel, Ames taught them the discipline that would serve them well at Gettysburg. General Howard brought Ames into the Eleventh Corps from the Fifth Corps, where he had been an aide to General

Meade. Ames replaced the popular General McLean. Ames made no secret of his contempt for "Germans," and he did not appoint a single German officer to his staff. He chose First Lieutenant Oscar J. Ladley of the 75th Ohio and the adolescent-looking, recently promoted Lieutenant Charles E. Doty of the 17th Connecticut as his aides de camp, selecting men from units that were considered "Yankee" regiments and were not labeled with the immigrant stigma.[23] Howard was well aware of Ames's antipathy toward his German regiments. In a letter to his wife, Howard acknowledged that Ames "does not have any fancy for German troops, is almost uncivil to them."[24]

General Adelbert Ames.
(Library of Congress)

Lt. Charles Doty with his sergeant's stripes. He was promoted in March 1863 to 2nd Lieutenant, Company F.
(Bridgeport History Center)

Twenty-eight-year-old Francis Channing Barlow, the new First Division commander, was always described as boyish looking. On May 24 he was chosen by Howard to replace Devens, who had been wounded at Chancellorsville. Barlow was a Harvard man, and an attorney by trade, from New York State, who believed emphatically in the Union cause. He had joined the 12th New York as a private and made a spectacular rise through the ranks. Barlow was promoted to colonel of the 61st New York at the beginning of the Peninsula Campaign and distinguished himself at Fair Oaks and Malvern Hill. He was severely wounded at Antietam and was not expected to live.[25] His wife, whom he had married the day before he left for the army, was the indomitable Arabella Griffiths Barlow, ten years older than her husband. A volunteer nurse for the U.S. Sanitary Commission, she nursed him back to health against the odds.[26]

Barlow was back in service as a brigade commander at Chancellorsville, but he and his brigade were detached from the Eleventh Corps when Stonewall Jackson's attack overwhelmed the unit, having been sent by Howard to reinforce General Daniel Sickles's Third Corps.[27] Barlow was never happy with his assignment to the Eleventh Corps, although Howard had requested him specifically to replace Devens in the belief that Barlow would make fighters out of the men who ran.[28] But Barlow never got over his disdain for the corps breaking at Chancellorsville and he never ceased to express his scorn for the Germans under his command. In his correspondence he disparaged his officers and men and felt that assignment to the Eleventh Corps

General Francis Barlow.

(Library of Congress)

was a stigma. He believed that the antidote to their deficiencies as soldiers was to institute his trademark command style of overly strict discipline and relentless training. After the war one of his subordinate officers wrote, "General Barlow had the happy faculty of making himself disagreeable to every officer and private of the Brigade."[29] Barlow retaliated for the perceived shortcomings of his new division assignment with utter contempt for the men he was assigned to lead and treated them with extreme disapproval and prejudice that he did not bother to hide. His letters home were peppered with derisive disdain, including "You know I have always been down on the Dutch and I do not abate my contempt now." He described his German troops as "these miserable creatures."[30] Barlow's contempt was generalized to encompass his entire command, singling out the German elements to be especially lacking. He believed them to be slack and disorderly soldiers and was not going to tolerate them. All orders were to be obeyed to the letter or consequences were severe. On June 2, 1863, Barlow wrote to a friend his description of his division:

> *Now I have command of the Division lately commanded by General Devens. It was the first to break on May 2nd and is in a most disgusting condition as to discipline and morale. But if hard knocks and a tight rein will make them fight, they will have to do it. One of the Brigades is wholly German and is commanded by Colonel von Gilsa (or rather commanded by a Major as Colonel von Gilsa is away and I have the next Colonel in rank in arrest). I expect to arrest them all the way down until I find some private soldier who will make them do things properly.*[31]

As the Army of the Potomac marched north in pursuit of General Lee it seemed Barlow was as much at war with his officers and men as he was with the enemy.

At the beginning of June the army readied itself for the new campaign. "June 6th the notable event was an order from General Barlow, directing every man to go to the brook and wash himself, and change his underclothing," William Warren wrote. "The weather was very warm and the earth very dry during this time."[32] Apparently being ordered to wash and change underwear left no doubt in the mind of even the lowliest private that a campaign was soon to commence. On June 8, Warren wrote, "At 11 o'clock of the morning of June 8th we received orders to pack up everything but our tents and be in readiness at any moment to march. We were ordered to have three days' cooked rations in our knapsacks. Heavy cannonading was heard in the direction of Fredericksburg and we thought sure we were in for another fight."[33]

William Warren, Company C.
(Courtesy of the William H. Warren Family)

The road to Gettysburg officially began for the men of 17th Connecticut on June 12, 1863. Prejudices were running deep throughout the army against the Eleventh Corps and exacerbating its disadvantages. The Eleventh Corps continued as the smallest corps in the Army of the Potomac, with just over 9,200 men. In the numbers game of the upcoming battle this would become a critical factor. Although new recruits to the Eleventh Corps had thinned the German ethnic character of the troops to less than half, the corps was still derisively referred to as the "German" corps.[34] The order of march put Major General Carl Schurz's Third Division in the lead at noon. The Second Division under Brigadier Adolph von Steinwehr rolled out at 1 p.m., with Barlow's First Division following thirty minutes later.

The first day's march was excessively hot, dry, and dusty. Water was difficult to find, many of the stream beds were dry, and the excessive dust raised by the marchers was choking. Conditions were brutal. On June 13, William Warren wrote, "We resumed our march at 4 a.m. We struck the Warrenton Turnpike, our destination being Catlett's Station. This place was reached at 5 p.m., after an afternoon of rapid marching. The day was excessively warm, and the dust blew in clouds. A large number of men were obliged to fall out through exhaustion, and two men of the 107th Ohio, in our brigade, died on the way."[35] The men marched well despite conditions. General Howard, wary after the Chancellorsville fiasco of how the corps would perform, took the opportunity to praise them on July 16: "The General Commanding the Corps is pleased to notice the excellent behavior of the troops under his command while on the very fatiguing and rapid march from Brooke's Station to this place. The corps has marched with very little straggling and some regiments without any men falling out of the Column of March. Credit is due to the officers in charge of the trains for the pains taken in causing no delay on the march."[36] All knew they were marching north toward a major battle. No one yet knew where or when it would occur.

On the march on June 16, William Warren wrote, "This morning at an early hour we resumed the march, and kept it up all day, bringing up at night at what is called Goose Creek. This was thirty-four miles from Centreville. The heat was intense, the dust unbearable. Much of the march was along a road shut in by pine brush which kept off all air. Our camp at Goose Creek was about four miles from Leesburg. The creek itself was liberally patronized by the foot-sore, dust-laden, weary soldiers."[37]

As the Eleventh Corps marched doggedly through the heat, dust, rain, and mud the disaster of Chancellorsville continued to loom over it. Captain Wilson French would write to his wife, Martha, on June 17th from Goose Creek, "I hope we will be able to whip them out this time, our orders are now forced marches, hard fighting, and short rations."[38] Captain French was carrying a carte de visite of one of his men, Corporal Andrew Couch, missing since Chancellorsville. On the back of the photographic card French had written in pencil, "Andrew Couch of my company. My favorite friend. He is missing in the last battle. I pray God he may return safe to us again." Corporal Couch would not return safe despite French's hopes, an example of one of the greatest tragedies of this war: there was no official mechanism for notifying families of the death of a soldier. Men killed in action often simply disappeared from their loved ones' lives. Notification relied on the eyewitness of comrades, or a company officer writing home, or the endless and inaccurate casualty lists published after battles. In the heat of battle many times men were simply listed as missing in action and it could take months, even years, to identify them as dead. Often their bodies were not identified, and graves simply marked "unknown." Tens of thousands of families suffered from the double loss of the death and unknown fate of a beloved soldier. Listed among the missing at Chancellorsville, the twenty-three-year-old Andrew Couch, a farm boy from Ridgefield,[39] had indeed been killed in action on May 2, 1863. Couch was the first Ridgefield resident killed in the Civil War.[40]

Corporal Andrew Couch, Company G, killed in action at Chancellorsville. (Captain Wilson French Collection)

The march went on. Captain French's last letter to Martha on the march to Gettysburg would be dated June 22, in which he wrote he was still "4 miles from America." As the army slogged ahead, hostility and conflict deepened within the First Division ranks as a result of Barlow's command. Almost every officer was a target for Barlow's ire. Any trifling or paltry deviation from strict orders was met with severe discipline. Arrests of officers were rampant. It might seem that a competent commander preparing troops for battle would understand that such a tyrannical approach to leadership, instead of building cohesion and élan in anticipation of combat, might damage his command relationships with his officers and men. This does not seem to have occurred to Barlow, who should have been well versed in the reaction to his tactics. He wrote home ingenuously that "There has been some murmur at my drawing the reins but I am told they are beginning to like me better—I have been very mild."[41]

On June 21, Lieutenant Colonel Fowler, serving in command of the 17th Connecticut, was ordered to punish stragglers. Fowler responded to headquarters that the men in question were not 17th Connecticut men. Fowler avoided arrest that day, but a few days later he was arrested along with Captain Enos Kellogg, Lieutenant Marcus Waterbury, and Lieutenant A. W. Peck of the 17th. All were charged with failure to prevent straggling. The order for arrest was issued by General Ames, who endorsed Barlow's methods. The issue was water. Marching conditions were alternately dry and

Three 17th Connecticut officers arrested on the march to Gettysburg. From left: Lieutenant Marcus Waterbury, Company I; Lieutenant Albert Peck, Company D; Lieutenant Francis Bliss, Company H. (Author's Collection and Bridgeport History Center)

dusty or wet and muddy. All the men were thirsty. Any officer who allowed men to step out of marching column to fill canteens for themselves and their comrades was brought up on charges for allowing straggling.[42] To our modern world, denying water to men marching for miles under difficult conditions and expecting them to be combat ready seems like madness. However, Ames and Barlow were of the same mind in this regard, and straggling was strictly prohibited. In addition to officer arrests, Barlow was well known to carry a heavy cavalry saber on the march and used it regularly it to strike stragglers. All the way north to Pennsylvania arrests continued. Other officers arrested from the 17th Connecticut included Captain James E. Moore, Captain John McCarty, and Lieutenant Francis Bliss.[43] It is unclear why Ames and Barlow felt that arresting numerous officers for petty charges would have a positive effect on discipline and obedience when, in fact, it could have only the opposite effect. No punishment made a bigger impression on the men of the 17th Connecticut than the arrest of their lieutenant colonel as they marched to Gettysburg on the way into battle. The men would be outraged.

On June 28, General George Gordon Meade issued General Order No. 67, announcing his appointment as commander of the Army of the Potomac, replacing Joe Hooker. Meade wrote, "The country looks to this army to relieve it from the devastation and disgrace of foreign invasion. Whatever fatigues and sacrifices we may be called upon to undergo, let us have in view, constantly, the magnitude of the interests involved, and let each man determine to do his duty." There could be no doubt in the mind of even the lowliest private that this march in pursuit of the Confederate army already invading Pennsylvania would end in battle.[44]

On June 28, Warren wrote,

> *We took up our line of march and proceeded to Frederickstown,* [present Frederick, Maryland] *a distance of twelve miles where we were obliged to halt for the night, as the town was so full of troops that we could not get through it. It is reported that Dr. Hubbard has been appointed medical director of our corps. June 29, we were aroused at 3 a.m. for roll call, and began our day's march at five o'clock with one day's ration of fresh meat. The weather was hot with frequent showers to make mud and wet us through. We made twenty-two miles by night, reaching Emmitsburg at six o'clock.*[45]

Dr. Robert Hubbard, surgeon of the 17th Connecticut, was appointed Medical Inspector of the Eleventh Corps. (USAHEC)

Private Timothy Spencer, Company K, who remembered marching barefoot to Gettysburg. (Bridgeport History Center)

The men still did not know where they were headed, except north, and rumors were rampant. In the brutal marching conditions men walked right out of their shoes. Some in the 17th Connecticut, including officers, were without footwear. On June 30, Sister Mary Jane Stokes, one of the nuns at St. Joseph's in Emmitsburg, described the Union men who entered the town that day: "The soldiers made their appearance here, as well as I can remember about three in the afternoon. We were going down to the barn . . . when we turned around, and here was a whole pack of them at the house behind us. The poor fellows looked half-starved, lank as herrings and barefoot."[46] Being barefoot is not often associated with the Army of the Potomac; that condition is usually perceived as a Confederate deficiency. However, many Northern troops went into the Battle of Gettysburg shoeless and hungry, thirsty, and exhausted after long, hard forced marches. These deprivations were not rectified until well after the battle. Timothy Spencer, Company K, would remember, "I believe I have walked as many miles barefooted as any other man in the regiment. Soon after the battle of Gettysburg began, while I was crossing a river, my shoes gave out and I lost them. As I could then procure no others, I went through the entire engagement barefooted, and did not get any shoes until the regiment reached Boonesborough Gap, near Middletown, Maryland some twelve days later."[47]

Emmitsburg, Maryland, sits just below the Mason-Dixon Line and the southern border of Pennsylvania. Founded in 1785, Emmitsburg was recognized as a religious center and symbol of Catholicism due to its association with Mother Elizabeth Seton, who in 1811 founded in Emmitsburg the first order of Catholic nuns in the United States, the Sisters of Charity, as well as the first Catholic school for girls in the nation. The town also had churches of Protestant worship along with the Catholic St. Joseph's College and Mount Saint Mary's Seminary School. The border town would serve as a crossroads for the armies several times during the war, and the citizens of Emmitsburg would alternately support and welcome both sides during the conflict.[48] As Federal troops entered the town on June 30, fire damage to the town was quite evident, with a conflagration having ravaged Emmitsburg on June 15. The flames had been visible eleven miles north in Gettysburg and had caused considerable consternation; the fire was initially thought to have been set by Confederates, but that was later disproven.[49] Both towns were on edge as the armies circled each other throughout the area.

The Eleventh Corps moved into a camp that covered the grounds of the present-day National Fire Academy and reached almost to what is now the Emmitsburg post office. General Howard made his headquarters at Mount Saint Mary's Seminary.[50] The *Emmitsburg Chronicle* printed an article in 1951 that described Emmitsburg during the Eleventh Corps occupation as seen by Union troops:

> *Small flags waved and dipped from the tower of the old Lutheran Church, used as a signal station by the army. Bearers of dispatches and squads of cavalry dashed madly through the town. The long roll of drums and the blood-stirring bugle calls filled the air; the fields were alive with soldiers. To the untrained eye it looked like a great mob, but it was not a mob in any sense, for in a very short time the men fell into orderly lines and in full marching swing, pressed forward across the fields toward Gettysburg, towards victory and also many of them--toward death. When the army began to arrive in town, the first thing the soldiers asked for was fresh bread. Nearly every house in the town was turned into a bakery and every woman who could bake was busy day and night, kneading bread while the soldiers needed more. The old-fashioned loaf was about three times bigger than the present baker's loaf. It was interesting to see a soldier, with a loaf under each arm, meet a squad of comrades. He would at once break the bread and hand it around. It would vanish quicker than the morning dew. No doubt it tasted to the poor fellows like the bread mother used to bake at home. The mother and the home that many a brave boy never saw again. The soldiers were well-disciplined and consequently well-behaved men and there was very little trouble between them and the people of town or country.*[51]

William Warren wrote, "We rested all day of the 30th of June at Emmitsburg. At night we had a good super [*sic*] of fresh bread, young onions, and milk—at our own expense."[52] Many soldiers made their way into the town with food on their minds. Fresh bread was especially popular and the people of Emmitsburg were very glad to sell it. Tom Bradley, of the 17th Connecticut's Company E, remembered on June 30 that he and his friend James Ainscow, a musician in Company K, "stopped at a bakers. Jimmy corresponded with the girl who waited on them and afterwards married her."[53]

A 17TH CONNECTICUT LOVE STORY

In 1887, Tom Bradley wrote two short descriptions to William Warren about his time in Emmitsburg. One of those descriptions was the intriguing statement, "stopped at a bakers. Jimmy corresponded with the girl who waited on them and afterwards married her." There was no other information included with Bradley's statement. Research has proved the statement to be true and uncovered the name of the young lady and the details of the affair.

James Ainscow, Company K musician, purchased bread from Annie McCullough in Emmitsburg on June 30, 1863, and returned after the war to marry her. (Bridgeport History Center)

Private James "Jimmy" Ainscow was born in 1842 in Manchester, England. He enlisted in the 17th Connecticut in August 1862 as a musician in Company K. On June 30, 1863, Ainscow and his friend Bradley, of Company E, purchased bread from a young Emmitsburg lady named Annie McCullough. Jimmy was indeed quite taken with Annie.

On June 1, Ainscow and Bradley, along with their regiment, marched from Emmitsburg and into battle at Gettysburg; both survived. On July 5, they departed Gettysburg with their regiment on the march in pursuit of the Confederate army. The march would take them again through Emmitsburg. Whether Jimmy would see his sweetheart as he and his regiment marched through town is not known. What is known is that he and Annie, after that fateful meeting on June 30, kept in touch through the rest of the war and Jimmy's service.

Privates Ainscow and Bradley would soldier on wherever their regiment's service took them. After Gettysburg, the Eleventh Corps would be broken up and the 17th Connecticut sent south to serve in South Carolina, Georgia, and Florida. On February 5, 1865, Ainscow and

Bradley would be with their regiment at a small action near St. Augustine, Florida, called Dunn's Lake. Both were captured and sent to Andersonville; both survived their imprisonment and were released after the war ended in May 1865.

In 1866 Jimmy returned to Emmitsburg. On September 25, 1866, James Ainscow and Annie McCullough, the young lady whom Jimmy and his friend had met and purchased bread from the day before the Battle of Gettysburg, were married in St. Joseph's Catholic Church in Emmitsburg.[54] Six children followed: Gertie in 1867, Charles in 1869, Anna in 1871, James in 1874, William in 1875, and Alice in 1877. Jimmy's work as a coach lamp maker and salesman would take the family to New York City, New Jersey, and Philadelphia.[55] On April 23, 1880, Annie would pass away in Philadelphia at age thirty-five. She is buried in an unmarked grave in St. Joseph's Catholic Cemetery in Emmitsburg, where she was baptized in 1845 and married in 1866.[56] Jimmy would not remarry. He would apply for a pension in 1901 and would pass away in New York City on June 27, 1903. He lies in a soldier's grave in Kensico Cemetery in Valhalla, New York, under a government stone marked "Musc, Jas. Ainscow, Co. K, 17th CT. INF."[57]

The evening of June 30 was clear. Campfires could be seen for miles around. The Sisters of Charity of St. Joseph had handed out bread and milk to hungry soldiers throughout the day. Troops bought all the whiskey and tobacco they could find. Many men availed themselves of the opportunity to have their confessions heard; Father Angelo Gandolfo heard confessions in the Stranger's Chapel and Father Burlando in his room.[58] The grounds of the town, convent, seminary, and college were flooded with soldiers, who by all accounts were respectful and polite. General Schurz and his staff occupied "the Asylum" (the White House) and General Howard took over the home of Father Burlando.[59] Schurz ordered the German band of the 45th New York to play for the priest and nuns of the academy. Colonel Leopold von Gilsa, commander of the First Brigade of Barlow's division, played the piano that evening.

Von Gilsa, who had been a major in the Prussian army prior to immigrating, had supported himself during hard times in America as a pianist in New York music and dance halls. He had been the colonel of the 41st New York and received command of the brigade prior to Chancellorsville. He was personally a brave officer, but he was detested by Barlow for his nationality, and Barlow deemed him a poor commander.[60] Von Gilsa himself had no use for Barlow's style of leadership. Howard also eyed von Gilsa skeptically and was wary of him. During the withdrawal from Chancellorsville, von Gilsa was violently furious. Howard sought to appease his volcanic anger by encouraging him to depend on God, to which the enraged von Gilsa responded with such a torrent of profanity that Howard, the "Christian General," thought him insane.[61]

As twilight fell on the last day of June 1863, the army settled down for the night, each man with his own thoughts, hopes, and fears. James Montgomery Bailey, Company C,

17th Connecticut, wrote about that night in a letter published in the *Danbury Times* in September 1863.

> *I well remember the night of the 30th of June. The sky was clear of clouds and filled with bright glittering stars. The moon threw a calm, mellow light over our camp, and the surrounding hills. We were lying at Emmitsburg in Maryland, near the Pennsylvania border. We felt that our marching was about done for the present, and that we were on the eve of a heavy struggle. The solemnity which always foreruns a battle, pervaded our minds, intensifying our thoughts of home, and weaving shadows of anxiety across our future. The conflict was imminent. All through the day flying rumors came on all sides. Lee had destroyed Harrisburg, routed the militia, and was rapidly advancing on us by way of Gettysburg. I stood leaning against a camp stake, gazing dreamily across the hill, with mind reverting to Chancellorsville and filled with anticipations of a second edition soon to be issued.*[62]

Private James Montgomery Bailey, Company C. Bailey would write of his wartime experiences under the pseudonym "High Private Manton." His articles were published in the *Danbury Times*, the newspaper he would own after the war. (Author's collection)

Captain James Moore and Lieutenant Milton Daniels, of Company C, both from Danbury, spent that evening together. They had both served in the 3rd Connecticut, a three-month regiment, Daniels as corporal in Company I and Moore as captain of the company. They had fought together at First Bull Run. In the summer of 1862 both men recruited for Company C in Danbury, Moore as captain and Daniels as lieutenant. The two were close. Moore, a striking man with a lantern jaw, dark curly hair, and sunken cheeks, was a forty-three-year-old mason and Mexican War veteran living on Elm Street in Danbury when the war broke out. He had married Jane Lewis in New York City in 1854 and was the father of four children. His youngest daughter, Ellen, had been born on August 2, 1862; on August 28, Moore was commissioned captain in the 17th Connecticut[63] and he departed with his regiment for the front on September 2. Moore was well thought of in Danbury. His service in the Mexican War and the 3rd Connecticut was well known, and he was respectfully referred to around town as "Captain." In the summer of 1862 Governor Buckingham issued a proclamation calling on the men of Connecticut to go to war. A draft was imminent if Connecticut did not fill its manpower quota. Many young men were finding it difficult to get work in a depressed economy, and these young men (and their parents), believing army service to be inevitable, wanted to serve with a man they knew and could trust, someone who had military experience

Danbury residents Captain James Moore and Lieutenant Milton Daniels would recruit and lead Company C. (Bridgeport History Center)

and was locally respected. For these reasons, Moore found it easy to raise a company within the town. Danbury men were eager to enlist in his company.[64]

Milton Daniels was a twenty-four-year-old married mercantile clerk with one son. He was living in Danbury when he first enlisted in 1861 as a corporal in Company I, 3rd Connecticut. When his three-month enlistment expired after First Bull Run, he reenlisted in Company E, 7th New York Cavalry until the following March, when he mustered out again.[65] In July 1862, he joined Moore in raising Company C in Danbury. Daniels's nineteen-year-old brother, William, an unmarried carpenter from Danbury, mustered into Company C as a sergeant. They left their widowed mother, Betsey, in Danbury. She would pass away on November 10, 1863, with both her boys away in the army. Before her death, Mrs. Daniels made a will leaving all her property to her sons, with the provision that "In case my said sons Milton H and William Leonard, now in the service of the United States, fall in battle or from any other cause should not return to their home," then all her property would go to her only grandson, Milton's boy.[66]

Spending the last night before the battle with his captain left an indelible memory on Lieutenant Daniels. He would write to William Warren from his home in Indianapolis in 1886:

> *On the night before the battle, we camped at Emmitsburg—the last night on earth for many of our comrades. I now wish I had the power of telling of the last night on earth of our dear old Captain James E. Moore, whose photo I now have before me. I can see ourselves under canvas; I believe it was what we called a dog tent. He says to me, "I am too utterly weary to rest and I want to talk to you." I said, "All right, Captain." He*

answered that he must talk about the upcoming battle that would surely be tomorrow. I said the battle was not expected until the day after; he said, surely on the morrow, and that next night would see me in command of the company—that he had been through the war with Mexico and so far through this, but that his days were now numbered—that the promotions would be many. Captain Moore said he was very weary and it would be a relief to be at rest. He asked me to attend to some matters for him—what to tell his family—and he had a fine Meerschaum pipe he wanted Quien to have. [Lt. Henry Quien, Company C, who had served with Daniels and Moore in the 3rd Connecticut at First Bull Run. He was the third of six sons, born in Germany, and was a hatter in Danbury. The men of the 17th, as well as Moore and Daniels, thought well of him.] *Well, I can't tell it, language fails, but we did not sleep that night.*[67]

The fields around St. Joseph College, the seminary and school in Emmitsburg where the Eleventh Corps camped the evening of June 30, 1863, photographed by Alexander Gardner, July 1863. (Library of Congress)

CHAPTER 4

July 1— Rendezvous With Destiny

Wednesday, July 1, 1863, began with General Howard ordering his corps to head north toward Gettysburg, Pennsylvania. General Schurz's Third Division would be ready to lead at 7 a.m., von Steinwehr's Second Division would follow by 7:30, and Barlow's First Division would be next at 8:15. Howard expected action, and he ordered all empty wagons, surplus baggage, useless animals, and "impedimenta of every sort" sent to Union Bridge, Maryland. Howard also impressed on his officers the need for speed. He ordered close marching, and shortening the column, when possible, with straggling forbidden.[1]

The 17th Connecticut began the march to Gettysburg with 17 officers and 369 enlisted men. This was down from its original strength of just over 1,000 men the September before.[2] William Warren wrote, "At 7:00, July 1, we were ordered into line, the objective point being Gettysburg, five or six miles distant [Emmitsburg was ten miles from Gettysburg[3]], Lieutenant Charles E. Doty, of Company F, was an aide on the staff of General Ames, Commander of our brigade . . . from his position on staff, and from that fact all orders communicated to our regiment during the fight were sent by him."[4] It was already seventy-two degrees by 7 a.m., and although it was cloudy throughout the day, it was humid.[5] The humidity, along with a morning shower, would make the day almost unbearable for soldiers in wool uniforms marching and fighting with little water.

As the morning went on, the temperature and humidity continued to rise, and the column was pushed hard. The Eleventh Corps bogged down behind the First Corps. Thousands of horses, wagons, artillery, and men had churned up the road, making it difficult for those following, and the march slowed. The marching column closed up on itself like a collapsing Slinky. Average marching speed for an army on the go was 2

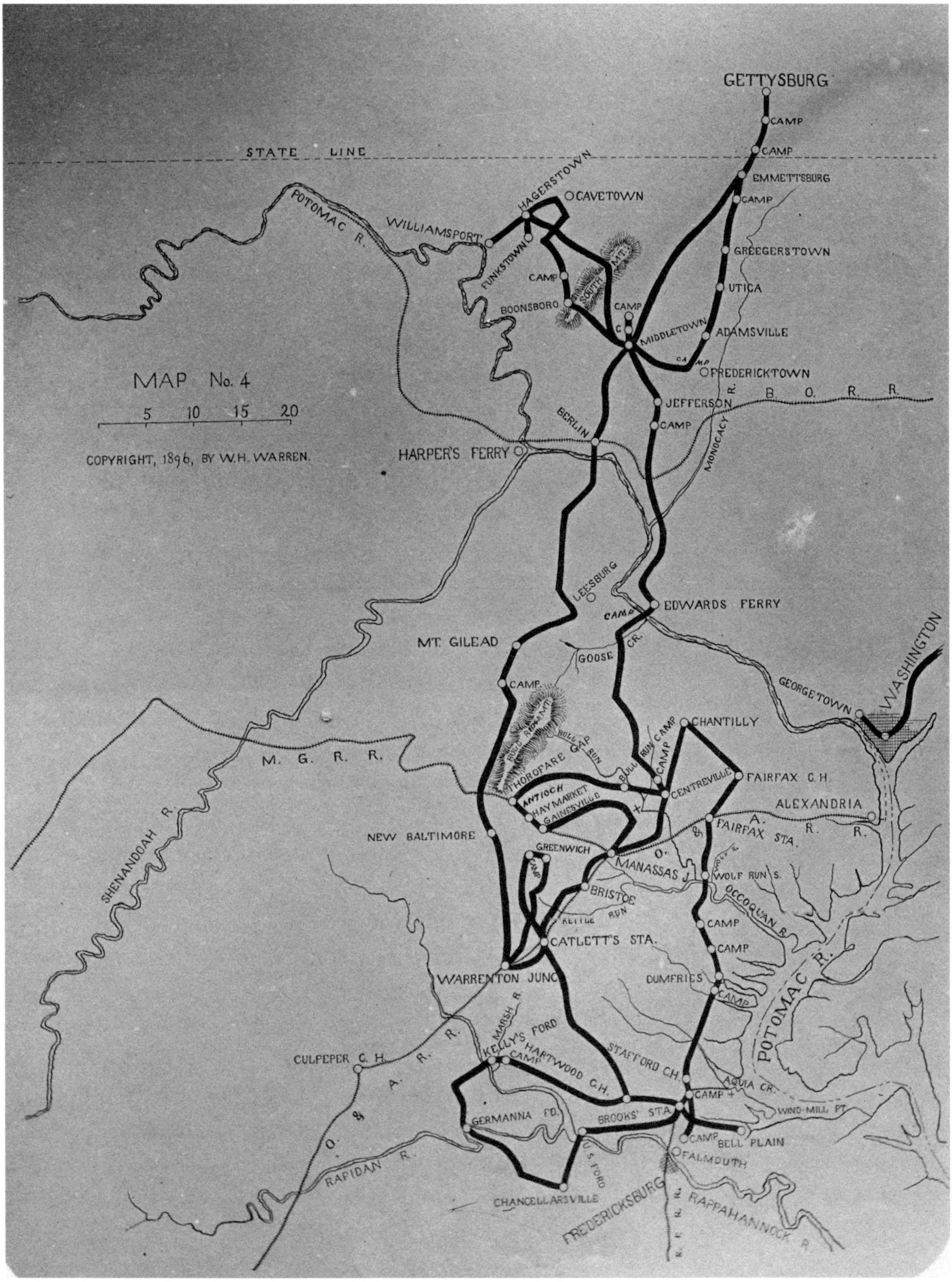

William Warren included this map in his manuscript showing both the regiment's route to Gettysburg and the route it followed after the battle as the Army of the Potomac pursued General Lee and the Army of Northern Virginia. (Bridgeport History Center)

to 2.5 miles per hour. A division marching in column was 2.5 to 4 miles in length, and a corps in marching column could be 7 to 15 miles long.[6] With time of the essence, Howard ordered Schurz, von Steinwehr, and four of the artillery batteries to take a right after passing Moritz Tavern on the Emmitsburg Road and to follow the Taneytown Road into Gettysburg. The route was longer but was free of the First Corps bottlenecks. Barlow's First Division continued along the Emmitsburg Road, the most direct route to Gettysburg, following the First Corps.[7] After issuing these marching orders, Howard turned command of the Eleventh Corps over to Schurz and went ahead to Gettysburg to find General Reynolds, the wing commander and ranking officer, and to determine where Reynolds wanted the Eleventh Corps deployed once it arrived.[8] Barlow was determined to drive his men forward and strictly enforce the no-straggling order. By the time the 17th Connecticut passed Moritz Tavern the men could hear the rumble of artillery north of Gettysburg. Soon the noise of musketry could also be heard. As the long column marched toward the sound of the guns there was now no doubt they were marching into a battle.

That morning Lieutenant Daniels was still worried about Captain Moore and his premonition of death, which they discussed the evening before during their sleepless night at Emmitsburg. Daniels wrote, "I thought daylight and a dash of cold water would bring him out all right, but not so, he tottered to the head of the company, and marched in silence, until way ahead we saw the puff of a shell, then the report, 'Now we are in for it.' Soon we heard the noise of battle, and the aide hurried from the front with orders to hurry up."[9]

Not all the men in the 17th had been ready to march that morning. Tommy Bradley, Company E, who had emigrated from Ireland and was working in a rubber factory in Newtown, Connecticut,[10] before he enlisted, was still on the prowl for a pair of shoes, having been unsuccessful the day before when he went with Jimmy Ainscow to buy bread in Emmitsburg. Bradley wrote in the third person remembering the morning of July 1:

> *While encamped near Emmitsburg, Thomas Bradley had no shoes to wear, so went into town to get a pair, but before he got back, the regiment had started on the march for Gettysburg. He was the right General Guide and carried the Guidon and when he went away he left it with the co. and when they left, they left it sticking in the ground. Major Brady came along, and seeing it there took it with him, and told Tommy that he could not have it again. Major gave it to Lieut. Col. Fowler, and he gave it back to Tommy. Major wanted to take it away from Tommy.*[11]

Despite Tom Bradley's mildly worded memory of leaving the guidon behind at Emmitsburg, one can only imagine what Major Brady's volcanic response must have been to such carelessness, never mind how he felt, or perhaps expressed himself, when Lieutenant Colonel Fowler returned the pennant to the man who had haphazardly left it behind. Tommy Bradley, perhaps conveniently, did not write about that.

As the grueling march toward Gettysburg continued greater numbers of men became overheated, footsore, and thirsty. Strict orders against straggling were brutally enforced. Many regimental officers were arrested for disobedience to orders due to their concern for the wellbeing of their men. Private William W. Paynton, Company A, described marching conditions on July 1 and the men's outrage when Lieutenant Colonel Fowler was arrested.

> *The morning of July 1 we again took up the line of march for the last time until we met the enemy on the field of Gettysburg. Soon after the start, an order was issued by General Barlow, our Division Commander, in which "Straggling was strictly forbidden—that the ranks must be kept closed up, and regimental and company commanders would be held accountable for the violation of said order." Aide-de-camps were constantly galloping from right to left of the line to observe any violations. The day was very hot and the men became thirsty; the water in their canteens was consumed quickly. A soldier belonging to the 17th Regiment, while crossing a brook that ran by the roadside stepped out of the ranks to dip a cup of water to quench his thirst. An aide, who was galloping along, saw the act, and immediately reported it to the General. In a few minutes we saw Lieut. Col. Fowler riding to the rear and surrendering his sword to Chaplain Hall, being considered under arrest. Soon after the column halted for rest. The boys of the 17th gathered about their beloved Fowler, and some of them, in their indignation, declared that if he was not released before the regiment went into action, they would not fire a shot. The Colonel told them not to do anything rash, but that if the Regiment went into a fight he would go with them, and as their commander too. The march was soon resumed, and orders were received from General Howard to hurry up the 11th Corps; we were put upon the double quick. Presently we saw Col. Fowler riding up to the front again and assuming command of the regiment; he had been released. By this time we could hear the booming of the guns at the front, and see the clouds of smoke that arose from the battle that had been in progress since early morning.*[12]

Chaplain Hall was ordered to take Lieutenant Colonel Douglas Fowler's sword after his arrest for allowing straggling. (Captain Wilson French Collection)

The arrest of an officer for a man stepping out of line for water on the arduous march to Gettysburg was not a scene unique to the 17th Connecticut. When the 13th Vermont Infantry dedicated its monument at Gettysburg on Hancock Avenue in 1899, they honored

Lieutenant Stephen F. Brown of Company K, who had arrived on the field without a sword. On the march to Gettysburg, Brown ordered a guard to stand aside to let his men drink from a well, after which he was placed under arrest and relieved of his sword. Brown seized a camp hatchet and carried it in the battle until he captured a sword from a Confederate officer. Determined to immortalize his action, the boys from Vermont commissioned the original design for the monument with Brown carrying the hatchet. When the Battlefield Commission objected to the design, the hatchet was replaced with the captured sword and the hatchet placed at Brown's feet. Later in the war Brown, since promoted to captain of the 17th Vermont, was severely wounded on May 12, 1864, at Spotsylvania Court House, Virginia, and suffered amputation of the left arm.[13]

The men of the 17th Connecticut marched toward a battle in progress. Hearing the sound of the guns and seeing the clouds of smoke in the distance, Private Payton, Company A, remembered,

> *The next hour was a trying one to the men of weak nerves, and many a poor soldier expressed in his blanched face a fear that would blush to speak, for there are none so brave but at the approach of battle feel a vague sense of impending danger and perhaps death. The bravado and bluster of camp life is all gone in the face of the enemy, and it is a remarkably courageous man that can look into the mouth of a twelve pound Parrott gun, or the muzzles of a regiment of infantry, and not feel a quiver of fear. For my part I felt that sense of uneasiness that is born of uncertainty and I wondered what would be my fate and how I should acquit myself in the struggle that was so near at hand.*[14]

As the 17th Connecticut marched through Gettysburg with its brigade, it turned down Washington Street. The men were fatigued, overheated, thirsty, and footsore, and knew they would soon be going into combat. Many citizens of the town were outside their homes passing water and food to the soldiers as the men hurried toward the mounting fury of the battle north of town. William Warren remembered that the regiment

> *marched about five or six miles without a rest, many of the boys falling by the roadside. The latter part of the march for a mile or two, was more than double quick, which made it very hard and tedious. When we did stop to rest, which was after we had marched through the town of Gettysburg, we dropped on the ground like dead men, very tired and exhausted. While we were passing through town the most intense excitement prevailed, as all knew, by the action of things that a fight was near at hand. The citizens would hardly venture out of their doorways but stood there handing us eatables and water. We went through in such a hurry as we could hardly stop to get anything to eat or drink; we were on business and soon had all we wanted.*[15]

Private J. Henry Blakeman, Company D, wrote,

Private J. Henry Blakeman, Company D. (Bridgeport History Center)

> *I must relate an incident that occurred the morning we passed through Gettysburg to enter the fight. A comrade and myself dropped from the ranks to get a drink of water from a tub placed in the yard by kind people of the town, and after drinking, were turning away, when a lady came to the door and said, "Ain't you hungry?" We of course, said, "Yes." The lady immediately ran down the cellar and brought up a cherry pie, which we divided and hurried on to overtake the regiment. When at Gettysburg, at the unveiling of our monument* [in 1884], *I recognized the house at once, but found the people who lived there in 1863 had moved to another part of the town. I finally succeeded in finding them—relating the circumstance—and afterward called on them with my wife, which call they returned at our hotel, making a very pleasant acquaintance.*[16]

General Howard, in command of the field after the death of General Reynolds, was on Cemetery Hill. He directed the arriving Eleventh Corps to move out of Gettysburg and into the open fields northeast of the town. Howard needed the Eleventh Corps to connect with the First Corps' battle line to protect the right flank. The First Corps had been in action since the morning, its line of combat fanning out in an arch northwest of the town and encompassing Seminary Ridge and the fields between the Fairfield Road, the Chambersburg Pike, Herr Ridge, Mummasburg Road, and the Newville Road. Schurz rushed two divisions forward to the north as Confederate general Robert Rodes's division formed on Oak Hill to the right of the Mummasburg Road. Rodes was in position to flank the First Corps as additional Confederate troops under General Jubal Early approached Gettysburg from the north.[17] Once General Barlow arrived on the field, he moved his division to the right of the Union line. Confederate general George Doles shifted his command to counter the Union buildup forming on the right as Barlow's division arrived. Barlow placed his division on Blocher's Knoll, named for the local farmer who owned the property. The knoll overlooked Rock Creek; just south of the knoll was the Adams County Alms House (also called the Poor House), a collection of buildings that would become one of the first of several Eleventh Corps field hospitals.[18]

Barlow's advance line formed an outward bulge, giving it an upside-down horseshoe effect that left gaps in the thin Union line. This placement left both of Barlow's

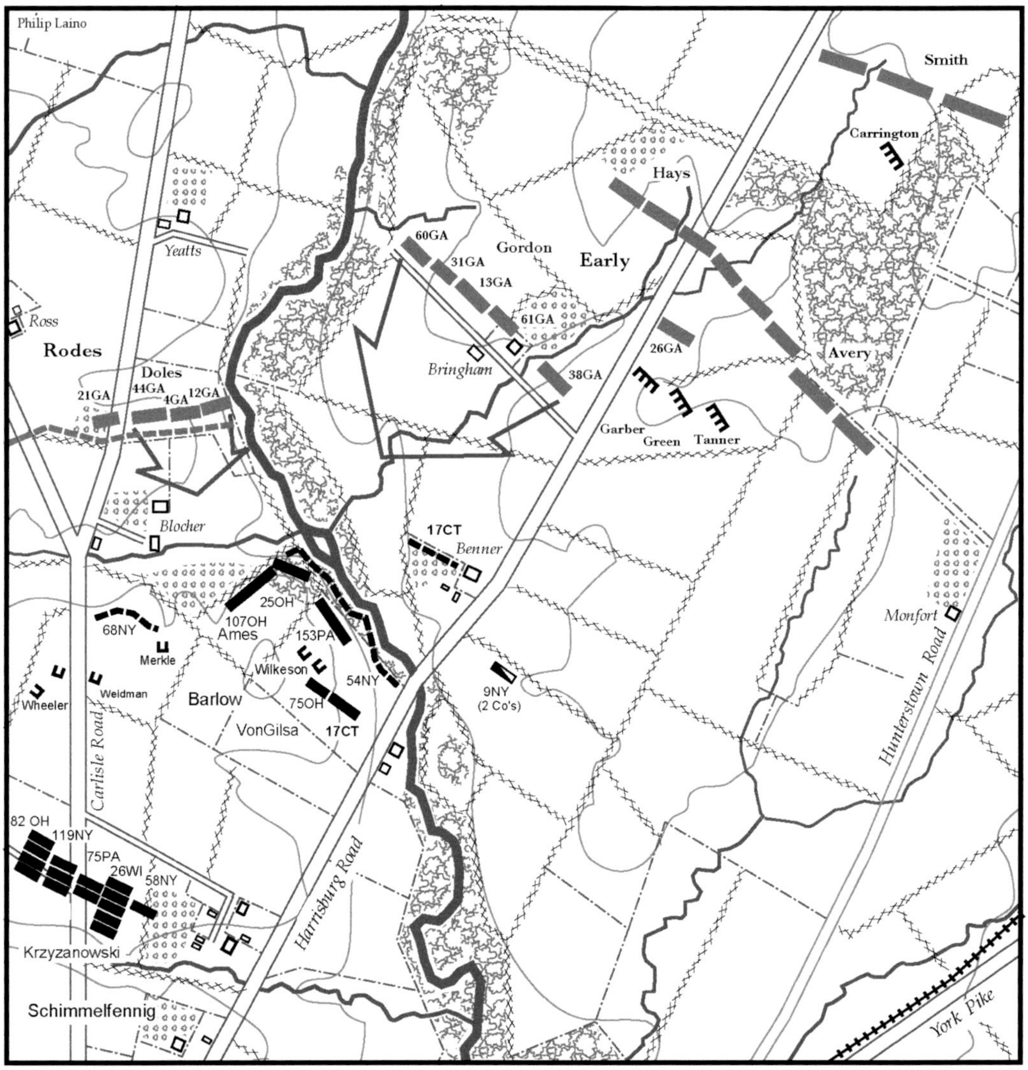

Barlow Advances to Blocher's Knoll

Barlow advanced his entire division to Blocher's Knoll. Part of the 68th New York, two companies of the 153rd Pennsylvania, and the 54th New York manned a skirmish line in the brush on the banks of Rock Creek. The rest of the 153rd Pennsylvania was on the knoll. Ames's brigade joined von Gilsa's and four guns of Wilkeson's battery. The 107th Ohio (458) faced Doles's infantry. The 25th Ohio (220) formed the apex of Barlow's position, and the 75th Ohio (269) and six companies of the 17th Connecticut (386 in total) formed a reserve. Four companies of the 17th Connecticut (A, B, F, and K) volunteered to advance under Major Brady and crossed Rock Creek to hunker down in the Benner Orchard. Gordon's brigade, in concert with Doles, began a two-pronged assault against the troops massed on the knoll.[19]

flanks unanchored and vulnerable to the Confederate onslaught that would hit both ends of his line; in military parlance, Barlow's aggressive move forward created a salient. The oncoming Confederates would attack Barlow from both sides and the front and would outnumber his men more than three to one. Artillery support on Blocher's Knoll consisted of four twelve-pound Napoleon guns of the 4th U.S. Artillery, Battery G, commanded by nineteen-year-old Lieutenant Bayard Wilkeson, whose horses covered the last two miles at a trot before the battery swung into combat.[20] Wilkeson unlimbered his four guns immediately and began firing on Doles to the left. Solid shot and shell screamed through the air. The 17th Connecticut and 75th Ohio were placed in reserve behind and to the right of Wilkeson's battery. Three regiments—the 107th Ohio, the 25th Ohio, and the 153rd Pennsylvania—were placed in a triangular formation at the apex of the knoll. Some of von Gilsa's regiment formed a skirmish line along Rock Creek below the hill.[21]

General Ames, commanding Barlow's second brigade, sent his aide, Lieutenant Charles E. Doty, to order a detachment of 17th Connecticut to secure a small bridge across Rock Creek below the knoll and act as skirmishers. Four companies were to take and hold a farmhouse across the creek. Lieutenant Colonel Fowler called for volunteers. Major Brady offered to lead them. Companies A, B, F, and K then proceeded immediately down the Harrisburg Road to the bridge near the brick farmhouse of Josiah Benner.[22]

Once these four companies crossed the bridge over Rock Creek, they were on the extreme right of the entire Federal line. These men of the 17th Connecticut were the only organized unit to engage the Confederates on the east side of Rock Creek during the first day's fight.[23] Their gallant action was conducted in the Benner orchard behind the house, where the Connecticut men were outnumbered and faced devastating Confederate pressure. Against the odds, and thanks in part to Brady's extraordinary leadership, when ordered to do so the skirmishers would withdraw with only minor losses and in good

Left to right: Captain John McQuhae, Company A; Captain Charles Hobie, Company B; Captain Henry Allen, Company F; missing is Captain McCarty of Company K. (Bridgeport History Center)

order, eventually reaching safety on the Union line on East Cemetery Hill. There Brady would assume command of what was left of the regiment.

Major Brady wrote in his after-action report of the battle on July 4, 1863,

> *The regiment arrived in Gettysburg between 1 and 2 p.m. of the 1st instant, and was marched with the other regiments of the brigade through and to the lower end of the town, and there halted for a moment. Four companies were immediately ordered out by Brigade General Ames, under command of Major Brady, to the right of the bridge at the lower end of the town, with instructions to throw out two companies as skirmishers, the other two to be held as a reserve, and to take and hold the brickhouse to the left and beyond the bridge. Two companies were thrown out and deployed as skirmishers as rapidly as possible to the right of the bridge, along the creek. The other two, held as reserve, were advanced in line, loading and firing as rapidly as possible, making at the same time a left wheel, so as to swing our right around the house, the reserve keeping near and conforming to the movements of the skirmishers.*
>
> *When near the house, the enemy opened upon us with shot, shell, grape, and canister, which retarded our advance for a moment, until Major Brady dismounted, went in front of the line of skirmishers, and led them on until quite near the house. The enemy, anticipating our movements shelled the house and set it on fire. We, however, held our ground, and held the enemy's skirmishers in check. Their loss up to this time was at least 5 to 1, most of the men in the four companies being excellent marksmen and having volunteered for this occasion. They consisted of Companies A, B, F, and K, commanded, respectively, by Captains McQuhae, Hobbie, Allen and McCarty. We continued skirmishing briskly until Major Brady received*

The Josiah Benner House in 1863. The four companies of 17th Connecticut skirmishers would be behind the house in the Benner orchard. (Gettysburg National Military Park)

> *orders from Brigadier-General Ames to draw in his skirmishers and return to town as rapidly as possible, and take command of his regiment. The order was obeyed, and we fell back in good order, skirmishing with the enemy, who advanced as we retreated, and tried to cut us off and capture us before we got to town, but we foiled them in this attempt by making a circuit and entering the town near the upper end, and soon joined the remainder of the regiment, which we found near the lower end of town. The loss in the four companies under Major Brady was 3 men killed, 1 captain and one lieutenant wounded, 1 sergeant and 3 men taken prisoners. I would here state that I had great difficulty in drawing in Captain McCarty's company (K), as they were so earnestly engaged and making such sad havoc among the rebels.*[24]

Back on Blocher's Knoll, the remaining six companies of the 17th Connecticut moved into line left of the 25th Ohio. Fowler, commanding the 17th, refused to dismount from his white horse despite his officers' entreaties to do so.[25] Wilkeson's gunners continued rapidly firing and Confederate artillery were returning the fire. Many of the men were restless and Fowler joked with them to "Dodge the big ones, boys."[26]

Barlow advanced with von Gilsa's brigade to halt the onslaught of Doles's Georgians on his left. Wilkeson's guns continued the duel quite effectively with artillery on Oak Hill to the left. Suddenly it became clear that Early's force was advancing southward on the Harrisburg Road. The rebel artillery converged on Wilkeson's four guns on the knoll, blasting away at them from both Oak Hill and the Harrisburg Road. Wilkeson's battery hotly returned fire in both directions. Doles's Georgians and General John B. Gordon's Georgians were soon converging on the knoll, catching Barlow in a vise. Brigadier General Harry Hays's Louisiana Brigade was right behind Gordon, and Colonel Isaac Avery's North Carolinians were to Hays's left. Barlow, who had been concentrating everything he had on Doles to his left, was caught unaware by Early's advance on the right. Gordon arrayed his Georgian Brigade (comprising the 60th, 31st, 13th, 61st and 38th Georgia regiments) to the front and right against the Federals on the knoll. Doles's Georgians (comprising the 21st, 44th, 4th, and 12th Georgia regiments) converged hard on Barlow's left. The Yankees were severely outnumbered.[27]

From the saddle, Wilkeson continued to fearlessly and effectively direct his battery against the Confederate assault. Gordon was finding it difficult to advance his Confederate brigade in the face of Wilkeson's fire. The nineteen-year-old lieutenant made for a compelling and visible target on horseback, and Gordon's two batteries trained every gun against the four-gun battery on the knoll. Wilkeson was struck and knocked off his horse, falling with a mortal leg wound. His horse was killed. Wilkeson was carried, or dragged himself, to the Alms House and died there that night.[28] Lieutenant Eugene Bancroft assumed command of the battery. One gun was disabled, and the rest began to withdraw. Barlow was also badly wounded trying to rally his thin, wavering line as the Confederate fury continued to converge on and swarm over the Federals.[29]

Lieutenant Wilkeson commanding Battery G, 4th U.S. Artillery, on Barlow's Knoll. (New York Public Library Digital Collection)

After he was wounded, Barlow's line was quickly overrun. Following the battle, he was quick to condemn his men, claiming they were well positioned to fight effectively but that his troops bolted as soon as the Confederate skirmishers advanced and no fight was made at all. These claims were proven untrue, but were consistent with Barlow's contempt for the men he led.[30] A reasonable examination of the overwhelming numbers of the Confederates and the vulnerability of the Federal position makes it evident no troops could have sustained this devastating blitz. Confederate general Richard Ewell reported an "obstinate contest." General Early described the fight as short and hot.[31] General Gordon later wrote that "under the concentrated fire from front and flank, the marvel is that any escaped."[32] Barlow was picked up by Confederates, taken into the woods, and left on a bed of leaves. He was then picked up by Union prisoners and carried to the Benner farmhouse, where the 17th Connecticut had earlier skirmished in the orchard. Barlow was told by Confederate surgeons who attended him at that field hospital that his wound was mortal.[33]

It was impossible for Barlow's First Division to withstand the Confederate onslaught. Whether he had realized it, and regardless of whether he admitted it, Barlow had placed his men in an untenable and indefensible position. The salient of his line created a vulnerable outward bulge, with both flanks in the air and indefensible, the thin Federal line woefully outnumbered by Confederates by more than three to one. The effect of Confederates converging on his line from three sides led to an inevitable catastrophe.[34] For the men in these Eleventh Corps regiments the scene was unbearably reminiscent of the humiliating May disaster at Chancellorsville that they had suffered two months earlier.

With the rebel yell, Doles's and Gordon's brigades attacked von Gilsa's three regiments along Rock Creek, throwing them into disarray and full retreat. Von Gilsa's men broke and ran, charging up the knoll. These same "Dutchmen" were the first to "run" at Gettysburg as they had at Chancellorsville. They ran through the Federals at the top of the knoll, breaking up the men there, with the Confederates following hotly after them. William Warren wrote after the war, "A German regiment came back hooting and halooing, right through our lines, which broke our regiment up and scattered us." In his diary he wrote, "The Dutchmen run right through our regt. And broke us up."[35] J. Henry Blakeman, Company D, wrote, "The rebel infantry advanced, and we formed in line of battle to meet them. No one who was there will forget the 'Mein Gott, let me go' of the Dutchmen of the first Brigade, who broke and rushed back on our line, and the vain endeavor of our men to stop them. Away they went like a flock of sheep with a dog after them."[36] The ethnic implications of the description of the action are clear. To the Yankee boys of the 17th Connecticut, it was the Germans who ran first. Indeed, despite the negative ethnic overtones of these writings, the six remaining 17th Connecticut companies on the knoll, along with the 75th Ohio, would make a stubborn, if very brief, stand against the Confederate assault that inevitably overwhelmed them.[37] Many officers and men would be killed, wounded, and taken prisoner; a lucky few fled through the town, escaping capture to reform at the foot of Cemetery Hill.

As von Gilsa's men fled through the 17th line at the top of the knoll, Lieutenant Colonel Fowler remained on his white horse despite his officers' entreaties to dismount. Fowler faced his Connecticut regiment toward the enemy and rode to the front of his men swinging his sword. He then gave his last order: "Now Seventeenth, do your duty. Forward, double quick! Charge bayonets!" With a yell the 17th charged to the top of the knoll. Many men of the regiment witnessed Fowler's horrific death. Hit in the head by artillery shrapnel, Fowler was killed instantly, his blood and brains flying onto Adjutant H. Whitney Chatfield, who was also on horseback alongside Fowler when he was struck. Chatfield's horse was killed. A ball went through Chatfield's hat, another passed through his sleeve, his haversack was torn to pieces, and the Revolutionary sword Chatfield carried (perhaps his grandfather's) was hit and its blade snapped off below the hilt.[38]

H. Whitney Chatfield was eighteen years old and working as a bank clerk when he enlisted as a private in Company G in August 1862. He was promoted to sergeant major in April 1863 and promoted again to lieutenant in June 1863 for his gallantry at Chancellorsville. On the afternoon of July 1, still stunned by Fowler's devastating death, Chatfield—covered in Fowler's blood and brains—joined Sergeant Major Betts in attempting to rescue Fowler's body in the face of the enemy, but they had to abandon it. Fowler's body was never identified or recovered. Young Chatfield was always a great favorite of the regiment. On February 5, 1865, at Dunn's Lake, Florida, Chatfield would be killed in a hand-to-hand encounter with the enemy. He was shot through the body trying to cut his way through Confederate attackers. He was twenty-one years old. His body was recovered and

Lieutenant H. Whitney Chatfield. (Connecticut Historical Society)

buried at Mountain Grove Cemetery in Bridgeport, Connecticut, with military and Masonic honors.[39]

Private William F. Otis, Company C. Warren noted this photograph was taken at parole camp in Annapolis, Maryland, after Otis was released from Belle Isle in Richmond. (Bridgeport History Center)

Almost immediately after Fowler was hit, Captain James E. Moore was killed. Captain Wilson French and Lieutenant Henry Quien were wounded, along with many others of the 17th. The fighting was desperate and hand-to-hand, with opposing color bearers often less than fifty paces apart.[40] Confederates were rolling up the Yankee brigade and taking prisoners. Any Federal who paused was scooped up by the advancing Confederates and captured along with the wounded. Amid the chaos Private William F. Otis, Company C, a hatter from Danbury, was captured while trying to retrieve the fallen Captain Moore's sword.[41] Otis would be imprisoned at Richmond's Belle Isle prison camp with other Federals captured at Gettysburg.

General Ames managed to control his battered brigade and retreat through the turmoil in fairly good order to establish a second line near the Alms House. Gordon's Georgians pushed the Federals off the knoll. More and more Confederates poured into the fight. General Harry Hays's fabled Louisiana Tigers pushed forward toward the Alms House buildings over the shrieking din and detritus of battle. Dead and wounded men and dead and wounded horses, equipment, and everything a soldier could drop was strewn across the field. The Tigers plowed through pockets of resistance as retreating Yankees stopped and fired periodically to try to delay the advance as they were pushed toward the town until the Federal retreat became a general rout.[42]

Major Brady's field report from July 4, 1863 summed up the action on the knoll:

> *The remainder of the regiment (six companies), under Lieutenant-Colonel Fowler, advanced with the other regiments of the brigade to the left and front of the town and directly in rear of the One Hundred and Seventh Ohio volunteers, in close column by division; were ordered to the front; notwithstanding the rush to the rear of troops directly in advance—until ordered by the brigade commander to fall back, which order was obeyed in good order, the men loading and firing as they fell back.*
>
> *Lieutenant-Colonel Fowler was killed when the regiment advanced and deployed. Captain Moore was killed about this time, and Captain French and Lieutenant Quinn* [sic] *were wounded and many of the men were killed, wounded and taken prisoners.*[43]

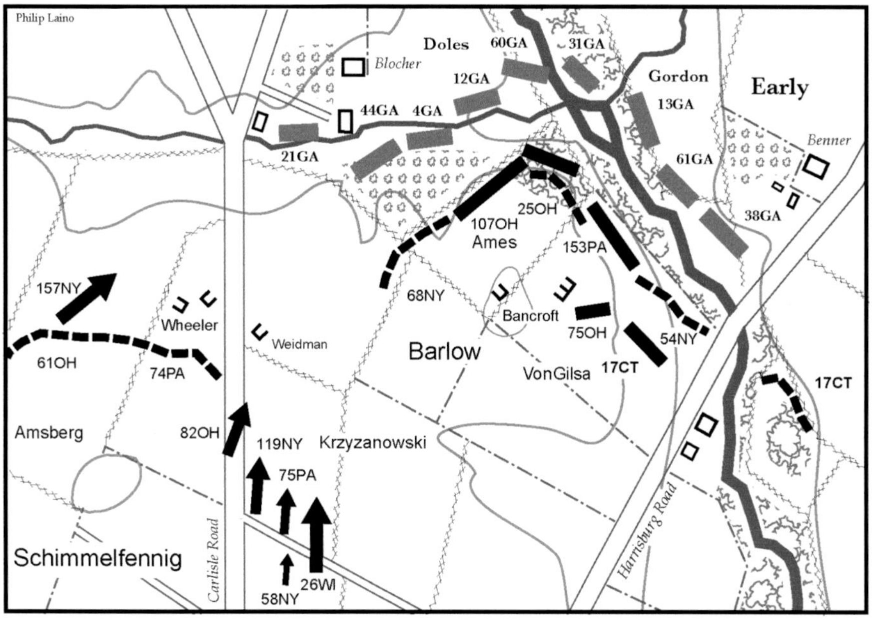

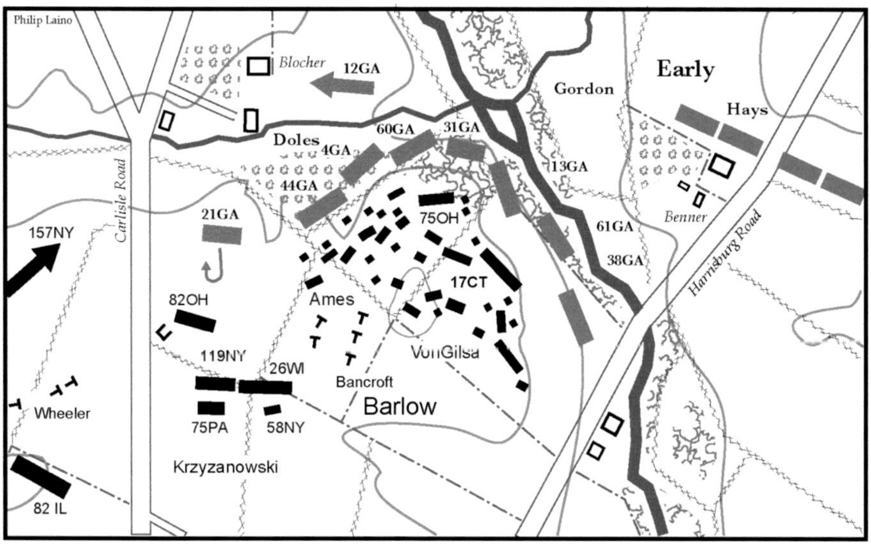

Top: the clash at Blocher's Knoll begins; bottom: Barlow's division is smashed and ousted from Blocher's Knoll.

Barlow's division was overextended and aligned in an awkward half circle with open flanks vulnerable to Confederate attack. The outnumbered line wavered and crumbled. Barlow was badly wounded and carried off. Many regimental commanders were killed or wounded. As Doles and Gordon pressed forward, Ames and von Gilsa's troops broke to the rear. Many Federal soldiers were killed, wounded, or captured. The 75th Ohio and six companies of the 17th Connecticut made a brief, courageous, and futile stand against the overwhelming numbers. Both regiments were flanked on both ends of their lines. The division began a full retreat as the Confederate tide rolled over it. Ames and von Gilsa's attempts to rally their men at the Alms House were futile and the Federals were swept from the field. Barlow's division suffered more than 45 percent casualties.[44]

Eleventh Corps resistance on Blocher's Knoll was finished. Walking wounded streamed toward the Alms House buildings and into the town, and many of the Eleventh Corps wounded were overtaken and made prisoners by the advancing Confederates and directed to the Alms House and other buildings in town. Federal soldiers packed the streets seeking to escape capture and attempting to locate and rejoin their regiments. Many became trapped in the alleys and narrow fenced yards behind the houses as they were hotly pursued by the Confederates. The streets became a churning, chaotic mass of confusion as both sides continued the fight. The blasting of artillery, gunfire, the screams of wounded men and wounded horses, the rebel yell, and the general roar of battle created a frightening pandemonium. Dr. Abraham Stout, assistant surgeon of the 153rd Pennsylvania, was captured trying to get through the town after leaving the Alms House. He was released by his captor and directed into town to open a hospital, which he did in the Trinity German Reformed Church at the corner of Stratton and High Streets. Stratton Street would become an escape route for fleeing Federals as well as a pathway for wounded to the Eleventh Corps hospital in this church.[45]

Dr. Stout gave a detailed account of how he opened the hospital at the church.

> [On July 1] *I was captured between the poor house and the town. Colonel D. B. Penn (7th Louisiana Infantry) saw me and dismounted. He walked by my side. . . . told me I was his prisoner, (and) taking me to the German Reformed Church, said to me, "You ought to take this church for a hospital." I said, "Yes. If it is not locked." But we found the doors unlocked and took possession. In less than half an hour, it was filled with wounded, mostly Union men. I was in attendance there three days . . . After that, we removed the wounded to the public school building.*[46]

The church had been built in 1851. It was a two-story brick building with a basement, an audience room, a gallery across one end with white plaster walls, and white-painted pews, pulpit, and woodwork.[47] This church and the public school next to it on High Street would be used as Eleventh Corps hospitals during the three days of Confederate occupation of the town. The church began receiving both Union and Confederate wounded as early as 11 a.m. on July 1.[48] Sixteen-year-old Eva Danner, who lived nearby on the town square, remembered that "The Wounded were carried into the lecture room of the church and there was so much amputating done there that the seats were covered with blood and they had to bore holes in the floor to let the blood run away." Another witness saw "men lying on boards on the tops of pews." Another noted that "The walls were splattered with blood and pews so badly soaked in it that later, they had to be replaced."[49]

As the shattered Federal units and artillery made their way into town pursued by the screaming Confederates, Major Brady described the combat and chaos in the streets prosaically in his July 4 field report. Despite his straightforward recounting of the regiment's role, his descriptions are gripping.

The location of the German Reformed Church on the corner of Stratton Street and High Street made it a natural destination for wounded Eleventh Corps soldiers seeing shelter in the town.
(Ron Pershio Collection)

When the regiment reached the town, the four companies under Major Brady were still skirmishing with the enemy and remained so until Brigadier General Ames sent an aide with orders for Major Brady to return with his command and assume command of the regiment, he being the only field officer of the regiment present. Upon arriving in town, Major Brady assumed command of the regiment and reported immediately to Brigadier-General Ames for instructions. The enemies were at this time advancing rapidly through the town. The regiment was immediately deployed in the streets and fired several volleys into the ranks of the enemy, which thinned their ranks and retarded their advance. We kept the enemy from advancing through the town until ordered to clear the street of our men for the purpose of planting a battery. The battery not being placed in position as intended, and the regiment being in line on the sidewalk, the enemy took advantage of this, and, with a superior force, rushed through

> *the main street, which compelled us to fall back, which we did reluctantly, but not without contesting the ground inch by inch.*
>
> *As we retreated, we loaded, halted, and poured destructive volleys into their ranks, which cleared the main street of them several times but we found the enemy too many for us. They poured in from every street in overwhelming numbers, which broke our ranks. Upon arriving near the battery on Cemetery Hill the regiment was halted and formed in line of battle fronting the town.*[50]

As the remnants of the 17th Connecticut escaped through the town and gathered on East Cemetery Hill, General Howard thought they were one of his German regiments. "Seeing the color sergeant and guard as they came between me and the stone wall, near the edge of the city I called out, 'Sergeant, plant your flag down there in that stone wall,'" Howard remembered. "Not recognizing me the sergeant said impulsively: 'All right, if you will go with me I will!' Whereupon I took the flag, accompanied by Rogers Howard's aide and the sergeant and his men, set it above the wall. That flag served to rally the regiment, always brave and energetic, and other troops."[51]

Second Lieutenant Albert Peck, Company D, wrote of the harrowing retreat through the town from Blocher's Knoll on the afternoon of July 1 and how the survivors were positioned on East Cemetery Hill by General Howard himself:

> *We were soon cut to pieces . . . we fell back into the town, where we met our skirmishers and formed in the side street for a while, but we did not remain there long, as the rebel force was too strong for us and we fell back to Cemetery Hill and reformed along a stone wall, near where the reservoir now stands, with but a fragment of our regiment left. I can tell you, the loss of the brave Colonel Fowler and Captain Moore took some of the zeal out of our boys for a while and when we were ordered forward after reforming on the hill, there was a little hesitation until, I think, General Howard took our colors and moved forward, and our boys followed with a cheer.*[52]

Lt. Albert Peck, Company D.
(Bridgeport History Center)

Major Brady described re-forming of the regiment on East Cemetery Hill.

> *About this time Major-General Howard, who was in the thickest of the battle, regardless of danger, asked if he had troops brave enough to advance to a stone wall across a lot toward the town, and said he would lead them. We replied, "Yes, the Seventeenth Connecticut will," and*

> *advanced at once to the place indicated, remained a few moments, and again advanced across another lot still nearer the town and behind a rail fence at the upper end of the town, which position we held until late in the evening, exposed to a galling fire from the enemy's sharpshooters, when the whole regiment was ordered out on picket and performed that duty until 2 o'clock of the 2d instant.*[53]

Lieutenant Peck wrote of picket duty that evening.

> *There was a detail of 100 men for picket from our regiment that night, but we were unable to furnish the full detail. . . . I was on the detail as subordinate; do not remember what other officer was with us. We were posted in an apple orchard close to the edge of town, with our videttes posted along by a board and rail fence. We were ordered to be very watchful and vigilant, as our troops were expecting to make an attack on town that night; I don't think I got any sleep that night.*[54]

Peck would not be the only sleepless soldier on Cemetery Hill that night. All were subjected to intense sniper fire from houses and other places of cover up and down the streets and fields. The "galling fire," as Brady termed it, was maddening and frightful in the way men were picked off at random. This firing from houses along Baltimore Street would harass the regiment for the next three days.

CHAPTER 5

Voices from the First Day of Battle

This chapter presents accounts written by the men of the 17th Connecticut about their experiences on the first day of the battle of Gettysburg, as compiled by William H. Warren. These are the words of the men who fought that day—men who lost friends, were wounded, were captured, suffered, and survived. The men would remember forever the trauma of Gettysburg. Their experience in battle would mark them indelibly. These accounts were their attempt to communicate and document what was difficult for them, or anyone, to express within the confines of written language.

These firsthand accounts are priceless. They comprise a sharing of the past with our present. The words of these survivors are a precious legacy from them to us in the twenty-first century. These men tried to communicate what they saw, thought, and felt on the battlefield. The memories of old soldiers are often criticized or devalued as distorted by time, emotion, and other factors. But this is as close as we in the present can come to witnessing the battle and understanding what they experienced. This is above all their story, their legacy to us. Rather than find fault with these words, rather than criticize as we examine and dissect them, it is more valuable to read them to gain an understanding of the magnitude of what these men experienced. Despite the limitations of language, individual writing ability, the fog of battle, or the vagaries of memory, their words bear witness to Gettysburg. Many of the accounts are straightforward and prosaic, documenting the experiences of what they saw, knew, and felt—and admitting what they did not know or remember. Some accounts are tinted with Victorian prose that seems to us labored, flowery, or posturing, but we must look beyond that. Some accounts are greatly flawed but still offer insight into the circumstances of the battle that can illuminate and enhance the record of the scholarship of Gettysburg. These accounts, compiled by Warren, are the unfinished work of his lifetime. He would continue to correspond, collect, compile, and edit these accounts from his comrades up to the time of his death in 1918. Warren would explain in the preface to his "Gettysburg Volume 3" his rationale for collecting the experiences of his fellow soldiers in the 17th Connecticut.

> *To secure the varied experiences of the wounded, of those taken prisoner, as well as to gather up the stories of those whose voiceless lips could speak no more their hardships and sufferings, while a work of love, has been a task exceedingly difficult and trying. I feel that no words of mine can portray the details of this battle, which we saw, and part of which we were, so have given the different accounts, as written by Comrades, who were also eye-witnesses, so that by the mouths of several every word may be established, and correct statements given.*

THE BATTLE OF GETTYSBURG AS SEEN BY THE WRITER

WEDNESDAY, JULY 1, 1863

William Henry Warren was born March 28, 1842. Warren was listed in the 1860 census as a railroad hand living in Danbury, Connecticut. In August 1862, as the Civil War raged, the twenty-year-old Warren enlisted in the 17th Connecticut Volunteer Infantry, joining Company C with other young men from Danbury. Warren, like many others, would see his Civil War service as the defining adventure of his life. To these men, their service in saving the Union was a source of immense pride. They went home to become active in veterans' groups that commemorated their service and honored their comrades who sacrificed their lives. Warren was taken prisoner on the first day of Gettysburg and sent to Belle Isle prison in Richmond. He was paroled on August 25, 1863, and returned to his regiment. He was mustered out of service on July 19, 1865, at Hilton Head, South Carolina, with the rest of the 17th Connecticut. Warren returned home to resume civilian life. In 1866 he married Delia Campbell Keeler and they had seven children. The 1880 census shows the family living in New Haven, Connecticut, and Warren's profession listed as painter.[1]

Private William Warren, Company C. (Courtesy of the William H. Warren Family)

William Warren never fulfilled his lifelong ambition to write and publish the regimental history of the 17th Connecticut Volunteer Infantry. He was unsuccessful in its completion but devoted himself obsessively to the task until his death. Warren was unceasing in his efforts to compile and collect accounts of the regiment's service and experiences. He corresponded widely with the officers and men of the 17th Connecticut, soliciting their written versions of events in camp, on the march, and on the battlefield. He compiled photographs, letters, firsthand accounts, and numerous other sources. Warren worked on the manuscript diligently until the end of his life. He passed away on June 5, 1918, and was interred in Wooster Cemetery in Danbury. His tombstone reads, "Father, William H. Warren, Co C 17th Inf. Conn Vols, Died June 5, 1918, AE 76."[2] Warren's account of his experiences on the first day of Gettysburg, July 1, 1863, described the difficult conditions of the march, how the men dropped to the ground in exhaustion after rushing through Gettysburg to the sound of the guns, their exhaustion, thirst, and hunger, and their dread that combat was imminent.

> *After passing through the town we halted in a meadow by the roadside, close column in mass, for a rest. Orders were then given us to load, and many of the boys discharged their pistols in the air to see if they were in working order as prospects were very flattering that we would soon have a chance to use them, for before we entered the town, it was passed through the lines that we were to have a fight here, and we could hear the discharge of musketry and artillery to our left and front. We could also see the cavalry fighting in our front and see that they were being driven back. Before we hardly had rested a moment in the meadow, Lieut. Col. Fowler wanted to know what companies would volunteer to go and feel for the enemy; he said he only wanted those companies who would volunteer, which were Companies "F" first, "A" second, "K" third and "B" fourth. We of company "C" thought there was no use of our going to feel for the enemy, for the cavalry that was in a small piece of woods about a mile in our front were, as I have said, being driven back and the fight had already commenced, so finally the companies did not go. We stayed in this lot about half an hour, lying flat on the ground, to try and get a little rest, then arose and double-quicked it out of the lot, and across the road into another lot. We were completely used up by this time. After fooling around about another half or three quarters of an hour, advancing and falling back, over fences and back again, flat on the ground and up again, rest became imperative.*
>
> *While we were resting, I took off my knapsack and threw it away, but took out my portfolio before I did so. While lying flat on the ground on our faces to avoid the enemy's fire as much as possible, solid shot (I think it was) struck about ten feet from us, digging a hole in the ground and throwing the dirt all around, then bounded over the regiment, burying itself in the ground in the next lot. The rebs had one battery in good range on us. After we got that shell introduction we got up and got out of that, over the fence into another lot, expecting every moment while on the move to get hit, but none of us did at that time.*
>
> *While our regiment was going across the open lot to the front where they were then fighting, a German regiment came back hooting and*

halooing, right through our lines, which broke our regiment up and scattered us, [These may have been men from the 153rd Pennsylvania, a nine-month German-speaking regiment of von Gilsa's Brigade that broke under heavy Confederate pressure.] *and while I was passing between an officer and his company, there being plenty of room between us, the officer (who I am very sure was drunk) raised his sword over his head, swinging it around, cursing and swearing at me, telling me to get out of that or he would split my head open. I will leave it to the reader to decide what I did. Finally, we managed to get as far as Barlow's Knoll where we made a stand and fired a few volleys. I had fired only a few times when feelings came over me that cannot be described. It appeared, as near as I can tell, that I stood there for some time all alone, no one as I could see near me, but enough went up with me. The rebs were near us and still advancing and with more men than we had. Finding myself in the above described position I fell back a few feet until I was stopped by an officer. The whole regiment was also falling back. Corporal Scott tried to rally portions of the regiment, and cried out to us, "Don't run, boys," so we stopped and I partly loaded my gun just where I was stopped, but before I got loaded the regiment or brigade again started to run, so of course I followed on. I had gone but a short distance when I saw Rufus Warren, who was ahead of me, fall the opposite way; he was running at the time but turning half way round he threw up his hands, crying, "oh dear, help me, help me," and fell to the ground. I was powerless to help him as we were all on the move to the rear with the rebs close to our heels and I did not know what moment I would share the same fate as he. I still kept moving on but had not gone but a short distance before a bullet cut a hole in my left trousers leg, just below the knee. I did not stop to investigate but kept on, glancing at my leg to see if the blood was running. The ball had not touched the flesh but simply torn a hole about three inches long and an inch wide. Bullets were then coming*

Corporal George Scott, Company C, tried to rally the men. (Bridgeport History Center)

Private Rufus Warren of Ridgefield was severely wounded on July 1. His left leg was amputated, and he died at the Eleventh Corps hospital at the George Spangler Farm on July 17, 1863.

in a shower and before I got across the field, I was hit in the right shoulder blade, which almost knocked me over. I thought surely, I was wounded, then I imagined the blood was running down my back, but I had made up my mind to keep on until I had crossed that large open lot and found a shelter, which I reached at length behind a haystack.

I was so exhausted that I had difficulty in arriving at the protection, where I threw myself on the ground more dead than alive. I found an officer there wounded in the back also a member of the 153rd Pennsylvania, who was wounded in the right leg below the knee. He was very weak from the loss of blood in crossing the field, and said to me, "My wound is a bad one," and I could see it was. Horses and men kept coming in while I lay there, one horse in particular attracted my attention, an artillery horse, having all his harness on, and a deep bad wound in him, from which the blood was running profusely. It pained him so he could not stand still but a moment at a time, so on he went and that was the last I saw of him. The rebel skirmishers and line of battle were steadily advancing while the bullets were coming thicker and faster. We soon found that our protection was of little avail and we must soon leave that position or run the risk of being killed for the battle was growing more and more fierce all the time. I therefore decided to move still further back and made for a barn shed about two rods away, leaving the officer to look out for himself. I reached the shed in safety and was soon joined by James Hannon, who came in saying, "Hullo, Bill, you here." "Yes," I replied, "and wounded in the back, I can feel the blood run."

In about half an hour the advance skirmish line, that nearly reached across the city, came up and we were all taken prisoners. One of the rebs

One of the thousands of dead horses on the Gettysburg battlefield. (Library of Congress)

with gun raised to his shoulder, full cocked, took deliberate aim at me and said with a very bad oath, "Go to the rear double quick or you will find a bullet after you." So we went without any further orders. Back of the skirmish line was a line of battle, and back of that was the rebel army. After passing these different lines we went over the same lot that less than an hour ago we had travelled under different circumstances; then we were going for a fight, now we were as docile as lambs. We reported to a Major. In crossing the field I saw John Benedict of Company "C" lying flat on his stomach on the ground, with all his accoutrements on, and as I passed I said, "Hullo, John, is that you? Are you wounded?" "Yes," he said, "help me, take off my knapsack and other things." While I stopped but a moment to help him, a reb saw me and told me with an oath to go to the rear or he would shoot me, so I said, "John, I am sorry I cannot help you but I have got to go to the rear or I will be shot." It made me feel bad to leave one of my own company in that position without assistance, but such was the case. I wished him all the good luck possible and left him, and I did not see him again until I returned home from the war.

The different sights I saw on the field are beyond description, of the wounded, dead and dying. I saw one man with his face on the ground and his stomach up, his head was under his body; another man lay partly on his side and from his mouth, nose and ears ran a pool of blood; also scattered here and there were those dead who had been killed in different ways, where about an hour before I was myself fighting perhaps side by side with those who are now sleeping in death. During all the excitement of getting into the fight and out of it, I lost everything I had, so in crossing the field again the thought came to me that I must get a rubber blanket, a tent and what other necessary things I could. I saw a rubber blanket and went for it but being mostly covered with blood and partly under a dead man, I left it and went for another. This one I found too dirty, so I discarded it and went for another one that had blood on one end. At a neighboring brook I washed the stains off and proceeded with it. On the other side of this brook was an open lot and here we formed in line near a stone wall adjacent to the road. Lieutenant Bartram joined us here. All the afternoon we lay here while prisoners were continually coming in and swelling our numbers. During the time we amused ourselves watching the rebel army advancing and stragglers going to the front. Some artillery passed us with the horses on a gallop as fast as they could go. One of the drivers, who seemed to be a good-natured, jolly sort of man, took off his hat and swung it with his whip over his head, and with a smile on his face said, "Whip you in your own state, hey? Whip you in your own state, hey?" He seemed to be very much pleased over it, but I wonder what he thought before he got through. From this lot we marched out into the road a little way, then turned into a barnyard where we stayed about two hours, then moved off on the road leading to Middletown, and marched into a very nice open lot, where the grass was about a foot high, where we stayed all night. Nearby was a red house and barn as we were just entering the lot, we marched in single file and were counted, our whole number being 3450 prisoners, taken all in one day. These figures were official. I received them from one of the officers who assisted in counting us. The bars were taken down and two rebel officers, one on each side of the entrances, counted us as we passed into the lot, putting a hand on each shoulder.[3]

There was a large number of prisoners, and I was one of them, being captured on the first day of the fight. A parole was offered us, which the enemy assured us was not legal, and if our people did not accept it and put us in the field and we were again captured, we would be shot. Only a small number of our regiment accepted this parole but we determined to go to Richmond and take our chances with starvation. We moved from Gettysburg July 4th, but only went a short distance on account of the road being crowded with the retiring enemy and its wounded.*[4]

*Warren and many others from the 17th Connecticut ended the first day of battle as prisoners of war. Many of these officers and men believed the parole the Confederates offered on the field was illegal, not officially sanctioned, and dishonorable. Warren, and others who left accounts of their capture experiences the first day at Gettysburg, noted that few Federal prisoners accepted the parole. The Confederates themselves, as Warren wrote, believed the parole would not be recognized and frankly told their prisoners if the Federal army did not recognize the parole, and they were again captured, they would be shot. During the Civil War the official protocol mandated that released prisoners had to be officially "exchanged" before they returned to the ranks.

LIEUTENANT (LATER CAPTAIN) MILTON H. DANIELS

Lieutenant Milton Daniels would survive the battle. Born in 1837 in Allegany County, New York, Daniels was a mercantile clerk living in Danbury with his wife and son when he enlisted in the 17th. His first enlistment was in 1861 as a corporal in Company I, 3rd Connecticut. When his three-month enlistment with the 3rd expired after First Bull Run, he re-enlisted in Company E, 7th New York Cavalry until the following March when he mustered out again. In July 1862, he and his former captain from the 3rd Connecticut, James Moore, raised Company C in Danbury for the 17th Connecticut. Moore was again captain of the company and Daniels was first lieutenant. Daniels would be promoted to captain on July 15, 1863,

Lieutenant Milton H. Daniels, Company C. (Bridgeport History Center)

following Gettysburg. Daniels's nineteen-year old brother, William, an unmarried carpenter from Danbury, also mustered into Company C as a sergeant.

The Daniels boys left their widowed mother, Betsey, behind in Danbury when they departed with the 17th Connecticut in September 1862. She would pass away on November 10, 1863, while both her boys were away in the army. Daniels served in the 17th until his resignation in March 1864. He was suffering from the effects of a shell wound received at the siege of Charleston (Fort Wagner). He stayed in Florida, working as clerk of the court at Enterprise, Volusia County; as a bookkeeper in Jacksonville; and in the boot and shoe business. His first wife, Amanda Hoskins, whom he married in 1858, passed away in Port Orange, Florida, in 1869. Daniels left Florida for Indianapolis in 1874 and worked there in life insurance and real estate. He was also a pension attorney and justice of the peace. In 1877 he married Charlotte S. Warren. He remained in Indianapolis and was involved in politics, veterans' affairs, the Masons, and other fraternal organizations. He passed away in 1904.[5]

Sergeant William L. Daniels, Company C. (Bridgeport History Center)

On June 30 Daniels described how his close friend and captain, James Moore, shared with him his premonition of death. Daniels sought to reassure Moore. The next morning on the march to Gettysburg, Moore was lethargic, and Daniels was deeply troubled by his captain's premonition.

> *Well, I can't tell it, language fails. . .* [Captain Moore] *tottered to the head of the company, and marched in silence, until way ahead we saw the puff of a shell, then the report, "Now we are in for it." Soon we heard the noise of battle, and the aide hurried from the front with orders to hurry up. Soon we reached the top of a hill and looking across the valley, we saw the battle (line) of the rebels and Reynold's corps. When we first saw them our boys were running, a duplicate of Bull Run, but they forced the rebs back, and it was pro and con until we were out of sight and in line of battle ourselves; we were in place at rest. Captain, Moore dropped on the ground, but in a few moments the rebels were giving us their*

Sergeant William Oscar Dauchy, Company C, was a married hatter from Danbury. He was killed in action the first day at Gettysburg. He was twenty-nine years old and left behind a widow and a seven-year-old son.[6] (Bridgeport History Center)

salutations, he sprang to his feet, but was instantly shot by two balls in the forehead. Then the Orderly Sergeant (William) Oscar Dauchy dropped, Quien was wounded in the right hand, then another and another, when we broke—every man for himself.

We rallied at Cemetery Hill. On calling roll of Company "C", we found missing every sergeant, every corporal but Corporal Scott, and only twenty-five of us out of sixty-five when we went into the field. Our brigade was rallied and placed in line immediately to the right of the road leading from Cemetery Hill through town, the regiment resting on the road, and the whole brigade immediately in front of cemetery Hill. General Adelbert Ames, our brigadier, had headquarters in the room over the main cemetery gate. We held this position the first night and the second day; we were withdrawn about 10:00 p.m. of the second, further back, to rest and eat a hardtack, that is those who had them. We cursed our quartermaster and begged of General Ames to make him bring us some rations; we must have gotten some but I do not remember how.[7]

*Yours, in F.C. & L.**
M. H. Daniels

*Daniels closed his letter to Warren with the traditional initials *F. C. & L.* for Fraternity, Charity, and Loyalty, the watchwords of the Grand Army of the Republic and the traditional closing among the brotherhood of comrades who fought for and saved the Union. Many of the letters among veterans are closed with these initials, which were important ideals to comrades corresponding with other members of the organization.

CORPORAL AARON W. LEE WOUNDED

Aaron W. Lee was born in 1831 in Ridgefield. The thirty-two-year-old farmer enlisted as a corporal in Company G, 17th Connecticut in summer 1862. Lee would be badly wounded at Gettysburg on July 1 but would live to return to his regiment. He would be promoted to sergeant in September 1864 and would be mustered out with his regiment in July 1865 at Hilton Head. After the war he returned to Ridgefield and his farm. The 1870 Ridgefield Agricultural Schedule Census lists Lee as farming 65 improved acres, with his farm worth $3,000 and equipment of $150 and another $1,000 in livestock. He was growing Indian corn and oats and was obviously a successful farmer. He would represent Ridgefield as first selectman and as the Republican state representative in 1877 and in 1880.[8] He remained active in veterans' affairs and

Corporal Aaron W. Lee, Company G. (Bridgeport History Center)

among the 17th Connecticut survivors. He passed away in his hometown on October 20, 1890, at age sixty.

Aaron Lee would write to his father, Edwin Lee, from his bed at Satterlee Hospital in West Philadelphia on July 15, 1863.[9] The hospital at Forty-fourth Street and Baltimore Avenue had opened June 9, 1862. It was a massive complex that would become the largest hospital in the world. The hospital had posted visiting hours and patient services, including nurses from the Sisters of Charity on call, plus a sutler's store, barbershop, a printing office, and a band.[10] Lee was transferred to Satterlee Hospital from the Eleventh Corps hospital at the Spangler Farm in Gettysburg.

> *WEST PHILADELPHIA HOSPITAL, JULY 15, 1863*
> *Dear Father*
>
> *As I am caged up in the Hospital at last and nothing to do but eat my meals and read the papers and think over matters and things. I will occupy a part of the afternoon in writing to you as I know you will be glad to hear how I am getting along. I got hit with a rifle ball in my left thigh going clean through and making an ugly sort of a hole but did not go deep enough to hit the bone. It is getting fine. We have first rate care here and good Doctors and plenty to eat—no reasons why a man should not be contented. I always had a dread of going to the Hospital. I always took them to be a sort of States Prison starved out butcher shop but I have come to the conclusion in the few days I have been here, it is a very comfortable place for the wounded soldiers. We get the best of care and everything for our comfort. There has been some hard fighting since the first.*
>
> *We left Emmitsburg on the 1st about 8 O'clock. We did not expect to get into a fight before the next day but when we got within 3 or 4 miles of Gettysburg hearing the bull Dogs barking and the order to Double quick, we knew then we were going right in. Just as we entered the town the Rebs sent a shell over our heads just to wake us up a little. We made quick time through the city and came to a halt just long enough to get our skirmishers out, then we started for the field of action on Double quick. In order to get to our position in line we had to cross the range of two Rebel batteries throwing solid shot and shell and some of the Boys said they threw Rail Road Iron. Well there was some tall time made and some pretty low brows until we got out of range of those batteries. However we got through without losing a man. There was a little rise of ground between us and their guns—the solid shot would strike the ground and throw a spray of dirt over us. We got our position on the point of a piece of woods. We had not been there but a few minutes when they opened on us again with shell and cut us up right and left. We got the order to change position which was done in good order. About this time the infantry came in sight. We got the order to charge. We started with a good will expecting to have a hand to hand fight with the 'Johnny Rebs.' Just as we got to the point of woods and about 5 rods*

from them the 153 Pennsylvania on our left broke and ran between us and the Rebs and mixing up with our regiment causing some little confusion for a minute but the boys went to work loading and firing as fast as they could. The first Corps was on our left. The Rebs began to turn their left and at the same time flank us on our right—some had to fall back—they had three men to our one engaged at that time, but was all done in good order. Things had got to be considerable interesting by this time. There were two lines of men drawn up from 8 to 10 yards apart. We had fallen back almost to the edge of the town. At this place some Major had rallied a few men around him and tried to have the whole line stop. I stopped at this place not noticing whether the regiment stopped or not and fired about 2 rounds before I missed our boys. By this time the Rebs were about three rods from us, we commenced to fall back again. I had just drawn a good sight on a strapping big Reb and fired and got hit myself at the same time. I looked around and seeing a barn close by I took my rifle for a crutch and drew myself for it. Here I saw Col. Harris of the 75th. He said they had taken the Alms house for a Hospital and I stopped there and in a few minutes the Rebs came in and took us prisoners. Edwin D. Pickett must have been wounded about the same time as I was. I did not think he would die that night. I lay down within six feet of him. The next morning I woke up and spoke to him but got no answer. I went to him and found him dead. The Rebs used us well while we were in their hands but our men took possession of the town before I was paroled. Our captain was paroled but he was not in the same Hospital with me. I suppose he is home now. He will go to Ridgefield before he comes back. [Lee refers to Capt. Wilson French of Company G, who was sent home by train to Bridgeport on July 8 to recuperate from his wounds. As a company officer, French was expected to correspond with and visit the families of the men of his company who were killed and wounded in the battle.]

Colonel Andrew Harris of the 75th Ohio would assume command of Ames's brigade on July 1 after Barlow was wounded and Ames assumed command of the division. Colonel Harris was well known to the men of the 17th, which was brigaded with the 75th Ohio. (USAHEC)

We had rather a rough time getting from Gettysburg here. We left about dusk—was on the cars all night—got into Baltimore about nine o'clock the next day. The Citizens of Baltimore came near killing us with kindness. We left about noon—got into Wilmington about sunset. Here men, women and children came flocking around the cars with baskets full of all kinds of provisions, tobacco and Ale, Beer, lemonade etc. We fetched up in Philadelphia about 10 o'clock the next day, the 9th. We came here and how long we shall be shut up here I don't know. I was in hopes I could have got a furlow to come home but there is a poor sight for it at present. I have not heard anything from the Regiment since I left Gettysburg.

I see by the paper the 11th Corps is at Funkstown [Md.]. *Gen. Mead* [sic] *is getting Lee in rather a tight spot. I hope he may never get out. I wish I could be with the Boys now. If I could have gone through these battles to the last day and then got hit I would not care so much. As it is I have lost all the fun this time but we have to take things as they come. Perhaps it was best I got hit the first day but I would liked to see the Rebs cross the river. If they get across they will probably have a fight tomorrow and I don't doubt that Mead* [sic] *will give them a good sound thrashing and learn them better than to trespass on free soil again. There were quite a lot of Rebs brought to this Hospital today. This Hospital covers about 12 acres of ground and a very handsome place. I believe I have taxed your patience long enough so I will close.*[11]

The Adams County Alms House (or poor house) consisted of several buildings and structures that housed the poor, insane, and other wards of the county. It was a working farm, infirmary, and asylum. Its location close to Barlow's Knoll, within sight of the first day's combat, made it one of the first Eleventh Corps hospitals at Gettysburg. Immediately after the battle began the Alms House offered shelter to the wounded, dead, and dying. (Gettysburg National Military Park)

THE DEATH OF ORDERLY SERGEANT EDWIN D. PICKETT

Orderly Sergeant Edwin Darling Pickett was a friend of Aaron Lee's from the same town, Ridgefield, and served with Lee in Company G. Pickett was twenty-eight years old when he died at Gettysburg. He left a wife, Sarah, and a two-year old son, Edwin William Starr Pickett. Edwin's brother Rufus Starr Pickett (who went by Starr) went to Gettysburg to recover his brother's body. According to Ridgefield diarist Anna Resseguie, news of Pickett's death reached Ridgefield on July 6. She wrote in her diary that Starr "searched some time among the dead at Gettysburg before he was found; his blanket was wrapped around him, his watch and pencil given by Starr were in his coat sleeve."[12] Starr brought Edwin's body home to Ridgefield. On the Sunday of his funeral, July 12, the churches suspended other services, and united in the tribute to his high personal character and his manly virtues.[13] Resseguie wrote that at Pickett's funeral, "a long precession of pedestrians, as well as carriages, followed his remains to the grave."[14] After the war it was Aaron Lee who proposed that Ridgefield's Grand Army of the Republic post be named for Pickett.[15]

William Warren would devote several pages in his manuscript to Orderly Sergeant Pickett's funeral, which he copied from an article printed in the local papers. On July 21, 1863, the *Norwalk Gazette* devoted an entire column to Pickett's funeral. The column was signed "Hieronymus." *"Seldom has a whole community been more deeply affected than was Ridgefield when it became known just after the Battle of Gettysburg that Edwin D. Pickett lost his life on the first day of that fierce contest."* Warren noted: *"His memory will be cherished while life lasts, by his fellow soldiers. . . . He left the richest of all legacies to his young wife and infant boy—the legacy of an unspotted name and of a record of noble daring and a noble death."*[16]

COPORAL JOHN BENEDICT WOUNDED

Corporal John Hempstead Benedict enlisted as a private in Company C, 17th Connecticut and was promoted to corporal in December 1862. He was listed in the 1860 census as a mason apprentice, boarding with the master mason he was apprenticed to in Danbury. Benedict would list his profession as mason/builder for the rest of his life. He passed away in 1921 at age eighty-one, and he is buried in Wooster Cemetery in Danbury.[17]

John Benedict wrote of himself in the third person in correspondence to William Warren.

Corporal John H. Benedict, Company C. (Courtesy Dale Call Collection)

Between Barlow's Knoll at Gettysburg, and the Poorhouse, were two open lots some 25 or 30 rods from the Knoll. While retreating across the open lot towards the Poorhouse, he was hit by a ball near the elbow, about (he thinks) 1:30 p.m. In trying to get over a fence and ditch both, he fell over and was rather in the rear of the rest, so someone cried out, "Come on, John." He started up in a hurry to get caught up and was loading at the same time, and then turned around to shoot, and while in the act of raising his gun to his shoulder, was struck. He kept on some two or three rods further and all the while losing blood, so by this time he began to feel faint and fell face foremost to the ground, with gun by his side that he had carried there in his left hand. He thinks he laid there about five minutes, but probably it was much longer as he became unconscious, and when he came to himself again he received a shot in the right leg, a wound about 14 inches long. The ball came from the direction of Barlow's Knoll.

Here he laid about half an hour, bullets flying thick and fast. The rebs on the Knoll came as far as Fence No. 1. then stopped and kept firing for a while, then ceased; then the prisoners came back over the field, of which W. H. Warren was one. The rebs that were at the fence were relieved there, and then moved off to some other part of the field, but while here they saw John and said to him, "We will take you back and lay you behind the fence, so if we fight this ground over again, you will not be so liable to be hit again," as he was lying there on low ground, so they carried him back over the ditch to fence #1, but he was wounded and fell near #2. They asked him, "What regiment?" "17th Conn." Said John. "Ha Ha!" that is right from Yankeedom," they replied; they thought they were fighting the

Sketch of Barlow's Knoll by Private Justus Silliman, Company H. (Bridgeport History Center)

Pennsylvania militia. The rebs asked John several questions about the army, as to what army it was, how many it numbered, where it was, etc. He gave them no satisfaction or consolation, so some of the officers said, "You are bad enough off now, being wounded, but if you were not wounded we would put an end to your existence soon." They then moved off.

Laid here by the fence until Friday afternoon, about dark. During Thursday some stragglers from the rebel army came along, and seeing John lay there in the hot rays of the sun, took four muskets and stuck the bayonets in the ground, then took a shelter tent and held it by the hammers of the guns. This formed a shade. All he had to eat this day was a piece of bread about as big as your hand that these stragglers had, which was simply flour and water stirred up together and baked which made it raw and solid. The rebs captured the flour in Gettysburg. Not a drop of water passed his lips that day and he suffered very much for the want of it. All the water he had Wednesday was a little that he had left in his canteen. He let his haversack hang from his neck and used it as a string for his wounded arm, then with the other hand and with one leg out stiff, he hitched along to a ditch that was about two feet deep, from two to four rods off. This took him about four or five hours to make the trip and get back again to his shade; he could not walk a step. He thought by getting to this ditch he might be able to get some water, but when he got there he found it was only mud and no water, so he took his tin cup and reaching over into the ditch filled it with mud, and putting it to his lips sucked out the moisture; it was thick and black, but he was willing to do anything to stop that hankering thirst. He had tried hard all day to get some water, by asking everyone that passed by him for some, but not a drink did he get.

John's feet had swelled so bad that the rebs could not pull his boots off, so they had to cut them off. Friday morning about 8 or 9 o'clock, a reb came along and said to John that he was looking for a canteen to get some water, and said, "Let me take yours and I will get you a canteen of water." So John did and expected never to see it again, but in about an hour he came back with it full; that did John more good than anything else. He stayed with John some two or three hours, and told him he would never go back into the rebel army again, but would go to New York or stay in the North somewhere. Finally, he said, "I guess I must go for there may be some rebel cavalry along by and by and take me for a deserter." The rebs detailed some of the Union prisoners to take care of the wounded. About 2 p.m. Friday, John was found by another party of men who gave him some bread. About 5 p.m. two Union men came with a wheelbarrow, and put a stick across the handles, then set John into it, facing the one wheeling him. The stick held up his legs, and while one wheeled the other held him up. He was wheeled to the Poorhouse shed, which was connected to the barn. Fred Goodale [Private Frederick W. Goodale, Company C, of Danbury] *came to see him as soon as he got to the shed and cut his coat and pants so that the wound could be dressed, which was directly done by two Union surgeons—one being a German, who handled him very carefully and tenderly. Inflammation set in and it swelled very badly so that it was thought at one time it would have to be cut off, but John begged so hard that one of them said, "We will do it up for you, and if we have to cut it off we can do it as well tomorrow." They then went off and that was the last John ever saw those two men. Towards evening a shower came up; laid here over night.*[18]

PRIVATE J. HENRY BLAKEMAN WOUNDED

James Henry Blakeman used his middle name all his life to distinguish himself from the many James Blakemans from whom he was descended, including his illustrious Revolutionary ancestors, in Stratford, Connecticut. He was born in 1841 in the Oronoque section of Stratford along the Housatonic River. Upon enlistment, Blakeman would list his profession as farmer and continue to do so his entire life. He and his cousin Selah Blakeman, and friends Stephen Crofut and Sylvester Rounds, from Huntington, would enlist in Company D, 17th Connecticut in August 1862. Crofut, a Stratford fisherman, was Henry's best friend and neighbor. The two had grown up together in Oronoque.

Private J. Henry Blakeman, Company D. (Bridgeport History Center)

From enlistment until Gettysburg, Henry, Stephen, Selah, and Sylvester were messmates and comrades. On the first day at Gettysburg the four would stand shoulder to shoulder on Barlow's Knoll. Stephen would be killed outright, and Henry and Syl Rounds badly wounded. Only Selah would survive unscathed to retreat with the regiment and fight the next evening on East Cemetery Hill. Henry would survive the war. He would spend eleven months in several hospitals until ultimately returning to his regiment in Florida as a musician for the rest of his enlistment. In 1866 he would return home to marry Amelia J. Burr, whom he had corresponded with throughout the war while she was a schoolteacher in Stepney. After the war he was a prosperous farmer in Stratford and prominent in civic affairs. He would hold almost every elected office in Stratford, was commander of the Elias Howe, Jr. GAR Post in Bridgeport, and would serve as a state legislator. He would remain active in civic and veteran affairs until his death in September 1918. Blakeman wrote to William Warren about his wounding in 1888.

Dear Comrade:— I well remember the hurried march from Emmitsburg the morning of July 1st 1863, and the singular feelings that creep through a person when the shot and shell begin to scream as they did when we reached Gettysburg—passed through the town and halted for a few minutes on the outskirts near the poorhouse, where most of the boys stripped themselves for business, then advanced and took position to support the battery that was shelling a rebel battery in the woods across Willoughby Run [actually Rock Creek]. *After a time, the rebel infantry advanced, and we formed in line of battle to meet them. No one who was there will forget the "Mein Gott, let me go" of the Dutchmen of the first Brigade,* [Von Gilsa's brigade, First Division, 153rd Pennsylvania] *who broke and rushed back on our line, and the vain endeavor of our men to stop them. Away they went like a flock of sheep with a dog after them, and in a very few minutes, we had business in earnest. While loading and firing to the best of my ability, (to use an Irish phrase) the first I knew I didn't know anything. Some unknown force seemed to whirl me around once or twice, the drop me all in a heap. How long I lay partly stupefied I could never tell, but when I tried to rise, someone close beside me said, "For God's sake, lie down," and taking a survey, I decided the advice was good, for our line had fallen back, and I was about halfway between the two lines of battle. The way bullets were flying from both ways was curious, thick as a hailstorm. I was shot through the left side—just grazing the top of the hip bone and passing close to the kidney. Almost the first sight to greet my eyes was the dead body of Stephen Crofut, shot through the head and lying only a few feet from me. We were playmates from boys and always tent mates while in the service.*

Very soon the rebel line came on and passed where I lay; then the bullets came all from one way, and I sheltered myself behind a large oak tree that stood very near where the 17th Regiment monument now stands on Barlow's Knoll. While lying there, a rebel soldier sought the same shelter, but an officer soon came up and said to him, "What are you doing here?" He replied, "I am wounded, Captain." "Where are you wounded," came next. And the fellow hunted his body over in vain for a scratch. The officer, covering him with his revolver, said. "You get out of here and into the ranks, or I will do something worse than wound you." It goes without telling that he got there. The officer then said to me, "In that barn (pointing to a barn some distance away) there are a lot of you

Stephen Crofut, Company D, was twenty years old when he was killed on Barlow's Knoll on July 1. (Courtesy of the Shelton Historical Society)

wounded men, and if you can, you had better get out there." So I made the trial, and before dark reached the barn designated. While on the way there, a rebel soldier, who I judged had rather be taking a prisoner to the rear than fighting in the ranks, undertook to escort me as guard, but the shot and shell from our batteries fell in there unpleasantly close and thick, and I could only move very slowly, so he commenced to hurry me, saying we should be killed in that place. I told him I could not go any faster and should not run away if left alone. He still kept urging me to hurry and getting a little further ahead until at last, when a shell came closer than usual, he took to his heels and I saw him no more. Bad as I was wounded and a prisoner too, I laughed to see that reb run.

As I said, I reached the barn and found it full of wounded Union soldiers. A rebel surgeon gave me a tab of lint, and a rebel soldier filled my canteen with water with which I kept the injured part wet, and that was all the surgical aid I received for four days . . .

Friend and Comrade Warren, if this little sketch is worth anything, use it as you like. Thanks for the photo; I find I have none on hand I care to send, but will have soon, and will forward one at once.[19]

Yours, in F.C.& L. J. H. BLAKEMAN
Late Co. D, 17th C.V.

PRIVATE JUSTUS SILLIMAN WOUNDED

Justus Silliman, Company H, wrote a long letter to his mother in New Canaan from the public school in Gettysburg, where he was a wounded prisoner, on Friday, July 3, 1863. Silliman was slightly wounded on Blocher's Knoll on the first day of battle when a bullet grazed his head. His description of July 1 is below. On or about July 4, Silliman would be moved from the public school to the Eleventh Corps hospital at the George Spangler Farm, and he would remain at the Spangler Farm caring for his friend Sam Comstock, who had been badly wounded on July 1. It was not unusual for slightly wounded men to nurse those who were more severely wounded. Silliman would go with Comstock to the Camp Letterman Hospital and would remain there with his friend until Comstock's death on September 27, 1863. Before Comstock passed, Silliman wrote home that he arranged for him to be embalmed and transported back to Connecticut. Silliman was able to obtain leave to accompany the body of his friend home and attend the funeral before rejoining his regiment.[20]

Private Justus Silliman, Company H. (Courtesy of New Canaan Museum and Historical Society)

Justus Mitchell Silliman was born in New Canaan, Connecticut, in 1842. His father, Joseph Silliman, died in 1850 when Justus was eight and his older brother, Joseph, was ten. The boys were raised by their mother, Martha Mitchell Silliman, and their maternal grandmother, Hannah Mitchell.[21] Silliman's mother, and especially his grandmother, made sure the Silliman boys never forgot they were the descendants of Yale-educated ministers of New Canaan's Congregational Church or the sons of one the most prominent men in New Canaan; the elder Joseph, who had listed his occupation as farmer, had served as town clerk, town selectman, head of the school board, member of the financial board of the Congregational Church, and for many years as justice of the peace. The family also raised two Black children, Thomas Peterson and Ann Paine, who had been brought to New Canaan from New York. Justus attended day school at the New Canaan Academy and then taught school in New Canaan. He enlisted in the 17th Connecticut in 1862 at twenty years old.[22] Justus would survive his wounding on Blocher's Knoll and muster out with his regiment in July 1865. After the war Silliman graduated from Rensselaer Polytechnic Institute with a degree in mechanical engineering. He was a professor at Layfette College in Easton, Pennsylvania, in charge of the Mining and Graphics Department and was prominent in his field.[23] He would marry Harriet Boughton and they would have two sons. Silliman would pass away on April 15, 1896, and be laid to rest in his hometown of New Canaan in Lakeview Cemetery.

In 1977 Thomas Boughton Silliman, Justus's oldest son, who lived to be 102, presented the New Canaan Historical Society, which his father helped found, with a collection 140 letters his father had written during the Civil War. In 1984 local historian Edward Marcus published *A New Canaan Private in the Civil War: Letters of Justus M. Silliman, 17th Connecticut Volunteers*.[24] This book has become a valuable classic in Connecticut's Civil War literature, and several of the letters contained therein are quoted in this volume.

Sergeant Samuel Comstock, Company H, was a New Canaan boy, the second child of nine. His father was Thomas Anthony Comstock and his mother was Polly Ann Lockwood Comstock, who died on March 17, 1854, after giving birth to her ninth child. The family farmed their property; the 1860 census listed Sam, then twenty years old, as a farm laborer. He enlisted as a sergeant in the 17th Connecticut in July 1862 with friends from New Canaan.[25] Sam Comstock would be badly wounded on July 1 on Blocher's Knoll. When Justus Silliman was transferred to the Eleventh Corps hospital at the Spangler Farm, he immediately began trying to locate Sam and found him in dire straits. Silliman found Sam amid a rainstorm lying in a puddle of water. He immediately made him as comfortable as he could and remained with him. Silliman wrote home that he expected Sam to have a long recuperation from his splintered leg, but he believed Sam would recover. He remained with Sam after both were transferred to the General Hospital at Camp Letterman. Sam died of his wound on September 27, 1863.[illegible] Silliman would accompany his body home and Sam would be buried in New Canaan at Lakeview Cemetery.[26]

*After Sam's death, his younger brother, Anthony Comstock, enlisted in Company H in honor of Sam. Anthony was nineteen years old and a pious young man who abhorred the behavior of his comrades when they swore, played cards, drank, and engaged in what he considered sinful and obscene behavior. He was unpopular with the regiment. When he received his whiskey ration, he dumped it out so other soldiers could not drink it. During the regiment's service in Florida, Anthony was made a clerk in the office of the provost marshal, the officer charged with maintaining order among both soldiers and civilians and overseeing all aspects of military law enforcement. After the war, Comstock went to New York City and made a career as the head of the New York Society for the Suppression of Vice. The first "Comstock Law" was passed by Congress in 1873. The act criminalized using the U.S. Postal Service to send obscenity, contraceptives, abortifacients, sex toys, personal letters with sexual content, or sexual information. Comstock became famous, and infamous, for prosecuting individuals, especially women, under the anti-obscenity laws named for him. He especially targeted anyone who disseminated any form of information on birth control, which was considered an illegal obscenity under the law.[27]

Hospital 11th Corps
Public School Gettysburg PA
Friday July 3rd 1863

My Dear Mother

You undoubtedly will have heard of the fight before you will have received this. I am a prisoner. The fighting still continues, but as I have leisure and have found part of an old school ledger and writing materials I thought I would improve the opportunity for using them.

We marched from Emitsburg Md to this place on the morning of July 1st. The roads were muddy and the march very tiresome as we were pushed forward in great haste. On arriving to within about three miles of the town we heard the cannonading and for the first time it entered our minds that we might soon have some fighting to do.

On our arrival at the city we found the 1st Corps engaged with the enemy and learned that its brave commander Gen [John] *Reynolds had been killed in the first charge. The citizens lined the streets holding cups of water for the thirsty, but we had no time to stop but passed through almost on the double quick and took our position on the right of the town. As soon as possible a portion of our force were sent out as skirmishers. These had left us but a few minutes when we were ordered to change position in all possible haste. We were obliged to pass through a raking crossfire from a rebel battery on our right, but most of their shells passed over us as we kept pretty close. After changing our position several times more in as many minutes most of us threw off our knapsacks and in ranks stretched ourselves on the ground to rest ourselves and escape the shells which were continually flying over us. Lt. Col. (Douglas)Fowler displayed great courage and coolness. I think our regt deserve credit. Gens. (Francis) Barlow & (Adelbert) Ames were present and set an excellent example to the men.*

My gun would not work so I dropped it and picked up another, this also missed fire (it had rained during the morning). Just then a man near me was shot. I seized his gun and had just fired at some rebs advancing on our left when I experienced a curious sensation in the head. On opening my eyes I found myself in a horizontal position and surrounded by Greybacks, our men having been forced back a short distance. I placed my cartridge box in front of my bruised noodle and lay a short time. Was then sent to a rebel hospital about three miles to the rear. Here we had every attention show us, our wounds promptly attended to and received kind treatment. Those who a short time previous had been hurling death at us, now assisted our wounded, bringing them water, crackers etc.

The hospital to which I was taken belonged to (Gen. Harry) Hayes brigade called the La (Louisiana) Tigers of (Gen. Jubal) Early's division. The rebels occasionally came in bringing sheep, chickens, etc. captured at the neighboring farmhouses. They all seemed perfectly confident of success as they were concentrating nearly the whole of their army of Va at this place. Occasionally some of the rebs would come up from the city with carpets, collars, shoes and other articles taken from the stores in Gettysburg.

I saw a portion of (Gen. Albert) Jenkins (Confederate) cavalry. They were finely mounted but poorly equipped. A squad of mounted riflemen also passed.

The rebels with whom I conversed seemed anxious to close the war and all were anxious to see Jeff Davis and Abe Lincoln hung and many looked forward to our next presidential election (1864) in hopes that it would either bring about reconstruction of the union or come to some terms of peace. There were several darkees around the hospital who were waiters on rebel officers. One of these was quite friendly and was a true union man. He said the rebels tried to make their case as good as possible but they were hard up.[28]

In the summer of 1884, when Silliman was a professor at Lafayette College, he corresponded with Colonel Noble, who was asked to head the Historical Committee of the Regiment in hopes of finally producing a regimental history. Few survivors responded to Colonel Noble's requests to assist the committee with information. Ultimately, the materials collected by the committee were turned over to William Warren who incorporated much of it into his manuscript. In the 1884 letter below to Noble, Silliman describes his experiences the first day.

Lafayette College, Easton, Pa.,
August 2nd, 1884

Gen'l W. H. Noble,

Dear comrade: I have hastily scribbled off some notes from some of my old war letters and shall be pleased if they prove to be of any assistance to you in writing up the history of the regiment. I am sorry I cannot give you a more connected account of what transpired during your absence from the regiment, and also for other intervals containing no record of the movements of the regiment. An outline of my connection with the regiment will but explain these omissions.

On Barlow's Knoll, July 1st, my rifle missed fire, when I sighted another which had been dropped by a skedadler, but the cap of this only exploded. Dropping this and laying hold of a third, wet with blood of one of our wounded, I fired on the advancing rebels, and turned to load, when I suddenly became unconscious and remained in this condition until the rebels occupied the grounds. I was wounded by a bullet, which glanced across the top of my head—scraping the skull. It proved to be but a slight wound. I was taken to the barn of J. Benner just across Rock Creek on the Harrisburg Road, and then occupied as the hospital of the Louisiana Tigers, where my wound was dressed by a rebel surgeon. The rebels were jubilant over their first day's success. A squad of cavalry came up from town—all wearing high paper collars and having their horses covered with bits of bright carpet.[29]

LIEUTENANT CHARLES E. DOTY, AIDE-DE-CAMP TO GENERAL AMES

Charles Doty in his sergeant's stripes. He was promoted to second lieutenant, Company F, in March 1863. (Bridgeport History Center)

During the Gettysburg Campaign, Second Lieutenant Charles Doty, Company F, was assigned as an aide-de-camp to General Adelbert Ames.[30] During the campaign and the battle it was Doty who brought Ames's orders to the regiment. After Gettysburg, Doty fell very ill. He was given a surgeon's certificate for leave near Williamsport, Maryland. Doty remained with the regiment in order to complete the company rolls, the only company officer remaining after the battle. He worked on the rolls whenever he could get away from headquarters, and he finished them at Warrenton Junction, Virginia. Doty remained extremely ill and both regimental surgeons, Drs. McEwen and Hubbard, endorsed a leave of absence for him because he was suffering from "intermittent fever" (perhaps malaria). His leave was refused. Ill and unable to obtain leave, Doty submitted his resignation, and it was accepted on August 4, 1863. He went home to Norwalk to recuperate and he returned to the regiment in September 1864 as a first lieutenant in Company I. He mustered out with the regiment in July 1865 at Hilton Head. After the war Doty married and had three children, two of whom lived. He was appointed postmaster of Norwalk in 1889 and served until 1892. He moved to Cleveland, Ohio, and died there in 1912. His death was attributed to "paralysis of the brain." He is buried in Norwalk Union Cemetery.[31]

> *Comrade Warren:—*
>
> *You ask me what regiment I refer to that all orders received at Gettysburg came through me. It was the 17th Connecticut. My being an officer in that regiment, General Ames always dispatched me, and if you remember, our regiment was rallied, as was the entire brigade that night of the first day, when we were literally crushed back. We each took a regiment to get together, and I naturally took the 17th Connecticut and rallied them in the street by the lumber yard* by hunting the officers left and requesting them by General Ames' orders, to form there, and as soon as the General got the other regiments formed, our whole brigade or that which was left of them, marched through the town and into the Cemetery Hill line in perfect order, and you know were nearly broken up in falling back. You will please not consider that I speak of myself so much in self-praise, for I abhor that, but what I state are facts, and no one more than Colonel Allen knew it better, and frequently requested me to give them, and in reply to his inquiries about the company volunteering to defend the bridge at Gettysburg* [Doty refers to Company F, one of the four companies detached over the bridge to the far side of Rock Creek below Blocher's Knoll.] *some years ago, I told him what I also give to you, and he said that was his own remembrance and asked me to go into all the detail, but I never get to it.*[32]
>
> *Yours, C.E. Doty*

*Several 17th Connecticut accounts mention a lumberyard. Its exact location is debated. Licensed Battlefield Guide Stuart Dempsey believes that this lumberyard "was a bit south of Coster Avenue off Stratton Street." According to Dempsey, "Today on the west side of Stratton before the railroad tracks there is a large open area where there used to be some old buildings that housed some Commonwealth offices 20 years ago. That now open lot is the area."[33] A lumberyard in this area can also be seen on the 1858 and 1872 maps, although those map locations do not agree.

LIEUTENANT ALBERT W. PECK DESCRIBES THE FIRST DAY'S COMBAT

Albert Peck was a twenty-four-year-old dry goods clerk living in a Bridgeport boardinghouse when he enlisted as first sergeant, Company D, on August 28, 1862. At the age of fourteen, Peck had left his home in Newtown for Bridgeport, where he worked in various dry goods enterprises. Before his enlistment he served in the state militia in both the Washington Light Guards and the City Guards. He was promoted to second lieutenant in November 1862. He would command the company at Gettysburg after twenty-seven out of the company's thirty-six men became casualties.

A youthful-looking Albert Peck in a frock coat without insignia, probably taken at enlistment. Peck mustered into Company D as first sergeant in August 1862. He would be promoted to second lieutenant in November.
(Bridgeport History Center)

Peck returned to Bridgeport and married Louisa W. Booth on December 27, 1865. He returned to the regiment in Florida and would muster out in July 1865. When he returned from the war he went back to clerking in Bridgeport and Newtown. He took over the "old home farm on Mt. Pleasant" and farmed it for the rest of his life. He was active in veterans' affairs and served as commander of G.A.R. Custer Post No. 46 in Sandy Hook, Newtown.[34] At age eighty, Albert W. Peck died at his daughter's home in Portchester, New York in April 1918. His obituary in the *Newtown Bee* was subtitled "Veteran of the Civil War and a Citizen Respected for his Sound and Lovable Qualities." Peck was buried in Newtown Village Cemetery. In 1918 two of Peck's sons—Dr. Charles H. Peck, an eminent New York surgeon, and Albert W. Peck Jr.—were serving with U.S. forces in France along with a grandson, Charles H. Peck Jr. A month before Peck passed in March 1918, his grandson died of pneumonia in the Roosevelt Hospital in France where his father, Charles H. Peck Sr., served as assistant director of general surgery.[35]

Peck's letter to Warren described all three days of Gettysburg. Peck's description of July 1 follows.

> *Dear Comrade:—*
>
> *Yours of the 5th instant came duly to hand. I am glad you were able to find something in my last to assist you in filling up your reminiscences of Gettysburg. You wish me to give my recollections of the first and second days fight.*
>
> *I was second lieutenant at the time in command of Company "D", which I think numbered 36 men for duty. I was the only commissioned officer in my company during the battle, as Captain Hubbell was A.A.G. on the staff of General Barlow and the 1st Lieutenant, Blinn, was absent, wounded.* [First Lieutenant Samuel E. Blinn was wounded and taken prisoner at Chancellorsville. He resigned in November 1863.]
>
> *While we were lying near the oak tree (as we were ordered to lie down while the rebs were shelling us) two of my men were wounded with a piece of shell—privates Alonzo Scranton and William S. Dewhurst. The later*

Lieutenant, later captain, William L. Hubble, Company D, served on General Barlow's staff during the battle. He was captured on July 1.[36] (Bridgeport History Center)

*was wounded somewhere in the neck. I called for two men to take them to the rear hospital. Sergt. John H. Foley and Corporal Gilbert Wordin took them to the rear. (I was sorry afterward that I sent two non-commissioned officers with them, as probably one private could have performed the duty just as well). I think the above named men were the first men wounded in the regiment during the first day's battle.**

Soon after I had sent my wounded to the rear, the Line Officers gathered around Colonel Fowler and tried to persuade him to dismount during the battle, but he refused, fearing he might be deemed cowardly. It was only a few minutes after this that the "Johnnies" were seen advancing through a piece of woods directly in our front, and we were ordered to fall in and were deployed in line of battle, and the command "Forward" was given, and our gallant boys advanced on the enemy with a will. But we were soon cut to pieces… and we fell back to Cemetery Hill and reformed along a stone wall, near where the reservoir now stands, with but a fragment of our regiment left… and when we were ordered forward after reforming on the hill, there was a little hesitation until, I think, General Howard took our colors and moved forward, and our boys followed with a cheer. [Several of the recollections that Warren collected in his manuscript mention General Howard personally guiding the 17th into position on Cemetery Hill and describe the general taking the colors and planting them where he wanted the regiment positioned.]

There was a detail of 100 men for picket from our regiment that night, but we were unable to furnish the full detail. I think Captain McCarthy or Kellogg was in command of the detail from our regiment—do not remember which. I was on the detail as subordinate; do not remember what other officer was with us. We were posted in an apple orchard close to the edge of the town, with our videttes posted along by a board and rail fence. We were ordered to be very watchful and vigilant, as our troops were expecting to make an attack on the town that night; I don't think I got any sleep that night.[37]

*With hindsight Peck had reason to regret the loss of manpower. Instead of the immediate loss of two men, he was now missing four in his already depleted company at the very beginning of the first day's combat. Company D casualties were very high. Peck notes Dewhirst (correct spelling) was wounded somewhere in the neck; Dewhirst would survive, return to the 17th, and be mustered out with the regiment at Hilton Head in July 1865.[38] Alonzo Scranton, a twenty-six-year-old carriage maker from Bridgeport, was struck in the back of his right jaw by a shot or a shell fragment. It went through his jaw and came out the front, cutting part of his jawbone out. He would also survive and be transferred to Company B, Veterans Reserve Corps, 4th Infantry, until discharged in July 1865.[39] Sergeant John H. Foley was also wounded July 1; he would survive and be transferred to Company F, Veterans Reserve Corps, 19th Infantry, and be discharged in July 1865.[40]

Sergeant John Foley, Company D (right), with his friend Sergeant Henry North. Foley was wounded on July 1. He would survive and be transferred to the Veterans Reserve Corps. (Bridgeport History Center)

PRIVATE ALONZO SCRANTON WOUNDED IN THE JAW

In the 1860 census Alonzo Scranton was listed as an unmarried twenty-two-year-old farmer living with his parents on their farm in Madison, Connecticut. His brother Leonard Scranton was a nineteen-year-old carriage maker living in Bridgeport in the home of brother-in-law, Charles K. Wilcox, the twenty-seven-year-old head of the household. Charles's brother, twenty-three-year-old Alvah Wilcox, also a carriage maker, lived in the home as well. Mary A. Scranton, sister to Alonzo and Leonard, was also living in the Wilcox home and was listed as a twenty-four-year-old teacher. The Scranton and Wilcox families were close and intertwined.[41] On August 21, 1862, Alva Wilcox married Sarah L. Dowd of Madison in Clinton, Connecticut.[42] Seven days later on August 28, Alonzo Scranton, Leonard Scranton, and Alvah Wilcox mustered into Company D, 17th Connecticut. Wilcox was made corporal, and the Scranton brothers were privates. All three men fought on Barlow's Knoll on July 1, where Alonzo was gravely wounded, struck in the back of his right jaw by a shot that first clipped another soldier before striking him. The shot went through Alonzo's jaw and exited out the front, ripping away part of his jawbone. Lieutenant Peck described Alonzo Scranton's wounding in the previous account. Alonzo would eventually recover after spending months in various

Leonard Scranton, Company D, was Alonzo Scranton's younger brother. Leonard was unhurt in the battle and mustered out with his regiment in July 1865. (Bridgeport History Center)

hospitals, and was transferred to the Invalid Corps. Scranton would finish his enlistment at Rock Island Prison Camp, Illinois, termed "Andersonville of the North."

William Warren documented Alonzo Scranton's wounding on July 1. The account is without attribution.

> *Alonzo Scranton was wounded on July 1st, 1863. A ball from a shell struck in the back of his right jaw—going through and coming out at the front—cutting part of his jawbone out. He was walked off the field soon after being wounded, by the help of Corporal John H. Foley and Willian Wirtz—one taking one arm and one the other—and was taken to the poorhouse where he remained about 24 hours, when he was recaptured by his own Company "D" they being the first company to reach the poorhouse. The same doctor that attended him here and took the ball from his face was also his physician while he and the writer were at the hospital at Windmill Point. He tells us that the man who stood next to him was knocked over by the force of the ball or shell that struck him, and he heard him say, "Oh, my God." Soon after (Scranton) was wounded and became unconscious, he tells me that he remembers two things very distinctly. One was that another regiment was marching up to the front, when a cannon ball struck one of the men in the stomach, tearing it open and passing clear through him. The other part that he remembers so distinctly was the shot and shell flying so thick and fast around him. Luther W. Lewis was with Scranton when he was wounded.* [Private Luther Lewis, Company D, was listed as a POW on July 1. He would be listed as paroled in August 1863.[43]] *A rebel guard came and asked him what he was doing there. He* [Lewis] *replied that he was taking care of his brother, so he went off and left them. On the 4th* [sic], *from ten to fifteen* [wounded men] *of Company "D" went all the way to Philadelphia on the cars arriving there about 12:30 midnight and went into a hospital. The hospital in which Scranton was six or eight months was called 24th and South.* [The South Street Hospital, located at 24th and South Streets in Philadelphia. This hospital was also known as the "Stump Hospital" for the large number of amputations performed there.[44]] *The ladies had charge of it and ran it until the Government took hold. Dr. North was Scranton's physician, and he procured a furlough for him.*
>
> *General Ferry, who is a Connecticut man, had all the eastern men transferred to the New Haven Hospital and gave Scranton the transfer paper to take with him. After some months stay, here, he went to Washington and was detailed by Provost Marshall Fry to go in the 4th Regiment Invalid Corps, stationed at Rock Island, Illinois where he stayed nine months, acting clerk of a camp of 10,000 rebel prisoners. Finally, he was mustered out and got his pay at the Paymaster's Office at Davenport, Iowa, which is just across the river from Rock Island Illinois, then he came home. He draws a pension from December 1st, 1880.*[45]

PRIVATE WILLIAM WURTZ WAS TAKEN PRISONER AND ESCAPED TO NURSE THE WOUNDED AT THE ALMS HOUSE

William Wurtz, sometimes spelled Wirtz, was born in Stuttgart, Germany. At the time of his enlistment in August 1862 he was working as a harness maker at the firm Calhoun Lacey and Company in Bridgeport. He enlisted in the 17th Connecticut with his brother, Charles, and his cousin Frederick Lindheim, who were working in the same harness-making and saddlery firm.[46] On July 1, the same bullet that struck Alonzo Scranton in the jaw would first cut through Wurtz's coat and the skin on his shoulder before striking Scranton. Wurtz would be taken prisoner. He escaped and would nurse both Union and Confederate wounded at the Alms House. After the 17th Connecticut returned to the Alms House on July 4, the wounded were transferred to the Eleventh Corps hospital at the George Spangler Farm. Wurtz would remain in Gettysburg and continue his nursing duties. Eventually Wurtz was given a pass to rejoin the regiment, which was not easy to locate. He was sent first to Baltimore and then to a parole camp in Alexandria, Virginia, where he met others from the regiment who had been captured at Chancellorsville. These men waited in Alexandria until they were transported by steamer back to the 17th Connecticut, which was then at Folly Island, South Carolina. In a bound, handwritten volume, William Warren recorded Wurtz's experiences at Gettysburg from an undated interview. The account is scattered over multiple pages and days that are bound out of order. Below is Wurtz's account of his experiences on the first day. The account was written in the third person in William H. Warren's handwriting.

> *On Barlow's Knoll, (Alonzo) Scranton who was a trifle in advance of Wm. Wurtz on a slight angle, a bullet struck Wurtz shoulder, cut (his) coat to the skin and took (the) skin off and was in the same range and path high enough, (that) the bullet struck Scranton in the jaw and he spun around 2 or three times. Wurtz's shoulder and Scranton's cheek was about on the same line.*
>
> *On the first day while the regiment was on the retreat from Barlow's Knoll, he stopped right back of the haystack and fired a few shots. While here he saw the rebs off to the right so he went into the Poorhouse yard and found many there wounded. Here, he was taken prisoner. He looked around and saw one of General Barlow's orderlies who had not seen the rebs coming, but turning around, he discovered them close at hand. Quick as thought he put spurs to his horse and laying down upon the horse's neck, Indian fashion, he rode off like lightning with about 20 rebs shooting at him. He kept on and came out all right. This was the same squad that captured Wurtz and others and ordered them to surrender and drop their guns which they did. The he went to the rebel Captain and asked him what he was going to do with them. The rebel captain replied, "We won't hang you," and laughed. They all fell in line and were marched off About 150 from different regiments. Soon a rebel major cavalryman on horseback rode up and said he was going to parole them. He rode to the right of the line and took the first 2 files or 4 men and told them to stay and help the*

wounded. These 4 men stepped to the right which left Wurtz on the right of the next file. He wanted to go with these 4 men so fell in line with them and thought he would take his chances with them as his feet were so sore he could go no further. Major said left flank and he marched them off and took no notice of Wurtz. While the officer turned to the left to the other squad, Wurtz stepped out of the ranks and went off with the 4. The other squad was marched off somewhere and that was the last he saw of them. Wurtz and his squad helped to take care of the sick and wounded all day and night. A rebel officer told this squad to get some pails and water and give the wounded laying on the field some water and take some bread and crackers with them. Some of the wounded had turned black laying in the sun so long. Their stomachs were bloated. Our forces on the 4th day regained the field and this detail all went back to their regiments.[47] [William Wurtz would remain at his nursing duties after the Confederate retreat on July 4. His account will continue in subsequent chapters.]

PRIVATE DEWITT C. RUSCOE CAPTURED

The 1860 census listed Dewitt Clinton Ruscoe as a twenty-year-old shoemaker from New Canaan and the oldest of eight siblings; in some records his name is spelled Rusco. He enlisted in Company H, 17th Connecticut, in August 1862 as a private. He was listed as wounded at Chancellorsville. He fought at Gettysburg and was captured on July 1. He would muster out with the regiment at Hilton Head in July 1865.[48] Ruscoe married Phoebe Provost in 1867 and the couple had four children. Ruscoe was active in civic and veteran affairs throughout his long life. He was a butcher, managed a market, and built up a large ice business. He served as commander of the S. P. Ferris Post, GAR, and was elected to the Connecticut House of Representatives in 1903 and 1905.[49] He died on January 31, 1928, at age eighty-seven, and is buried in Lakeview Cemetery in New Canaan.[50]

Private DeWitt Ruscoe, Company H. (Courtesy of the New Canaan Museum and Historical Society)

While writing about our march through town, he says:— "I would have given all I had or ever would have if I could have been landed out of that place but there I was and there I meant to stay . . . An order, as I suppose, came to Colonel Fowler from General Barlow to have the fence rail torn down, so Colonel called on some of our regiment to go and tear it down. Now I don't say this for any praise of mine, only that I want to say that I was shaky on entering the city, but soon we had arrived where the shot and shell were flying into our ranks. . . . I can say I was the only man out of Company H, if I mistake not, that got up out of the regiment and advanced to the rail fence and helped to tear it down. Captain Kellogg motioned for us to come in and join the regiment, after we had torn down about what we needed.

Captain Enos Kellogg, Company H. (Bridgeport History Center)

Now while all this was being done I did not feel any more afraid than I do at the present time writing this which is over 22 years since it happened; but the order came to charge. . . . when one of our boys, Comrade Levi Dixon. . . . used words at the time which he does not use nowadays, and I was close to him and heard him use these words: "Give them H. . . Boys." He meant business too at the time, and it was in that dreadful charge where so many brave boys gave up their lives for their country and where Levi Dixon of Company "H" lost one of his legs. I have often spoken to him about the words he used on that occasion. Many of our boys were made prisoners, myself included.[51]

Private Levi Dixon, Company H, was an eighteen-year-old shoemaker from Poundridge, New York, when he enlisted in the 17th Connecticut. He was severely wounded in his right leg on July 1. Dixon's biography in Find-A-Grave states, "Enlisted August 1862 from New Canaan. Wounded July 1, 1863, Gettysburg, Pa. His shattered leg was amputated by a Confederate surgeon, and he was later recaptured by the Federal army. He was discharged in Oct. 1864. He lived in Stamford after the war."[52] The *Medical and Surgical History of the War of the Rebellion* confirms that a Confederate surgeon amputated Dixon's leg but does not give the location. Dixon was transferred to the Eleventh Corps hospital at the George Spangler Farm with other Eleventh Corps wounded after the town of Gettysburg was back in Federal control. Later he was moved to Camp Letterman General Hospital and there underwent surgery on August 28 and September 3 to remove bone fragments from his stump.[53] After his discharge on October 10, 1864, Levi Dixon returned to live in Stamford. He continued his profession as a shoemaker. He married Matilda Jane Caldwell Dixon and they had one son, Alden Ferris Dixon. Dixon would pass away in 1919 and be buried in Woodland Cemetery in Stamford.[54]

LIEUTENANT HENRY QUIEN WOUNDED

Captain Henry Quien was a popular and respected officer who appears in many of the accounts left by veterans of the 17th Connecticut. Quien—whose name is often misspelled as Quinn—was born in Germany in 1841, the third of six brothers. His parents immigrated to Danbury and Henry became involved in the hat trade. He answered

Lincoln's first call for enlistments in the spring of 1861 and joined Captain Moore's Company I, 3rd Connecticut. He fought at First Bull Run with Captain Moore and Lieutenant Milton Daniels. Two of Quien's brothers also served. The elder, George, served as a second lieutenant in Company K, 23rd Connecticut. The younger, Christian, enlisted as a sergeant in Company A, 11th Connecticut and would be promoted to second lieutenant in Company F in 1864.

Lieutenant Henry Quien, Company C. (Bridgeport History Center)

After his three-month enlistment in the 3rd Connecticut ended, Henry returned to Danbury. He married Mary Collins in August 1862 right before enlisting a second time as a second lieutenant in Company C, 17th Connecticut. Quien was shot in the hand on July1 but did not leave the field. After Moore was killed, Lieutenant Quien was in command of the company. Quien would be promoted to captain in August 1864. On February 5, 1865, Quien and a number of officers and men would be taken prisoner at Dunn's Lake in Florida. Quien would be sent to Andersonville and released in April 1865. He would be discharged in May 1865 and return home to Danbury.[55]

Quien prospered as a hatter in Danbury. He was involved in veterans affairs and would partner with his brother Christian and Frank T. Benedict in insurance and real estate. Quien and Mary had seven children together before her death in 1875. In 1876 Quien would marry his younger sister-in-law, Elizabeth Collins. Upon her death in 1892 he married a third time, to Augusta E. Kinner, on November 26, 1892. Henry would die in November 1900 at the age of fifty-nine, the first of the six Quien brothers to pass away. He was survived by Augusta and four of his children. He is buried in Wooster Cemetery in Danbury.[56]

In 1895 Quien gave Warren a brief description of his wounding, which occurred shortly after Daniel Purdy, of his company, was shot next to him. Private Purdy, Company C, was the only son of Almon Purdy, a miller, and Deborah Purdy. Purdy was shot through the lungs and upon his death was buried in a marked grave on the Spangler Farm property.[57] No family member came to retrieve his body. Daniel was later disinterred from the Spangler property and laid to rest in Gettysburg National Cemetery, Connecticut Plot, Section B, Site 6.

> *As I have said before, when we were going into the fight, we got all mixed up by the Pennsylvania Regiment* [153rd Pennsylvania], *so Daniel Purdy said to Lieutenant Quien, "Where shall I shoot?" Quien put his hand on his shoulder and said, "Go in there." He had taken his hand from his shoulder when Purdy was shot through the stomach. He was taken back to a hospital. After this he had no use for his body below the chest but was*

apparently paralyzed. He died at the hospital and was buried near the stone wall by the cemetery, afterward being removed inside the (National) cemetery.

(From Henry Quien—July 13, 1895)[58]

PRIVATE JOHN C. COLLINS WOUNDED

John Collins, born in Ireland in 1833, was a married day laborer from Stamford when he enlisted in Company B, 17th Connecticut.[59] Collins was wounded at Gettysburg on the first day. An account of his wounding is below. The account is undated and written in the third person.

> *He was a cook for the officers, besides taking care of their horses. About the time our regiment was going into the fight at Gettysburg, the Chaplain* [Chaplain William K. Hall[60]] *said to him, "Get those horses to the rear and get them something to eat." Just then an Irish officer swung his sword around to rally his men. That got the horses excited, and while trying to quiet them he fell, and one of the horses stepped on him. He managed to get the horses back to a barn near Cemetery Hill, where he met Dr. Hubbard,* [Dr. Robert Hubbard, the regimental surgeon for the 17th Connecticut and medical inspector of the Eleventh Corps] *who said to him, "John what are you doing here?" "I have got my horses in here." Replied Collins, "and have got hurt." "Well, said Dr. Hubbard, get one of them and follow me, or we will be gobbled up." They both went to the rear as fast as they could, but stopping near a barn, where the Doctor established a hospital. He had just got a Lieutenant upon a table to cut his leg off but was obliged to stop and put the officer into an ambulance, and take him to the rear, as shot and shell came so thick and fast that they had to leave again for the rear, and Dr. Hubbard established another hospital further back. At this hospital Collins again told Dr. Hubbard that he was hurt. "Well, said the Doctor, "I have my hands full, as you can see, you go to the rear and I will attend you as soon as I can."*[61]

Private John Collins, Company C. (Bridgeport History Center)

John Collins is listed in several sources as being wounded at Gettysburg on an unspecified date, the presumption being July 1. It is not known if Hubbard was the surgeon that ultimately attended to John. As noted, Hubbard certainly had his hands full on July 1 and it may have been any time within the three-day battle that John received care for his injury and the injury was recorded. He is listed on the roster for

Spangler Farm wounded as "Collins, John, Pvt., 17th CT, B, lower 3rd right leg & knee, water dressing."[62] This description of the injury is consistent with John's description. But there is more to John's story. On August 29, 1863, the *Hartford Courant* reprinted a story from the *Stamford Advocate*, titled "Narrow Escape." This short article described Collins's wounding:

> *Narrow Escape.—We saw a few days since a Roman Catholic Prayer Book, which had been carried in the breast pocket of John Collins, a member of the 17th C.V., at the battle of Gettysburg. A Minnie ball penetrated Collins' clothing and passed through the prayer book to the 199th page. Between this page and the next, is a picture of our Savior teaching a child. On this picture not the slightest impression of the ball is visible. The book is treasured as having been the providential means of saving the life of its owner. Collins was wounded in the leg and hip at the same battle.—Stamford Advocate*[63]

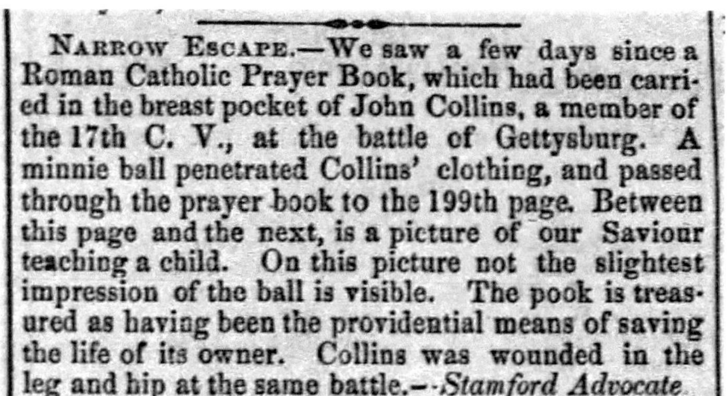

NARROW ESCAPE.—We saw a few days since a Roman Catholic Prayer Book, which had been carried in the breast pocket of John Collins, a member of the 17th C. V., at the battle of Gettysburg. A minnie ball penetrated Collins' clothing, and passed through the prayer book to the 199th page. Between this page and the next, is a picture of our Saviour teaching a child. On this picture not the slightest impression of the ball is visible. The pook is treasured as having been the providential means of saving the life of its owner. Collins was wounded in the leg and hip at the same battle.—*Stamford Advocate*

***Hartford Courant* reprint from the *Stamford Advocate*, August 29, 1863.** (Author's Clipping)

The story of John Collins's prayer book is extraordinary, but not unique in the annals of the Civil War; Bibles and prayer books and all manner of personal effects saved the lives of those who carried them. Another of the 17th Connecticut men would be saved from a chest wound by something he carried: Charles Stiles Wells, Company D, had a thick stack of writing paper folded in his breast pocket on the first day of battle that prevented a bullet from entering his chest. In the torrent of flying lead, he was hit again in the thigh. Wells kept his leg but was discharged for disability in November 1864 after a long recuperation in Union hospitals. After he and other wounded from the 17th Connecticut were transferred to the hospital at the George Spangler Farm, Stiles Wells gave a piece of the writing paper that saved his life to J. Henry Blakeman, who penned a remarkable July 4 letter to his mother in Stratford. Henry described to his mother how the stack of paper saved Wells's life: "I got this sheet of paper of Stiles Wells. It was in a small portfolio in his breast and a ball passed through the whole fifty thickness but did not hurt him and it probably saved his life. He was afterwards wounded in the leg."[64]

CORPORAL GEORGE DICKENS *(WAS NOT)* WOUNDED

There is no date or attribution attached to this account. We may presume that William Warren wrote and edited this account from information, oral or written, he received from George Dickens or John Bouton, or both. Perhaps the last line in Dickens's account was contributed by George W. Bradley, Dickens's brother-in-law. This may be a later account that Warren edited heavily, adding dialogue to make it more interesting. It is certainly a "quirky" account, as George Dickens was never wounded despite the title of the entry that Warren gave.

Corporal George Dickens, Company C. (Bridgeport History Center)

Notwithstanding the edits, and based on evidence from various other sources, there is no reason to doubt the substantial truth of the account. As a result of his actions at the German Reformed Church in Gettysburg, where this account takes place, George would remain in Gettysburg at this church hospital as a nurse during the three days of battle. He would go with the wounded when they were transferred to the Eleventh Corps hospital at the Spangler Farm and continue his nursing duties there. Dickens was crucial in helping families coming to Gettysburg locate the wounded and dead of the 17th Connecticut for disinterment and transfer to Connecticut for burial. Some sources list him as captured on the first day; however, this may be a function of recordkeeping, as the German Reformed Church was in Confederate hands July 1–4 and the wounded Union men, doctors, and nurses there were prisoners until the Confederate evacuation. Beginning July 4, once the town was back in Union control, the process of consolidating the wounded and evacuating them from makeshift hospitals such as this church and the Alms House began. Eleventh Corps wounded scattered at various places around the battlefield were transferred to the large Eleventh Corps hospital site at the George Spangler Farm.

George Dickens was born in 1835. He is listed in the 1860 census for Danbury as a married hatter with two children: Sarah, thirteen, and Lucius, seven. The Dickens family would contribute four sons to service during the Civil War, with George joined by brothers Milo (Company E, 1st Connecticut and Company B, 1st Connecticut Heavy Artillery); William (Company A, 11th Connecticut as a wagoner), and Clark (Charles) (Company G, 17th Connecticut). George enlisted as a corporal in Company C with other friends and family from Danbury. Later in the war he was reduced to private at his own request. He would muster out at Hilton Head in July 1865 with his regiment.[65]

George returned to Danbury after the war and resumed his profession as a hatter. His first wife, Eunice Bradley Dickens, died in 1870. Their daughter, Sarah, apparently also died sometime before the 1870 census. Living in the Dickens's home was a Jane Booth, thirty-eight, and her son Arthur Booth, six; she was presumably a widow keeping house for George after his wife's death. By the 1880 census, George had remarried to Alice B. Bradley in 1872. Alice, the widow of William B. Bradley, had a daughter, Ida.

Eighteen-year-old Ida worked in the same hat factory as George. George, Alice, and Ida would live as a family until George's death in 1904. George Dickens was a respected veteran in the Danbury community until his passing. He had many friends and family members among Danbury's close-knit society.[66]

> *George Dickens and John Boughton (sic) were fast friends and tent mates. They agreed between them that when they went into a fight and either one of them should get wounded the other one would take care of him as best he could under the circumstances. John was wounded the first day on the retreat back through the town. George saw him and said, "What's the matter, John?" "I am wounded, "he replied. George asked where and John said "in my arm." "Can you get along alone," asked George. "I don't know," replied John. "I will try to get you back into the town," said George. So he took hold of John and helped him back into the town where he got him comfortable quarters in one of the pews of the little church, by going up four or five steps to get inside. After making John as comfortable as he could, he left him for a few minutes and then returned and asked him if he would like a canteen of water fresh and cool. "Yes," said John. So he took his canteen and went across to a brick house and filled it and returned it to him saying, "John, now I guess I shall have to leave you." "If you must, all right," said John. Then George started to go out and got as far as the front door when he was met by a rebel who said to him, "You had better not go out of here; better take off your traps and set them there in the corner. So George said, "If you want them more than I do you can have them," and at the same time taking them off. George then went back into the church and sat down in the pew beside John. In a little while someone said, "There is a file of men with a corporal coming to pick up all men not wounded, and those that are wounded but can walk." So George on the impulse of the moment, putting into action the first thought that came into his mind, went out into the aisle and picked up a bloody rag, wrapped it around his left ankle, and then went back and sat down beside John, with his foot turned over on the side and his head bent way*

The German Reformed Church on the corner of Stratton and High Streets would become an Eleventh Corps field hospital for many of the 17th Connecticut. (Gettysburg National Military Park)

over looking down at his foot in about as hard a looking, woe-be-gone way as possible. The corporal came and in turn asked each one what was the matter with him. When he came to John he said he was wounded in the left arm, just below the elbow, by a Minnie ball; then he tapped George on the shoulder and said, "What's the matter with you?" He did not even look up, but finally said in a low grumbling voice, "Nothing much, only I guess my leg is all broke to pieces," so he passed on. He picked up a few men and then went out of the building. George then took off the bandages but soon the same thing was repeated, with about the same results as above. Soon after this George went out into the vestibule and asked the Doctor what he should do or if he could use him as a nurse. He said he did not know but he had about all he would be allowed to have and did not know whether they would need any more or not. The doctor was a German and a Union man. He told George to tie a white cloth around his arm, and that would then show that he was a nurse; then he told him to gather up all the bloody rags and put them in a pile. He then asked the doctor what he should do with them, "Take them across the road," said the doctor, "and throw them over the fence into the lot." He picked up an armful and went out to the door, and there stood a rebel guard. The situation of things out of the doors made George a little fearful about going outside, but he finally plucked up courage enough and went across the road; coming back about midway of the road, a Minnie ball struck about two feet from him. He jumped up in the air and ran for the door. The guard said, "By God! That was a pretty close call, wasn't it," laughing. George said, "About as close as I want it." After the war was over he found that it was his brother in-law that fired that shot, George W. Bradley. (George (Dickens) was here (in Gettysburg) about three months helping the doctors.[67]

PRIVATE GEORGE W. BRADLEY FIRES A SHOT

George F. Bradley is named in the account above as being responsible for a shot that came near to ending his brother-in-law, George Dickens. How these men decided George Bradley was the one who fired the shot seems like a postwar embellishment that made a better story of the incident, but one never knows. The 1860 census lists George Bradley as a seventeen-year-old apprentice mason boarding in the home of Able Parsons, a Danbury master mason. George Bradley enlisted in Company C, 17th Connecticut, along with two of his brothers. In addition to George, the youngest of the three, David Bradley would enlist

Private George F. Bradley, Company C. (Bridgeport History Center)

and be discharged for disability in December 1863. Lewis Bradley, the oldest, a hatter from Danbury, was taken prisoner on July 1. Lewis was released in August and served out his enlistment. George Bradley served his enlistment unscathed and mustered out with the regiment in July 1865 at Hilton Head.

PRIVATE JOHN W. BOUTON WOUNDED

John W. Bouton (sometimes spelled Boughton) was George Dickens's good friend. The two served together in Company C and Dickens would stick closely to Bouton after Bouton was wounded on July 1. John Bouton was listed in the 1860 census as a twenty-three-year-old carpenter with a wife, Frances, nineteen years old, and an eight-month-old daughter, Emma. He enlisted with other Danbury men in Company C. Despite his wounding at Gettysburg, John would muster out with the regiment in July 1865 at Hilton Head.[68]

Private John Bouton, Company C. (Bridgeport History Center)

On Sunday, May 29, 1892, William Warren interviewed John Bouton, who gave him the particulars of his wounding on July 1. Warren left a handwritten account in a bound volume tagged "Miscellaneous information on the events of the Civil War and on individuals of the various companies of the 17th Conn. Regiment gathered by William H. Warren."

> *JOHN BOUGTON WOUNDED: He was wounded as we fell back near the poor house barn. The first one he saw after being wounded that he knew was George Dickens who said to him, "are you hurt," his blood was running down his left arm. The doctors call it "fore left arm" which is just below the elbow. John had his gun and knapsack in his right hand. The bullet was in his arm until the third day then taken out by a rebel surgeon. It was very painful. Dr. Hubbard came along to where they were. George saw him first. Hubbard asked if he was wounded. Dr. said, "take good care of it and wet it well with water." So he would put it under a faucet and let water run on it for hours at a time. (So John told me.) He was with the company (Company C) in the fight . . . There were rebel wounded prisoners in the same hospital.*[69]

LIEUTENANT DAVID S. BARTRAM CAPTURED

David Sanford Bartram, twenty-eight, was married carriage maker from Redding with two children when he enlisted in Company G, 17th Connecticut in August 1862. Bartram mustered in as first sergeant and in June 1863 he was promoted to second lieutenant. He was captured on July 1. Bartram, like many others captured that day,

Lt. David Bartram, Company G, before his promotion. He was captured July 1. (courtesy of Sheila Bartram Hislop)

refused the parole offered on the field, believing his captors were offering him a dishonest and dishonorable parole that was not legal. Bartram spent the next twenty months in nine Rebel prisons, including Richmond's Libby for ten months; Danville, Virginia; Macon and Savanah, Georgia; and Charleston, South Carolina. Bartram was finally paroled at Wilmington, North Carolina, on March 1, 1865.[70] In 1886 Bartram wrote to William Warren describing his experiences. His account of July 1 is below. Bartram also supplied Warren with his prison diaries, parts of which Warren transcribed into his manuscript.

The censuses of 1860, 1870, and 1880 all show David and his wife, Harriet D. Hull Bartram, living next door to David's parents, Aaron and Harriet. David and his wife were the only living children of their respective parents and from the census it appears the family remained close. The 1860 census lists both David and his father as carriage makers. Subsequent census records list them both as farmers. David's daughter, Nellie Bartram, remembered in an interview in the 1940s that "When my father came back, there was nothing doing in the carriage business, and he got him a job in a shirt factory in Danbury. He wasn't very strong after the war, and he didn't do much farming."[71] David and Harriet would have seven children. David was a respected citizen in Redding. He held several town offices and was elected constable for several terms. He was active in the Nelson L. White GAR post in Redding.[72]

On Wednesday, July 6, 1898, the *Danbury News* reported that sixty-four-year-old David S. Bartram, a prominent and well-known citizen, had died the day before at his home of pneumonia. The paper also reported that Mrs. Bartram was taken ill at the same time and was in critical condition. Harriet Bartram died the day after her husband's death. The *News* reported, "The death and funeral of David Bartram and wife was a very sad affair. Two of his daughters are deranged over the death of their parents. One has been taken to the sanitarium at Westport, and the other will be taken in a day or two. Mr. Bartram will be much missed." David and Harriet lie in Hull Cemetery in Redding.[73]

Friend Warren:—

I attended officers' call at seven a.m. July 1, 1863 at Emmitsburg, Maryland and the orders were to have the men fall in, stack arms and be ready to march in one hour, or at eight o'clock. By the time we had made half the distance to Gettysburg, the sharp reports of artillery could be heard in our front, indicating that the ball had commenced. About that time word came back that Reynolds was killed, and our Corps

Commander, Howard, left us and went to the front. My opinion is that we arrived at Gettysburg at one p.m. The first wounded person I saw was an officer from the First Corps whom they were carrying into a hotel on the market square. As we passed along we moved through the town at a double quick, out nearly opposite the County Almshouse, when we turned into a field at the right, and while there shell and Minnie balls were singing around us quite smart. At that point Gen. Ames came to Colonel Fowler and asked for four companies for skirmishing, and before the request had hardly been made, Captain C. H. Hobbie of Company B called out to Company B to fall in.

General Ames and Colonel Fowler both told him he was not fit to go, as his wound that he got at Chancellorsville had not healed up, and besides he had just taken a French leave from the hospital, before he was fit to do so, where he had been sick with the measles. He said that he was bound to go in and get satisfaction. Major Brady had command and not Colonel Allen, as reports say, [at Gettysburg Colonel Allen was in command of Company F, one of the four companies sent across Rock Creek as skirmishers] *and they went out on the right of the road and not a man, I think, was wounded at that point, as they were not under fire. The other companies with the brigade, passed through a gate just beyond the Almshouse to the left of the road, across the field, up the slope to the Oak Grove, were the monument now stands, then we were ordered to tear down the fence at our right, and after a little time our regiment was sent to the rear a short ways, where we laid down, as a reserve for the brigade, and under a shell fire from both flanks and in front, and when we were ordered from that point to the Oak Grove again, there is where we lost the most men in our regiment, Colonel Fowler and Captain Moore, with a host of other dear comrades, near the same point. I saw General Barlow of our Division when he was wounded, when we were driven back from Barlow's Knoll. When we got back as far as the Almshouse, he told all that he could to go or we would be taken prisoners. I passed out the front door to the gate and there I found Corporal A. W. Lee of my own company, badly wounded. He asked me to carry him into the house. I did so, bound up his wound as best I could, started out again, but had barely stepped out of the door when I was ordered to surrender. I asked a rebel officer for permission to stay and take care of the*

Captain Charles Hobbie, Company B, was wounded at Chancellorsville and had been hospitalized for measles. He took "French leave" from the hospital, meaning he left without permission, against doctor's orders, to lead his company at Gettysburg.
(Bridgeport History Center)

wounded, but was refused, and was told to get to the rear under guard, and I and others crossed the field again in about the same tracks that we crossed twice before, to the grove. There I saw Colonel Fowler's and Captain Moore's bodies, and pinned their names to both of them, but was not allowed to look around to help or to say a word to the boys, (we) were driven across the river to a house on the same road that the Almshouse stands on [the Harrisburg Road across Rock Creek], *and just at night moved a short distance to the right, and corralled in a clover field.*"[74]

David S. Bartram

PRIVATE FREDERICK G. LINDHEIM WOUNDED

Private Frederick G. Lindheim, Company G, in civilian clothes.
(Bridgeport History Center)

Fred Lindheim (spelled alternately as Lindhiem, Lindhien) was born in Wurttemberg, Germany, in 1840. In August 1862 he was working in the saddle shop Calhoun Lacey and Company in Bridgeport when he enlisted in Company G, 17th Connecticut with his cousins Charles and William Wurtz. Lindheim was wounded on July 1. He never returned to the regiment. On March 7, 1865, he was transferred to Company H, Veteran Reserve Corps, 21st Infantry. He was discharged on July 6, 1865. After the war he listed his profession as varnisher. He married and became a naturalized citizen on March 9, 1866, in the New Haven U.S. District Court. His naturalization papers note he was an ex-soldier. On November 21, 1876, tragedy struck Fred and his wife, Caroline, when two daughters, four-year-old Elizabeth and two-year-old Caroline, died the same day. Because of his wounds Fred qualified for an invalid pension on January 16, 1866, and collected that until his death on November 29, 1907, at age sixty-seven. He, Caroline, and their two daughters are buried in Evergreen Cemetery in New Haven.[75] In an undated, handwritten account Lindheim gave William Warren the particulars of his wounding.

Wounded at Gettysburg the first day in the hip, while in line of battle with his company. It has pained him more or less every day since and can tell in advance about the different changes of weather by the feeling of his leg. The wound affected the leg so badly that he was not able to stand on it. It seemed that it was partially paralyzed, so he crawled on hands and knees for a short distance and laid down as his legs refused to carry him any further. The wounded lay thickly over the field all the p.m. The rebel advance also crossed the field and the officer in command said to his

> *men, "Come on boys, don't be stepping on those men." In the evening the rebs took the wounded off the field. He was taken back (he thinks) as far as the poor house barn and left outside, as the barn was crowded full to overflowing. The doctors were constantly cutting off legs and arms. He lay here on the ground for two days and three nights and then was recaptured by our forces. Tents were put up to be used as hospitals and ambulances went around and picked up the wounded. He was in one of these tents.*[76]

PRIVATE JOHN L. HAYES WOUNDED CARRYING THE COLORS

John L. Hayes, eighteen, was living in Norwalk when he enlisted as a private in Company F, 17th Connecticut. He was badly wounded on July 1 while carrying the U.S. colors. After the war the 1870 census listed him as working as a bookkeeper and having a wife and two children. He and his wife, Nellie, would eventually have five children. When John passed in 1894 at age fifty-one he was buried in Cypress Hills Cemetery in Brooklyn.[77] In 1885 he wrote a letter to R. Lorenzo Ells, who had been a Lieutenant in Company A. Ells was active with the GAR and the 17th Connecticut Survivors Association, and he was appointed to the 17th Connecticut monument committee and would become chair of the 17th Connecticut Historical Committee.[78] Ells forwarded this letter to William Warren sometime after he received it. In the letter Hayes wrote an account of his wounding. Several sources listed Hayes as wounded in the abdomen; eyewitness accounts to his wounding state he was shot in the leg. The record of Spangler Farm wounded states: "Hayes, John, L., Pvt., 17th CT, F, flesh wound right thigh, water dressing."[79] Reading Hayes's account of his wounds it is evident that due to the trajectory of the bullet both descriptions are true. After the battle Hayes was transferred from the Alms House to the Eleventh Corps hospital at the Spangler Farm. Hayes returned to duty on January 23, 1865, with his transfer to the Veterans Reserve Corps, 16th Infantry, Company C. He was honorably discharged on July 6, 1865.[80]

> *Friend Ells:-*
>
> *In relation to the matter referred to at our meeting, I submit the following:*
>
> *After the regiment had arrived at Gettysburg the men dropped their knapsacks and prepared for immediate action. I went to Captain Allen, telling him that I was going in and wanted a rifle (being Adjutant Clerk I had turned mine in to the Quartermaster's Department months before). He told me Company "F" was one of the companies ordered out as skirmishers—that I had better fall in and find a musket on the field as he had none. I did so and commenced marching into position—the rebels firing artillery during the time. I picked up a rifle during the marching, with accoutrements.*
>
> *After we had halted and faced to the enemy, I took my position in Company "C" to the left and rear of the colors. Lieut. Col. Fowler called*

Captain Henry Allen, Company F. (Bridgeport History Center)

me and gave me his picture. After the rebels had commenced their terrible fire and our line had crumbled away, I saw through the smoke that the national colors were falling near me; I grabbed them, throwing down my musket. I felt exhausted by our march that day from Emmitsburg and the excitement of battle and concluded to divest myself of a rubber blanket that was tied around me, and whilst holding the colors up with my left hand and throwing the blanket over my shoulder and head with my right, I was severely wounded, the ball entering my right thigh, striking the bone, passing up through the groin and lodging in the pit of my stomach. I shouted for someone to take the colors, but in the smoke, noise and confusion no one responded, until presently Jimmy . . . ,[probably James (Jimmy) Ainscow, a musician from Company K, whose account of the flags follows] *I don't remember his other name, helped me up and leaning on his shoulder with my left arm, I carried the flag in my right to the Poorhouse where I fell on my hands and face—the colors going down with me. I afterwards found myself in the Poorhouse, lying on one of the dining-room tables. As I was throwing the rubber blanket over my head, Corporal Burns, with the State colors in his left hand was swinging his cap over his head with his right shouting at the top of his voice, "Rally around your colors, boys. Rally around your colors," perhaps not more than ten men near him, as everything at that time had gone to pieces and the rebels had gotten very close to us. A good many wounded on their way off the field and some killed. I judged the wounded from seeing them put a hand to an arm, head, or leg in such a manner as to lead me to believe they were shot. I noticed one blackened eyed soldier, I think of Company "C", wounded sitting up as we were approaching him and crying for someone to help him up; a ball struck him again and he needed no help. To the left of us about 1500 feet the state colors were being carried off the field.*

After I laid on the table in the Poorhouse a short time, D. S. Bartram came and said, "Boys we are all taken prisoners." Corporal Perry was there, [Robert N. Perry, Company F, of Norwalk] *wounded in the arm, he said, and one of Company "D". When you record, don't forget that the brave dead Corporal of Company "B": shouted to his death, "Rally around the colors boys, rally around the colors."*

(The above is a true copy of a letter sent to Lieut. R. L. Ells, as he is Chairman of the Historical Committee and he sent it to me, William Warren.)

SERGEANT MAJOR BETTS—THE FIRST DAY OF BATTLE

C. Frederick Betts, born September 11, 1846, was only fifteen years old when he mustered in as a corporal in Company C, 17th Connecticut in August 1862. Apparently, no one did the math on his age at enlistment. A month before the Battle of Gettysburg, Betts, then only sixteen, was promoted to sergeant major. On September 1, 1863, ten days before his seventeenth birthday, he was promoted again, to second lieutenant in Company A. His final promotion, at age eighteen, was to captain of Company F in March 1864, replacing Captain Henry Allen, who had been promoted to major. Captain Betts would be taken prisoner at Dunn's Lake, Florida, on February 5, 1865, and sent to Andersonville. He was paroled in April 1865.[81]

Betts's first name, which he always abbreviated to the initial, was Carmi after his father. He always went by C. Frederick or Fred Betts. He was the youngest of the family and remained very close to his unmarried older sisters, Julia and Mary. He wrote to them throughout the war. Part of his letter to his sisters after the battle—describing Colonel Fowler's death and the attempts to recover his body at Gettysburg—would be published in the *Norwalk Gazette* on July 14, 1863. Betts would live part of his adult life in New York City, and he joined the Grand Army of the Republic there in 1880. He gave his occupation as broker. He never married and died at age fifty-four in his sisters' home at 84 Main Street in Norwalk on May 22, 1901. The cause of death was listed as paralysis of the brain.[82]

Betts's account of his experiences at Gettysburg covered the three days of the battle and the aftermath. The first day's account is below. The rest of his account follows in subsequent chapters.

> *The following is a true copy of a letter written by C. Frederick Betts, of Co. A, to Lieut. Col. Henry Allen, giving his experience at Gettysburg.*
>
> *"Starting from Emmitsburg early in the a.m. my first vivid impression was produced by an Aide who came galloping down the road with orders to hasten forward, and soon afterward I heard heavy firing. We pushed on at almost a double quick and with a brief halt for water in the square, passed through the town and out toward Seminary Ridge beyond and to the right of the Poorhouse grounds. Here we learned of Reynold's death and of the consequent change in commanders through our corps. At about eleven o'clock, as I recollect, three* [sic—four] *companies of the 17th were sent out as skirmishers, and as volunteers had been called for, the regular division formation was broken. Shortly after, the Regiment was ordered to the left and deployed in column of Divisions as reserve to our Brigade. This formation you will remember was especially awkward owing to the absence of the Companies skirmishing, and to this fact was due, in my opinion, the temporary confusion which followed the order to deploy and advance. Several companies missed their usual place in line and rushed hastily up the hill to close the break. At this time our gallant Fowler who, during the vigorous shelling which preceded our advance had jokingly cried, "Dodge*

the big ones boys", rode to the front where he was joined by Gen. Ames and staff, and after a brief glance at the numbers of the enemy, ordered us to fall back. It was at about this time that the Regt. suffered its heaviest loss for the first day.

Our colors, which were on the top of the Knoll, apparently attracted the special fire of the rebels. Capt. Moore fell in the advance and, if memory serves me right, it was here that Quien, who then took his place in Co. C, was shot in the hand. My duties as Sergt. Major took me from right to left constantly conveying orders and endeavoring to prevent the fleeing members of some Penn. Regiment, who justified their flight by saying "Our time ish out," from breaking through our lines and though many of our best men fell, one after the other while holding our colors aloft, I failed to get their names and Company. As we turned to fall back, Col. Fowler, who had just been left by Gen. Ames, brought in the rear of our Regt., and as he, with Adjt. Chatfield and myself started down the slope, we saw slowly following in the rear, the advance line of rebel skirmishers, a light battery on the ridge, which was shelling us and making things quite lively. We had not gone far, when to our horror we saw Col. Fowler falling from his saddle as his horse galloped away. Chatfield, who had just had his light sabre cut in two by a ball, hastily dismounted; poor Fowler was dead. It seemed to us that the hole in his head could hardly have been made by a fragment of a shell which had just burst above us, as it looked round and clearly marked, however, this was not time for speculation, so calling back one of our Regt. Co. E, whose name I cannot recall,* [Corporal Roscoe Perry, Company E, who claimed in his account that he was the last man to see Fowler's body and would become a POW on July 1] *we endeavored to lift his corpse upon the adjt.'s horse, but we found it impossible to do so, as his weight was beyond our strength, and after several attempts, we reluctantly left him.*

*This was the 153rd Pennsylvania, a German-speaking regiment posted as skirmishers below Blocher's Knoll along Rock Creek. Some of its men believed their nine-month enlistments had expired on June 22; in reality, the term had a few more days to run. Major John Frueauff had gathered the men around him on July 1 and told them their enlistment obligation had been fulfilled and that if any man in the ranks did not wish to go into battle he should step out of line. No man did.[83]

The boyish Adjutant Chatfield was well liked by the regiment. He was killed on February 5, 1865, at Dunn's Lake, Florida. His body was brought back to Connecticut and interred in Mountain Grove Cemetery in Bridgeport. (Buck Zaidel Collection)

At this time the rebel line had advanced within hailing distance, and the requests we received were more vigorous than polite. Chatfield, mounting his horse, escaped by a close shave to our right. Our friend of Co. E [Corporal Perry] *was captured before he left that field, while I, scaling a fence in front of us, tore across the next field towards a stone wall of the Poorhouse. On the way there, I saw trotting along with the American colors on his shoulder, Jimmy* [sic—Betts means John Hayes, Company F] *Hayes, of Co. F, who just about that time received a shot through his leg which floored him. I ran over to raise him but found him too badly hurt. A comrade from Co. C, I think ran up at the same time, and in view of the fact that he carried a musket and I had none, agreed with me that I had better take the flag, and so taking up the old colors, as I had at Chancellorsville, I continued my trot towards the shelter of the Poorhouse. Inside the walls of the barnyard, we found Gen. Ames and staff. We waited for orders which soon came in the shape of several shells bursting over our heads—a piece of one striking the staff of our colors* [The U.S. colors of the 17th Connecticut that are preserved in the state capitol at Hartford have battle damage consistent with Betts's description.[84]] *and making us start back through the town. I recall a futile attempt to dislodge some skirmishers from a lumber yard, under direction of Gen. Ames, and a halt for a few minutes in support of a single "Napoleon", hauled by a rope through the street, but have no connected recollections of when the small remnant of our Regt. was reformed on Cemetery Hill and assigned to its first position in line to the right of the road and overlooking the town. I recall the visit of Gen. Howard in the p.m. who found our Brigade a trifle out of line, and jumping his horse over the stone fence, led us forward to the next fence under a (hatline?) from sharpshooters.*

The Bachelder brothers were born in Maine and relocated to Bridgeport, Connecticut. The two oldest enlisted in Company D, 17th Connecticut: Melvin (left) as a private and Cyrus as a sergeant. They are pictured with the 17th Infantry insignia prominently displayed on their caps. Melvin, the youngest of the brothers, was a coppersmith.[85] (Maine State Library)

I recall also, the trip Theodore Brotherton, of Co. F, and I think Batchelder, of Co. D and myself, across the hill for a box of ammunition and the return with it, and can still hear the thud of the ball which passed through poor Batchelder's body and left him, as we thought, dead in the grass, and remember plainly the dangerous, but well performed duty of the detail sent to carry him to the rear, but the fatigue and excitement of the day seem ever present as I try to fill in the details of the nights alterations of*

> *rest and alarm. Nor can I remember now to whom the American colors were given.*

*There were two Bachelder brothers in Company D. Sergeant Cyrus T. Bachelder, listed as a POW July 1, and Private Melvin C. Bachelder. In the July 7 casualty list printed in the *Norwalk Gazette*, Sergeant Cyrus Bachelder was listed as wounded.[86] The wounding Betts describes here does not square with the facts and Bachelder certainly was not killed. Sergeant Bachelder was taken prisoner on July 1 but released when the Confederates retreated. Corporal Theodore Brotherton, Company F, of Norwalk, was not listed as wounded.[87] Sergeant Bachelder's rank would be reduced to private on March 12, 1865, possibly for ill health, and he was discharged on July 5, 1865.[88] The description Betts gives above about Bachelder and Brotherton cannot be verified by the author.

STEPHEN WILCOX, COMPANY F

In 1862 Stephen R. Wilcox, twenty-two, of Norwalk was a married carpenter with an infant son. Wilcox enlisted in Company F as a corporal. At Gettysburg he served as a private having been reduced in rank. By September 1863 he would again be wearing his corporal stripes, and he kept them until the end of the war when he was mustered out with the regiment in July 1865. Wilcox would be slightly wounded on July 2.[89] He remained in Gettysburg after the Federal army left in pursuit of Lee and performed nursing duty at the Camp Letterman General Hospital. Following is an excerpt from the letter Wilcox wrote his brother-in-law, Walter Clark, on August 1, 1863, describing his experiences on July 1.

> *I was sick before we got here and then they marched us twelve miles in the morning and never gave us but one rest and that was for about twenty minutes. We marched right thru the town and filed thru the lot and unslung some of our knap sacks and put them in a pile. Then Lieut. Col. Fowler asked who would volunteer to go out as skirmishers. Capt Allen marched his men right out and then called for Company A and K. We then went up the road and filed off into a lot and deployed as skirmishers and advanced to a stream and forded it. It was about up to our knees and then we stopped where we was for further orders. In a few minutes we got over the fence and advanced across a wheat field and got almost on the batteries of the Rebs when the Rebs made a charge on our division and our skirmishers were ordered back. We fell back a little ways and I saw the Adjutant coming towards us. He said that the Lieut. Col. was dead and showed us where his brains were spattered on this arm. He said that Capt. Moore was dead, the two best men in the regiment. We could see the Rebs coming out of the woods and they drove our men and then in a minute I saw our men charge on them but they was to much for us and we had to fall back fighting, as we fell back in good order, what little there was left of us. Some of the companies came out with four men and some of them with more.*[90]

CAPTAIN WILSON FRENCH WOUNDED

This account was written in the third person. It was probably from an interview given by Captain French to William Warren after the war. This account is undated but most likely from the 1880s. There is documentation in the French family papers that Warren visited French several times at his home in Stratford to interview him for the manuscript.[91]

Captain Wilson French, Company G. (Captain Wilson French Collection)

Wilson French, thirty-three, was a saddler and harness maker living in a rented house on Mill Hill in Bridgeport when he enlisted in Company G, 17th Connecticut as a first lieutenant in August 1862. French had been active in the local militia. He and Captain James E. Dunham were responsible for recruiting Company G. Recruiting ads for Company G published in the *Bridgeport Standard* in the summer of 1862 bear both their names. French would leave behind his wife, Martha, and two children when he departed in August 1862 with his regiment.[92]

At Chancellorsville French was the officer on the picket line with Companies G and I on the extreme right of the Union flank when Stonewall Jackson struck with 26,000 screaming Confederates and rolled up the Eleventh Corps.[93] It is possible that pickets in French's Company G fired some of the first Union shots of the disastrous battle. After Chancellorsville, Captain Dunham left the regiment and French was promoted to captain. French was wounded the first day at Gettysburg; his account of his wounding follows. Captain French would carry the shell fragment that wounded him in his arm for the rest of his life. He returned to his regiment in the fall of 1863 and served as the provost marshal of St. Augustine, Florida. Captain French was taken prisoner on February 5, 1865, at Dunn's Lake, Florida, during an ambush in which a number of officers and men were captured. French was sent to Andersonville, where Colonel William Noble, captured on Christmas Eve 1864, was the highest-ranking prisoner. French would be released from prison in late April 1865 after Lee's surrender at Appomattox. Shortly after he returned home in the summer of 1865, he was ordered to Washington to testify at the trial of Henry Wirz, the commandant at Andersonville.[94]

After the war, Wilson French moved to Stratford, Connecticut, with his wife and two children. Their home still stands on Broadbridge Avenue. His son died of tuberculosis in 1869. After the war he and his wife had two more children, a daughter and a son. French would become a partner in Wells and French, a saddlery and bridle business. Martha Bouton French would die in 1910 after breaking her hip. In 1912, a still vigorous Wilson French would campaign for Theodore Roosevelt's Bull Moose Party, leading a parade in Stratford.[95] He would pass in 1916 at age eighty-six, remembered for his modesty and quiet dignity.

Dr. Robert McEwen was an assistant surgeon with the 17th Connecticut. (Captain Wilson French Collection)

He (Captain French) was wounded the first day on Barlow's Knoll at the elbow of right arm, by a piece of explosive shot, as the Doctors called it. He had his arm raised to full length over his head, with sword in hand, when he was wounded. He looked around for someone to take his place while Henry Waite assisted him back to the Dutch Reform Church, which was then being used for a hospital. On the way they met Dr. McEwen. As French could not move his arm, the Doctor cut his coat sleeve open and dressed the wound, then told him to go to the hospital as above stated.

He [Captain French] *stayed in this hospital till the morning of the 4th, then a field hospital was established back of Cemetery Hill. Those able to go home were sent there on furlough, while others were sent to this hospital. Captain says, "I do not know who sheathed my sword, I could not."* [Captain French's sword is in the collections of the Stratford Historical Society.] *The class and back rooms were used by the Doctors for amputation rooms. French went into one of these rooms with sword and belt on. When the amputation was over, the men went back into the audience room. There were a good many ahead of him who had their arms and legs taken off. Finally, his turn came, and he told the doctors that he wanted his wound dressed. They replied that they wanted to take his arm off. French said, "You will never take it off as long as I am alive." The Doctors talked in German a while, and then dressed it, and said they would look at it in the morning, but they never saw the wound after that.*

Waite was detailed as nurse, so kept Captain well supplied with cold water and that was all he did for the wound. There were about 5,000 wounded men in different buildings from the first day's fight.[96]

(From Capt. French.)

French was technically a POW while at the hospital in the German Reformed Church while the Confederates held the town. With the pervasive inaccuracy of casualty information on July 4, Major Brady reiterated that status when he wrote the regiment's after-action report, "Captain Wilson French and Lieutenant Bartram are the only officers known to have been taken prisoners. The former was wounded in the first day's engagement. We are not aware that either of them was paroled."[97] Captain French was not in Confederate hands and had already been transferred to the Eleventh Corps hospital at the Spangler Farm. He was listed on the hospital rolls as "French, Wilson, Capt.,

17th CT G, right elbow joint, water dressing, fracture."[98] Lieutenant Bartram would spend the next twenty months in nine Confederate prisoner camps.[99] Captain William Hubbell, Company D, whose capture was not noted in Brady's report, would be incarcerated with Bartram in Libby Prison.[100]

As soon as the railroad was repaired after the Confederate withdrawal, the medical corps began sending wounded men by the hundreds to large general hospitals in Philadelphia, York, Washington, and Baltimore. Among the first to be sent from Gettysburg were wounded officers like Captain French who were ambulatory. These men were given leave to recuperate at their homes. On July 9, the *Bridgeport Evening Standard* reported, "We hear that Captain French, of the 17th arrived home last evening. He was shot in the arm."[101] A year after the battle, French would write to his wife, Martha, reminiscing about the night he turned up unexpectedly on their doorstep dirty, bloody, wounded, and in very bad shape. In an undated, handwritten, third-person account by Warren, French gave the statement, "Wilson French on the way to Gettysburg and while there did not have his boots off for 14 days, and then not until he got home on July 8 by being wounded. His boots and stockings had to be cut off and then the skin and the toenails came off with the rest."[102]

PRIVATE HENRY E. WAITE, MEDICAL ORDERLY

As a wounded officer, Captain French had a private assigned to him as a nurse. Private Henry E. Waite, Company K, was the sixteen-year-old son of a Bridgeport woodworker when he enlisted in the 17th Connecticut in 1862. Waite enlisted to escape a difficult homelife with an abusive and alcoholic father.[103] Dr. Hubbard was well aware of Waite's difficult homelife and took Henry under his wing. Hubbard wrote to his wife,

> *I may send also $40 to Mrs. Thomas Waite from her son as I find tonight that he was intending to send that to his father who is in habits a drunkard & in politics a copperhead and with such a character would make poor use of the money. So in case it comes to you, it will greatly oblige me by seeing that the money is put into Mrs. Waite's hands who is a poor broken-hearted worthy woman. Her son is very well and is acting as orderly to the Medical Staff of the regt. I shall take good care of him & see that his mother, if possible, has the benefit of his pay.*[104]

Private Henry Waite, Company K, detailed as a medical orderly and nurse. (Sean Summers Collection)

Waite would muster out with the regiment at Hilton Head in 1865. He remained active with the 17th Connecticut Volunteer Survivors Association and in veterans' affairs for the rest of his life. In 1885 Waite earned a medical degree from the Eclectic Medical College, City of New York. He was licensed to practice medicine in multiple states and became a manufacturer and inventor of "Electro Medical" and "Electro Surgical Devices." His company, Waite &

Bartlett, was known nationwide.[105] Waite held many patents and was a pioneer in the field of X-rays. His company laid the groundwork for modern radiology and his son, Harry Fuller Waite, followed in his footsteps. The younger Waite was acclaimed as the greatest American developer of X-ray equipment during the "Golden Age of Radiology" (1900–40) and he designed mobile X-ray units used by the American Expeditionary Force in Europe during World War I.[106]

Dr. Henry E. Waite died in 1917 at age seventy-one from heart failure and was interred in Mountain Grove Cemetery in Bridgeport. He was laid to rest by his surviving comrades from the 17th Connecticut.[107] It can only be wondered how his nursing duties as an adolescent private soldier, who enlisted to escape an abusive homelife, influenced his career in the medical field. Waite's training and practice as an eclectic physician is a testament to the rejection of the "heroic medicine" of the Civil War years. Eclectic medicine refuted such harsh and toxic medical practices and replaced them with botanical and more benign substances and physical therapy practices. In the mid-nineteenth century Waite's company manufactured many devices that today would be considered quackery, but the company also pioneered X-ray and fluoroscope technologies that were carried on by Waite's son and formed the foundation of modern internal diagnostics. X-rays allowed physicians to examine the internal body, eliminating a surgeon from probing with a bloody finger, or metal rod, to locate bullets and determine the extent of shattered bones on the battlefield. This was something that Civil War surgeons could not even imagine.

FROM VIRGINIA TO GETTYSBURG AND BACK

William Wallace Paynton was listed as a married hatter when he enlisted in 1862 in Company A, 17th Connecticut as a private. Paynton was promoted to corporal on September 1, 1864.[108] Paynton returned to his profession as a hatter after the war and lived in both Connecticut and New York. In 1889, William Wallace Paynton applied for a federal soldier's pension and received it. In the 1910 census he would be listed as living in the home of his daughter, Catherine, and son-in-law Samuel McDowell, in Fishkill, Dutchess County, New York. His age was listed as seventy and his wife, Margaret was listed as age sixty-five, the pair having been married twenty-eight years. Despite the 1910 census listing, Paynton was also listed as being as an inmate at Fitch's Home for Soldiers in Darien, Fairfield County, Connecticut.[109] Paynton may have entered residence at the Fitch's Home sometime in 1910 or even earlier, living separately from his wife. He was certainly a long-time resident at the soldiers' home and would remain in residence there until his death in 1920. Following his death, Margaret applied for a soldier's widow's pension and received that until her death in 1924.[110]

Fitch's Soldiers' Home was founded by Darien businessman and philanthropist Benjamin Fitch, who was appalled at the costs of war when he saw men returning home maimed or leaving widows and orphans indigent after sacrificing their lives for the Union. Fitch, a lifelong bachelor, decided he would build them a sanctuary. President Lincoln and Secretary of War Edwin Stanton endorsed the idea. On July 4, 1864, three thousand people gathered for the dedication of Fitch's Home for the Soldiers and Their

Fitch's Home for the Soldiers and Their Orphans in Noroton Heights as it appeared in 1906.
(Author's collection)

Orphans in Noroton Heights. "It is proposed to raise for the permanent endowment of the Home, a sum of $100,000, and to provide for the support of upward of 80 disabled soldiers, and the support and education of their children," the *Hartford Daily Courant* reported. The home opened the following year. It was the first of its kind in the country. The home would serve veterans and their families until 1940 when it closed its doors and transferred the veterans to Rocky Hill.[111]

William Wallace Paynton remained active in veterans affairs and among the 17th Connecticut survivors. He wrote about his experiences and William Warren incorporated some of his memories into his manuscript. Paynton would title his writing about the battle *From Virginia to Gettysburg and Back*, and would divide his account into chapters.

Paynton edited his account of the battle over the years. It is apparent that a private soldier could only acquire some of the information Paynton detailed regarding the larger scope of the battle long after his experiences in combat. It is not an unusual observation that these men, writing about their experience years later, studied the battle to enhance and more accurately portray the larger events surrounding their regimental experience. On the front of the handwritten copy book with his memoirs, Payton wrote, "Dedication—To my Friend and Comrade, William Warren, Co. C 17th Reg and Conn Vols, These "Recollections" Are Respectfully Dedicated by the Author, W. Wallace Paynton, Late Corporal Co A 17th Reg & Conn Vols, Soldiers Home, Noroton Heights, Conn, Oct 1st 1909."[112] Following is Paynton's account of the first day of battle beginning with the march from Emmitsburg to the retreat and battle line formed on East Cemetery Hill. This part of Paynton's account closes with the sharpshooting that would plague the regiment over the next two days while in that position.

FROM VIRGINIA TO GETTYSBURG AND BACK
Written by W. W. Paynton

Company "A" was the first company on the right; Lieut. Col. Fowler approached us and advised us to lay off our knapsacks; we could get them again on our return, they would be a burden to us. Alas, we did not return that way; that was the last time the gallant Fowler ever addressed the boys of his old company "A". Shortly after our deploying to the right, the brigade was ordered to advance and to charge the enemy. But a few rods had been covered, when Fowler was struck in the head by a shot and killed instantly. The Adjutant, Chatfield, who was by his side, had his horse killed under him, and one bullet through his hat, another through the sleeve of his coat, while the hilt and a few inches of blade was all he had left of his sword. The charge was repulsed, the brigade fell back. Capt. James E. Moore, of Company "C", was killed and our Color Sergeant E. D. Pickett, Corp. Henry Burns and 33 others of the regiment fell in this charge. Adjt. Chatfield and Sergt. Major C. F. Betts attempted to rescue Fowler's body, but after dragging it some distance were compelled to abandon it, and it never has been recovered yet.

A messenger was sent to Major Brady to retire the skirmish line in as good order as possible. A running fire was kept up with the rebel skirmishers; Captain McCarty of Company "K", however did not relish the idea of retiring. He called to the Major to come back and rally the line. He did not understand that the Major had orders to retire, so he tried to keep the line together, but a panic was on hand. The army was falling ack. Soon we re-entered the town and joined the retreating columns of the Corps in it[s] flight. All was confusion and disorder. Every street was filled with panic-stricken soldiers of all branches of the service. Each one seemed bent on his own safety. In some cases, artillery men had abandoned their guns and left them to fall into the hands of the enemy. In passing up one street, I observed a howitzer that had been thus abandoned. A few blocks below was a large public square. Into this square the rebels were crowding, yelling, and making for that gun. Just as I came opposite to where the gun was, some "Yankee" boys ran out to the gun and finding it loaded they fired into that crowd of yelling rebels, and reloaded and fired it several times, until I turned off into another street and lost sight of them. At last Cemetery Hill was reached, and here at the Gate House General Howard and staff were stationed and ordering the 11th Corps to file to the right into the cemetery. The 17th regiment was advanced to a position behind a stone fence near the brow of the hill, with artillery at our rear. During the next two days that Lee occupied the town, the public buildings and churches that were used as hospitals were filled with rebel sharpshooters—those demons of modern warfare, who would send their death dealing messengers into the ranks of our artillery and infantry.[113]

A SALOON AT GETTYSBURG NEAR EAST CEMETERY HILL

Corporal William O. Merritt was an unmarried hatter from Norwalk when he enlisted in Company A. Merritt would survive the war to be mustered out with his regiment. In 1896 he wrote William Warren his account of a saloon near East Cemetery Hill after the regiment retreated from Barlow's Knoll.

> *The Regiment fell back the first day to the foot of Cemetery Hill. Nearby, was a liquor saloon which had been deserted, probably when the fight opened. The proprietor, as it would seem, got out in a hurry, for everything was left just as he got through with it. When Wm. O. Merritt came along there, an officer came out of the saloon and stopped him, told him to come inside and act as sharpshooter. About 40 others had been stopped for this purpose. Merritt readily saw if he did, the house would be a target for the rebs to shoot at, so watching his opportunity, he made his way out, and went up the hill into our lines, behind our breastworks, the rebs firing at him all the way, while the boys of our Regiment were hollering at him to lay down, but he kept on safely into our lines.*
>
> *From Wm. O. Merritt, August 26, 1896*[114]

Merritt may have been referring to the Wagon Hotel as the saloon that was held by Union soldiers. The Wagon was located south of town at the foot of Cemetery Hill where the Emmitsburg Road joins Baltimore Street. Union soldiers from the Eleventh Corps had passed the hotel on their way into battle on the morning of July 1. Confederate sharpshooters continually harassed the Union line from houses on Baltimore Street including the Rupp, Winebrenner, McCreary, and Welty houses, along with the Rupp tannery.[115] Union sharpshooters from the Eleventh Corps positioned inside the Wagon Hotel returned fire at the Confederates for the next two days. The hotel suffered several solid shots from artillery and two Union soldiers were killed there. After the battle, the carpet was taken up and underneath a door in the floor were found kegs of liquor.[116] Today a gas station/convenience store is on the site of the old hotel.

The Wagon Hotel, circa 1886, at the junction of the Baltimore Pike and the Emmitsburg Road.
(Library of Congress)

CHAPTER 6

Those Who Carried the Colors on the First Day

The colors of a regiment were its most sacred and valuable symbols. To carry them was an honor, to lose them a disgrace. Men carried and followed the colors in battle no matter the odds, through triumph or tragedy. The men who carried the colors were the bravest of the brave. Color bearers were unarmed, they could not fight back, and they were frequently killed or wounded. To be a color bearer was the greatest honor. It took great courage to carry the flags unarmed and under fire, to advance, and to stand fast. Regiments carried two flags—the American flag, also referred to as the national colors, and a regimental flag that identified the unit and state. An armed color guard, comprising six or eight corporals, accompanied the flag bearers. The color guard's task was to protect the flag bearers and to take up the colors should a flag bearer be wounded or killed. Regulations stated the two regimental colors were carried side by side on the march and in battle. The colors were each carried by a designated color sergeant.[1]

The colors constituted the greatest target and the greatest prize on the battlefield. The colors and those who carried them were often the only means of communication through the smoke, thunderous noise, and chaos of battle. The colors led the regiment where voices, drums, or bugles could not be heard amid the roar of artillery and clamor of musket fire. The colors were powerful symbols and rallying points for the regiment. Men were trained to follow their colors through the worst. To lose the colors was the ultimate dishonor. To capture another regiment's colors was the greatest triumph on any battlefield. The significance and powerful symbolism, as well as the communication power of the colors, was paramount to any regiment. During the Civil War the colors were revered, and men were willing to fight—and die—for them.

Two flags were presented to the 17th Connecticut. Before the regiment left Bridgeport, the ladies of Norwalk presented it with a regimental flag purchased from F.

F. Rice at the cost of $65. The second was a national flag that was financed by LeGrand Lockwood.[2] That flag was presented to the regiment as a gift from Company F, also known as the Lockwood Guards, from Norwalk. LeGrand Lockwood was a wealthy businessman and railroad executive who was elected treasurer of the New York Stock Exchange in 1863. Lockwood financed Company F in 1862, spending $1,000 to outfit the unit. Company F used part of that money to buy the national flag for the regiment. The sleeve on the staff was inscribed "17th Connecticut/by/Lockwood Guard/Norwalk, Conn." Gerry S. Caughman, author of *Qui Transtulit Sustinet: Connecticut Battle Flag Collection*, a history of Connecticut's regiments and their flags, wrote of the regiment's U.S. flag: "The flag is one of the most beautiful in the Capitol collection. It is doubtful the large hand-embroidered stars could be duplicated today."[3] The national flag of the 17th Connecticut bears battle damage consistent with descriptions of the men who carried it on July 1. Caughman notes, "Also the bottom of the staff of this national color is mismatched and there are missing stars."[4]

On September 17, 1879, on the seventeenth anniversary of the Battle of Antietam, the city of Hartford hosted "Battle Flag Day" in honor of the soldiers and sailors of the Civil War. The entire city was decorated, and the celebration was immense. Veterans from every Connecticut regiment took part in the parade and presentation ceremonies. All of Connecticut's battle flags were presented and encased at the new capitol building, where they remain on display in the Hall of Flags. The *Hartford Courant* covered Battle Flag Day extensively. The *Courant* reported the condition of the 17th Connecticut's flags: "Seventeenth-One national, poor, looped; one state, very bad, can't be unfurled."[5] In 1985 the regimental flag of the 17th Connecticut was removed from the cabinets in the Hall of Flags where it had been placed in 1879. The flag was twisted around the staff and was in terrible condition. "Only the bottom of the finial survived the war. It looks as though the top was shot off in battle," Caughman wrote.[6] In 2002 the 17th Connecticut's U.S. flag was conserved. "It was mounted on China silk with the missing portions dyed a little lighter than the original flag," Caughman wrote. "It was covered with a sheer layer of nylon and the three layers were then stitched together. It is on exhibit in the Hall of flags at the Capitol."[7] In her book, under a photograph of the staff of the national flag, Caughman wrote, "Note the damage to the staff and the bent brass mounting rod which was more than likely caused by a bullet."[8]

Combat on the first day of Gettysburg on Barlow's Knoll was devastating to the Union men who were outnumbered by more than three to one by the Confederate attackers. Confederate general John B. Gordon described the Federal resistance to the overwhelming onslaught: "The enemy made a most obstinate resistance until the colors on portions of the two lines were separated by a space of less than 50 paces, when his line was broken and driven back."[9] Despite the blitz by the Confederates, the Union regiments preserved their colors. For the rest of his life Gordon remembered the hand-to-hand combat by two flag bearers. The Union flag bearer was probably from the 25th Ohio but remains unidentified. "This lion-hearted color-bearer . . . stood firmly in his place, refusing to fly, to yield his ground, or to surrender his flag," Gordon wrote. "As the Confederates crowded around him and around the stalwart men who still stood firmly by him, he became engaged in personal combat with the color-bearer of one of my Georgia regiments. What his fate was I do not now recall, but I trust and believe his life was spared."[10] In 1880 Lieutenant Colonel Jeremiah Williams of the 25th Ohio wrote to John B. Bachelder, the great nineteenth-century artist and historian of the battle: "During the first day's engagement the forces of Gen. Gordon (Confederate) were in such close conflict with the regiment . . . that the flag-bearers struck each other with their flag-staffs!"[11]

William Warren collected several accounts from men who carried, or witnessed who carried, the flags on the first day of the Battle of Gettysburg. It is almost impossible, however, to say with certainty what the sequence was of who carried the regimental and the U.S. colors or even who all the flag bearers were. The accounts were written well after the war. Despite the time lapse, these witness accounts can be compared, and their similarities bear witness that each of the men mentioned *did* carry the flags at some point during the first day's battle, and in doing so several were wounded and others made the ultimate sacrifice.

Multiple accounts, articles, and books about the 17th Connecticut regimental flags on the first day of Gettysburg describe the death of Sergeant Edwin D. Pickett of Ridgefield, whom sources identify as the third man to be killed carrying the regimental colors.[12] The author's efforts to determine the identity of the first two men killed carrying the regimental colors before Pickett have not been successful.

In Volume 3, page 607, of his eighth edition Warren wrote:

> ***Regimental Flags***
> *Since the close of the war there has been considerable controversy, by members of the regiment, as to who carried the flags into the fight at Gettysburg, and who brought them out. The following statements, as given to me by different comrades who claim they either saw, or had a part in the transaction, are enough proof to show how the flags were cared for.*[13]

The accounts that Warren collected and put into his manuscript were not sequential and were scattered throughout his "Gettysburg" volume. Below is the author's best attempt to assemble the accounts in a readable and sequential order and identify the men who wrote the accounts and carried the flags on the first day's battle.

PRIVATE WILLIAM F. OTIS

William F. Otis, Company C, was listed as a prisoner on July 1, 1863. He wrote on July 27, 1894:

> *The state flag was on the left of the regiment and the United States flag on the right. Corporal Burns carried the state flag and Sergeant Cyrus T. Batchelder carried the United States flag into the fight of Gettysburg. Burns*

was wounded and William F. Otis, who saw him fall, ran for the flag. C. Fred Betts was also on the same mission and succeeded in getting there first, so he bore the flag off the field.[14]

Private William F. Otis, Company C. (Bridgeport History Center)

PRIVATE JOHN L. HAYES

John L. Hayes, eighteen, was living in Norwalk when he enlisted as a private in Company F, 17th Connecticut. He was wounded carrying the national colors. He wrote this account in 1885 in a letter to R. Lorenzo Ells, a lieutenant in Company A. Ells forwarded this letter to William Warren sometime after he received it and Warren included it in the manuscript. This account appeared in the last chapter in its entirety; the portion about Hayes carrying the flag is reprinted here so that the reader may compare this with other accounts of the flags on July 1.

> *After the regiment had arrived at Gettysburg the men dropped their knapsacks and prepared for immediate action. I went to Captain Allen, telling him that I was going in and wanted a rifle (being Adjutant Clerk I had turned mine in to the Quartermaster's Department months before). He told me Company "F" was one of the companies ordered out as skirmishers—that I had better fall in and find a musket on the field as he had none. I did so and commenced marching into position—the rebels firing artillery during the time. I picked up a rifle during the marching, with accoutrements. After we had halted and faced to the enemy, I took my position in Company "C" to the left and rear of the colors. Lieut. Col. Fowler called me and gave me his picture. After the rebels had commenced their terrible fire and our line had crumbled away, I saw through the smoke that the national colors were falling near me; I grabbed them, throwing down my musket. I felt exhausted by our march that day from Emmitsburg and the excitement of battle and concluded to divest myself of a rubber blanket that was tied around me, and whilst holding the colors up with my left hand and throwing the blanket over my shoulder and head with my right, I was severely wounded, the ball entering my right thigh, striking the bone, passing up through the groin and lodging in the pit of my stomach. I shouted for someone to take the colors, but in the smoke, noise and confusion no one responded, until presently Jimmy. . . .* [Private James (Jimmy) Ainscow, a musician from Company K] *I don't remember his other name, helped me up and leaning on his shoulder with my left arm, I carried the flag in my right to the Poorhouse where I fell on my hands and face—the colors going down with me. I afterwards found myself in the Poorhouse, lying on*

one of the dining-room tables. As I was throwing the rubber blanket over my head, Corporal Burns, with the State colors in his left hand was swinging his cap over his head with his right shouting at the top of his voice, "Rally around your colors, boys." "Rally around your colors," perhaps not more than ten men near him, as everything at that time had gone to pieces and the rebels had gotten very close to us. A good many wounded on their way off the field and some killed. I judged the wounded from seeing them put a hand to an arm, head or leg in such a manner as to lead me to believe they were shot. I noticed one blackened eyed soldier, I think of Company "C", wounded sitting up as we were approaching him and crying for someone to help him up; a ball struck him again and he needed no help. To the left of us about 1500 feet the state colors were being carried off the field.

Corporal Henry Burns, Company B, a shoemaker from Norwalk, was killed carrying the state colors on July 1, 1863. (Image courtesy of Garry Wilkinson)

CORPORAL JAMES C. MAYNE

Corporal James C. Mayne, Company G, whose name is often spelled *Main* in various records, wrote his account of the death of Corporal Burns and how he picked up the state colors in a letter to Cyrus Raymond, Company H. Private Raymond was listed as missing on early casualty lists. He was wounded and captured on July 2. On August 8, after his release, he was admitted to the United General Hospital at Annapolis, Maryland, with "Rubeola" (probably German measles).[15]

Mr. Cyrus Raymond-

I can tell you who picked up the colors that Corporal Burns had, as I did it. Burns was shot over the right eye, as the order to retreat was given, and fell over on the colors, and I had to roll him over to get them.

J. C. Mayne[16]

Corporal Mayne's account was corroborated in a brief statement by Captain Wilson French, Company G, found in Warren's handwriting in a separate volume in the manuscript: "James C. Main, Company G, saved the colors the first day at Gettysburg so says Captain French."[17]

JAMES AINSCOW, COMPANY K

Private James Ainscow, a musician in Company K, wrote to William Warren in 1896 about the U.S. colors. Ainscow is the "Jimmy" referred to in several accounts. Ainscow helped Hayes to the Alms House after Hayes was wounded carrying the colors:

When Batchelder dropped the colors, John Hayes picked them up and was wounded. Then C. Fred Betts picked them up and carried them off the field. While in his hands a shell exploded and carried away three stars in the blue field. (The stars were worked on with silk.) The staff was shot away about 6 in. below the bottom of the flag. Betts carried the colors off the field by the aid of this 6 in. stump.[18]

Private James Ainscow, Company K. (Bridgeport History Center)

Sergeant Cyrus Bachelder served in Company D alongside his brother, Private Melvin Bachelder. Both brothers were born in Maine and enlisted in the 17th Connecticut in Bridgeport in 1862. While carrying the U.S. colors the first day on Barlow's Knoll, shortly after Colonel Fowler was killed, Bachelder went down when a shell struck a fence rail and sent it crashing into his chest. As the regiment fell back Bachelder was taken prisoner. He was paroled after the battle and returned to the regiment.[19] (Author's Collection)

SERGEANT MAJOR C. FREDERICK BETTS

In 1884 C. Frederick Betts wrote a detailed letter about his experiences at Gettysburg to Colonel Henry Allen. Betts had been promoted to sergeant major in June 1863 when he was sixteen years old; he would later be promoted to captain of Company F. He was taken prisoner at Dunn's Lake, Florida, on February 5, 1865, and sent to Andersonville. He was paroled in April 1865. The following excerpt pertains to Betts's account of the flags.[20] Betts's full account of the action on July 1 is in chapter 5.

Our colors, which were on the top of the Knoll, apparently attracted the special fire of the rebels. . . . My duties as Sergt. Major took me from right to left constantly conveying orders . . . many of our best men fell, one after the other while holding our colors aloft, I failed to get their names and company. As we turned to fall back, Col. Fowler, who had just been left by Gen. Ames, brought in the rear of our Regt., and as he, with Adjt. Chatfield and myself started down the slope . . . We had not gone far, when to our horror we saw Col. Fowler falling from his saddle as his horse galloped away . . .

At this time the rebel line had advanced within hailing distance, and the requests we received were more vigorous than polite. Chatfield, mounting his horse, escaped by a close shave to our right . . . I, scaling a fence in front of us, tore across the next field towards a stone wall of the Poor House. On the way there, I saw trotting along with the American colors on his shoulder, Jimmy [sic; Betts means John Hayes of Company F, who was wounded while carrying the flag; Jimmy refers to James (Jimmy) Ainscow,

> *who went to Hayes's assistance. Both Hayes's and Ainscow's accounts make this clear.] Hayes, of Co. F, who just about that time received a shot through his leg which floored him. I ran over to raise him but found him too badly hurt. A comrade from Co. C (sic), I think ran up at the same time, and in view of the fact that he carried a musket and I had none, agreed with me that I had better take the flag, and so taking up the old colors, as I had at Chancellorsville, I continued my trot towards the shelter of the Poorhouse. Inside the walls of the barnyard, we found Gen. Ames and Staff. We waited for orders which soon came in the shape of several shells bursting over our heads—a piece of one striking the staff of our colors and making us start back through the town . . . the fatigue and excitement of the day seem ever present as I try to fill in the details of the night's alternations of rest and alarm. Nor can I remember now to whom the American colors were given.*[21]

ALBERT PECK, COMPANY D

In 1887, Lieutenant Albert Peck, Company D, wrote an account of the Battle of Gettysburg. "I was second lieutenant at the time in command of Company D, which I think numbered 36 men for duty," Peck wrote. "I was the only commissioned officer in my company during the battle, as Captain Hubbell was A.A.G. on the staff of General Barlow and 1st Lt. Blinn, was absent, wounded." (Lieutenant Samuel Blinn, Company D, had been wounded and captured at Chancellorsville.) In summarizing the results of the battle, Peck would address the issue of who carried the flags—specifically, the men who carried the national flag on the first day's battle:

> *Sergt. Cyrus T. Batchelder carried the national colors into the first day's fight, but for some reason dropped them and they were picked up by Private Daniel S. Garrit, of Co. "D"* [alternate spellings are Garrett, Garritt], *who turned them over to Captain Betts of Co. "A" until after we reformed in the town, when Garrit claimed them and brought them safely back to Cemetery Hill and carried them through the rest of the battle. I received a letter from Colonel Allen some time ago, in which he stated he had received a letter from Betts in which he claimed to have picked them up, but I wrote to Garrit about it and he says he picked them up and met Betts, who asked him for them, and he gave them to him without thinking, but after the regiment reformed in the town, he claimed them and Betts gave them to him. I know Garritt carried them back to Cemetery Hill, as he was with me.*[22]

In his account of the first day's fight, Peck also described the retreat from Barlow's Knoll through town and how General Howard took the colors at Cemetery Hill to position the regiment, "*General Howard took our colors and moved forward, and our boys followed with a cheer.*"[23]

THOMAS A. MARSH, COMPANY D

In 1902, Thomas A. Marsh, Company D, wrote to William Warren about his wounding on Barlow's Knoll while carrying one of the regimental flags. Marsh, born in Kent, England, in 1835, was a married farmer from Easton with an infant daughter when he enlisted. His brother-in-law Charles Quick enlisted with him in August 1862. Marsh was gravely wounded by multiple bullets minutes after taking the flag.[24] Marsh would spend months in various hospitals until he was transferred on August 30, 1864, to the 159th Company, Veterans Reserve Corps, 2nd Battalion. He would be discharged for disability on August 12, 1865.[25] Marsh's account of taking up the flag and being immediately wounded is in the third person:

> *He was wounded the first day on Barlow's Knoll. The color corporal of his company being wounded, Marsh was ordered to take his place, and had but just commenced his new duties, when he was wounded by bullets knocking to pieces the cap off his left shoulder. He had three bullets taken out, besides other pieces of lead from his shoulder and side. He carried one bullet in his body 17 years, then had it taken out because it troubled him so much. Another bullet was taken out in Philadelphia, a foot or more, down the side of his body from where it went in. Another was taken out in the New Haven Hospital. The three bullets were about six inches apart from each other. After being wounded he started to go to the rear, but when a few rods away, he fell to the ground exhausted and unconscious.*[26]

There is no reason to doubt Marsh's description above. However, the second half of his account becomes quite fantastical until it reverts to the believable when Marsh describes being taken to a Confederate hospital. Perhaps whoever found the unconscious Private Marsh was having some fun with the wounded man, or he hallucinated, or he simply believed what he relayed to Warren and Warren included this implausible portion of the account in the manuscript. The following is inexplicable and although there were several rumors of Confederates drinking whiskey mixed with gunpowder at Gettysburg, the idea of General Longstreet caring for a wounded private on Barlow's Knoll and offering him the explosive beverage is beyond bizarre.

> *Laying there about two hours he was taken prisoner by General Longstreet, himself, who made himself known to Marsh. The General dismounted a rod or two away and walked up to Marsh, who asked him for a drink of water. General said, "I have not got anything but gun powder and whiskey in my canteen. We have to give it to our men to make them fight your men." The General then called a man from the ranks and told him to get Marsh some water to drink from the brook and then take him to the hospital, which was a rebel division hospital, about 5 miles from Gettysburg. While laying on the ground the two hours, there had been considerable fighting done, for all around him lay dead rebels. Marsh was in this hospital till*

> *the A.M. of July 4, when all the men that were able to walk were called out into line by a reb doctor who told them that they would have to walk to Richmond.*[27]

Several men of the 17th Connecticut were photographed with the regimental flags and Warren included them in the photographic volume of his manuscript. These photographs with commentary follow.

Corporal William Humphries, Company C (Bridgeport History Center)

William Humphries was born in Ireland in 1834. He became a naturalized citizen on October 3, 1865, in Danbury Superior Court. He was a hatter by trade, and active in veteran and civic affairs. He served three terms as the doorkeeper at the Connecticut State Senate, and served as a burgess, street commissioner, and health inspector in Danbury. He died July 16, 1917, at age eighty-two. His obituary stated he was a color bearer at Gettysburg.[28] Warren wrote in his photographic index, "While the regiment was returning home from the war and were marching up Chapel Street in New Haven to the state capitol on the public green, with colors flying, a photographer asked him [Humphries] to come into his gallery and let him take his picture of which this is a copy."[29]

James Middlebrook, Company D, was a married farmer from Trumbull who wrote home to his wife on July 9, 1863, about the fight on Barlow's Knoll. He served as a nurse at the Eleventh Corps hospital at the Spangler Farm after the battle. "We went into the fight the first of July & our brave Lieut Col fell & quite a number of our Co were wounded & some killed. The morning after the fight there were only 10 men of the Co there, we went to the front under a perfect shower of shot and shell and when we got there they poured it into us being the Color Company & the wonder is we did not all fall."[30]

James R. Middlebrook, Company D. (Bridgeport History Center)

Middlebrook was promoted to corporal on January 30, 1864; his picture with the flag was taken after this promotion. Warren notes in his picture index, "On the margin of his card was written, regimental flag, presented by the Lockwood Guard."[31] Shortly before his muster out in July 1865, Middlebrook wrote to his wife, "Make up your mind to travel some when we get home. I think of going to that place long to be remembered—Gettysburg."[32]

Robert Perry was born in Scotland in 1843 and was working as a dyer when he enlisted in the 17th Connecticut in 1862 as a private. He was wounded on July 1. Shot through the left shoulder, he was later transferred from Gettysburg to the U.S. General Hospital in Germantown, Pennsylvania.[33] He would be promoted to corporal on January 1, 1865, and would muster out with the regiment at Hilton Head in July 1865. The 1870 census listed Perry as married to Sarah, with whom he had three children. He died in 1879, age thirty-five, and is buried in Norwalk's Union Cemetery.[34]

Robert N. Perry, Company F, was wounded on July 1. (Bridgeport History Center)

CHAPTER 7

July 2—Holding the Line

Just after 4 a.m. on June 2 a humid dawn began to break over the town and fields of Gettysburg. By 7 a.m. it was already warm and muggy. Soldiers and citizens knew it would be a hot day in more ways than one.[1] The first day of battle had ended with the Confederates in control of the town and Union troops driven back south of the town. As the sun rose, the Eleventh Corps was hunkered down along Cemetery Ridge to the east and south of Gettysburg. The second day of battle would be a long and crowded one for soldiers and civilians. After the war, when the men remembered and wrote about the events of July 2, the times they used were approximate. It is exceedingly difficult to pinpoint time with any exactitude during the battle and there was no such thing as synchronized watches or daylight saving time. On July 2, 1863, in Gettysburg, morning twilight began at 4:11 a.m. and sunrise was at 4:44 a.m. Evening began with sunset at 7:41p.m., with darkness at 8:14 p.m.[2] The weather conditions, the smoke of battle, and the intensity of the experience could all affect the soldiers' estimations of time.

After a sleepless night, the men on East Cemetery Hill began the day hungry. The only provisions available had been what they carried from Emmitsburg in their haversacks and those rations were mostly gone. As was the case of all soldiers during the war, erratic and deficient diets resulted in debilitating conditions that affected health on campaign and in battle. Vitamin C deficiencies pervaded the army and caused symptoms of scurvy, or the scorbutic taint, as it was referred to in the Civil War. Most men during their service, at one time or another, suffered from extreme fatigue, swollen joints, bleeding gums, and the debilitating early effects of scurvy. Even without the symptoms of scurvy, the men on Cemetery Hill were hungry and dehydrated. More significant for the coming night fight on East Cemetery Hill was the "nyctalopia," or night blindness common to soldiers in the Civil War resulting from a lack of vitamin A.[3] It is fair to state that people of the Victorian age could not see as well at night as we in the twenty-first century. Night actions were rare in the Civil War and the July 2 fight on East Cemetery Hill would be hellacious; men who saw perfectly well during the day would become almost blinded by the dark as night descended. For these soldiers, July 2 would become both the longest day and an endless night.

After the harrowing retreat through town the evening before, Lieutenant Albert Peck, Company D, remembered that the regiment was unable to furnish a full detail of the requested of one hundred men for picket after they reached the new position. Peck wrote, "We were posted in an apple orchard close to the edge of town, with our videts posted along by a board and rail fence. We were ordered to be very watchful and vigilant, as our troops were expecting to make an attack on the town that night; I don't think I got any sleep that night."[4] The relentless and nerve-racking sharpshooting from houses facing the Federal line again erupted with the morning light, and would continue until the Confederate withdrawal on July 4. The Federals would try their best to return the harassment, with several notable incidents remembered by the men of the 17th Connecticut. By the morning of the third day, Major Brady, who was sporting a painful shoulder wound from the attack the night before, was so exasperated, in pain, and probably overwrought with the Confederate sniping that he yelled at his men, "For God's sake, can't you keep those fellows quiet?"[5] Constant sniping took casualties and frayed the nerves of all throughout the next two days. Private William Fields, Company F, wrote, "Saw the following on a.m. of the 2nd day while at the stone wall: The rebel

This battlefield sketch from Alfred Waud shows houses in town where Confederate and Union sharpshooters traded fire. In front of the house on Baltimore Street, to the left, lies a dead soldier. Several of the houses along Baltimore Street along the Union lines on East Cemetery Hill were filled with Confederate sharpshooters. Confederate fire plagued Federal regiments like the 17th Connecticut and the Union artillery batteries that were within view of these houses. (Library of Congress)

sharpshooters were in different houses. One house had a hospital flag on which was full of sharpshooters and they had a good range on our regiment. [Corporal] Darius B. Rockwell, Company F, was hit. It was sure death to anyone who exposed themselves. Finally, it got so bad that our folks opened batteries on them and cleaned them out which broke it up."[6]

On the morning of July 2, the hungry and thirsty men who were left in the 17th scrounged for anything they could find. The lucky ones had some hardtack, or a little water left in their canteens; most did not. The regiment was still in the position where General Howard had led them when they reached Cemetery Hill after the tumultuous retreat through town the evening before. When the 17th Connecticut roll was called on the morning of July 2, it revealed the regiment had lost 145 of the 386 men it had gone into battle with. The casualties included 17 killed, 73 wounded, and 55 missing or captured.[7] That morning, Lieutenant Milton Daniels, Company C, recalled that "On calling roll of Company C we found missing every sergeant, every corporal but Corporal Scott, and only twenty-five of us out of sixty-five when we went into the field."[8]

The position of the regiment would change several times during the day. According to Major Brady, on July 1 General Howard had advanced the 17th

> *across another lot still nearer the town and behind a rail fence at the upper end of the town, which position we held until late in the evening, exposed to a galling fire from the enemy's sharpshooters, when the whole regiment was ordered out on picket and performed that duty until l2 o'clock of the 2nd instant, when we were relieved and took a position behind the rail fence and 150 paces further to the right of the place we occupied before going out on picket. We remained in this position, exposed to the enemy's batteries and sharpshooters, until 7 p.m., when we were ordered to the extreme right, behind a stone wall on each side of a lane, below the battery opposite the cemetery entrance.*[9]

Because of the several position changes noted in Brady's official report, some confusion surrounds the exact location of the regiment during the attack the evening of July 2. Fueling the questions are Brady's own words and those of Colonel Harris of the 75th Ohio, who was commanding the brigade.[10] Harris, writing after the war, stated that General Ames (who assumed command of the division after Barlow was wounded) ordered the 17th Connecticut to von Gilsa. In the same letter Harris wrote, "the 17th Connecticut having returned to join my right."[11] Regardless of how this is interpreted, the move of the 17th Connecticut left a gap between the 107th and 25th Ohio that was not filled at the time the Louisiana Tigers attacked Harris's line. As this book is concerned with the personal reminisces of the men who fought this battle, the purpose here is not to engage in that controversy, but to acknowledge that the position of the 17th Connecticut in the battle line has not been determined without argument. Also acknowledged is that the present-day monuments, although physically set in stone, do not always precisely mark the position of a regiment. It is possible that men who fought on East Cemetery Hill may not have known themselves, amid the ferocity of the attack and the trauma and chaos of combat, exactly where they were in the line and who was around them in the darkness and smoke. Much of the analysis of the line positions came after the battle, some of it immediately after, but for some the contentions were never definitively settled (see Appendix D: Alternate Maps for the Brickyard Lane Deployment).

Line positions were not the only source of disagreement. Immediately after the battle, accusations against the Eleventh Corps erupted again, or continued, in similar vein from Chancellorsville and the day before on Blocher's Knoll. Nevertheless, the survivors of the 17th Connecticut remained adamant that on July 2 they stood their ground under the Confederate assault, and there is ample evidence to back this claim. Any intimation that the regiment did not hold its ground prompted postwar venom from the 17th Connecticut survivors toward those who dared defame the regiment. In one restrained statement, Lieutenant Peck wrote to William Warren, "On the eve of July 2nd, when the Tigers charged, I was right in the center of the Regiment during the whole engagement, and as far as I could see, <u>not a man</u> left his position until after we were relieved by Gen. Ames' order." Warren annotated Peck's statement with his own postscript: "He [Peck] writes this to contradict statements made by Guides who tell the public in their lectures that two companies of our Regiment during this charge broke and fell back."[12]

What is well documented regarding the 17th Connecticut's location on East Cemetery Hill is that the regiment did change position several times on July 2; that the regiment, along with the 75th Ohio, made a stand at the bottom of the hill under attack by General Hays's Louisiana brigade has also become accepted scholarship. The 17th Connecticut and the 75th Ohio, positioned alongside each other behind a low stone wall, stood fast under intense assault and did not break even when the 54th and 68th New York regiments on the right of the 17th Connecticut gave way, and the 107th Ohio and 25th Ohio on the left of the 75th Ohio buckled under pressure from 5th and 6th Louisiana regiments.[13] It also must be recognized that with the breaks in the Federal line, Confederates surged around and past the 75th and the 17th where they stood, got behind the two Yankee regiments, and briefly fired into them from the rear as they made their mad scramble in the murky darkness up the hill to attack the artillery.

Visitors and historians today trying to envision the lines of attack and defense on East Cemetery Hill must understand that the landscape there is some of the most disturbed and churned up land on the battlefield and bears no resemblance to its 1863 appearance. The construction of Wainwright Avenue, which approximates the path of the Brickyard Lane, was the first major disruption to the 1863 landscape on East Cemetery Hill.[14] The fields where the Louisiana and North Carolina troops crossed is now the location of two schools and their attached parking lots and playing fields. The substantial overgrowth between Wainwright Avenue and the school playing fields obscures almost all of what remains of the 1863 viewshed.

Wainwright Avenue with the 17th Connecticut monument to the right. The dense foliage shows just how much of the viewshed is obscured. The elevated retaining wall is topped by a metal guardrail that was placed along the avenue when it was built. (Library of Congress)

The construction of the avenues on the battlefield took place between 1882 and 1917. The avenues were to serve as the park's main interpretative system, and they continue to be the central routes for touring the battlefield today. Wainwright Avenue replaced the path of the Brickyard Lane or Winebrenner Lane (named for the tannery owner with a house and business on Baltimore Street where the road egressed into the town). This lane was a wagon path that allowed farmers and others with heavy loads to skirt the east side of Cemetery Hill, rather than take the Baltimore Pike up and over the hill, as they made their way into town.[15] Construction of Wainwright Avenue significantly and forever altered the terrain and views of July 2, 1863, by drastically regrading the area. Further changes were the subsequent paving of a school parking lot over Winebrenner Run, the creation of the retaining wall under the roadbed facing the Confederate assault, and the obscuring of a freshwater spring that was across the lane to the right of the 17th Connecticut's position in front of the 54th New York.[16] In several firsthand accounts by soldiers of the 17th seeking water, it may be this spring that they speak of, or Raffensperger's Spring, in addition to Menchy's more prominent spring, visible on most maps of the battleline. Menchy's spring is to the right of the 17th position down the Brickyard Lane.

This glass-plate view from July 1863 shows the terrain over which the Louisiana Tigers charged the Union position. The view was taken from Cemetery Hill at about the position of the right gun of Wiedrich's Battery. The German Reformed Church is visible at right; to the left of the church, behind the trees, is the roof of the public school. Both the school and the church served as hospitals during the battle. (Library of Congress)

Most firsthand accounts of the second day's battle from the 17th Connecticut describe the town as clearly in view. Especially prominent landmarks in Gettysburg, visible from the battle line at the base of East Cemetery Hill, were the German Reformed Church on the corner of Stratton and High Streets and the school with its bell cupola, to the right of the church and also on High Street. The sightlines went both ways: Several wounded Union soldiers being held as prisoners in the school described watching the Louisiana Tigers during the day of July 2, resting, smoking, and cooking over their campfires. Several 17th accounts described watching the assault begin in the twilight as Hays's Brigade formed up. J. Henry Blakeman, wounded on July 1 and taken behind the lines to a Confederate field hospital, recalled, "The next day, July 2nd all the wounded prisoners were taken in ambulances—carried into the town of Gettysburg and put into a school-house and church on the edge of town . . . From the windows of our prison, we saw the Louisiana Tigers form and start on the charge that the 17th Regiment helped to repulse with such slaughter on the evening of the 2nd. It can easily by imagined we were somewhat anxious as to the result of the fight."[17]

On July 4, several accounts from battleline state that a squad from the 17th was ordered to enter and search the town to verify that the Confederates had evacuated. As the squad advanced, a Union doctor come out of the German Reformed Church and waved his hat as a signal for all clear.

At first glance the terrain over which the two brigades of Hays's and Hoke's (Avery's) infantry would charge during the night attack on July 2 (5th, 6th, 7th, 8th, and 9th Louisiana and 6th, 21st, and 57th North Carolina) seemed a deadly proposition for the

This 1863 glass plate taken from the Baltimore Pike and looking toward Culp's Hill shows the landscape that the North Carolina Brigade advanced over toward the Union line. Colonel Avery's North Carolinians advanced to the left of Hays's Louisiana Tigers during the assault. (Library of Congress)

This later stereoview portrays Culp's Hill, with the base of Cemetery Hill in the foreground. This is the landscape over which three North Carolina regiments advanced to engage von Gilsa's Brigade, which was posted to the left of the 17th Connecticut. The monument in the bottom left marks the position of von Gilsa's 41st New York, which was placed to the right of Menchey's Spring across the lane. The stone wall and fence along Brickyard Lane is in front of the monument. (Library of Congress)

attackers, with strong advantages for the defenders. Although the Union line looked formidable, it was extremely thin. The Federals would be outnumbered in the coming fight by two to one. The two Eleventh Corps brigades reported only 1,150 men fit for duty on July 2 compared to an estimated strength of Hays and Avery of 2,100.[18] In addition, as twilight began to settle on Cemetery Hill the Union line there did not expect to be attacked. Casualties the day before on Barlow's Knoll had reduced most of the Federal regiments to below half of what they were when they entered the battle. Without enough manpower to secure the line, Colonel Harris, commanding the brigade, had three of his regiments on the extreme right: the 107th Ohio, 17th Connecticut, and the 25th Ohio. The three regiments formed a bend to the east along the Baltimore Pike, creating an elbow on the left of the thin Union line that descended along the Brickyard Lane. The infantry, artillerymen, and horses there were in full view of and vulnerable to Confederate sharpshooters in the houses along Baltimore Street.

The Union batteries on Cemetery Hill appeared formidable, but had weaknesses. The three-inch ordnance of Wiedrich's and Ricketts's batteries, placed on the hill the previous day for long-range support of the troops north of town, were not suited to fire anti-personnel cannister without fouling the rifled tubes, although the gunners certainly did when the time came.[19] Compounding this weakness, the placement of the batteries at the geographical crest of the hill, rather than the military crest, gave the tubes superior long-range sight and power, but prevented them from effectively protecting themselves in a frontal, close-encounter attack. The artillery had blind spots at the bottom of the hill, and the artillerists were unable to depress their guns sufficiently to ward off a close-range charge. In artillery speak, "these batteries had no point blank."[20]

Union infantry was placed below the hill and below and out of the sight of the artillerists. The daunting open ground over which the Confederates planned to charge also afforded the attackers some unexpected advantages. Because of the swales, marshy bottoms, and stone walls bisecting the fields, along with the darkness that fell on the attack, the ground offered cover and concealment that would not have been there in full light. Conversely, the stone walls along the Brickyard Lane were low and did not offer their Union defenders solid cover.[21] Apparently there had been no thought, as on Culp's Hill, to entrenching or reinforcing the existing walls. At one point during the attack, due to the rolling terrain, Federals were able to see only the flashing muzzles along the base of the hill and could hear the attackers but could not see them. The growing darkness also provided the Confederates with some cover from the relentless Union artillery fire. As the attack progressed the inability of the tubes to depress far enough negated their effectiveness until it seemed that the Confederates were right on top of the infantry and then on the artillery.[22]

On July 2 the action began at first light for the 17th Connecticut in an orchard. Lieutenant Peck wrote of that morning,

> *The Rebel pickets began to move around the fences about four o'clock in the morning and commenced firing on our boys and our boys fired back. I can tell you it was pretty close shaving in the orchard for three or four*

> *hours. We had to hug apple trees pretty close to keep from getting hit, but I do not remember of any of our men getting hit. I remember carrying fresh cartridges to some of the boys in my soft hat along the rail fence where some of our men were posted. The bark was well peeled off from some of those apple trees before we got relieved. The Rebel pickets got sort of a crossfire on us and we had to change our positions once in a while. I believe we were relieved just before noon and I was not sorry as it got to be pretty hot there.*[23]

Peck remembered the roar of the dueling artillery, the racket of sharpshooting on both sides, and the heat of the day:

> *It was very warm that day and we crawled up under the fence to keep from getting sunstruck. I finally thought I would raise up my head a little and see if I could see any Johnnies dying in the grass—when "zip"—came a Rebel bullet, which I thought was meant for me and it made my hair stand up a little, and I concluded I could see well enough by looking between the rails.*

He also recalled the men of the regiment retrieving water:

> *Our men used to get their drinking water at Menchey's Spring which was located near Culp's Hill and just over the fence from the lane that ran from the town to Culp's Hill. One man would take as many canteens as he could carry conveniently and start on a run down the hill and fill his canteens and then run back with them and very likely the Rebel Sharpshooters would keep firing at him all the way, but they did not get hit very often and we had to keep somebody on the way for water most all of the time.*[24]

Throughout the day the artillery dueled. In the late afternoon to the south the din and roar of battle from the Peach Orchard, Cemetery Ridge, The Wheatfield, and Little Round Top could be heard clearly on East Cemetery Hill. The relief that each of the attacks were repulsed was palpable, and rumors ran rampant. Peck recalled, "*A union courier or dispatch bearer was sent around our whole line of battle and we could hear the men cheer as he rode along. He reported the capture of General Longstreet with six thousand prisoners, but it turned out that Longstreet's Adjutant General was captured instead of Longstreet. The fight ended just before night.*"[25] The powerful rumor that Longstreet was either killed, captured, or wounded, made its way throughout the Union army before it was finally put to rest.

July 2 was the bloodiest day of the three-day battle, and the second-bloodiest day of the war, after Antietam. General Lee's entire strategy for July 2 was stymied by poor staff work, delays, and lack of coordination between his generals. Yet with all the flaws, the Confederates came within a hair's breadth of breaking the Union line at its left flank and center. General Meade had used his interior lines to throw most of his reserves at

This stereoview shows part of the terrain that some of the Confederate regiments would cross to attack East Cemetery Hill. (Author's collection)

Lee's late-afternoon attacks and the Confederate assaults had been blunted. By evening Meade's right was seriously vulnerable, and the challenges of day were not yet over.[26] As the noise of battle quieted to the south and daylight began to fade, the Union line on East Cemetery Hill did not yet believe it would face a nighttime assault.

The Confederate plan of attack on East Cemetery Hill had its merits, but in the twilight at the end of the day on July 2, the timing crucial to Lee's strategy was already lost. General Richard S. Ewell, commander of the Corps, had been instructed by Lee to begin his assault on Meade's right when Longstreet began his assault on Meade's left. Ewell was to start "a simultaneous demonstration . . . to be converted into a real attack should the opportunity offer."[27] By dark that evening, Longstreet's attack, which had been late in getting underway, had been repelled and was all but over when Ewell began his demonstration with an opening bombardment from Benner's Hill. Three brigades from General Edward Johnson's division were to attack Culp's Hill; Hays's and Avery's brigades would assault Cemetery Hill, with Gordon's brigade in reserve. General Rodes, to the west on Long Lane, would move against the salient in Meade's line from the other side.[28]

Confederate artillery under Major Joseph Latimer, the nineteen-year-old "Boy Major" artillery chief for Johnson's division, was instructed to support the attack on Culp's Hill by shelling Union-held Cemetery Hill. Latimer had few choices for the placement of his artillery and chose Benner's Hill along the Hanover Road, which overlooked the town and the Union position. Between 4 p.m. and 5 p.m. Latimer's batteries went into action against Federal artillery.[29] Benner's Hill was a commanding artillery platform, but as such, was also a perfect target for Federal artillery. As Latimer opened his batteries, Federal guns on Cemetery Hill begin to pound him back.

On July 3, a wounded Justus Silliman, Company H, would pen a letter from the public school on High Street where he was being held prisoner: "At about four o'clock yesterday PM the fight was renewed with great fierceness. The cannonading and musketry firing was terrific and the sound of shells rushing through the air was continuous and resembled somewhat that of a tremendous waterfall."[30]

Latimer's fire began to take a toll on the Union batteries. A twenty-pound shell exploded under the left gun of Captain James Cooper's 1st Pennsylvania Light Artillery Battery B and killed or wounded all five men working the piece. The gun remained functional. A new gun crew manned the piece and hurled shot back at Benner's Hill before their wounded and dead comrades were removed. Another of Latimer's hits struck an axle of another of Cooper's guns; its crew continued firing until the gun gave out. One of Lieutenant George Breck's rifled guns was struck on the axle and disabled, and to his unit's rear one of the caissons was struck and exploded.[31] Amid the hellish blitz, Colonel Charles Wainwright, in command of the Union artillery on Cemetery Hill, was observing the fire from Wiedrich's Battery when a Confederate shell burrowed into the ground at his feet. Wainwright stoically remembered, "I waited quietly to see if it would drive out the hole it entered when it burst, or would it break straight up. It never occurred to me that should it come right up it would certainly hit me, until it had safely blown out its entrance." At the wall across from the cemetery gatehouse, Wainwright and Ames consulted when Wainwright saw another twenty-pound shot strike a line of infantry. He remembered the shell "taking the line sideways it literally ploughed up two or three yards of men, killing or wounding a dozen or more. Fortunately, the shot did not burst, for it struck so near where we were sitting it covered us with dust."[32]

This real-time battlefield sketch by Alfred Waud shows the retiring of disabled Union artillery on Cemetery Hill. (Library of Congress)

Shells arced screaming and shrieking over the fields. Below East Cemetery Hill, the 17th Connecticut remained unscathed by the barrage above them. Peck remembered,

> *While our brigade were lying on East Cemetery Hill beside a stone wall, the Rebels opened a Battery on us . . . nearly a mile away, and shelled us for about an hour, and we were ordered to lie down, and we lay pretty close to the ground and could hear the shells bursting over our heads and the pieces came quite as close as we wanted them to. Our batteries on the hill, just above us soon replied to the Battery which was located on Benner's Hill and soon drove it away and blew up one of their caissons. They soon returned to their position but were driven away from it three times. I so not remember that any of our brigade were killed or wounded by their shells.*[33]

The 17th had hunkered down and was fortunate. Other infantry and the artillery higher up the hill were not. The atmosphere was one of shrieking shrapnel, the boom and roar of the big guns, smoke, and flashes from the cannon muzzles. The screams of wounded and dying men and horses rent the air. Elsewhere on the hill Confederate overshots rained shrapnel into Evergreen Cemetery. Exploding shells cracked headstones and took casualties, killing, maiming, and mortally wounding men seeking shelter among the tombstones. One famous casualty was Captain Frederick Stowe, a member of General von Steinwehr's staff and the son of Harriett Beecher Stowe, author of *Uncle Tom's Cabin*. Stowe was struck in the head by a shell fragment and taken to the division field hospital in or near the cemetery, where he was tended to by Dr. Robert Hubbard, surgeon of the 17th Connecticut.[34] Stowe would be evacuated to the Eleventh Corps hospital at the Spangler Farm, where the shell fragment would be extracted on July 3 by Dr. Brinton. Stowe was sent from Gettysburg with other wounded in mid-July to a military hospital in New York City. Stowe would suffer from headaches, loss of hearing, chronic inflammation, and alcohol addiction following his wounding. He would disappear after arriving in San Francisco in 1870 and was never heard from again.35

On Benner's Hill, Latimer was being pummeled as Federal artillery started to tell against his position. Available batteries from all over Cemetery Hill, from the Eleventh, First, and Twelfth Corps, maneuvered to return fire with everything the Federals had. Latimer knew he could not hold the position. His casualties were fifty artillerymen and thirty horses.[36] He requested permission from General Johnson to pull his guns off the hill. Johnson ordered Latimer to withdraw but leave four guns on the hill to support the coming infantry advance. Soon after evacuating his guns, a shell exploded near Latimer. It killed his horse and mortally wounded the Boy Major. Latimer was evacuated with the Confederate retreat from Gettysburg, but he died on August 1 at Harrisonburg, Virginia.[37]

Late in the afternoon, as the artillery continued to roar and sharpshooters engaged in their deadly work, louder and more terrible sounds of battle erupted from the south with the fury of Confederate attacks at the Peach Orchard, the Wheatfield, and Devil's

This sketch by press artist Edwin Forbes shows the scene at the Evergreen Cemetery gatehouse at 6:30 p.m. on July 2. The cemetery was the center of the Eleventh Corps position. The large script in the center denotes this is the crest of the hill. Forbes annotated the locations of the ring of rebel batteries firing from the distance on the Union center. On the far left Forbes wrote: "*the rebel battery in wheatfields*." Forbes's notations of the limbers and caissons behind the Union artillery in action, the road to Gettysburg (the Baltimore Pike) in front of the cemetery gatehouse, and the infantry behind a stone wall, gives an eyewitness view of the situation. (Library of Congress)

Den. The sharp clatter of musketry was continuous under the crashing roar and thunder of the cannonading. After twilight, General Hays's Louisiana brigade began to form in preparation for their attack on Cemetery Hill. The 5th and 6th Louisiana formed up in the streets of Gettysburg and in the fields below the town.[38] Avery's brigade formed in the fields of the Culp Farm. Avery would move southwest toward the northern face of Culp's Hill and then wheel to the west and attack the southern end of the Union line below the Baltimore Pike. General Ewell's plan was for Gordon's Georgians to support Hays and Avery and to reinforce them as necessary. General Doles, positioned along Long Lane, was to move forward and support the Tigers as they pushed through the salient, or elbow, on the right of the Union line.[39] About this time to the east, gunfire and the furor of battle erupted on Culp's Hill as Johnson's men began their assault on Brigadier General George Greene's depleted Twelfth Corps brigade.[40] Greene's men held the breastworks the old general had them construct despite the displeasure of his superiors. Greene's fortifications would save Culp's Hill for the Union.

Lieutenant Peck remembered the start of the fight on Cemetery Hill.

> *About six o'clock p.m. or perhaps a little later, our regiment was moved from the position on the side of East Cemetery Hill down to the right and foot of the hill and was posted along a low stone wall beside the lane, where our monument now stands. Two companies under command of Captain Henry P. Burr of Company E were ordered to get over the fence by the lane and advance out part way between the lane and Culp's Hill, with orders to fall back on the line with the regiment—if they were attacked.*

> *We had been in our position but a short time when firing commenced in our front, which was probably on the two companies who had been sent out from our Regiment, and very soon our men got orders to commence firing and opened fire by order of our Major. We had been firing but a few minutes when the Major ordered us to cease firing, saying that we were firing on our own men. The men stopped firing for a moment, but we soon saw the long line of gray coming up and the boys began firing again and kept it up.*[41]

The Confederate assault moved forward. Hays's brigade, with the 5th Louisiana on the right and followed to the left by the 6th, 9th, 7th, and 8th Louisiana regiments, led the advance. The Louisiana Tigers assaulted the left and center of the two Ohio regiments (the 107th and the 25th) along the Baltimore Pike and the Federal regiments along the Brickyard Lane, including the 75th Ohio and 17th Connecticut. Colonel Avery, leading the North Carolina regiments, ordered his officers to dismount and make the charge on foot. Avery remained mounted and began to advance with his 6th North Carolina. Avery's three regiments, the 6th, 21st, and 57th North Carolina, swept in an arc toward the right of the Federal line behind the walls and fences of Brickyard Lane.[42] Avery urged his men forward as artillery ripped into their ranks. Despite the terror of the artillery, the descending darkness offered some cover to the attackers' advance. The closer the Confederates got to the front of the hill, the sooner the power of the artillery would be negated because the tubes were unable to depress far enough in their front to be effective.[43] The Confederate attack at the bottom of this hill would also be shielded by the bow of the hill as the infantry was out of sight from the gunners at the top. Avery ordered his advancing regiments to wheel toward the right of the Union line. He was then struck in the neck by a musket ball and fell from his horse mortally wounded. Amid the darkness and the smoke of battle, Avery's men were unaware their colonel was down.[44]

About that time the 17th Connecticut was ordered to the right. Major Brady's after-action report described the move: "*7:00 p.m. when we were ordered to the extreme right, behind a stone wall on each side of a lane, below the battery opposite the cemetery entrance. Two companies were advanced to the grain field near the woods, through which the enemy were rapidly advancing. We covered the wall on each side of the lane by compelling about 300 stragglers, who had no commander, to fall into our line.*"[45] One must question where Brady found three hundred "stragglers who had no commander." This "orphaned" regiment was probably the 74th Pennsylvania.[46] The 17th Connecticut was apparently moved by General Ames's order. Whether the order was misconstrued by Brady, or badly given by Ames, no unit moved in to seal the gaping hole in Colonel Harris's line created when the 17th moved to the right. Harris, commanding the brigade, was appalled: "In moving the 17th C.V. . . . their place at the wall was left vacant, thus endangering the left flank of the 75th O.V.I. and the right flank of the 25th O.V.I. Before I could make any arrangements to remedy this breach in the line the attack of the enemy on Cemetery Hill was made."[47]

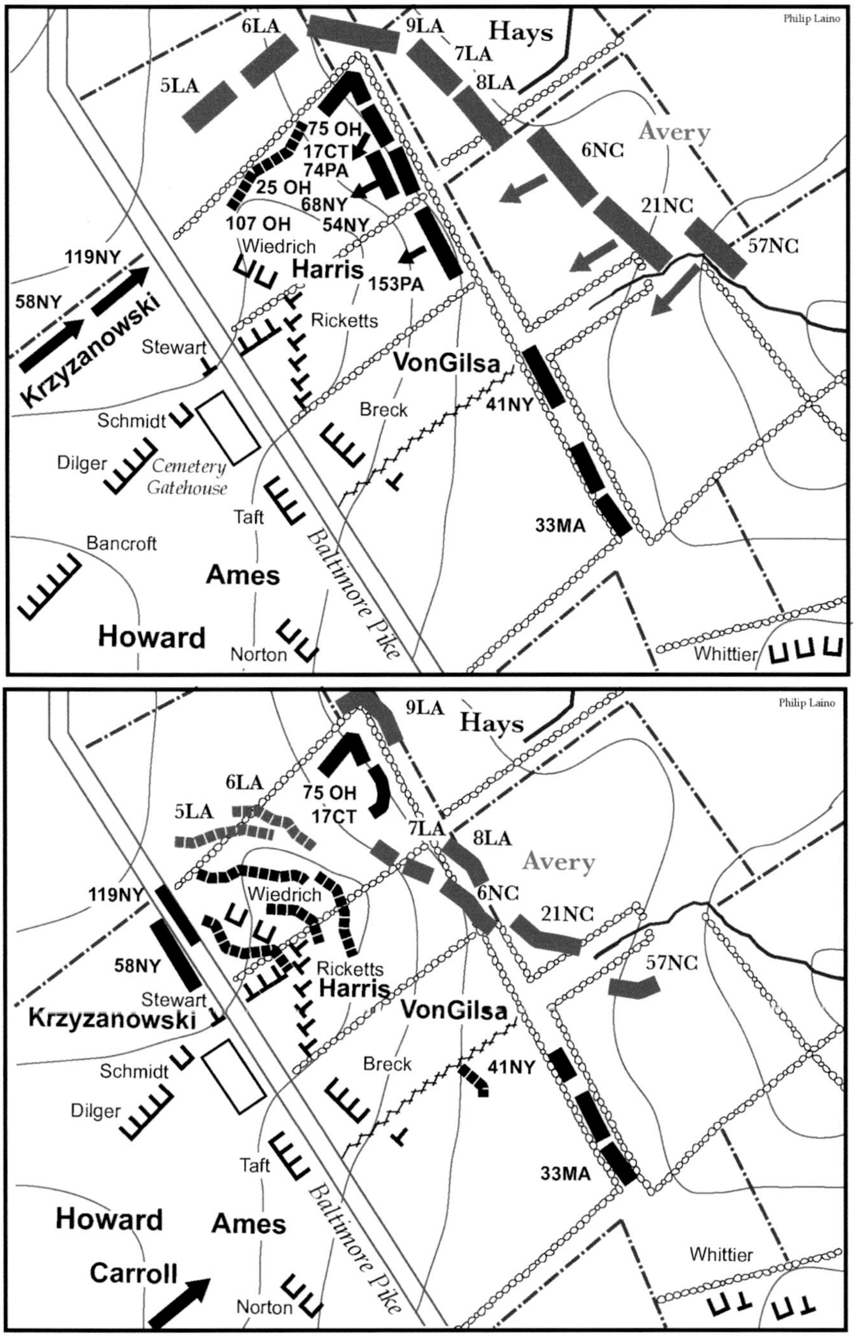

Hays and Avery Charge Up East Cemetery Hill.

Top: Hays's and Avery's brigades assault East Cemetery Hill on the night of July 2. The 5th and 6th Louisiana storm through the gap between the 107th and 25th Ohio. The 68th and 54th New York break under the Confederate attack. The 153rd Pennsylvania and 41st New York withdraw. Bottom: The 75th Ohio and the 17th Connecticut make a stand at the bottom of the hill. The 5th and 6th Louisiana charge Wiedrich's guns. The 7th Louisiana and 6th North Carolina charge Ricketts's guns.[48] (Maps by Phil Laino)

Suddenly, in the growing darkness the Confederate infantry was face to face with the Union infantry and too close for Union artillery to have much effect on the attackers.[49] Brutal hand-to-hand combat ensued. The 5th and 6th Louisiana stormed through the gap in the salient between the 107th and 25th Ohio. The Tigers swarmed Wiedrich's battery. On von Gilsa's line to the right along Brickyard Lane, the 68th and the 54th New York broke for the rear. Amid the vicious close-order combat, and the confusion, darkness, smoke, and noise, the 7th Louisiana and 6th North Carolina blasted past the collapsed line of von Gilsa's units to charge Ricketts's guns. The 17th Connecticut and the 75th Ohio continued to stand at the northern base of the hill, with the enemy getting around them and briefly firing into them before madly charging up the hill to the artillery.[50] The 57th North Carolina continued to be pelted by the artillery. Lieutenant Edward Whittier, commanding Greenlief Stevens's 5th Maine Battery, moved three guns on McKnight's (Stevens's) Knoll from his right to the left to rip into the rebels with everything he could hurl at them.[51]

From the 17th Connecticut's position on Brickyard Lane, Major Brady reported that as soon as the 17th reached its position at the wall and got the stragglers into line,

> *We had no more time to form behind the wall before the enemy were discovered advancing rapidly upon our right and a full brigade obliquely toward our left. When within 150 paces of us, we poured a destructive fire upon them, which thinned their ranks and checked their advance. We fired several volleys by battalion, after which they charged upon us. We had hand-to-hand conflict with them, firmly held our ground, and drove them back. Soon after, some of our troops on our left giving way, the rebels succeeded in getting in our rear. We again drove them back and held our position. It was during this conflict that Major Brady was wounded by a fragment of shell, which hit him upon the right shoulder.*[52]

Stevens's Battery in action against the Confederate assault on Cemetery Hill. (Library of Congress)

For the 17th Connecticut and the 75th Ohio troops along the low stone wall at the lane, the artillery was both friend and foe. William Paynton, Company C, watched Gilbert Reynolds's battery discharge a gun and wait for the effects of the shot. Paynton claimed it exploded in the midst of a wagon train and took out men and horses. Another shot from the same gun left the muzzle and immediately exploded, hurling a fragment into a soldier of the 75th Ohio, tearing off his leg below the knee. Paynton witnessed Colonel Harris run to his man to bind his wound; the soldier died on his way to the hospital.[53] The instances of hand-to-hand conflict the regiments had with the Louisiana Tigers were numerous and desperate on both sides. Paynton had been one of the skirmishers assigned to Captain Burr. They had barely returned to the regiment when "we could hear the rattle of musketry and see the flash of powder; we could hear the yells of the rebs and the shouts of the boys in blue as they fought hand to hand over the fence. Our major was wounded in the shoulder and in his agony at the pain from it, he thrust the point of his sword into the heel of one of Co. A's men who was barefoot."[54] Based on an examination of casualty lists this man may have been Abijah Hagar, wounded in the heel.[55] The incident demonstrated another instance of just how poorly shod, or barefoot, so many men were at Gettysburg. In the bedlam, Paynton's messmate, Calvin Nobles, would be killed. His body never found or identified. Paynton himself would be separated from the regiment, writing "*I found myself in the midst of a Pennsylvania regiment.*"[56] Private Moses W. Wheeler, Company C, wrestled doggedly with one of the attackers, and was dragged across the wall and taken prisoner.[57] Wheeler was somehow able to escape. In a short, undated, unattributed account in Warren's Gettysburg volume, it was recorded that *"Moses A. Wheeler was taken prisoner the second day at Cemetery Hill where the Louisiana Tigers made the charge at the stone wall just before dark. He was taken back through the town and (re)joined our party on the third day."*[58]

Corporal George Scott, the only noncommissioned officer to answer the roll from Company C that morning, would find himself grappling with a rebel captain over the wall and would take him prisoner. Captain Burr of Company E would snatch a rebel flag out of the hands of an unidentified color bearer. The flag did not survive but Burr took the man prisoner.[59] Sergeant Major Betts remembered, "*Capt. Burr captured the rebel color bearer and 'got hunk', as he said for Chancellorsville, where he was captured.*"[60] To the right of the 17th as the Tigers rushed the stone fence in front of the 75th Ohio, William Southerton witnessed, amid the screaming and swearing, the flashes of musketry "*There stood the major of the Tigers! Right on top of the wall! He carried their flag! A flash of steel! Lorenzo Dowler stabbed the major through with his bayonet. The rebel fell headlong over the rocks as a force of his men sprang to the top of the wall . . . The Tigers' flag! What a scramble as the flag was torn into pieces! Our boys pounced upon the rag as if a piece of it would be the greatest badge of bravery, they would ever get their hands on.*" This captured rebel flag was presumably torn to pieces and never identified.[61] The next morning Lieutenant Peck would walk among the dead and debris of the battlefield from the night before and would pick up "*a couple of white stars that had been torn from a rebel flag and a piece of flag also.*"[62] In the fight for Cemetery Hill, men and flags were literally shredded to pieces.

Colonel Wainwright replaced Cooper's Battery with Ricketts's six rifled guns. Ricketts placed four of his guns in Cooper's lunettes, the earthworks around the cannon. As the gunner on Ricketts's second piece moved his gun into position, he found a severed hand in the lunette in front of the gun."[63] Wainwright ordered Ricketts to "*fight your battery to the last*." In stubborn obedience, the battery would "expend every round of cannister, and then fire case shot without the fuses, "rotten shot" that burst at the mouth of the gun, to halt the rebel charge."[64] As von Gilsa's men scrambled up the hill in a panic, in the dark and the confusion they stumbled into Ricketts's lunettes and the canister from the battery tore into them. The Tigers gained the wall between the batteries and poured fire into the gunners. A few of Ricketts's crew were caught up in the growing panic when Ricketts screamed at them, "*Die on your own soil boys before you give up your guns!*"[65] Ricketts's left piece was spiked by the enemy, who killed, wounded, or took prisoner every man assigned to it. While the left half of the battery was engaged in hand-to-hand fighting with the attackers, the right half of the battery kept firing.[66]

At Wiedrich's Battery, to the left of Ricketts, "*One of the first Rebels to reach the guns threw himself over the muzzle and called out to the gunners, 'I take command of this gun.' The German gunner replied 'Du Sollst sie haben!' (You shall have it!) He pulled the lanyard and blew the rebel to kingdom come. Nothing remained by a spray of blood and small bits of human flesh spattered here and there.*"[67] Adjutant Peter Young remembered the 107th Ohio was ordered to "*fall back upon the battery and hold that at all hazards*." The battery was silenced as hand-to-hand combat engulfed the guns. The gunners fought with everything they had. Next to Young in the melee was Sergeant Geibel, the 107th color bearer, who was shot down. Young reached to save the colors from the oncoming enemy. "*Having scaled the stone-fence on our right, found the rebels up to and among our guns, yelling like demons at the supposed capture . . . I ran forward, revolver in hand, shot down the color bearer (8th La. Tiger Regt. As it proved by the description on the vile rag) and sprang for the colors at the same time a rebel, seeing his comrade fall sprang forward and caught them but fell to the ground, where I wrested them from him.*"[68] As Young turned toward his men he was shot in the left lung and arm. He kept to his feet and made it back to Sergeant Major Henry Brinker, who caught him in his arms as Young fell.[69] Lieutenant Peck would write, "*The rebels discovered the gap in the brigade and passed around our left and broke through and got into Wiedrich's and Ricketts's Batteries, on top of Cemetery Hill, but were soon driven back by the gunners with stones and gun swabs and by the infantry supporting the batteries . . . Adjutant Young, of the 107th Ohio, succeeded in capturing a stand of Rebel colors during the action and was afterwards made a captain and appointed on General Ames's staff. Adjutant Young was severely wounded during the engagement.*"[70]

Hays was encouraged by the breaching of the enemy line and his men's attack on the batteries. He expected Gordon's Brigade in support to exploit and consolidate the Confederate breakthrough. In the darkness Hays saw a line of troops nearing the action from the west and at first believed it was Rodes coming to support him. It was instead Colonel Wladimir Krzyzanowski's Eleventh Corps brigade and Colonel Samuel "Red" Carroll's Second Corps "Gibraltar Brigade," rushing to push the Confederates off the

Alfred Waud's sketch shows the ferocity of the close-quarter combat as the Tigers charged the Union batteries in the dark. Gun crews used everything they had to fight the enemy off the guns: rammers, spikes, fence rails, stones. Officers discharged their sidearms at point-blank range. Primed cannons were fired into the faces of the enemy. Flag bearers on both sides were shot down in succession. (Library of Congress)

artillery and the Union line. Major Tate, 6th North Carolina, on the hill with only about seventy-five North Carolinians and a dozen Louisianians, saw no hope for support in the darkness around him and began to withdraw. He stated, "*The enemy stood with a tenacity never before displayed by them.*" Samuel W. Eaton, 57th North Carolina, wrote, "*We were under desperate fire, only a few got to the batteries and could not hold them . . . there was harder fighting today than ever I knew before.*"[71] At the bottom of the hill part of the 6th Louisiana and most of the 9th had been held back by the 75th Ohio and 17th Connecticut. The 57th North Carolina had been pounded by the artillery on the flank and had not penetrated the Federal line. The 41st New York and 33rd Massachusetts had held the right end of the line. With Carroll's brigade rushing to the guns to crush the rebel attackers, Hays had no hope of holding his ground without reinforcements and reluctantly gave the order to withdraw.[72]

As Hays withdrew, dozens of Yankee prisoners slipped away in the darkness to make their way back up East Cemetery Hill to find and rejoin their regiments. Colonel Carroll's 14th Indiana and 7th West Virginia charged in and cleared Ricketts's Battery. These regiments, along with the 4th Ohio, pushed the rebels off the hill.[73] The gunners rushed back to their pieces to quickly reload, but the darkness helped to protect the withdrawing rebels. Captain Seymour observed, "*Had it not been for the darkness, the enemy would have, no doubt, cut us up terribly with his re-captured artillery as we fell back down the hill.*"[74] "Red" Carroll's Gibraltar Brigade had made a thrilling and successful

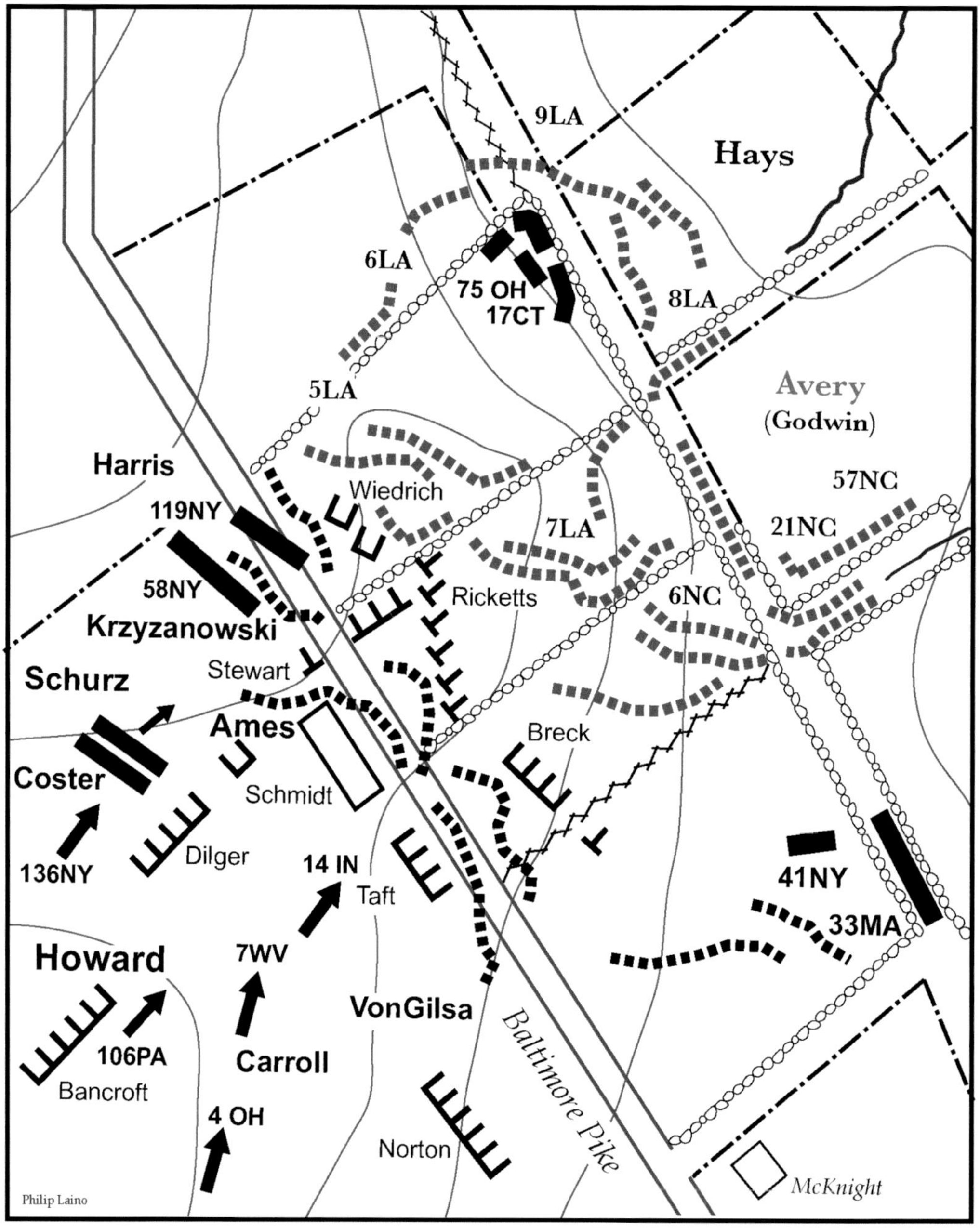

Union Reinforcements Arrive and The Confederate Assault Fails

Colonel Wladimir Krzyzanowski leads the 119th New York across the Baltimore Pike and into Wiedrich's battery. The 58th New York follows them, with Coster's Brigade behind. Carroll's Brigade, with the 14th Indiana in front, attacks the enemy at Ricketts's battery. Carroll's 7th West Virginia and the 4th Ohio charge in behind the 14th Indiana. General Hays at first believed the men pouring in from the Baltimore Pike were his reinforcements from Rodes's Division and ordered his men to hold their fire. When he realized these men were Yankees, he ordered his men to withdraw behind the stone wall at the base of East Cemetery Hill. Realizing no reinforcements were coming, Hays was forced to recall his men and abandon the attack.[75]

(Map by Phil Laino)

counterattack. These men believed, as did many, that they saved East Cemetery Hill from "the incompetent, cowardly" Eleventh Corps. They certainly helped, but it was the Eleventh Corps itself, at the crest of the hill, that had obstinately fought the attackers. Carroll's men met a stalled assault that had reached its peak and were the force that sent it tumbling back down the hill.[76]

Finally, as the batteries ceased firing and the smoke of battle cleared, a full moon rose from behind Culp's Hill. The light of the moon revealed the shocking detritus and destruction on East Cemetery Hill and the fields in front of it. The field groaned and moaned with human wreckage and debris as comrades, ambulance crews, and medical personnel sorted through the field trying to alleviate the suffering. Colonel Harris stated, "*We gathered up the dead and cared for the wounded of both friend and foe.*"[77]

Major Brady reported,

> *After the enemy had been driven back, the firing ceased, excepting occasional shots from their sharpshooters. We were relieved by the Fourth Ohio Volunteers and were ordered to change front to the left behind a wall running at right angles to the one we had just occupied and fronting the town where the enemy entered on our left. We remained at this wall all night and during the whole of the 3d instant, exposed to a crossfire of the rebel batteries and their sharpshooters. With the latter our best marksmen exchanged shots and succeeded in dislodging many of them.*[78]

Even before the guns fell silent on the second day, recriminations against the Eleventh Corps "Dutchmen" erupted again, just as they had at Chancellorsville and on the first day at Gettysburg. After the attack was repelled, Carroll's Brigade formed along Brickyard Lane in the dark and Carroll sent a courier to Howard. The courier found General Ames instead. Ames ordered the aide to tell Carroll to hold his position and added that he had no confidence in the men of the Eleventh Corps. Carroll himself then rode up to Cemetery Hill to find Howard, who also stated the same about the men he led.[79] Second Corps reinforcements were welcomed by the men of the Eleventh Corps and were a relief to the batteries. Those reinforcements hit the line as the rebel attack was stalled and began receding. With only about seventy-five North Carolina men and a dozen Louisianans in the batteries at the crest of the hill and no reinforcements to sustain them, Major Tate had begun to withdraw his men just as Carroll's 7th West Virginia and 14th Indiana, with the 4th Ohio following, cleared them from the guns and forced them down and off the hill. Lieutenant Peck wrote regarding the 17th Connecticut, "*The 4th Ohio Regiment came in from our right on the double quick and dropped down in the grass in our rear, ready to assist us if we needed them, but we did not need their assistance as our boys held their position until the danger was past.*"[80] It would be the 4th Ohio that relieved the 17th Connecticut on the Brickyard Lane when the regiment was ordered withdrawn.

The maligning of the Eleventh Corps, however unjust considering the facts of the battle, would never cease. After Gettysburg the corps would be disbanded. Ames's

Brigade, with the 17th Connecticut, was transferred to South Carolina. The rest of the corps would be combined with the Twelfth Corps and transferred to the Army of the Cumberland in the western theater.[81] For years the argument would rage that Carroll's Brigade had saved the Eleventh Corps on East Cemetery Hill. Some of the controversy played out in the pages of the *National Tribune*, the newspaper dedicated to veterans of the Civil War. On November 24, 1892, an article appeared in the *Tribune* titled, "*At Gettysburg. Lieut. Peck Tells What Carroll's Brigade did in the Battle.*" Peck took aim at the 4th Ohio's earlier claims in the *Tribune* that Carroll's Brigade had rescued the guns of Wiedrich's Battery and saved the day for the Eleventh Corps. In his article, Peck quotes the *Official Records* in support of the Eleventh Corps' defense of its batteries:

> *At Weidrich's battery, General Ames by extraordinary exertions arrested a panic, and the men with sponges, staffs, and bayonets forced the enemy back. At this time he received support from Gen. Schurz. Effective assistance was also rendered at this time by a portion of Gen. Steinwehr's command at points where the enemy was breaking through. This furious onset was met and withstood at every point and lasted less than an hour.*

Peck goes on to describe the Louisiana Tigers' breakthrough in the gap created by moving the 17th Connecticut to the right:

> *Before other troops could be put in place of my regiment the Tigers broke through and got on the flank of the 25th and 75th and forced them back, and succeeded in reaching the batteries, where they only remained a few minutes, when the troops rallied, and with the assistance of the men of the batteries and supports from the Eleventh Corps they were repulsed, not by Carroll's Brigade, but by Ames Brigade, and other help from our Corps. During this charge, Adj's Young, of the 107th Ohio (Ames's Brigade), captured the colors of the 8th La. Tigers, as shown by the official report of Capt. John Lutz, 107th Ohio, page 720.*

Peck goes on to say, "*I am not going to claim that Carroll's Brigade was not wanted on this occasion, for I am convinced after reading the official records, that they were wanted.*" In his last paragraph Peck extends the olive branch and requests an end to the controversy: "*Comrades, truth is truth, and history is history. Give us the facts. Look up the records and bring forward your evidence in a fair and manly way. Let us at least be comrades. It is glory enough to have taken any part in the historic battle of Gettysburg.—A. W. Peck, First Lieutenant, Co. D, 17th Conn., Newtown, Conn.*"[82]

The night of July 2 ended two very costly days for the Eleventh Corps. Colonel Harris's Brigade (Ames's Brigade) would incur over 55 percent casualties.[83] Yet the Confederates had gained nothing. East Cemetery Hill remained in control of the Union. Supply trains, Federal ammunition, the artillery reserve, and the Baltimore Pike—the road to Washington—were secure. The Confederates had failed to penetrate the Union line. They had come within a whisker of success several times that day, ending with the attempt on East Cemetery Hill. Any single breakthrough could have been a decisive step toward a Southern victory, but repeated Confederate failures to spearhead and consolidate a breakthrough ended all such hopes. The Union line on East Cemetery Hill was held chiefly due to an Eleventh Corps defense. Had the Confederates achieved an unwavering breakthrough there, the third day at Gettysburg would have turned out very differently. General Meade would probably not have held his council of war at the Leister House that night; he and his commanders would have been way too busy dealing with the breached line. If the Union had lost Cemetery Hill on July 2 to a strongly reinforced breakthrough, Meade would have had a fight on two fronts, and would have lost the ability to use his interior lines to rush artillery and infantry support where it was most needed. The Baltimore Pike would have been within Confederate control along with Union supply and ammunition trains. Had Cemetery Hill been lost on the night of July 2, Gettysburg could have become a Union defeat on July 3. The Eleventh Corps, despite the slurs against it, defended East Cemetery Hill tenaciously and ultimately kept it for the Union.

In 1873, John Bachelder, the great artist-historian of the Battle of Gettysburg, wrote in his book *Gettysburg, What to See—How to See It*, about the fight on Cemetery Hill:

> *On the spot where we stand occurred a scene on the night of the 2d, which embodied the magnificent charge, the firm defense, the fierce seething struggle of armed men, frenzied with the maddening influences of war. They fought with cannon, muskets, pistols, handspikes, rammers, clubs, stones, anything with which an attack could be made, or defense given. Here in this immediate vicinity, occurred instances of personal bravery and intrepidity seldom surpassed.*[84]

(Library of Congress)

CHAPTER 8

Voices From the Second Day of Battle

This chapter presents firsthand accounts from 17th Connecticut men about their experiences on the second day of the battle, Thursday, July 2, 1863. The accounts comprise the experiences of the survivors, the wounded, the prisoners, and the men who nursed their wounded comrades.

WILLIAM WARREN, PRISONER

William Warren was taken prisoner on July 1 on Barlow's Knoll. On July 2 he woke up in a field and began his first day in captivity. Warren kept a diary the entire time he was in the army, including his time in prison. His entry for July 2 follows:

> *Gettysburg, Thursday, July 2, 1863*
>
> *This A.M. I arose at pleasure, having nothing particular to do, and got breakfast, after which, I passed up and down the line talking to the rebs who were guarding us. I enjoyed it very much, as I found the men that were in the field very pleasant and very accommodating. I changed canteens with one of them. In the P.M. we marched through several lots for about half a mile and halted on the side hill in a wheat field where we staid the rest of the day. P.M. there was considerable excitement over the talk about paroling, as the Rebs gave each of our officers a sheet of paper to enroll our names on, then separate each regiment and give the paper back to them again. Our officers where then taken from us and not allowed to speak to us again; it was so strongly reported, that we believed it, that our parole should be, by paroling each regiment then take us as a body into our lines and let us go where we chose; if our Government would accept*

Private William Warren, Company C. (Courtesy of the William H. Warren Family)

Private Theodore S. Morris, Company C, was a nineteen-year-old farmer from Danbury when he enlisted in the 17th Connecticut. He was taken prisoner on July 1 at Gettysburg and paroled on August 21, 1863. He was taken prisoner a second time on February 5, 1865, in Florida and was sent to Andersonville. Fresh meat followed the armies on the hoof and had to be slaughtered. On July 2, Morris volunteered for butcher duty and returned to his fellow prisoners with fresh meat. (Bridgeport History Center)

us under such circumstances, as paroled prisoners, all right, but if not, the Rebs will not take us back again, but leave us to shirk for ourselves.

Some accepted this offer and went through all right without any trouble. After we heard how nicely they got out of their troubles, the rest of us were sorry we did not follow suit and go with them, but not a single man in Co. C thought it was best, after talking it all over, to accept that kind of parole, as it was not a proper way of doing business, so thought we would be lawfully and properly recalled by going to Richmond. We hardly knew what to do for the best; we could have our choice. After getting into our lines, they [the men who took the Confederate parole] *had nothing to show that they were paroled prisoners; we thought they ran a great risk.*

P.M. very heavy cannonading and some very near to us, and some too close we thought, so we picked up what we possessed of this world's goods and all commenced to fall back but had not gone but a short distance before we were stopped by the guard. After dark, a call was made for butchers, so T. Morris of Company C responded to the call; they said they had some cattle for us and if we wanted anything to eat we must butcher it. He brought back with him, for ten of us, a hind quarter and half liver. It was after nine o'clock before we had supper, but what did we care; we had plenty of time to eat and also to sleep.[1]

J. HENRY BLAKEMAN, WOUNDED PRISONER

For many of the Union wounded who fell into Confederate hands on July 1, the day began in various Confederate-held field hospitals scattered over the town, farms, and fields of Gettysburg. Private J. Henry Blakeman, Company D, was shot in the left side on Barlow's Knoll July 1 and was one of the wounded prisoners transported from a Confederate field hospital to the public school building on High Street on July 2. In 1888 he wrote to William Warren a multiday account of his experiences at Gettysburg. Blakeman's account of July 2 follows:

> *Stratford. April 30, 1888*
>
> *As I said, I reached the barn* [an unidentified Confederate field hospital on July 1] *and found it full of wounded Union soldiers. A rebel surgeon gave me a tab of lint, and a rebel soldier filled my canteen with water with which I kept the injured part wet, and that was all the surgical aid I received for four days. The next day, July 2nd, all the wounded prisoners were taken in ambulances—carried into the town of Gettysburg and put into a schoolhouse and church on the edge of town, under fire of our artillery, apparently, hoping we would be killed by our own guns, but not a shot struck the buildings during the two days we were there. From the windows of our prison, we saw the Louisiana Tigers form and start on the charge that the 17th Regiment helped to repulse with such slaughter on the evening of the 2nd. It can easily be imagined we were somewhat anxious as to the result of the fight, and more than some glad to see the skirmishers come through the streets on the 4th of July, and to know were with friends again. I am sure I am not indebted in any large amount to the "Johnnies" for board, for in the three days I was with them, they only gave me three crackers and a little water.*[2]

Private J. Henry Blakeman, Company D. (Bridgeport History Center)

The school building on High Street next to the German Reformed Church on the corner of High and Stratton Streets. Wounded Union prisoners held in this building witnessed the charge of the Louisiana Tigers against Cemetery Hill on the evening of July 2. (Photo by author)

JUSTUS SILLIMAN, WOUNDED PRISONER

After he was wounded on Barlow's Knoll, New Canaan private Justus Silliman, Company H, described being taken to a field hospital belonging to General Harry Hays's brigade. The location of this hospital is difficult to determine. Greg Coco, in his book *A Vast Sea of Misery*, stated it to be the Elizabeth Weible Farm; the house is still standing on Shealer Road.[3] Another possible location is the Josiah Benner Farm, across Rock Creek on the Harrisburg Road, where four companies of 17th Connecticut skirmished with Confederates in the property's orchard before retreating through town to East Cemetery Hill. Years later, in writing to William Warren, Silliman identified the Benner Farm as being the site he was taken to by Confederates after he was wounded. On July 2, the Confederates transported Silliman and other wounded into the town of Gettysburg to the school building on High Street. While being held in this prison hospital, Silliman wrote a long letter to his mother. Silliman concluded his letter just as Confederate guns opened their bombardment against the Union lines preceding Pickett's Charge on July 3. The first part of the letter described his experiences on July 1 and his wounding on Barlow's Knoll. Silliman's July 2 experiences, from that letter, follow:

Private Justus Silliman, Company H. (Image courtesy of New Canaan Museum and History Center)

> *I remained at the hospital till Thursday noon* [July 2] *when I with the other captured wounded were sent to this hospital in ambulances, some of which formerly belonged to the Garabaldi Guard* [39th New York] *and were captured at Harpers Ferry. The other ambulances resembled our butcher wagons at home. The rebels had thousands of muskets which they had captured from us the day previous, collected in stacks in the street. I saw a rebel cannon which had been struck in its mouth by one of our shots and flattened out, the rebels had buried all their dead but many of ours still lay where they fell.*
>
> *The city* [Gettysburg] *was apparently deserted by the citizens, they having fastened themselves in and taken to their cellars for protection. The rebels seem to be having a good time generally and their rail fence gait told of empty whiskey barrels. They appeared perfectly happy and inclined to treat everybody with attention.*
>
> *We were taken to this hospital which with a German Dutch reformed church was at the east end of the town and mostly occupied by wounded of the 11th Corps. Nurses were not abundant, and I have done what I could to relieve the suffering. Several of our own surgeons are in attendance but*

> *to their shame are more neglectful to our wounded than were the rebel doctors. They will remain for hours at the windows watching the progress of the battle while our wounded were in agony for want of proper attention. We are in full view of the battlefield, the rebel line of battle being within a few rods in front of our hospital. Our own line is also in full view. They occupy a line of hills which they have fortified.*
>
> *At about four o'clock yesterday pm the fight was renewed with great fierceness. The cannonading and musketry firing was terrific and the sound of shells rushing through the air was continuous and resembled somewhat that of a tremendous waterfall. The La brigade were in a hollow in front of us, where they lay close until nearly dark though they had their skirmishers out nearly all day. These were occasionally picked off by our sharpshooters. Bullets frequently whistled around our hospital but I have not heard of any one being injured by them.*
>
> *Just at dusk we saw those infallible La tigers make preparations for a charge. They stealthily formed in line under cover of a hill and slowly and in excellent order advanced toward our lines till within a short distance of them when with a loud yell they rushed forward on the double quick. The clash was tremendous, but short, and Jacksons picked men retreated back panic stricken and with their ranks terribly thinned. Then it was that we were gladdened by the cheers of our men. The fight raged till nearly nine o'clock.*
>
> *I am quite anxious about Sam* [Comstock] *and would like to know how he fares. The wounded were almost starving for something to eat, as the citizens are afraid to venture out.*[4]

Silliman and Sergeant Sam Comstock had enlisted together in Company H with other New Canaan boys. Comstock was the second of nine children from a farming family. He was badly wounded on July 1 on Blocher's Knoll. When Silliman wrote this letter to his mother he did not know his friend's whereabouts or his condition. When Silliman was transferred to the Eleventh Corps hospital at the George Spangler Farm he located Sam in a rainstorm lying in a puddle. Silliman immediately did his best to make Sam as comfortable as he could. He remained with Sam when both were transferred to the General Hospital at Camp Letterman. Sam died of his wound on September 27, 1863, and Silliman accompanied his body home to be buried in New Canaan at Lakeview Cemetery.[5]

In 1884 Justus Silliman, then a professor at Lafayette College in Easton, Pennsylvania, was contacted by Colonel Noble at the behest of the 17th Connecticut Historical Committee. This committee was formed after one of the reunions in an unsuccessful attempt to produce a regimental history and remove William Warren from the process. The committee put out a call for correspondence from the veterans of the regiment regarding their experiences in the war. Colonel Noble, then General Noble, was chosen chairman. William Warren would record in Volume 3 of his history the failure of this committee: "He (Colonel Noble) wrote to many of the boys for their experiences, but very few responded to his call, as he so informed me. But there is one of Co. H that responded and as I am the only individual of the regiment that is writing the history, Col. Sent me his letters, which filled several sheets of foolscap paper. The following is a portion of the letters."[6]

A postwar image of Justus Silliman when he was a professor at Lafayette College in Easton, Pennsylvania. (Dale Call Collection)

Justus Silliman was one of the few to respond to General Noble's call for information. He also granted permission for Noble to distribute his sketch of Barlow's Knoll. Silliman had an engraved printing plate made. He wrote Noble that the 17th Connecticut Volunteer Association was welcome to the plate for $20 and noted that any number of prints from it could be made. In this same letter, Silliman stated he had no diary of his army life and could not provide Noble with a "minute account" but that he did have several letters that he would look over and send notes from. Noble was welcome to take from the accounts anything that might be useful.[7] Following is Silliman's 1884 account of July 2.

> *July 2nd by J.A. Silliman*
>
> *On the 2nd of July at noon, the wounded soldiers in this hospital* [Twenty-one years after the battle, Silliman identified this hospital as the Benner barn. In the 1863 letter to his mother, he did not name the location he was taken after being wounded.] *were sent to the Gettysburg Schoolhouse, which had been occupied by our forces as a hospital at the opening of the battle but was now within the rebel lines. Here I remained until the 4th. We rode in the ambulances which had been captured from the "Garibaldi Guards." A little north of the Almshouse we saw in the road a brass cannon—the muzzle of which had been struck by one of our solid shot and flattened into the form of an egg. I afterwards saw one of our own guns, in the muzzle of which a solid shot had been lodged. The first rebels had collected the muskets captured on the first day of the fight and piled them in the center of the square. These however, they left in their hasty retreat on the night of the 3rd. No citizens were to be seen on the streets as we passed through, but many of the rebels we met were hilariously drunk. The school building to which we were taken was on the rebel line of battle and in full view of our own line, about 60 rods distant, and directly in front of the position occupied by the 17th Conn. Vol's. The Louisiana tigers were just in front of us a little to the left. The men were stretched on the ground under cover of a low ridge and spent the afternoon eating, sleeping and card playing. They had skirmishers out just at*

the brow of the hill—several of whom were killed by our sharpshooters. Just after dark, after the battle had been raging for some time on the left of our lines, the Tigers having been ordered to charge quietly formed in line, crept stealthily to the crest of the ridge, and then with a wild yell sprang to their feet and started on a full run for our lines. The yells of the rebels, however, were soon completely drowned in the huzzahs of our boys, and in a short time the fragments of what was left of the brigade came back at a lively pace.[8]

LIEUTENANT MILTON DANIELS

On January 14, 1880, Milton Daniels, Company C, wrote to William Warren from his home in Indianapolis. Daniels's letter described all three days at Gettysburg, the aftermath of the battle, and the pursuit of Lee's army. Daniels's account of July 2 follows:

We rallied at Cemetery Hill. On calling roll of Company "C", we found missing every sergeant, every corporal but Corporal Scott, and only twenty-five of us out of sixty-five when we went into the field. Our brigade was rallied and placed in line immediately to the right of the road leading from Cemetery Hill through town, the regiment resting on the road, and the whole brigade immediately in front of Cemetery Hill. General Adelbert Ames, our brigadier, had headquarters in the room over the main cemetery gate. We held this position the first night and the second day; we were withdrawn about 10:00 p.m. of the second, further back, to rest and eat a hardtack, that is those who had them. We cursed our quartermaster and begged of General Ames to make him bring us some rations; we must have gotten some but I do not remember how.

. . . Now after I was ordered to the right with Companies C and D, while we were marching on the hillside, I was at the head in a captain's place and the orderly of Company D was at my side, a shot came—touched my coat—and took him in the side; he dropped dead. Soon the whole regiment was to the right behind a stone wall where brush had grown up by it. We had not been there long before we saw the rebs coming through to a peach orchard in a field of wheat. The battery in our rear was giving them a warm reception with grape and canister, firing over our heads. I remember the lead wadding from one shot killed one of our men, which demoralized us worse than the enemy in front. On came the enemy into the meadow in

Milton Daniels in a postwar photograph from about the time he wrote his 1886 letter to William Warren. (Bridgeport History Center)

our front. We, the 1st Brigade, 1st Division, 11th Army Corps, sent them our compliments from our Enfield rifles, at will. Here I want to compliment Companies C and D in my command, for the coolness displayed. Only about half a dozen of the enemy broke through but the dead in front were in heaps. I think we lost none right there.

We had two men, one in Company C, George Wood, Jr. the other Wm. Curtis, from Newtown, who were particularly noticeable for coolness for positions of trust. George was deaf; Bill liked Commissary, but at this battle they redeemed themselves from all traits of not being good soldiers. It proved we had been fighting the Louisiana Tigers. While the Tigers were coming across the meadow, George and Will were sitting down behind the stone wall, and you would have supposed they were shooting at a target. I saw George shoot taking a dead rest, and heard him say, "He won't come any farther, will he, Bill?" Then Bill shot and said, "I got that fellow, George." And they kept it up that way perfectly oblivious to danger themselves.

Corporal George Scott, who was acting orderly, had it hand to hand with the enemy as they charged the fence. He shot a fellow and took a captain prisoner. He had caught a Tiger; we did not know what to do with him; it was dusk and we had not men to spare to send him to the rear, and I never knew how he was disposed of; I have often wondered; speculated much. We were kept in line there all night.[9]

A postwar photograph of Private George Wood Jr., whom Daniels remembered for his coolness under fire. (Bridgeport History Center)

Corporal George Scott, Company C, was a forty-six-year-old laborer from Danbury when he enlisted in the 17th Connecticut. On July 2, he took a Confederate captain prisoner during the hand-to-hand fight at the stone wall. Scott would be promoted to sergeant after Gettysburg on July 15. (Bridgeport History Center)

CORPORAL WILLIAM WALLACE PAYNTON

Corporal William Wallace Paynton, Company A, dedicated his personal recollections of the war to William Warren in 1909. Paynton was then a resident of the Old Soldiers Home (Fitch's Home for Soldiers and Orphans) at Noroton Heights in Darien, Connecticut. Warren would save the handwritten copies Paynton gave him in a copy book. He would also transcribe some of those accounts into his typed manuscript. It appears that Paynton worked on his recollections and edited them over a number of years. Paynton jumbled some of the events of July 2 and July 3; however, his recollections are valuable in understanding the experiences of a common soldier, and several of the incidents Paynton wrote about on July 2 were corroborated in the accounts of others from the regiment. Paynton's first account began with the regiment's position after reaching Cemetery Hill late on July 1 and described the night combat of July 2. In the second account Paynton described Confederates shooting at 17th Connecticut men from a hog pen behind a house. The deadly sharpshooting that the regiment was exposed to all three days from Confederates occupying the houses along Baltimore Street was remembered by the men for years afterward.

(Following the retreat from Barlow's Knoll through the town),

> *At last Cemetery Hill was reached, and here at the Gate House General Howard and staff were stationed and ordering the 11th Corps to file to the right into the cemetery. The 17th regiment was advanced to a position behind a stone fence near the brow of the hill, with artillery at our rear. During the next two days that Lee occupied the town, the public buildings and churches that were used as hospitals were filled with rebel sharpshooters—those demons of modern warfare, who would send their death dealing messengers into the ranks of our artillery and infantry. Several men belonging to a battery that was posted in our rear had been hit by them. Our boys would hold a cap on the end of a ramrod just above the level of the fence to see them send a bullet through it. On that afternoon there was a party of five (the writer was one of the number) doing picket duty in the field adjoining. We were all together under an apple tree, excepting one man who stood as outpost. We were annoyed very much by frequent shots striking the ground around us, and also the three under which we were. No one was hit as yet, but we did not like to be shot at in that way and not know where it was from…*
>
> *There was another chap who had done a good deal of mischief. He had a position at the foot of the hill close under a rail fence; frequently a curl of smoke would issue from under the fence, and the next instant some of the artillery men would be hit. It was determined to drive him out; so the Lieutenant in charge told the sergeant to drop a shot down there and stir that reb up a little. The sergeant sent a shot direct to the spot, and there were no more artillery men wounded from that quarter.*

. . . From the time the duel opened until it closed it was one incessant roar. The ground on Cemetery Hill was torn and ploughed by the rebel shot and shell, and trees were cut in two; it was a fearful time for at least three quarters of an hour. From the position occupied by the 17th Regiment a good view could be had of nearly the whole line of batteries . . . The effect of their shots in the Cemetery was frightful to behold. Beautiful monuments and pillars of marble were broken and destroyed, while the horses of the artillery and the artillerymen who were killed and their mutilated and swollen bodies gave evidence of the terrible battle that was raging. The infantry, in the meantime, were forcibly the idle spectators of the fight. It was not safe to even raise one's head above the stone fence, for rebel sharpshooters were on the alert to pick off a "Yank" on sight. About the middle of the duel four ammunition wagons, were seen moving from one point to another, as if going to supply a battery. An officer, mounted on a white horse, seemed to be in charge. A battery was posted in the rear of the 17th Regiment. I think it was the 1st Independent Battery of New York. The officer in charge of a section ordered a shot to be sent after that wagon train. As the gunner discharged the piece we watched for the effect. It landed straight in the midst of that train, and exploding then blew the whole train to pieces, and I have been informed either killed or wounded every man and horse belonging to it. Another case was that of a shell from the same gun exploding as soon as it left the gun, and a fragment of several pounds weight struck a soldier of the 75th Ohio Regiment on the leg, below the knee, and tore it from him, only a shred of skin to hold it. Col. A. Harris ran to bind his wound, I learned the poor fellow died on his way to the hospital.

At last the firing ceased, and for a short time it was deathly still, but it was only the stillness that precedes the storm. . . . About this time a small party of 17th Regiment under command of Captain Burr of Co. C, myself among the number, were ordered to advance to a position at the base of Cemetery Hill, to the edge of a grain field, and deploy as a skirmish line, but to make no demonstration, only to act as a corps of observation, and if attacked in front to make the best of their way to the main line again. There was a sort of a gulch at the end of the grain field, as if caused by a washout. We could not see above the top of the grain unless we stretched ourselves up on the bank. While we were there, the regiment was moved with the brigade down the slope of the hill to meet the oncoming division and while the struggle was going on we were idle spectators and auditors of the conflict. We could hear the rattle of musketry and see the flash of powder; we could hear the yells of the rebs and the shouts of the boys in blue, as they fought hand to hand over the fence. Our Major was here wounded in the shoulder, and in his agony at the pain from it, he thrust the point of his sword into the heel of one of Co. A's men who was barefoot. [Many in the regiment remembered being barefoot during and after the battle. Based on an examination of casualty lists, the man Major Brady accidentally stabbed may have been Abijah Hagar, Company A, wounded in the heel.[10]]

But presently I thought I heard a noise in our front and raising myself a little, I something that made my blood chill. It was the advance column . . . I immediately called Captain Burr's attention to it and he ordered us to fall back as best we could. As we turned to fall back, I saw my old messmate, Calvin Nobles, who was next in line to me, fall, shot by a rebel bullet, and that was the last time I ever saw him. I fell just then and all the world was a blank to me; he had been my constant companion for months, and a truer comrade or more faithful soldier I never knew.

Comrade ______ of Co. C was the next man to him, and as he made toward the point where the Regiment was, I took a course toward the top of the hill. I expected a shot in my back every step I took, but I reached the top in safety, and as I clambered over the fence, I found myself in the midst of a Pennsylvania Regiment that had taken the place vacated by the 17th Connecticut. "Well, fall in here with my file closers; your regiment is down yonder." I did so but I had hardly taken my place when that yelling horde of rebs came tearing over the fence and crushing down those Pennsylvanians like so many toys, made a rush for our artillery. In the melee I was knocked over and nearly trampled to death. Presently, as I arose, a reb shouted to me, "Throw down that gun, you are a prisoner."

Private Calvin Nobles, Company C, was killed amid the darkness on July 2 and his body never identified or recovered. Nobles was an unmarried locksmith from Norwalk when he enlisted. He was twenty-three years old when he was killed in action at Gettysburg. (Bridgeport History Center)

A sickening feeling came over me at these words; of all the fears that I had on becoming a soldier, that of being a prisoner was the worst. I believe I would rather have lost an arm or leg than be a prisoner. The whole story of the horrors of Libby and Andersonville passed through my mind in a moment; my wit saved me. Feigning to be shot, I dropped suddenly to the ground, holding fast to my musket by the strap; I lay there for some minutes in fearful suspense. At last the surging mass had so far passed by me as to allow me a chance to rise, but I did not. I began a sort of crawl, still holding to the strap of my musket and dragging it after me. I must have made a few rods, when I then arose, and seeing a regiment of Union boys close at hand I joined them and fought the battle out in their ranks. The rebs were finally repulsed in this attack . . . after the fight was over, it must have been nearly ten o'clock; I made my way to a fence at the rear and curled up beside it for a nap. When I awoke in the morning I found a bedfellow, W. B. Newcomb of my own company. While we sat there wondering where the regiment was, or how to find it, we saw another one of our boys approaching, John McCorkle, of Co. C, right general guide.

Presently a voice was heard from the other side of the fence asking, "Soldiers, where do you belong?" I answered, "to the 17th Conn." "Do you know where your regiment is?" "No." "Do you know where they were before the fight last night?" "Yes, but don't know in what direction to look for them." The voice then said, "right over there, and go immediately to your regiment." I turned immediately to see who the speaker was, and found it was General O. O. Howard, our Corps Commander, and he pointed with his left hand the direction for us to take. We found it as he said, and when we arrived the number was thirteen in Co. A.[11]

John McCorkle (or McCorkell), born in Ireland, was an unmarried hatter living in Bethel when he enlisted at age nineteen. He would be promoted to corporal in August 1863 and then to sergeant in January 1865. He would muster out with the regiment at Hilton Head.
(Bridgeport History Center)

In another account, Paynton described how Confederate sharpshooters, who were harassing the Union line from houses along Baltimore Street, were driven from a hog pen on July 2.

HOW THE SHARPSHOOTERS WERE DRIVEN FROM THE HOG PEN

By W. W. PAYNTON

During the afternoon of the (2nd) of July, 1863, a party of five of Company A, 17th Regt., C.V. were posted in a field directly in front of the line occupied by the regiment, on the brow of Cemetery Ridge. There were a few apple trees in the field, and they were under one of these trees. The party consisted of Calvin Nobles, Jas. Hurlburt, Ed. Maloney, St. Clair Guthrie and W. W. Paynton. We were annoyed very much by some rebel sharpshooters, who kept up quite a brisk fire on us for some time, without harm, however, but their shots fell in very close proximity to us. We were unable to discover for a good while just where they came from. At last Ed. Maloney saw a curl of smoke come up from what seemed to us a hog pen at the rear of a house about sixty yards distant. There was evidently more than one of them, as two and three shots came together frequently. We began to consider some plan to drive them out. Finally, it was decided that we all load up, and that four of us fire simultaneously right into that hog pen, while one of us reserve his fire to see the effects of the volley. It was left to myself (Paynton) to hold the reserve fire. The other four boys discharged their pieces dead into the pen, and the smoke had hardly cleared away when the three or four rebs began clambering out. Just as the last one was throwing his leg over the top board of the pen, I drew bead on him and he went over sooner than he expected to, and in a different manner. It was plain to be seen that he was hurt badly, for his comrades returned to assist him to a place of safety, but we made it so hot for them that they were obliged to leave him to his fate and look out for themselves. We were not troubled by those chaps anymore that day.

This photograph of Baltimore Street was taken November 19, 1863, the day Lincoln gave the Gettysburg Address at the Soldiers' National Cemetery. It shows several of the houses along Baltimore Street that were occupied by Confederate sharpshooters. The Rupp House is on the left; the Rupp Tannery smokestack is the tall structure behind the house. Confederates fired from the house and tannery and into the Union line. To the right is the Welty House, which is still on Baltimore Street but unrecognizable due to renovations; it is now one of the two bed-and-breakfast rentals for the Brickhouse Inn. Behind Welty is the McCreary House, which no longer exists. The last house is the Winebrenner House. Brickyard Lane exited out onto Baltimore Street alongside this home. The Winebrenners also had a tanning business there. The Winebrenner house still exists as Mr. G's Ice Cream. All three of these houses, and others along Baltimore Street, sheltered Confederate sharpshooters during the battle. (Library of Congress)

LIEUTENANT ALBERT PECK

SECOND DAY AT GETTYSBURG

By Albert W. Peck

As soon as it was light on the morning of 2nd of July, we could see the Johnnies moving along the fences in our front, keeping out of sight as much as possible. It was not long before "zip" came the bullets from them, and our boys promptly returned their fire, although it was difficult to see them. Our boys took shelter behind the rail and board fences and apple trees, and once in a while the bullets would peel the bark from the trees, and there were a good many close shaves. Some of the boys got out of ammunition, and I recollect carrying some cartridges to some of them in my hat. I recollect noticing one of our boys in particular, Lieutenant George Shaw (then a Sergeant) who was stationed behind an apple tree, and the Johnnies had got a range on him and were trying their best to sting him—their bullets cutting the bark from the tree—but they did not hit him, and he was blazing away at them as fast as he could load and fire.

The Johnnies finally got a crossfire on us from the vicinity of the old tan yard, [Peck may be referring to the Rupp Tannery, from where Confederates had a crossfire on the Union skirmish line until it pulled back.[12]] *and it got so hot that we were finally relieved and moved back to our old position behind the stone wall. I think it was sometime during the morning of that day that two or three of the Johnnies were seen in an open field near town and quite a number of the boys fired at them. There were a good many shots fired at some of them who were firing from the corner of a large church in town; in fact we fired at every Johnnie that came in site within reach of our rifles. I had a rifle some of the time that day and fired a number of shots to keep myself busy. I believe Major Brady claimed to have hit one reb that nearly the whole regiment fired at. He was a long way*

Lieutenant Albert Peck, Company D, in a photograph taken later in the war, showed some marked maturity and aging compared to his enlistment photograph.
(Bridgeport History Center)

Sergeant George Shaw, Company D, dueled with Confederate sharpshooters from behind an apple tree.
(Bridgeport History Center)

off, in one of the large fields, walking, and some one of our shots brought him down. The next occurrence I recollect on that day was the opening of a rebel battery in a wheat field nearly a mile away. They shelled our brigade for nearly an hour, I should think, until our batteries on the hill drove them off. I think they returned to their position again but were finally again driven off and had one of their caissons exploded. I think the rebs only opened on us with three guns—one of which was a Whitworth. We noticed the shell from that came much quicker than from the others. We hugged the ground pretty close, and some of the shell burst over our heads, but I do not remember that any of our brigade were either killed or wounded, although we were very much exposed. I do not think we should have gotten off so well if we had been under fire from our own batteries so long. I think our artillery was far superior to theirs, at least that posted near us on Cemetery Hill, as we had a fine chance to notice the effect from those batteries of their firing.

I think I told you in my last about the breaking up of the squad of rebel cavalry. I was posted in the lane at the foot of the hill, when Captain Kellogg was ordered to make an advance in front of our line to find the enemy, and saw his men get over the fence when he ordered them to advance out and shoot. One of his men was wounded and the rest of the detail fell back over the fence. The Captain should have gone over the fence and moved out with his men, instead of staying in the lane and ordering his men to advance, but it was a dangerous spot, as the rebel sharpshooters were lurking in the grass behind fences and trees.

There was a detachment of the 25th Ohio Regiment sent out soon after in the same direction and for the same purpose. They moved out as skirmishers quite a distance, but did not encounter the enemy, and returned. The Johnnies did not expose themselves in our immediate front, as they probably did not like to draw the fire from our batteries. My next recollection on that day is about the assault on the 12th Corps on our right, who occupied the piece of woods on our right and front known as Culp's Hill. There was terrific fighting there all that afternoon until nearly dark, and our batteries kept shelling the woods constantly and the rattle of musketry was incessant. Just previous to the attack on the 12th Corps, there was very heavy fighting on the left, near Round Top and the Devil's Den, when Longstreet's Corps tried to capture Round Top. We could hear the fighting there but could not see it as it was on the other side of the hill, nearly two miles away. I recollect

Captain Enos Kellogg, Company H. (Bridgeport History Center)

the report that came from there, that Longstreet was captured with six thousand prisoners. We could hear our boys cheering quite plainly all along the lines as the news came in.

Just before dark our regiment was moved from the stone wall on the side hill to the foot of the hill near the lane, with a low stone wall in our front. We had not been in our new position long when firing commenced on our picket line, and the pickets were driven in. Our boys commenced firing, when Major Brady ordered them to cease firing as we were firing on our own men; the firing ceased for a moment, when the boys saw the rebel line approaching and commenced firing again, and the batteries on the hill above us opened on them with grape and cannister, which passed over our heads. I fired quite a number of shots with my revolver at the rebs, as it was the first and last chance I ever had to use it on them. I think this assault on our Corps lasted about an hour, which was a charge by the Louisiana tigers on our batteries. They did not break through our regiment but got through somewhere on our left and nearly captured some of our guns above us but were finally repulsed.[13]

ALVAH WILCOX MORTALLY WOUNDED

Corporal Alvah Wilcox was twenty-three-year-old carriage maker living in Bridgeport in 1862. On August 21, 1862, he married Sarah L. Dowd. Seven days later Alvah enlisted in Company D with his good friends, the brothers Leonard and Alonzo Scranton. Twenty-one-year-old Leonard Scranton was also a carriage maker; Alonzo was a farmer.

Corporal Alvah Wilcox, Company D, was mortally wounded on July 2. (Bridgeport History Center)

The three friends were together from their enlistment until July 1 at Gettysburg, when Alonzo Scranton was gravely wounded on Barlow's Knoll, shot through the face and jaw. On July 2, Alvah would be wounded on East Cemetery Hill; he was initially taken to a field hospital in or near the Evergreen Cemetery gatehouse. Leonard Scranton would survive the battle unscathed. After the battle both Alonzo and Alvah were transferred to the Eleventh Corps hospital at the George Spangler Farm. Wounded Alonzo would nurse Alvah, who would die in Alonzo's arms on July 7.

Both Scranton brothers gave postwar accounts of Alvah's wounding to William Warren. One account is described in the manuscript without attribution, but was most likely given by Alonzo: "*Alva Wilcox was wounded July 3 (sic), 1863 at Gettysburg by a sharpshooter, while on his way up Cemetery Hill; ball went through his left arm into his body and passed downward around to the left side.*"[14]

Leonard Scranton also described Wilcox's wounding: "*A shot struck his right arm and went right through his body and he died on the 6th. He was shot while going into the fight and when he was found he lay on his back reading his bible. He was taken to the field hospital and died there.*"[15]

Leonard Scranton, Company D. (Bridgeport History Center)

Wilcox's wounding and death also made a strong impression on Lieutenant Peck, who wrote to Warren in 1886 about the incident. Peck was deeply impressed by Alvah, who had served as a corporal in his Company D. From Peck's letter:

> *I had a detail of two men posted along the lane in front of Cemetery Hill during the second day's fight with orders to keep a sharp lookout in our front, to discover any movement of the enemy. The day was very hot and we had to lie close to the rail fence in our front, to keep from getting hit by the rebel sharpshooters, who lay in the gras and wheat fields in our front. I thought I would take a look over the rail in front of me and raised my head a little, when zip came a bullet so close it made my hair stand up some and made me more cautious in exposing myself when it was not necessary. When I was relieved and while returning to my company, I was told by someone that one of my men had just been wounded by a rebel sharpshooter and was then lying in the field near our batteries on Cemetery Hill. I went up there at once and soon discovered Corp. Alva E. Wilcox, of Company D, suffering from a bullet wound through the left shoulder, which had also penetrated his abdomen. I at once called two or three comrades and we put the Corporal into a rubber blanket and carried him to the field hospital just inside the Cemetery gate. One of the Drs. Probed his wound and said he would be all right in a day or two; he was all right, but he died, and was mustered out on the other side on July 6th. He was one of our bravest and best.*[16]

Peck's 1906 *Civil War Reminisces* included a longer description of Alvah Wilcox's wounding:

> *I was finally relieved from duty in the lane and took my men back on the hill and dismissed them, and while going up the hill I met Capt. Henry Allen from our regiment who informed me that one of my men was wounded and lay in the grass on top of the hill, so I looked him up and soon found it was Corporal Alva E. Wilcox, who had been wounded up by a Rebel sharpshooter and the bullet had gone through his left arm*

> *near the shoulder, and had passed through his arm and had lodged in his abdomen, causing a mortal wound.*
>
> *I soon found three men from Company D and we got him into a woolen blanket and the four of us carried him to the field hospital which was just inside the gate of the Cemetery. I stayed a short time to let the surgeon probe the wound. He said the wound was not dangerous and that he would be all right in a few days. Poor fellow, he was "all right" in a few days as he was dead and buried. I had to return to my company soon, as I was the only commissioned officer in my company, and I bid him good-bye and went back to my company.*
>
> *I have since been told by a member of my company who was wounded in the battle that Comrade Wilcox had been detailed by Major Brady to take the place of the second man who had either been killed or wounded by a rebel sharpshooter in the same place, and it would seem a great pity that the Major would want to expose the third man to meet the same fate. When I found Comrade Wilcox he was lying on his right side and sitting up a little and had a Testament in his hand which he was reading. He looked very pale. He was a large man and probably weighed 175 lbs. We had about all we could carry to get him over to the Cemetery as it was quite a long walk. I saw his headstone in the Evergreen Cemetery since the war . . . I wrote a letter to his wife and got a reply to my letter. Comrade Wilcox was one of our bravest and best men and was a great loss to the Company.*[17]

Further descriptions of Alvah Wilcox's death, his first two burials, and the final return of his body to Connecticut, will follow in the appropriate chapters.

WILLIAM T. FIELDS, COMPANY F

In December 1885, William Warren spent several evenings with William T. Fields at the latter's home in New Haven recording Fields's experiences at Gettysburg. Warren's handwritten account is transcribed below. Several sources list Fields as an eighteen-year-old painter who enlisted in Company F in Norwalk on August 12, 1862. The 1860 census from New Rochelle, New York, where Fields was born and spent his childhood, shows that his father and older brother were both painters. His mother had passed away earlier in 1860. William was listed as thirteen years old in that census. William's birth date, carved on his tombstone in Grove Street Cemetery in New Haven, is given as October 11, 1846. It is likely that when William enlisted in Norwalk in August 1862, he was only fifteen years old. Fields served out his enlistment and was mustered out with the regiment at Hilton Head, South Carolina, on July 19, 1865. The 1870 census shows William living as an unmarried boarder in the New Haven home of a widow and working as a clerk in the Tradesmen's Bank. By 1885, when Warren visited with his old comrade, Fields was the president of the Tradesmen's Bank and at the time of his death was a successful financial broker.[18]

Fields's account covered July 1–5. The bulk of the account focused on the second day of the battle. Because Warren interviewed Fields over several evenings, the events Fields described are not in exact order and his descriptions switch back and forth between the events of the morning and the evening of July 2. Warren noted this with A.M. and P.M. The account was found in Warren's handwriting.

> *William Fields, Company F, saw the following on a.m. of 2nd day while at the stone wall. The rebel sharpshooters were in different houses. One house had a hospital flag on it which was full of sharpshooters, and they had a good range on our regiment. (Corporal) Darius B. Rockwell, Company F was shot. It was sure death to anyone who exposed themselves. Finally, it got so bad that our folks opened batteries on them and cleaned them out which broke it up.*
>
> *A.M. of the 2nd day opened with sharpshooting. In the P.M. a member of an Ohio regiment (he thinks) was shot. His regiment was in the rear of the 17th and marching to the rear and one of the rebel sharpshooters in some house dropped him, being the only one in the regiment hurt. He lay in the hot sun for 15 or 20 minutes before anyone dared go to him. Then a call was made for volunteers. Two men from the 17th with a rubber blanket rushed out and put him onto it and took him to the hospital back over the same stone wall that only a few moments before his regiment had passed over. They were going double quick.*
>
> *P.M. of 2nd day a rebel battery was off to the extreme right of Cemetery Hill which opened fire upon our regiment and the Ohio regiments, and the battery on the hill. That fire continued for ½ or ¾ hour much to the annoyance of the regiment, then our batteries opened fire on them, dropping shell right into them and in 15 minutes they hitched up their batteries and left.*
>
> *A.M. of the 2nd day the 17th was ordered to advance a little to the foot of cemetery hill and took position in a lane, then were under fire of sharpshooters for several hours and the regiment returned on their stomachs.*
>
> *Later in the P.M. the position of the regiment changed to right angle with what it was in the A.M. Later in the P.M. while making coffee orders came to prepare for action immediately. It was here that Capt. Kellogg gave the order to advance out and shoot.* [Warren noted, "see A. W. Peck's letter about this."] *Still later P.M. the position was changed again. The regiment now faced Gettysburg at the foot of Cemetery Hill at about dark. Some of the rebs in front of the regiment were taken prisoners while others were killed and others retreated which closed the fight for the night.*
>
> *About dark of 2nd day our skirmishers in great numbers were driven in, the rebs tight to their heels and firing into them. Some of our men got excited and fired into our skirmishers. The 17th lay back of the stone wall and it was here behind this wall that the regiment had a fight with the*

Louisiana Tigers. Just as soon as our skirmishers were out of the way our regiment fired just as fast as they could. Some of the Tigers came right up to the opposite side (of the) stone wall, firing continued so long it got to be dark. Could not see one man from another. All the time the 17th was firing the artillery back of them, upon the hill was constantly firing into the rebs. Capt. Burr had a hand-to-hand fight with one of the Tigers and took him prisoner. The rebs broke through on the right of the regiment and went to their rear and so on up Cemetery Hill and had a hand-to-hand fight with the gunners. During the hottest time of this fight, when it seemed that the regiment could not hold out any longer, the 25th Ohio came down Cemetery Hill on double quick and filled in right back of the 17th and laid down. The ammunition of the 17th was very low being 2 days in action. The 25th supplied them or divided. [Fields may mean the 4th Ohio of Carroll's Brigade, which charged behind the 14th Indiana and the 7th West Virginia to clear the Confederates from the batteries and East Cemetery Hill as the attack stalled and was receding. The 4th Ohio would take the place of the 17th Connecticut in line that night after the attack ended. The 25th Ohio had been out on picket earlier on July 2 along with the 17th before the 17th changed position.]

During this time Henry Allen was directly back of Wm. Fields. A. W. Peck was very near and had been using his revolver. Allen asked Peck to let him take it and Peck did so. While Allen was shooting with the revolver he was shot in the right hand. Fields turned around and saw Allen's hand all blood. Allen cussed and swore around and says, "Give them hell boys." And he went to the rear. This fight lasted from about dark till about 9 P.M. Quiet rest of the night which ends the second day.[19]

Captain Henry Allen, Company F, was wounded July 2 on East Cemetery Hill. (Dale Call Collection)

At the end of Fields's account William Warren wrote: "Wm. Field's account as he gave it to me at his home evenings in December 1885 on Gettysburg."

STEPHEN WILCOX WOUNDED

In 1862 Stephen R. Wilcox of Norwalk was a twenty-two-year-old married carpenter with an infant son. He was not related to Corporal Alvah Wilcox, Company D, who was mortally wounded on East Cemetery Hill on July 2. Stephen Wilcox enlisted in Company F as a corporal. At Gettysburg he served as a private after having been reduced in rank. In September 1863 he would again be wearing his corporal stripes, and he kept them until the end of the war when he was mustered out with the regiment in July 1865. At Gettysburg he was slightly wounded on July 2. Wilcox stayed in

Gettysburg after the Union army left in pursuit of Lee. He served nursing duty at Camp Letterman. On August 1, 1863, he wrote his brother-in-law, Walter Clark, a letter about his circumstances at the hospital and described how he was wounded on July 2.[20]

General Hospital, Gettysburg, PA, August 1, 1863

Dear Brother Walt,

I read your kind and ever welcome letter yesterday and I am glad to hear from you that you are all well. I hope that you may be fortunate enough not to get drafted. I expect that they will have some fun in Norwalk when they commence to draft which I suppose has commenced this week. I hope that Rhodes will not have to come. If he does, I would like to have him in my regiment. The 11th Corps is broken up and our division I hear will go in the 2nd Corps under command of General Howard. The 2nd division is going in the 12th Corps. Three division is to be under command of General Carl Schurtz. It is an independent command. He is to guard the railroad from Manassas to the Rappahannock.

I have had the office of Ward Master in a ward of Rebs but there was so much work to do that I gave it up. I felt sick. I feel rather weak. [This was at Camp Letterman General Hospital, near the railroad tracks north of town along the York Pike.] *I don't have any appetite and don't feel well myself but my drink-atite is as good as ever. Yesterday I went to town and got all the whiskey and gin cock-your-tails that I wanted and felt better. I should like to be in New York with you again. I think that your young Steve Wilcox and myself would have a jolly good time. I think I shall not stay here long. I shall get on to the regiment if I don't find something else that suits me better to do.*

You say that you don't know how I was wounded nor how bad. I was wounded but only slightly. I was on picket. I went out at dark the first day and at daylight the second about three o'clock. I could see the Rebs moving about over in the wheat and grass fields. We commenced to point our rifles at them and send them a message of lead. As soon as the balls began to fall thick around them, they would drop down in the grass out of sight and whenever one of them showed himself we fired at him. There was one of them coming across the lot on horseback. I put my rifle to my shoulder and fired and Mr. Reb rolled off like a pumpkin. I don't know whether I killed him or not, but his horse made tracks and got out of the way. Every once in a while, you could see four men carry a wounded one off the field on a stretcher. Pretty soon they began to shoot right, I reckon out of the houses and everywhere they could get under cover. They shot one of the 107th Ohio boys right in back of me and then in a few minutes another was wounded close on the other side of me. I sat close by a fence like this [small sketch of fence, not provided] with no protection but one of the posts. They shot the fence all to pieces and the post that I was behind was hit four times. When they hit me, I was sitting at the foot of the post loading my last round of cartridge. The Rebs had the range of me from the houses and had me in a crossfire. I was turned a little to one side. The ball went thru my [rubber] blanket and just grazed my back in two places. It struck just below my shoulder and went in and cut four holes in the back of my blouse. It cut my cartridge belt almost in two. If I had been turned a little further around it would have went right straight thru me and that would have been the last of our Steve for it would have cut my gizzard string and started the claret.

There was another Corporal hit by a ball, and it went thru this thigh. He was close to me when I was hit. I left and it was not long before they hit him. I went back where we lay before on picket and the small balls rained around and passed me with a whiz.

I went in the house and got the chance to make me a cup of coffee, the first thing I had eaten in thirty-six hours. After I got the coffee down I felt better. I went into the next room and one of the boys helped me to dress my wound. I never had it dressed but twice, but my back was so lame and stiff for three or four days that I could hardly stir. . . .

There were a great many wounded and taken prisoners. We fought well and bravely but the 11th Corps never gets any credit for what it does. The 11th and 1st Corps done most of the fighting and lost almost all of their men but the 11th Corps is no more. [After Gettysburg, General Meade proposed dissolving the Eleventh and distributing its elements among several other corps. On August 5 the War Department issued the orders. The 17th Connecticut would be assigned to the Tenth Corps and the Department of the South, and it continued to be brigaded with the 25th, 75th, and 107th Ohio regiments until the end of the war.[21] It is amazing that when Wilcox wrote this letter, dated August 1, this private was already aware that the high command would dissolve the Eleventh Corps.]

I am glad to hear that Frank Gilbertson is safe and well. I have a very bad headache today and do not fell very well but I think I shall feel better in a day or two. I got a letter from Rhodes and Mary. She says that they had some fun there. I should like to be there to see the fun. Well, Walt, I think I have scribbled enough to keep you busy reading for some time. Write soon as you hear from me again and believe me ever yours.
Brother S.R. Wilcox[From the margins of the letter] From your humble servant, Steve Wilcox[22]

SERGEANT MAJOR C. FREDERICK BETTS

At sixteen years old, C. Frederick Betts was sergeant major of the regiment at Gettysburg. In 1884 he wrote to Colonel Henry Allen a long letter describing his experiences during the battle. The portion of his letter describing July 2 follows.

Captain Henry Burr, Company E, who said "he got hunk for Chancellorsville" after the hand-to-hand combat at East Cemetery Hill. (Bridgeport History Center)

July 2nd, the day was varied only, I think, by the sharpshooters who, from different locations, endeavored to pick off anyone bold enough to show a head above the stone fence, except by an artillery duel between Battery I, 1st NY [Wiedrich's Battery] *and a rebel battery across the valley. During this p.m. a column of rebel infantry came out of the woods on our right and defiled through the fields far in our front and just before dark, came gradually up in line to the wall behind which we lay, and although finally repulsed, broke through the line to the left of us and left some of their dead among the guns on the hill behind. It was during this charge that Lieut. Col. Allen was wounded, and that Capt. Burr captured the rebel color bearer and "got hunk", as he said for Chancellorsville, where he was captured.*

It seems to me that it was on this day that our Brigade commanded by Major Harris, of the 75th Ohio, was reinforced by a Brigade from Second Corps commanded by a Maine Colonel [Colonel Samuel Sprigg "Red" Carroll's Gibraltar Brigade of the Second Corps; Carroll hailed from Maryland, not Mainc.] *and I recall the feeling of intense satisfaction I felt when those full regiments filed in behind our line and lay down out of range.*[23]

This panorama shows the crest of East Cemetery Hill. From left to right are the monuments to Ricketts's Battery, Cooper's Battery, the 4th Ohio in the distance, General Hancock, and the 14th Indiana. (Library of Congress)

CHAPTER 9

July 3— The Final Struggle

On July 3 another humid morning dawned with heavy summer clouds covering the sky.[1] The regiment began the day in its new position facing the town. After the harrowing assault the night before was repulsed, the 4th Ohio replaced the 17th Connecticut at the stone wall on the Brickyard Lane. Major Brady wrote in his July 4 report:

> *We were relieved by the Fourth Ohio Volunteers and were ordered to change front to the left behind a wall running at right angles with the one we had just occupied, and fronting the town, and where the enemy entered on our left. We remained at this wall all night and during the whole of the 3d instant, exposed to a crossfire of the rebel batteries and their sharpshooters. With the latter our best marksmen exchanged shots and succeeded in dislodging many of them.2*

The men of the regiment recorded various experiences during the third day. The accounts reflected the diverse personal circumstances of the wounded, the prisoners, and the men who remained on the firing line. On July 3, the men were mostly witnesses to events rather than combatants, except for the constant fire coming from houses along Baltimore Street that plagued them throughout the day. Another day of continuous sharpshooting took a physical, emotional, and mental toll on the men. July 3 would see the longest firefight of the battle, a seven-hour battle on Culp's Hill to the northeast of Cemetery Hill. And the tremendous cannonading of the artillery that afternoon that preceded Pickett's Charge would shake the earth the men lay upon.

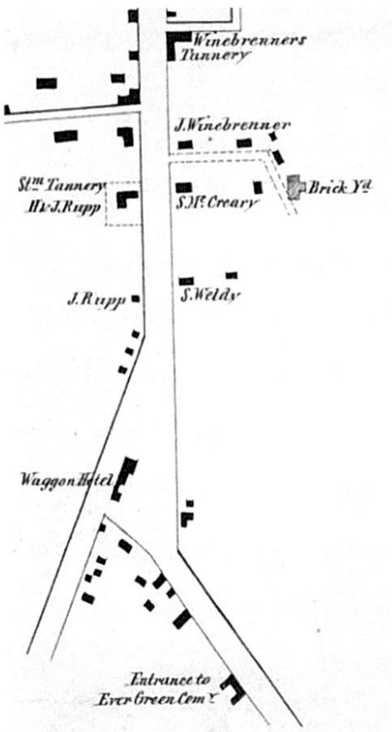

This diagram of Baltimore Street, taken from an 1858 map of Adams County, shows the houses from which Confederate sharpshooters fired into the Union artillery and infantry. From the top right side of Baltimore Street are the Winebrenner Tannery, the entrance to Brickyard Lane off Baltimore Street, the John Winebrenner home, the Samuel McCreary home, and the Solomon Welty home. The McClellan house where Jennie Wade was killed (the only civilian killed during the battle) is the small, unmarked square before the larger Catherine Snyder House (also unmarked) across from the Wagon Hotel. (Library of Congress)

MILTON DANIELS, COMPANY C

We rested until four a.m. of the third day, when were placed a few rods to the right; we held this position returning the fire of the sharpshooters as best we could. I remember Major Brady saying, "For God's sake, can't you keep those fellows quiet?" I remember two incidents that made a strong impression on us all. The enemy was firing on us from the houses of the town. Out of one house came two shots in quick succession; we returned the fire, but soon after learned that we killed a young woman in the house while she was kneading bread.

The other incident was this: A boy came to me and said, "Lieutenant, I have lost my regiment and I want to join your company for the present, and if I fight well and do my duty, will you give me a good report to my Captain?" I replied, "Certainly, I will, my boy." Now away to our right was a rebel sharpshooter hidden behind a pile of fence rails, who kept one of our guns silent for some time, shooting every man that tried to load it. I said to the boy, "Perhaps you can get that chap," explaining to him the situation. The sharpshooter shot at a cannoneer; the boy shot at him, but in a moment, as it were, a shot came back between the second and third rails of the fence and struck him in or near the heart. I was standing just behind him; if it had not struck him it would certainly have got me. He had nothing about him to show who he was, except he was an Indiana boy.[3]

The unidentified Indiana boy killed in front of Lieutenant Daniels may have been from the 14th Indiana, one of the three regiments of Samuel Carroll's Second Corps Gibraltar Brigade, that charged the night before on East Cemetery Hill to help clear

Confederates off the batteries. The soldier may have been separated from his regiment in the dark and confusion. Several members of the 17th had also become separated from the regiment during the night action and made their way back in the morning.

The young woman to whom Lieutenant Daniels refers is Mary Virginia Wade, known as Jennie, the only civilian killed during the Battle of Gettysburg. On the morning of July 3, news about a young woman being killed flew through the Union lines and the town. Daniels mistakenly presumed she was killed by Union fire; however, the consensus among historians is that Wade was killed by a Confederate bullet fired from the area of the Rupp Tannery. Jennie's death was known by many immediately after the battle. In an entry for July 4 in his *Reminisces*, Lieutenant Albert Peck wrote, "*Our army took possession of the town on July 4th and captured quite a number of prisoners. I think the only citizen killed in town during the battle was a young lady named Jenny Wade, supposed to have been killed by a Rebel sharpshooter.*"[4]

During the battle, Jennie, her mother, her eight-year-old brother, Harry, and a disabled six-year-old boy the family cared for stayed at a small house on Baltimore Street with Jennie's sister, Georgia McClellan, who had given birth to a son, Lewis Kenneth, on June 26. Georgia's husband, John Louis McClellan, was away with his regiment in the Union army. The house was a duplex, with the McClellans renting the northern half. The other half was occupied by widow McClain and her four children.

On the morning of July 1, as the battle began north of Gettysburg and the fighting crept south and into the town, Jennie had taken her brother and the young boy she cared for and left her home on Breckenridge Street. She brought the children to her sister's home on the southern edge of town, believing it was safer.[5] It was not. The little brick house on Baltimore Street became part of the Union line, and rebel artillery and rifle fire from the houses and tannery on Baltimore converged on Union targets on Cemetery Hill, including this house. Rebel infantry fired from houses all along Baltimore Street. The little brick house was caught in a crossfire. Bullets struck the house and around it continuously. Union men in its vicinity were wounded and killed. The thud of bullets hitting the house and the cries from wounded in the garden made rest impossible.[6] Despite the danger, Jennie continued to fill the water bucket from the well for hordes of thirsty Union men.

On the morning of July 3, twenty-year-old Mary Virginia Wade was instantly killed while kneading dough for bread for Union soldiers. (Library of Congress)

During the battle Jennie baked constantly to feed soldiers who appeared at the door for food and water. Early on July 3, Jennie was kneading dough in the kitchen as her mother lit the fire for the day's baking. At about 8:30 a.m. a bullet tore through the paneled kitchen outer door on the north side of the house, and the open door between the parlor and kitchen, striking Jennie in the back below the left shoulder blade. The

A 1903 photo of the house on Baltimore Street where Jennie Wade was killed. The bullet came through the door and struck her in the back, killing her instantly. The house was damaged by more than 150 bullets during the three-day battle, including a ten-pound Parrott shell that went through the roof and attic of the house and lodged in the far brick wall without exploding. (Library of Congress)

bullet passed through her heart and killed her instantly. The bullet that went through her body lodged in the front of her corset. Her hands were still covered in dough. Union soldiers brought Jennie's blanket-wrapped corpse, and the family, into the more protected cellar on the McClain side of the house. Leaving her family safe in the McClain cellar with Jennie's body, Mrs. Wade returned to the kitchen and resumed baking for the men.[7]

WILLIAM WARREN, PRISONER

The morning of July 3, William Warren was a prisoner in Confederate hands. His account of that day again explains why he and his fellow prisoners decided not to take the parole the Confederates offered them.

> *We arose from our couch (mother earth) about daylight and cooked breakfast to keep it from spoiling, which was fresh meat. About 1:30 all prisoners fell in line—one in one lot and some in another—to see who would accept the parole, as the rebs told us, all who wished (could) take the parole on the field and go into our lines, but they advised us not to take it, as it would not be legal, and if we were taken prisoners again, we would be shot, so our company got together and talked the matter over,*

and finally came to the conclusion that the longest way round is the shortest way home, so concluded to go to Richmond.

About one half of our regiment accepted it [the parole] *by stepping out to the front, but not one man of Co. C accepted; there was a great deal of hard work done studying the situation for a little while, but after talking the matter over thoroughly all came back with the exception of about one dozen. Those that accepted the parole left us and went off to another field by themselves; that was the last we saw of them, for about dark they were taken to Carlisle. Today the rebs told us we could write home once more before we left here, but to be very careful what we wrote, as they should open every letter and read it before it was mailed and if there was anything in them they did not like, the letters would be destroyed, so as to make sure my letter would go, I wrote the following: "I am a prisoner of war, taken at the battle of Gettysburg, and I am going to Richmond so do not expect to hear from me in some time. The Rebs are giving us plenty to eat and that is good." (The whole thing was a lie for they almost starved us to death.) About a month after my folks received the letter. About five P.M. one day's rations were weighed out of ½ pint of flour and ½ pint of meal.*[8]

LIEUTENANT ALBERT PECK, COMPANY D

Around daybreak, Union Twelfth Corps artillery began firing from Culp's Hill. Southern batteries opened up and the Confederates prepared to attack.[9] The longest continuous firefight of the three-day battle began that morning on Culp's Hill. Along Baltimore Street, as soon as it became light, the Confederates began shooting from the houses and into the Union line, and the Federals returned fire. The sharpshooting would continue the pattern of the previous two days. Early that morning, Lieutenant Albert Peck walked over East Cemetery Hill and surveyed the carnage from the night before. In 1887, Peck wrote to Warren about what he saw that morning. In 1906 he would record his recollections of that day in his *Reminisces*. Both of Peck's July 3 accounts follow, beginning with the 1887 letter to Warren.

I remember seeing a rebel color bearer laying dead near our batteries next morning; I also saw a large dead reb who had a straw hat on, his sleeves were rolled up. He had no coat on. He wore a U.S. belt with a U.S. plate turned down. I picked up a couple of white stars that had been torn from a rebel flag and a piece of flag also. I do not recollect that our regiment was engaged at all on Friday. We were ordered to stand at arms and watch the front. During the fearful artillery firing that preceded the charge of Pickett's Division we could hear the shells coming from nearly all directions, and the constant rattle of musketry and yelling of the Johnnies, but we could not see any of the fighting, as it was on the other side of the hill and could not be seen from our position. We were standing at arms all the afternoon waiting orders to move on, but they did not come.[10]

A Confederate infantryman wearing a U.S. belt plate turned upside down, as described by Lieutenant Peck, depicted on the Coster Avenue mural in Gettysburg by artists Mark H. Dunkelman and Johan Bjurman.
(Photograph by author)

In 1906 Peck wrote in his recollections for July 3:

> *July 3rd, 1863. We were up early on the morning of the 3rd, and I went up to the top of the hill where the batteries were and I saw a young Rebel color bearer lying dead near one of our batteries. I also looked over the fence into the apple orchard and saw a big burly Johnnie lying there dead. He had on a broad brimmed straw hat and two gray shirts. He had his sleeves rolled up and above his elbows and he wore a U.S. belt around his waist with the U.S. turned bottom side up. He evidently meant business and was going for one of the batteries just over the fence, but he did not get there as he got a Union bullet just below his belt which evidently put him out of business. It was reported that a whole Rebel Division lay near the town all day July 2nd waiting to capture the batteries on East Cemetery Hill that night.*[11]

Peck described the fury of the fight that took place on Culp's Hill that morning.

> *There was heavy fighting in the woods on Culp's Hill early in the morning. The 12th Corps under General Slocum were trying to retake the breastworks which the Johnnies had taken from them the night before and they succeeded in retaking them after three or four hours of fierce fighting in which the artillery and infantry were both engaged. We were lying but a short distance from where the battle was raging and could see some of the troops between the trees, and could also see some of the signal corps, near*

the outside of the woods. Our Corps was not engaged. We could see troops belonging to Johnson's division of the Rebel Army marching along a road to re-enforce the troops at Culp's Hill, nearly a mile away, and could see our batteries occasionally drop a shell into their ranks and they would stop and turn back once in a while.

Quite a large squad of Rebel Cavalry rode out across a large open field in our front and stopped at a small white house. It was probably some General and his staff. At any rate, someone sent a notice up to one of the batteries on top of the hill and they opened two or three guns with shell on them, and this soon broke them all up and they very soon started on a gallop for a piece of woods about half a mile away.[12]

Much of what Peck described was sketched in real time by the artist-journalist Edwin Forbes, who was at Gettysburg reporting on the battle for *Frank Leslie's Illustrated Newspaper*. During the Civil War the technology to reproduce photographs in print publications had not yet been developed and photography did not have the ability to capture action scenes. Illustrated newspapers such as *Harper's Weekly* and *Frank Leslie's* sent sketch artists out into the field. These men were on hand to sketch action, such as combat, as it occurred. These sketches were then turned into woodcuts that could be printed in illustrated news publications. At 10 a.m. on July 3, Edwin Forbes sketched the activity taking place on the battlefield along with detailed notes of the action. Forbes later turned this sketch into an oil painting. His detailed notes document quite a bit of what Peck described in his recollections.

Artist Edwin Forbes's real-time panoramic sketch of the simultaneous actions at Gettysburg at 10 a.m. on July 3 is described in his notes that flow across the sketch. ***Notes across the top of the drawing from left to right:*** **Artillery shelling the rebel infantry in the woods to the right; Union artillery caisson explosion; Union artillery on the brow of the hill; Rebel shells bursting; Cemetery left of house, front and center of white grave markers; the town is over the hill beyond; Union artillery caissons behind infantry in the rear; fight for possession of wooded hill; Culp's Hill smoke ascending among the trees.** ***Notes in the middle of the sketch from left to right:*** **Back of the battle numbers of ambulances coming along; reserves lying down; men supplying infantry in line of battle; infantry marching.** ***Notes on the bottom left of the sketch:*** **Wounded men coming back; line of battle; cooking coffee, sitting, and lying, Artillery park; Baltimore Pike, July 3, 10 a.m.** (Library of Congress)

HOW A SUPPLY OF WATER WAS OBTAINED

BY W. W. PAYNTON, COMPANY A

July 3 was the hottest of the three days of the battle. Humidity was high and there would be a thunderstorm about 6 p.m.[13] For men lying on the battle line all day thirst was relentless. Water was a precious commodity, but filling canteens under enemy fire was a dangerous proposition. Corporal William Paynton, Company A, related the following to William Warren in one of his written sketches.

> *During the terrible artillery duel that took place on the third day at Gettysburg, the men in Co. A suffered intensely for water. Posted behind a stone wall on the brow of Cemetery Ridge, it was all one's life was worth to raise his head above the top of the wall or in any manner show himself, as the situation was completely covered by Lee's sharpshooters, who occupied tops of buildings in the town, used as hospitals, and other places of advantage, But at last, Paddy Ford, offered to take half dozen canteens and go up to a spring on the hillside, in full view of the sharpshooters, and fill them and return with them or die in the attempt. So he crawled to the spring, and lying flat beside it, he filled the six canteens. Within arm's length of him lay a dead rebel who had been killed in some previous part of the battle. Paddy looked at him for a moment and reaching out he rifled his pockets of their contents, and then returned to the lines. Shots fell thick and fast all around him, but none struck him. The boys whose canteens were filled would not give a drop away except to their most intimate chums. Finally I said, "Boys, give me half dozen canteens. I may as well be shot as die of thirst, I am going to the spring for water, if I never come back you may know where to look for my body." So I started in the same manner as had Paddy, and reached the spring in safety. I filled the six canteens and received the same compliments from the Rebs as he did, with the same results. After I had got the water, I took a look at the dead Reb! He lay flat on his back, and a hole in his waist belt told where the deadly mini ball had found its way to his young life, for he did not appear more than 16 or 17 years of age. I looked at his upturned face for a moment, and in my fancy, I could read his life's story. How that he had been reared in some far away Southern home—the only son of his mother and she a widow, perhaps—how she had given him to the service of his country, although in a mistaken cause, she was anxiously awaiting the close of the war and the return of her boy. But I also noticed that Paddy, in his visit had not taken all that the boy's pockets contained; a gun wrench was left sticking half out of one pocket, and I reached in and took it. It was just the thing I wanted most, next to water. I brought it home with me in 1865 but had the misfortune to lose it afterwards. I returned to the lines as safely as I went, and our thirst was soon satisfied.*[14]

FRANK S. MIDDLEBROOK, COMPANY F

Corporal Francis S. Middlebrook also remembered the water incident on July 3 with Paddy Ford from Company A. Middlebrook sent a short, undated account to William Warren that was recorded in the manuscript. Middlebrook was promoted to sergeant major in August 1864. After the war he would return to Norwalk, marry, and was listed in various census records as a paint salesman and wine broker. He was active in veterans' affairs and was the commander of the Buckingham Post GAR in Norwalk when he died in 1906.[15]

> *Middlebrook thinks it was the P.M. of the third day, when Paddy Ford was going to the spring for water, with several canteens, under cover of the rifle pits, which were on a right angle with the line of battle; in returning, he came back on the other angle, thus he did not get hurt, but several canteens were shot away being under fire from the sharpshooters.*[16]

Private Patrick "Paddy" Ford, born in Ireland, was a married twenty-seven-year-old laborer when he enlisted in Company A of the 17th Connecticut in 1862. In 1884, when the 17th Connecticut monument was dedicated on Barlow's Knoll, Ford was remembered fondly in the dedication program, where he was referred to as "the jolly Paddy Ford of Company A."[17] Ford would muster out with the regiment at Hilton Head in 1865.[18]

JUSTUS SILLLIMAN, WOUNDED PRISONER

Private Justus Silliman, wounded in the head on Barlow's Knoll on July 1, was still incarcerated with other wounded men of the 17th Connecticut and Eleventh Corps in the common school building on High Street. In a letter from July 3 written from the schoolhouse to his mother in New Canaan, Silliman described what he witnessed on the third day of the battle from his place of confinement.

> *A Georgia brigade now occupy the ground where the La brigade lay yesterday. We cannot watch the fighting today as the rebs have been ordered to shoot any of us who make their appearance at the front windows, so we are obliged to keep pretty close. There is a rebel general in front of the hospital watching the progress of the fight and giving orders, he is dressed in citizen clothes, wears a straw hat slouched over his head and uses a cane in lieu of a sword. This is the old Gen [Jeb]sic Stuart. Eual [General Richard Ewell] is riding around town with his one leg, being followed by an attendant carrying his crutches. At this moment the rebel battery has opened a very heavy fire directly in front of us and our guns are replying with interest. The firing has now become general all along the line and bullets and fragments of shell are rattling against our hospital, making a great racket. One shell from our battery entered a house adjoining but*

> *did not explode. This is all at present. Do not worry about my head for it is a very slight affair, it aches a little but is merely a scratch. It was very providential that while so many were taken I was spared.*[19]

The "old" General Steuart in front of the school-hospital on High Street to whom Silliman refers was the father of General George Hume Steuart (nicknamed "Maryland" Steuart), whose troops attacked Culp's Hill that morning and were repulsed. "Old" General George H. Steuart had served in the War of 1812. The elderly general had followed the Confederate army to Gettysburg and encountered Gettysburg physician Dr. John W. C. O'Neal on the road near Cashtown, where O'Neal rode with the general for a bit until the old man needed to rest before making his way to Gettysburg. Dr. O'Neal left him at a house in McKnightstown.[20]

The mansion estate of "Old" General George H. Steuart in Baltimore was confiscated by the U.S. government in 1861 for hospital purposes. The hospital held up to 1,400 patients and was often called Steuart's Hospital, until 1863, when the name was changed to Jarvis Hospital. In an interesting twist, some of the men from the 17th Connecticut wounded at Gettysburg who were incarcerated in the schoolhouse were sent to Jarvis/Steuart's Hospital in Baltimore to recuperate from their wounds after the battle. J. Henry Blakeman, Company D, was one of these men. He would write several letters home to Connecticut from that hospital.[21]

In August 1884, Justus Silliman, then a professor at Lafayette College, sent letters to General William Noble about his experiences at Gettysburg. In his remarkable account below Silliman described how he climbed into the steeple of the schoolhouse to witness Pickett's Charge on July 3.

> *July 3rd, By J. M. Silliman*
>
> *On the morning of the 3rd the rebels informed us that they had orders to shoot any of us if we appeared at the windows, (of the school building on High Street) so in order to watch a battle, I climbed to the cupola, from which I had an excellent view of the field. Even at that height, the bullets were whistling around my ears and the noise of shot and shell in the air resembled that of a mighty torrent. Another brigade occupied the position held by the La. Tigers and met with similar repulse when they charged our lines. Some members of the 17th were the first to enter our hospital on the morning of the 4th, and soon after, the wounded who were half famished, were supplied with food.*
>
> *Lafayette College, Easton, PA., Aug 14/84.*[22]

Lieutenant Albert Peck wrote a description of the artillery barrage and Pickett's assault in his 1906 *Reminisces*:

> *After the firing stopped on Culp's Hill, there was nothing more doing until about two o'clock in the afternoon when the Rebels opened a heavy fire of*

This woodcut from an 1858 map of Adams County shows the Common School on High Street next to the German Reformed Church where wounded Eleventh Corps men were held prisoner during the battle. Justus Silliman, Company H, watched the attack of the Louisiana Tigers on East Cemetery Hill from this building on the evening of July 2. On July 3, Silliman climbed up into the school's steeple to watch the day's action. The school building is still on High Street. The school bell is now in Unity Park on Lefever Street, off Baltimore Street at the entrance to what was Brickyard Lane during the battle.
(Library of Congress)

artillery all along their line. There were supposed to be about one hundred and fifty guns engaged on their side and about the same number on our side, and the air was full of shell coming from nearly all directions, and the fire seemed to be especially directed to our batteries—inside of the cemetery. After the artillery firing had nearly ceased, a long line of Rebel Infantry was seen approaching from the woods beyond Seminary Hill. The artillery from the Round Tops, from the Cemetery and from all along the line opened on them as the line approached, and soon our skirmishers and infantry were engaged and our artillery were engaged too, and there was great excitement for a while. We could not see Pickett's men as they were on the other side of the hill, but we could hear the cheers and the racket and see the horses flying back and forth and the men carrying dispatches with foaming horses and could see some of the aides with their arms in a sling. General Howard's Head Quarters were just inside of the Cemetery Gate in the Porter's Lodge, and in a very exposed position, as a great deal of the artillery fire was directed to the batteries within the cemetery. Howard had eighteen guns there that did terrible execution among Pickett's men.

We were ordered to stand at arms and watch the front and be ready to move at a moments notice. A good many shells came over our heads, but I do not think any of our men were hit by them. General Howard said that a shell burst in one of the regiments in the cemetery—killing and wounding twenty-seven men but not a man left the ranks without orders. The solid shot and shell did a great deal of damage in the cemetery, killing and wounding a great many men and horses, breaking down monuments and fences and headstones.

Lee's Army commenced to retreat on Friday night, soon after Pickett's charge, which was a bad failure and was a great loss in killed, wounded

> *and prisoners. It was said that Pickett only had fifteen thousand men and General Longstreet was almost sure he would be defeated and was opposed to making the charge.*[23]

Peck underlined the words in the last sentence of his account for emphasis. The account was written many years after the battle and reflects, that over the years, Peck read about and researched the battle he had fought in as a young officer. Peck came to the underlined conclusion as have many historians today.

CHAPTER 10

The Glorious Fourth

Drenching summer downpours began the night of July 3 and rain became torrential on the Fourth of July. The thunderstorms probably sounded tame after the tremendous cannonading of July 3. The wounded, the prisoners, the men lying on their arms on the battle line, and the retreating Confederates were all drenched. The dead in shallow burial trenches were uncovered and left exposed in the mud of the driving rain. The streams and creeks swelled their banks. On July 4 Rock Creek overflowed its banks and became so high and swift at the Second Corps hospital at the Jacob Schwartz Farm that ambulatory wounded close to the creek scrambled to higher ground. Hospital attendants and anyone able to help tried to evacuate the helpless wounded who were trapped by the rising water. There were reports that at as many as twenty wounded were drowned.[1]

On July 4, J. Henry Blakeman and others were moved from the schoolhouse hospital on High Street to the Eleventh Corps hospital on the George Spangler Farm. Blakeman wrote home to his mother, "Here we have to lie on the ground and last night we had a terrible rain so I am as wet as water can make me."[2] Dr. Daniel G. Brinton, surgeon in chief of the Second Division, Eleventh Corps, wrote in his diary, "A heavy rain came . . . and as we laid many (wounded) in spots without shelter some indeed in the barnyard where the foul water oozed up into their undressed wounds, the sight was harassing in the extreme."[3] Surgeons operated under the overhang of the Spangler barn, only partially protected, as water poured down on them and their patients.[4] The survivors all had to deal with the mud, mire, and miserable, sodden conditions in their various states and circumstances.

WILLIAM WARREN, PRISONER

William Warren began the Fourth of July as a prisoner. The Union men were offered a parole by their captors. Many Yankees refused to accept the parole that they deemed dubiously legal. The Union boys understood their refusal of parole meant walking the long road to Richmond, where they would have to wait in captivity to be legally exchanged.

Today is Independence Day, but I do not feel very independent; I should think I was rather dependent, as I am a prisoner of war and dependent upon someone to get me out of this scrape. It is also a holiday, but what difference does that make to me; as long as we are prisoners, our days will be all holidays; I mean we will not have our daily duty to perform, but will lay off on our oars—living on the fat of the land in the Southern Confederacy in the "Sunny South," where we can relieve our minds from business and spend a few summer months at the Capitol on the banks of the James River, with nothing to worry about—knowing that our board and hotel bills will be paid, also having guards to carefully watch over us in our daily walks and midnight slumbers, to keep away all harm. Reader, just stop and think what valuable and highly esteemed citizens of our country we are, to demand so much attention. What makes the difference; I cannot demand that attention today? I return to my copy book again and read as follows: "Being a prisoner of war I am almost starved and wet through two or three times over by the heavy storm. One year ago today, I was at a celebration in Bridgeport, a free man, not a soldier; plenty to eat and drink, plenty of money, a pleasant day and all I could ask for; now I have none of these things. But compare the difference one short year has brought forth—who knows the events of the coming year; no one but God! About daylight we prepared ourselves for a move which came in a short time. We marched through four or five lots, to be counted off, then stopped about one hour in a low meadow close by the side of the road.

It rained very hard all the A.M. it was soon over, but there we stood and took it. During all this time, the Rebel army was falling back, and they wanted all the road to themselves; It was full of all kinds of teams that they could possibly raise to carry off their wounded. It was a bad night to see them and to hear their groans, as we could plainly see the whole thing. Men were piled in wagons like sheep—not a place vacant, and every wounded man that could walk was obliged to, to make room in the wagons or carts,

William Warren described the misery of Confederate army as it retreated from Gettysburg in the driving rains of July 4. All suffered in the wretched weather and mud, especially the wounded. (New York Public Library Digital Collections)

for those that were worse off than they were. They brought with them a few ambulances; their other conveyances were business wagons, two and four wheeled carts, and in fact all kinds and descriptions from a first-class wagon down to an old rickety farmer's cart just ready to drop down. Their horses were anything and everything from a mule to an old plug—anything that could stand up, and they made it go and took it along with the rest. They stole on the road all their horses and wagons that they had. For a mile or two each side of us, every house, barn, shed and anything that would hold a wounded man, was filled to overflowing, besides tents that were put up and filled. After waiting about one hour, we marched out onto the road and marched till dark, then stopped for the night. Many of the boys traded off all the spare things they had to get something to eat as our meals were very limited and we were very hungry.[5]

THOMAS MARSH: WOUNDED PRISONER ESCAPES

On July 1, Tom Marsh, Company D, was terribly wounded after retrieving the colors from the wounded color corporal of his company. A bullet pierced his left shoulder, shattering the bone. Three bullets were removed from his body including pieces of lead from his shoulder and side. One bullet was removed in a Philadelphia hospital after the battle. The surgeon found that bullet a foot or more down the side of his body from where it entered. Another was removed after he was transferred to Knight Soldiers' Hospital in New Haven, Connecticut. The third bullet he carried for seventeen years before he finally had it removed.

On July 1, after he was wounded, Marsh remembered lying on the ground for about two hours with dead rebels around him. Marsh was evacuated from the battlefield to a hospital he remembered being a "rebel division hospital, about 5 miles from Gettysburg."[6] He remained at this unidentified hospital behind Confederate lines until the morning of July 4. Apparently, despite his wounds, Marsh was able to walk. The following account of July 4 was given to William Warren and written in the third person in 1902:

Marsh was in this hospital till the A.M. of July 4, when all the men that were able to walk were called out into the line by a rebel doctor who told them that they would have to walk to Richmond. While this rebel doctor was at one end of the line, a doctor from a New York regiment was at the other end. He said to them, in a quiet way, "If you don't get out of this I'll boot you all out." He was asked where they should go. The doctor in reply asked them if they knew where the spring was. Marsh said that he knew. There were about 40 able to walk. The New York doctor told them to go as easy and quietly as they could to the bushes, which they did, and made good their escape into our lines. After a day or two all the wounded were sent to Philadelphia by rail.[7]

Thomas Marsh was listed on the Spangler Farm patient list as "Marsh, Thomas, Pvt., 17th CT, D, flesh wound upper 3rd left shoulder, water dressing."[8] A water dressing was the most extensive therapy offered to patients at the Eleventh Corps hospital at the Spangler Farm. Mostly this consisted of keeping the wound wet in some way, shape, or form. Marsh, with three bullets in him, but not in danger of imminent death, nor having a limb that needed to be amputated to save his life, was treated with a water dressing until his evacuation to Philadelphia.

The surgeons at the Spangler Farm used a triage system developed by Dr. Jonathan Letterman, the medical director of the Army of the Potomac. The wounded were sorted into three categories. Some wounded were made comfortable, if possible, and left to die. Others were scheduled for surgery as quickly as it could be performed. The third group was left until further treatment could be conducted, and Marsh was among this group. Marsh was not deemed in need of immediate surgery but was one of the early evacuations from Gettysburg. Once in the general hospital at Philadelphia his wounds were treated surgically. He was then transferred to Knight Hospital in New Haven, Connecticut for anther surgery. After months of hospitalization, Marsh was transferred on August 30, 1865, into 159th Company Veteran Reserve Corps, 2nd Battalion. He was discharged for disability on August 12, 1865. Thomas Marsh was one of the lucky ones. He would return to his wife and farm in Easton, Connecticut, to raise his family. Marsh would pass away in 1913 at seventy-seven years old. He was buried at Oak Lawn Cemetery in Fairfield, Connecticut.[9]

W. W. PAYNTON, COMPANY A

William Wallace Paynton recorded in his memoirs his experiences on July 4. He was among the 17th Connecticut men who were ordered into Gettysburg as the Confederates were retreating. His account begins with the return of Colonel Noble, who was wounded at Chancellorsville and absent from the Gettysburg battle.

> *On the morning of July 4th it was discovered that Lee had begun the withdrawal of his army. Preparations were immediately made to invest(?) the town. In the midst of a heavy shower of rain we were ordered to charge and take possession of the town. Just as we were about to start, we were pleased to see the tall form of our Colonel William H. Noble take his place at the head of the regiment. While at his home in Bridgeport, Conn., he learned of the advance of Lee toward the North, and though still suffering from the wound in his arm received at Chancellorsville, determined to come to the front and share with the boys of the 17th the dangers and glories of the campaign. He succeeded in reaching us only after the battle was practically ended, and he was welcomed by the boys right heartily. He has kindly given me, in a recent letter, the circumstances of his journey to the regiment, and I will incorporate it as part of this article.*
>
> *He says:—"When I first heard of Lee's advance, I started from home for Washington. I could get no order how to reach the regiment—hazed*

around—got a horse on pay charge to go across the country—came near being captured with a hundred army teams and guard at Tannallytown. [Tenleytown, a neighborhood in Washington, D.C.] *Finally got permission to go by rail with horse to Baltimore and reported to General Schenck for directions to meet the regiment. Got this and the next morning started by rail for Westminster, twenty-two miles away, which I only reached the third of July about Breakfast time, and started for Gettysburg by the Baltimore Pike, and got there after detention by a furious thunderstorm, after Pickett's Charge.*

In a few minutes the Second Brigade, with Col. Noble in command started on the charge. The brigade at this time numbered scarcely the force of a full regiment. We were obliged to break into an irregular line as we advanced into the town, and some taking one street and some another, but keeping in as near a parallel as possible. Scores of rebel soldiers came out of hiding places beneath stoops and outhouses, and surrendering as prisoners, said, "We uns are tired of the war and don't want to be exchanged." As we passed a certain house that had a high stoop in front, I suspected there might be a party hiding there, so I peered in under it, and sure enough there were six of the "Johnnies" there. I called to them to come out and surrender, at the same time pointing my musket at them; they shouted, "Don't shoot, we uns will come out," and right glad they were to do so.

Colonel Noble, wounded badly at Chancellorsville, rushed to Gettysburg from his home in Bridgeport when battle seemed imminent. Arriving late on July 3, he immediately took command of the brigade, while Major Brady remained in command of the regiment. General Ames, the brigade commander, was moved up to division commander to replace wounded General Barlow.

(Author's collection)

Finally, we reached that part of the field where the regiment started on that fatal charge on the first day of battle; what a sight met our eyes! The dead lay for the most part where they had fallen—their features unrecognizable. Accoutrements were scattered in every direction; muskets were piled up in heaps as high as haystacks in various places; broken gun carriages ad caissons, wrecks of ammunition wagons and the swollen and distorted, putrefying bodies of horses killed during the battle, were to be seen whichever way one looked. While viewing this scene of death and carnage, a column of rebel cavalry was seen approaching from the brow of a hill to our right. Perceiving us. The started at a full gallop to charge on us. Colonel Noble instantly formed us into a hollow square and waited the onset. They advanced to within twenty-five or thirty yards of us and seeing no sign of our breaking the retreat was sounded and they galloped off again as they came. Soon after we returned to our old position on Cemetery Hill, and preparations were at once begun for the pursuit of Lee. Regiments were mustered to ascertain the strength of the army. The dead were buried, and scouting parties were sent out in all directions to hunt up and bring in the stragglers and report them.[10]

MILTON C. DANIELS, COMPANY C

Lieutenant Milton Daniels.
(Bridgeport History Center)

Lieutenant Milton Daniels survived the battle unscathed. He would be promoted on July 15 to captain. He was wounded at Fort Wagner, South Carolina, on August 19, 1863, and would resign from the regiment on March 6, 1864. On July 4, Daniels was one of the officers who led a squad into the town of Gettysburg to determine if the Confederates had withdrawn. Daniels's biggest fear was that his brother, Sergeant William Daniels, who was missing, had been killed on the first day of battle. Many of the men who were missing were either taken prisoner the first day or were, indeed, among the dead on Barlow's Knoll and many would remain unidentified. Several of the men of the 17th who were either freed prisoners or wounded remembered seeing Lieutenant Daniels at the head of the squad. They also remembered that the first question he asked them was if they had seen his brother. Daniels's agitation, perhaps grief, and anger can be felt in his account as he describes taking shots at the enemy and his desire to shoot the Confederate sergeant of the picket post that his squad captured. Although he relates these incidents in a rather flippant manner, many years later, his worry and anguish for his brother are obvious. The brothers were close, and Daniels was devastated by the possible loss of his brother.

In the gray of the morning of the 4th, I was detailed to command the skirmish line of 20 men, 10 from the 17th and 10 from the 107th OVH with a 2nd Lieutenant from the 107th. We deployed just to the right of the town and advanced slowly and wondered why the enemy did not fire upon us. Soon we saw a white flag wavering from a church door for us to come on. We went, and found the flag was waved by one of the 75th Ohio surgeons. The enemy had evacuated. (The incidents going through town would fill a book if well told). We went through the town and established our line near and to the right of the seminary. In a minute or two a cavalry general came up and formed a line a few rods in advance. I was mad, began to growl, but just then General Ames came up—asked what the matter was. I told him and he gave us orders to advance to the Poorhouse, we did so and found thousands of our wounded, and a happier crowd than they is seldom seen, to think they were in our lines again. We captured a picket post of the enemy; we saw them before they saw us.

Now I will say that I supposed Brother Will was killed in the first day's fight and had been taking a gun often for a shot myself, and saying at the time, "Here is for Will, boys." When we saw the picket post, I took a gun and was about to shoot the sergeant in command; he threw up his hands and says, "You have got me, Lieutenant." He proved to be from Baltimore, a fine specimen of manhood, and I have always been glad that I did not shoot him. After we took these men, we were relieved and ordered to take our prisoners to the rear. We took it leisurely back through the town and stopped at a well on the sidewalk to take a drink, as it was the first water for many hours, we stayed with it until we had enough. Just then Colonel Noble came up—it was the first any of us had seen of him since Chancellorsville.[11]

Sergeant William Daniels, Company C, was taken prisoner on July 1. No one knew his whereabouts and he was feared killed. He would be promoted to first sergeant on July 15 while still a prisoner. William would be promoted again to first lieutenant on August 22, 1864 and would muster out with the regiment at Hilton Head in July 1865.
(Bridgeport History Center)

WILLIAM T. FIELDS, COMPANY F

In December 1885, William Warren interviewed William T. Fields in his New Haven home over several evenings. Fields, a former private in Company F, was in 1885 president of the Tradesmen's National Bank in New Haven. Warren took handwritten notes of Fields's memories of the battle; Fields's brief account of July 4th follows.

> *4th Day*
> *Col. Noble came this A.M. and told the boys to get their coffee and then they marched into the town of Gettysburg where we took a few prisoners. Left Gettysburg at night and went over a portion of the field that Pickett had charged over and a night long to be remembered of dead horses, wounded, the stench and, etc. When Pickett retreated, he left on one field over 1000 of his dead. This field was on the left of Emmitsburg Road leaving Gettysburg."*[12]

FRANK S. MIDDLEBROOK, COMPANY F

Frank Middlebrook with his sergeant major stripes. He was promoted August 28, 1864.[13]
(Bridgeport History Center)

Corporal Frank Middlebrook gave William Warren a rather lighthearted, undated account of his adventures in town on July 4 after the Confederates evacuated. Unfortunately, Middlebrook left no indication as to the identity of the young lady, mother, and grandmother whom he wrote about. This account brings up some interesting questions about the informality of the army during the Civil War in its dealing with civilians, and adherence to orders and discipline. In Middlebrook's case, he was not in any hurry to rejoin the regiment after being dismissed from picket duty, and it is unlikely he suffered any ill consequences for his deviation. His account brings into question just how much food he had to share with the family he met and where he got it—not to mention that the Confederates had cleaned out most of the townspeople's food in houses and gardens, and especially coveted that precious substance, coffee. It is possible Middlebrook did have coffee with him that he had been unable to boil up during the battle. His mention of sitting alone at a table with a young lady in her home could certainly be construed as very racy behavior during the Civil War, even if the girl's mother did eventually enter the room. After the war Middlebrook married his wife, Helen, in 1868.[14] Perhaps after his marriage it was his wife who compelled him to stop writing to the "very pretty girl, with curls" from Gettysburg.

> *On the a.m. of July 4th, after the 17th had charged into the town, a number was put on picket, Middlebrook was one. After a while they received orders to rejoin the regiment again. While going back, Middlebrook stopped at a house to get something to eat; he went upstairs and there found an old lady who told him to go downstairs and help himself. In the pantry he found two loaves of bread. While there he heard a noise behind him; he turned around to see what it was and there stood a very pretty girl, with curls, about 18 or 19 years old. After explanations were made, she invited Middlebrook to have something to eat, but as they were nearly out of food, Middlebrook gave them some of his rations. Fresh vegetables were gathered from the garden, ham and eggs were fried and some good coffee made. Middlebrook and the daughter sat at the table alone but her mother coming in, Middlebrook was introduced to her, and a very pleasant conversation passed between them all. Middlebrook and the young lady promised to write each other, and to seal the contract he kissed the*

grandmother, mother, and daughter. Correspondence was kept up for about two years, then forever stopped.
From F. S. Middlebrook[15]

PATRICK WADE, COMPANY K

Patrick Wade was born in County Galway, Ireland, on March 18, 1844. He came to Bridgeport, Connecticut, with his parents and siblings in 1849 and received his education in the local public schools. In 1858 he became an apprentice in the mechanical department of the local Democratic paper, the *Bridgeport Farmer*. This newspaper was anti-Lincoln and had Southern leanings, and after the First Battle of Bull Run the newspaper offices in Bridgeport were wrecked in a pro-Union riot. Nathaniel Morse, one of the *Farmer*'s editors, had to flee, reportedly running along the roof to an adjoining building to escape the rioters. In 1862, at age seventeen, Pat Wade enlisted in Company K of the 17th Connecticut. It is unclear if he was working at the paper at the time of his enlistment, as the publication had to shut down for a period after the riot. Wade was promoted to corporal on May 16, 1863, after the Battle of Chancellorsville. He survived the war and mustered out with his regiment in July 1865.[16]

Pat Wade was a seventeen-year-old printer's apprentice when he enlisted in Company K, 17th Connecticut. (Bridgeport History Center)

After the war, Pat Wade returned to the printing business and was employed by the local Republican newspaper, the *Bridgeport Standard*. He remained employed by the newspaper until his death. Wade had a talent for the mechanical functions of the publishing and printing business. He was the superintendent of the mechanical department and became a stockholder and a director of the paper. After the war, Wade was heavily involved in veterans' affairs and the 17th Connecticut Survivors' Association. The *Standard* was the publisher for the association's reunion and monument dedication publications and other printed materials. When he passed away at age fifty-five in 1899, Pat Wade was well respected and well liked. He and his wife, Catherine, never had children. When Pat made out his will before his death, he made sure Catherine was his executor and received everything he owned. While so many of his comrades were buried in Bridgeport's Mountain Grove Cemetery, Pat was interred in St. Michael's Cemetery, the place of rest for Catholics in Bridgeport.[17]

In March 1886, Wade wrote to Milton Daniels in Indianapolis about his experiences on July 4, 1863, in Gettysburg. Daniels sent Pat's letter on to William Warren, who included it in his manuscript.

Comrade Daniels:—I received your very welcome letter and was more than pleased to hear from you. My recollections of that memorable 4th of July A.M. at Gettysburg is as follows—

After being detailed, we marched from the position of the Regt. on East Cemetery Hill to the meadow below and deployed as skirmishers. After advancing a short distance we met a skirmish line from some German Regiment (whose name or number I do not remember) and you requested the officer in command to advance his line to the fence beyond, halt, lay down, and you would advance our line to a fence further on. How well I remember the cowardly action of that officer and his men. Then came your order to forward 17th, and carefully we picked our steps toward town. After we got about half way, we saw an officer which afterwards proved to be a doctor come out of a church or school, which was being used as a hospital, and wave his hat. The order to forward double quick was immediately given, and away we went over fences and gullies. On reaching the town, then commenced the fun—the citizens pointing out to us the barns, sheds, etc., where rebs were hidden away. The prisoners we captured were sent back to our regiment, which then occupied the public square in town. And here I make the claim, and, I think, without fear of contradiction that our skirmish lines were the first Union troops in the town of Gettysburg that A.M. What do you say?

After sending the prisoners back to the rear, we started for the poor house. On reaching the top of the first knoll from the town, we discovered

The ground that the skirmishers of 17th Connecticut went over toward the town on the morning of July 4 was the same ground that Jubal Early's men charged over the night of July 2. The German Reformed Church is at the far right. Several of the accounts of July 4 mention seeing a Union doctor come out of the church to signal the men as they approached the town.
(Library of Congress)

the rebel cavalry in force near Rock Creek, and as their bugler sounded a charge, we fell back a few paces and occupied the first house on the left-hand side, and there awaited their coming; but they came not! If they did, we could have given them a warm reception (although few in numbers) as there were two men to every window fronting that way. And just here I want to call your attention to the audacity of the orderly who came riding up full speed from the town and reaching the top of the knoll, where we had left, was fired upon by the cavalry. How quickly he dismounted and getting in the shade of his horse, led him to safer quarters. On reaching the poor house we found a number of our members who were prisoners and wounded; the names of those I remember now were Wm. Wirtz, Co. D, and J. M. Silliman, Co. H, prisoners, and Levi Dixon, Co. "H" who had his leg shot off. There were many more whose names I cannot recall. On our way back to town, I captured a drummer boy from a Georgia Regt. who had a very nice drum, which by the inscription, was presented to him by the ladies of some town in Georgia; I gave it to the first Union drummer boy that I met, and have ever since regretted my hasty action, as it would have been highly prized as a memorial by one of our own drum corps. On reaching the center of the town you gave a few of us permission to get something to eat, so we started down a side street—stopped at a prominent residence, and after a good deal of knocking and pounding at the basement door, was answered by a young lady who assured us that herself and mother lived in the cellar during the battle. We informed her that the fighting was over and Lee had been whipped. We soon had a fire going; we furnished the coffee and sugar while she supplied us with radishes and lettuce fresh from the garden. We exchanged names and promised to write to them, but promises were made to be broken, at least it was so on my part. I tried to find the house when there two years ago, as I wanted to thank the family for their kindness and make their acquaintance anew, but I was unsuccessful, and yet the place was changed very little, and the battlefield remains the same as we left it twenty-three years ago. I would advise you if you ever come east, not to return without paying Gettysburg a visit.

And now about the officers and men of our regiment. Gen'l Noble is alive and well. Capt. Dunham, Lieuts. Ruggles and Norris, Dr. Gregory and Quartermaster Hayes are dead; Capt. Waterbury is in the insane retreat since last summer; Major Brady, Capts. Hobbie, McQuahae, McCarthy, Kellogg, Burr, Hubble, Quein, Wood, French, Gray and Drs. Hubbard and McEwen are alive and well. Lieuts. Craw (Cave), Harvey, Clancy, North, Knapp, Doty, and Mills are still in the land of the living. Drum Major Tom Hearn is dead, and many, yes very many of the old boys are dead and gone. At our reunion last year we reported fourteen (14) who had died during the past year.

Write soon, your Comrade, P. Wade, Jr.[18]

ALBERT PECK, COMPANY D

At the time of the Battle of Gettysburg, Albert Peck was a second lieutenant in Company D. He was the company's only remaining commissioned officer during the battle and thus assumed command of the company. Lieutenant Peck wrote to William Warren a letter of his account of July 4 titled, "Fourth Day at Gettysburg." Peck also wrote about his July 4 experiences in his 1906 *Reminisces*. Both of Peck's accounts for July 4 follow.

> *Fourth Day at Gettysburg by Albert W. Peck, Newtown, Conn. Jan 2nd, 1886*
>
> *Dear Comrade:—*
>
> *Yours of Dec. 30th is received. In reply would say I have not forgotten the promise I made to you at the Reunion, but I do not think I can tell you anything about Gettysburg that will be new. I was on picket in front of Seminary Ridge and in front of the brick Seminary on July 4, the last day of the fight. Capt. Kellogg was in command of the detail from our Regt., with Lieut. Hubbell of Co. C* [sic, Co. E] *and myself as subordinates.* [Peck is referring to James E. Hubbell, Company C, of Westport. Hubbell was a first sergeant at Gettysburg and would be promoted to second lieutenant September 1, 1863.[19]]
>
> *The headquarters of our post was in a small schoolhouse nearby. Our videttes being posted along a rail fence. The Rebel pickets were posted along a rail fence at the base of Seminary Ridge, and I think their headquarters were either behind the ridge or at a small brick house near their line. We could see them march their relief down the hill from the ridge. The Johnnies kept up a regular fire on our boys, and we replied promptly, although I do not think anyone was hit on either side, as we were too far away for doing much damage. Occasionally a shot would come from one of the Johnnies secreted near what looked like a post out in the middle of a large lot, and we watched carefully to see if we could discover where the shot came from. I finally suggested that two or three of us had better fire at what we supposed was the post, at the same time. We did so, and we saw a Johnnie get up lively and go for a tree nearby, so we were not troubled much more by him. We supposed his former position had become rather warm for comfort. The Johnnies stopped firing for a while, and we wondered what had happened as a large number of them appeared in sight from behind*

Lieutenant Albert Peck in a late-war photograph. (Bridgeport History Center)

the ridge, and we soon saw a squad of rebel cavalry approaching our lines. When about halfway between the two picket lines, they halted and we discovered that they had a flag of truce. They were soon met by a delegation from our lines, when a consultation followed the result of which we did not learn at that time, but afterwards heard that Gen. Lee requested Gen. Meade to remove the women and children from the town as he intended to shell it, but Meade did not scare worth a cent, and Lee withdrew his pickets that night.

There was a well near the brick house where we supposed the officers commanding the picket line had their headquarters, and there seemed to be an old-fashioned windlass to draw the water. We saw the Johnnies try to draw water a number of times during the day, but I do not think they got much, as our boys would let them get the bucket part way up, when they would send some minnies after them, and they would let the bucket drop and seek shelter behind the house. Of course, this seemed like fun to our boys, but probably it was not much for the thirsty Johnnies. During the flag of truce, we noticed the rebel pickets carrying rails and placing them in piles. We wondered what they were doing that for, but soon discovered when hostilities were commenced that the bullets began to come from behind the pile of rails. We imagine their former position was rather hot. It rained most of the day and we got pretty well drenched, and about sun-down, our Capt. thought we ought to be relieved and detailed me to go down to headquarters for a relief.

When I got into town it was quite dark and I did not succeed in finding our headquarters. There were no lights in the streets and there seemed to be no one around, so after wandering around a long time, I was afraid to attempt to find my way back to the picket lines, in the dark, for fear of being captured by the Johnnies. While passing along the sidewalk I saw a door standing open and went in and asked if they could let me stay there all night? They told me they had all they could accommodate, but if I could sleep on the lounge, I might stay, and as I was very wet and tired, I at once accepted their kind offer, and after partaking of a hearty supper, I bunked on the lounge and had a good night's rest for the first time since the commencement of the fight. I awoke early next morning and ate a good breakfast and after offering to pay my bill, which was generously refused, I started out to look up the pickets. I soon met Capt. Kellogg

Captain Enos Kellogg, Company H, of New Canaan was the officer in charge of the detail that night who sent Peck back into town with the request that his men be relieved.
(Bridgeport History Center)

and his command, and after explaining why I did not obey his orders, I returned with the regiment to Cemetery Hill, our former position. The name of the family who so generously and kindly entertained me that night at Gettysburg was Comfort. I do not remember the first name. I took pains to look the family up when I was there with our Association to dedicate the Monument to our fallen heroes who left their precious bones on that bloody field, and succeeded in finding them, and was at once recognized by the Father of the household and had the satisfaction of returning my thanks for his comfortable entertainment.[20]

The Henry Comfort house, where Lieutenant Peck slept the night of July 4, sits opposite Jennie Wade's birthplace on Baltimore Street. The house is the right half of a double house. At the time of the battle Henry Comfort was fifty-seven and his wife, Marie, was fifty. The Comforts, like so many of their neighbors on Baltimore Street, took in wounded soldiers. At least one man, Captain John Costin, Company F, 82nd Ohio, is believed to have died at the Comfort house in mid-July. The Comforts sheltered Captain Costin's wife and young son in their home when they came from Ohio to nurse Costin before his death.[21]

Maria Comfort was friends with the Wade family. In 1861, she was photographed sitting between the Wade sisters. The three are immaculately dressed and their arms entwined. Georgia Wade, twenty, is on the right; Maria, forty-eight, is in the middle; and Jennie, eighteen, is on the left, clasping Maria's hand. If the sitters in this beautifully

The Henry Comfort home on Baltimore Street is the house on the right. This is probably the home in which Lieutenant Peck spent the night of July 4. When Peck returned to Gettysburg in 1884 for the dedication of the 17th Connecticut monument, he found the family and thanked them for their long-ago hospitality that dark, rainy night in 1863. (Photo by author)

composed photograph had been unknown, a viewer may have assumed it was a mother posing with her daughters. This photograph remains the only known image of Jennie Wade and has been reproduced many times in cropped format showing only her. Maria Comfort's son, Charles, was a carpenter, and he is believed to have been the one to finish the coffin used to bury Jennie Wade after she was killed on July 3.[22]

In 1906, in his *Civil War Reminisces*, Peck again detailed his experiences of July 4, 1863. He wrote that one of his men reported for duty that morning without his gun or equipment. Peck left out this incident when he wrote to Warren in 1886, probably because he was speaking of a comrade who was still alive, and it was not proper to cast aspersions on fellow soldiers. Veterans did not speak ill of other veterans even if they were shirkers. However, Peck's exasperation with the man was evident in his personal reminisces.

> *The Battle of Gettysburg, Penna., July 4, 1863*
>
> *I was a 2nd Lieutenant and was the only commissioned officer in Company D during the battle of Gettysburg and was in command of my company during the whole battle. My Captain, William L. Hubbell was detailed as provost marshal on General Barlow's staff and was taken prisoner during the first day's battle and went to Libby Prison in Richmond and was gone about six months.*[23]
>
> *On the morning of July 4th we made coffee for breakfast for the first time since Wednesday night. ___ ___ reported for duty this morning, without any gun or equipment, and I asked where he had been during the battle. He said, "Over there." and pointed somewhere, I could not tell where. I knew very well it was somewhere out of danger as he was never known to be around where there was any fighting to be done.*
>
> *Colonel Noble reported for duty on the morning of July 4th and took command of the Regiment and was ordered to take the Regiment through the town and place them on picket—out near the Chambersburg Pike—in front of the Brick Seminary. I was detailed for picket on that day under Capt. Enos Kellogg of Company H. We were posted near a small brick school house where there was a Rebel picket post, and there was a well near the school house. The pickets used to come out there to draw water. We would let them get the bucket about half way up the well and then we would fire at them. It was awful cruel to keep the Johnnies from getting a drink, but I think they fired at us whenever they got an opportunity. It rained hard about all day and we got pretty well soaked through. There was one Johnnie that lay out in the middle of a*

William L. Hubbell, Company D, captured on July 1. (Author's collection)

large lot and he looked like an old bar post. He kept firing at us every little while. Finally, I picked up a rifle and loaded it and got two other men to join me and we were all to fire at the supposed bar post at the same time and we did so and very soon we saw a Johnny jump up and run for a tree, so we did not see him much more, nor the bar post either.

After we had been here a short time, a flag of truce with a small squad of Rebel cavalry came out about half way between the two picket lines and halted. In a few minutes a squad of Union cavalry came out and the two squads met and held a consultation. The pickets on both sides ceased firing and a large lot of Johnnies came out from an old railroad cut near the Seminary and watched the truce. We saw some Johnnies piling up rails, probably to protect themselves from our bullets. We also saw them relieve their pickets. As soon as the truce was over and the men had returned to their lines the firing began again. None of our men got hit and I don't think we hit any of the Johnnies as they were too far away to get hit.

Just before dark—Capt. Kellogg sent me up town to Head Quarters to see if we could not get relieved from picket as we were wet through. It was very dark when I got up town and there seemed to be no one in the streets and I could not find Head Quarters. I finally went along until I saw a door standing open and I knocked on the door. A lady came to the door and I asked her if I could stay there all night. She said her house was full and she had no room but said there was a sofa in the room and if I could sleep on that I could stay. I told her I could sleep on that nicely, so I stayed and she gave me a good breakfast the next morning. I offered to pay her for my lodging and meal but she would not take anything from me. When I left there in the morning I gave her my address and name and rank. Her name was Comfort. I do not remember her husband's name, but met him there some years after the war.

The reason why I did not go back to my picket post that night was because it was so dark I could not find the way back and was afraid of being captured by the Johnnies. I met the Captain coming in with his picket next morning and after explaining the matter to him he said it was all right.[24]

WILLIAM WURTZ, COMPANY D PRISONER AND NURSE

Private William Wurtz, a German-born harness maker from Bridgeport, had been captured and escaped July 1 when he joined a group of Union prisoners detailed to care for the wounded. Wurtz's account was handwritten by William Warren. It is not known when Warren transcribed it.

July 4th
This A.M. the poorhouse farm was full of rebs, Wurtz went towards the barn and the first man he saw was Pat Wade, they shook hands, and he

said, "Pat I am very glad you have come, how did you get here?" This was about daylight. Wurtz told Wade to go in the barn and there he found a squad of men, mostly from the regiment. They captured what rebs they could that were there. The rebs said they were glad to be captured as they had got tired of it. Wurtz was then recaptured. Luther Lewis was captured with Wurtz and paroled.[25]

JUSTUS SILLIMAN, COMPANY H WOUNDED PRISONER

On July 4, after it was determined that the Confederates had evacuated the town, wounded from the Eleventh Corps, including those of the 17th Connecticut, that were scattered in field hospitals all over Gettysburg began to be evacuated to the Eleventh Corps hospital at the George Spangler Farm. Justus Silliman was one of these men. He wrote a letter to his mother from the Spangler Farm on July 7 describing the Fourth of July:

> *Our forces entered the town at daylight on the morning of the fourth, the rebels having left in great haste the night previous after having ransacked all the stores and many private residences. I saw Capt Kellogg early in the morning. I do not think the rebels can count us as prisoners as we were not to my knowledge paroled and were recaptured. I took a short walk, saw orderly Cave* [First Sergeant Thomas P. Cave, Company H] *who told me there were but ten men left in our Co and not a hundred in the regt. He told me of Sam's being wounded* [Sergeant Sam Comstock, Company H], *also that Col. Fowler had been killed and Gen. Francis C. Barlow was wounded. I saw Col. Noble who arrived very timely and has command of the brigade. Gen Ames commanding the division, our regt is commanded by Capt Mc Carty.*[26]

Years later, Silliman wrote to Colonel Noble about finding Confederate correspondence on July 4. William Warren included the excerpt of the letter in his manuscript:

> *On the 4th of July I found some rebel correspondence and this being the day of Vicksburg's surrender, I read you the following extract from the letter of a Southern Lady: "I reckon I can give you nothing now from Vicksburg that you will not get through the papers. Our brave garrison is still holding out; the earth around is covered with dead Yankees, and it is said the atmosphere can hardly be breathed. Our men will die before they will capitulate. It will be as the brave Pemberton has said, "When the last pound of bacon, beef and flour, the last grain of corn, the last coon, the last hog and possum and dog, have been consumed, and the last man shall have perished in the trenches, then and only then, will we give up Vicksburg."*[27]

Silliman also described what he learned at the public school on July 4 before he and others were evacuated to the Eleventh Corps hospital at the Spangler Farm.

> *I have since learned that it was our division which repulsed the La and Ala brigades on the 2nd and 3rd, they were also the first to enter town on the 4th. When our forces took possession of the town the inhabitants opened their houses and acted as though just released from prison . . . Our men captured prisoners in every part of the city, almost every corner, garret and cellar contained a skulking butternut. The guard of our (Confederate) hospital fell asleep during the night and in the morning awoke a prisoner.*[28]

UNWRITTEN HISTORY

On October 8, 1896, an article titled "Unwritten History," with the subtitle "Squad of 17th Conn. First Learned of Lee's Retreat at Gettysburg," was addressed to the editors of the *National Tribune.* The article appeared on page three in a featured column called "Fighting Them Over—What Our Veterans Have to Say About Their Old Campaigns." The *National Tribune* was a newspaper published for veterans of the Civil War. The paper defined its raison d'etre under its original 1877 masthead as: "A Monthly Journal devoted to the interests of the Soldiers and Sailors of the late war, and all Pensioners of the United States." The newspaper also served as the voice of the Grand Army of the Republic and became a weekly publication in 1881. The newspaper changed its name several times, eventually becoming the *National Tribune, the Stars and Stripes* of the American Expeditionary Force during World War I. A final name change to *Stars and Stripes* took place in 1963. It is currently an independent newspaper reporting on the activities of the Department of Veterans Affairs, veterans' organizations, and veterans' legislation. The *Tribune* used Lincoln's words from his second inaugural under its masthead: "To care for him who has born the battle and his widow and orphans."[29] These words became the motto of the U.S. Department of Veterans Affairs.

Students of the battle will undoubtedly notice some creative writing in the article, but it reiterates, for the most part, the sum of the eyewitness accounts by various men in the 17th Connecticut. The article reflects the writing style of the times and its genre. William Warren included part of the article in his manuscript, but he was probably not the author. The article was signed, "Veteran, New Canaan, Conn," which calls to mind Justus Silliman, but Silliman had passed away in April 1896 while living in Easton, Pennsylvania. The article may have had more than one contributor, but the primary writer is probably Patrick Wade, Company K.

Though ostensibly written in the third person, the article slips into first person several times. The writer notes that "*the detail consisted of Lieut. Milton H. Daniels, Co. C; Serg't Patrick Wade of Co. K and 10 privates.*" Farther down in the article it states, "*When we deployed Lieut. Daniels had the right of the line and I had charge of the left.*" Pat Wade definitely participated in this detail, though he was not yet a sergeant at Gettysburg and he never lived in New Canaan. Wade's obituary from 1899 echoes some of the wording of this article, and its inaccuracies, which are not glaring. Wade was highly esteemed by his regimental comrades, his business associates, and his community. If Wade truly is the author, he did a good job with the article, representing the service of a fine Connecticut regiment, in a publication that celebrated veterans and their service.

FIGHTING THEM OVER—What Our Veterans Have to Say About Their Old Campaigns—UNWRITTEN HISTORY. Squad of the 17th Conn. First Learned of Lee's Retreat at Gettysburg.

Editor National Tribune: The 17th Conn. Bears a record as noble as that of any other regiment in the service. The official war documents show that it was engaged in many a desperate struggle, and that it had borne the conflict like every regiment which Connecticut sent to the front, bravely and well. It numbered among its members men from all over the state although it was recruited chiefly in Fairfield County, but it represented the State in its many battles and the State is justly proud.

The regiment was recruited and organized during the month of August 1862 and a month after the first roll of the recruiting drum had been sounded, it started for Washington, 1,000 strong. This was on September 3, and upon its arrival in Washington the regiment was joined to the Army of the Potomac. The regiment was officered as follows: Colonel, Wm. H. Noble, Bridgeport; Lieutenant-Colonel, Charles Walter, Bridgeport; Major, Allen G. Brady, Torrington; Adjutant, Albert H. Wilcoxson, Norwalk; Quartermaster, Hanford N. Hayes, Bridgeport; Surgeon, Robert Hubbard, Bridgeport; First Assistant Surgeon, Robert C. McEwen, Stamford; Second Assistant Surgeon, Elijah Gregory, Bridgeport; Chaplain, William H. Hall, New Haven; Sergeant-Major, Theodore Gray, New Haven; Quartermaster-Sergeant, John S. Ward, New Haven; Commissary-Sergeant, Josiah L. Day, Danbury; and Hospital-Steward, Jesse S. Nash, Bridgeport.

The first battle in which the regiment took part was that of Chancellorsville on May 2, 1863. During the battle the regiment was called upon to charge frequently, and while they were several times driven from the positions which they had taken up, it was only by superior numbers. The loss to the regiment in this battle was 120 officers and men.

The regiment engaged in the Battle of Gettysburg from July 1 to 4, the loss in this battle being 198 officers and men. The regiment served for 12 months with the Army of the Potomac and was then transferred to the Department of the South.

Besides these two battles other notable events in which the regiment was engaged were the battle of Welaka and Saunders, Fla., and the battle of Dunn's Lake, Fla.

The regiment returned with 446 less than when it started; that number being killed, captured, died of disease or discharged.

There is a chapter in the history of this regiment which has never before been published, and yet it is a chronicle of one of the most important of the acts accomplished by the members of the 17th, for which credit has never been given. It was a squad of men, under two officers, from this regiment which furnished the information that Lee had retreated, and which recaptured Gettysburg after days of fighting outside the town. North and South alike were waiting for the result of the three-days' battle, and 80,000 soldiers along the Union lines were listening for the sound of the guns and the rattle of musketry, when they heard the cheer which told them that Lee had retreated, and that the Northern army had been victorious.

That cheer came up from the squad from the 17th, and it was heard all over the country. It was the cheer of men who at the command had taken their muskets and stolen across a part of the meadows, where the day before not a man could show himself without being either killed or wounded. These men did not know where they would meet the enemy, or when they would be shot by the sharpshooters which for three days kept the place clear. It took brave men to move steadfastly along under such conditions, and yet there was no faltering. The news which the squad brought to the waiting army and States well repaid them for their bravery.

Among the men of that squad was Serg't Patrick Wade. His story, as told to the writer, is very interesting. Wade said that the regiment fought the first day on the north of the town of Gettysburg, on a spot known as Barlow's Knoll. The 17th occupied the left center of the line. During the day we were driven back by superior numbers through the town and to a position outside of and overlooking it. This was on East Cemetery Hill and was the line the regiment held until after the battle.

We had opposed to us, in the town, the famous Louisiana Tigers, and on the night of the 2nd they charged us with fixed bayonets. It was the brigade of which our regiment was a part that destroyed the Tigers for after their charge they ceased to exist or to be recognized as a body in the Southern army. The 17th held their line in spite of the charge and drove the Tigers back with great loss.

After Pickett's desperate charge, which came late on the afternoon of the 3rd, there was little or no firing and this quiet continued during the night, with the exception of an occasional discharge on the picket-line. This stillness of the enemy looked suspicious for it was a common saying that when the enemy was quietest they were up to their greatest tricks, and we suspected from this that they were working up some kind of mischief. The rank and file were not the only ones who suspected that there was something unusual going on within the lines of the enemy.

This suspicion extended to the officers in command of the brigade and the division. Early on the morning of the Fourth of July, 1863, an order came from Gen. Ames, commanding the First Division, to Gen. William

H. Noble, commander of Ames's Brigade, to send out a skirmish-line consisting of 10 men under a Lieutenant and Sergeant.

General Noble had joined the regiment, having arrived on the battlefield the night of July 3, his first appearance with the regiment since his wounding in the arm at Chancellorsville, Va., on May 2. The order commanded the skirmish-line to go out into the meadows at the foot of East Cemetery Hill, and proceed toward the town, feeling for the enemy.

The detail consisted of Lieut. Milton H. Daniels, of Co. C; Serg't. Patrick Wade, of Co. K, and 10 privates. We started out at 3:45, deployed in the meadows and started for the town.

The journey was what may be considered a forlorn hope. It was a hazardous one. For three days the fire from the enemy's sharpshooters in the town had been so severe that a man who showed himself for a minute dropped back, dead or wounded. There were some white faces in the squad when we started, and it was the first time in any army experience that I felt as though the odds were greatly against us. However, it was the first duty of the soldier to obey orders and so we started.

Before our start it was distinctly understood that there was to be no word spoken, and that all commands were to be given by signs of the hand, these signs being agreed upon and understood. When we deployed Lieut. Daniels had the right of the line and I had charge of the left. The meadows being low, damp ground, and the days being very hot, a heavy fog had risen during the night and had settled over everything, making it almost impossible to see 300 feet ahead. We kept close together, for the fog was too thick for the usual distance between the skirmishers.

We continued to advance, going forward about 100 feet and then lying flat on our faces and listening, trying to hear some sound from the enemy. Then we would advance again. We knew well that we were treading on dangerous ground, as the Louisiana Tigers and Hoke's Brigade, of Early's Division, lay between us and the town, a position which they had occupied for three days. We passed over that portion of the ground where the rebel line had been stationed. We knew it by the trampled grass and by the bits of cracker and bread which had been dropped.

When we came to this deserted line we felt as if we were being led into a trap. This was the line which for three days had been occupied by one of the most celebrated brigades in the rebel army, and yet where was the enemy? There was no sign of him, except the long grass which had been trampled flat, or the pieces of cracker, an empty canteen, and all the refuse left by a line which had been sleeping on its arms. We knew that we were nearing the town. It was less than half a mile away, and yet since we had started we had seen no signs of the enemy.

Suddenly the fog began slowly to lift, and we saw the cupola of a little church. We knew that this was on the edge of the town, for we had seen it during all the three days of the fight. We advanced a little farther and discerned objects moving about in the yard. Another advance and we saw that these objects were men, some clad in gray and some in blue. They discovered our advance, and some stopped to look under the fog, while others happened away.

Shortly afterward an officer appeared in the middle of the street waving his hat, We increased our pace to a double-quick, and in a few minutes reached the officer, who informed us that Gen. Lee had been retreating since 3 o'clock in the morning.

This officer also informed us that the barns and cowsheds all over the city were full of rebels, asleep, who had crawled into them the night before, and had been left behind. We started toward the center of the town, on the way going up to the barn doors and pounding on them with the butts of our muskets, making all the noise possible, and commanding the Johnnies to come out at once, and to leave their guns behind. Each man as he appeared was laughed at for being caught napping.

We kept on, and as soon as the hospital was reached, we gave three cheers, which were echoed back to our lines. This cheer was heard by Gen. Ames, sitting in his Headquarters at the Cemetery gate, and it was the first intimation to our boys that the battle had been won.

Gen. Ames, knowing that the town had been reached, ordered Gen. Noble to charge with his brigade into Gettysburg. By this time our skirmish-line had reached the center of the town, which was marked by a large square, and looking down the Baltimore Road we saw Gen. Noble at the head of his brigade, with our regiment in advance. We had with us 18 prisoners, which we had captured in barns, and sent them back to be turned over to Gen. Noble, while our line continued out through the town to the Harrisburg road.

Here to our chagrin, we discovered a regiment of rebel cavalry drawn up in line to cover Lee's retreat. With a handful of men against a regiment of cavalry it was a question what was best to be done. Seeing a house a short distance away, we ran for it and commenced to fire out of the windows at the cavalry, which had started on charge toward our retreat.

After going a short distance however, the bugle sounded to the right, and we saw the line wheel about, recross Rock Creek to a little bridge, and shortly after disappear behind Seminary Ridge.

From the house we continued for a short distance to the Alms House, which had been turned into a hospital, in which were many wounded. Here we found a few of our regiment which had been captured on the first day of the fight and had been left to take care of the sick. They were very much surprised to see us, supposing that we, too, had been captured.

We reminded them that prisoners very seldom have guns in their hands and assured them that they were no longer prisoners. Although they had been in back of Lee's line, this was the first intimation they had of that General's retreat. We returned from the hospital to the town, where we met our regiment. We turned over a total of 46 prisoners, which we had captured that morning.

Our regiment fought the battle of Gettysburg with empty stomachs. One the night of the 1st we were to draw three days' rations, and so at noon we had eaten everything we had in our haversacks, expecting to draw our rations in time for supper. The fighting began in the afternoon though, and our supply trains were sent to Westminster, some 20 miles back of our lines, before we had drawn any rations. From the morning of July 1st until the afternoon of the 4th we had nothing to eat but what scraps of food we could pick up by foraging during the lulls in the battle; and what water we had to drink came from a well which was constantly dipped dry and was in so much demand that it was necessary to wait several hours before we could fill our canteens.

The strain on our nerves when we left our regiment on that skirmish may well be imagined. We were half starved, thirsty, and very nervous from the constant strain of three days of firing and three nights of alarm, and then to start out on what seemed to be a mission the result of which could hardly be anything but death, it is no wonder we proceeded with the greatest caution. There was not a man in the party who would not have volunteered to go out, but those that went who were chosen, and all arrived safely with the news that the battle, which was the turning point of the civil war, had been won by the Northern army.

Of that squad of 12 who went out to Gettysburg on the morning of July 4, 1863, there are now but three left alive. These are Lieut. Milton H. Daniels, of Co. C, who at that time hailed from Danbury but who is now from Indianapolis; myself, Serg't Patrick Wade, of Bridgeport, a member of Co. K, and Private John H. Grannis of Saybrook. To the comrades of the 17th is due the credit that it was a squad of 12 of her men who sent back to the waiting army the news that the battle was over. It was news which the Union Generals and army waited for; it was news which the President and his officers at Washington waited for; it was news which every family in the land prayed for; and the 17th was the first to bring it."—Veteran, New Canaan, Conn.[30]

CHAPTER 11

Broken Bodies and Wounded Men

This chapter explores the various hospital sites associated with the 17th Connecticut and the Eleventh Corps. It examines the experiences of the wounded of the regiment, and those who participated in their care. Thousands of wounded were scattered among the dead almost everywhere on the field of the first day's fight where the First and Eleventh Corps engaged the enemy. Field hospitals and field aid stations sprang up in barns, farmhouses, outbuildings, yards, orchards, and anywhere shelter, water, and care could be offered. At every "hospital" location, whether held by Confederates or Federals, surgeons and medical personnel did all they could to tend to the wounded of both sides.

It is often difficult to determine exactly which wounded were taken to which location or where their caregivers served. Scant records exist, and documentation if it can be cross-referenced, is sometimes contradictory. Casualty lists and hospital records were notoriously inaccurate.[1] The first day at Gettysburg was so tumultuous, chaotic, and frenzied that no words can really describe the cauldron in which these men found themselves. Some of the missing were dead and were never accounted for or found. Some of the missing were prisoners. Unless surviving comrades witnessed another man's fate, there was really no way to know for sure what had happened. In the aftermath, even months after the battle, company officers were still corresponding with widows and families to confirm deaths or provide information about what other men in the regiment were able to remember and piece together about the fate of the missing and dead.[2]

The Battle of Gettysburg was a medical calamity before the fighting even began. On June 19, to move the army faster through Virginia, Joe Hooker ordered a reduction in the number of medical supply wagons. Dr. Jonathan Letterman, the medical director of the

Army of the Potomac, tried to salvage the situation by creating a reserve medical supply train in Washington. As soon as he knew battle was imminent, Letterman ordered the wagons brought up to Westminster, Maryland, twenty miles from Gettysburg. On June 28, George Meade became the new commander of the Army of the Potomac, replacing Hooker. On July 1, with battle looming, Meade ordered his corps commanders to send all wagons except ammunition and ambulances to the rear.[3] The commander's first priority was that nothing obstruct the flow of ammunition to the army. As the battle commenced on July 1, there were very few medical supplies available to treat the wounded. This created a horrific situation for casualties and medical personnel. In his report on the operations of the medical department at Gettysburg, Letterman noted, "The expediency of the order, of course, I do not pretend to question, but its effect was to deprive this department of the supplies necessary for the proper care of the wounded, without which it is as impossible to have them properly attended to as it is to fight a battle without ammunition."[4]

Dr. Jonathan Letterman was a career army doctor who is recognized as the "Father of Battlefield Medicine." His evacuation, triage, and care systems are still used today in emergency and mass-casualty situations. Letterman became medical director of the Army of the Potomac in 1862. In his new position, Letterman found chaotic and antiquated procedures and red tape that obstructed every measure of care in the army's

Dr. Jonathan Letterman (seated, second from left), medical director of the Army of the Potomac, with his staff. (Library of Congress)

medical department. Letterman would revolutionize procedures for battlefield care, including evacuation of the wounded, by creating a trained ambulance corps that answered to the medical department and not the quartermaster department. He instituted the triage system of evaluating and sorting the wounded into three categories to improve survival: mortal wounds, slight wounds, and surgical cases.[5] Letterman created protocols for forward first aid stations, long-term recovery hospitals on the battlefields, and evacuation and treatment systems based on established procedures. These reforms became collectively known as the Letterman System and tremendously improved treatment and survival for the sick and wounded.[6] By the time of Gettysburg, Letterman's evacuation procedures alone ensured that wounded were removed from the battlefield within hours of the battle ending.[7] All the wounded were off the field by July 4, unlike previous battles where the wounded lay on the field for days.[8]

At Gettysburg the first tier of care received by a wounded man was at a field-dressing station located close to the fighting. Medical personnel bandaged the wound and administered whiskey for shock and morphine for pain if available. If the wounded man was unable to return to the fight, he would be removed to a field hospital by ambulance or stretcher bearers. A field hospital could be a farm, field, barn, tent, house, church, or public building located away from the fighting. Field hospitals often came under fire or had to relocate during the battle. Here the wounded would be triaged.[9] Surgical cases would be operated on as soon as possible, receiving priority care. Most surgeries during the Civil War and at Gettysburg were amputations done under anesthesia—chloroform or ether, with chloroform being preferred, as combustible ether made surgery hazardous by lantern or candlelight. After the battle, all wounded, Union and Confederate alike, were treated without regard for which side they fought. Wounded Confederates in Union hands might wait for evacuation off the field, as Union boys in Confederate hands would, and they might have to wait for surgery. Medical care was remarkably comparable for the wounded on both sides at Gettysburg and during the war. Lieutenant William Wheeler of the Thirteenth New York Battery wrote in a letter home, "Utterly as I detest a living active rebel, as soon as he becomes wounded and a prisoner, I don't perceive any difference in my feelings towards him and towards one of our own wounded heroes."[10]

As soon as the battle began, refuge was needed for the wounded. Houses, barns, outbuildings, yards, and fields immediately began to serve as aid stations and field hospitals. For the 17th Connecticut and the Eleventh Corps on July 1, the Adams County Alms House, or Poor House, a complex on the Harrisburg Road near Blocher's Knoll, would become one of the first and most prominent field hospitals on that part of the battlefield. Other surrounding farms and homes such as the Blocher Farm, Benner Farm, and Crawford house and barn also soon overflowed with wounded from both armies. As the fight escalated, surrounding houses and farms along the Harrisburg Road and other connecting roads and farm lanes served the wounded and prisoners. When the First Corps and the Eleventh Corps began to buckle under Confederate pressure, Gettysburg public buildings, private homes, churches, and even the county courthouse all became hospital space to shelter the wounded. The total casualties for the battle are difficult to pinpoint with surety. However, "safe numbers" indicate that 7,739 men from both sides were killed outright. Wounded totaled 26,706. The missing comprised 10,887.[11] These numbers are conservative. Of the wounded, as many as 4,000, or probably more, died very soon after the battle. Of the missing, some were killed, most were captured, and others became the unknown dead.

When the Confederates retreated on July 4, they took many wounded high-level officers, and wounded men they deemed could survive the journey, in the retreat trains, some seventeen miles long, winding down to the Potomac. The Confederate army left behind a handful of medical doctors and about 5,456 of their wounded unfit for travel. The Army of the Potomac began its pursuit of the Confederates July 5. During the battle more than 650 Union medical personnel were on duty.[12] After the battle, Dr. Letterman left with the army, taking the bulk of his medical personnel with him, expecting that the army would be fighting another battle within the next few days. He left behind 106 surgeons and placed Dr. Henry Janes, a volunteer surgeon from the 3rd Vermont, in command of "all field hospitals" around Gettysburg.[13] Janes had under his charge about sixty different hospitals and over 20,000 Union and Confederate wounded needing attention.[14] Gettysburg, a town with less than 2,400 in population, was overwhelmed.

It soon became apparent that the medical department had to do something to consolidate the wounded left behind in numerous locations. When the Union army left Gettysburg, it left six ambulances and four wagons from each corps to transport wounded from field hospitals to the railhead on York Road.[15] As soon as the burned railroad bridges were repaired, the wounded, both Union and Confederate, were evacuated by rail to permanent hospitals in cities all over the East Coast. On July 20, Camp Letterman, a large general hospital, was established near the battlefield on the Wolf Farm property, along York Road near the rail line.[16] The property sat on high ground and had good drainage, a reliable source of water, and shade. Proximity to the railroad provided for the transportation of men and supplies and the location was accessible to ambulance transport. Construction began on July 16; four days later, Camp Letterman General Hospital opened with 400 tents, each capable of holding twelve patients.[17] By July 25, 16,125 wounded patients had been transported from Gettysburg to permanent military hospitals. Approximately 4,217 men, too seriously wounded to be evacuated, remained. Camp Letterman General Hospital remained open until November 20, the day after Lincoln's Gettysburg Address.[18] Dr. Cyrus N. Chamberlain,* who oversaw all Sixth Corps field hospitals, later assumed charge of the U.S. General Hospital at Camp Letterman.[19]

*Dr. Cyrus Nathaniel Chamberlain (1829–1899), U.S. Volunteers, an 1850 graduate of Vermont Medical College, has long been confused with Dr. C. R. Chamberlain, who graduated from the Homeopathic Medical College of Pennsylvania in 1853. It was Dr. C. R. Chamberlain, in partnership with Franklin Benjamin Lyford, who operated as an embalmer at Gettysburg after the battle. The assumption made in many publications about the aftermath of Gettysburg is that the men were one and the same. They were not. The separate identity of both doctors was established by scholar and researcher Barbara Franco in her unpublished Gettysburg Surgeons Database.[20]

SURGEONS OF THE 17TH CONNECTICUT

The 17th Connecticut had three surgeons assigned to the regiment: Surgeon Robert Hubbard, Assistant Surgeon Robert McEwan, and Assistant Surgeon Elijah Gregory. Gregory was ill but Hubbard and McEwan served during the battle. Even with the accounts of the men they tended to, it is impossible to pinpoint the movements of these doctors during the battle. The combat and casualty situation was fluid and chaotic, and these doctors were on the move, especially on the first day of battle. Field-dressing stations were set up as soon as possible. On July 1, these dressing stations had to move to avoid being overrun, shelled, or captured. From Private John Collins's account, we know Hubbard moved at least three times on the first day, initially to avoid capture.[21] On the battlefield these doctors treated all wounded, regardless of regimental designation. This included any wounded Confederates. After the battle, Dr. Hubbard served at the Eleventh Corps hospital at the George Spangler Farm and also tended wounded patients in town.

The three surgeons of the 17th Connecticut dealt with every health and medical situation imaginable during their service. They served with valor and were committed healers. They, like their medical generation, learned from the wounded they cared for during the Civil War. Like most physicians in antebellum America, these doctors had little or no experience in the treatment of gunshot wounds and little to no surgical experience. The Civil War changed medicine forever in America. It was the war that would make good doctors into surgeons. Surgery, before the Civil War, was infrequently used as a treatment by practicing physicians except in medical schools and in cases of extreme emergency. During the war tens of thousands of surgeries were performed, almost 95 percent of them under anesthesia. The most performed surgery was amputation, which would save many, many lives. After the Civil War surgery became a standard medical practice whenever and wherever needed in patient treatment. Many wounds to the extremities were complex and untreatable due to the pulverizing force of the minié ball. Amputation removed the complex, untreatable damage to a limb and created a simpler, more easily treatable wound that vastly increased the chances of survival for the wounded. Today, the wounds our service members experience in the Middle East from IEDs are so destructive to the human body that they are reminiscent of the wounds of Civil War soldiers. Even modern medicine, which has come so far since the Civil War, cannot save such damaged limbs, and many times amputation is utilized as the most optimal treatment.

SURGEON ROBERT HUBBARD

Dr. Robert Hubbard of Bridgeport was the regimental surgeon, enlisting at the formation of the regiment in August 1862. During the Battle of Gettysburg he served on General Howard's staff as the medical inspector of the Eleventh Corps. Several men of the 17th left recollections of Dr. Hubbard serving on the field. After the battle Hubbard remained one of the surgeons at the Eleventh Corps hospital at the Spangler Farm, and he cared for a wounded officer, and probably other wounded of the regiment and corps, in town at the office of Dr. Taylor and Dr. Cress on Baltimore Street where the Adams County Library now stands. Hubbard probably tended wounded at other sites as well.[22]

When he enlisted as surgeon with the 17th Connecticut in the summer of 1862, Hubbard was a well-regarded physician in Bridgeport with a wife and small son. He had been educated at Yale and carried on a thriving practice with his partner, Dr. Nash. When the army left Gettysburg in pursuit of Lee on July 5 Hubbard would be left behind. He rejoined the Eleventh Corps later in July. When the corps was broken up after Gettysburg, Hubbard was sent to Lookout Mountain, Tennessee, where he served as staff surgeon to General Hooker and participated in several western theater battles. Dr. Hubbard resigned his commission in December 1863 due to broken health, which would take him years to rebuild. After the war Dr. Hubbard continued his successful medical practice in Bridgeport. He served in the Connecticut General Assembly and unsuccessfully ran for Congress. He also served as president of the State Medical Society. He died in 1897 from head trauma after falling on the stairs to his office in Bridgeport, Connecticut.[23]

Dr. Robert Hubbard. (Bridgeport History Center)

ASSISTANT SURGEON ROBERT MCEWEN

First Assistant Surgeon Dr. Robert McEwen was a graduate of Williams College and the College of Physicians and Surgeons in New York City. In 1859 he traveled to Europe and South Africa. For a short time in South Africa he was a commissioned surgeon in Her Majesty's service. He returned home in 1860 to practice medicine in Stratford, Connecticut, where he resided with his parents. In the summer of 1862, he enlisted as an assistant surgeon with the 17th Connecticut. In September 1863 he resigned his commission due to ill health. After the war he resided and practiced medicine in Saratoga Springs, New York, at 1 Franklin Square, a large Greek Revival home. He was the consulting doctor for the famous Hathorn Spring.[24] When he died in 1893 at age sixty, his widow, Sarah, purchased the substantial property next door and ran the mansion as the Adirondak Lodge from 1894 to 1918. It was an "exclusive boarding house with broad piazzas and private baths." Both properties still survive in the historic heart of Saratoga Springs as office, retail, and residential units.[25]

Dr. Robert McEwen. (Captain Wilson French Collection)

ASSISTANT SURGEON ELIJAH GREGORY

Second Assistant Surgeon Dr. Elijah Gregory was born in Danbury in 1833. He began practice there and graduated from Yale College of Medicine in 1856. Dr. Gregory practiced medicine in North Salem, New York, where he married Josephine Shepard in 1857. He left New York after his health broke down and returned to Connecticut to rest and reactivate his practice in Bridgeport in the fall of 1861. In the summer of 1862, he was commissioned assistant surgeon in the 17th Connecticut. Throughout his enlistment, Dr. Gregory's health was precarious. In June 1863 as the army moved toward Gettysburg, Dr. Gregory was very ill. On June 24, Dr. Hubbard wrote to his wife by the light of a campfire, "*Dr. Gregory will go to the hospital for a week or two—he has miasmatic fever* [probably malaria] *with periodical neuralgia.*"[26] Despite his ill health, Dr. Gregory was the only doctor, of the three originally commissioned, to serve his entire enlistment. He mustered out with the regiment at Hilton Head in July 1865. He returned to practice medicine in Bridgeport after the war and died at age forty-three in 1877. He is buried in Center Cemetery in Bethel, Connecticut.[27]

Dr. Elijah Gregory. (Bridgeport History Center)

THE ADAMS COUNTY ALMS HOUSE

The Adams County Alms House, referred to as the "Poor House" in numerous battle accounts, served as an immediate hospital location for the Eleventh Corps because of its proximity to the fighting on Barlow's Knoll. This collection of buildings, and its attached farm and cemetery, housed the indigent, needy elderly, mentally ill, destitute women and children, and "unfortunates" of Adams County. Residents were referred to as "inmates" and were expected to work daily if they could do so.[28]

This glass stereoview shows the Adams County Alms House as it appeared in 1863. The prominent building just behind the fence with the white lathing is the insane ward. (Gettysburg National Military Park)

This stereoview of the 17th Connecticut monument on Barlow's Knoll, dedicated July 1, 1884, shows the open ground surrounding the location. The Alms House (Poor House) complex would have been clearly visible from the fighting at this position with the town of Gettysburg behind it. (Author's Collection)

The Alms House buildings were located approximately where the Adams County Agricultural and Natural Resources Center (Ag Center) is now on the Harrisburg Road. In 1818 the site commissioners began purchasing land along the Harrisburg Road, and the Alms House opened in 1819. Approximately 150 acres formed the core of the complex, with more acreage added over the years to accommodate crops and pastures. The buildings immediately became a hospital site on July 1, as the property was directly in the path of the Eleventh Corps retreat route and was overrun by Ewell's Confederates.[29] In 1961, after the opening of a new nursing facility, Green Acres, on the Harrisburg Road, the remainder of the buildings were demolished and the land was sold for business development.[30]

When the Civil War came to Gettysburg on July 1, 1863, it also came to the Alms House. "*The location of the inmates was not recorded as the officials had little time to move the elderly and mentally ill,*" *historian Elise Morey wrote.* "*It is likely they retreated to the basements of some of the buildings for shelter.*"[31] The Alms House remained in Confederate control throughout the battle, and the Union wounded there were prisoners as well as patients. On the morning of July 4, after the Confederate withdrawal, a squad of Federal soldiers that included members of the 17th Connecticut would return to the Alms House. With the Federal return, the Union wounded and prisoners on the property were freed and the Confederate doctors, medical personnel, and wounded, in turn, became prisoners.

CORPORAL AARON LEE, COMPANY G, WOUNDED JULY 1

Aaron W. Lee was a born in 1831 in Ridgefield. He was a farmer when he enlisted as a Corporal in Company G, 17th Connecticut, in the summer of 1862. Lee was wounded and became a patient at the Alms House on July 1. Despite his wound, he was determined to return to the regiment, and he did. Thus, in his words, "*He cheated the Invalid Corps out of a recruit.*" Lee would be promoted to sergeant in September 1864 and would be mustered out with the 17th in July 1865 at Hilton Head.

Lee wrote to William Warren in 1886 about his experiences as a wounded prisoner at the Alms House.

> *After the first flash of battle had passed away, I was in that state of mind I could view the two lines of battle calmly and my only thoughts were those of gaining the battle but just before reaching outskirts of the city a Minnie ball went zip through my thigh. I stepped back of a building where some mounted officers stood, and they directed me to the Almshouse, and to hurry or I would be taken prisoner. Two of the 17th met me at the gate and went with me into the dining-room. David Bartram went out and got a piece of shelter tent and was in the act of bandaging my leg, when a rebel officer came in and ordered all who could walk to the rear. I was feeling a little weak from loss of blood and did not get up. About nine o'clock that night I was told that some of the 17th were upstairs. I borrowed a cane from an old man and limped and hobbled upstairs. I found Henry DeForrest and E. D. Pickett, both wounded.*
>
> *Pickett was in great pain from a wound in the groin. I asked one of our rebel guards to go out and get a blanket or two, as there were plenty lying around. He brought three or four. I made him as comfortable as I could and he said he felt easier. By this time the house was filled with the wounded. About twenty feet away, at one end of the hall, I found a place to bunk myself. On the morning of the 2nd I was awakened by the firing of the batteries. Looking to where Pickett lay, he was in the same position I left him the night before. Just then a rebel officer came up the stairs. I asked him about the man I pointed to. He put his foot on his arm and shook him a little and said, "He is dead," so was at once carried out.*

Corporal Aaron Lee, Company D. (Bridgeport History Center)

Private Henry DeForrest, Company G, was wounded the first day and taken to the Alms House. DeForrest survived his wound and was transferred to the Veteran Reserve Corps. (Bridgeport History Center)

> *I remained there a prisoner until the 4th. About 12 o'clock Captain Burr comes up the street with a squad of men, and those of us that could be moved were taken to the field hospital in the orchard* [the Eleventh Corps Hospital at the George Spangler Farm[32]]. *From there I went to Philadelphia—arriving on the night of the 9th—and then, for the first time, my wound was dressed. Gangrene set in and I had a pretty tough time of it; the doctors gave me up and said I could not live, but I did not agree with them. I had made up my mind that I was going to pull through and I did. After getting so I could walk on crutches, the doctors wanted to transfer me to the Invalid Corps, but I rebelled and got a furlough for 20 days, and through the kindness of Lieutenant Governor Roger Averill and General O. S. Ferry, I was transferred to New Haven* [Knight Soldiers Hospital]. *By this transfer the Invalid Corps was cheated out of a recruit, and I returned to my regiment at St. Augustine, Florida, arriving on the 6th of June 1864.*[33]

Captain Henry Burr, Company E, one of the officers of the 17th Connecticut who led a squad to liberate the Alms House on the morning of July 4. (Bridgeport History Center)

Roger Averill, lieutenant governor of Connecticut. (Bridgeport History Center)

Lee described how he was slated to enter the Invalid Corps, which he did not want to do. He wanted to return to his regiment. Incapacitated or wounded soldiers no longer fit for active duty were often transferred to the Invalid Corps until they completed their enlistment, serving as cooks, clerks, guards, or other light-duty posts, freeing up healthy soldiers to fight. The name "Invalid Corps" was viewed as derogatory. The word *invalid* meant to nineteenth-century men they were no longer "valid" or "whole" individuals; thus the term was despised. Compounding the dislike of the word, the Invalid Corps' initials, I.C., were used in the army to refer to equipment and arms that had been inspected and condemned. This did little to promote the popularity of the Invalid Corps name, nor did the fact that healthy soldiers referred to the Invalid Corps as the "Cripple Brigade."[34]

In 1864, the Invalid Corps was renamed the Veterans Reserve Corps, a move intended as a morale boost for those men who were serving in it. Many wounded or ill soldiers fought hard against transfer to the Invalid Corps, or Veterans Reserve Corps. Aaron Lee was one of these men. To avoid this transfer, Lee sought out the assistance of Connecticut lieutenant governor Roger Averill, a Danbury native. Averill was accessible to, and supportive of, Connecticut soldiers and their families. Many men felt they could count on his help, and he proved them right. William Warren felt he was important enough to the soldiers of the 17th Connecticut to include his photograph in the manuscript.

CORPORAL JOHN BENEDICT, COMPANY C, WOUNDED JULY 1

After he was wounded on Barlow's Knoll, Corporal Benedict lay helpless and suffering on the battlefield until Friday, July 3, when he was finally brought to the Alms House shed in a wheelbarrow. He was treated at the Alms House and transferred to the corps hospital at the Spangler Farm. On July 20, he was sent to the U.S. General Hospital in York, Pennsylvania. Benedict's account of his wounding is given in chapter 5. He was listed on the casualty and hospital registers as "*wounded in the left arm and lower 3rd right thigh.*"[35]

> *Laid here by the fence until Friday afternoon, about dark. During Thursday some stragglers from the rebel army came along, and seeing John lay there in the hot rays of the sun, took four muskets and stuck the bayonets in the ground, then took a shelter tent and held it by the hammers of the guns. This formed a shade. All he had to eat this day was a piece of bread about as big as your hand that these stragglers had, which was simply flour and water stirred up together and baked which made it raw and solid. The rebs captured the flour in Gettysburg. Not a drop of water passed his lips that day and he suffered very much for the want of it. All the water he had Wednesday was a little that he had left in his canteen. He let his haversack hang from his neck and used it as a string for his wounded arm, then with the other hand and with one leg out stiff, he hitched along to a ditch that was about two feet deep, from two to four rods off. This took him about four or five hours to make the trip and get back again to his shade; he could not walk a step. He thought by getting to this ditch he might be able to get some water, but when he got there he found it was only mud and no water, so he took his tin cup and reaching over into the ditch filled it with mud, and putting it to his lips sucked out the moisture; it was thick and black, but he was willing to do anything to stop that hankering thirst. He had tried hard all*

Corporal John H. Benedict, Company C. (Courtesy Dale Call Collection)

day to get some water, by asking everyone that passed by him for some, but not a drink did he get.

John's feet had swelled so bad that the rebs could not pull his boots off, so they had to cut them off. Friday morning about 8 or 9 o'clock, a reb came along and said to John that he was looking for a canteen to get some water, and said, "Let me take yours and I will get you a canteen of water." So John did and expected never to see it again, but in about an hour he came back with it full; that did John more good than anything else. He stayed with John some two or three hours and told him he would never go back into the rebel army again but would go to New York or stay in the North somewhere. Finally, he said, "I guess I must go for there may be some rebel cavalry along by and by and take me for a deserter." The rebs detailed some of the Union prisoners to take care of the wounded. About 2 p.m. Friday, John was found by another party of men who gave him some bread. About 5 p.m. two Union men came with a wheelbarrow, and put a stick across the handles, then set John into it, facing the one wheeling him. The stick held up his legs, and while one wheeled the other held him up. He was wheeled to the Poorhouse shed, which was connected to the barn. Fred Goodale [Private Frederick W. Goodale, Company C] *came to see him as soon as he got to the shed and cut his coat and pants so that his wound could be dressed, which was directly done by two Union surgeons—one being a German, who handled him very carefully and tenderly. Inflammation set in and it swelled very badly so that it was thought at one time it would have to be cut off, but John begged so hard that one of them said, "We will do it up for you, and if we have to cut it off we can do it as well tomorrow." They then went off and that was the last John ever saw those two men. Towards evening a shower came up; laid here over night.*[36]

DICK TAYLOR'S DEATH AT THE POORHOUSE

Private Richard D. Taylor, Company C, was a married hatter from Danbury. He was mortally wounded July 1 during the fighting at Blocher's Knoll. His body was never identified. His wife filed for a widow's pension on August 12, 1863. His name is inscribed on the soldiers' memorial in Wooster Cemetery in Danbury.[37] His body is probably interred among the unknown dead in the Soldiers' National Cemetery at Gettysburg. This account of Taylor's death at the Alms House was in Benedict's 1887 letter to Warren. Warren noted that "*John Benedict gave me this as coming from John McCue.*"

John McCue was shot in both legs while in the charge going up Barlow's Knoll, and he says that Dick Taylor was shot at the same time in the bowels, and died that night; they both fell together, side by side. For some time while in the army, Dick had lost his voice, and could only speak in

> *a whisper, but after he was wounded, he could speak as loud as anyone, and during the night Taylor and McCue conversed with each other about themselves and their condition. During the night Dick told McCue that he thought he was dying, but McCue dropped to sleep and in the morning when he awoke, he found Dick was dead.*[38]

WILLIAM WURTZ, PRISONER AND NURSE

On July 1, William Wurtz (often spelled Wirtz), Company D, was slightly wounded when he was struck in the shoulder by a piece of shell or a minié ball that then passed through Private Alonzo Scranton's jaw. Wurtz was captured, escaped, and became a nurse at the Alms House all in one day. Scranton, who was seriously wounded by the bullet that skinned Wurtz's shoulder, became one of the patients at the Alms House. After the Confederate retreat on July 4, when the Alms House was recaptured by a squad from the 17th Connecticut, Wurtz remained on nursing duty.

> *On Barlow's Knoll, (Alonzo) Scranton who was a trifle in advance of Wm. Wurtz on a slight angle, a bullet struck Wurtz shoulder, cut coat to the skin and took skin off and was in the same range and path high enough, the bullet struck Scranton in the Jaw and he spun around 2 or three times. Wurtz shoulder and Scranton's cheek was about on the same line.*[39]
>
> *On the first day while the regiment was on the retreat from Barlow's Knoll, he stopped right back of the haystack and fired a few shots. While here he saw the rebs off to the right so he went into the Poorhouse yard and found many there wounded. Here, he was taken prisoner . . . Soon a rebel major cavalryman on horseback rode up and said he was going to parole them. He rode to the right of the line and took the first 2 files or 4 men and told them to stay and help the wounded. These 4 men stepped to the right which left Wurtz on the right of the next file. He wanted to go with these 4 men so fell in line with them and thought he would take his chances with them as his feet were so sore he could go no further. Major said left flank and he marched them off and took no notice of Wurtz. While the rebel officer turned to the left to the other squad, Wurtz stepped out of the ranks and went off with the 4. The other squad was marched off somewhere and that was the last he saw of them. Wurtz and his squad helped to take care of the sick and wounded all day and night. A rebel officer told this squad to get some pails and water and give the wounded laying on the field some water and take some bread and crackers with them. Some of the wounded had turned black laying in the sun so long. Their stomachs were bloated. Our forces on the 4th day regained the field and this detail all went back to their regiments. He (Wurtz) asked Col. Noble if he should stay back or go with the regiment. Colonel told him he had better stay and do what good he could (for the wounded).*"[40]

SERGEANT COMSTOCK, COMPANY H, WOUNDED

In 1884 Justus Silliman, who had served in Company H and was wounded at Gettysburg, wrote to General William Noble this brief account of the wounding of his friend Sergeant Samuel Comstock. The account confirms conditions at the Alms House Hospital and that both Confederate and Union surgeons were tending to the wounded there and performing surgery.

> *Of Company H, Sergt. Comstock, who had been wounded a short distance below Barlow's Knoll lay upon the field until the 2nd, when he was taken to a barn adjoining the Alms House, where a rebel surgeon extracted the bullet. On the morning of the 4th he was removed to the 11th Corps Hospital, which had been established on the premises of George Spangler, about two miles below the town, on a road connecting the Baltimore pike with the [Taneytown?] Road.*[41]

JOSIAH BENNER FARM

Just below Barlow's Knoll, across Rock Creek on the Harrisburg Road, was the two-story brick house of Josiah Benner. In the front of the property was a stone springhouse that predated the American Revolution. Confederate general Richard Ewell rested near here and was said to have bathed the stump of his amputated leg in the cool spring water.[42]

On July 1, immediately upon arriving on the battlefield, four companies of the 17th Connecticut were dispatched across Rock Creek to this property as skirmishers under the command of Major Allen Brady. As the atmosphere became increasingly "hot," the Yankees kept near the house and used it for cover. Confederate artillery tracked

The Josiah Benner farmhouse on the Harrisburg Road as it appeared in 1863. The picket fence surrounding the house remembered by the veterans is visible in the photograph. (Gettysburg National Military Park)

their movements and shelled the house. The house caught fire, but the flames were extinguished. Eight artillery shells struck the house; one remains embedded in the back of the house under the eaves.[43] As the Confederate onslaught rolled through, Brady and his men were forced to retreat through the town.[44] This house, barn, and its yard became a Confederate-controlled hospital site for the wounded from Barlow's Knoll and the Eleventh Corps. The most prominent Eleventh Corps patient, General Francis Barlow, was treated in the Benner House. Barlow was told his wounds were mortal by the Confederate surgeons who tended to him.[45]

It is probable that wounded of the 17th Connecticut were treated by Confederate surgeons at this location but it is difficult to accurately identify which men. Possible wounded men treated at the Benner farm who left accounts are Justus Silliman and J. Henry Blakeman. These two men could also have been treated at the Elizabeth Weible Farm, farther behind Confederate lines.

PRIVATE JUSTUS SILLIMAN WOUNDED

Long after the war, in a letter to General Noble dated August 2, 1884, Private Justus Silliman, Company H, briefly described his wounding on July 1 and identified the field hospital he was taken to as the Benner Farm. However, in a letter to his mother written on July 3, 1863, while he was being held as a wounded prisoner by the Confederates in the hospital-school on High Street, Silliman identified the hospital he was taken to on July 1 as belonging to Hays's Division. Undoubtedly other wounded members of the regiment were with him at whatever location he was initially tended to. It is quite possible that in his postwar study of the battle, Silliman determined he was taken to the Benner barn. Either the Benner Farm or Weible Farm are plausible Confederate hospital locations for Silliman on July 1. His 1884 description to General Noble follows:

> *On Barlow's Knoll, July 1st, my rifle missed fire, when I sighted another which had been dropped by a skedadler, but the cap of this only exploded. Dropping this and laying hold of a third, wet with blood of one of our wounded, I fired on the advancing rebels, and turned to load, when I suddenly became unconscious and remained in this condition until the rebels occupied the grounds. I was wounded by a bullet, which glanced across the top of my head—scraping the skull. It proved to be but a slight wound.* ***I was taken to the barn of J. Benner just across Rock Creek on the Harrisburg Road****, and then occupied as the hospital of the Louisiana Tigers, where my wound was dressed by a rebel surgeon. The rebels were jubilant over their first day's success. A squad of cavalry came up from town—all wearing high paper collars and having their horses covered with bits of bright carpet.*[46]

The Benner barn as it appeared in 1863. (Gettysburg National Military Park)

PRIVATE LEVI DIXON, COMPANY H, WOUNDED

Nineteen-year-old Private Levi Dixon's right thigh was shattered on July 1 when a Confederate minié ball slammed into him. Dixon was taken to a nearby field hospital where a Confederate surgeon amputated his leg. A description of Dixon's case would appear in the monumental *Medical and Surgical History of the War of the Rebellion.* The book confirmed that a Confederate doctor performed a circular flap amputation on either July 1 or 2 but did not state the location the surgery was performed at or the surgeon's name.[47] Dixon's wounding was witnessed and described by several members of the regiment, and several of those recollections William Warren transcribed into his manuscript. Levi Dixon would spend many months in various Union hospitals until his discharge for disability on October 10, 1864.

After the war Dixon was a popular member of the 17th Connecticut Survivor's Association. For many years he was well known in Stamford as the beloved school janitor at Center School. The article about his retirement from the school in the *Daily Advocate* stated,

> *His obliging disposition and good nature made him popular, especially with the boys. Another source of popularity was the war stories he used to tell the pupils. Mr. Dixon is a veteran of the Civil War and lost a leg at the Battle of Gettysburg. Nothing pleased him more than to get a group of boys and girls together and regale them with war stories. Often, he would appear in the classrooms fully equipped as a soldier and give a graphic illustration of some point of history.*[48]

In May 1884, Levi Dixon returned to Gettysburg as a member of the "locating committee" of the 17th Connecticut, who were planning the unveiling and dedication of their monument on Barlow's Knoll for July 1 that year. The committee was scheduled to meet with the Gettysburg Battlefield Association for the approval of the placement of the monument. When they arrived in Gettysburg, the veterans hired a carriage and a guide to visit the battlefield. The Stamford newspaper reported:

> *They soon found the old brick house which the Confederates used as a hospital, and where Dixon's leg was amputated. The house seems but slightly altered in the 21 years since that day, and the old barn stands there yet. Even the half broken picket fence was readily recognized.* [The 1863 photograph of the Benner house shows the picket fence around the house.] *Nearby on Barlow's Knoll the veterans walked the ground of their first day's fight. They found the large oak tree they all remembered gone, but the stump still there. Dixon brought home a piece of it and also come home with a minie ball he found. The veterans also remembered the old pole bridge over Rock Creek that was now replaced by a "covered" wooden structure.*[49]

ELIZABETH WEIBLE FARM

The exact location where Justus Silliman, Company H, and J. Henry Blakeman, Company D, and other wounded 17th Connecticut men were treated on July 1 is impossible to know with certainty. Based on their accounts, they may have been treated at the Benner farm, as Silliman stated in his 1884 letter to General Noble, or they may have been treated at the Elizabeth Weible farm on Shealer Road. The Weible farmhouse is still there but the barn is long gone. There were three farms in proximity that became Confederate field hospitals: Elizabeth Weible's farm; the Shealer farm, located diagonally across and down Shealer Road from the Weible farm; and, behind the Shealer farm, the Henry Montfort farm on Hunterstown Road. The three farms made the area an obvious location for treatment of the wounded from Barlow's Knoll streaming behind Confederate lines on July 1. Records indicate that over three hundred wounded were treated at the Montfort and Weible farms, and some of that number were treated at Shealer.[50]

The Elizabeth Weible farmhouse as it appears today, on Shealer Road. The barn is long gone.
(Photograph by author)

Based on their accounts, Silliman and Blakeman may have been treated at the Weible Farm. Several wounded on the first day claim that they were taken "*several miles*" behind the lines, including Silliman and Blakeman. Without giving too much credibility to the accuracy of the distance calculated by a wounded man, this statement about distance indicates these men were not cared for at the Alms House or the Benner farm near Barlow's Knoll but may have been treated farther behind Confederate lines. The late Gregory Coco, in his book *A Vast Sea of Misery*, pinpoints this hospital location as the Elizabeth Weible Farm[51] in part because Silliman's account identified the hospital he was taken to on July 1 as belonging to Hays's Division. "*The hospital to which I was taken belonged to Hays brigade called the La Tigers of Early's division.*"[52]

During the war, both sides afforded medical treatment to all wounded without consideration for their allegiance. A Union man in a Confederate hospital might have to wait his turn after the Confederate wounded, and vice versa, but there are very few instances of any wounded being refused treatment, even from noncombatants whose homes and farms were invaded and often devastated. Silliman attested to good treatment by rebel doctors and personnel: "*Was then sent to a rebel hospital about three miles to the rear. Here we had every attention shown us, our wounds promptly attended to and received kind treatment, those who a short time previous had been hurling death at us, now assisted our wounded, bringing them water, crackers, etc.*"[53]

Blakeman, shot in the left side, slowly made the trip to the hospital under his own power. In his description of his treatment by Confederates, he was more ambivalent than Silliman. "*I reached the barn and found it full of wounded Union soldiers. A rebel surgeon gave me a tab of lint, and a rebel soldier filled my canteen with water with which I kept the injured part wet. And that was all the surgical aid I received for four days.*"[54]

Both Silliman's and Blakeman's accounts describe wounded Union prisoners as being taken from this hospital location on Thursday, July 2, in wagons and ambulances, to the school building on High Street in Gettysburg. There they remained until they were liberated after the Confederate withdrawal on July 4.

BLOCHER FARM

The Blocher Farm property served as home to two generations of that family. Blocher was the original name of the little knoll above Rock Creek that is now known as Barlow's Knoll. The small stone and wood house in the front of the Blocher property alongside Table Rock Road (known as the Newville Road at the time of the battle) was the home of John Blocher, a widower, who lived alone in the one-and-a-half-story home. This structure is the only original structure on the property. During the battle the farmhouse and barn were the home of John's son, Reverend David Blocher, and his wife. Father John's small house was used by the 17th Pennsylvania Cavalry as they picketed the Carlisle Road on the morning of July 1. The property fell into Confederate hands as Doles's Brigade advanced to attack the Eleventh Corps forces on the knoll. The houses and farm buildings served as a Confederate aid station. According to the Historic American Building Survey in the Library of Congress, John's house was purported to be the site of a meeting between General Robert E. Lee and his corps commanders on the evening of July 1.[55]

The John Blocher home on Table Rock Road is the only original building that remains on the Blocher farm. (Photograph by Author)

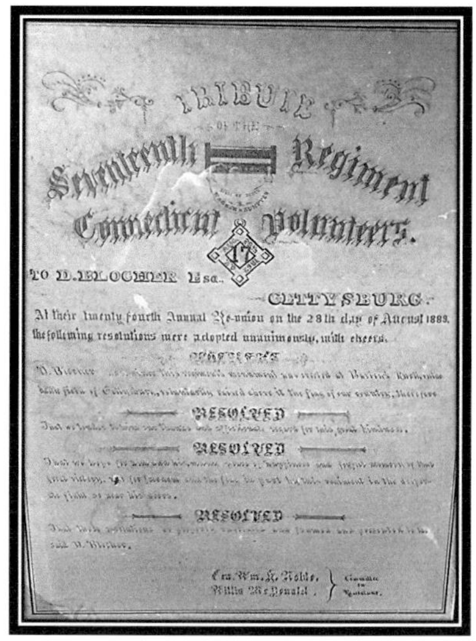

Tribute of the Seventeenth Regiment Connecticut Volunteers.

To D. Blocher Esq.

Gettysburg.

At their twenty fourth Annual Re-union on the 28th day of August 1889, the following resolutions were adopted unanimously, with cheers.

At right: The set of resolutions presented to David Blocher from the 17th Connecticut in 1889. (Image courtesy of David Malgee)

The S. G. Elliot burial map shows twenty-eight Confederate burials on the property, deemed to be a high estimate. Two of the Confederates were identified: Lieutenant Colonel David R. E. Winn, killed leading a charge on Barlow's Knoll, and Josiah H. Law. After the war a feud erupted between David Blocher and the Winn family when they tried to retrieve Colonel Winn's body. Blocher refused the family unless they paid for the exhumation. An old story goes that Blocher kept on his mantle a part of Winn's jaw that contained a gold plate or bridge for his teeth. Blocher wanted $10 from the family for maintenance of the grave and would include the bridge when the money was paid and the body was shipped home. In the 1870s a negotiated price of $5 was agreed upon and Colonel Winn was sent home to his family in Georgia.[56]

David Blocher had a much better relationship with the men of the 17th Connecticut. In 1884 the regiment erected their monument on Barlow's Knoll. In 1885 the surviving members of the 17th Connecticut erected a wooden flagpole on the spot where their beloved Lieutenant Colonel Fowler was killed on the first day of the battle. The flagpole immediately became a landmark of the first day's battlefield and for years the national colors were raised by David Blocher. When the 17th Connecticut dedicated their second monument on East Cemetery Hill in 1889 the survivors honored David Blocher during the ceremony for his contribution to the regiment in raising the flag. In thanks, General Noble presented Blocher with "a handsome framed set of engrossed resolutions."

THE LUTHERAN SEMINARY HOSPITAL

On July 1, the cupola of Schmucker Hall was used as an observation post by Brigadier General John Buford. As the fighting swelled, the buildings on Seminary Ridge were pressed into use as hospitals. The Lutheran Seminary Hospital treated nearly seven hundred men from both sides. Seriously wounded men were housed in the basement until flooding required them to be moved to the upper floors. The seminary was the last temporary hospital in Gettysburg to close; it was shuttered on September 7 after its

Alfred Waud sketched the Lutheran Theological Seminary, on the crest of Seminary Ridge, on July 1, 1863. The main academic building in the center is Schmucker Hall, referred to as "Old Dorm." Schmucker Hall was flanked on either side by two large brick homes occupied by Reverend Dr. Charles Krauth and Reverend Dr. Samuel Schmucker. All three seminary structures would serve as hospitals. In the foreground is the Chambersburg Pike (Buford Avenue). The house on the far left is the Elias Sheads house known as the Oak Ridge Seminary for Girls run by Elias's daughter, Carrie. This home would also become a hospital on the first day of battle.

remaining Union wounded were transferred to Camp Letterman and the Confederate prisoners were sent to various Union prison camps.[57] On September 1, Colonel George McFarland of the 151st Pennsylvania, who had his leg amputated and had been at the hospital since the first day, wrote, "*Today the rebs go, tomorrow the 'one armed' and the next day the 'one legged' Union men. 60 or 70 were to go today but could not get off. So by Monday (September 7) the whole thing may be cleared out.*" Colonel McFarland was finally able to leave for home on September 16. He was the last patient at the Lutheran Seminary hospital.[58]

The Lutheran Theological Seminary served mainly as a First Corps hospital. Confederate wounded and several high-ranking Confederate officers were also treated there. From July 1 until the Confederate withdrawal, Union doctors and wounded were considered prisoners until the fortunes of war reversed. Two captured Confederate surgeons treated wounded here until they were sent to prison camps.[59] Records show that at least three men from the 17th Connecticut, wounded on Barlow's Knoll, were taken to this hospital for treatment.

SERGEANT CYRUS BACHELDER, COMPANY D, WOUNDED

Sergeant Cyrus Bachelder.

(Author's Collection)

Sergeant Cyrus Bachelder, Company D, was listed as wounded on the first day of battle. Bachelder was carrying the flag on Barlow's Knoll when Lieutenant Colonel Douglas Fowler was instantly killed, struck in the head by an artillery shell. An exploding shell fragment struck and shattered a fence rail, sending it careening. The rail hit Bachelder in the chest and knocked him down. The regiment fell back and Bachelder was captured. He was taken, with other wounded prisoners, to a hospital in a nearby barn. On July 2 he was transported to the Seminary. After the Confederate retreat, wounded prisoners were effectively paroled and Bachelder returned to the regiment.[60]

PRIVATE FRANK BENSON, COMPANY C, MORTALLY WOUNDED

According to documentation in the October 21, 1863, pension claim made by Frank Benson's widow, Private Benson suffered a gunshot wound on July 1. On July 4, he was transferred to the Seminary from an unstated location for treatment of that wound. The widow's pension file states on July 16, 1863, Benson died there of the wound and complications from pleurisy.[61] This record seems straightforward. However, Benson's case highlights the difficulty in keeping accurate records during battle. Benson also appeared on the list of Spangler Farm wounded as "*Benson, Frank, Pvt., 17th CT, C, lower 3rd right thigh, compound fracture, splints.*"[62] Benson was included on a list of men who died at the Eleventh Corps hospital compiled by Gettysburg resident J. G. Frey.[63] Private Frank Benson's body, however it got there, lies buried in the in the Connecticut section of the Gettysburg Soldier's National Cemetery, gravesite CT-A-10.

The stone marker for Private Frank J. Benson, Company C, Gettysburg National Cemetery. (Photo by author)

PRIVATE WILLIAM S. DEWHIRST WOUNDED

On July 1, Private William S. Dewhirst was admitted to the Seminary hospital after he received a saber wound on Barlow's Knoll. Wounds from swords, sabers, and bayonets requiring medical treatment were exceedingly rare during the Civil War, comprising less than 0.4 percent of all wounds.[64] The *Medical and Surgical History of the War of the Rebellion* listed Dewhirst's case in the section on the treatment of Wounds and Injuries of the Head: "*Denhurst (Dewhirst), H. (William S.), Private, Co. D, 17th Connecticut Volunteers. Sabre-cut of the scalp. Gettysburg, July 1, 1863. Admitted to Seminary Hospital, Gettysburg, same day. Transferred to South Street Hospital, Philadelphia; thence to Knight Hospital, New Haven, Connecticut on March 24, 1864. Returned to duty April 21st, 1864.*"[65] (It is obvious by the mistakes in the spelling of his name that the transcriber read the Ws in Dewhirst's first and last names as Ns.) The wound must have been a serious one. Dewhirst spent many months in various hospitals before returning to duty.[66] He mustered out with the regiment at Hilton Head on July 19, 1865. After the war, Dewhirst returned to his farm in Trumbull and would live until 1903, when he died at the age of seventy-one.[67]

THE TRINITY GERMAN REFORMED CHURCH

By the afternoon of July 1, the Confederate onslaught pushed toward the town. Despite stubborn fighting by the First and Eleventh Corps, the Confederates were in control of much of Gettysburg. As retreating Federals flooded the town, pursued by the Confederates, every public building and church in Gettysburg was opened as a hospital. Many private homes would also shelter wounded. Bodies of dead men and dead horses littered the streets. Piles of amputated limbs were soon seen under the windows of buildings serving as operating theaters. The horrors of the situation were indescribable.

Dr. Abraham Stout, assistant surgeon in the 153rd Pennsylvania, recounted,

> *(On July 1) I was captured between the Poor House and the town. Colonel D.B. Penn (7th Louisiana) saw me and dismounted. He walked by my side . . . told me I was his prisoner, (and) taking me to the German Reformed Church, said to me: "You ought to take this church for a hospital." I said, "Yes, if it is not locked." But we found the doors unlocked and took possession. In less than half an hour, it was filled with wounded, mostly Union men. I was in attendance there three days . . . after that, we removed the wounded to the public school building.*[68]

Private Reuben Ruch of Company F, 153rd Pennsylvania, Dr. Stout's regiment, was wounded on Barlow's Knoll. He wrote, "*I found the church full . . . I should call it a slaughterhouse. There must have been ten or twelve amputation tables in one room . . . they were all busy . . . the doctors had their sleeves rolled up to their shoulders and were covered with blood. I saw all I wanted to of the part, and I climbed the stairs to the floor above.*"[69]

The shrieking chaos in the streets was echoed within the walls of the church. Eva Danner, a sixteen-year-old who lived on the square in Gettysburg, remembered, "*The*

This 1863 stereoview of Trinity German Reformed Church shows the church on Stratton Street looking south from York Street. The church's location at the corner of Stratton and High Streets made it a natural destination for wounded Eleventh Corps soldiers seeking shelter in the town. (Gettysburg National Military Park)

wounded were carried into the lecture room of the church and there was so much amputating done there that the seats were covered with blood and they had to bore holes in the floor to let the blood run away." Other citizens remembered "men lying on boards on the tops of pews," and the walls of the church spattered with blood, the pews so badly soaked in blood they later had to be replaced.[70]

CAPTAIN WILSON FRENCH, COMPANY G, WOUNDED

Captain French was struck in his right arm while his sword was raised over his head. He was taken prisoner as the Confederates engulfed Barlow's Knoll and directed to a field hospital. Assistant Surgeon Robert McEwen encountered French on the field and dressed his arm. French was then directed to the German Reformed Church. Private Henry E. Waite, Company K, was assigned as a nurse. After the Confederate withdrawal, French was transferred to the Eleventh Corps hospital at Spangler Farm. He was evacuated by rail on July 8 and sent home to Connecticut to convalesce. French gave several interviews to William Warren after the war, all of them written in the third person.

Wilson French, Company G.
(Wilson French Collection)

> *He was wounded the first day on Barlow's Knoll at the elbow of right arm, by a piece of explosive shot, as the Doctors called it. He had his arm raised to full length over his head, with sword in hand, when he was wounded. He looked around for someone to take his place while Henry Waite assisted him back to the Dutch Reform Church, which was then being used for a hospital. On the way they met Dr. Ewen. As French could not move his arm, the Doctor cut his coat sleeve open and dressed the wound, then told him to go to the hospital as above stated.*
>
> *He (Captain French) stayed in this hospital till the morning of the 4th, then a field hospital was established back of Cemetery Hill. Those able to go home were sent there on furlough, while others were sent to this hospital. Captain says, "I do not know who sheathed my sword, I could not.*" [French's sword is in the collections of the Stratford Historical Society.]
>
> *The class and back rooms were used by the Doctors for amputation rooms. French went into one of these rooms with sword and belt on. When the amputation was over, the men went back into the audience room. There were a good many ahead of him who had their arms and legs taken off. Finally, his turn came, and he told the doctors that he wanted his wound dressed. They replied that they wanted to take his arm off. French said, "You will never take it off as long as I am alive." The Doctors talked in German a while, and then dressed it, and said they would look at it in*

> *the morning, but they never saw the wound after that. Waite was detailed as nurse, so kept Captain well supplied with cold water and that was all he did for the wound.*[71]

French spoke to William Warren a number of times over the years about his wartime service. In another recollection he talked about how Barney Marshall, Company D, was wounded and entered the German Reformed Church with him. Marshall was wounded in the neck and the ball had to be surgically extracted. Private Marshall apparently recovered quickly and returned to the 17th Connecticut to be mustered out with the regiment in July 1865. Marshall's listing at the Spangler Farm reads, *"Marshall, Barney, Pvt., 17th CT, D, flesh wound back of neck, ball extracted."*[72]

Warren described Marshall's wounding.

> *He was wounded in the back of the neck so badly that he could not turn his head. He and Capt. French went into a church, and into the inside of the alter rail. Captain was very much impressed with the way Marshall held his head.*
> *(From Capt. French)*[73]

BEST FRIENDS PRIVATE GEORGE DICKENS AND PRIVATE JOHN BOUGHTON, COMPANY C

George Dickens was a married hatter from Danbury, one of four Dickens brothers to serve in the Civil War. His best friend was John Boughton, a carpenter, also from Danbury. They enlisted together in Company C and made a pact that if one of them was wounded the other would care for him. On Barlow's Knoll on July 1, John Boughton was struck in the left forearm. George got Boughton off the field and to the German Reformed Church, got him into one of the pews, and went to get him a canteen of water. He encountered a Confederate, who advised him not to go into the street but to remove his equipment and go back into the church. When a Confederate squad came to the church to round up prisoners George pretended to be wounded. Determined to remain with his friend, Dickens subsequently asked one of the German doctors if he could stay in the building as a nurse and the doctor told him to tie a white cloth around his arm, and that would then show that he was a nurse.[74]

John Boughton wrote his account in the third person:

> *He was wounded as we fell back near the poor house barn. The first one he saw after being wounded that he knew was George Dickens who said to him, "are you hurt," his blood was running down his left arm. The doctors call it "fore left arm" which is just below the elbow. John had his gun and knapsack in his right hand. The bullet was in his arm until the third day then taken out by a rebel surgeon. It was very painful. Dr. Hubbard came along to where they were. George saw him first. Hubbard asked if he was wounded. Dr. said, "take good care of it and wet it well with water."*[75]

Stereoview of the German Reformed Church used as an Eleventh Corps Hospital offered shelter for many wounded from the 17th Connecticut. (Gettysburg National Military Park)

The surgery performed by a Confederate surgeon to remove the ball from John Boughton's arm on July 3 most likely occurred at the German Reformed Church.

George Dickens remained at this church hospital serving as a prisoner nurse until the Confederate retreat. He then went with the wounded, who were relocated to the Spangler Farm, and remained there as a nurse there for the next three months. At the Spangler Farm, Dickens proved himself of service to the wounded, and to grieving families coming from Connecticut and other states who wanted to bring home their boys. He assisted families who came to Spangler in the identification and recovery of their dead that had been buried at the hospital site. These accounts are in the next chapter. William Warren left a brief, handwritten character sketch of George Dickens in his papers. He wrote, *"George Dickens, tall, large, well built, stocky, very erect, well liked, good character, with a kind disposition."*[76]

THE PUBLIC SCHOOL ON HIGH STREET

This two-story school building on High Street appears much today as it did during the battle; the cupola was removed, and the school bell is located in Unity Park off Baltimore Street. The school was completed in 1858 as Gettysburg's first consolidated public school for the education of both males and females. The school became a hospital on the first day of battle for Union cavalry and First and Eleventh Corps wounded. Confederate wounded were housed on the second floor and Union men on the first.[77] Both Justus Silliman and J. Henry Blakeman, wounded and taken prisoner on July 1, were transported to this hospital by Confederates on the morning of July 2. Both left accounts of their time in this building.

The public school on High Street would serve as a hospital from the first day. The building retains much of its 1863 appearance except for the removal of the cupola. (Photograph by author)

WOUNDED PRISONERS JUSTUS SILLIMAN AND J. HENRY BLAKEMAN, HOSPITALIZED AT THE PUBLIC SCHOOL

On July 3, Justus Silliman found an old school ledger. He used the paper for a letter to his mother in which described how he and other wounded were transferred to this hospital on July 2 by the Confederates using captured Union ambulances. Silliman described seeing thousands of captured muskets the rebels had collected and stacked in the street. He described a rebel canon he saw "*which had been struck in its mouth by one of our shots and flattened out*" and how the rebels had buried their dead, but that Union dead lay where they fell. Silliman noted that there were few nurses, and he did what he could to help other wounded. Silliman also had harsh words for the doctors in attendance.

> *We were taken to this hospital which with a German Dutch reformed church was at the east end of town and mostly occupied by wounded of the 11th corps, nurses were not abundant, and I have done what I could to relieve the suffering, several of our own surgeons are in attendance but to their shame are more neglectful to our wounded than were the rebel doctors. They will remain for hours at the windows watching the progress of the battle while our wounded were in agony for want of proper attention, we are in full view of the battlefield, the rebel line of battle being within a few rods in front of our hospital, our own line is also in full view. They occupy a line of hills which they have fortified.*"[78]

On night of July 2, from this hospital, Silliman witnessed the attack of the Louisiana Tigers on East Cemetery Hill.

> *At about four o'clock yesterday PM the fight was renewed with great fierceness, the cannonading and musketry firing was terrific and the*

> *sound of shells rushing through the air was continuous and resembled somewhat of a tremendous waterfall. The La brigade were in a hollow in front of us, where they lay close until nearly dark though they had their skirmishers out nearly all day. These were occasionally picked off by our sharpshooters. Bullets frequently whistled around our hospital, but I have not heard of anyone being injured by them. Just at dusk we saw those infallible La tigers make preparations for a charge, they stealthily formed in line under cover of a hill and slowly and in excellent order advanced toward our lines till within a short distance of them when with a loud yell they rushed forward on the double quick. The clash was tremendous, but short, and …picked men retreated back panic stricken with their ranks terribly thinned. Then in was that we were gladdened by the cheers of our men. The fight raged until nearly nine o'clock.*[79]

J. Henry Blakeman, wounded on Barlow's Knoll on July 1, recalled in an 1888 letter to William Warren how he, like Silliman, was transported to the High Street school on July 2. Blakeman also witnessed the attack of Hays's Brigade on the Union line at East Cemetery Hill. He wrote about watching the attack from the hospital building and how relieved the wounded Union prisoners were on July 4 when Union skirmishers liberated them. Unlike Silliman, Blakeman was not complimentary of his treatment at the hands of the Confederates.

> *From the windows of our prison we saw the Louisiana Tigers form and start on the charge that the 17th Regiment helped to repulse with such slaughter on the evening of the 2nd. It can easily be imagined we were somewhat anxious as to the result of the fight, and more than some glad to see the skirmishers come through the streets on the 4th of July, and to know we were with friends again. I am sure I am not indebted in any large amount to the "Johnnies" for board, for in the three days I was with them, they only gave me three crackers and a little water.*[80]

In 1884 Silliman, then a professor of metallurgy at Lafayette College in Easton, Pennsylvania, corresponded with General Noble. Silliman recounted that he witnessed Pickett's Charge on July 3 from the cupola of the public school hospital.

> *On the morning of the 3rd the rebels informed us that they had orders to shoot any of us that appeared at the windows, so in order to watch a battle, I climbed to the cupola, from which I had an excellent view of the field. Even at that height, the bullets were whistling around my ears, and the noise of the shot and shell in the air resembled that of a mighty torrent.*[81]

JEREMIAH CULP CARPENTRY SHOP ON YORK STREET

The Jeremiah Culp carpentry shop on York Street was identified as a Confederate hospital by the writings of Liberty Hollinger, a sixteen-year-old who lived with her family at the point of the Y intersection where the York and Hanover Roads meet. Her father, Jacob, owned a warehouse on the corner of Stratton Street, which the Confederates broke into and raided. Liberty and her family remained in the cellar of their home on York Street during the battle and the family cared for several wounded. The Hollinger property and Culp carpentry shop were just east of the square. Liberty Hollinger wrote,

The Jeremiah Culp home and carpentry shop on York Street. (Author's photograph)

> *There was an emergency hospital in a carpenter shop not far from our house. The Carpenter's bench was used as an operating table, and (my sister) who had gone there several times said that there was a big pile of legs and arms outside the window. On Saturday afternoon (July 4) a Confederate surgeon came into our yard . . . Mother . . . invited him to eat with us. But he very politely declined, . . . as he (said) he was too weary and heartsick from amputating limbs all day. We could see on his knee-high boots how he had tried to get rid of the blood stains which had splashed on them while he was at work.*[82]

The Culp house was empty during the battle because the family had left the home, but Jeremiah Culp purportedly returned at some point during the battle to work on a coffin said to be for Confederate brigadier general William Barksdale. The coffin was left behind unfinished when the Confederates retreated. Maria Comfort, who was photographed with Jennie Wade and her sister in 1861 and who lived nearby on Baltimore Street, stated that her son, Charles Comfort, finished the coffin, which was then used to bury Jennie Wade.[83]

SERGEANT OSCAR ST. JOHN, COMPANY F, PRISONER AND NURSE AT A CONFEDERATE HOSPITAL

On August 30, 1890, Oscar St. John, Company F, wrote an account of his experiences in Gettysburg to William Warren. As a captured prisoner, St. John assisted a Confederate surgeon in a house in Gettysburg. It is impossible to definitively document this location, but we can examine the possibilities. St. John gives the doctor's name as Fontane.

Sergeant Oscar St. John, Company F. (Bridgeport History Center)

The only doctor located in records with this name was Dr. John B. Fontaine of the 4th Virginia Cavalry.[84] He may have been serving as a brigade surgeon with Confederate cavalry, perhaps that of Fitzhugh Lee and/or Jeb Stuart. It is possible that Dr. Fontaine may have come into town, at least from July 2 through July 4, and taken over a house for surgery.

That said, there is no positive identification of Dr. Fontaine as the surgeon St. John worked with, despite the similarity of his name with that of the surgeon identified by St. John. The accuracy of the location in town where Sergeant St. John served as a nurse cannot be fixed with certainty as the Culp woodshop. There is no reason to doubt St. John's account that he was detailed to assist a Confederate surgeon in a house in the town. St. John's account illustrates how many private homes in Gettysburg were used to treat the wounded.

Oscar St. John was a twenty-three-year-old sailor from Norwalk when he enlisted in Company F, 17th Connecticut. He had already seen service in the navy as a master's mate on the war sloop *Pensacola* and the gunboat *Anacostia*. In 1861 he enlisted for three months in Company G, 3rd Connecticut, and in August 1862 he enlisted in the 17th Connecticut with the rank of sergeant. St. John was mustered out with the regiment in Hilton Head in July 1865. During his service with the regiment in Florida he suffered greatly from scurvy, which affected his eyes. While in Florida he married Mary Delores Sanchez in St. Augustine on May 29, 1865. After the war St. John would become a very successful captain, ship owner, and businessman in East Norwalk, Connecticut. He and his wife had fifteen children, thee of whom died young. St. John died of a cerebral hemorrhage on September 4, 1912, at age seventy-four.[85]

> *When the charge was made at Cemetery Hill, the rebs retreated from that and went back through the town . . . St. John was taken prisoner on the street that runs from the square to Cemetery Hill and paroled on the field. Dr. Fontane used one of the houses on the square for a hospital, and St. John was there helping for three days and on the a.m. of the fourth he joined the regiment and reported for duty.*[86]

In the same account St. John gave Warren the following description of an encounter with Confederates.

> *St. John had the privilege of the city, given him by the white cloth on his arm, as a badge; he asked one of the Louisiana Tigers what troops they were and if they were in that charge? They replied they were. St. John then asked what troops they had been engaged with? They replied "a lot of G. D.*

> *... Nutmegs from Conn. 17th Regt." They cussed them and then said they would not run, nor could not make them run; they clubbed their muskets on us. St. John says, "Of all the swearing I ever heard, that night beat all." (From O. St. John, Aug. 30th, 1890)*[87]

OFFICE AND HOMES OF DR. TAYLOR AND DR. CRESS ON BALTIMORE STREET

Dr. Robert Hubbard, surgeon for the 17th Connecticut and medical inspector of the Eleventh Corps, tended wounded at various locations throughout Gettysburg from July 1 until he left the town on July 14. Several of these locations can be determined with accuracy, such as the Spangler Farm, and the offices of Doctors Taylor and Cress on Baltimore Street. These offices and homes no longer exist and were replaced in 1913 by the large classical post office building that is now occupied by the Adams County Library.[88]

On July 7, Dr. Hubbard wrote to his wife that he had been left behind when the army departed to follow Lee.

> *Gettysburg Pa July 7, 1863*
>
> *My own dear Nellie,*
>
> *You will doubtless be surprised to learn that I have been left behind & that the Army have advanced in pursuit of the enemy. After the terrible fighting on Friday & the complete route of the Rebel Army Genl. Howard with himself and part of his staff thought they would have a little tilt in charging on the rebel picket which they left to keep up appearances & in the fray Capt. Griffith of the staff was seriously wounded & Genl. Howard requested me to remain with him until out of danger & at the same time take general charge of all our Corps Hospitals.*[89]

On July 5, General Howard and his staff, along with cavalry assigned to his headquarters, were on the Fairfield Road about two miles from Gettysburg as the Sixth Corps departed following General Jubal Early's retreat. Howard's party encountered the Confederate rear guard and in the ensuing scuffle Captain James J. Griffiths, Howard's aide de camp, was seriously wounded.[90] As Dr. Hubbard wrote to his wife, he was personally assigned by General Howard to oversee the care of Captain Griffiths, as well as supervise all of the Eleventh Corps hospitals, including the George Spangler Farm.

Captain Griffiths was taken into Gettysburg, probably to Dr. Taylor's home on Baltimore Street, for care. Doctors Taylor and Cress were in partnership and treated an unknown number of wounded in homes, churches, and public buildings in Gettysburg.[91] Hubbard also boarded at the Taylor home as he cared for Captain Griffiths and oversaw his responsibilities at the Spangler Farm, traveling back and forth daily.[92] Hubbard may have tended to other wounded at this location as well as at other places in town. On July 10, 1863, Captain Griffith died. The cause of death was listed as "*gunshot wound penetrating cavity of peritoneum.*" Dr. Hubbard wrote to his wife that he was arranging to have the body sent home to Philadelphia for burial and he would soon leave Gettysburg to rejoin General Howard's staff, if he could find them. His host, Mrs. Taylor, "*expresses great regret at my intended departure.*" In this same letter to his wife, Hubbard explained he was quite anxious to be at the next fight with Lee's army, which he thought would occur if Lee could be prevented from crossing the Potomac River.[93]

THE EVERGREEN CEMETERY GATEHOUSE AND GROUNDS

On July 1 and 2 Evergreen Cemetery was the epicenter of the Union battle line. The Evergreen Cemetery Gatehouse, stable, and grounds served as aid stations and offered refuge to wounded men during the battle. Barns and structures nearby the cemetery also sheltered the wounded.

The cornerstone of the cemetery gatehouse, one of the most beautiful and prominent landmarks in Gettysburg, was laid on September 1, 1855. Elizabeth Musser and Peter Thorn, who had both emigrated from Germany and settled in Gettysburg, were married that day. On February 9, 1856, Peter Thorn accepted the position of cemetery caretaker for an annual salary of $150. He and Elizabeth moved into the north side of the gatehouse rent-free, and Elizabeth's parents, John and Catherine Masser, lived on the other side. Peter was responsible for mowing and caring for the grounds, digging all the graves, and arranging removals to other cemeteries. On August 16, 1862, Peter enlisted in the 138th Pennsylvania Infantry, in which he would serve for three years. Elizabeth assumed, with some help from her father, Peter's caretaker duties in the cemetery. Before the battle, Elizabeth's workload averaged five burials a month. At the time of the battle, Elizabeth was the mother of three sons, and was six months pregnant with her fourth child.[94]

On Wednesday morning, July 1, as the Confederate army clashed with the First Corps on Seminary Ridge, Elizabeth went upstairs in the gatehouse and looked west to see "*them fighting on the ridge near McMillian's house . . . while they were fighting on the ridge the Union soldiers came from all directions.*" Elizabeth baked bread to feed the soldiers who came to the house. She and her parents "*had all the tins and cups and tubs and everything outside filled with water. All the time our little boys were pumping and*

Photograph of the gate to Evergreen Cemetery, taken shortly after the battle in July 1863 by Timothy O'Sullivan. (Library of Congress)

carrying water to fill the tubs . . . and worked and helped this way until their poor little hands were blistered."[95] As the Union lines re-formed on Cemetery Hill later in the afternoon, they brought up their artillery to fire in the direction of the Alms House. A Union officer requested a man to go out with him to show him the roads, and Elizabeth went despite protests that it was too dangerous. Elizabeth showed him the Harrisburg Road, York Pike, and Hunterstown Road. When she returned to the gatehouse she wanted to go upstairs to see if the Union had held or gained ground. As she came down the stairwell a shell cut into the window frame and went through the ceiling. She did not return upstairs.[96]

General Howard made his headquarters in and near the gatehouse. One of his officers requested that Elizabeth make supper. She had given away all her bread that morning and questioned the officer about the suitability of what she could prepare. He assured her it was good enough for wartime. Still uncertain about preparing supper, Elizabeth visited her neighbor, Captain Meyer. She had stored some hams at his house for safekeeping. She arrived at the house just after dark and could not find the family. What she did find were many wounded soldiers. She became so upset she quickly left and went home without any of the meat she wanted to prepare for supper.[97] When Generals Howard, Sickles, and Slocum came in about midnight for supper she fed them pancakes.

On July 2 at first light the guns opened, and Elizabeth, her children, parents, and neighbors went into the cellar—seventeen people in all. After several hours of the terrible cannonading, the door burst open and they were told, "*This family is commanded by General Howard to leave this house and get as far in ten minutes as possible. Take nothing but the children and go*!" As they fled down the Baltimore Pike a shell burst behind them. No one was hurt and they hurried faster to the Musser farm, which they found full of soldiers and wagons.[98] Elizabeth and her father returned to check on their property about midnight that evening, which Elizabeth recounted.

> *We had fat hogs and we wanted to look after them. When we got to the stable, we could hear the wounded men holler and go on, laying around the house,—in the cellar too . . . we could not get near the house for wounded and dead . . .My father got a man to take us into the cellar where six wounded men were, and they had our bed clothes spread all around. The poor wounded men were crying and going on so that we did not want anything then. They called their wives and children to come and wet their tongues. Then we went down the pike again.*[99]

When the family retuned on July 5, they found devastation all around them. There was no glass left in the gatehouse windows and some of the frames were knocked out. Their pump was broken. Fifteen soldiers were buried beside the pump shed. All the family bedding and everything left in the cellar was full of blood and mud. Then Elizabeth received orders from the president of the cemetery association, David McConaughy, to begin burying the dead. She, six months pregnant, and with some help from her elderly father, dug the graves and buried 105 soldiers. Around the house fifteen horses lay dead. In a field next to the cemetery lay nineteen more.[100]

The cemetery, and the area surrounding it, was a dangerous place to be during the battle. Later visitors were shocked at the destruction. Dead horses and the debris of battle littered the cemetery. Iron fences around graves and gravestones were broken and damaged. Pennsylvania College professor Michael Jacobs, who wrote one of the first accounts of the battle, noted, "*People assumed that the tombstones were knocked down from the fighting, unaware that the monuments had been laid down by order of General Howard. Not only was this done out of respect for the dead, but also as protection for the soldiers. A monument struck by a shell created hundreds of projectiles that greatly increased the risk of injury.*"[101] The two tallest obelisks, to the Smyser and McPherson families, were two of the monuments taken down by Howard's orders, undoubtedly because these tall monuments were easily sighted by Confederate artillery.[102] Howard's action protected many of the monuments and prevented more of the stones from becoming shrapnel.[103]

At 3:30 p.m. of July 2, while the roar of fighting from the Peach Orchard, The Wheatfield, and Little Roundtop went on and artillery dueled on both sides, fifty-five guns from A. P. Hill and Richard S. Ewell's artillery opened on Cemetery Hill. Within minutes the atmosphere was charged with hot iron destroying whatever was in its way. Round shots whooshed overhead and slammed into the ground. Shells shrieked, screamed, and burst, killing and maiming. In the cemetery shot plowed into the ground, monuments and gravestones were smashed, and caissons, ammunition wagons, and cannons were struck and exploded. Men and horses were killed and wounded. Shrapnel flew and cracked through the cemetery as men took cover behind headstones. A shell fragment struck Captain Frederick Stowe, son of the famous writer Harriet Beecher Stowe, in the head and seriously wounded him. Stowe was brought to the field hospital where Dr. Hubbard tended to him. Surgeon Henry Van Aernam wrote, "*The situation of our hospital was that the shells that passed over our line of battle, either in front or right our left, would fall (near the hospital) . . . the shells were frequent and familiar visitors. There were five horses killed by shells right about the hospital—two men were wounded, and several horses wounded.*"[104]

Dr. Hubbard treated wounded here for several days. As part of General Howard's staff, Hubbard was on hand in and around Howard's headquarters. Private John Collins, Company B, who had charge of the officers' horses, wrote that as he retreated from Barlow's Knoll on July 1 one of the horses panicked and stepped on him. He found Dr. Hubbard at a barn near Cemetery Hill and tried to explain he had been hurt. Hubbard told him to get the horses and follow him or they would be captured. They stopped at a barn where Collins says that Hubbard was performing an amputation and was obliged to put the officer he had operated on in an ambulance to the rear as "*shot and shell came so thick and fast that they had to leave again for the rear.*"[105] Perhaps it was at this point that Collins was saved by his Catholic Prayer Book, carried in his breast pocket, that stopped a ball from penetrating his chest.[106] Hubbard was then treating wounded at yet another hospital location, according to Collins, who tried to tell the doctor again he had been hurt. Hubbard advised him to go to the rear until he could attend to him and resumed his work.

This field hospital was probably in or near the cemetery as mentioned in several accounts. This location was a natural place for Dr. Hubbard to station himself to be near his corps commander and close to his regiment. From Elizabeth Thorn's account, the stable and the gatehouse were used for the wounded, and there were wounded men all around the property. This most probably was Dr. Hubbard's last stop on the field on July 1 and it is logical that he remained here until at least the morning of July 4.

On July 2, this "field hospital" was described as just inside the cemetery gate by Lieutenant Peck, Company D, 17th Connecticut, who called a squad to carry one of his wounded company members to the hospital:

> *one of my men had just been wounded by a rebel sharpshooter, and was then lying in the field near our batteries on Cemetery Hill. . . . Corp. Alva E. Wilcox, of Company D was suffering from a bullet wound through the shoulder, which had also penetrated his abdomen. I at once called for two or three comrades and we put the Corporal into a rubber blanket and carried him to the field hospital just inside of the Cemetery gate. One of the Drs. Probed his wound and said he would be all right in a day or two; he was all right, but he died and was mustered out on the other side July 6th. He was one of our bravest and best.*[107]

CORPORAL ALVAH WILCOX, COMPANY D, MORTALLY WOUNDED

Corporal Alvah Wilcox, Company D. (Bridgeport History Center)

Corporal Alvah Wilcox was wounded by a sharpshooter's bullet on July 2 on Cemetery Hill. The wound was severe, and one account stated that Wilcox was paralyzed. The wound described by Lieutenant Peck went through Wilcox's shoulder and penetrated his abdomen. Wilcox's wound was what Civil War surgeons referred to as a "sucking wound." This type of wound caused the lungs to collapse and suffocated the soldier. During the war army surgeons searched for a way to treat these wounds. Such wounds were immediately deemed mortal by examining surgeons and were often left untreated. Dr. Benjamin Howard observed it was the "sucking," the negative pressure in the thorax created by the chest wound, that was the cause of the fatal lung collapse. The doctor found that if he closed the wound with metal sutures, followed by alternating layers of lint or linen bandages, and sealed it with collodion it crated an airtight seal that he referred to as "hermetically sealing." However, during the Civil War and before knowledge of germ theory, Howard's procedure had little effect on the mortality rate of such wounds.[108]

Dr. Howard performed his experimental surgery of "hermetically sealing" the chests of at least ten wounded men at Gettysburg. Dr. Howard primarily treated wounded at the Fifth Corps hospital at the Jacob Weikert Farm on the Taneytown Road; he performed nine of the ten "hermetic sealing" surgeries there. Two of those surgical cases were documented as being transferred to the Seminary Hospital. Corporal Wilcox's surgery was listed as the wound being sealed on the field. The Medical and Surgical History of the War of the Rebellion documents, "*CASE.—Sergeant(sic) Alva C. Wilcox, Co. D, 17th Connecticut Volunteers, received a gunshot wound of the lung at Gettysburg, Pennsylvania, July 3(sic), 1863. The wound was hermetically sealed on the field by Assistant Surgeon B. Howard, U.S.A. Death resulted on July 7. The case is reported by the operator.*"[109] Dr. Howard probably performed Wilcox's surgery on July 3. The surgery was likely performed at the field hospital in or near Evergreen Cemetery. All ten of the men Dr. Howard performed this surgery on died, including Wilcox. Two patients died at the Seminary Hospital, and seven perished at the Fifth Corps Hospital on the Taneytown Road. Wilcox, transferred to the Eleventh Corps Hospital at the Spangler Farm, died there on July 7. These men who underwent this experimental surgery are only surgical footnotes in medical history, but Dr. Howard's procedure for treating chest wounds by sealing them would eventually lead to the standard practice for their successful treatment in modern medicine.

WILLIAM WURTZ, COMPANY D, PRISONER AND NURSE

Private William Wurtz, the German born harness maker, was captured on the first day and escaped in the confusion as a group of prisoners he was part of were marched away by a Confederate officer. Wurtz joined a small group of Union prisoners detailed to care for the wounded at the Alms House. On July 4 a squad from the 17th Connecticut advanced through Gettysburg and "liberated" wounded and medical personnel, including Wurtz, who had been prisoners at the Alms House. There Wurtz encountered Corporal Patrick Wade, Company K. Wurtz then walked over to Cemetery Hill to see his company. He also went up to the cemetery field hospital and left his account of seeing the wounded Alvah Wilcox. The account was written in the third person.

> *On the 4th day after Wm. Wurtz came back on the field from seeing Pat Wade (at the Almshouse), he saw Alva Wilcox. Wurtz came back to the company which was laying on a hillside. He saw A. W. Peck and asked where the company was. Peck said, "Here, what is left of them." Only about 4 or 5 others. He went up near Cemetery Hill and saw Dan Garrett holding Alva Wilcox. Wilcox had a fine gold watch which he handed to Garrett and said, "I want to leave this with you." Wurtz talked with Wilcox and asked him where he was wounded. He put his hand to his chest but did not say a word.*[110]

Beginning on July 4, Eleventh Corps wounded from the Alms House, the German Reformed Church, the school building on High Street, and the field hospitals and dressing stations in and near the cemetery were moved to the Spangler Farm. Corporal Alva Wilcox would be one of those evacuated to Spangler. William Wurtz would continue nursing duties at Spangler until he left Gettysburg to rejoin the regiment.

THE ELEVENTH CORPS HOSPITAL AT THE GEORGE SPANGLER FARM

The George Spangler Farm was located between the Taneytown Road and the Baltimore Pike. The farm was 156 acres with a stone house, large Pennsylvania bank barn with an attached wagon shed, a separate stone kitchen, various outbuildings, and a good water supply. These attributes all made it an excellent site for a large hospital. At the time of the battle the Spangler family consisted of George, forty-eight; his wife, Elizabeth, forty-five; and their children Harriet, twenty-one; Daniel, twenty; Sabina, nineteen; and Beniah, fifteen. The farm was taken over from July 1 as a hospital. The six family members remained on the property; for the next five weeks while the hospital was in use, they would share one upstairs bedroom.[111]

Beginning July 1, the buildings and the surrounding fields were full of wounded. On July 2, the farm's fields closer to the battle lines on Cemetery Hill became the site for the Union artillery and ammunition reserve, filled with more than 114 cannons with limbers and caissons, nearly 1,500 horses, ambulances, wagons for reserve ammunition, other support materiel such as forges to repair equipment, and over twenty-three hundred men.[112] Rock Creek provided water for the animals; each horse needed about ten gallons each day. The fields provided fodder for grazing (grass or hay); each animal needed twelve to fourteen pounds a day. Horses also required twelve to fourteen pounds of grain (oats, barley, corn) for nutrition and each animal produced ten to fifteen pounds of manure and two gallons of urine each day.[113] This strategic location allowed the artillery reserve to rush ordnance to wherever it was needed on the Union line. This factor alone marked the property as vital to the conduct of the battle.[114]

Union surgeon Dr. Daniel Brinton estimated that there were about one thousand wounded at the Spangler Farm on July 4. As many as two thousand wounded were

The George Spangler Farm in a postwar photograph by William H. Tipton. (Gettysburg National Military Park)

treated at the Spangler Farm in early July. The numbers are almost impossible to fix with accuracy because Eleventh Corps wounded, beginning on July 4, were transported to the farm from all over the battlefield. The 17th Connecticut's wounded were transferred from the Alms House, German Reformed Church, the public school building, and other small homes and hospitals. As wounded flooded the farm, they were put anywhere there was space once all of the buildings were full. The farm would come under artillery fire on the afternoon of July 3 as Confederate cannons on Seminary Ridge bombarded the Union line before Pickett's Charge. Confederate overshots exploded precariously close to the barn. Surgeons operated night and day the first five days of July. Four operating tables were placed under the overhang of the barn to partially shelter them from the terrific rains that began on July 4. As soon as the railroad bridge was repaired over Rock Creek, doctors began evacuating wounded to large general hospitals in York, Philadelphia, Baltimore, and elsewhere on the East Coast. On July 20, Camp Letterman General Hospital was established on the York Pike near the railhead. By July 25, 16,125 wounded had been evacuated out of Gettysburg. Approximately 4,217 remained because they were unable to travel, and those men were transferred to Camp Letterman.[115] The Eleventh Corps hospital at the Spangler Farm closed on August 6, 1863.

DOCTOR DANIEL BRINTON, SURGEON-IN-CHIEF, SECOND DIVISION, ELEVENTH CORPS

Dr. Brinton performed surgery and tended to the wounded at the Spangler Farm from July 1 to July 5 when he departed with the army. He wrote in his diary,

> *During the day (July 1) the medical officers were busily engaged in choosing and arranging a hospital. Its location was altered twice owing to the approaching fire of the enemy, but finally it was definitely established in a large barn 1 mile back from the cemetery. The wounded soon began to pour in, giving us such sufficient occupation that from the 1st of July till the afternoon of the fifth, I was not absent from the hospital more than once and then but for an hour or two. Very hard work it was, too, & little sleep fell to our share. Four operating tables were going night and day. On the 4th of July, which in it surrounding gloomy enough, was livened by our belief that we had a great victory, the number in the hospital was 1000. A heavy rain came over in the afternoon and as we laid many in spots without shelter some indeed in the barnyard where the foul water oozed up into their undressed wounds, the sight was harassing in the extreme. We worked with little intermission, & with a minimum amount of sleep. On one day I arose at 2 AM & worked incessantly till midnight. I doubt if ever I worked harder at a more disagreeable occupation. On the afternoon of the 3rd we were exposed to a sharp fire of shells. Several horses & one man were killed close to the hospital. Shells fell within 20 ft of the room where we were, and we were much in fear that the barn would blaze*

> *which would have been an unspeakably frightful casualty. Fortunately, we did not have this to record.*[116]

MAJOR GENERAL CARL SCHURZ, THIRD DIVISION, ELEVENTH CORPS

Major General Carl Schurz, commander of the Third Division of the Eleventh Corps, visited the Spangler Farm hospital where his wounded were being treated on July 4.

> *I saw long rows of men lying under the eaves of the buildings, the water pouring down upon their bodies in streams. Most of the operating tables were placed in the open . . . partially protected against the rain . . . There stood the surgeons, their sleeves rolled up . . . their bare arms as well as their linen aprons smeared with blood . . . around them pools of blood and amputated arms or legs in heaps . . . a surgeon, having been long at work . . . put down his knife, exclaiming that his hand had grown unsteady, and that this was too much for human endurance, hysterical tears streaming down his face.*[117]

J. HENRY BLAKEMAN, COMPANY D, WOUNDED

J. Henry Blakeman was wounded on Barlow's Knoll on July 1. He was in line with his cousin Selah Blakeman, Sylvester Rounds, and his best friend, Stephen Crofut. As the Confederate onslaught rolled over Barlow's division, Blakeman was shot through the left side. Stephen Crofut was killed, shot in the head. Sylvester Rounds was shot in the left shoulder. Of the four, only Selah Blakeman escaped unharmed to re-form with the survivors on East Cemetery Hill. Blakeman was able to walk to a barn where he was seen by a Confederate surgeon. On July 2, he and other Federal wounded prisoners at that location were loaded into wagons and ambulances and taken to the public school building on High Street. On July 4, after the Confederate army evacuated the town and the Union wounded and doctors were no longer prisoners, many of the Eleventh Corps wounded were brought to the hospital at the Spangler Farm. Once they arrived, ambulatory wounded began searching for men and friends from their regiments. Many men were laid on the bare ground in and around the farm buildings without cover or shelter. Amid the lashing rain on July 4, J. Henry Blakeman wrote home to his mother in Stratford, Connecticut:

> *11th Corps Hospital near Gettysburg*
> *July 4, 1863*
>
> *Dear Mother*
>
> *I think I shall have a chance to send a letter this afternoon and knowing your intense anxiety will write a little. You know we have had a terrible fight and men are slain by hundreds but thanks to our preserver I escaped with my life though pretty severely wounded. I was hit the first day before I had time to fire my gun, taken prisoner and kept one day*

and then taken to the city and the next day our folk took the town and I was taken to our hospital some three miles back. Here we have to lie on the ground and last night we had a terrible rain so I am as wet as water can make me but that is good for the wound. I was struck by a rifle ball in the left side between the hip and ribs passing through the flank. Dr. says he thinks it did not enter the cavity and if not it will heal soon. Do not worry about me for it will do no good. I don't mind it much can get up and walk around quite spry and have a good appetite. I can hardly bring my mind to tell you that Stephen was killed by the same volley that wounded me. He was within three feet of me was shot through the head and killed instantly. Stephen was liked by the whole co. and will be much mourned. I know it will almost kill his mother but reality is better than suspense and what I tell you you can depend upon. I saw Selah yesterday morning for a few minutes he escaped unhurt. Our Regt is badly cut up they numbered only eighty yesterday. Co. D. only five besides Lieut. Peck. Col. Arrived yesterday morning and had command of the Brigade. Col. Fowler is killed Maj Brady is wounded and Capt Burr in command of the Regt. I lost everything I had but my canteen and a little water. Even lost my cup. I got this sheet of paper of Stiles Wells. It was in a small portfolio in his breast and a ball passed through the whole fifty thickness but did not hurt him it probably saved his life. He was afterwards wounded in the leg. Sylvester is hurt in the shoulder not seriously. There are twelve of us from Co. D here together wounded they say this morning that the Rebs are getting off as fast as possible and I guess they are pretty badly whipped. The 11th Corps did not run much this time as their cas.(casualties) plainly shows. I cannot tell you where to direct to me now for I don't know where we shall be taken. I will write again as soon as I am established in a hospital. Don't worry about me I am feeling as well as circumstances can permit. So with much love and many good wishes for your welfare I remain your son in good spirits. Henry P.S. Tell them I was hit face toward them no reb saw my back. Henry[118]

Private Stephen Crofut, Company D, killed July 1 on Barlow's Knoll. (Shelton Historical Society)

Blakeman spent the next eleven months in different Union hospitals before returning to his regiment at St. Augustine, Florida, in 1864. Sylvester Rounds who was wounded in the shoulder, next to Blakeman on Barlow's Knoll, would eventually be transferred to the Veteran Reserve Corps. Stephen Crofut's body was never found. He was probably interred as one of the unknowns in the Soldiers' National Cemetery. Stiles Wells, who was saved from a chest wound by the thick wad of writing paper in his pocket, one sheet of which Henry Blakeman used to write his letter to his mother, was listed on the Spangler Farm hospital rolls as, "*Wells, Charles, S., Pvt., 17th CT, D, flesh wound lower 3rd right thigh, water dressing.*"[119] Wells was discharged for disability on November 28, 1864.

SERGEANT SAMUEL COMSTOCK AND PRIVATE JUSTUS SILLIMAN

Sergeant Sam Comstock, Company H, was wounded on Barlow's Knoll and lay on the field until July 2. He was taken to the Alms House where a Confederate surgeon operated and extracted the bullet.[120] On July 4, Comstock and Private Justus Silliman were transferred to the Eleventh Corps hospital at the Spangler Farm. Silliman had been very worried about Comstock. Like so many other ambulatory wounded, once at Spangler, Silliman began searching for friends and others from his regiment. Silliman found Comstock in deplorable condition. He would do everything he could for his friend and other wounded men. Silliman remained at Spangler with Comstock until they were both transferred to the Letterman General Hospital on the York Pike later in July.

> *Tuesday, July 7th*
>
> *My Dear Mother*
>
> *I am sitting beside Sam, within our own lines in the 11th Corps hospital situated about two miles east of town, our wounded are very numerous and occupy a barn and farmhouse and several acres of ground. Our forces entered the town at daylight on the morning of the fourth, the rebels having left in great haste the night previous after having ransacked all the stores and many private residences. I saw Capt Kellog(g) early in the morning. I do not think the rebels can count us as prisoners as we were not to my knowledge paroled and were recaptured . . . It has rained here every day for a week and makes it distressing for many of the wounded who have lain on the wet ground without any shelter. I searched for Sam as soon as I arrived here. It was raining quite hard and I finally found him laying out in the storm in a puddle of water. I procured a stretcher, and with the assistance of others finally got him in comparatively comfortable quarters where he still remains. He lay on the field of battle all night and part of the next day, when he was taken to the poor house where he remained until the fourth, when he was recaptured and sent to this place. The bullet entered his hip just below the backbone and was cut out at the side of his leg, the bone is some splintered but it is believed not broken. He is rather weak but has a good appetite and is in good spirits, his wound is doing well and pains him scarcely any, and although it will be a long time before he is able to walk I have but little doubt that he will in the end come out all right.*

Silliman assisted other wounded men from the 17th Connecticut who were at this hospital and described the death of Confederate general Lewis Armistead.

> *The rebel Gen Armstead who was wounded and a prisoner was taken to this hospital and has since died. He was rather past middle aged, he is from Va and one of the reb wounded says he was one of the best disciplinarians in their army. He was wounded in the breast and leg.*[121]

By this time Private Silliman's head wound was healing well. He remained at Spangler and took on nursing duties for men who were more grievously wounded. He described many of the patients he attended to and remained especially devoted to his friend Sam Comstock. In this letter to his mother, Silliman described conditions at the Spangler farm hospital and some of the men he cared for.

> *Field Hospital 11th Corps*
> *Gettysburg, Pa. July 15th/63 Wed.*
>
> *My dear Mother*
>
> *We yet remain at this hospital though more than a thousand have been sent to Baltimore and other cities. I could have gone soon after the fight but have stayed here to take care of Sam and suppose have lost what little chance I had of furlough. Sam is doing well though is quite weak and tired of lying so long in one position. He is in comfortable quarters and has good attention, though thousands of our wounded died solely for want of timely care they are now enjoying a great many luxuries. The Christian commission are doing good work.*
>
> *In our tent there is a man of Co. C of our regt Joseph Lockwood [sic, Whitlock] from Ridgefield. He has his right arm amputated, but it was so long a time neglected that I think he will die in consequence. His father arrived this morning he is doing his best to save him but I think is shortening his life by too much excitement and worrying.*
>
> *Ten o'clock P.M. Have been very busy this afternoon attending to the wounded. One poor fellow who occupied this tent has left this world of suffering and gone to Jesus in whom he trusted. He was a fine intelligent man, was superintendent of the sabbath school in the town at which he enlisted, his name is John Edmonds, Co H 1st Ohio light artillery. He leaves a mother and sisters to whom he a short time previous had dictated a letter. He had his leg amputated twice. Joseph Edmonds [sic, Whitlock] is apparently dying his father is a pious man and seems resigned. He has another son here who received a flesh wound in his leg. J.W.'s arm was amputated seven days after it was shattered and the mortification in consequence is now killing him. There is a German here from Tiffan [Tiffin] Ohio, shot through the lungs the same bullet passing through his legs. He cannot recover as he breathes partially through his wound . . . There were at first three thousand wounded in our hospital hundreds have had limbs amputated. The barn more resembled a butcher shop than any other institution. One citizen on going near it fainted away and had to be carried off.*

> *I left off to write a letter for Mr. Whitlock to his wife, his son died a few minutes after I had finished writing.*
>
> *The groans of the wounded are sounding through the camp night and day. I will not shock you with the details of the terrible sufferings of these martyrs for their country. Neither will I write of the scene I witnessed in passing over the battlefield.*[122]

The man who died was Private Joseph Whitlock of Company C. Silliman refers to him alternately as Joseph Edmonds or JW. The Spangler Farm hospital register lists him as, "*Whitlock, Joseph S. Pvt., 17th CT, C, bone fracture lower right arm, died July 16, bones extracted & hand amputated.*"[123] Joseph's brother, Private Nephi Whitlock, was also at the Spangler Farm, listed as "*Whitlock, Nephi, Pvt., 17th CT, C, flesh wound upper 3rd left leg, water dressing.*"[124] The Whitlocks' father came from Connecticut to the Spangler Farm to care for his sons. He did not bring Joseph's body with him when he returned to Connecticut. Joseph was first buried at the Spangler Farm and subsequently disinterred and reburied at the Soldiers' National Cemetery. Nephi was transferred to into the 159th Company Veteran Reserve Corps, 2nd Battalion. He was discharged on July 24, 1865.[125]

After the war, Nephi Whitlock spoke to William Warren about his and his brother's wounding and Joseph's death. A brief handwritten account was in Warren's manuscript:

> *Joseph and Nephi Whitlock, Company C, my copy reads (Warren's notes) James Kyle (Corporal James Kyle, Company C) carried him into a church which was then being used for a hospital. Joseph Whitlock, his brother, was wounded in the shoulder, it got flyblown and maggots got into it and it mortified. His father came after him.*[126]

PRIVATE WILLIAM WURTZ, COMPANY D NURSE, DESCRIBES THE MAGGOTS

William Wurtz, who evaded capture July 1 at the Alms House, remained there until the morning of July 4 caring for the wounded. Wurtz continued his nursing duties at the behest of Colonel Noble, who advised him to remain behind when the regiment left Gettysburg and do what he could for the wounded. Wurtz stayed with the wounded at the Spangler Farm for at least a week before leaving to rejoin the regiment. Wurtz gave an undated account to William Warren in which he discusses the maggots that infested almost every wound and every dead body at Gettysburg. Wounded men were often beside themselves because of the wiggling maggots chomping on the dead flesh of their wounds. Men begged the surgeons to do something to eradicate the "worms," which wiggled sickeningly and could actually jump. One wounded Alabama soldier described first the flies and then the maggots that tormented the wounded: "*Great Green flies in swarms of millions gathered in the camp, grown unnaturally large, fattened on human blood . . . fever smitten, pain-racked, there came to us another terror, we were to be devoured wile living by maggots—creeping, crawling in among the nerves and devouring the soldier while yet alive.*"[127]

Turpentine was often used on wounds to remove maggots. Sometimes turpentine was administered when a caregiver took a mouthful and spit it onto the wound. Other substances were also used, such as chloroform, which Wurtz describes. Often there were not enough medical personnel for "maggot patrol," and maggots were just left, as they could not be avoided, much to the dismay and disgust of the wounded. Later in the war it was discovered that maggots only eat the dead and decaying flesh of a wound and, therefore, are beneficial and can be life-saving.[128] Sometimes referred to as "nature's surgeons" modern medicine grows maggots in a sterile environment and they are used today in the treatment of burn victims. In the Warren manuscript, Wurtz referred to himself in the third person when he gave an account of his assignment to use chloroform to eliminate maggots from wounds.

> *"Wurtz had charge of . . . about 18 wounded . . . and 3 of them were rebs and one was a captain from Florida who had a watch, he was afraid our folks would take it from him. About every ½ hour he (Wurtz) had to mark the wounds with chloroform to keep out maggots. Wurtz was there a week and then got through and then he got a pass to find the regiment."*[129]

CORPORAL ALVAH WILCOX, COMPANY D, DIES IN ALONZO SCRANTON'S ARMS

Alonzo Scranton, Alvah Wilcox, and Scranton's brother Leonard enlisted together in Company D in August 1862. Wilcox's brother Charles was married to the Scrantons' sister Emily. The three men were extremely close. Alonzo Scranton was shot in the jaw on July 1 on Barlow's Knoll and sent to the Alms House. Alvah Wilcox was shot in the lungs on July 2 on East Cemetery Hill. On July 3, Dr. Benjamin Howard performed his experimental surgery on Wilcox in the field in an attempt to "hermetically seal" the "sucking wound" in his chest. After the Confederate withdrawal, Scranton and Wilcox were transferred to the Spangler Farm hospital. Alonzo, despite his own wound, nursed Alvah. On July 7, Alvah died in Alonzo's arms. This undated and unattributed account describes Wilcox's wounding and death and gives accounts of two other wounded men at Spangler.

> *Alva(h) Wilcox was wounded July 2, 1863, at Gettysburg by a sharpshooter, while on his way up Cemetery Hill. A ball went through his left arm into his body and passed downward around to the left side. He was taken to the barn where Alonzo Scranton was, and died at 12.30, midnight, and was buried about seven or eight o'clock on the a.m. Alonzo Scranton was doing all he could for him, being straddle of him, and turned him over just before he died. He had a lighted lantern in his hand and that, I believe, was all the light there was. Someone called for this lantern, but Dr. Hubbard told them to let him have it. Wilcox died gradually, or in other words, commenced to die from the time he was wounded-from his feet up. Dr. Hubbard gave Alonzo Scranton a white blanket to wrap around Wilcox after he died and he was buried with it.*[130]

Alonzo Scranton was active in assisting other wounded from his company besides Alvah Wilcox and gave William Warren several accounts of other wounded men.

GEORGE R. HAYES, COMPANY D, WOUNDED

Private George Hayes was with Alonzo Scranton at the Spangler Farm. He was listed as "*Hayes, George R., Pvt, 17th CT, D, fracture left leg and arm, water dressing.*"[131] Scranton gave Warren a description of Hayes's wounds:

> *Geo. R. Hayes received at this fight five or six flesh wounds, in the left leg, arm, shoulder, and other places, and got well from them all, but finally died with Small Pox at Baltimore. He remarked to Scranton that they had not killed him as yet, nor were they going to. He was one of a squad of sick and wounded men that went to Baltimore direct from Gettysburg, while other squads went to Philadelphia.*[132]

George Hayes died at Jarvis Hospital in Baltimore on October 5, 1864. His place of burial is not recorded. An entry for him in Find-A-Grave lists him as "lost at war."[133]

CORPORAL FRED H. CARPENTER, COMPANY D, WOUNDED

Fred Carpenter was another wounded member of Company D who was with Alonzo Scranton at the Spangler Farm and probably witnessed Wilcox's death. Scranton and Carpenter were transported to a hospital in Philadelphia together. Carpenter was listed as "*Carpenter, Frederick H., Cpl., mid 3rd left forearm, water dressing, fracture.*"[134] Carpenter returned to the regiment and was captured at Dunn's Lake, Florida. He was sent to Andersonville and was released on April 11, 1865. He was officially discharged on June 8, 1865. Writing of himself in the third person Carpenter gave William Warren this statement:

> *"Fred H. Carpenter was also wounded in the wrist and was in the barn with Wilcox and Scranton; he went to Philadelphia, in the hospital there, and was treated by Dr. Murray who was a practicing physician there."*[135]

Private Frederick H. Carpenter, Company D, wounded July 1.
(Bridgeport History Center)

THE SANITARY COMMISSION AND THE CHRISTIAN COMMISSION AT THE SPANGLER FARM

Many of the wounded at the Spangler Farm, and elsewhere in Gettysburg, encountered volunteers and nurses from the U.S. Sanitary and U.S. Christian Commissions. Members of both organizations were universally praised by the grateful wounded and fellow caregivers alike. The volunteers of these organizations did everything possible for the material and spiritual comfort and care of the wounded.

General Meade's orders before the battle commanded all supply wagons to halt on the approach to Gettysburg. Only ammunition and ambulances accompanied the army as it marched toward battle.[136] As a result, after the battle every kind of supply was needed but unavailable, including food. Acute hunger among the soldiers and wounded was endemic. Many had nothing to eat for several days. Both during and immediately after the battle surgeons were able to operate at hospitals around the field, as adequate supplies of anesthetics had accompanied the ambulances. Once a patient was out of surgery, however, there were no supplies to feed, clothe, shelter, or nurse them or their wounded comrades. Help was needed on all fronts and the Sanitary and Christian Commissions willingly and ably supplied it.

The United States Sanitary Commission (USSC) and the United States Christian Commission (USCC) were the two great civilian relief organizations of the Civil War. They came to Gettysburg as soon as they could after the battle. They brought with them much-needed supplies for the care and comfort of the wounded and the devastated town. Members of the USSC arrived on July 4 and established a distribution point at White Run School House several miles from Gettysburg. The commission immediately began distributing supplies and food to the hospitals in the area. On July 7 when the railroad reopened, the USSC took over the Fahnestock Store in Gettysburg on Baltimore Street.[137]

The United States Sanitary Commission was established in 1861 at the beginning of the war. Its mission was to supply for the soldiers what the government could not or did not. Women and the relief organizations they comprised all over the North were the commission's driving force, but the organization's official leadership consisted of prominent men. The Sanitary Commission's inspection committees traveled to military encampments to enforce hygiene, sanitation, and diet policies and procedures for the benefit of the soldiers.

The United States Christian Commission was founded in 1861 after the Battle of Bull Run to meet the spiritual and moral needs of soldiers. The USCC grew into a powerful and more practical organization that not only supported and sponsored chaplains, clergy, and religious literature for the armies, but like the USSC, stockpiled material goods for the care and keeping of soldiers and the wounded. At Gettysburg the USCC main storehouse was at the John L. Schick store on Baltimore Street. The Christian Commission was active at the various field, division, and corps hospitals after the battle and at Camp Letterman.[138]

THE SANITARY COMMISSION COLLECTED MAIL FROM THE WOUNDED

At Spangler Farm, before he was evacuated to Philadelphia, Alonzo Scranton was able to send word home of his wounding and Alvah Wilcox's death. William Warren wrote in his manuscript that: "*A MAN FROM THE New Jersey Sanitary Commission came there and gathered from the boys all the letters and mailed them. Scranton wrote one to his wife* [to be] *and one to Wilcox's brother, and both came on to Gettysburg.*"[139]

Alonzo sent letters to Charles Wilcox and Harriet S. Davis, whom he married in 1865. They later traveled to the battlefield to find Alonzo and to attempt to bring Alvah Wilcox's body back to Connecticut, a trip detailed in chapter 12.

A LETTER TO THE FATHER OF A SON WHO DIED AT SPANGLER FARM FROM CHRISTIAN COMMISSION VOLUNTEER PASTOR J. M. HINSON

Daniel Purdy was a twenty-one-year-old unmarried hatter from Danbury. He was shot through the lungs on July 1 on Barlow's Knoll. He was listed on the Spangler hospital register as "*Purdy, Daniel H., Pvt., 17th CT, C, flesh wound left shoulder & lungs, dead, water dressing.*"[140] Daniel would linger, mortally wounded, through the first two weeks of July. Reverend J. M. Hinson, the pastor of the Port Richmond M.E. Church in Philadelphia, was a volunteer at the Spangler Farm. Pastor Hinson ministered to the wounded and to Daniel Purdy and was with him as he died of his wounds. Reverend Hinson wrote of Daniel's death to his father in Danbury. Private Purdy would be buried at the Spangler Farm and was subsequently disinterred and reburied in the Soldiers' National Cemetery.

> *Philadelphia, July 23rd, 1863*
>
> *Mr. Alson Purdy, Dear Sir:—*
>
> *It becomes my painful duty to send you sad tidings. I was a delegate of the U.S. Christian Commission to the battlefield at Gettysburg; among the sufferers, I found your son; he was shot through the lung. His mind was fixed on home and heaven. When I first met with him, I inquired about his home and relatives, he said, "I have a father and mother and two little sisters; how I would love to see them". He asked me to pray with him; I complied. He said, "I feel comfortable in my mind, a good hope. A telegram was sent to you and I asked him in case you did not come, what word he had to leave for you. He said "Tell father his son done his duty as a soldier for his country and his Lord. (Just here I would mention that he prayed with one of his dying companions). Tell mother not to worry and take good care of the children; tell the girls to love and obey their parents, both in sight of God and man".*
>
> *He received as good care as the time and circumstances could afford. While your son has fallen, his messages to you are words of comfort, and you should not mourn as those having no hope. He died July 14th, about four o'clock p.m. at the 11th Corps Field Hospital near Gettysburg.*
>
> *Yours obediently, J.M. Hinson, Pastor of*
> *Port Richmond M.E. Church, Phil.*[141]

Amid so much death and devastation, young Daniel Purdy's death stood out in the memories of many. In 1864 the New York State Relief Agency, whose agents were at the

Eleventh Corps hospital at the Spangler Farm, issued its report on the work the agency had done on behalf of the wounded at Gettysburg. The report poignantly described Daniel Purdy's death with the belief that "death was not dark to him."

> *Another soldier, Daniel H. Purdy of Fairfield County, Conn. At nine o'clock at night he was reported to be dying. By the light of a candle held in a reversed bayonet, some of his fellow-soldiers, and a clergyman and others gathered around his tent where he lay upon a bundle of hay. A prayer was offered up by the clergyman that the way of death might not be dark to him. When the prayer ceased, young Purdy astonished the group around him by quoting text upon text, of the most beautiful of all the promises of the Christian religion; while repeating these, his ear caught the sound of a familiar hymn sung in a neighboring tent and his face became radiant with devotion—death was not dark to him.*[142]

The *Danbury Times* printed a tribute to Private Purdy and other members of Company C who gave their lives at Gettysburg. William Warren copied it into his manuscript:

> *The following letter was copied from "Danbury Times". It records the death of another of Co. "C", C.V., who fell at the battle of Gettysburg, and sealed with his life his devotion to his country. The same volley that sent his captain and others of his company to their long home, also laid him low. Though so young, he had the courage of a man and the heart of a true patriot. Just before passing away to his eternal rest, he raised himself up and cried, "stick by the old flag, boys," and with these words on his lips, he died. Moore, Douchy, Bronson, Barnum, Blackman, Taylor, Benson, Warren, Whitlock, Delavan and Daniel H. Purdy of Co. "C", 17th C.V., are the victims of this cruel war, slain at Gettysburg. But they have not died in vain! The Republic still lives, and their homes and firesides are still safe from the ravages of an unmerciful foe: blessed be their memories.*[143]

PRIVATE JAMES MIDDLEBROOK, COMPANY D, NURSE AT SPANGLER FARM

James Middlebrook was a married farmer from Trumbull. He would serve as a soldier-nurse at the Spangler Farm through July. Before he got to Gettysburg, Middlebrook had been seeking a transfer to the Invalid Corps and made no secret of it. He discussed this with J. Henry Blakeman, who was also seeking transfer to the Invalid Corps for the same reason. Both Middlebrook and Henry Blakeman were impaired by severe hernias.[144] They were very badly "ruptured" in the lingo of the day. Hernia was considered a valid reason for discharge or transfer to lighter duty. Later in the war, after thorough physical exams became the norm at induction, hernia was the number one reason for rejection of prospective recruits.[145]

Middlebrook fought with the regiment on the first day on Barlow's Knoll and escaped unscathed. In a July 9 letter to his wife, on U.S. Christian Commission letterhead, he explained that Major Brady excused him after the first day's battle to take on nursing duties. Perhaps his condition was the reason.

> *Gettysburg, Pa. in the 11th Corps Hospital*
> *July 9, 1863*
>
> *Dear Wife,*
>
> *I almost blame myself for not writing to you sooner, but the fact is I have not had time to do it until now, I came here July 2 by permission of our major because I did not think it prudent for me to stay with the Regt as I am. I went into the fight on the first day and this makes 2nd time I have lost all my things. Thank God I am safe. When I came here I thought to do something for the soldiers & am now doing all I can for them. Dressing wounds, giving them water & waiting on them to make them as comfortable as we can. Our hospital is a large barn & is full. Some 200 on our first floor where I am & under the barn as many more and lots of them in tents around outside. There are some men in the barn with arms and legs off & it is enough to make ones head bleed to witness the amputations.*
>
> *I feel it is my duty to do all I can for them. I cannot see them suffer shall stay as long as I can stand it. Now members of the Christian Commission are here from Philadelphia & Baltimore & citizens from other places doing all they can to comfort. Not withstanding may God bless them. You know nothing of the Horrors of War & cannot without you go to see for yourself— we went into the fight the first of July & our brave Lieut Col fell & quite a number of our Co were wounded & some killed. The morning after the fight there were only 10 men of the Co there, we went to the front under a perfect shower of shot and shell and when we got there they poured it into us being the Color Company & the wonder is we did not all fall—*
>
> *There are a number of ladies here every day & one who belongs to some Regt who wears the soldiers uniform throughout, one Lady was here with the American Costume on yesterday. One in our company died in the barn the other day. Corporal Wilcox a fine man was shot in the arm & breast. The Ball remaining in his stomach. I*

James Middlebrook, Company D, photographed in his lieutenant's uniform in 1865.
(Courtesy of the William H. Warren Family)

have not had a blanket to sleep under of my own since the Battle. I found one on the way here from the Battlefield but gave it to a wounded man to cover him—have not had a change of clothes since—must go somewhere and get some soon. The folks at home don't know how much they might do for the soldiers & never know it—will write you again soon. Is growing dark & I must close—Good Bye.

Write Soon
Ever your affectionate
Husband Jas Middlebrook[146]

One of the most fascinating elements of Middlebrook's letter is his reference to a lady "*who belongs to some Regt who wears the soldiers uniform throughout,*" and "*one Lady was here with the American Costume on yesterday.*" Who were these women? A lady in a soldier's uniform—who could this be? A lady wearing the "*American Costume*" was a term for dress reform, or a woman wearing bloomers or pants. Who could this be?

Marie Tepe, one woman who wore the uniform of her regiment, was in Gettysburg on July 9 when Middlebrook wrote this letter. Tepe, or "French Mary," was the vivandière of the 114th Pennsylvania Zouaves and served during the battle; she then remained behind to nurse casualties. Marie wore a Zouave uniform with a shortened skirt and pants underneath. Awarded the Kearny Cross for bravery at Fredericksburg, Marie advanced into battle at Gettysburg with her regiment and cared for the wounded. After the battle, Marie nursed the wounded at the Jacob Weikert Farm on the Taneytown Road.[147] This was within easy walking distance of the Spangler Farm. Marie was photographed twice while at Gettysburg. The Tyson brothers photographed her in their Gettysburg studio in her uniform shortly after the battle. Between July 9 and 11, 1863, Philadelphia photographer Frederick Gutekunst photographed Marie leaning against a post in a view of East Cemetery Hill.[148] Perhaps on one of the days she was photographed, Marie stopped by the Spangler Farm hospital site.

Dr. Mary Walker as she appeared during the Civil War.
(Library of Congress)

Dr. Mary Walker was presumed by some historians to have been a volunteer doctor at Gettysburg. Dr. Walker was the only woman to be awarded the Medal of Honor. The doctor wore a military frock with a skirt and pants beneath. Liberty Hollinger, a sixteen-year-old who lived on York and Hanover Streets just east of the town square, purportedly remembered Dr. Walker on the street wearing "*a low silk hat with bloomers, and a man's coat and collar.*"[149]

We will never truly know the identities of the two women whom James Middlebrook described in his July 9 letter, but it is fascinating to speculate.

SCENES IN AND AROUND THE ELEVENTH CORPS HOSPITAL

On the morning of July 5, as the survivors of the regiment were awaiting orders to march from Gettysburg in pursuit of Lee's army, William W. Payton, Company A, was assigned to a squad searching out stragglers from the regiment. The detail included a search of the Spangler hospital site. Paynton describes the Spangler Farm hospital and the areas of the battlefield he walked over:

Sergeant George Ruggles, Company K, would be promoted to lieutenant after Gettysburg. (Bridgeport History Center)

> *On the morning of July 5th, I was detailed as one of a scouting party to go in search of stragglers belonging to the regiment, and report with them to the Provost Marshall of the Regt., Lieut. Geo. R. Ruggles of Co. K. There were three of us, in charge of Sergt, Thos. B. Wood all of Co. A. We were directed to take the road leading to the 11th Corps Hospital, some two miles in the rear, and to scour the country on either side, bring with us any soldiers of our Regt. who were found not having been detailed as an attendant at the Hospital. We were to meet at the hospital, which was a large barn. I took to the fields at the right but did not find any soldiers of the 17th Regt. until I reached the hospital. There was a large orchard in the rear of the barn, and under nearly every tree was a shelter tent, or a rude shelter of boards constituting an improvised hospital and occupied by one or more wounded soldiers.*
>
> *While strolling around amongst these, I came upon an old friend that had been one of our "Big-Six" mess at Brooks Station, Va., the winter of '63; he was in attendance upon Corp. W.W. Westlake of Co. A. who had been wounded in both legs, and both had been amputated above the knees. I stopped to speak a few words of cheer and encouragement to Westlake, who was a good, brave boy, having just been promoted and was a popular comrade as well as a good soldier. He died in a few days later during a second amputation. As I turned to leave my old mess-mate wanted me to take him with me; he said he was sick—that he was sick of the situation. He had straggled away, and a surgeon had detailed him to attend Westlake, but he said he was unfitted for the task, and he wanted to return with me to the regiment. He said he had been there two days and nights and had not had a mouthful to eat, he was almost starved. I gave him all the "Tack" I had, which was three, and we started together from the orchard to meet the rest of the detail. Just then I saw another chap, a member of Co. C that I thought might as well go with me, so I approached him and said, "What are you doing here?" he replied that he was detailed by a surgeon as nurse in the hospital. I looked him over and made up my*

mind that he was lying. "Is that so?" says I. "What are you doing with that waist belt and cartridge box on?" He still maintained that he was detailed nurse. Then I asked him where was the hospital badge which all field nurses wear, consisting of a strip of white cotton cloth tied around the arm above the elbow. This was a "stunner" to him, and when I told him of my mission, and unless he could take me to the surgeon that detailed him to verify his statement, he must go with me to the Regt. I brought my musket to a charge and ordered him forward, and he wilted, and I took him to the Regt.

On our way out to the road, I saw a man standing in the doorway of the barn, whom I thought I knew. As I approached him I found that he was a member of Co. F. Wilber F. Morgan, and a townsman of mine. He had been wounded in the arm and suffered amputation above the elbow. He appeared cheerful and seemed to be doing well; soon as possible, he obtained a furlough, and, while at home, his wound broke out bleeding afresh, and he bled to death.

On our way out we passed a corner of the barn, and I noticed two large hogsheads that stood close to the roadside. Curiosity prompted me to look into them; I was horrified to find them filled with human limbs, arms, legs, hands and feet that had been amputated from the bodies of the brave boys in blue, that their lives might possibly be saved. I turned away with a shudder; such is war! We passed through that part of the battlefield on our return, known as Devil's Den, where some of the hardest fighting took place. There were several places between the jagged rocks where some Union soldiers lay dead. His comrades not yet having opportunity to bury him. In a sort of glen, we found a group of soldiers cooking coffee; I asked them if they could spare a cup to my companion, which they did, also some hard tack.

We then moved on toward the front. I reported my two men to the Lieut., upon arriving, and they, with other stragglers, were placed in a company by themselves at the rear of the Regt. Just as a joke, more to impress on the mind of one of these men the danger of straggling I reported him to the Lieut. as a deserter. The Lieut. took the joke and scratching his name on a memoranda it was allowed to stand that way until just before leaving Gettysburg that evening; he came to me and begged for me to go to the Lieut. and tell him that he was no deserter and ask to take his name off his book as such. I thought he had suffered enough, so I went to Ruggles and told him that joke had worked a cure, and he crossed off the word "deserter", and my old mess-mate was happier. He earnestly protested that he would never leave his company again, but in less than three days he was missing, and we did not see him again for months. Poor fellow! I pitied him. He ought to have staid at home with the women folks and helped make bandages for the soldiers at the front.[150]

JOHN BENEDICT AND JOHN MCHUGH: WOUNDED FRIENDS HOSPITALIZED TOGETHER

Corporal John H. Benedict was wounded July 1 on Barlow's Knoll. He was laid under a shed at the Alms House until July 5 when he was transported to the Eleventh Corps hospital at the Spangler Farm in an ambulance with his friend Private John McHugh, who had been shot in both legs on July 1. Both men were from Danbury and served in Company C. They would be hospitalized at Spangler together. *"John Benedict gave me this as coming from John McCue, while they were in the hospital together—both being in the same tent while at Gettysburg,"* Warren wrote in his manuscript. *"The two Johns were in the hospital together for twenty days* [at the Spangler farm], *being cared for all the time by the Sanitary Commission citizens, and citizens' doctors, as well as army doctors; they worked night and day and did all they could for the wounded."*[151]

Private John McHugh (or McCue) was born in 1835 and emigrated from Ireland sometime in the late 1850s. He was working as a hatter in Danbury when he enlisted in Company C, 17th Connecticut in 1862. He was shot in both legs on July 1 on Barlow's Knoll. He was listed on the Spangler hospital rolls as *"McHugh, John, Pvt, 17th CT, E(sic), flesh wound left knee & upper 3rd right leg, water dressing."*[152] McHugh was lucky to keep both legs and survive. After multiple hospitalizations he was sent back to the regiment, promoted to corporal in March 1865, and mustered out with the regiment in July 1865 at Hilton Head.

McHugh married twice and had nine children. Despite finishing out his enlistment with the regiment, he remained handicapped for life due to his wounds. When he was admitted to the Soldiers' Home in Togus, Maine, at age sixty, his admittance record states *G.S.W.B. Legs*, (gunshot wound both legs) as the explanation instead the usual degree of disability. He was receiving $12 a month as a pension and in 1895, later raised to $14. He died August 14, 1907, *"found drowned in creek south of home (the Soldiers' Home)."* The ledger of the Soldiers' Home states *"Body taken to Boston by Son, 15.8.07."* McHugh is buried in Mount Benedict Cemetery in West Roxbury, Massachusetts, with some of his children listed on the stone including an infant and a toddler.[153]

McHugh and Benedict were transported together to the United States Hospital at York, Pennsylvania. After some months, McHugh was transferred to Knight Hospital in New Haven, Connecticut. Benedict, who had been listed on the Spangler hospital rolls as *"Benedict, John H., Cpl., 17th CT, C, left arm & lower 3rd right thigh, arm splinted,"* remained hospitalized in York, where he faced a long, difficult recovery.[154] In January 1864, after months of pain, Benedict was finally deemed well enough for a two-week furlough. On February 5, Benedict was readmitted to the hospital, this time as a member of the 108th Company Veteran Reserve Corps, 2nd Battalion. John Benedict remained in the 108th until the end of the war and served as the clerk at the York hospital. He was discharged on July 29, 1865.

Benedict gave William Warren an account of visiting the graves of three fallen comrades at the Spangler graveyard before he was evacuated from Gettysburg to York:

> *A day or two before John Benedict left Gettysburg, he walked out to the place where Daniel Purdy, Frank G. Benson and Joseph Whitlock were*

> *buried beside a fence. On the 20th again, the two Johns were taken by rail to the general hospital at York, Penna. While there John Benedict kept improving until the next March, 1864, when he went on duty as clerk in the surgeon's office, which position he held until the close of the war—then the hospital was broken up and John came home.*[155]

The three 17th Connecticut men buried by the fence—Daniel Purdy, Frank G. Benson, and Joseph Whitlock—along with other Union dead buried on the Spangler Farm, were removed in late 1863 or early 1864. They now rest in honor in the Soldiers' National Cemetery.

The graves of Daniel Purdy, Frank G. Benson, and Joseph Whitlock in the Connecticut section of the Soldiers' National Cemetery. (Author Photos)

SURGEON'S CERTIFICATE FOR JOHN H. BENEDICT

When Benedict sent his 1887 letter to Warren, he attached his surgeon's certificate from the attending doctor at the general hospital in York. Warren's transcription of the document follows:

> *U.S.A., General Hospital, York, Pa.*
> *February 4th, 1865*
>
> *John H. Benedict, Corporal Company C, 17th Regiment, C.V., Age 23 years, was wounded in the Battle of Gettysburg, Penna., July 1st, 1863, in the right arm, by a Minnie ball striking and breaking right humerus in middle, passing downwards and breaking the internal condyle; and gunshot flesh wound of right leg striking the popliteal space, passing upward and escaping about the middle of the inside of the thigh. Received while lying faint from loss of blood from wound of arm. Wound of entrance of missile remained open until about the middle of November. The wound of arm healed early, previous to October 6th considerable inflammation was excited about the joint. The patient suffers much pain; sensation in the fourth finger is entirely wanting. Partial ankyloses of the joint exists from bony deposit; extension not being complete and the patient able to flex the forearm only to a point at right angle with humerus. Furloughed January 14, 1864. Readmitted February 5, 1864.*[156]

THE ENDURING IMPORTANCE OF THE GEORGE SPANGLER FARM AND WHAT IT TEACHES US TODAY

The Eleventh Corps hospital at the George Spangler Farm closed on August 7, 1863, five weeks after the battle, when the last wounded were evacuated. Wounded unable to travel were taken to Camp Letterman General Hospital on the York Pike. The six members of the Spangler family emerged from the small upstairs bedroom they had all shared while their farm served as a hospital. The sickening wreckage they faced and had to deal with can only be imagined: The smell and the filth of blood-soaked buildings. The destruction of all their crops and fields. Their farm equipment gone, and outbuildings damaged. The suffocating smells from decayed flesh and human feces that hung in the atmosphere and were inescapable. Their fences gone to firewood. Their property a graveyard. Yet these tough Pennsylvania farmers persevered. They cleaned, repaired, rebuilt, and replanted.[157]

In 2008, the George Spangler Farm and eighty acres surrounding it was purchased by the Gettysburg Foundation. The barn, house, summer kitchen, and several outbuildings were rehabilitated and renovated to their Civil War appearance. The Spangler Farm today represents the best surviving example of a farm used as a field hospital during the Civil War. This historic jewel is a place of reverence. It honors the sacrifices of the wounded and dying, and the brave and compassionate men and women who cared for them. The Spangler Farm teaches us about battlefield medicine, the care and comfort of the wounded, and the lessons of coping with horrific loss as lives are recovered and rebuilt. The Spangler Farm holds a singular place in the history of the Battle of Gettysburg and our American story.

The Spangler barn as it appeared 2008 before its restoration. (Photograph by Author)

CAMP LETTERMAN UNITED STATES GENERAL HOSPITAL

On July 5, the Army of the Potomac departed Gettysburg in pursuit of Lee's army. Anticipating another large battle, Dr. Jonathan Letterman left Gettysburg on July 6 with the bulk of his surgeons and medical personnel. Letterman left behind 106 surgeons to care for over 20,000 wounded Union and Confederate men in and around Gettysburg. These wounded were scattered in sixty to one hundred different hospital sites. It soon became impossible to adequately supply so many dispersed field hospitals, and conditions deteriorated. As soon as the wrecked railroad bridges became functional, wounded by the thousands were evacuated to major hospitals all over the East Coast. By July 25, 16,125 wounded had been evacuated from Gettysburg.

The General Hospital at Camp Letterman opened on July 20 on the Wolf Farm on the York Pike. The hospital was positioned on a hill with consistent breezes, a good water supply, and access to the railroad. Those wounded who were unable to travel, approximately 4,200, were transferred to Camp Letterman. These men came to Letterman to recuperate or die. Letterman Hospital closed on November 20, the day after the dedication of the National Cemetery and Lincoln's Gettysburg Address.[158]

Men from the 17th came to Letterman as patients and nurses. Sergeant Sam Comstock died there. His devoted friend Justus Silliman came here to nurse him. Levi Dixon, wounded on Barlow's Knoll, his right leg amputated in the field by a Confederate surgeon, underwent two painful surgeries on his stump at Letterman. Dixon lived to return home to Connecticut after stays in several hospitals.[159] James Newton, Company E, wounded July 1 when a bullet fractured his left foot, was at Letterman. He too would be lucky enough to receive a discharge and return home after a long convalescence in other hospitals.[160] John Seerey, Company K, who enlisted at sixteen, was shot in the left

Hospital tents at Camp Letterman Hospital. (New York Public Library Digital Collections)

leg on July 1. His leg was shattered, and he would lose it to amputation. He would be transferred to Letterman on August 8. After a long recuperation at other hospitals, he would be discharged to return to Connecticut.[161]

Of the men of the 17th Connecticut, Justus Silliman, would leave the most eloquent writing about his experiences at Letterman. His family tried to send him things from home that would bring him comfort during the time he nursed there. His primary concern was the condition of his friend Sam Comstock. Silliman remained hopeful until the end.

> *Letterman Hospital*
> *Gettysburg, September 3/63 Th*
>
> *My Dear Brother*
>
> *. . . You have probably received the letter I wrote after the reception of the box. Sam enjoys the wine very much he has regular rations of whisky prescribed but takes the wine instead which is much pleasanter and more beneficial. I supposes this will shock certain members of the temperance society to hear of it but I hope they may survive the offense. Sam appears to be improving very slowly . . . his leg is still suspended in a sling, and he is obliged to remain in one position, but he is in good spirits tough weak and thin . . .*[162]

> *Letterman Hospital*
> *Gettysburg Sept 25th 1863 Friday 7 PM*
>
> *My Dear Mother*
>
> *. . . Of the ten boys who tented with me at Bridgeport but one remains with the company.*[163]

> *Sept 26th 7 PM*
>
> *I have just returned from visiting Sam he is failing rapidly and is liable to drop away at any moment. He seemed disinclined to talk and wished to sleep I have made arrangements so that I can have him embalmed. The cost of embalming will be $15.00, Box 5.00, Expressage would cost about 24.00 but I went over to see Gen'l Terry today and when I wish it I can obtain from him transportation to my regt. with permission to go to New Canaan which he says will give me about four or five days there. He has no authority to grant furloughs but manage it in that way so to amount to amount to the same thing. He was very kind to arrange it in that way. So if nothing happens to prevent I shall have Sam's body embalmed and will leave with it for home as soon as I can procure sufficient money.*[164]
>
> *Your affectionate son*
> *Justus*

Sergeant Samuel Comstock died at Letterman Hospital on September 27. Justus was able to bring Sam home to New Canaan, where he was buried in in Lakeview Cemetery. He was twenty-one years old. Justus Silliman returned to the regiment at Folly Island, South Carolina, and would muster out with the rest of the 17th Connecticut on July 19, 1865.[165]

CAMP LETTERMAN TODAY

Camp Letterman was a place that caregivers and wounded men alike believed would never be forgotten. It was a place where many gave "the last full measure of devotion." Many patients died there, while countless others fought the fight of their lives. For them, the real battle began at this place after the guns of Gettysburg fell silent. In many ways this eighty-acre tent hospital was remarkable. It was part of Letterman's concept for battlefield wounded. It was once the largest hospital ever built in the United States. It was a storied place, hallowed ground, a place that should have long been honored and remembered. But time has not been kind to this ground. The butcher and meat area of Gettysburg's Giant supermarket is today situated where the operating tents of the hospital once stood.[166] The granite and bronze stone that marks the hospital location on busy Route 30, across from McDonald's, is ignored by cars whizzing by. The land behind the marker is unkept, desolate, treeless, ugly. It was once a trailer park, demolished years ago for a commercial land sale. The development that surrounds the location is less than attractive.

Sadly, preservation efforts have been unsuccessful. Among the complex factors affecting Camp Letterman's priority as a preservation goal is that this ground is not deemed, per se, battlefield land. This important and remarkable piece of hallowed ground continues to languish, and erode, and await the bulldozer. Once lost, history will never reclaim it. This ground, and the Americans who suffered and died here, and those who came to bind the wounds of those brave men here, deserves more. Perhaps someday it may receive justice. Until then we must not forget the men and women who here served and suffered.

The Camp Letterman Hospital Marker on Route 30. The wreath was placed on Remembrance Weekend by the Blue and Gray Hospital Association to honor the memory of the wounded and the medical personnel of Camp Letterman. (Photograph by author)

CHAPTER 12

Aftermath—The Survivors and the Honored Dead

The aftermath of the battle saw the exodus of the armies but brought a new invasion to Gettysburg. Hundreds, perhaps thousands, of people arrived at the devastated town of 2,400 inhabitants, which was overwhelmed with dead and wounded. The wounded outnumbered the townspeople almost ten to one. Citizens who had fled the battle were some of the first to arrive after the armies departed. Food, shelter, water, and material sustenance to support the living were in short supply or nonexistent. Farms, fields, and homes were wrecked. Others who flocked to the battlefield had varied motivations. Relief workers, nurses, the Sanitary Commission and Christian Commission were helpers who came to serve. Anguished family members flooded the town searching for loved ones among the wounded and the dead. The town and battlefield became a bonanza for embalmers and coffin makers, relic hunters, and those who sought to profit from the aftermath of battle. The curious, Gettysburg's first great wave of tourists, arrived to gawk at the gore and destruction. They often sought souvenirs of the great battle to take home.

As the armies marched away, wounded who could be evacuated were sent off by the thousands to hospitals in York, Philadelphia, Baltimore, and other cities. Union men taken prisoner were marched off with their Confederate captors. Confederate prisoners were sent to Northern prison camps unless they were medical personnel. Then they stayed until their services were no longer required and they too were shipped off to prison to await exchange or parole. As soon as groups left, others came to take their places in the harsh and shattered environment.

Those who came were struck first by the overpowering smell: putrid air polluted by dead horses and dead men and the vast amount of human waste and effluvia. Human and horse flesh rotted in the July heat. Torrential summer rains uncovered and exposed

This engraving by sketch artist Francis H. Schell, titled "Citizens Flock to See the Battlefield," appeared in *Frank Leslie's Illustrated Newspaper*. (Library of Congress)

shallow graves. The hospitals were charnel houses of amputated limbs and maggot-infested wounds. Flies, millions of them, blackened the landscape. The thick, sickening atmosphere was inescapable and intensely palpable. As early relief workers approached hospitals, they would have smelled them before they saw them. They were stunned by the sights and sounds. Cornelia Hancock, a twenty-three-year-old Quaker nurse from Salem, New Jersey, would be the first female nurse to enter the Second Corps hospital at the Jacob Schwartz Farm on July 7. She described her approach to the hospital:

> *As we drew near our destination, we began to realize that war has other horrors than the sufferings of the wounded or the desolation of the bereft. A sickening overpowering, awful stench announced the presence of the unburied dead, on which the July sun was mercilessly shining, and at every step the air grew heavier and fouler, until it seemed to possess a palpable horrible density that could be seen and felt and cut with a knife.*[1]

In addition to the inescapable odors and frightening sights, hospitals were loud, unruly, disturbing areas of sensory overload. In their misery and distress the wounded shouted, groaned, cried, and screamed. A Christian Commission delegate reported of the Second Corps hospital at the Jacob Schwartz farm,

> *The men were in terrible condition. They were upon the damp ground, many of them with nothing under them . . . there was an unusually large number of amputations, the stumps lying directly upon the ground. Many of the men, perhaps most of them, were in want of clothing. Suitable food was not to be had. The surgeons were overworked . . . (the) Rebels, most of them severely wounded . . . (were) shrieking and continually crying for assistance . . . Destitute of clothing, many of them naked, lying in the mud . . . cursing, praying, begging their visitors to put an end to their suffering.*[2]

Private Justus Silliman witnessed the disturbing sights and sounds of the Eleventh Corps hospital at the Spangler Farm. "*The groans of the wounded are sounding through the camp night and day,*" Silliman wrote in a letter home. "*I will not shock you with the details of the terrible sufferings of these martyrs for their country. Neither will I write of the scene I witnessed in passing over the battlefield.*"[3] Fannie Buehler, who lived on Baltimore Street and who nursed wounded in her own home, remembered the loud and anguished cries of the wounded coming from the open windows of the courthouse across the street. A band came every afternoon to play patriotic songs to mask the anguished sounds of suffering and soothe the wounded and the neighbors. Buehler remembered that the sights, smells, and sounds coming from the courthouse hospital were "*too horrible to describe.*"[4]

The indescribable scenes on the battlefield that Justus Silliman spared writing home about were often beyond the words of those who witnessed them. For the armies, it was a relief to march away from the battlefield even if it meant another large-scale battle.

Private William Fields, 17th Connecticut, Company F, the future New Haven bank president, remembered the regiment leaving Gettysburg on July 5.

> *Left Gettysburg at night and went over a portion of the field that Pickett had charged over. The night was one long to be remembered of dead horses, wounded, the stench & etc. When Pickett retreated, he left on one field over 1000 of his dead. This field was on the right of Emmitsburg road, leaving Gettysburg.*[5]

Lieutenant Albert Peck, Company D, also wrote of the departure from the field.

> *Sunday, July 5th, 1863: There was no fighting at Gettysburg today, as the Rebel Army had retreated, and our troops occupied the town and we lay quiet most of the day and looked over the battlefield some. We left Gettysburg about 5:30 PM with orders to march to Middletown, Md. But only marched to Rock Creek that night and went into camp there. We were very glad to get away from Gettysburg on account of the awful stench from dead horses and dead men there. It rained quite hard during the night and we lay on the ground with no protection but our blankets.*[6]

Dr. Daniel Brinton recorded the scene in his diary.

> *The afternoon of the 5th I passed in strolling through the town and visited the scene of battle on our right where the 12th Corps had made a most valiant stand. The trees were scored with bullet marks, in some instances whole trunks were torn in two by cannon shot. The dead had just been buried but the ground bore abundant evidence of the desperation with which the fight had been carried on."*[7]

IN PURSUIT OF LEE'S ARMY

The Army of the Potomac arrived at Gettysburg with a battle strength of 94,119. It left Gettysburg in pursuit of the Army of Northern Virginia with about 70,500. Total casualties for the Union army were 23,594 killed, wounded, missing, and captured.[8] The 17th Connecticut had suffered a casualty rate of 51 percent killed, wounded, and captured during the battle. Of the 386 (William Fox lists 369[9]) men who had gone into battle the first day, fewer than 197 of the survivors were able to leave the battlefield in pursuit of the enemy.[10] Some of the survivors remained to care for the wounded. Those that remained in the 17th Connecticut, able to march away, were in very rough shape. The men had stripped off their equipment before going into battle on July 1, and now everything was gone except for what they carried. Many of the men were barefoot, including some officers. All were hungry. The rains had turned the roads into a quagmire. They sloshed through the mud and slept in it. The survivors were grateful to be alive. On July 5, the 17th Connecticut left Gettysburg about 5:30 p.m. in pursuit of the enemy, heading south on the Emmitsburg Road toward the Mason-Dixon Line. As they marched away from Gettysburg, many never forgot the sights they passed on the fields Pickett's division had crossed to attack Cemetery Ridge on the afternoon of July 3.

Edwin Forbes painted this scene of the Union army marching on the road to Emmitsburg in the rain in pursuit of Lee's army. (Library of Congress)

PRIVATE TIMOTHY C. SPENCER, COMPANY K, BAREFOOT

Timothy Spencer was a farmer from Bethel, Connecticut. After the war he gave William Warren this account about his lack of shoes during the battle.

> *He says, "I believe I have walked as many miles barefooted as any other man in the regiment. Soon after the Battle of Gettysburg began, while I was crossing a river, my shoes gave out and I lost them. As I could then procure no others, I went through the entire engagement barefooted, and did not get any shoes until the regiment reached Boonesborough Gap, near Middletown, Maryland some twelve days later."*
>
> *From T. C. Spencer*[11]

Private Timothy Spencer, Company K. (Bridgeport History Center)

LIEUTENANT MILTON H. DANIELS, COMPANY C, BAREFOOT

Lieutenant Milton H. Daniels assumed command of Company C after Captain James E. Moore was killed July 1. As he marched away from Gettysburg, Daniels believed his younger brother William, a sergeant in Company C who was among the missing, to be dead. Unknown to Lieutenant Daniels, William had been captured at Barlow's Knoll. As Lieutenant Daniels and the regiment marched south down the Emmitsburg Road, William was being marched through Fairfield and the Monterey Pass, headed toward the Potomac with other Union prisoners enroute to captivity in Richmond.[12] Daniels wrote to William Warren with his account of leaving Gettysburg in 1884.

Lieutenant Milton Daniels and his brother, William Daniels.
(Bridgeport History Center)

> *On the night of the 5th about dark, we commenced the chase of Lee, and soon got lost in a corn field, where we stayed until morning. It had rained all night. We slept like logs in the fresh plowed ground, and in the morning we looked anything but Holiday Soldiers. Over half of us were barefoot, without knapsacks, coats, hats or capes, but all seemed to feel pretty well, and wondering if the old Wooster Guards would admire us.* [The Wooster Guards were a militia company in Danbury and the first to pledge their service to the state when Lincoln called for 75,000 volunteers after Fort Sumter.[13]] *Now we had to follow the macadamized road which was literally covered with blood from our bare feet. One half of the army was barefoot. I remember one incident in which Albert Peck, Company D, took a hand. We were at Emmitsburg after the battle and were wondering if we could not get shoes of some kind at the stores. We met an old F.F.V.* [F.F.V. was an abbreviation for First Family of Virginia. Daniels uses the term to demonstrate how superior this gentleman reacted toward Yankee soldiers.], *we called him, and he laughed at us for our appearance, and made the remark that he had two pair at home; we offered to buy his. (We had no money.) He would not sell as we were not his sort. We then compelled him to take his off. I put them on but they were so big I could not wear them; I think I gave them to George Dickens.* [Daniels is probably mistaken here. George Dickens remained behind as a nurse to the wounded according to several accounts.] *We, Peck and myself, found some black cotton hose in a store, and each got a pair, and I tell you they helped for some miles wonderfully. In three days we drew shoes, socks and full supplies; one of the boys drew shoes and socks for me; Oh, how good they felt. It seemed as if I could march the earth over.*[14]

PRIVATE WILLIAM W. PAYNTON: INCIDENTS IN PURSUIT

William Wallace Paynton wrote his memoirs and dedicated them to William Warren. His recollections spanned the entire service of the regiment. He recalled several incidents during the pursuit of Lee's army.

> *Rations were issued, ammunition served out, and late in the afternoon of July 5th we started on the march in pursuit of Lee. I will relate one or two instances right here to illustrate the condition of the Potomac Army—as to its fitness to follow Lee's Army to the Potomac River.*
>
> *The 17th Regiment was probably in as good order (and surely no better) as any other for the march. The long tramp we had taken to reach Gettysburg had worn out the shoes that were new, or nearly so, when we started, so most of us were barefooted and footsore. Our clothing was also very much worn, and most of us had left our knapsacks on the battlefield, containing our surplus. Comrade J. B. Hurlbut* [James Hurlbutt, an unmarried bookbinder from Norwalk who enlisted at age eighteen in Company A and mustered out with the regiment in July 1865 at Hilton

Head] *who had become my messmate since the death of Nobles, had in some way, secured a pair of men's fine boots during the last two days that we remained at Gettysburg. He could only wear one of them, however, as his right foot had been injured during the fight and was badly swollen. I was also barefoot, and in the same fix with him, with the difference—my left foot was sore. So he divided the boots with me, he taking the left and I the right, and in this condition we left Gettysburg.*

Another soldier of Co. F, 17th Regiment, had on a pair of pants so badly ripped that they would hardly hold together. On passing through one of the streets of the town, a lady saw his plight and calling him, took him in the house and presented him with a good pair of Union soldier's pants that had belonged to her son who was killed at Antietam. This was but a fair sample of the condition of the greater part of the Army of the Potomac; and yet it was far better than the condition of the rebel army that was hastening as fast as it could to reach the Potomac and cross into Virginia. Why should we not follow them and overtake them if possible, and either destroy them or suffer defeat in the attempt?*

We did not go far the first day, but at eve on the next, the 7th of July we halted at the foot of the South Mountain, near Middletown, Maryland. By this time I was nearly barefoot again. The roads over which we marched had been badly broken up by the heavy ammunition wagons and caissons and the boot that I had on when I started was completely worn out. I was not only barefoot but hungry. We only had one day's rations of hardtack and coffee issued on the 5th and that we consumed, and none had been issued since. We could not forage, and the only food we had was the grains of wheat that we had shucked out with our hands, pulled from the grain fields we passed through. As we came to a halt that night, I threw myself on the ground and declared that I did not care whether I ever got up again or not; I was totally demoralized. Sergt. Waterworth of my company tried to encourage me by offering to share with me the remaining crumbs of hardtack in his haversack, but I refused, as I knew his condition to be not better than my own. To add to the discomfort, the weather was of the drizzly sort and I was wet as well as hungry and tired. While I lay thus on the ground so utterly indifferent as to what became of me, a brass belonging to the 33rd Mass. Regiment struck up that beautiful old Scotch melody, "Coming Through the Rye." The strains of music so revived me that I felt like getting up and dancing a jig; I verily believe that music saved me from mutiny. I have often wondered since where the wind came from to produce the music, if the 33rd Mass. Regiment were as short of rations as the 17th Conn. In a few moments a forward movement was ordered, and I got up and tramped along a mile or so, when we made camp for the night. Rations of raw fresh beef could be had for the going to the foot of the mountain after it, but both Hurlburt and myself were too tired, so we went supperless to bed.[15]

*A search of Gettysburg records, with the assistance of Tim Smith, the Director of Education at the Adams County Historical Society, yielded no identity of a Gettysburg mother who lost a son at Antietam. However, it is entirely probable that a woman gifted the soldier with a pair of Union trousers as described by Paynton in his account.

SERGEANT MAJOR C. FRED BETTS

In 1884, Fred Betts wrote a multiday account about his experiences at Gettysburg to Colonel Henry Allen. Allen sent it to William Warren, who included it in his manuscript. Betts had enlisted from Norwalk in August 1862 when he was fifteen years old as a corporal in Company A of the 17th Connecticut. He turned sixteen a month later and was a sergeant major at Gettysburg. He was promoted to second lieutenant in September 1863 and in March 1864 he was promoted to captain of Company F. Betts was captured on February 5, 1865, at Dunn's Lake, Florida, and sent to Andersonville. He was paroled on April 21, 1865. Betts remained unmarried and was extremely close to his two older sisters in Norwalk. He spent most of his professional life after the war in New York. He died in 1901 at age fifty-four from "paralysis of the brain." He is buried in Norwalk's Union Cemetery.[16]

> *Early in the a.m. we started on our march, stopping quite often for the wagon train and artillery to pass, as the rebel army seems to be rapidly falling back. About two p.m. we stopped until five, for the wagon trains to pass. On our line of march we passed a hotel called "Oak Grove Inn". We then marched up through Blue Ridge; after reaching the top and standing around about for one hour, we about faced and filed right, into an open lot where we encamped for the night it being about ten p.m. Two of us, each one having a rubber blanket, agreed to sleep together for the night; my comrade laid his blanket on the ground, while I spread my blanket over us; this made it very comfortable—the blankets keeping all moisture from the ground, as well as the dew (as the dews were very heavy most every night). In the night I woke up being so cold and damp, and to my surprise, found no blanket over us, someone had stolen it; I never saw it again.*
>
> *Nearby was a hotel used as a summer resort, and back of it was a ten-pin alley. Our officers got their breakfast at the hotel. The weather being rainy and the mud being deep, it was very hard walking, besides we forded several streams. We stopped marching for the day about ten p.m.*"[17]

LIEUTENANT DOTY'S DILEMMA—ILLNESS AND RESIGNATION

During the battle, Lieutenant Charles E. Doty, Company F, was on the staff of brigade commander Adelbert Ames. After the Confederates overran Barlow's position on the knoll, it was Lieutenant Doty that Ames dispatched from the crumbling battle line at the Alms House to recall Brady and companies A, B, F, and K from the Benner Farm across Rock Creek. It was a miracle that Doty was able to deliver the order unscathed and that Brady got his companies across the creek and through the town in a fighting retreat. Doty, like so many of the men of the 17th after the battle, was suffering from illness.

Despite endorsements from both Dr. Hubbard and Dr. McEwen to receive leave for illness, Doty's request was refused. He was the only officer left in Company F. He eventually was forced to resign his commission, which he did so reluctantly, and returned home to recuperate. In September 1864 he returned to the regiment and was commissioned again as a second lieutenant. Doty would muster out with the regiment at Hilton Head on July 19, 1865.

Lieutenant Charles Doty, Company F, as he appeared at enlistment in his sergeant's stripes. Doty was promoted to second lieutenant in March 1863. (Bridgeport History Center)

> *After the battle was over, and when near Williamsport, an order came to clean out the camps of the sick and wounded. The officers that were sick were sent to Washington hospitals. Lieut. Doty was one. Dr. McEwen gave him a certificate and advised him to go, as Capt. Henry Allen and Lieut. Knapp had already gone, which would leave Co. "F" without an officer. One day while Lieut. Doty was visiting Co "F" to see some of the boys, he was told by them that orders had been received to make out the muster and pay-roll, and there was no officer to do it, so Lieut. Doty felt it his duty to stay and help the boys out in their trouble, so as often as he could get away from headquarters, he would help them on the rolls. The rolls were completed while on the march from Williamsport and finished at Warrenton Junction. Soon after, Lieut. Doty was taken down sick again with intermittent fever; he would not go in a hospital, so lay in his tent. He sent for a leave of absence, which was endorsed by Dr. McEwen and Dr. Hubbard, but was refused, as no more officers were allowed to leave. He found he could not get a leave of absence that way. So he sent in his resignation, which Major Brady kept for some time. Finally, after being urged by Lieut. Doty, it was forwarded and accepted and he came home for about six months, and then returned to the service again.*
>
> *(From C. E. Doty, Mar. 12/'86)*[18]

THE PRISONERS

Among the exodus from Gettysburg that began on July 4 were the Union prisoners marched away by the Confederate army. The estimated number of captured Union troops was 2,358; presumed missing were 2,405 men, some of whom were dead and others captured. It is estimated that 3,500 to 4,000 Federal prisoners were sent to Richmond.[19]

Federal prisoners captured on July 1 were marched up the Carlisle Road about five miles from Gettysburg and offered parole. Many men, like those of the 17th Connecticut, refused the offered parole because they believed it was illegal. Those that took the terms of parole were sent up Carlisle Road toward Harrisburg. Federal prisoners who rejected parole were guarded behind Confederate lines in an open field south of the Fairfield

Road along the banks of Willoughby Run. On July 4 General Lee's proposed exchange of prisoners was refused by General Meade. On July 4 the prisoners were gathered into infantry formation under guard by Pickett's Division and began their march toward Richmond through Fairfield, Pennsylvania. As the Confederate army retreated, guard duty would be taken over by General John Imboden's cavalry brigade on July 9.[20]

Federal prisoners were marched through the Monterey Gap to Hagerstown and Williamsport, Maryland. They reached the Potomac River on July 5 and crossed it on old ferries holding 60–200 men each. The column's crossing took twenty-four hours. Prisoners were then marched to Martinsburg, West Virginia, and then to Winchester, Virginia, reaching the latter July 12. Prisoners, many of them barefoot and starving, were force-marched down the Valley Pike, a macadamized road that made for very hard marching. They camped around Mount Jackson on July 15 and marched 22 miles the next day to Harrisonburg. On July 17, after a hellish forced march of another 19 miles, they were bivouacked outside Staunton on the railhead to Richmond. Between July 18 and August 6, it is estimated 3,500 to 4,000 prisoners were shipped in ramshackle rail cars, some of them open, 135 miles to Richmond. Officers were sent to Libby Prison, a converted tobacco warehouse in the city of Richmond, and enlisted men were sent to Belle Isle in the James River to await parole.[21]

Two of the 17th Connecticut officers who were missing, and presumed dead for weeks, were Captain William Hubble, Company D, and Lieutenant David Bartram, Company G. Searchers who came to the battlefield from Connecticut in an attempt to discover their fate returned home without any answers. As friends and relatives hunted for them on the battlefield, both officers were walking south with the rest of the prisoners toward incarceration at Richmond. James Middlebrook wrote home to his wife on July 18, from his post as a nurse at the George Spangler Farm, that "*Mr. Hatch of Bridgeport has been here but did not see him, neither did he take the trouble to enquire about the Co to know who was dead or alive. Came to see about Capt. Wm Hubble supposed to be killed.*" Dr. Hubbard wrote to his wife on July 10, "*Capt. Hubble I fear is killed. He was on Genl. Barlow's staff & I saw the Genl. This morning who is severely wounded and he told me that he (Hubbell) was killed although did not seem to possess any definite information. He may be a prisoner & safe. The rebels captured considerable number of our men.*"

William Hubbell, Company D, was serving on General Barlow's staff when he was captured on July 1. (Author's collection)

An April 11, 1991, article in the *Redding Pilot* reprinted an interview with Nellie Bartram, Lieutenant David Bartram's daughter. Nellie was three when her father went off to the Civil War in 1862. She remembered, "*After the battle of Gettysburg, my mother and my uncle went to Gettysburg to see if they could get any word of him (my father) that was two weeks after the battle.*" The family may have believed David was dead. In the same article, Nellie remembered, "*My uncle was looking for shoes that my father wore. They were specially fixed with iron heels, but they couldn't find them or any trace of my father so they came back home."*[22] Nellie does not state so, but the presumption must be that her uncle, David's brother Walker Bartram, and his sister-in-law, Nellie's mother, presumed David dead. They traveled to the battlefield and searched in unmarked graves, trying to identify David by his unique shoes. Years later on the page of a scrapbook found by family members, Walker Bartram pasted two stamps, one Confederate and one Union. Under the Union stamp was his faded, handwritten explanation: "*This stamp was taken by W. B. Bartram from an envelope containing several dropped by a soldier on the battlefield of Gettysburg which was fought July 1, 2, 3rd of July 1863. Lieut. D. S. Bartram was taken prisoner on the 1st & taken to Richmond where he was kept confined and starved for 20 mos. He was finally released on the 1st March 1865. Eleven months of this time in Libby Prison the other nine months in eight different prisons and pens. At one time in Charleston under guns of Fort Sumpter.*"[23]

Lieutenant David Bartram, Company G, was captured July 1 and reported missing. Bartram was confined in nine different Southern prison camps for twenty months before his parole on March 1, 1865.[24] (Sheila Bartram Hislop)

LIEUTENANT DAVID BARTRAM COMPANY G—HIS PRISON DIARY

A copy of Lieutenant Bartram's prison diary for 1863 was included by Warren in his manuscript. Bartram described his capture and his incarceration in Libby Prison in Richmond. The unfortunate Bartram would spend twenty months in nine different Confederate prisons and would not be paroled until March 1865.[25]

> *David Bartram's Prison Diary from July 1 to August 1, 1863*
>
> *The following diary was kept by him while a prisoner of war in a rebel prison, during the year 1863.*
>
> *July 1st. Was taken prisoner about 4 or 5 p.m. July 1st. The rebs are making out our paroles. 7:30 p.m. there has been hard fighting since 4 p.m. July 3rd. A parole was offered us this a.m. on conditions, but would not accept of it. Fighting commenced about 4 o'clock this a.m. and there has been very hard cannonading most of the day; received rations for the first time. July 4th about 200 officers are prisoners. 5 p.m. we are all nicely started on our march, as we suppose to Richmond. Rained hard all night. July 5th. Saw General Lee; marched until 12 o'clock p.m. July 6th. Oh! What a night. There has been no sleep now for two nights. We are now at Monterey Springs, Maryland, where we are having our paroles made out. July 7th. Passed through Hagerstown at 10:30 a.m., at 1.15 p.m. we*

The infamous Libby Prison, a converted tobacco warehouse in Richmond where imprisoned Union officers were incarcerated. (Library of Congress)

halted. July 8th. We crossed the Potomac and at 1.30 a.m. we first stepped foot on Virginia soil, as prisoners of war. July 9th. Still on the banks of the Potomac and still nothing to eat, until Captain Wm. L. Hubble went and bought something, we had a good dinner. Marched 15 miles and passed through Martinsburg. July 10th. Started on our march at 9 a.m. and marched until about 6 p.m. and then encamped some miles from Winchester. July 11th. We lay still all day; made some bread; this place is called Washington Springs. July 12th. About 9 a.m. found us on the move again. Marched about eight miles, passing through Winchester, and went into camp about one mile south of the village. July 13th. It has rained in torrents most of the day; 7 p.m. and have just halted for the night just outside of Strasburg. July 14th. Passed through Strasburg, Woodstock, and Edinburgh, and halted 9 miles from Mt. Jackson at 7 p.m. Marched 24 miles. July 17th. Started at 7, passed through Mt. Washington and Mt. Gidney. July 19th. Staid last night in Libby Prison. Preaching today; it has been an awfully long day. July 20. Exchanged this a.m. $5.00 U.S. money for $17.00 or 19.00 (cannot make it out) Confederate money. Had religious services and are to have them twice every day. July 21st. Up early and took a bath and washed my shirt, had hard thunder shower this p.m. July 22nd. Richmond papers this morning have news from the New York papers of the 18th. Nothing new. July 23rd. Got dried apples, sugar, coffee and soap today, and so had stewed apples and coffee for supper. July 25th. Nothing new, only we had good soup for supper (coffee, rice and stewed apples) with hot beans which we bought ourselves. July 26th. Had two sermons; commenced to cook today for ourselves. July 28th. Got in a new lot of eatables. July 29th. Am about sick.

August 1st. Have been in prison one month and hope and pray that I will not be here another one.[26]

WILLIAM WARREN, COMPANY C PRISON DIARY

Private William Warren left a rich and detailed account of his capture, forced march, transport, and imprisonment at Belle Isle in Richmond. Just before he was captured on July 1 a bullet cut through Warren's pants below the knee. He was then struck in the right shoulder by a spent bullet or shell fragment that knocked him down. Hurting and convinced he was bleeding, he became quite agitated. He sought shelter in a "barn shed," probably at the Alms House, and was captured as the Confederates overran the field. During his captivity, Warren kept close to other members of Company C. He and most of the men with him from the 17th Connecticut were paroled in August after a difficult five-week imprisonment at Belle Isle. This prison camp was located on a small island across from Richmond in the James River. Warren's diary entries are detailed and compelling. His descriptions of his transport, wartime Richmond, and the prison camp are fascinating. His account is a rich addition to records of the Gettysburg experience.

Private William W. Warren, Company C. (Courtesy of the William H. Warren Family)

Belle Isle was in the middle of the James River across from the Confederate capital of Richmond. It housed enlisted prisoners. This sketch by a prisoner shows the tents of the overcrowded prison camp guarded by Confederate artillery, with Richmond in the distance. (Library of Congress)

<u>*On the Road – Monday July 6, 1863*</u>

Marched again this a.m. and reached the town of Waterloo about noon, where we stopped sometime for troops and wagons to pass and were called up in line to be counted off for rations, then started on our march again, wading brooks, going through mud over shoe, and but very little in the road, but across lots. Our progress was very slow as we were passing through the town of Waynesborough, the town clock struck nine; this was something unusual for us to hear, it immediately reminded us of home. Before we got out of hearing, it struck ten; we were one hour going one mile, marched all night until daylight. There was something very peculiar about this night's march; I have never been able to learn the cause of it. My idea is that our army was following up the rebs very close, closer than they could cross the river to get out of the way. If the prisoners had stopped for the night in camp, I think we would have been captured before a.m. Circumstances and talk make me think that the above is correct. Our march during the night was composed of stops every few moments—to a rod or two and stop, then again, several rods and stop, then again a rod or two, and so it was all night long. We being very tired and sleepy we would drop to sleep while marching, and then one of those awful stops or halts would come, bringing us all together, or in other words, running into the man ahead of you, ca-thump; this, of course, would wake us up, then without losing any time we would drop on the ground, where we stood, in groups, laying close to each other to keep warm—no matter what condition the ground was in—even if mud was over (our) shoes--we would lie, sit or any way to get asleep, all in a heap, until the front commenced to move, then the first one that woke up would punch another one, and he someone else, and so on down the line until we all got started once more, but before we fairly got under good headway, another halt, then follow suit as above described. We drew rations of meat and flour. Weather, a wet and dreary day.

<u>*Near Hagerstown, Thursday, July 7, 1863*</u>

About daylight I woke up, after having two or three hours sleep, and cooked some breakfast. Then we started again on a march, being about one mile from Hagerstown. Quite a place. Yesterday, there was a cavalry fight here. I saw several horses and men lying dead on the ground—the men were stripped of their clothing and left naked. The prisoners that were captured were locked up in the courthouse, all the stores were closed. While marching through the town, ladies stood in the doorways making different remarks, such as, "Where there is Union, there is love!" "Cheer up boys, McClellan is behind", "Three cheers for the Union", and other remarks that I have forgotten. The rebs did not like it, and told them, with an oath, to shut up their heads. Marched within a mile of the Potomac and encamped for the night.

Near the Potomac, Wednesday July 8, 1863

I was obliged to get up before daylight, as I was drowned by the rain. Our officers went to the Potomac to cross, so reported; very soon we started, but marched only a short distance and stopped about half an hour, then about faced and marched back to our old place, where we stayed all day. Reported that some of our officers were drowned. The rope attached to the boat broke; this is why we came back. Other reports are, that the citizens from town sent some rations of bread, and the rebs sold it for 25 cents a loaf, also that our government sent us some rations, but the rebs would not let them come through. Weather: rained all night and most all day; about dark it cleared off.

Near the Potomac, on the Maryland side, Thursday, July 9, 1863

Arose about daylight to get our rations, and cooked them, ready for a move. At 1 p.m. we started, and marched about half a mile, to the banks of the Potomac. We were then divided into the three squads and told to stand by the side of the road, so that horses and wagons could pass. Marched through the town of Williamsport and crossed the Potomac at this place; also crossed over a canal that runs parallel with the Potomac, and by its side. We move down the road to the bank of the river, where we find our pontoons, fastened to a rope, equally divided across the stream each pontoon carrying 45 men as a load. We used the four, going from one to the other, while crossing the swollen, rushing, foaming, river to the opposite side. These pontoons were being used constantly for the transporting of the rebel army and Union prisoners across the Potomac. The rebs had a great deal of trouble with these boats to get them properly rigged so they would work, which took a great deal of time. The rope had to be made very secure, strong and fast—more so than usual, caused by the heavy storm. They also ran a ferry boat across which took about 20 men and three or four teams; this was run by a big wire rope stretched from shore to shore, about an inch or two in diameter and about ten or twelve feet from the water; then two other smaller ropes fastened from the main rope to the boat by pulleys. I crossed about 10 p.m. in one of the pontoons, then lay down by the fire and went to sleep. I sold my fly tent for $2.00, Confederate money. The rebs have no tents only what they get from us.

We were very hungry, so we asked most every reb we saw for something to eat. There was one thing we were anxious about, and also talked about every day, that as long as we were on this side of the Potomac, (Maryland), there was a chance for us to get away, but after we crossed the river, we gave up all hope of escaping, and the remark was made several times in my presence, that all hopes were now gone of trying to get away, for we were in the land of the rebels, as well as in the hands of the rebels, so we were resigned to our fate, and made the best of it. Rations: one days rations of meat and flour. Weather: Pleasant.

On the banks of the Potomac in Virginia, Friday, July 10/'63

We left here late in the a.m. as all the prisoners did not get over until daylight. Marched three miles beyond Martinsburg, were we expected to draw rations.

Camp near Winchester, Saturday July 11th, 1863

Marched out in two ranks expecting to draw rations, but in vain, as they were all drawn before we reached there—we being at the end of the line. There was two hours spent in vain, counting over the bread. It was baked by the citizens of Martinsburg for our special use, but the rebs had the first handling of it, so we had only what they had a mind to give us, which was not much. The loaves differed in size and shape; some being wheat loaves, some shortcake, and some rye biscuit. We were counted off in squads of 100 each, then the squads divided into four companies of 25 men each. The Sergeant that counted us off did not count himself in, so when we drew rations, he took his, and that left one man without any, which according to my luck was me, but I happened to get hold of a small ration of fresh meat. It was fight for dear life, and the one that got the most was the best fellow. I bought a small loaf of bakers' bread for which I paid $2.00; we were in a very bad fix for rations; we have not had a mouthful from the rebs weighed out to us in two days and marched from 15 to 25 miles each day. All I had to eat was to cut some green grass, put it over the fire in a kettle of water, and boil it until it was tender enough to eat without any seasoning whatever, as salt was a very scarce article with us and, I think, the rebs too, but they would once in a great while weigh us out a little. Many and many a time, when they gave us flour, have I mixed it up thin in cold water, (no salt) and spread it on a plate or half canteen, then baked it over a fire until I thought it was done; generally, it would be about half baked, or, in other words, half raw and heavy as lead, but we had to eat it or go hungry. Marched till late at night, camping out on the outskirts of Winchester. Drew rations of bread.

Camp near Winchester, Va., Sunday July 12, 1863

Marched through Winchester this a.m. and encamped about two miles beyond. P.M. Drew two days ration of flour and meat, which we were told must last until we reached Mount Jackson, 42 miles distant, or nearly half-way between Winchester and Stanton. Weather looks like a storm.

Camp near Strasburg, Monday July 13, 1863

We started early this a.m. but no sooner had we got in line and fairly under way, before one of those dubious halts took place, which comes unexpected and leaves the same way. It was nearly two hours before we again started; in the meantime, it began to rain. After leaving Winchester, we reached Middletown in a little while and found the stream beyond the town swelled so high as to prevent fording, consequently we had to go further up the stream to cross, and after a tedious time in water up to our knees part of the way, besides mud over shoe and raining all the time, we succeeded in getting around on the pike again, which is a macadamized road and was in tip top order. Marched until night, then encamped just outside of Strasburg, Evening: a shower but pleasant through the night.

Tuesday July 14th, 1863

Marched within five miles of Mt. Jackson and halted for the night.

Camp near Newmarket, Wednesday, July 15, 1863

Marched within a short distance of the town and halted for rations. P.m. Marched ten miles further and halted for the night, beyond Newmarket. Here Wm. Otis bought a loaf of bread for 50c and two doz. Biscuit, for which he gave $2.00. Drew two day's rations of flour and meat; part of the meat was bacon. Our rations today were a little better than they formerly have been.

Thursday July 16, 1863

Started in good season(?) and marched within 23 miles of Stanton, Va. Just as we turned off the road to go into a lot, where we were going into camp for the night, it commenced to rain, and for an hour it never rained harder in the world, then it slacked up long enough for us to draw rations and eat supper, when it began again and kept it up all night. No sleep tonight for us—the worst and most tedious night I ever witnessed in the army, and well I remember that night as Wm. Otis, Monty. Bailey and myself were chums. We agreed when taken prisoners, that us three would stand by each other, and what one had we all had. After we got into camp, us three gathered what wood we could find, and built a fire, but it rained so hard we hardly kept it burning. Two of us would sit up at a time; one to be company for the other, while the third one lay down to sleep if he could. Our camp was on a side hill, so we laid down on one side, with a canteen under our shoulder, another under our hip and the third under our foot, with a stream of water running under us, and between the canteens. This is the truth and nothing but the truth. This way we slept as long as we could, or until we got so cold that we woke up—not a dry rag on us—then we would get up and go into the fire and one of the others would try it for a while; this is the way we spent the night, wet through, chilled through, tired through and hungry clear through. No one, only those that were there, can possibly realize what a bad night it was. Drew rations of cracker and bacon. Heavy rain all night.

Private William Otis, Company C, was a prisoner with William Warren. Otis was captured on July 1 trying to save Captain Moore's sword. Warren noted on a handwritten page that the *Bridgeport Standard* had published an account of this on July 9, 1863. Warren wrote that this photograph of Otis was taken at the parole camp in Annapolis, Maryland.[27] (Bridgeport History Center)

Friday, July 17, 1863

Thank God daylight has once more come; what a wretched night to have spent—up and down all night. At daylight it began to clear away; I felt sick all the a.m. Went into camp about 5 p.m. within four miles of Stanton. The town of Harrisburg [sic, Harrisonburg], which we passed through, is the finest village I have seen in Virginia, and evinced more evidence of life and Southern Aristocracy; the ladies were good looking and dressed in style. Wm. Otis bought three pounds of cheese, $3.00; pint of peanuts 50c, and two dozen small cakes $2.00. I borrowed a five dollar Confederate note of Corp. Weed, of Co. H. At night we drew rations of hard-tack and bacon.

Camp near Stanton, Saturday July 18, 1863

Marched through Stanton, which we found to be quite a place, and turning to the right, marched about one mile and encamped by the railroad, being searched, our tents and rubber blankets taken from us before entering the lot. There is a splendid spring at the lower end of this lot—clear as crystal and cold as ice! I saw a passenger train for the first time in nine months; we expect to leave here tomorrow. Weather: good and pleasant.

Staunton on the R.R., Sunday July 19th, 1863

At 10 a.m. it was announced that 700 men would be transported to Richmond, and the first that got in line would go first, so of course there was a scattering, running, jamming and a great deal of swearing as the line was being formed. Eight of Co. "C" succeeded in getting in line, and all were marched down to the depot and embarked—part on platform and part on box cars. They were rickety old things; the box car I was in had no roof, only the frame and well do I now remember while sitting on the frame, that it swayed first one side, then the other, that I was frightened *and expected every moment to be cast into the next field by the track. The inside of the car was full to overflowing (same as all the rest). We moved very slow as the cars would not permit of fast travel; the roadbed was also in very poor condition; there was also a halt every little while. The scenery, however, was truly remarkable, especially after passing beyond the Blue Ridge; the road skirted the summit of a high ridge giving a splendid view of the valley beneath the distant mountains. It was very tedious riding, nevertheless, and night brought no relief, as it was so crowded, that sleep of any account was out of the question. So the time wore away while we went jogging on to Richmond. We left Staunton at just eleven a.m., the distance to Richmond being 136 miles. The first station we arrived at was Fishersville, 129 miles to Richmond. The second station was Waynesborough, 124 miles to Richmond; about half-way between Fishersville and Waynesborough, we stopped about half an hour going up grade. Passed through four tunnels between two stations; the first tunnel we were seven minutes passing through, I timed it by my watch, and were running pretty lively too. After we came out, I was standing on the platform and was obliged to look almost straight up to see the top of the mountain. The third station was 115 miles to Richmond; passed a signboard marked "Blair's Park 24 ½ miles". There were two trains on the side-track here—one a passenger train, just arrived, loaded mostly with soldiers. This is the Virginia Central R.R.; the name of the passenger train engine was "Hero"; the name of the other engine was "C.S.C." Name of the fourth station was Iva; fifth station Charlottesville, quite a place; sixth station, Shadwell, here was a brick building and several other wooden buildings, minus the insides. Here we run on the side-track and waited about one hour for another train. Between this station and the next, we stopped to get wood; they burnt chestnut and oak. At five p.m. we were just 90 miles from Richmond. Seventh station, not known; eighth station, Lindsays, did not stop here; ninth station Gordonsville, another road branched off here and went to Culpepper. Several tents and barracks were put up here around and near the depot and filled with wounded. Arrived here about dark and stayed about one hour, for the officers to get their supper, so it was reported, then went on, stopping at the different stations along the road until we arrived at Richmond. I bought two blackberry pies for $1.00, Confederate money, and sold one to R. G. Seymour for $1.00, Confederate money; they were very thin—hardly more than the top and bottom crusts, and hardly berries enough to color the crust; they were poor things but being very hungry I bought the first thing I could get hold of.*

<u>Richmond, Monday July 20th, 1863</u>

We reached Richmond this a.m. at just 3:20 but were not allowed to get out of the cars until about six or seven o'clock, then were marched down to Libby Prison, then about face and went into a building called Castle

Castle Thunder was a converted tobacco warehouse at Cary and 19th Streets in Richmond used as a prison. (Library of Congress)

Thunder. The first floor was packed with tobacco from floor to ceilings, as solid as stone. We stopped in the middle of the street and in front of the building, awaiting orders, and while waiting, men, women and boys came to see us and looked at us as though we were curiosities, and some said they thought the Yankees had horns and they came to see them; they were taught so by their superiors. Some of them had baskets of bread—four small loaves about as large as your fist for $1.00. Just here I remember a circumstance that happened under my observation. Some of the boys were buying some bread of a woman and offered her $1.00 Confederate money, which she refused, stating she wanted greenbacks; she run their money way down below par, and swore about it. This consequently made quite a stir and a rebel officer came to see what was the excitement, and after an explanation he told her she must never refuse their money again; he reprimanded her very strongly with oaths and sent her off.

We were packed into Castle Thunder like sheep in a pen; it was full before we got there, so the reader can imagine how it was after about 3,000 more were in there. Here we stayed about two or three hours; during this time, we were examined, our haversacks and canteens taken from us, then were sent downstairs as we were searched, then came back again, then rations were issued to us. They were a good many rations short, so the boys of the 17th did not get any, nor those that were behind us. I bought $2.00 worth of bread while in the street, and gave a man that I owed, 75C worth of bread, to cancel my indebtedness with him. We stayed here only a short time longer, and was marched out into the street, and through part of the city until we came to the bridge that spans the James River. It is all enclosed like a long box; on the top, the cars run; under it and in the enclosure is a carriageway, and on either side are foot paths. We marched across this bridge, then across another bridge, then turned *to the right and came back a little ways, which brought us on Belle Island, and we were then divided off into squads of 90 men each. Sergt. Daniels had command of the squad I was in. There are large iron works on this island running bull blast, called "Belle Island Iron Works". While we were in Castle Thunder, a prisoner set in the window facing the street, the sash being up. A guard was walking his beat back and forth and the prisoner was talking with his comrades in the room, and while talking, he took from his mouth a chew of tobacco and without thinking and still talking, carelessly threw it out of the window, without looking to see where it was going to strike, but unfortunately it struck the guard on the head, so he, without saying a word, fired at him. The bullet went through his right arm at the elbow; his wound was dressed by some of his comrades; I never saw the man after that. Another circumstance I well remember. While we were being examined on the second floor in Castle Thunder at the head of the stairs, a man just ahead of me said something to the man that was examining him; what it was, I did not hear, although I was watching the whole proceeding. He grabbed the man by the back of the neck and, with a kick, shoved him down the stairs end over end. When it came my turn, I had nothing to say, but was speechless.*

Belle Island, Tuesday July 31st, 1863

Arose from our couch of mother earth at 11 a.m. and drew ratings of fresh meat and soft bread—one loaf of bread for eight men, and seven pounds boiled fresh beef for 90 men. About four p.m. drew another ration of bread and soup—one loaf for eight men and from half to a pint of soup to one man, or six pails full for 90 men, made of red beans and James River Water. The above are one day's rations for each and every day.

JAMES MONTGOMERY BAILEY, COMPANY C: IMPRISONED AND PAROLED

James Montgomery Bailey, Company C, was captured on July 1. He refused the parole offered by the Confederates and found himself marching south to Richmond after the rebel retreat. After he was released and returned to the regiment, Bailey wrote a series of articles under the name "High Private Manton" about his experiences at Gettysburg, his capture, and imprisonment. The articles were published in the *Danbury Times*, the newspaper Bailey purchased and published after the war. Bailey's articles were printed in the *Times* in the fall of 1863 under the title *Under Guard, or the Sunny South in Slices.* This excerpt of "Slice 11" covers Bailey's release from Belle Island and transport back to Northern soil through Petersburg and City Point, and ultimately to Camp Parole at Annapolis, Maryland. Camp Parole was the location released Union prisoners of war were sent to await exchange and return to their regiments. Bailey's experiences speak for many in the regiment who were captured on July 1. In this excerpt Bailey's observations of his imprisonment and Civil War Richmond are vivid. In contrast to William

Warren's prosaic diary, Bailey's jocular and humorous account was clearly written for publication. Readers who wish to explore all High Private Manton's *Slices of the Sunny South* may do so on the 17th Connecticut website at www.17thcvi.org.[28]

Private James Montgomery Bailey, imprisoned with William Warren, penned his army experiences under the name "High Private Manton" for the *Danbury News*. Bailey later bought the paper in 1870. After the war he was a well-known publisher, author, and humorist. (Author's collection)

> *Slice Eleventh (November 26,1863)*
> *Before going further in my narrative, it will be well to give you an insight in minor details of our living on Belle Isle, and I believe I can do it in no better way than by the history of a single day. About sunrise we would awake, stretch ourselves, and sigh a regret that dreams are naught but dreams after all; and taking our cups we would go to the sunken barrel at the end of our street, and have a wash. Returning to our tent, the time till breakfast, between 9 and 10 o'clock, would be spent. In laying around, counting the moments, and wondering when the meal would be ready. About half an hour before time the most anxious of the crowd would man the earthwork on the cook shanty side, and gaze eagerly at the movements of the cooks, envying every mouthful they took, and cordially damning them, sotto voice, for their tardiness. By the time the pails were placed out filled with meat, the crowd would have become quite dense, but this last named movement dispersed them as so many bayonets could not, and each man retired to his own quarters to await his ration. In an instant, all would be life in our tent. Daniels was the third Sergeant to draw and everything required must immediately be got in readiness—the blanket to bring the bread, the dish for the salt, and meat, and men to bring them in. Daniels drew for one hundred men, receiving 12 ½ loaves of bread, weighing 2 lbs each and 17 lbs of meat including bone, which invariably managed to be no small item in the weight. The hundred were divided into six squads, with a man from each to draw their ration from Daniels. When divided up each man would receive four ounces of bread, two of meat, and about twelve grains of salt to season it. The meat would be eaten slowly, every morsel accompanied by a sigh, and when at last it would be finished, we would lay quietly down, with our hunger but half appeased. The interval till supper, between three and four P.M., would be spent in our tent, the sun being altogether too hot to admit of promenading, even if our weakened state would have allowed us. Some of the boys got to making rings of the bones, and in this employment passed the time, but I was never noted for making anything but blunders, thus this interesting occupation*

was denied me. But there was one branch of service in which we could all indulge, stupidity or rank exempting none, and that was the assassination of that disagreeable vermin known as lice. I will not shock the sensibilities or my readers by relating the deeds of violence committed nor by giving the size and voracity of our bodily ailments, but I will simply assert that they were thick and that if they did not carry us off out of sight, it was not on account of any physical disability. Between these foes and thoughts of food we would divide our attentions till the fast increasing crowd at the earthwork reminded us it was near supper time. This meal would pass off like the preceding one. The same ration of bread would be dealt out to us but instead of meat we would get nearly a pint of bean or rice soup, made from the water of the James River plentifully seasoned with gravel and about as weak as Southern reasoning. The boys designated it as condensed James River, and as for the beans and rice they principally existed in the name and imagination. About 6 P.M. the atmosphere would cool off, and then we would come out of our tents like so many juvenile crabs out of their holes, and interchange opinions with one another. I generally turned in about 8 o'clock but would [unreadable line] seldom get to sleep till nearly midnight, and then the day would end.

Wednesday morning, Aug.29th I was taken with chills and fever and concluded I was in for a systematic course of the shakes and I looked forward to about as dreary a future as my particular star ever blessed or cursed me with. But the future is not known to any great extent to any man; and I rejoice to say that in the case mentioned I met with a heavy disappointment. About four o'clock that afternoon the doctor made his appearance in quest of the sick. Three weeks before that time I would have looked upon his visit as a signal for going off, but of late he had made similar calls, sorting out the sick and sending them over to the city to the hospital, so I attached no importance to this. But a few minutes after someone came in the tent and said that the sick were being paroled as fast as they were being taken out. Upon this I went to the entrance to see for myself. The camp was very quiet which confirmed my impression that there was no sign of going off on this move, but yet in plain contradiction to this was the paroling of the sick. What was it for? I asked myself. It had not been done to others sent to the hospital. I enquired of some that were leaving if they believe a squad was going to City Point, but they were as ignorant as myself. I could get no satisfaction from any one and was in doubts as what course to pursue. I wanted to return to our own lines, but I did not want to go to the hospital, for there would be no telling when I would get away. In despair I called Otis and gave him the particulars and we held a council of war. It is needless to give the minutes but suffice to say we hit on the following plan which I concluded would work. I was to put on the excessive drooping style and lean heavily on him while he carefully piloted me out to the paroling tent. After that he could take care of himself, the only thing necessary was to get that little embankment between him and the camp. After that the sailing was remarkably smooth, and we would run the risk for City point.

The plan was acted upon and worked admirably. We succeeded in passing the guards and Doctor's scrutiny all right and in ten minutes were paroled and waiting our turn to cross over to the city. I must apologize for playing the sick one on the Confederates, but the reader will least believe that the end sanctified the means. I own to being of an artless disposition not given to deceiving but will not deny that on that occasion I veered slightly from my usual course.

It is impossible to analyze my emotions as we crossed the river and looked my last on the white tents and familiar surroundings of the Belle Isle camp. A feeling of enthusiastic gratitude was struggling in my heart with dubious doubts as to how the apparent deliverance would end. I could not bring myself to believe that I was really going home and I dared not indulge in hopes for fear of their being blasted. As soon as we struck the other shore a woman came up to us with bread to sell. She gave four small loaves for a dollar and would take nothing but greenbacks in payment. A friend of mine managed to get four of the loaves, although he had no money, which he kindly shared with us. Probably Otis can explain the bit of financiering. From the place of landing we were marched to the Palmer Prison on Cary Street and left in the upper story for the night, first giving us a ration of bread. This move precluded all idea of a hospital, but yet I did not feel like hoping too strongly. There was a large number of prisoners on Belle Isle, and we might have been removed to make room. Ah, how obstinate is the human mind when it takes the notion. It looks upon every blessing in the light of a nightmare and being well acquainted with fickleness of the beast, exhibits no haste to mount it. So much for humanity, especially the feminine portion of it, bless their dear souls.

It was uncomfortably warm in that loft and for some time I could not get to sleep and when I did it was a poor affair and did not amount to much. At 2 o'clock A.M. we were aroused and taken out into the street, receiving a ration of bread as we passed out. From there we were marched to the depot of Richmond and Petersburg Rail Road, and loaded. At 3 ½ o'clock we started, crossed the river, and Richmond and its agony were out of sight. At dawn we passed a number of earth works but they were empty and had evidently been so for some time. The riding was tedious in point of time, but the prospect ahead was glorious enough, that is at times, for I must confess that had not as yet lost all dread of the result. "Oh dear," thought I. "If I were only at City Point," but I wasn't at City Point so I continued to dangle my legs over the car-side, and stare at the sunny scenery.

At 9 o'clock or so we reached Petersburg, twenty-two miles from Richmond. After a delay of an hour or so, we shipped aboard the branch road for the Point. The cars on this route deserve special notice. Although the most of them were originally designed for freight, yet adverse circumstances have conspired to render them open. The Yankees that rode in these were compelled to straddle the splinters in order to keep off the track. A passenger car was attached to the end of the train filled with citizens, mostly ladies, bound for the North.

At 11 o'clock we rounded the bend at the Point, and the next moment were in front of the New York, flying the stars and stripes. I have said that we were paroled as sick; well, God knows we were sick but no outsider would have believed the fact had he been in sound of the cheer that went up from those weak stomachs at the sight of the old Flag. Of course I cheered with the rest and in attempting to thank God I wondered whether any difficulty would be experienced in exchanging then I sat down and waited till the rolls were examined gazing anxiously at the boat and inwardly estimating the quantity of grub she contained. At last all was arranged and we were marched on board, each boat shoved off amid many "thank Gods" and tears of gratitude. I stood at the rail and gazed at the fast receding place till it disappeared from view and then I felt safe and free—yes free! How blessed that simple word seemed to me as I kept repeating it to myself, with my eyes bent down on the water, and my thoughts lifted up to God.

And now, reader, my prison experience is over and we must part, but before closing I beg leave to thank you for your company, which you have so kindly given me on the painful road I have guided you over; and in the end I offer a prayer that you may never be placed UNDER Guard, nor see, as I did, Sunny South in Slices.

Many of the Union enlisted men captured at Gettysburg and sent to prison in Richmond were released on parole after about five weeks at Belle Isle. They were sent to Camp Parole to await exchange and return to their regiments. (Library of Congress)

CORPORAL HORACE Q. JUDD, COMPANY G: A PRISONER LEFT BEHIND

Horace Q. Judd was a twenty-one-year-old divinity student when he enlisted as a corporal in Company G, 17th Connecticut. He married Ellen E. Crofut on August 31, 1862, at the home of T. Frank Brinsmade, known as Blythe Hall, located on the green in Washington, Connecticut. The service was performed by visiting clergyman Henry Ward Beecher.[29] Horace's mother was a Stowe so he and the famous man were probably related. The next day, Horace left his bride to join his regiment in Bridgeport. On September 3, 1862, the 17th Connecticut broke camp and left by train for the front. It would be three long and difficult years before Horace and Ellen saw each other again. At Gettysburg, Corporal Judd was captured on July 1. He was extremely ill during the ensuing forced march to the Potomac. After he was transported across the river with other prisoners, the Confederates pronounced him unfit for travel, diagnosed typhoid fever, and sent him back across the river. Judd was taken to a hospital in Hagerstown, Maryland, by Union troops. His recovery would be a long one. On July 4, 1864, he was transferred to the 159th Company Veterans Reserve Corps, 2nd Battalion and honorably discharged on August 12, 1865. After the war, Horace and Ellen began a family together and he began his life's work as a prominent and respected Methodist minister. He served in parishes throughout Connecticut and New York. On March 22, 1920, he died at age seventy-nine.[30] He is buried in Center Cemetery of his hometown, Bethel, Connecticut.[31] Judd's story follows in two retellings. William Warren's account from his manuscript appears first. Following Warren's description is the account Reverend Judd wrote to Warren in an 1888 letter giving the details of his imprisonment and illness in his own words.

> *While the regiment was on the retreat the first day, he (Corporal Judd Company G) was captured. About five or six of the boys went off to the right, where they found a battery, and remained with it too long, were also captured. There had been a squad of rebels gone in between the battery and the town, and so captured battery and all. But, the battery, seeing they were captured, limbered up and started off on a dead run and got away, while the rest were taken prisoners. He went with us prisoners as far as Williamsport, where we all crossed the river. He had been complaining for days about being unwell, so after he had crossed the river, the rebel surgeons examined him and pronounced him unfit to march, and said, "This man has got the typhoid fever, send him back over the river into Williamsport."*

Reverend Horace Q. Judd after the Civil War. Judd was captured at Gettysburg on July 1, 1863. (Gunn Historical Museum)

He came back over the river again, and the rebs left him to take care of himself the best he could.[32]

LETTER FROM REV. HORACE Q. JUDD

Following is about one-half of a letter that Judd had printed in a newspaper while he was preaching in Woodbury, Connecticut.

It was my misfortune to be included as a prisoner of war. Our regiment had been ordered to throw our knapsacks and haversacks in a pile in a field before going into battle, and hence when taken prisoners we had no blankets and no rations. The next morning we were turned into a field without shade or shelter and kept in the broiling July sun for three days, and our rations consisted of a pint of wheat flour to be stirred up in water and baked as best we could without salt, and once in two days a small piece of poor beef without salt. In our march from that field for Richmond, we passed through the camp of the rear guard of the Confederate Army and their wagons were full of supplies of all kinds—the products of foraging among the rich towns and farms of Pennsylvania, but no portion of it came to the prisoners. Thousands of blankets must have been gathered up by the Southern men on the field of Gettysburg, but not one ever covered a Union soldier again,—and as night came on we lay down on the march, exposed to rain and sun by day and dew or rain by night. Many were taken sick, myself among the number. My sickness proved to be typhoid fever and resulted in my being left at Williamsport on the Potomac. After the Confederate Army evacuated the place I fell into the hands of our own army and was placed in a field hospital at Hagerstown, Md. In a few weeks we were transferred to a United States General Hospital at Chester, Penna. Here were several hundred Confederate prisoners, sick, wounded and convalescent, and all of them being cared for as tenderly as though they were Union solders. Indeed, they ate from the same table—fared the same in all respects as Union soldiers—and even received the tender care of our Christian Commission, being supplied with articles of underwear, stockings and shoes included of which many were destitute when they came there. They went out of that hospital reluctantly, many of them declaring to me that they would rather stay there than go back to the South. In all my intercourse with the Southern soldiers they admitted the universal kindness of the Northern people toward them, and many were glad as they told me, to fall into our hands as prisoners of the war. Thousands upon thousands gave themselves up to our army, knowing that they would be treated humanely, and were glad to become captives for the sake of the rest and abundant food they were sure to receive at the North.

> *All honor to the brave men who fought for the Lost Cause. Many of them did not deserve the hardships which they endured, and my sympathy always flows out to the rank and file of the Confederate Army, I have, however, no sympathy for some of the leaders in that vain and wicked attempt to subvert the best Government the sun ever shone upon.*
>
> *Yours truly, H.Q. Judd*
> *Woodbury, Conn, February 20, 1888*[33]

TRANSPORTING THE WOUNDED

When the Army of the Potomac left Gettysburg to pursue the retreating Confederate army, Dr. Jonathan Letterman ordered 106 surgeons to remain behind with the wounded. Each corps was required to leave behind six ambulances and four wagons to assist in transporting over twenty thousand wounded dispersed in more than one hundred hospital locations to the railroad depot.[34] Wounded men able to be transported by rail began leaving Gettysburg on July 7. Railcars designated for transporting the wounded from Gettysburg were stocked with hay for relatively short trips to hospitals in Harrisburg or York. Water coolers, tin cups, bedpans, and urinals were stocked for longer trips to New York and Maryland. Before the wounded left Gettysburg, the United States Sanitary Commission fed them and gave them water.[35] By July 22 rail transport had evacuated over sixteen thousand wounded men from Gettysburg. The remaining wounded, unfit for travel, numbered more than forty-two hundred. These wounded were transported from hospitals dispersed throughout Gettysburg and the surrounding area to Camp Letterman General Hospital on the York Pike.[36]

Transporting as many wounded as possible out of Gettysburg was an immediate priority. The horrific conditions in Gettysburg after the battle can neither be adequately described or conveyed to twenty-first century Americans. In the nineteenth-century world, there was no indoor plumbing, central heating, or refrigeration. Most Americans had to grow and slaughter their own food. Bathing was only an occasional activity and washing clothing was a monumental, labor-intensive task. The magnitude of the environmental disaster after the battle sickened people who were otherwise quite used to foul odors, the blood and offal of slaughtered animals, and the sights, sounds, and smells of the times. To these hardy citizens there were no words to describe the horror of the battlefield. There is no accounting of the number of civilians who perished after the battle due to foul and poisoned water supplies or contagious disease. They were many. One of the most disgusting aftereffects of the mass casualties of both human and horse flesh were the flies, millions upon millions, that blackened bodies and surfaces and spread disease. Within ten minutes of a man being killed the flies would lay their eggs and the maggots would hatch, part of the natural cycle of the decomposition process. In a world without refrigeration, maggots were a common occurrence on food, meat, and even hardtack. All manner of bugs were common in homes as well as hospitals. Maggots, flies, mosquitoes, fleas, and lice were common to nineteenth century living, especially among the armies and the hospitals.

Maggots were especially loathed by the wounded men, all of whom suffered from these disgusting "worms" invading their wounds. An understanding of the beneficial effects of maggots as "nature's surgeons" did not occur until later in the war. Maggots devoured the dead and gangrenous flesh of wounds and left the healthy behind. Still, even after this was discovered, the wounded were horrified and tormented by the "worms" that crawled through and feasted on their damaged bodies. Doctors and caregivers tried their best to eradicate the creatures, a seemingly hopeless task, with chloroform and turpentine and other topical solutions applied directly onto the wounds. One surgeon noted, "*In 12 hours the wound is literally covered with maggots and in 24 hours the stump looks as though a swarm of bees had settled into it.*" Another wrote, "*The maggot does damage in the wound, not by attacking living tissue, but by the annoyance created by the continued sensation of crawling.*" Often wounds were infested even before they could be dressed. A patient account from Gettysburg recalled, "*My wounds were in a frightful condition. They had not been dressed, and the maggots were crawling into them.*"[37]

PRIVATE J. HENRY BLAKEMAN, COMPANY D, TRANSPORTED TO JARVIS HOSPITAL, BALTIMORE

J. Henry Blakeman, Company D, was transported out of Gettysburg from the Spangler Farm to Jarvis Hospital in Baltimore, Maryland. Henry had been shot in the left side on Barlow's Knoll on the first day. In mid-July Henry wrote home about the maggots in his wound. Perhaps these "surgeons of nature" saved his life. He spent the next eleven months recovering in different Union hospitals on the East Coast. Henry was lucky. He finally returned to the regiment at St. Augustine, Florida, in the summer of 1864.

Private J. Henry Blakeman was transferred to Jarvis Hospital in Baltimore. He would spend eleven months in various hospitals before returning to the regiment in St. Augustine, Florida. (Bridgeport History Center)

Jarvis U.S. General Hospital, Baltimore Md,
July 17, 1863

Dear Sister,

. . . last Monday we were brought here. Before we came here we saw pretty hard times, lying on the ground with only a shelter tent for five days. I was wet through and had not half enough to eat. I wore the same shirt that I was wounded in all bloody for nine days and half that time it was full of maggots and wore the same pants till I got here...

The Rebs flanked me but I guess I shall be good for another dig at them yet.

Henry[38]

PRIVATE FRANCIS H. FERRY, COMPANY C, TRANSPORTED TO PHILADELPHIA

Another 17th Connecticut man who was evacuated out of Gettysburg was Private Francis H. Ferry, Company C. Ferry was an unmarried tinsmith from Bethel. He was shot on July 1 on Barlow's Knoll. He was listed on the Spangler Farm hospital rolls as "*Ferry, Francis H., Pvt., 17th CT, C, fracture right forearm, ball extracted.*"[39] On July 9, Ferry would be sent by train to the U.S. General Hospital in Philadelphia. After a long recovery in August 1864 Ferry was transferred to 159th Company, 2nd Battalion, Veterans Reserve Corps.[40]

Private Francis H. Ferry, Company C. William Warren noted this photograph was taken in Philadelphia while Ferry was recovering from his wound. (Bridgeport History Center)

WOUNDED JOHN BOUGHTON AND HENRY SMITH RETURN TO CONNECTICUT

Apparently not all the wounded waited to be transported out of Gettysburg. John Boughton (spelled Bouton on some records) was listed as a patient at the Spangler Farm along with Private William Henry Smith, Company C, an eighteen-year-old hatter from Bethel. Boughton had been shot in the upper left forearm and the ball was extracted. Smith had been wounded in the right shoulder. When the wounded were being evacuated from Gettysburg to other hospitals, John wanted to go back home to Connecticut. Smith joined him. In 1892 Boughton gave Warren an account of their leaving Gettysburg. It's difficult to estimate the timing of the trip as both men were listed as being patients at the South Street Hospital in Philadelphia by July 8.[41] However, there is no reason to doubt that sometime after the battle they got home to Connecticut and returned. After recuperating from their wounds at various hospitals, both John Boughton and William Smith returned to duty and mustered out with the regiment at Hilton Head on July 19, 1865.

John Boughton, Company C. (Bridgeport History Center)

> *John said to Henry Smith (Co C) "I AM GOING HOME." Smith quickly responded, "I am with you." Then John went in search of the doctor's office and got a pass for two days. They looked over their money and they only*

> *had $8.00 between them. The doctor told them to get the medical director to sign the pass and then the guards would pass them out without trouble.*

The medical director mentioned may have been Dr. Hubbard, the medical inspector for the Eleventh Corps, who was working out of Dr. O'Neal's office on Baltimore Street as well as at the Spangler Farm where the two men were patients.

> *They took the Camden & Amboy Railroad. Their money carried them as far as New York and they landed at Castle Garden and from there they walked to the 27th Street depot. On the way there they were met by one of the Sanitary Commission who asked them several questions where they came from and where they were going, then they took them into a restaurant and gave them their breakfast then they were escorted to depart and their tickets bought and seen onto the train for home. At Norwalk they took the 11 a.m. freight train for Danbury. Mr. Parsons, conductor, called for tickets and as they had none he asked where they came from and where they were going. He passed them.*[42]

THE BUSINESS OF DEATH AT GETTYSBURG

Prior to the battle Gettysburg, the county seat, had been a prosperous and progressive town. After the battle the town was wrecked physically and economically, and families did whatever they could to survive. Families opened their homes first in compassion to the wounded, and then to the families and visitors searching for loved ones. The incoming hordes needed places to stay and there was not enough hotel space to accommodate them, so they turned to private homes. These travelers needed meals and other necessities. They needed transportation to the hospitals and laborers to disinter and transport their dead. Carriage makers and carpentry shops began churning out coffins, of which there was an enormous shortage. Undertakers and embalmers, at great profit to themselves, flocked to the town to accommodate families who wanted to ship home their beloved dead. Family and farm carriages and wagons were turned into hired transport for the living and the dead. Townspeople provided guide services to family members seeking the likely places where their loved ones were hospitalized or buried. Service industries that surrounded the recovery of the dead blossomed in Gettysburg and its surrounding areas.[43]

Engraving by Alfred Waud for *Harpers Weekly* titled "The Lost Found." (Author's collection)

JUSTUS SILLIMAN, COMPANY H, WRITES HOME OF SERGEANT SAM COMSTOCK'S DEATH

Private Justus Silliman, slightly wounded, remained behind to nurse his friend Sam Comstock, who was slowly dying at Camp Letterman. Silliman wrote his brother and mother from Camp Letterman with updates on his and Sam's condition. Just a few days before Sam died, Silliman was making arrangement to contract the services of an embalmer, purchase a coffin, and bring Sam home to New Canaan for burial.

US General Hospital
Gettysburg August 2nd 1863

My Dear Brother

. . . Since the Battle, Gettysburg has been an extensive coffin mart and & embalmers harvest the field. The coffins were stacked on the streets blockading the sidewalks. These coffin speculators made an enormous profit but their harvest is now over, as the commander of this post has issued orders prohibiting the disinterring any bodies during the months of August and Sept as it endangered the health of the residents . . .

Your affectionate brother
Justus[44]

September 26 6 PM

I have just returned from visiting Sam he is failing rapidly and is liable to drop away at any moment, he seemed disinclined to talk and wished to sleep. I have made arrangements so that I can have him embalmed. The cost of embalming will be $15.00, box $5.00, Expressage would cost about $24 but I went over to see Gen'l Terry today and when I wish it I can obtain from him transportation to my regt. with permission to go to New Canaan which he says he will give me about four or five days there. He has no authority to grant furloughs but manage it in a way so as to amount to the same thing. He was very kind to arrange it in that way. So if nothing happens to prevent I shall have Sam's body embalmed and will leave with it for home as soon as I can procure sufficient money...*

Your affectionate son
Justus[45]

*Silliman may have been referring to General O. S. Ferry. Ferry was from Bethel, Connecticut, and in 1861 left the House of Representatives to become colonel of the 5th Connecticut. By 1863 Ferry was a general. He was well known to Fairfield County men and families. After the war, Ferry was a U.S. Senator. General Ferry is mentioned several times in Warren's manuscript as helping wounded 17th Connecticut men after the battle. Alonzo Scranton, Company C, wounded on the first day, stated: "*General Ferry, who is a Connecticut man, had all the eastern men transferred to the New Haven Hospital and gave Scranton the transfer paper to take with him.*"

THE EMBALMERS

More than seven hundred Union bodies were transported from Gettysburg from the end of the battle to early 1864, along with perhaps a dozen or two dozen Confederates. At least six "embalming surgeons" set up businesses in or near Gettysburg after the battle. Often these embalmers were medical doctors or even army surgeons who used embalming as a side business to supplement their income. In the aftermath of the battle their services were in high demand.[46]

Embalming was not unknown before the Civil War. As far back as ancient Egypt human cultures had sought to preserve the dead. The Civil War regularized embalming in America. During the war it became a necessity to embalm corpses before transporting them home to families by freight. Corpses not embalmed, or those poorly prepared, were a transportation nightmare on trains. Charles Wilcox, in searching for the body of his brother, 17th Connecticut corporal Alvah Wilcox, would experience travel on a train forced to halt to unload rotting bodies as effluvia leaked from their coffins. Only embalmed bodies were allowed to be shipped, and devastated families who wanted their dead to come home gladly paid for these services. Besides allowing remains to be transported by rail, embalming also allowed loved ones to see for themselves the remains of their beloved dead. Obviously, no one wanted the wrong cadaver. However, mercenary embalmers were known to embalm even poorly decayed remains for shipping to grieving families.[47]

In the 1860s embalming used fluid of zinc chloride and arsenic to preserve a body. Blood was not drained, and embalming fluid was hand-pumped into the corpse. The body was cleaned, dressed, and placed in a coffin. For transport the coffin was lined with zinc or copper. Sometimes coffins with ice compartments were also used, with the ice being replaced during shipment. Often the embalming procedure did not reach all parts and extremities of the body and coffins had to be equipped to contain leakage and odor. During the war a newer procedure evolved in which "fluid with pounded glass and chemicals was injected into the blood vessels, and the body was bled at the neck. This made the body hard and stony but preserved its appearance, sometime for years."[48]

After the battle there were embalmers who pitched tents in and around Gettysburg and practiced a brisk and profitable business. Dr. Bunnell would embalm Rufus Warren, Company C, who was wounded on July 1 and died at the Spangler Farm hospital. (National Museum of Civil War Medicine)

The cost of embalming at Gettysburg varied, usually $15–25 for an enlisted man and $50 for an officer. In order to get a body home there were a host of other necessary costs. If family members traveled to the battlefield, they needed round-trip train tickets, meals, and lodging. There were often costs for locating the body, disinterment, transportation to the embalmer, the coffin, a new uniform, and express fees for the train. Once the body arrived at its hometown, there were funeral expenses for the church service, the services at the cemetery (including the digging of the grave), the cost of a marker, and the cost of boarding and feeding guests. Sometimes even the church bell ringer at the funeral needed to be paid. As embalming became prevalent in America the embalmer became an undertaker who made all the arrangements comprising these fees and expenses.[49]

THE SEARCH FOR THE WOUNDED AND DEAD

Newspapers all over the North printed calls for help for the wounded. The *Norwalk Gazette* published an article on July 21, 1863, titled "Duty to Our Wounded." It called for donations from Norwalk citizens to the Christian Commission. The article did not neglect the Confederate wounded prisoners in Union hands.

> *Thousands of our brave soldiers are lying today before the eyes of their countrymen, wounded, torn and maimed in the recent carnage of Gettysburg. Other thousands are prostrate under the power of disease wasting away, parched by fevers and thirst. They are husbands and fathers, brothers and sons . . . They have enlisted, fought, bled and suffered for our common Country, Government, Law and Union—How much do we owe them? There are thousands of our captive enemies who have been cast upon our mercy, sick and wounded, far from their homes and friends. When they were in arms against the country that had nurtured them, and the Constitution to which they had sworn allegiance, it was our painful duty to smite them in support of Order and Government, God's ordinances. But now that they are cast down, helpless and suffering, Christian charity says "Love your enemies, bless them that curse you." Love may disarm them and turn their hatred to penitence, and their curses to blessings. How can we render succor and sympathy to our friends, and relief to our enemies? There are various agencies which we may employ: but the most favorable present opportunity is afforded by the Christian Commission.*[50]

Friends and family members of the 17th Connecticut, if they had the means and stamina, came to Gettysburg in search of their wounded and dead. Sometimes they were successful and returned to Connecticut to prepare for a funeral and bury their loved one close to home. Some who made it to Gettysburg returned to Connecticut in grief after seeing their loved one die. Yet those families at least had the consolation of knowing with certainty what had happened to their loved ones; others searched in vain and returned to Connecticut without knowing the fate of their soldier.

Joseph and Nephi Whitlock's father came from Ridgefield to the Spangler Farm to tend both his sons who were wounded on July 1. Joseph, who suffered an amputation, died, and was buried at the Spangler Farm. He was later disinterred to the national cemetery. Nephi survived but spent months in hospitals before being transferred to the Veteran Reserve Corps. Their grieving father returned to Connecticut without either of his boys, but he knew for certain what had happened to both.

Searching for the wounded and dead was a grim duty and could be undertaken only by the strong and those with financial means. It was a point of honor to reclaim the cherished dead and bring them home for a decent burial among family and friends. William Warren included several accounts from family members of their trips to recover loved ones. The local Connecticut newspapers printed stories of these seekers and their grueling errand.

Many of the men of the 17th Connecticut who fell on the first day would never be identified or recovered. We presume that they lie buried in unmarked graves in Gettysburg National Cemetery. The condition of the dead on the first day's field was frightful. When Samuel Weaver, the superintendent of exhumation charged with moving the Union dead to the national cemetery, wrote his final report on March 9, 1864, he noted the insurmountable difficulties in identifying many of the dead and mentioned specifically those on the first day's field.

> *Before we commenced our work, the battlefield had been overrun by thousands of sorrowing friends in search of lost ones, and many of the graves opened and but partially or carelessly closed. Many of the undertakers who were removing bodies, also performed their work in the most careless manner, invariably leaving the graves open, and often leaving particles of the bones and hair lying scattered around. These things are frequently to be seen on every part of the battlefield . . .*
>
> *The bodies were found in various stages of decomposition. On the battlefield of the first day, the rebels obtained possession before our men were buried, and left most of them unburied from Wednesday until Monday following, when our men buried them. After this length of time, they could not be identified. The consequence was that but few on the battlefield of July 1 were marked. They were generally covered with a small portion of earth dug up from along side of the body. This left them much exposed to the heat, air, and rains, and they decomposed rapidly, so that when these bodies were taken up, there was nothing remaining but the dry skeleton. Where bodies were in heavy clay soil, or in marshy places, they were in a good state of preservation. Where they were in sandy, porous soil, they were entirely decomposed. Frequently our men were buried in trenches—the numbers in a trench amounted to sixty or seventy bodies.*[51]

For friends and family members of who came to Gettysburg seeking the wounded and dead, determining reliable information was a source of great anxiety. Casualty lists were often extremely inaccurate. Family members frantically scanned these notices in newspapers, the local telegraph, or post office for mention of loved ones They could bring relief or terror to the families back home, but there was no guarantee all was well if a loved one's name did not appear on a casualty list. Sometimes, names appeared when men had been hurt, but the wound was not even enough for them to leave the ranks, causing families great distress until they could get more solid, reassuring information. The casualty lists misspelled names, and first names were often wrong or missing, a distressing problem when many last names in the regiment were the same or similar. 17th Connecticut Captain Henry Allen, wounded on July 2, had his name misprinted in his own brother-in-law's newspaper, the *Norwalk Gazette*, as Harvey Allen.[52] Thc July 7 casualty list appearing in the *Gazette* was almost certainly compiled by Homer Byington, Captain Allen's brother-in-law, who was at Gettysburg and was the publisher of the paper. Byington was also a war correspondent for the *New York Tribune*. He sent the first casualty list to the *Tribune* on Monday, July 6; the Gazette printed that list July 7 and stated that the list was copied from the *Tribune*. Many of the casualties listed did not even show first names. Some had first initials. Captain Hubbell, taken prisoner, was listed as "*probably killed, evidence strong*."[53]

The search for the missing and the dead would go on for months, with company officers trying to account for their men and substantiate their fate for families. If there were no eyewitness accounts to a man's death or capture, in some cases there could be no certainty of their fate, and these men would be presumed killed. This was especially true of the dead on the first day's field, where unburied bodies lay for days in the hot July sun before being hurriedly and inadequately buried. Many would never be identified. Some families were luckier than others. Captain Wilson French, Company G, would turn up on his wife's doorstep on Old Mill Hill in Bridgeport on the night of July 8, still muddy and bloody from the battlefield, before Martha French had an inkling he had been wounded. As a wounded officer who was ambulatory, French was sent from Gettysburg on one of the first trains north. Years later, French gave William Warren some particulars about his condition upon returning home. In a handwritten, undated notation Warren wrote: "*Wilson French on the way to Gettysburg and while there did not have his boots off for 14 days, and then not until he got home on July 8 by being wounded. His boots and stockings had to be cut off and then the skin and the toenails came off with the rest*."[54]

Captain Henry Allen, Company F, wounded July 2 on East Cemetery Hill. (Dale Call Collection)

Connecticut papers printed the first casualty lists on July 6 and 7. Many lists were copied from paper to paper, compounding misspelled names, missing names, typeset errors, or mistaken conclusions about the living, the wounded, and the dead. Newspapers, with all their inadequacies, were the way nineteenth-century Americans got their news. For better or worse, they were crucial to learning the fate of loved ones.

A. Homer Byington, the publisher of the *Norwalk Gazette* who reported from Gettysburg for the *New York Tribune*, had a special relationship with the 17th Connecticut, not only because it was the local Fairfield County Regiment, but also because he was married to Captain Henry Allen's half-sister. The story of how Byington earned the Gettysburg reporting scoop by telegraph is cloaked in mystery and myth and has been greatly romanticized. We do know that before the battle Byington and other war correspondents were aware that Lee had crossed the Potomac and that a pitched battle was inevitable. However, they did not have enough information to follow the armies. On June 30 Byington was in Lancaster, waiting for the next day's Philadelphia newspapers to decide where to go next. On July 1 he was at Hanover after the cavalry battle there. The telegraph had been cut by Confederates and somehow it was repaired, either by Byington's contrivance or by the army, and Byington had sole access to it for a brief time. He was at Gettysburg on the night of July 2 and witnessed part of the battle for East Cemetery Hill in which the 17th Connecticut played a role. On the evening of July 3 Byington certainly sent a telegraph message with news of the battle to the *New York Tribune*. It was intercepted by the War Department. Lincoln was at the telegraph office as the message came in from Hanover. "*Who is Byington*?" the president had telegraphed back to Hanover. "*Ask the Secretary of the Navy*" was the response. This telegram caused Gideon Welles, Connecticut politician and U.S. Secretary of the Navy, to be awakened at midnight. Welles knew Homer Byington well as a Connecticut Republican and could vouch for him. The dispatch was meager with information. Amid the confusion and the conflicting intelligence reports being received, Lincoln, though hopeful of Union victory, was at first skeptical of the good news. Byington's telegraph beat Meade's official report to Washington by about six hours. Despite his "scoop," Byington did not have contacts at headquarters, and as a single reporter subject to the "fog of war" he did not have the bigger picture. Byington's information was limited, as was the initial casualty list he submitted.[55]

By July 4, more accurate battle information arrived, and by July 5 and 6 all the major newspapers were reporting a Union victory and sorting out the many rumors. It would seem that with Byington on hand the 17th Connecticut should have had an edge in more accurate casualty reports back to Fairfield County, but this did not prove so. Byington's *Norwalk Gazette* was subject to the vagaries of communication and chaos that affected every phase of battle reporting. Despite Byington's access to the Hanover telegraph, the best information family members received, and much of the accurate information about casualties published in the local newspapers, was from the men themselves, who wrote home to family and friends who then often submitted their letters to be printed in the newspapers.[56]

THE DEATH AND BURIAL OF SERGEANT EDWIN PICKETT, COMPANY G

Sergeant Edwin D. Pickett, of Ridgefield, was a married twenty-eight-year-old clerk with a two-year-old-son. He was mortally wounded on July 1, shot down carrying the regimental colors. Pickett's brother traveled to Gettysburg and brought him home to be buried in Ridgefield. Fellow Ridgefield resident Corporal Aaron Lee, Company G, had been shot in the leg; he witnessed Pickett's death at the Alms House.[57]

Pickett's body was buried near the Alms House, probably by Confederates in control of the first day's field, or perhaps by Union burial parties after the Confederate withdrawal on July 4. Apparently, Sergeant Pickett's body was not easy to find. News of Pickett's death reached Ridgefield on July 6. Anna Ressenguie, the daughter of the owner of the Keeler Tavern in Ridgefield, wrote of Edwin's death and funeral in her diary on July 12: "*The funeral of Eddie Pickett whose remains were brought home yesterday, is attended at our church this afternoon. A long procession of pedestrians, as well as carriages, followed his remains to the grave. His brother Starr searched some time among the dead at Gettysburg before he was found. His blanket was wrapped about him, his watch and pencil given by Starr were in his coat sleeve.*"[58] On July 16, 1863, an account of Pickett's funeral and eulogy appeared in the local papers and William Warren transcribed it into his manuscript.[59] Pickett is buried in Ridgefield's Hurlbutt Cemetery. The carving at the top of his stone is a hand bearing a flag; the inscription, obscured by dirt and wear, states, "*A Christian Patriot is sleeping here.*"[60]

CORPORAL AUGUSTUS BRONSON, COMPANY C, RETURNS HOME

Augustus Ezra Bronson was born in Danbury on December 27, 1835. In the spring of 1861, the schoolteacher enlisted in Company I, 3rd Connecticut Infantry. His captain was James Moore, also of Danbury. Bronson was captured at First Bull Run. He was sent to Richmond's Belle Isle and transferred to other Southern prisons, including one in New Orleans, before he was paroled in June 1862. After his release that summer, he enlisted in the 17th Connecticut, Company C, as a sergeant under Moore, his former captain. His older brother, Orrin Bronson, and his brother-in-law, Lewis Bradley, who was married to their sister Sarah, also joined Company C of the 17th Connecticut as privates.

On Wednesday, July 1, August Bronson was shot in the head on Barlow's Knoll. Both Orrin Bronson and Lewis Bradley were captured. Augustus died Sunday, July 5. He may have died at the Alms House hospital, which was the closest location to his wounding. His widowed brother-in-law Truman Judd, who was married to Bronson's sister Betsey, who

Brothers-in-law as well as brothers in arms: Lewis Bradley (left) and Sergeant Augustus E. Bronson, Company C. Lewis was married to Augustus's sister Sarah. Sergeant Bronson's older brother, Private Orrin Bronson, also served in Company C. (Bridgeport History Center)

had died the year before, came to Pennsylvania to bring Augustus back home to Connecticut. Bronson is buried in Upper Starrs Plain Cemetery near his father's home in Danbury. The funeral eulogy to Bronson was published in the *Danbury Times* and William Warren later transcribed it into his manuscript.

> *But he is gone; his body reposes among his native hills. The spot where it lies is sacred and will ever be held in grateful remembrance by his appreciative countrymen. He lived a patriot and died a patriot; his bereaved friends have the sympathy of all true loyalists. In his death his country loses a brave and valiant soldier, but*
>
> *How then can man die better, than facing fearful odds, for the ashes of his fathers and the temples of his gods?*

The last quote is from Thomas Babington Macaulay's poem about Horatius, the brave Roman soldier who defended a bridge over the Tiber River against the invading Etruscans to save Rome. His heroic stand allowed the Roman army to escape safely across the river and destroy the bridge to prevent invaders from crossing. The Civil War generation knew this story well and was steeped in the classical literature of heroism and sacrifice. It believed that there was no higher honor than to sacrifice one's life for a sacred cause, to die a hero's death, a good death. This belief, and such words, did much to comfort families. The idea of heroic sacrifice rationalized the mass casualties that were suffered during the Civil War as being justified for a higher, holy cause, for God and country. The classical Latin words so often spoken and inscribed on the tombs of the honored dead, "*Dulce et decorum est pro patria mori,*" translate as "*It is sweet and fitting to die for one's country.*" The full quote from Macaulay's poem exemplifies this belief:

> *Then out spake brave Horatius,*
> *The Captain of the Gate:*
> *To every man upon this earth*
> *Death cometh soon or late.*
> *And how can man die better*
> *Than facing fearful odds,*
> *For the ashes of his fathers,*
> *And the temples of his gods*[61]

CAPTAIN MOORE'S BROTHER BRINGS HIS BODY HOME

Captain James Moore of Company C was beloved by the regiment. In 1884, the 17th Connecticut monument on Barlow's Knoll was sited to mark the place where his men believed he was killed. Moore was forty-two at the time of his death. He had fought in the Mexican War, where he served as a flagbearer. In 1861 he was commissioned a captain in Company I, 3rd Connecticut, a three-month regiment. He led his company at First Bull Run. In the summer of 1862 when the 17th Connecticut was forming, Moore again was commissioned a captain in Company C. Danbury men from the old 3rd joined him; Milton Daniels and Henry Quien were among the company officers. Moore was a respected man with military experience and the citizens of Danbury had confidence that their sons would be in good hands under his leadership. William Warren left a handwritten character sketch of him in his manuscript:

Captain James Moore, Company C. (Captain Wilson French Collection)

> *James E. Moore: Tall, slim, 6 ft. or more, good disciplinarian, but at the same time he had a winning way about him that the company all liked, so much so, that we all called him the father of the company, and he would often call some of the boys to him and give them good fatherly advice. Full of grit and not afraid of anyone, especially when he thought he was in the right. A very conscientious Episcopalian Christian. He lived and talked his religion in the army. Exemplary man.*[62]

Several men in Company C remembered that Moore had a premonition of his death in the upcoming battle. Lieutenant Daniels, who was close to Moore and had served with him in both the 3rd Connecticut and the 17th, remembered Moore's demeanor on the evening of June 30, and how he thought would die on July 1. Daniels remembered:

> *I thought daylight and a dash of cold water would bring him out all right, but not so, he tottered to the head of the company, and marched in silence, until way ahead we saw the puff of a shell, then the report, "Now we are in for it." Soon we heard the noise of battle, and the aide hurries from the front with orders to hurry up. Soon we reached the top of a hill and looking across the valley, we saw the battle of the rebels and Reynold's corps. When we first saw them our boys were running a duplicate of Bull Run, but they realized and forced the rebs back, and it was pro and con until we were out of sight and in line of battle ourselves; we were in place rest. Captain Moore dropped on the ground, but in a few moments the rebels were giving us their salutations, he sprang to his feet, but was instantly shot by two balls in the forehead.*[63]

Possibly the last 17th Connecticut man to see Captain Moore was Lieutenant David Bartram. Bartram described how he was taken prisoner at the Alms House and marched back across the same path used in the regiment's retreat. He recognized the bodies of both Moore and Lieutenant Colonel Douglas Fowler and stopped and put their names on both. Moore was hastily buried on the field. Captain Moore's brother came to Gettysburg and was able to identify him and bring his body back to Danbury, perhaps because Bartram had tagged the body. Unfortunately, Fowler's body would never be found.[64]

On July, 12, the *Danbury Times* reported that Captain Moore's body was brought home to Danbury for his funeral service. His brother, J. E. Moore, had traveled to Gettysburg and retrieved the body from a marked grave on the battlefield. The *Times* published a detailed article on Moore's funeral. He is buried in Wooster Cemetery in Danbury.

> *The body of our late Captain James E. Moore, who was killed at Gettysburg while gallantly leading us to the front arrived here on Saturday a.m., accompanied by his brother, Mr. J.C. Moore, and was taken in charge by a committee of arrangements previously appointed. The box containing the remains was enveloped in the National Flag, and immediately removed to the late residence of the Capt., on Elm Street., where it lay until about three p.m. Sunday when two Masonic Lodges of Bethel and Danbury, the Jackson Cadets, and a company of returned Volunteers under the command of Capt. John W. Bussing, with draped colors and muffled drums, escorted them to the First Congregational Church, where the funeral services were to be held. The remains were met at the door of the Church by the Pastors of the Episcopal and Congregational Churches, who headed the procession as it marched along the aisles, the Rev. J. L. Townsend reading the burial services in accordance with the Episcopal. At the conclusion of the Burial Service, the choir sang, "Send them home tenderly." Elder A. N. Gilbert then proceeded to deliver the funeral discourse, taking his text from Acts 5th Chapter, 38 and 39 verses. The address was a stirring one and listened to with marked interest. The closing prayer was made by Rev. G. M. Stone, and the exercises of the church were closed by the choir singing the hymn, "Cease Ye Mourners, Cease to Languish Over the Grave of Those Ye Love."*[65]

THE SEARCH FOR LIEUTENANT COLONEL FOWLER'S BODY

One of the great mysteries of the 17th Connecticut at Gettysburg was what happened to Lieutenant Colonel Fowler's body. Despite many efforts, his body was never identified nor recovered. Fowler was beloved by the men of the regiment, and the dramatic circumstances of his death almost overwhelmed them on the field. Once the survivors of the regiment reached East Cemetery Hill there was some reluctance to advance until General Howard himself took the flag and led them into position.[66]

Douglas Fowler was born in Guilford, Connecticut, in 1826. He was one of six sons of Richard Fowler and Polly Hart. All six brothers served in the Civil War—five for the Union and one for the Confederacy.[67] Fowler was a locksmith by trade. In 1853 he married Melissa Jane Nash, who passed away after the death of their infant daughter in 1855. In 1861 when the war broke out, the thirty-five-year-old widower was living in

Norwalk. He served as captain of Company G in the 3rd Connecticut and fought at First Bull Run. When his three-month enlistment expired in August, he enlisted in the 8th Connecticut in September 1861 as the captain of Company H. Fowler, disgusted with regimental politics, resigned his commission in the 8th Connecticut in January1862 over differences of opinion regarding promotion. In August 1862 he recruited Company A out of Norwalk for the 17th Connecticut and was again commissioned captain in a three-year regiment. After Lieutenant Colonel Walter was killed at Chancellorsville and Colonel Noble badly wounded, Fowler was promoted to lieutenant colonel over Major Brady, who had led the regiment at Chancellorsville. Brady would lead the 17th at Gettysburg after Fowler was killed on July 1.

Lieutenant Colonel Douglas Fowler was killed July 1 while commanding the regiment.
(Captain Wilson French Collection)

On July 1, to the fury of the men of the 17th Connecticut, Lieutenant Colonel Fowler was arrested because one soldier stopped to dip a cup in a stream for water during the hurried march to Gettysburg. W. W. Paynton remembered,

> *The boys of the 17th gathered about their beloved Fowler, and some of them, in their indignation, declared that if he was not released before the regiment went into action, they would not fire a shot. The Colonel told them not to do anything rash, but that if the Regiment went into a fight he would go with them, and as their commander too.*[68]

As the Eleventh Corps marched toward the sound of the guns booming north of Gettysburg, Fowler was indeed released to lead the 17th Connecticut into battle.

The stunning and spectacular violence of Fowler's death was the stuff of nightmares even in the midst of vicious combat. Fowler's death would never be erased from the minds of the men. In the memory of the survivors of the 17th Connecticut everything about Fowler before his death became important; the last words he said to individuals, his last drink from a canteen, Fowler's final words as shot and shell began to shriek over the regiment on Barlow's Knoll. A Norwalk boy, Private John Hayes, Company F, who would be horribly wounded soon after witnessing Fowler killed, remembered, "*After we had halted and faced to the enemy, I took my position in Company 'C' to the left and rear of the colors. Lieut. Col. Fowler called me and gave me his picture.*"[69]

Lieutenant Peck remembered Fowler refusing to dismount, "*The Line Officers gathered around Colonel Fowler and tried to persuade him to dismount during the battle, but he refused, fearing he might be deemed cowardly.*"[70]

Sergeant Major Frederick Betts remembered Fowler joking with the men under fire, with the words, *"Dodge the big ones boys."*[71]

Fowler was instantly and horrifically killed when shot or a shell struck him in the head. Almost immediately, despite the regiment being forced back with great casualties, there were attempts to save Fowler's body.

> *Lieut. Col. Fowler approached us and advised us to lay off our knapsacks . . . Shortly after our deploying to the right, the brigade was ordered to advance and to charge the enemy. But a few rods had been covered, when Fowler was struck in the head by a shot and killed instantly. The Adjutant, Chatfield, who was by his side, had his horse killed under him, and one bullet through his hat, another through the sleeve of his coat, while the hilt and a few inches of blade was all he had left of his sword. The charge was repulsed, the brigade fell back...Major C. F. Betts attempted to rescue Fowler's body, but after dragging it some distance were compelled to abandon it, and it never has been recovered yet.*[72]

Adjutant Whitney Chatfield wrote home after the battle and a portion of his letter was reprinted in the *Norwalk Gazette.* "We think there can be no doubt of Col. Fowler's death. Adjutant Chatfield writes to a friend that, 'Lieut. Col. Fowler was shot dead while riding by my side, his blood and brains flying all over my coat.'"[73]

Adjutant H. Whitney Chatfield was riding beside Fowler when he was killed. (Connecticut Historical Society)

Sergeant Major Betts wrote home to his sisters after the battle; a portion of his letter also appeared in the *Gazette.* "*When I started to retreat, the Regiment had all gone, and Col. Fowler was just ahead of me, when to my horror I saw him reel and fall from his saddle. I ran to him and found that he was dead, a ball passed entirely through his head. I tried to carry him off the field, but the weight was too much for me. When I left the Rebs were not 10 feet from me.*"[74]

In 1884, Betts wrote a more elaborate recollection of Fowler's death in a letter to Colonel Henry Allen about his experiences at Gettysburg.

> *Our colors, which were on the top of the Knoll, apparently attracted the special fire of the rebels. Capt. Moore fell in the advance and, if memory serves me right, it was here that Quien, who then took his place in Co. C, was shot in the hand...many of our best men fell, one after the other while holding our colors aloft . . . As we turned to fall back, Col. Fowler, who had just been left by Gen. Ames, brought in the rear of our Regt., and as*

> *he, with Adjt. Chatfield and myself started down the slope, we saw slowly following in the rear, the advance line of rebel skirmishers, a light battery on the ridge, which was shelling us and making things quite lively. We had not gone far, when to our horror we saw Col. Fowler falling from his saddle as his horse galloped away. Chatfield, who had just had his light sabre cut in two by a ball, hastily dismounted; poor Fowler was dead. It seemed to us that the hole in his head could hardly have been made by a fragment of a shell which had just burst above us, as it looked round and clearly marked, however, this was not time for speculation, so calling back one of our Regt. Co. E, whose name I cannot recall, we endeavored to lift his corpse upon the adjutant's horse, but we found it impossible to do so, as his weight was beyond our strength, and after several attempts, we reluctantly left him. At this time the rebel line had advanced within hailing distance, and the requests we received were more vigorous than polite. Chatfield, mounting his horse, escaped by a close shave to our right. Our friend of Co. E was captured before he left that field, while I, scaling a fence in front of us, tore across the next field towards a stone wall of the Poorehouse.*[75]

The "friend from Co. E" whom Betts mentioned as being captured trying to save Fowler's body was Corporal Roscoe Perry. Perry was a shoemaker's apprentice from Westport when he enlisted in the 17th Connecticut. While the regiment was in St. Augustine, Florida, Perry was looking for someone to do his laundry, and found Margarita Antonia Capo.[76] After the regiment mustered out at Hilton Head, South Carolina, Perry returned to St. Augustine, and on October 27, 1865, he married Margarita. They had seven children in ten years. Perry would die in 1901 and is interred at Evergreen Cemetery in St. Augustine.[77]

Corporal Roscoe Perry, Company E, as he appeared after the war. (Courtesy of Paul Knight)

In 1895, Perry wrote a letter to Captain Enoch Wood about his attempt to recover Fowler's body. Perry was captured after Sergeant Betts jumped the brook to escape the Confederates who surrounded them. The brook may have been the Alms House Run. Perry was sent to Richmond with the other captured men of the 17th Connecticut. Perry's letter is remarkable and richly detailed.

St. Augustine, Fla, June 8, 1895
Capt. Enoch Wood,
127 Main St., Norwalk, Conn.

Dear Sir and Comrade:—

Yours of the 4th inst. came duly at hand and I was pleased to hear from you. In regard to our Captain [sic] Fowler's death, I would say that I was the last man who had possession of his body. If you remember, Captain, when we retreated to Cemetery Hill, we left our dead and wounded on our first field of battle. We were ordered to support the 2nd Rhode Island Battery, which we did until we were completely routed from that position. It was at that time of our falling back that someone of the 17th had Colonel Fowler by the collar, trying to get him off; I cannot remember the comrade's name but think it was the Sergeant Major (Betts). I took hold of the collar of his coat with my right hand, and we got about two hundred yards or more away with him, but being hard pressed by the enemy, we were compelled to drop him. I had my canteen shot away and had bullets all through my clothing and rubber blanket. I had only one wound in the hand, received from a spent bullet in the commencement of the fight.

At the point of our leaving the Colonel, we came to a swift running brook. The comrade whom I assisted commenced to cry and said, "My God, Perry, we cannot get him off; save yourself." He having no accoutrements but a sword, jumped across the brook and cleared it, but I having my gun, etc., could not do it, but fell partially in with my back against the bank on the opposite side. Before I could straighten up I was surrounded by one of the hardest crowds I ever saw. One little fellow about 18 years old came riding up and levelled a revolver at my head and said, "Throw down that gun." As I had my gun in my left hand, I slipped my right up to the lock, pulled and away she went; that was my last shot at Gettysburg. The bullet, I believe, did its work for the fellow fell off his horse shot through the throat, and dropped beside our Colonel. My captors then were bound to kill me. One tall fellow made for me to pin me to the ground with his bayonet, but the lieutenant in charge, seeing me covered with blood and brains from dragging the Colonel, caught his gun and said to him, "For God's sake, don't kill a wounded man." I believe that saved my life, for I was ordered to the rear, while the main body passed on. I sat down there and saw our beloved Colonel stripped of everything he had; a masonic pin, his watch, boots, coat, and in fifteen minutes there were not a dozen men in the 17th that could have recognized him.

About this time the prisoners of the 17th were looking over the fields for friends, and I found several from my company. I do not remember how many of us there were, but about 96, I think, officers and men. We were ordered from the field and out into another one of wheat and green

> *apples, and we staid there under guard until July 4th without anything to eat but wheat and green apples. On July 4th we drew rations, one half pint of flour, no salt, bread or anything else; we mixed wheat, apples and flour together and started for Richmond. There were a good many of our boys left on the field, and a trench was dug and the boys both blue and gray, were buried there, near the ground where we left the Colonel. I have never been to Gettysburg since, but I could go and put my foot on the ground where we left him, but his remains can never be found for there are hundreds buried in the same grave. I told this to Colonel Wm. H. Noble on Folly Island, when I got back, and have told others the same.*
>
> *Our post is organized, and it is prospering; we have a good deal to contend with, but we are holding our own. I had the honor of naming the post after our Adjutant Chatfield and have been Post Commander two terms. I am pleased to give you the details as to the Colonel's death. Kindly remember me to the members of the Post in your place named after him. It is unnecessary for me to repeat how much we all loved Fowler and missed him at that awful fight. Remember me kindly to all the 17th boys. I shall be pleased to hear from you all again.*
>
> *Yours in F. C. & L., Roscoe Perry*[78]

An undated, unsigned entry in the Warren Manuscript about Fowler's body was probably from Adjutant Whitney Chatfield. Chatfield was killed on February 5, 1865, in Florida at Dunn's Lake. Warren may have copied this account after the war from other information he had access to. Some of the particulars about Fowler's body concur with Roscoe Perry's 1895 letter to Captain Enoch Wood.

> *Lt. Col. Fowler's Burial*
>
> *After the news had reached Norwalk that he was killed, a party of men went from there to Gettysburg and looked for his body but could not find it. A Drum Major was taken prisoner was sent back over the same field and found Fowler's body just where he had laid it, by the side of the fence, naked. From the time this Drum Major had left him to the time he came back again, which was possibly a short time, the rebs had stripped him of his clothing. He had a Masonic Ring on his finger and a gold pin on his bosom that the ladies of Norwalk pinned on when he left there. He also had a gold watch in his pocket and $75 in money.*
>
> *(The above particulars are given by the Adjutant)*[79]

Along with the first printed casualty reports of the battle, the *Norwalk Gazette* printed an obituary for Colonel Fowler on July 7, 1863. The obituary lauded Fowler's patriotism and sacrifice. The article ended with "*We trust that when the remains of the heroic Fowler shall be brought home for interment, Norwalk and vicinity will take occasion to pay them such respect as his brave deeds and heroic death in defense of our Liberties so justly entitle them.*"[80]

When news of Fowler's death reached Norwalk, there was every expectation that his body would be brought back to Connecticut and an elaborate hero's funeral would take place. On Thursday, July 9, Captain Enoch Wood and Captain James L. Russell, both of Norwalk, arrived at Gettysburg to search for Fowler's body. Wood had resigned his commission as captain of Company F, 17th Connecticut in March 1863 due to ill health. Russell had served with Fowler in both the 3rd and 8th Connecticut regiments. Russell had been severely wounded at Antietam and had been discharged in January 1863. After searching for Fowler's body for three days the two former captains returned to Norwalk without success. On July 14, the *Norwalk Gazette* printed the following report of their search.

> *Lieut. Col. Fowler.*
>
> *Captains Enoch Wood and James L. Russell have been to Gettysburg for the purpose of trying to obtain the body of Lieut. Col. Fowler but have returned without succeeding in their object. They send us the following report.*
>
> *Messrs. Editors.—Knowing the deep interest felt in this community as to the fate of Lieut. Col. Fowler, we feel it to be our duty to give the public some account of the results of our mission to Gettysburg where we proceeded last Tuesday in hopes of recovering the body of our late friend. Although we did not succeed, it will be some satisfaction to his many friends to know that every effort was made to accomplish that end.*
>
> *After many delays on the road, we arrived at Gettysburg about 8 o'clock on Thursday morning. We immediately proceeded to the Hospital of the 11th Corps, where so many of our brave boys lie wounded. After visiting those belonging to the 17th we procured the services of Serg. Lees and Privates Turney and Downs, all of Co. E of the 17th, we proceeded at once to the spot where Col. Fowler is supposed to have fallen. We here found about sixty graves, forty-six of which we knew to be those of our men, the others were mostly those of the enemy. Two only out of this number were marked, one of which was that of Capt. James E. Moore, (whose body had been removed the day previous by his brother) the*

Captain Enoch Wood, formerly of Company F of Norwalk. He resigned on March 23, 1863, due to health issues. Wood and Captain James Russell would undertake a mission to Gettysburg to search for Douglas Fowler's body. (Captain Wilson French Collection)

other was of a Lieut. Gamble of a Ga., Regt. We opened all of these graves with the exception of the Rebel Lieut. but found no traces whatever of our lamented friend. After diligent search for some distance around this particular locality, we very reluctantly returned to town, feeling that we had done all we could do under the circumstances.

It may be well to state (as we were reliably informed by those participating in the engagement) that at the time Col. Fowler fell, his Regt. were obliged to retire before an overwhelming force of the enemy, leaving the field in the possession of the Rebels, who held the ground until Friday night and virtually until Sunday morning, as their pickets did not retire until that time. This we think establishes the fact that all our men who fell there were buried by the enemy. We have the authority of a citizen living near for saying, that the Rebels cut the name of Capt. Moore on the board that stood at the head of his grave; this citizen saw our men before they were buried but had no knowledge of seeing any officers.

Now it seems to us, that if Col. Fowler's body had been there the Rebels would undoubtedly have marked the spot where he was buried as they did that of Capt. Moore.

We still cling to the hope that he may be only wounded and a prisoner, at the same time we fear that our hopes will not be realized.

In the loss of Col. Fowler, the Union has lost one of its bravest defenders—a soldier by nature, a true patriot and a warm hearted friend.

Enoch Wood,
James L. Russell.

South Norwalk, July 13th, '63.[81]

In June 1896, Enoch Wood sent the following description about the search for Fowler's body to William Warren. The regret that Fowler was never recovered or identified lingered through the years in the memory of the veterans of the regiment.

Capt. Enoch Wood spent three days looking for Fowler's body and had opened over 100 graves. He saw the open grave where Capt. Moore was buried but his brother had been there and took the body home. In his search a big trench was opened where the dead were laid head and foot. With all their clothes on, even to shoes, while a knapsack was placed over their faces. The trench was filled with about a foot of dirt. The writer was an eye-witness of the trench.

(From Capt. Wood June 20, 1896)[82]

There were many factors that contributed to Fowler's body never being identified. Wood and Russell logically began their search at the location of Fowler's death and the area where Captain Moore's brother recovered his body the previous day. We know from accounts that in the attempt to save Fowler's remains, the body had been dragged away from the location where the lieutenant colonel was killed. Corporal Perry wrote that he and Sergeant Major Betts dragged Fowler as far as a brook when they were surrounded by Confederates. Perry dropped the body and was captured while Betts jumped across the stream and escaped. This brook may have been the Almshouse Run, which was on the far side of the Alms House complex almost at the edge of town. This is a significant distance to drag a body and far from where the regiment's dead lay and would have been interred on the field.

Several accounts state that Fowler was stripped, as were many of the Union bodies on the first day's field. Perry stated he saw Fowler in this condition soon afterward, and that Fowler was unrecognizable. The dead from July 1 had reportedly lain in the hot July sun several days before they were buried. If so, as Captain Wood believed, this would also have affected any identification attempts. Lastly, the devastating head wound that instantly killed Fowler may have made it impossible to identify his remains. Adjutant Chatfield's description of the gory mess that spattered him after Fowler was struck makes it obvious that the wound would have been a factor in identification of the body. Fowler's youngest brother certainly believed this was the case. In 1922, Edward Fowler, who had fought with the 14th Connecticut at Antietam, wrote to his niece Minnie about his and his brothers' service in the Civil War. Edward starkly described to his niece, "*An unexploded cannister shot struck Douglas and took the top of his head off above his mouth. The enemy took possession of the field 5 min after he was hit. That was the reason he was not identified, and his body never found.*"[83]

Lieutenant Colonel Douglas Fowler probably lies in the Gettysburg National Cemetery as unknown. Fowler's sacrifice at Gettysburg was never forgotten by the men of the 17th Connecticut. They remembered him as the bravest of the brave. His heroic death has hallowed the ground wherever his body rests.

PRIVATE STEPHEN CROFUT, COMPANY D—NEVER FOUND

Lieutenant Colonel Fowler was not the only soldier sought for and never found. On August 1, 1863, J. Henry Blakeman wrote to his mother the details of Stephen Crofut's death. Henry was Stephen's best friend. They had been born within months of each other in the Oronoque section of Stratford. Henry was wounded in the same volley that killed Stephen. Henry was evacuated from Gettysburg and sent to Jarvis General Hospital in Baltimore. Stephen was the only son of a Stratford fisherman, and his death at Gettysburg shattered his family. Stephen's body was never identified or recovered and is probably among the unknown in Gettysburg National Cemetery. Several of J. Henry Blakeman's letters home, including the following, referenced details of Stephen's death to be passed on to Stephen's family.

Private Stephen Crofut, Company D, was killed July 1.

(Bridgeport History Center)

Jarvis Hospital, Baltimore Md.
Saturday, Aug 1st, 1863

Dear Mother.

I will write what I know concerning Stephen's death. As you know, we lay for twenty or thirty minutes supporting a battery and while lying there the officers called for volunteers to pull down a fence that was thought might be in our way and was somewhat exposed to the enemy's shells. Selah, Stephen and myself and some others went and pulled it down. After lying down again the battery was firing, Stephen says "those are ours, give it to them." These were the last words I heard him say as just then we moved towards the Rebs and my attention was directed to them. He must have been hit at the same moment that I was for as soon as I got up I saw him lying near me and under his head a large puddle of blood. I did not go to him for one look at his face satisfied me that he was dead and I could hardly move myself. I suppose he was buried by the Rebs as they held the field and our boys that were over the field afterwards said the dead were all buried.[84]

Henry's words "*our boys that were over the field afterwards said the dead were all buried*" refer to members of the 17th Connecticut, who on July 4 were sent back over the first day's battlefield. It is probable that the description Henry wrote to his mother was received from his cousin Selah Blakeman, who was among the squad. These men were sent to determine that the Confederates had withdrawn from Gettysburg, and they liberated wounded Union prisoners and medical personnel in the town and at the Alms House hospital.

PRIVATE RUFUS WARREN'S UNCLE BRINGS HIS BODY HOME

On July 1 on Barlow's Knoll, William Warren witnessed his friend Rufus Warren's wounding. The men, who were not related, both served in Company C of the 17th Connecticut. William Warren was retreating with the rest of the regiment as the Confederates overwhelmed the Federals on the knoll. William Warren would include his account of Rufus Warren's wounding in his manuscript. The following excerpt was probably copied from his Civil War diary.

Private Rufus Warren, Company C, wounded on July 1. Warren died at the Eleventh Corps hospital at the Spangler Farm on July 17 after his leg was amputated. His uncle traveled to Gettysburg to bring his nephew home to Ridgefield for burial. (Bridgeport History Center)

I had fired only a few times when feelings came over me that cannot be described. It appeared, as near as I can tell, that I stood there for some time all alone, no one as I could see near me, but enough we up with me. The rebs were near us and still advancing and with more men than we had. Finding myself in the above described position I feel back a few feet until I was stopped by an officer. The whole regiment was also falling back . . . I was stopped, but before I got loaded the regiment or brigade again started to run, so of course I followed on. I had gone but a short distance when I saw Rufus Warren, who was ahead of me, fall the opposite way; he was running at the time but turning halfway round he threw up his hands, crying, "oh dear, help me, help me," and fell to the ground. I was powerless to help him as we were all on the move to the rear with the rebs close to our heels and I did not know what moment I would share the same fate as he.[85]

Rufus Warren was shot in the left leg and suffered a compound fracture. He was probably taken to the Alms House and subsequently transferred to the Eleventh Corps hospital at the Spangler Farm. The Spangler Farm hospital register lists him as "*Warren, Rufus, Pvt., 17th CT, C, compound fracture mid 3rd left leg, died July 17, amputated, upper 3rd*."[86] Warren would be buried in a temporary graveyard for those who died at the Spangler Farm hospital. The Elliott burial map shows some 185 Union and 20 Confederate bodies buried there, which is probably a high estimate.[87] Bodies buried at Spangler were usually wrapped in blankets and placed in crude coffins made from wood found on the farm. Graves were marked with the name of the dead, written in pencil, carved, or painted on a board.[88]

It was to this graveyard that Rufus Warren's uncle, Hiram O. Nash, came to find his nephew and bring him home to Connecticut. Warren's family had been frantically scanning the Connecticut papers for news of his whereabouts and information about his condition. On July 11, Starr Picket returned to Ridgefield with the body of his brother Edwin, killed on the first day. He brought news to Warren's family that Rufus was alive at the Spangler Farm and had suffered an amputation. Hiram Nash wanted to leave immediately for Gettysburg, but the draft riots in New York halted communication and travel. On July 17, Nash left Connecticut. After a long train trip delayed by an accident, he reached Baltimore, located the provost marshal, obtained a pass, and left for Gettysburg. When Nash arrived at the Spangler Farm, Corporal George Dickens of Company C, serving as a nurse,

Corporal George Dickens, Company C, nursed the wounded at the Spangler Farm and helped a grateful Hiram Nash to locate his nephew's body. (Bridgeport History Center)

was instrumental in helping him locate Warren's body. Nash left a moving and meticulous account of his journey to Gettysburg.

> *We closely observed the papers after the battle but so imperfect and meagre were the accounts that we could learn nothing of his welfare until the return of our friend, Rufus S. (Starr) Pickett, who recovered the body of his deceased brother, who was also killed on the first day. He informed us that Rufus was wounded and in the hospital; this was the 11th. Then the riot going on in New York prevented the ordinary means of travel. Again, we heard that he was still living. On the 17th I set out with the intention of seeing him alive if possible. My wife took me in the carriage to Sanford's Station (on Danbury & Norwalk R. R. as it was then). Reached New York City at 10:30 a.m., remained there until 7:50 p.m. as nothing could be gained by leaving sooner. Passed over to Jersey City and designed reaching Baltimore at 4 o'clock the next a.m. On reaching the crossing of the Susquehanna at Haver-de-grace, we were delayed seven hours by an accident which occurred to a train, as an engine being off the track, and we did not reach Baltimore until 11 o'clock. Found the Provost Marshall, obtained a pass, and left the city at 3 o'clock p.m. Delayed nearly six hours at Hanover Station, left at midnight and reached Gettysburg about daylight Sunday a.m. Here the railroad terminated.*
>
> *Learning of the probable direction of the 11th Corps Hospital, we set out, some eight or ten of us, on the Emmitsburg Turnpike some two miles, until we reached the Taneytown Road, which turned to our right about half a mile and brought us to the camp. With indescribable emotion we approached the camp, and soon with intense solicitude we inquired the fate of our poor nephew, and was met with the answer by George Dickens, a member of his company, that he expired on the morning of the 17th about the time we left our home. We were conducted to his grave which we found decently marked with a head-board, name, company, date of death, etc., This we secured and brought home with us. We returned to the village and made all necessary preparations. Went about and around the village and saw the destruction and ravages of the war. We went again in the p.m. to the hospital and learned of the following facts of the case of the deceased: "He was wounded by a cannon ball in the left leg, which had to be amputated just above the knee, which was done on the 4th with much fortitude. Upon the inquiry of the nurse as to what he should say to his friends, if any of them should appear, "Tell them," says he, "to live as Christians and meet me in heaven." And what should I say to the Regiment, should I see them again? "Tell them to be praying men and stand by the flag of the Union to the last."*
>
> *Arose early the next morning, the 20th and went with a friend and took up the body, which cost $1.00, had it conveyed to the office of Dr. Bunnell,*

where it was disinfected, then covered with charcoal and chloride of lime, then put into an air tight coffin with gutta percha edges, with long screws thickly set, then put into a large box and tan bark closely packed between; this being done, it was taken to the express office ready for transportation.

Went over the field where Rufus fell; he was in the hands of the rebels for a while, who robbed him of all he had, and $7.00 in money.

Left at 3 p.m. for home; was delayed on the road and did not reach Baltimore until 11 a.m. the 21st and left for New York at 1 p.m. reaching there at 10 p.m. 196 miles in nine hours. Reached home the next day, the 22, at 11 a.m. The corpse arrived the next day, the 23, and was brought to my house.

The funeral was the following Sunday, the 26th; the services were held in the M.E. Church in the p.m. It was thronged within and without; the pulpit was beautifully decorated with Union flags neatly trimmed with black crepe. Danbury friends came over en masse with a file of soldiers, music and a draped flag. The singing was appropriate. Rev. W. C. Hoyt, Presiding Elder of the Bridgeport District, offered prayer. Rev. C. P. Ford pastor of the church, delivered a patriotic, war time address. Rev. A. N. Gilbert followed in an exaltation admired by all. On moving from the church to the grave the procession was under the direction of H. A. Scott and E. W. Keeler as marshals. The pall bearers were Eldridge Northrop, Frank W. Lockwood, William Northrop, Alonzo Brown, _______ Couch, Henry Benedict and _______ _______, all unmarried. The slow march of 100 carriages, with a long line of citizens on foot, the waving flag deeply draped in mourning, the soldiers in rank and file with glistening arms, the low sound of the muffled drum and the solemn repeated toll of the bell of the Episcopal Church, conspired to render it one of the most impressive and interesting services of the kind ever witnessed in the place. The remains were lowered by eight young men, mentioned above, there to rest by the side of his respected and departed mother. Three volleys were fired over his grave, and the services here ended.

So died our nephew, who was one of our family, at the age of 21 years, 7 months and 18 days.

Hiram O. Nash, Ridgefield[89]

Reverend Hiram O. Nash of Ridgefield traveled to Gettysburg to bring home the body of his beloved nephew, Rufus Warren. (Bridgeport History Center)

William Warren included an itemized list of expenses for the retrieval, preparation, and transport of Rufus Warren's body and his funeral expenses in Ridgefield. Nash had listed the expenditures in his diary and his son shared them with William Warren.

The following is an exact copy as taken from the diary of Rev. Hiram O. Nash, Ridgefield, Conn. His son lent it to me after his father's death. Some lines he had two items on as I have copied it:[90]

<u>"Expenses in obtaining the body"</u>
Fare to Norwalk $0.47
New York $1.00—City 5 cts $1.05
Eating 28 cts—to Baltimore $6.45 .... $6.73
Hanover Junction $1.45
Gettysburg $1.00
When there (in Gettysburg) board $1.00
Taking up body $1.00
Disinfection $15.-coffin $32 .... $47.00
Conveyance to Dr. Bunnell's (the embalmer) thence to
Express Office $5.00
Express through (for the body?) $23.00
Returning to Hanover Junction $1.00
Baltimore $1.45—Eating .20 .... $1.65
New York $6.45—Supper .19 .... $6.64
Lodging .50—city fare .5 .... $0.55
Norwalk $1.00—Ridgefield - $1.40 .... $2.40
Stage .38—Shaving .10 .... $0.48
Stamps and writing home $0.09
<u>For time 6 days .... $4.14</u>
.. $104.65

A monument of beautiful Italian marble now, Dec. 21st. marks the grave on which is inscribed "Rufus Warren, Son of Burr and Eliza Warren, was wounded in the battle of Gettysburg, PA. 1st July 1863, and died on the aged 21 years." 7 months and 18 days, soon after the funeral his father was notified of all particulars, but no answer was ever received from him.

<u>"Additional Expenses"</u>
First Cost—$104.65 .... $104.65
To Jones or James Gilbert—Coffin Handles $0.94
Dr. De Forest—tolling bell $0.50
James E. Mead, digging grave $2.50
A.?. Gilbert, Undertaker attendance $2.50
Papers Executed, and sent to friends
Postage stamps & Letters $1.00
<u>E. B. Price, Grave Stones .... $30.00</u>
Total $142.09
<u>Sent to him by his request of sundry articles & at sundry times .... $8.89</u>
.. $150.98

CORPORAL ALVAH WILCOX'S DEATH AND REBURIALS

One of the saddest of the many sad stories associated with the 17th at Gettysburg was that of the wounding, death, and reburials of Corporal Alvah Wilcox, and of the loved ones he left behind. Pieces of Alvah's story have been recounted in previous chapters and will be completed here with the account of his older brother, Charles, who traveled to Gettysburg with Alonzo Scranton's fiancée, Harriett Davis, to find the wounded Alonzo and to bring Alvah's body home. Wilcox was wounded on July 2 on East Cemetery Hill "*by a sharpshooter, while on his way up Cemetery Hill; a ball went through his left arm into his body and passed downward around to the left side.*" He was put into a blanket by members of his company, directed by Lieutenant Peck, and carried to the "field hospital," described as being within the cemetery gate. The *Medical and Surgical History of the War of the Rebellion* lists Wilcox as receiving surgery for his wound "in the field," probably at this cemetery hospital, in which Wilcox's sucking chest wound was "hermetically sealed" by Dr. Benjamin Howard.[91]

A prewar image of Alvah Wilcox. Wilcox's first name is often spelled "Alva" in the Warren Manuscript and other official records. (Bridgeport History Center)

On July 4, Wilcox was transferred to the Eleventh Corps hospital at the George Spangler Farm. He was found there by his longtime friend Private Alonzo Scranton, who had been shot in the jaw on July 1. Alonzo did all he could for Alvah but the situation was hopeless. Wilcox died in Scranton's arms on July 7.

> *Alva Wilcox was wounded July 2, 1863 at Gettysburg by a sharpshooter . . . He was taken to the barn where Alonzo Scranton was . . . Alonzo Scranton was doing all he could for him, being straddle of him, and turned him over just before he died. He had a lighted lantern in his hand and that, I believe, was all the light there was. Someone called for this lantern, but Dr. Hubbard told them to let him have it. Wilcox died gradually, or in other words, commenced to die from the time he was wounded-from his feet up. Dr. Hubbard gave Alonzo Scranton a white blanket to wrap around Wilcox after he died and he was buried with it.*[92]

After Alvah Wilcox's death, and before his evacuation from Spangler on July 8 to the South Street General Hospital in Philadelphia,[93] Scranton was able to write a letter home to Connecticut that was mailed by a New Jersey Sanitary Commission volunteer. This letter would bring Charles Wilcox, Alvah's brother, and Harriett Davis, Scranton's future wife, to Gettysburg in search of the two men.

In 1888, Alonzo Scranton gave William Warren an account of this trip to Gettysburg. To observe decorum and propriety, Warren titled the entry, "*Mrs. Alonzo Scranton's Trip to Gettysburg*." Harriett, or Hettie, did not marry Alonzo until after his discharge from the Veterans Reserve Corps in 1865. At the time she made this trip, Harriet was a single woman, undertaking a difficult journey, escorted by a married man who was not her relative. The remarkable account of their journey is below:

> *"MRS. ALONZO SCRANTON'S TRIP TO GETTYSBURG."*
>
> *On the following Thursday, after the battle of Gettysburg, a letter was received from Alonzo Scranton by C. K. Wilcox, who was brother to Alva Wilcox, and brother-in-law to Alonzo Scranton* [Charles was married to Scranton's sister, Emily] *giving the particulars about Alva's death. Mr. Wilcox did not let Mrs. Scranton see the letter but told her of the contents. The next a.m., Mrs. Scranton, in company with Mr. Wilcox, left Bridgeport, by rail, almost eight o'clock and reached New York about eleven o'clock, and went direct to Philadelphia, by rail, and from there to Baltimore by rail, reaching there in the a.m. and then direct to Hanover Junction, which was about 20 miles from Gettysburg. Here the passenger train would go no further until the next a.m., as it was then night. But on another track stood a freight train composed of cars which were loaded with grain for army horses at Gettysburg. In some of these cars bags were piled up to make room for some of the passengers who thought they must reach Gettysburg as soon as possible, in order to see their friends. Many went so that all the available room inside was covered as well as the platforms outside. Reached Gettysburg the following a.m. early. They both went to work to procure a coffin for Alva, but tried in vain not a coffin, or anything like one; or even a board, could be bought in Gettysburg, so about five p.m. of this same day, they both took the train for Baltimore, where they procured a coffin—went back to Gettysburg and had Alva dug up, put in the coffin and buried in the cemetery until winter, then Mr. Wilcox went to Gettysburg again and had Alva dug up the second time, then took him to Madison, Conn. for his last burial. I think he was taken into the church.* [Charles had his brother removed from his first burial at Spangler Farm, and on July 16, 1863, Alva was reburied in Evergreen Cemetery.[94]]
>
> *On the train that Mr. Wilcox and Mrs. Scranton were on, going from Gettysburg to Baltimore, there were two bodies that were so decayed that they were running out of the coffin, and the train was stopped twice to bury different ones because the smell was so bad they could hardly breath. Finally, it got so bad that a stop was put to it, and no more bodies were removed from the field. And while they were on their way to Baltimore to get a coffin, the order was issued to this effect; so you see they were just too late. This train was composed of box cars with seats in, and all loaded with rebel prisoners except one for passengers. Just before the train*

reached Baltimore it stopped to give the prisoners some sandwiches and coffee, so Mr. Wilcox said to Mrs. Scranton, "I believe I will go and see the rebel prisoners, as I have been so busy I have not had a chance to see them today." So he went and looked around, and finally leaned up against a car, and he saw a woman give the prisoners some sandwiches. This woman went to a policeman and told him that there was a rebel spy in the car, and then the inquiry was, "Where is he? Where is he?" "There he is" said the woman, at the same time pointing to Mr. Wilcox. Some conversation was exchanged between the policeman and Mr. Wilcox, which resulted in his arrest. Mr. Wilcox said that he had a lady with him, so the policeman called on Mrs. Scranton, and told him it was her brother-in-law. The three went to Barnum's Hotel where a room was procured for Mrs. Scranton, and Wilcox was taken to the Provost Marshall's office, where he found many others were confined for similar circumstances and petty things. Here he was confined on a Sunday a.m. from four o'clock until eleven o'clock. While on the road to Gettysburg, Wilcox met Joseph King, an officer who was stationed at Baltimore who said to him, "If I can do anything for you, let me know." So after he was confined, he sent for him, who had him released. Monday Wilcox got a coffin and went back to Gettysburg, where he stayed one night and two days, and from there, back to Baltimore again, where they stayed until Saturday. During this time they were in search of Alonzo Scranton. They could not telegraph on account of the riot in New York, so wrote a letter and received an answer on Saturday, and found he was in Philadelphia; they took the train and arrived there Sunday night and stopped at the Continental Hotel. Monday a.m. they got a ten days' furlough for Alonzo, and they took the train for Bridgeport.

As the train neared Gettysburg on which were Mr. Wilcox, and Mrs. Scranton, the stench from the battlefield was so very bad that the Drs. that were on the train gave the ladies some medicine and put camphor on their handkerchiefs to be held to the nose. Chloride of lime was scattered through the town and where they stopped, which was at a private house (Adams they think the name was), the folks there told them that the blood ran in their own door yard, while men lay on their doorsteps and around in the yard; some of them were all drawn up and cracked open before they were buried. After Mr. Wilcox reached home, he was taken sick with a fever, and Mrs. Scranton did not get over the effects of it through the whole summer. (From Alonzo Scranton, May 5th and 6th 1888)[95]

After brother Charles located a suitable coffin he had Alvah disinterred from the temporary graveyard at the Spangler Farm. We presume Charles had Alvah embalmed but there is no record of who the embalmer was. Unfortunately, the saga did not end there. Because of the obstacles to transporting his brother's body to Connecticut, Charles had to leave Alvah in Gettysburg. The town and surrounding area had become so unhealthy that ultimately General Orders No. 2 was issued, forbidding the disinterment of corpses from the battlefield and its environs during August and September of 1863.[96]

Instead of being freighted home to Connecticut, Corporal Alvah Wilcox was reburied in Evergreen Cemetery on July 16, 1863, Permit #422.[97] Alvah's grave in Evergreen may have been dug by Elizabeth Thorn, the six-months-pregnant cemetery keeper who took over the duties of her husband while he was serving in the Union army. Elizabeth Thorn, with some help from her father, dug 105 graves after the battle. In the winter of 1864, Charles Wilcox returned to Gettysburg and finally brought Alvah home to be buried in West Cemetery in Madison, Connecticut. Alvah Wilcox's stone marker at Evergreen Cemetery still remains.

Corporal Alvah Wilcox's military stone in the Civil War section of Evergreen Cemetery, where graves were dug by Elizabeth Thorn. (Photograph by author)

Sarah L. Dowd Wilcox, who married Alvah seven days before he enlisted, was a bride for one week and a widow for fifty-one years. Sarah received a widow's pension of $8 a month. In 1911 Sarah was declared insane, and a conservator was appointed to manage her affairs, including her widow's pension, which had increased to $12 a month.[98] Sarah died on January 2, 1914, and would be buried alongside Alvah and her parents in West Cemetery. The stone is marked Dowd-Wilcox.[99]

GETTYSBURG NATIONAL CEMETERY

On July 11, 1863, Pennsylvania governor Andrew G. Curtin toured the battlefield and was appalled at the destruction, the raw and foul air, the scarred earth and trees, the farms and fields devastated. Especially shocking was the landscape littered with horrible sights of the human dead in various, inadequate graves that barely covered their remains. Nineteenth-century Americans were keenly aware that the dead, hurriedly and inadequately buried everywhere in little mounds and shallow trenches, would be in the way of spring plowing.[100] Families and their agents, along with undertakers and souvenir seekers, flocked to the battlefield. In their searches for loved ones, graves and burial trenches were disturbed and then hastily and carelessly covered over, causing more havoc on the farms and fields. Some of the dead were uncovered and recovered

Panorama view of Gettysburg National Cemetery in 1913 on the 50th anniversary of the battle. (Library of Congress)

multiple times; others were left uncovered. To prevent this, General Orders No. 2 was issued by the army's Department of the Susquehanna: "*During the months of August and September 1863, no corpses will be allowed to be disinterred from any of the burial grounds, cemeteries, or battleground of Gettysburg. The health of the wounded soldiers and citizens of the community requires the stringent enforcement of this order, and any violation of it reported to these headquarters will meet with the summary and severe punishment.*"[101] This order was enforced until the first frost in October made it safer to remove bodies.

Pennsylvania had passed a law in 1862 requiring the commonwealth to care for its wartime wounded and dead. Under this law Pennsylvania paid the costs of exhumation, a zinc-lined coffin, and transportation for any soldier from the state whose remains were claimed.[102] By the middle of July 1863, well aware of this law and desiring to honorably bury the dead of the battle, several proposals were made for the creation of a cemetery to honor Pennsylvanians killed or who died of wounds at Gettysburg. Former army surgeon and New York relief agent Theodore Dimon held a meeting with Gettysburg attorney David Wills—whom Governor Curtin had appointed the relief agent for Pennsylvania—at which he proposed that an "all inclusive" cemetery be created on the battlefield, for Union men who had fought and died from all the Northern states.[103]

Despite a rival proposal from local attorney David McConaughy, who was president of Evergreen Cemetery and who was buying land adjacent to Evergreen for a cemetery plan of his own, Governor Curtin approved the proposal of Wills and Dimon. Work began in conjunction with the other Northern states on a plan of design. Through the mediation of local community leaders, McConaughy sold the land he had purchased to the state for use as a soldiers' cemetery. Scottish-born William Saunders, an employee of the U.S. Department of Agriculture, was hired as the landscape architect. His plan was simple yet elegant, with the goal of burial by state in a semicircular pattern, with officers and men on equal footing—the low stones blending into and achieving unity with the landscape.[104]

When cooler weather arrived in October, David Wills had broadsides and advertisements printed calling for sealed bids for the removal of the dead from the battlefield and into coffins, to be reburied to strict specifications in the new soldiers' cemetery. The bids were opened on October 22 and Frank W. Biesecker was selected to complete the contract for $1.59 a body.[105] Samuel Weaver was hired as superintendent of exhumation and the work began on October 27, 1863 and continued until March 18, 1864. In his final report to David Wills, Weaver reported the total number of bodies removed to the soldiers' cemetery was 3,512, and 979 bodies were unidentified. If an unidentified body was discovered to have a regiment or state, that body was buried in the appropriate state section. Weaver's report states "*There was not a grave permitted to be opened or a body searched unless I was present.*" All articles found on the bodies were packed and labeled; there were 287 labeled packages for friends or relatives to claim.[106]

The new cemetery was to be the honored resting place for only Northern heroes. No Confederates were knowingly interred there. If a Confederate body was uncovered in the exhumation process it was covered over and left where it was. Samuel Weaver made note of this in his final report:

> *In searching for the remains of our fallen heroes, we examined more than three thousand rebel graves. They were frequently buried in trenches, and there are instances of more than one hundred and fifty in a trench . . . It may be asked how we could distinguish the bodies of our own men from those of the rebels. This was generally very easily done. In the first place, as a general rule, the rebels never went into battle with the United States coat on. They sometimes stole the pantaloons from our dead and wore them, but not the coat. The rebel clothing is made of cotton and is of a grey or brown color. Occasionally I found one with a blue cotton jean roundabout on. The clothing of our men is of wool, and blue; so that the body having the coat of our uniform on was a pretty sure indication that he was a Union soldier. But if the body were without a coat, then there were other infallible marks. The shoes of the rebels were differently made from those of our soldiers. If these failed, then the underclothing was the next part examined. The rebel cotton undershirt gave proof of the army to which he belonged. In no instance was a body allowed to be removed which had any portion of the rebel clothing on it . . . I here most conscientiously assert, that I firmly believe that there was not a single mistake made in the removal of the soldiers to the Cemetery by taking the body of a rebel for a Union soldier.*[107]

There are twenty-two identified bodies in the Connecticut section of Gettysburg National Cemetery. Five of them are 17th Connecticut men. Four of these men—Private Frank J. Benson, Company C; Private Joseph Whitlock, Company C; Daniel H. Purdy, Company C; and James Flynn, Company E—died at the Spangler Farm and were disinterred from marked graves.[108] The fifth, John W. Metcalf, was killed July 2 on East Cemetery Hill. Many of the men killed the first day, including Lieutenant Colonel Douglas Fowler, were never identified. These men are most likely buried as unknowns in the national cemetery. Captain James Moore, Edwin Pickett, and August Bronson were among the few to be identified from the first day's field and brought home by family members to be buried in Connecticut.

The Connecticut section in Gettysburg National Cemetery.
(Photograph by author)

Of the twenty-two marked graves in the Connecticut section two, perhaps three, are Confederate graves. In Section A, Grave 5, marked as "S. Carter, A, 15 Regiment C.V.," most likely belongs to Lieutenant Sidney Carter, Company A, 14th South Carolina. Carter was wounded in the chest during the attack on Seminary Ridge on July 1. Carter's trusted slave, Dave, stayed with him until July 3. Carter knew he was dying, and as the Confederate army retreated he gave Dave his watch and personal effects, telling Dave to relay to his family that he would meet them in heaven. Carter died at Cashtown in Federal hands on July 8, 1863. Dave walked several hundred miles back to the Carter home in South Carolina. The watch that Carter wanted to go to his young son was lost, but Dave delivered Carter's personal effects and last words to his widow and family.[109]

Section A, Grave 5 in the Connecticut section of Gettysburg Military Cemetery, marked as S. Carter, A, 15 Regiment C.V., is most likely Lieutenant Sidney Carter, Company A, 14th South Carolina. (Photograph by author)

In Section B, Grave 8, marked "Corp. ______ Williams, D, 20th Regiment C.V.," probably holds Corporal David Williams, Company D, 20th North Carolina, killed July 1 during the attack of Iverson's Brigade. He was originally buried on the John Forney farm.[110] In Section B, Grave 10, marked "William Cannells," has two possible identities. When his body was exhumed, this man was listed as having on his person "letters, $8 rebel money, diary, &c."[111] He could be 3rd Lieutenant Ira T. Connell of Company G, 30th North Carolina, who was killed or died July 3 or 4. He was originally buried along the Fairfield Road. The other possible identity is Corporal William Cannell of Company F, 16th Maine, who was killed July 1.[112]

A third Gettysburg invasion took place when the national cemetery was dedicated on November 19, 1863. The town was once again swamped with visitors. David Wills invited President Lincoln to the ceremony. After the main oration by Edward Everett, the principal speaker, the president was asked to give a "few appropriate remarks." The president did so with the elegiac and immortal 272 words of the Gettysburg Address.

For those who came to the dedication of the honored resting place of the Union dead, one of the most disturbing features had to be the several thousand Confederate graves that were scattered over the landscape in all directions. Small, barren mounds and rises in the earth marked the long prominent burial trenches that had begun to settle. On February 2, 1864, the *Gettysburg Star and Sentinel* printed an article on the disposition of the Confederate dead:

> *There appears to be considerable feeling in and around Gettysburg that a place be set apart for the burial of the Confederate dead who are now buried promiscuously over the battlefield, or in the vicinity. The recent rains have washed the places where they are buried, and the bones are exposed; besides which, in a short time the land will be put under cultivation, and no trace of their last resting place will be left. Common humanity would dictate the removal to some spot, not in or about our own National Cemetery, but the purchase of ground somewhere, where Southern friends may, when the rebellion is crushed and all is peace, make their pilgrimage here.*[113]

The bones of Confederate dead disturbed by the farmer's plow. (Library of Congress)

The idea was almost treasonous to some Northerners, who believed only Southern sympathizers would advocate for honorable graves for traitors. Certainly, the state of Pennsylvania would not bear the cost for the decent burial of traitors to the Union. There were few families in the South that had the resources or means to retrieve their dead, and there was little Northern sympathy for any such initiative in a nation sick of the war. It was not until 1870 that a movement was underway in the Southern states to gather and transfer Gettysburg's Confederate dead. The Ladies Memorial Associations from Virginia, Georgia, and North and South Carolina contracted Dr. Rufus B. Weaver, the son of Samuel Weaver. The difficult process was fraught with financial and political turmoil. Dr. Weaver was never fully reimbursed but did the work ethically and diligently. In the years after the battle many of the graves had been lost or destroyed. Identification was problematic in many instances, but between 1871 and 1873 Dr. Weaver managed to examine, box, and ship to the South 3,320 remains from 116 separate sites. Weaver struggled for years to try to claim what he was owed by the Ladies' Associations, but the claims were never settled.[114]

THE VETERAN RESERVE CORPS

The army was not done with the many wounded who ultimately recuperated but would never be considered "whole" again. Uncle Sam needed manpower and was reluctant to release any man who could serve a purpose in support of the army. After Gettysburg many of the surviving wounded of the 17th Connecticut were transferred directly into the Invalid Corps to complete their term of enlistment. The Invalid Corps was created in 1863 as a military reserve organization within the Union army to allow partially disabled, infirm soldiers to perform light duty, freeing able-bodied soldiers to serve on the front lines. Based on the extent of a soldier's wounds or illness, they were assigned to one of two Invalid Corps battalions. The first carried weapons and fought in combat. The second was made up of men with more serious impairments, who served as nurses, cooks, and prison guards. The Invalid Corps was known as the "Cripple Brigade" or the "Inspected and Condemned" after the IC initials that Army inspectors stamped on faulty goods and supplies. This rendered it unpopular among wounded soldiers, who felt less than whole as "damaged goods" and felt "condemned" to service in the Invalid Corps. The word *invalid* itself was considered an insult in the nineteenth century. For a man to be called *in-valid*, no longer a valid man, meant he was useless, less than whole. In 1864 the Invalid Corps was renamed the Veteran Reserve Corps (VRC) to eliminate this stigma and to rebrand the corps as honorable service.[115] When the Veteran Reserve Corps was called out to man the defenses of Washington at Fort Stevens against General Jubal Early's raid on July 11 and 12, 1864, one story went that an officer of the Veteran Reserve Corps was asked if his men would stand. To which he replied, "*Well, we can't run.*"

As the Gettysburg casualty lists were being printed in Connecticut newspapers, Provost Marshall James E. Dunham was printing advertisements to recruit wounded Connecticut officers and soldiers into the Invalid Corps. Dunham, the former captain of the 17th Connecticut's Company G, had resigned his commission on May 8, 1863, for the safer, more politically expedient position of Connecticut Provost Marshal of the 4th District. And indeed, many of the 17th Connecticut wounded, some after many months of convalescence, would be transferred to the corps to finish out their enlistments before receiving an honorable discharge. Others, like Corporal Aaron Lee, would do everything in their power to return to the regiment, disdaining service in the Invalid Corps. Wounded officers, honorably discharged for disability and always in demand, were solicited to receive commissions. Major Brady, wounded in the shoulder on July 2, would never return to the regiment. Brady was discharged for disability in October 1863; loathe to leave the army, he mustered into the Veteran Reserve Corps 20th Infantry as a major. Brady would court controversy

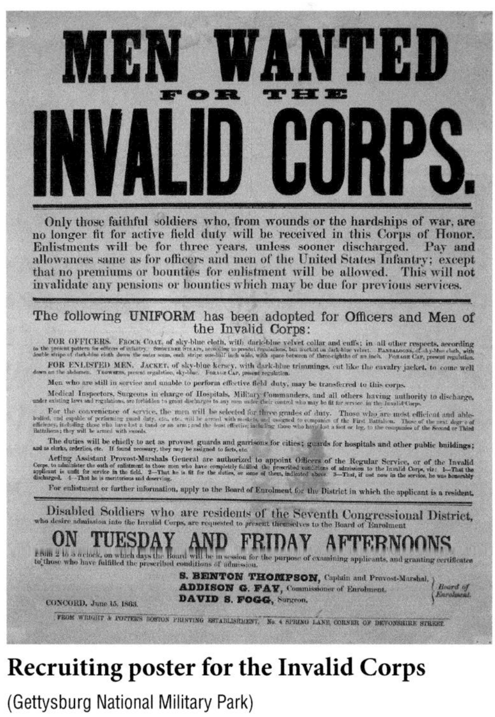

Recruiting poster for the Invalid Corps

(Gettysburg National Military Park)

as the provost marshal of Point Lookout Prison Camp. By war's end Brady was breveted colonel and would remain in the army until 1867.[116] Many of the surviving wounded of the 17th Connecticut who fought at Gettysburg would finish their enlistments as clerks, nurses, and guards in the VRC.

THE MISSING

The tens of thousands of unknown dead of the Civil War were a heartbreaking national tragedy. The army had no formal procedures or protocols for notifying families in the event of a soldier's death. There was no central graves registration process. There were no official identification tags or discs like the dog tags that became universal military protocol during the First World War to provide body identification. After battles, families searched for the fate of their loved ones in the notoriously inaccurate casualty lists published in local newspapers or telegraphed and posted in public locations. Record keeping was a fragile construct that depended mostly on company rolls and descriptive lists made out by the company clerks and officers. Eyewitness accounts from comrades of men killed in battle, wounded, or missing were solicited, sometimes for months, even years, after a battle occurred in order to determine the fate of the missing and dead.

In mass casualty situations, like the first day at Gettysburg, where many company officers were casualties themselves, regimental and company record keeping broke down and uncertainty about the fate of the missing might never be established. As we saw in preceding accounts, immediately after the battle men like Sergeant William Daniels, Company C, Lieutenant David Bartram, Company G, and Captain William Hubbell, Company D, were listed as missing and presumed dead until their status as prisoners was established well after the battle. Searchers from Connecticut traveled to Gettysburg to examine graves and hospitals for Bartram and Hubble only to return home without any information. Some men of the 17th Connecticut, such as Private Calvin Nobles, Company A, who was killed in the darkness during the attack on East Cemetery Hill on the night of July 2, were listed as missing, presumed killed, no further record. For grieving families this lack of certainty was devastating. From a more practical standpoint the death of a soldier had to be established beyond a doubt before a soldier's pension could be received. Calvin Nobles's mother was finally able to apply for and be granted a pension for her son's death in 1880.[117]

For months after the battle, company officers interviewed possible witnesses and searched for information to answer inquiries from grieving widows and family members seeking pensions after the deaths of their husbands and sons at Gettysburg. The pension act of July 14, 1862, increased pension rates and provided potential eligibility for pensions to every person in military or naval service since March 4, 1861 (who could prove disability), their widows and orphans, and for dependent orphan sisters.[118] The pension process was often difficult to negotiate without legal assistance. The pension procedure relied upon the Adjutant General's Office or the Navy Department to confirm details of death or disability for each application from records submitted by the regiment. Any uncertainty or lack of definitive records regarding the death of a soldier could halt the process. Pension regulations prohibited payments to "any person who in any manner aided or abetted the rebellion." A widow had to have positive proof of the death of her husband. She had to prove marriage with official documentation, had to have official registrations for the birth of any children she claimed were eligible, and had to present documentation with sworn statements that she had been loyal to the United States and had never supported the rebellion. Often the pension application required sworn, notarized statements from neighbors or community members who knew the deceased soldier and his wife and children, as well as a positive, official identification of death.[119]

On December 18, 1863, Captain Burr of Company E was called on to present a signed statement for a pension application for the widow of George Gurnsey and her minor son.

Camp of the 17th Regt. C.V.
Folly Island S.C. Dec. 18th 1863

This certifies that George H. Guernsey of Westport, Ct. was a member of Co. E. 17th Regiment Conn. Vols. Was wounded at the Battle of Gettysburgh Pa. July 1st, 1863, and died from the effects of his wounds at U.S. G. Hospital West Philadelphia, Pa. August 9th 1863. Final Statements sent to Adjt. Genl. Washington.

H. P. Burr
Capt. Co. E.
17th Regt. Conn.[120]

On January 29, 1864, Captain Milton Daniels, Company C, was called on to present a signed statement for a pension application for Anna Delevan, the widow of Smith Delevan. There was some uncertainty as to the circumstances of Delevan's death. He was wounded on July 1 and listed as dying of wounds on July 15 at Gettysburg.[121] A National Archives hospital register lists Delevan as dying of wounds on July 22 but also states that there was no record of him being at a field hospital.[122] Captain Daniels determined Private Delevan was killed immediately in action.

Camp 17th C.V.
Folly Island, S.C.
January 29th 1864

This is to certify that Smith Delevan a private of my company was killed at the battle of Gettysburgh, Penn. July 1st, 1863, while engaged in action—it was at first reported that he died in hospital, but was afterwards found to have been killed immediately so reported members of my company that were taken prisoner and saw him.

M. H. Daniels
Capt. Co C 17th C.V.[123]

THE HIDDEN COSTS OF THE WAR

Not all the wounds of war are visible. In 1886 the congressional Committee on Military Affairs took up the case for the relief of James Roach, Company E, 17th Connecticut, and submitted a report (H.R. 228) with testimony to "remove the charge of desertion" from Roach, based on insanity. It declared that Roach was not responsible for his acts, and he continued insane until his death on January 6, 1865, of inflammation of the brain.

Private James Roach, Company E, was a thirty-eight-year-old married tailor from Westport. He died in the regimental hospital at St. Augustine, Florida, and is listed as dying of disease. He may be buried at St. Augustine National Cemetery. Roach's Find-A-Grave entry states he was "lost at war."[124]

The report from the Committee on Military Affairs featured testimony from First Sergeant George C. Lees, Corporal James A. Perry, Captain Burr, Captain Hubbell, Corporal Rufus Wakeman, and regimental surgeon Dr. Sabine Stocking. All confirmed that in the words of Sergeant Lees,

> *that for nearly a year he (Roach) performed all the duties required of him . . . a month previous to his death his mind was utterly gone, and in that state he died . . . that it is his firm belief, based upon close observation previous to and subsequent to the battle of Gettysburg, that James Roach was not sufficiently sound of mind to comprehend a soldier's duties, or be responsible for his actions; that the officers of the regiment considered he was feigning sickness for the purpose of procuring his discharge; consequently he was treated with undue severity . . . he (Lees) was satisfied at the time and subsequent events confirmed . . . that Roach's sickness and mental derangement was unfeigned and real.*[125]

Corporal Perry stated in his testimony that he *"witnessed manifestations of insanity in Roach during the campaign in Virginia and previous to the battle of Gettysburg; that he believes, from close observation, that Roach was of unsound mind and not responsible for his acts; that his insanity and death were caused by the necessities of the service, together, perhaps, with a nervous and excitable temperament, which he seemed to possess."*[126]

The Committee recommended that the bill pass, concluding that James Roach was not responsible for the act of desertion before he died, and that the evidence was clear and conclusive based on the statements of the 17th Connecticut men who gave testimony.

Doctor Sabine Stocking, the 17th Connecticut's regimental surgeon, gave testimony on the insanity and death of Private James Roach. (Bridgeport History Center)

We will never know what the true sacrifices and costs of war were to many of the survivors who did not manifest physical wounds. The unseen costs of war took a tremendous toll on Civil War veterans, as they do in every war. War's horrible effects on the mind—including the effects of posttraumatic stress and the distress of alcohol and addiction in coping with wounds seen and unseen—are still not well understood. War is not kind to the human psyche. Wounds that are unseen can be as deep and terrible as those that are visible.

Epilogue

Monuments and Memory

The great generation of men that returned home from the Civil War in 1865 bears remarkable parallels with the great generation that returned home from World War II in 1945. Franklin Roosevelt said, "*There is a mysterious cycle in human events. To some generations much is given. Of other generations much is expected. This generation of Americans has a rendezvous with destiny.*" Much was expected from both these great American generations and their "rendezvous with destiny." The Union men of the greatest generation of the nineteenth century understood that they protected and saved the nation amid its greatest crisis, and that their service and sacrifice conveyed to their posterity a country reunited and renewed as a stronger and greater nation.

For the survivors of the 17th Connecticut, and other veterans of the Civil War, their service remained the defining adventure of their lives. The experiences of the veterans of this greatest of American wars affected them profoundly. Their crucial role in saving the Union was a source of immense pride. These men returned home in 1865 and resumed their civilian lives. They married their sweethearts and began families. They contributed to their communities. They became active in veterans' groups and fraternal organizations, and for the rest of their lives commemorated their service and honored their comrades who sacrificed their lives. Almost all of them would join the Grand Army of the Republic (GAR), creating one of the most powerful forces in American politics. The GAR was founded on the principles of "Fraternity, Charity, and Loyalty," and it fought for and guarded pensions for veterans, wives, and the children of those who died in service. They promoted patriotic education and supported political candidates, mostly Republican, who would support and promote their political agendas. The veterans named their local GAR posts after their fallen comrades. Their wives and daughters supported them in the Women's Relief Corps. These veterans created monuments throughout the nation: on battlefields where they fought, in the towns and cities where they lived, in cemeteries where the beloved and honored dead were interred. Commemoration and remembrance became powerful forces in their lives and

1902 Bridgeport Encampment of the 17th Connecticut Survivors Association. William Henry Warren is sitting in the front row, third from right. (Courtesy of the William H. Warren Family)

the landscape of the nation. Because their service was a source of enormous pride for them and their heirs, they took measures to protect their legacy in bronze and stone. Regimental histories, publications like the *National Tribune*, and patriotic writings and books celebrated the sacrifices of the fallen, the service of the veterans, patriotism, devotion to the nation, and "Americanism."

The veterans of the 17th Connecticut gathered annually in reunion on August 28 each year, beginning in 1867. The August reunion date commemorated the day when the regiment was mustered into service. The regimental veterans' badge that the veterans designed for themselves, and wore proudly, combined the Eleventh and Tenth Corps symbols, the two corps to which the regiment was assigned. On the double brass parallel bars suspended from the ribbon was inscribed "Chancellorsville and Gettysburg." The crescent moon symbol of the Eleventh Corps bore the inscription "Siege of Forts Wagner & Sumter." In the center of the Tenth Corps symbol was a large 17, and inscribed around the square was Aug. 28, 1862, C.V.

The badge of the 17th Connecticut Volunteer Regiment. (Author's collection)

On July 12, 1865, James Middlebrook wrote from Hilton Head, South Carolina, to his wife in Trumbull that the regiment would soon be home. In the letter Middlebrook discussed traveling with his wife after he returned. "*Make up your mind to travel some when we get home. I think of going to that place long to be remembered—Gettysburg.*" [1] The members of the regiment would return to Gettysburg over the years to dedicate their monuments and remember and honor the ultimate sacrifice of their comrades who never came home.

THE 1884 MONUMENT DEDICATION ON BARLOW'S KNOLL

On July 1, 1884, twenty-one years after the battle, the survivors of the 17th Connecticut and their guests gathered on Barlow's Knoll to dedicate their monument. The excursion began on the morning of June 30, as ferryboats arrived at the Pennsylvania Railroad depot at Jersey City. Once the survivors of the 17th Connecticut and their guests were assembled, more than two hundred people, the party purchased tickets on a special train that would take them to Pennsylvania. They arrived at Gettysburg at sunset. The next morning the ladies assembled in front of the Eagle Hotel and embarked in carriages for Barlow's Knoll. The men assembled with two bands and other guests. They marched in parade to the battlefield. A covered viewing stand, accommodating one hundred people, had been erected near the tablet to be unveiled.[2] The monument dedication booklet described the scene:

> *At a signal given, the two flags covering the Tablet were removed by Miss Minnie Moore, daughter of the late Capt. James E. Moore, who fell on this spot during the battle of July 1st, 1863, and Miss Fannie Noble, a daughter of Gen. W. H. Noble, while a large national ensign was drawn to the top of a thirty-six foot pole erected near the Tablet. At the same time one gun was fired from the cannon of the Corporal Skelly Post, G.A.R., and the band played the Star Spangled Banner, amid great applause.*[3]

The dedication booklet estimated more than seven hundred people gathered on Barlow's Knoll for the ceremony. Gettysburg battlefield photographer William H. Tipton was on hand to photograph the dedication. His photograph shows an immense crowd surrounding the monument, making it almost impossible to pick out individuals who attended.

In the Lewis Leigh Collection at the United States Army Heritage Education Center at Carlisle, Pennsylvania, there is an original photograph of the monument dedication in the papers of General William Noble. The back of the photograph bears the following handwritten description:

> *The Monument of the Seventeenth Regiment Connecticut Volunteers—to the Men of the Regiment who fell in battle at Gettysburg July 1st, 1863—the first day of the great battle. Frances' great-grandfather, General William Henry Noble was the Colonel of the Regiment—and it was known as*

The 17th Connecticut monument dedication on Barlow's Knoll, July 1, 1884. (Gettysburg National Military Park)

the Fairfield County Regiment—as the soldiers all came from Fairfield County, Connecticut.

The Monument was unveiled July 1st, 1884—twenty-one years after the battle—by Frances' grandmother—Fannie Sheldon Noble. The picture represents the scene just after she had unveiled the Monument by drawing aside the flag which draped it. The grey haired gentleman seated in the center at the front of the canopy is great-grandfather Noble. The gentleman seated at his right is Governor Lounsbury of Connecticut—who was a private soldier in the Regiment—the one at his left—is Rev. Dr. William K. Hall of Newburgh, New York who was the Chaplain of the Regiment. Grandmother and great-Aunt Nettie are seated near them but cannot be seen in the crowd.

The battle of Gettysburg lasted three days. The 1st day, all of the Union Army had not overtaken General Lee's Army and the 1st and 11th Army Corps had to fight alone and had a very hard, desperate fight—but that night—the rest of the Union Army arrived, and the Confederate Army had the hard time and retreated during the night of the 3rd day and when the 4th of July arrived it dawned very gloriously for the Union. The Regimental Veteran Association of the 17th always keeps a flag flying by this monument because their Lieut. Col. was instantly killed there.

The Regiment has another monument,—a shaft—in the battlefield—to mark the spot where they fought the last day. This monument was erected to them by the State of Connecticut. It is at the foot of Cemetery Hill.[4]

The dedication booklet featured the sketch of Barlow's Knoll made by Private Justus M. Silliman, Company H, and was labeled "*A Few Days After the Battle of Gettysburg, 1863*." The sketch shows a landscape that can only be imagined today and had changed dramatically by the time of the dedication. The description of the sketch in the booklet read:

Barlow's Knoll

The grove, consisting mostly of oak and hickory, has been entirely cut off. The oak tree crowning the knoll was a prominent landmark to all the members of the Seventeenth Connecticut Volunteers who were engaged in the fight. This oak was severely shattered by lightning some time after the battle. The stump of this tree was removed in fragments as memorials of the battle. The fences in the foreground were torn down by our men just before the engagement. In a trench, about a rod to the left of the oak, the rebels buried about seventy men. There were also four graves, two of which appear in the sketch, while the others are under the rails nearby, which also cover the dead in the trench. The Memorial Tablet was placed twenty or thirty feet to the right of the oak.[5]

Private Justus Silliman's sketch of Barlow's Knoll from the Warren Manuscript. (Bridgeport History Center)

The men of the 17th well remembered the oak tree portrayed in Silliman's sketch. In May 1884, the monument locating committee went to Gettysburg to finalize the placement of the marker on Barlow's Knoll; among its members was Stamford resident Levi Dixon, formerly of Company H. Wounded on July 1, Dixon had his leg amputated at Gettysburg by a Confederate surgeon. The *Stamford Advocate* reported on the chosen site for the monument,

> *Nearby on Barlow's Knoll is the spot where the Seventeenth received such a murderous fire from the enemy. The large oak tree whose trunk and limbs were shattered by shell and Minnie balls is gone, but the stump is still there. Mr. Dixon brought home a piece of it, and together with a Minnie ball picked up on the field, together with other balls and pieces of shell, has placed the relics in the mineral case in the Stamford High School. A neighboring clump of woods, standing in 1863, is gone and its absence alters considerably the general aspect of the scene vividly stamped upon the memory of the visitors. The stumps of the trees are yet there, however.*[6]

After the dedication of the monument William Warren wrote, "*In July 1884 when the regiment dedicated their monument, near this tree, the boys dug around the roots, then cut them off as deep down as they could, most every man bringing home a piece with him. My piece was shaped into a wine glass, and a few other small things.*"[7]

THE 1885 FLAGPOLE MARKS THE LOCATION OF COLONEL FOWLER'S DEATH

In 1885 the surviving members of the 17th Connecticut erected a wooden flagpole on the spot where their beloved Lieutenant Colonel Fowler was killed on July 1, 1863. The pole immediately became a prominent landmark on the first day's battlefield. For years, the national colors were raised by David Blocher, the farmer whose family originally owned Barlow's Knoll, called Blocher's Knoll during the battle. At their annual August 28 meeting, the veterans unanimously adopted a set of resolutions honoring David Blocher's service. In October 1889 when the 17th Connecticut returned to Gettysburg to dedicate its second monument on East Cemetery Hill, the survivors presented Mr. Blocher with "*a handsome framed set of engrossed resolutions.*"

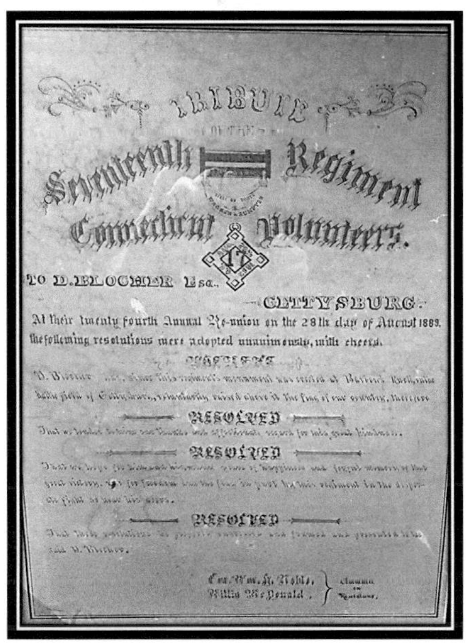

The 1889 framed set of resolutions presented by the 17th Connecticut to David Blocher in 1889. (David Malgee Collection)

The resolutions read:

> *TRIBUTE OF THE Seventeenth Regiment Connecticut Volunteers TO D. BLOCHER ESQ., GETTYSBURG. At their twenty-fourth Annual Reunion on the 28th day of August 1889. The following resolutions were adopted unanimously. With cheers. RECOGNIZES: D. BLOCHER who has since this regiment's monument was erected at Barlow's Knoll on the battlefield of Gettysburg voluntarily raised above it the flag of our country, therefore, RESOLVED: That we tender to him our thanks and affectionate regard for his good kindness, RESOLVED: That we hope for him and his, many years of happiness and joyful memory of that great victory made for freedom and the flag in part by this regiment in the desperate struggle so near his doors. RESOLVED: That these resolutions be properly engrossed and framed and presented to said D. BLOCHER.*

The first wooden flagpole came down in a storm in the mid-1890s and a steel pole replaced it. That pole, in turn, was replaced by the existing pole in 1921. In 1922 at the Annual 17th Connecticut Survivors meeting, the members voted to procure a designation plate for the pole, which marks it today. At that time there were fewer than forty surviving members of the regiment and only twelve attended the reunion and voted on the plaque appropriation.[8]

The plaque on the 17th Connecticut flagpole reads "*Erected by the 17th Conn Vols. Assn.*" The 17th Connecticut monument can be seen in the background. (Photograph by author)

In 2017 Company F, 14th Connecticut funded the restoration of the flagpole. In 2018 the restoration was completed by the National Park Service. On July 1, 2018, on the 155th anniversary of the first day's battle, a living history and rededication ceremony, organized by Company F, 14th Connecticut was held to honor the 17th Connecticut and all who fought at Gettysburg.[9]

THE 1889 DEDICATION OF THE MONUMENT ON EAST CEMETERY HILL

In 1889, the survivors of the regiment returned to Gettysburg to dedicate a second monument at the foot of East Cemetery Hill where they fought on July 2. On October 22, 1889, veterans of the 17th Connecticut and the 27th Connecticut traveled together to Gettysburg to dedicate monuments. The 17th Connecticut monument was a granite shaft, almost 20 feet tall, erected on Wainwright Avenue at the base of East Cemetery Hill. The location may mark the position of the regiment during the night fight on July 2, 1863; however, the terrain and views that the veterans would have remembered from their position on July 2 had been almost totally obscured by overgrowth. The construction of Wainwright Avenue significantly altered the height and pitch of the old Winebrenner farm lane, or Brickyard Lane, which it replaced. The fields across which Hays's brigade of Louisiana Tigers attacked the Union line on East Cemetery Hill were developed for the parking lots and sports fields of two school buildings now there.

The 17th Connecticut monument on Wainwright Avenue commemorating the fight on July 2, 1863. (Photograph by author)

At left: The national and Connecticut state colors flying above the 17th Connecticut monument on Barlow's Knoll. (Photograph by author)

THE GREAT REUNION OF 1913

As the fiftieth anniversary of the battle approached, the remaining men of the 17th Connecticut Survivors Association who were able made plans to travel and participate in the great reunion. The local Connecticut papers covered preparations, and on June 28, 1913, the *Bridgeport Evening Farmer* noted the sweltering weather in Gettysburg with the headline "*Hot Time in Gettysburg for Veterans*."[10] Between July 29 and July 4 more than fifty thousand old soldiers from every state would attend.

On June 28, as the veterans made plans to depart for the great reunion, the front page of the *Bridgeport Farmer* announced, "*Survivors of the 17th Conn. Will Keep Flag Flying Forever at Gettysburg*." The survivors had been concerned about their legacy on Barlow's Knoll and had made provisions to preserve it. In the article, Sergeant Samuel Thorp, of Company K, wounded on the first day at Gettysburg, explained that when he and his comrades arrived in Gettysburg, they would finalize arrangements for a fund to keep the flag waving in perpetuity.

> *On Barlow's Knoll where the 17th made its stand and checked the Confederate advance for the time being, has been erected a monument. There is also a tall flagstaff and from this the Stars and Stripes waves every fair day. A man who owned a farm close by, some time ago made an arrangement with the 17th Conn. Veteran Association to keep the flag flying. He has since died but his son looks after the flag.*
>
> *Since the war many surviving members of the 17th regiment have prospered in business and when Sergeant Thorp and his old comrades go to Gettysburg, they will complete arrangements for a fund to keep the flag waving forever.*
>
> *Money subscribed by the veterans of the 17th Conn will be invested and the earnings used to keep a new flag forever on the staff beside the monument of the 17th. Barlow's Knoll is visible from all railroad trains entering Gettysburg and tourists always remark on the flag which waves there. The veterans of the 17th have kept the colors there since their monument was dedicated.*[11]

Sergeant Samuel Thorp, Company K. Thorp was wounded at Gettysburg on July 1. He was shot in the left arm on Barlow's Knoll.
(Bridgeport History Center)

The Great Reunion would be front-page news nationwide for the next several days. The *Farmer*'s front page reported, "*Sweltering Veterans Evacuate Gettysburg—Thousands of Old Soldiers, Satisfied with Brief Visit, Hasten to Comforts of Home Life—Connecticut Delegation Finds Tents Occupied by Other Visitors*."[12] On July 5, the *Bridgeport Times* ran a front-page article titled, "*Capt. French Back From Gettysburg—Oldest Member of*

Captain Wilson French in 1914. (Captain Wilson French Collection)

Bridgeport Party First to Return, But Had a Good Time." Captain Wilson French was an active man until his death in 1916. In 1912, the year before the reunion, the local papers reported that French had led a campaign parade for the Bull Moose Party of former president Theodore Roosevelt. When he returned from Gettysburg, French was interviewed about his trip. He stated he had been ill almost the entire time at Gettysburg and came home rather than go to the hospital there. Questioned about the camping quarters for the veterans, French stated, "*The Connecticut party did not arrive at the camp until 11:30 Monday night and when we got there we had some difficulty locating our tents. Then we found we had no cots or blankets. I got a cot and blanket for the tent I was assigned to and went in search of a water bucket. When I returned, I found a party of Virginians had taken possession of my tent, cot, blanket and all.*" The paper printed a few other complaints, but it concluded the article with the captain's quote that "*I had a delightful time while I was there though.*"[13]

THEY FOUGHT THE GOOD FIGHT

As the new century rolled forward, the old veterans became fewer. The storm clouds of world war began to gather in Europe. Those survivors who were able still answered the call. Each Decoration Day, now Memorial Day, they gathered for ceremonies in cemeteries and town greens. Each August 28 they continued to gather for their annual reunion, where one of the sad duties of the survivors was to read and record the roll of those old veterans who passed away during the year.

William Warren addresses schoolchildren and the public at a Decoration Day ceremony in Oak Grove Cemetery in West Haven, Connecticut in 1912. (Courtesy of the William H. Warren Family)

During his long life of service, J. Henry Blakeman would hold almost every office in his hometown of Stratford, Connecticut. He would serve as a state representative right up to his death. He remained active in his church, the GAR, and many organizations. On his last Memorial Day, in 1918, he led his comrades in the parade. Many of the Civil War veterans participating that year had to be driven on the parade route in automobiles. The Bridgeport newspaper photographed the event with Henry proudly front and center. J. Henry Blakeman passed away on September 21, 1918, at age seventy-six. He lies in Putnam Cemetery in Stratford with his family. The cenotaph over the empty grave of his best friend, Stephen Crofut, who was killed on July 1 on Barlow's Knoll as he stood shoulder to shoulder with Henry, is on the other side of the cemetery. Stephen's body lies with the unknown dead in Gettysburg National Cemetery.

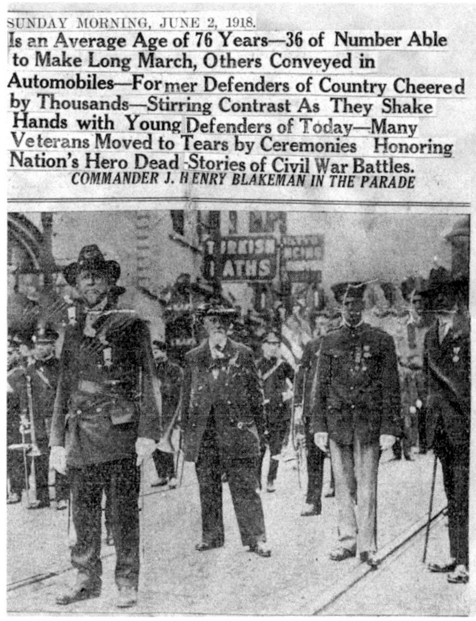

J. Henry Blakeman marching in the Memorial Day parade. (Bridgeport History Center)

Henry's cousin, Selah Blakeman, would also remain vigorous and energetic well into old age. He was well known in the community and continued to be active in both national and local GAR affairs. Selah and his wife never had children. His beloved niece, Harriet Blakeman, the daughter of his youngest brother, would often be

Left: Selah Blakeman at the 17th Connecticut monument on Barlow's Knoll. Right: Blakeman at the 17th Connecticut monument on East Cemetery Hill. Both photographs circa 1913. (Selah Blakeman Collection)

with her uncle, helping him with veterans' affairs and the affairs of the 17th Connecticut Volunteer Association. As Selah's eyesight failed, Harriet Blakeman began keeping the association's books, and she eventually became the group's treasurer. On December 19, 1924, Selah G. Blakeman passed away at his home in Shelton. The Shelton newspaper titled his obituary, "*Colonel Selah G. Blakeman, Civil War Veteran is Dead—Shelton's 'Grand Old Man' Dies at Midnight, Aged 83.*"[14]

THE LAST REUNION

In 1936, Harriet Blakeman sent out invitations for the regiment's seventh-fifth reunion, to be held the next year. The final reunion would take place at Norwalk's Roton Point Park. The invitation noted that "*A most urgent appeal is hereby made to* ***every*** *member to attend* ***this*** *year.*" No member of the regiment would live to attend: the last survivor, Edward Pinkney, died on December 14, 1936. On August 30, 1937, the *Norwalk Hour* reported, "*The final reunion of the 17th Connecticut Volunteers Association was held Saturday at Roton Point Park when the secretary of the association was ordered to close the books of the group and make provision for the presentment to a historical organization for preservation. The association voted also to turn over all of its funds for the perpetuation of a custom observed by the regiment since the close of the Civil War, that of keeping its regimental flag continuously aloft over the battlefield of Gettysburg out of respect for the many members of the regiment who lost their lives there.*"[15]

It would not be until 1964, that Harriet Blakeman liquidated the funds of the association and closed the books forever. On October 21, she enclosed a check for $908.06 to the Gettysburg Battlefield Preservation Association (GBPA) with the request that it use the funds to purchase battlefield land. She wrote that she felt "*that the purpose of the GBPA is one every man of the 17th Regiment Connecticut Volunteers could support with enthusiasm.*" Harriet also inquired about the flagpole on Barlow's Knoll, a subject near and dear to every member of the 17th Connecticut: "*Is the National ensign still flying*

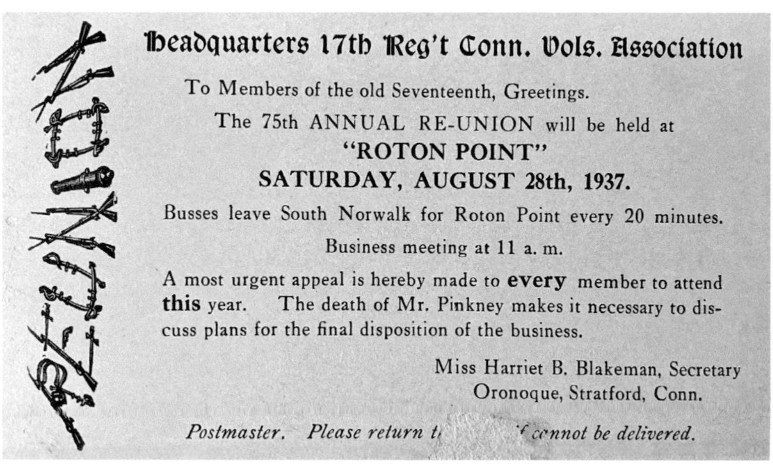
REUNION

Headquarters 17th Reg't Conn. Vols. Association

To Members of the old Seventeenth, Greetings.

The 75th ANNUAL RE-UNION will be held at

"ROTON POINT"

SATURDAY, AUGUST 28th, 1937.

Busses leave South Norwalk for Roton Point every 20 minutes.

Business meeting at 11 a. m.

A most urgent appeal is hereby made to **every** member to attend **this** year. The death of Mr. Pinkney makes it necessary to discuss plans for the final disposition of the business.

Miss Harriet B. Blakeman, Secretary
Oronoque, Stratford, Conn.

Postmaster. Please return t[illegible] cannot be delivered.

The invitation to the final reunion of the 17th Connecticut Volunteer Association in 1937 after the death of the last survivor, Edward Pinkney. (Author's collection) *from the flagstaff at Barlow's Knoll? The 17th Regiment Connecticut Volunteers erected this flagstaff, having received permission from the United States Government. I hope that it is being used every day.*"[16]

On October 24, 1964, Blakeman received a prompt reply from R. D. Hoffsommer, acting executive director of the GBPA. He thanked her for the check. "*I applaud your wisdom in choosing GBPA as the recipient, and I feel sincerely that the men of the 17th would do the same, for it will help preserve for posterity the field they have made sacred to all Americans by their valor and sacrifice.*" In answer to her query about the flagpole, he wrote, "*As I drive from Harrisburg to Gettysburg, one of the first things I see on the field is the flag flying from its tall staff at the 17th's position on Barlow's Knoll. It constitutes one of the guiding marks on the battlefield. The Government is faithful to its promise. We shall be equally faithful in the use of your generous contribution.*"[17].

A gathering of veterans at the Elias Howe Jr. GAR Post in Bridgeport. Third from right is Selah Blakeman, peering through his glasses at the camera with his dimming eyesight. Blakeman wears his 17th Connecticut Veteran's medal proudly alongside the five-pointed bronze GAR medal. (Bridgeport History Center)

Acknowledgments

There are more people than I can count or thank for making this book possible. However, one person whom I can never thank enough, for both his confidence in me and his belief that this book was worth taking a chance on, is Kevin Drake. On a late-August day in 2017, Kevin and I were speaking on the phone and the conversation turned to our favorite topic, Gettysburg. I asked him if he had time to see something I thought was one of the best Connecticut Civil War items I could think of. He said sure, and we took a quick trip to the Bridgeport Public Library. Elizabeth Van Tuyl, the archivist, pulled the thirteen volumes of the Warren Manuscript for us. As we looked through the volumes, I told Kevin I thought Warren's manuscript would make a great book someday. He agreed, and the rest is history—or at least this book. Elizabeth and her predecessor, Mary Witkowski, supported my numerous trips to the library over the years to pore through William Warren's volumes.

To my editor, Ted Hirt, I owe my deepest thanks. Born in Stamford, Fairfield County, Connecticut, Ted is an attorney by profession. He is a reenactor with Battery B, 1st Rhode Island Light Artillery, a living historian, researcher, and a Gettysburg Licensed Town Guide. With his deep passion for Gettysburg's history, his unique skill set, and his proficient editing, Ted's suggestions for improving the manuscript made this a better book. Ted's generosity, knowledge, and editing expertise cannot be overstated. Any errors in this book are mine alone.

I was introduced to the 17th Connecticut regiment when Ann Wardman, then of Stratford, called Shelton High School in 2005 and subsequently dropped off forty-two Civil War letters from Company D's Selah Blakeman for me to read. I soon became acquainted with Selah's cousin J. Henry Blakeman and their Company D messmates Stephen Crofut and Sylvester Rounds. On July 1, 1863, all four stood shoulder to shoulder on Barlow's Knoll; Stephen was killed and Henry and Sylvester were badly wounded, both needing months to recover. Only Selah Blakeman was unscathed, able to fight the next day on East Cemetery Hill. On July 5 he marched away with what was left of the regiment in pursuit of General Lee's army.

These four men were all from Stratford. Carol Lovell, the former curator of the Stratford Historical Society, was instrumental in welcoming me and assisting my research on the 17th Connecticut at the historical society. The members of Stratford Historical Society hosted history presentations by me on numerous occasions. In 2013 Carol called me and said she had received copies of Captain Wilson French's Civil War letters. Once school was out that afternoon, I drove down to the historical society to see six volumes of transcribed letters and documents, almost six hundred! I soon met Susan Richardson Curry—Captain French's great-great-granddaughter—her aunt Betty Richardson, and the rest of the family. The historical society debuted a program in 2014 titled *One Family's Civil War*, and from that time I had access to a treasure trove of letters about the French family, the 17th Connecticut, Bridgeport, and Stratford during the 1860s, and made many wonderful lifelong friends.

I owe a great deal of gratitude the descendants and keepers of the 17th Connecticut regiment: Sue Curry and her husband, Michael; Betty Richardson, her late husband, Don, and her late brother-in-law (and Sue's dad), John; and Lieutenant David Bartram's descendant, Sheila Bartram Hislop, who sent me articles and a precious photograph of David in uniform. Charlene Henderson searched out and posted hundreds of obituaries on Find-A-Grave for the 17th Connecticut and kindly assisted in burial research. Charlene passed suddenly in the fall of 2021 and her support and passion for this project was greatly missed as I completed my final edits. Although I have never met him, Bob Rosati has located so many of the graves of the members of the regiment. I have used his work numerous times over the years. To Jim Fielden of Cleveland, descendant of Roland E. Perry, 75th Ohio, "sister" regiment to the 17th Connecticut, I owe a debt of gratitude for the regimental hospital registers that he transcribed from the National Archives and shared with me. I know I'll see him at the Spangler Farm. To William H. Warren's great-grandsons, Alan Deane Draper and David Warren Draper, thank you for contacting me and sharing William Warren's family history and his legacy.

I also owe a great debt to Dale Call, descendant of Private Benjamin Brotherton, Company E, wounded at Chancellorsville, who since 1997 has labored to expand and keep the legacy flame of the 17th Connecticut alive on his incomparable blog and webpage. Over the years his generosity in sharing the information he has collected and published on the regiment has made it possible for descendants and researchers alike to know and honor these men. I cannot ever thank him enough.

I owe a huge debt of gratitude to all the authors whose works have contributed to this book. The late Gregory Coco's pioneering research into the aftermath of battle produced many publications that I have reread many times over the years, including *A Vast Sea of Misery* and *A Strange and Blighted Land*. Coco's works on the common soldier and the dead of Gettysburg are an invaluable legacy. Other valuable works were: Busey and Busey's *Union Casualties at Gettysburg, A Comprehensive Record*; James Pula's *Under the Crescent Moon with the XI Corps in the Civil War*; Scott Mingus's *Louisiana Tigers in the Gettysburg Campaign*; Charles Hamblen and Walt Powell's *Connecticut*

Yankees at Gettysburg (and thank you to Walt for his kindness in consulting with me on the manuscript); Harry Pfanz's *Gettysburg: Culp's Hill and Cemetery Hill*; John Archer's *The Hour Was One of Horror*; Michael Dreese's *Torn Families, The Hospital on Seminary Hospital*, his works on the flag bearers, and more; Ronald Kirkwood's superb *Too Much for Human Endurance,* on the importance of the George Spangler Farm as a refuge for the wounded and a strategic asset in the battle; and Phil Laino's magnificent opus, the revised and expanded *Gettysburg Campaign Atlas*, which was priceless in giving me insight into and understanding of the before, during, and after of Gettysburg. Several of Phil's maps enrich this volume. All these books and authors deserve a special mention for helping me research this book.

Special thanks go to Barbara Franco, independent scholar, researcher, and founding director of the Seminary Ridge Museum. Barbara was generous in sharing her research on the doctors, surgeons, and nurses who cared for the wounded after the battle and in reviewing my writing in this area; her phenomenal and comprehensive database on the doctors and surgeons of Gettysburg, once published, will be a tremendous addition to the scholarship of the battle.

I thank Licensed Battlefield Guide Stuart Dempsey, who always answered my emails, for his generosity in sharing his knowledge over the years, and his Eleventh Corps tours of the battlefield. I thank Tim Smith, author, Licensed Battlefield Guide, and Director of Education of the Adams County Historical Society, who assisted me both directly and indirectly over the years simply by being a foremost historian of the battle and town and doing the job he loves for Adams County. Over the years, Tim's tours of the battlefield and the town, and especially of East Cemetery Hill, have been instructive and enlightening in helping me to understand the second day's battle. I concur wholeheartedly with Tim that East Cemetery Hill is often treated as the redheaded stepchild of the Gettysburg battlefield. At Gettysburg National Military Park, I thank retired historian John Heiser and museum curator Greg Goodall for help with research and images.

My thanks must also go to the following individuals and organizations: Ken Rich, who was always helpful to me when I reached out with obscure questions; Jake Wynn, formerly of the National Museum of Civil War Medicine; the local Connecticut historical societies who have always supported my research for this project and so many others, including the Shelton Historical Society, Seymour Historical Society, Derby Historical Society, and the Connecticut Historical Society. My appreciation also goes to all my comrades at the Civil War Round Table of South Central Connecticut and the Housatonic Civil War Round Table who have hosted many of my programs on the 17th Connecticut and other Civil War topics. My deepest thanks to Bob O'Brien, Phil Vitiello, and Dave Pelland.

Of course, I must pay tribute to William Warren and the men of the 17th Connecticut, who contributed their firsthand accounts to his manuscript. For many years, my interest in the Civil War has become more focused on the authentic experiences of the citizen-soldiers and their families. I'm not really interested in the "numbers games" of history. As I age, I have become less concerned with the statistics and grand strategies of war and more engaged with the authentic experiences of people like me, who, trapped in years of upheaval and national events, made history from the bottom up. I don't discount numbers and statistics, but Mark Twain's saying about "lies, damn lies, and statistics" makes sense to me. Statistics and numbers can obscure more than they reveal, and numbers are especially prone to obscuring the humanity, and the inhumanity, of events.

William Warren set out to write a regimental history. He never completed that task, but the material he gathered about the rich variety of the experiences of the individuals of the regiment forms a precious legacy much deeper and meaningful than a regimental history. With this book, I hope that I have shared the experiences of the individuals who lived, fought, and sacrificed at Gettysburg in a compelling and engaging manner that casts new light on the lives of these citizen-soldiers. All honor to those volunteer sons of the 17th Connecticut.

Last but not least, thank you to Nick, for driving me through forty-nine states over the years, and for tolerating my quirks and quests to find history everywhere. May we continue to seek and find, live long and prosper, until we too pass into history.

APPENDIX A

Colonel Noble's History of the 17th Connecticut Regiment

Written by Bvt. Brig.-Gen. William H. Noble,
Late Colonel of the Seventeenth Connecticut Volunteers

Record of service of Connecticut Men in the Army and Navy of the United States
During the War of the Rebellion.
Connecticut Adjutant-General's Office
Contributors: Smith, Stephen R.; Camp, Frederick E.; Barbour, Lucius A.; White, George M.
Press of the Case, Lockwood & Brainard Compamy
1889
https://cslib.contentdm.oclc.org/digital/collection/p128501coll2/id/177208/

HISTORY

OF THE

SEVENTEENTH REGIMENT C. V. INFANTRY.

WRITTEN BY BVT. BRIG.-GEN. WILLIAM H. NOBLE, LATE COLONEL OF THE SEVENTEENTH CONNECTICUT VOLUNTEERS.

THIS regiment was almost wholly enlisted from the sons of Fairfield County. The appointment of its Colonel, William H. Noble of Bridgeport, and the order for its rendezvous as the county regiment at what is now the Seaside Park of that city, were made by Governor Buckingham at the earnest request of leading citizens of the county. The hour was dark, and there was desperate need of soldiers in the field. It was doubted whether the county alone could fill a regiment as rapidly as the whole State, but the men of Fairfield County took the risk. They pledged the Governor to have their good men and true as quickly at the front as any Connecticut regiment. Well did Fairfield County fulfill that promise.

Its Colonel was commissioned on the 22d day of July, 1862. Within thirty days the regiment could have marched to the front a thousand strong. To it, Norwalk furnished two companies, A and F; Stamford, Company B; Danbury, Company C; Bridgeport, Company D and parts of three others; Westport, Newtown, and Bridgeport made up Company E; Ridgefield, Redding, and Bridgeport, Company G; New Canaan, Company H; Greenwich, Company I. Company K was furnished mostly from Fairfield and Bridgeport. Every town of the county sent a squad of soldiers to the regiment, which was mustered into the United States service on the 28th day of August, 1862, and left for the front by rail on the 3d of September following.

Its departure was a rare scene of patriotic devotion and affection at parting. The date of its moving had become known throughout the county. On the 3d of September, from all its towns there thronged to Bridgeport, filling its seaside camp and the city, the kindred and friends of the regiment. They showered Godspeeds and blessings on their sons, and braced their hearts to the parting by pledges to keep all right and bright at the firesides of the county.

The regiment thought it was going straight "to fight mit Sigel," as General Franz Sigel, commanding the Eleventh Corps, Army of the Potomac, had by permission of the War Department early won the consent of the regiment to join his force. On its arrival at Baltimore, however, it found that city alarmed by raids of the enemy's cavalry, and the regiment was stopped by General John E. Wool, then commanding, and after a delay of a day or two was ordered to encamp as auxiliary to the garrison of Fort Marshall. This was an important earthwork and barracks just east of Baltimore, overlooking the city and harbor, and commanding a wide sweep of country.

Neither the work given the regiment, nor the duties imposed, nor their military association, were pleasing. It therefore sought, through its Colonel, a transfer to its original destination, Sigel's Corps. This action coming to the knowledge of General Wool so angered him that, late on the night of Oct. 14, 1862, he peremptorily ordered its Colonel to have the Seventeenth Regiment outside of Baltimore before noon of the 15th, or take the consequences At half-past eleven the next day, the regiment and all its belongings were speeding by rail to Washington. Arriving there at night, they were ordered next morning to Fort Kearney, one of the northwest defenses of the Capital. After about a fortnight at this fort, on November 5th a welcome order came for the regiment to report to General Sigel, at Gainesville, Va. His corps then held Thoroughfare Gap of the Bull Run Mountains.

On reaching Gainesville, the Seventeenth was united with the Second Brigade, First Division, of this Corps. This Second Brigade was made up of four regiments of Ohio men — the Twenty-fifth, Fifty-fifth, Seventy-fifth, and the One Hundred and Seventh. Later on, the One Hundred and Fifty-seventh New York was added, making, with the Seventeenth Connecticut, six regiments, which served through the rest of the war close together in Virginia, on Folly and Morris Islands, S. C., and in Florida. All were, either together or in detachments, in Florida under the command of Colonel Noble.

Soon after the Seventeenth Connecticut joined the Eleventh Corps, it moved to Hopewell Gap, in the same mountain range, thence after a fortnight to Chantilly, Va., and on December 6, 1862, it began a tedious seven days' winter march, through slush and snow, towards Fredericksburg, Va. The corps was held as a reserve to the advance of General Burnside's Army of the Potomac.

After the disaster at Fredericksburg, the Seventeenth spent its winter in camps at Stafford Court House, Belle Plain, and Brooke's Station, Va. All these posts were near landings on the Potomac and the railroad from Aquia Creek to Falmouth.

On the last of April orders were given to make ready to move with the corps (now under command of General Howard) in the disastrous campaign of Chancellorsville. This was the first telling work the regiment had faced. The weather was excessively warm, and before Chancellorsville was reached all had got into light marching order, and the road was strewn with surplus impedimenta. The Eleventh Corps crossed the Rappahannock at Kelly's Ford on pontoons, and the Rapidan at Germania Ford by a temporary bridge and by fording. On the field of Chancellorsville the Seventeenth was stationed near the extreme right of the line. Two of its companies were on picket in the Wilderness when Stonewall Jackson surprised and routed the Eleventh Corps, whose commander was two miles away at the Chancellorsville House. This was the first trial of the Seventeenth under fire. It lost in the battle (killed, wounded, and missing) 120 men. Lieutenant-Colonel Charles Walter was instantly killed. He had been captured at first Bull Run, and was only released from his imprisonment in time to receive the appointment of Lieutenant-Colonel of the regiment. Colonel Noble was severely wounded and his horse shot under him. Horace Greeley, on page 357 of his "American Conflict," singles out for commendation the hopeless rally of this regiment under Colonel Noble, in face of defeat and retreat all around them.

After the withdrawal of General Hooker from this battle-field, the regiment and its corps rested near Brooke's Station until the Army of the Potomac began that following of Lee's advance which resulted in the battle of Gettysburg. It reached that battle-field in the fiercest of the first day's fight. The regiment was pushed forward to the extreme right. Two of its companies, as volunteer sharpshooters, were sent to its outmost flank. The regiment was struck by an overwhelming force, under Confederate General Gordon, at Oakhill, now Barlow's Knoll. Here it lost most of its thirty-nine men who fell in that battle. The entire number of killed, wounded, and missing in the action was 198. Lieutenant-Colonel Douglas Fowler was instantly killed; Captain Wilson French was severely wounded; Major Allen G. Brady was severely contused and disabled by a shell-splinter breaking the scapula.

On that Oakhill now stands the regiment's monument to its dead in the battle Looking from Cemetery Hill northward over the field of Gettysburg, it is a conspicuous landmark. Around it sweeps the new military boulevard which is to encompass the entire battle-field.

Overwhelmed and repulsed by the superior force of the enemy, the Eleventh Corps retreated to Cemetery Hill. Here the Seventeenth in its brigade line was posted at its northern foot. This place it held through the next two days of the battle. Its position was many times charged upon, but the enemy neither broke through nor disordered its ranks.

On the 6th of July the regiment and its corps, with the rest of the army, began that following of the Confederate force which ended in its escape across the Potomac. It was several times close upon their pickets, and at Hagerstown, Md., was right on their breastworks, thrown up to hold off our attack while making ready to get over the Potomac. When the Union army, after two days' delay, advanced, the enemy had crossed that river. The Eleventh Corps soon after passed over on pontoons, and marched, rested, and renewed their tattered clothing, worn from Gettysburg. A few unimportant movements were made and several positions briefly held.

Early in August, 1863, at Catlett's Station, Va., the division (then Gordon's) was ordered to take rail for Alexandria and there embark for the Southern Department. The transports reached Folly Island, Aug. 12, 1863. The brigade under General Ames was soon transferred to Morris Island. It there saw the first gun fired in Gillmore's bombardment of Sumter, and its southwest wall battered into sand heaps. The regiment was many times, for several days, in the siege works approaching Fort Wagner. Two of its men were killed and several wounded. For two weeks, in and out of said works, the regiment was constantly under fire from Forts Wagner, Moultrie, and Johnson, and the batteries near Charleston. Shell and round shot reached nearly the whole of Morris Island. The regiment met here the Sixth and Seventh Connecticut, worn by long and hard service in this department. General Terry commanding these and other troops, was the next in rank under General Gillmore. He had made ready to assault Wagner in three columns, when its evacuation over night was announced.

On Morris Island, before the fall of Wagner, the Seventeenth, with all the regiments of its division, had volunteered to make a night assault upon the walls of Sumter. But the claim of the navy to that honor relieved it from the chance of death or glory. Both might have been the outcome from such an assault.

After Wagner fell, until about February 23, 1864, the Seventeenth with all its division remained camped on Folly Island. A brief expedition to St. John's Island had been the only event. At that date an order came for Ames's Brigade to embark for Florida. The disaster at Olustee threatened to be followed up by an effort to drive our forces out of that district On arrival at Jacksonville, General Seymour, commanding, gave General Ames a division, of which the First Brigade was under General Hawley, the Second under Colonel Noble. After about a month without incident, the whole force at Jacksonville was broken up. All re-enlisted regiments were sent north to the Army of the Potomac; the Seventeenth relieved the Tenth Connecticut at St. Augustine; the Ohio boys remained at Jacksonville. From this time to the end of the war the Seventeenth's headquarters were at St. Augustine. One company usually garrisoned the old Fort

San Marco; the rest were scattered on raids and at posts. The regiment had been but a few days at St. Augustine when all but that garrison were ordered to Volusia, seventy-five miles up the St. John's River, and to hold posts at Welaka and Saunders below. Right away these two out-of-way posts were captured, and their force of thirty-nine men and two officers were taken to Andersonville. The two companies left at Volusia, by pluck and strategy held on till relieved.

Soon after, General Gordon, then commanding Florida, placed in charge of Colonel Noble all the territory east of the St. John's River. This brought Lieutenant-Colonel Wilcoxson in immediate command of the regiment and of St. Augustine. Generals Birney, Gordon, and Hatch, who severally commanded Florida during 1864, sent the regiment and other forces under Colonel Noble on various raids through Florida. The results of these raids, though successful, were of no great military importance, but they subjected the regiment to the trying effects of the climate, and planted the seeds of lasting disease.

On the 24th of December, 1864, when returning across the country from a court martial at Jacksonville to St. Augustine, Colonel Noble was captured by guerrillas and taken to Macon and Andersonville, Ga. Lieutenant-Colonel Wilcoxson, thus left in command of the regiment, was, about Feb. 4, 1864, on an expedition to Bradock's Farm, on the South of Dunn's Lake, some fifty miles from St. Augustine, mortally wounded while endeavoring to escape from Dixon's Cavalry. At the same time Adjutant Chatfield was instantly killed, and thirty-two men and two officers and a lot of army teams captured. The men were taken to Andersonville.

From this time, the regiment served without any important occurrence through the winter of 1864–5, and the following spring to about June, 1865, when it was ordered to rendezvous at Jacksonville, preparatory to discharge and departure for home. The Seventeenth was mustered out at Hilton Head on the 19th of July, 1865.

Thus passed out of the service and into history one of those Connecticut regiments whose entire conduct and capacity conferred immortal honor on the State, and contributed so essentially to uphold the authority of the Nation.

ENGAGEMENTS.

Chancellorsville, Va., May 2, 1863.
Gettysburg, Pa., July 1–4, 1863.
Morris Island and Fort Wagner, Aug., 1863.
Welaka and Saunders, Fla., May 19, 1864.
Dunn's Lake, Fla., Feb. 5, 1865.

APPENDIX B

Regimental Roster

SEVENTEENTH REGIMENT C. V. INFANTRY.

Field and Staff.

Name and Rank.	Residence.	Date of Enlistment.	Date of Muster in this organization.	Remarks.
Colonel.				
William H. Noble,	Bridgeport,	July 22,'62	Aug.29,'62	Wd. May 2, '63, Chancellorsville, Va. Cap'd Dec. 24, '64, St. John's Co., Fla. Pro. Brig.-Gen. by bvt. Mch. 13, '65. Par. Apr. 8, '65. M. o. July 19, '65.
Lieutenant-Colonels.				
Charles Walter,	Bridgeport,	Aug.27,'62	Aug.29,'62	Killed May 2, '63, Chancellorsville, Va.
Douglas Fowler,	Norwalk,	July 14,'62	Aug.28,'62	Pro. from Capt. Co. A, May 2, '63. Killed July 1, '63, Gettysburg, Pa.
Albert H. Wilcoxson,	Norwalk,	July 16,'62	Aug.29,'62	Must. Adj. Pro. Capt. Co. I, Nov. 15, '62. Pro. from Capt. Co. I, Sep. 1, '63. Wd. and cap'd Feb. 5, '65, Dunn's Lake, Fla. Died Mch. 6, '65, Tallahassee, Fla.
Henry Allen,	Norwalk,	Aug.11,'62	Aug.28,'62	Pro. from Capt. Co. F, to Maj. Mch. 5, '64; Lt.-Col. May 20, '65. M. o. July 19, '65.
Major.				
Allen G. Brady,	Torrington,	July 18,'62	Aug.28,'62	(See Lt.-Col. 3d C.V.) Pro. from Capt. Co. B, Aug. 29,'62. Wd. July 2,'63, Gettysburg, Pa. Disc. dis. Oct. 21,'63. Must. Maj. 20th Regt. V. R. C. Nov. 23, '63; Lt.-Col. and Col. by bvt. Aug. 7, '65. Disc. Dec. 15, '66.
Adjutants.				
William L. Hubbell,	Bridgeport,	July 23,'62	Aug.28,'62	Pro. from 1st Lt. Co. D, Nov. 15, '62; Capt. Co. D, June 4, '63.
H. Whitney Chatfield,	Bridgeport,	Aug.20,'62	Aug.28,'62	Pro. from Sergt.-Maj. June 4, '63. Killed Feb. 5, '65, Dunn's Lake, Fla.
Quartermasters.				
Hanford N. Hayes,	Bridgeport,	July 25,'62	Aug.29,'62	Resgd. July 18, '63.
John S. Ward,	Bridgeport,	July 22,'62	Aug.29,'62	Pro. from Q.M.-Sergt. Oct. 24, '63. M. o. July 19, '65.
Surgeons.				
Robert Hubbard,	Bridgeport,	Aug.11,'62	Aug.29,'62	Resgd. Dec. 28, '63.
Sabin Stocking,	Glastonbury,	Aug.29,'62	May 31,'64	Pro. from Asst. Surg. 8th C. V. May 31, '64. M. o. July 19, '65.
Asst. Surgeons.				
Robert C. McEwen,	Stratford,	Aug.16,'62	Aug.29,'62	Resgd. Sep. 30, '63.
Elijah Gregory,	Bridgeport,	Aug.16,'62	Aug.29,'62	M. o. July 19, '65.
Henry S. Turrell,	New Milford,	———	Feb. 13,'64	Cap'd May 19, '64, Welaka, Fla. Par. Nov. 18, '64. M. o. July 19, '65. Must. 1st Lt. and Asst. Surg. U. S. A. June 26, '75.
Chaplains.				
William K. Hall,	New Haven,	Oct. 27,'62	Oct. 28,'62	Resgd. Nov. 6, '63.
George Burnham,	†Hilton H'd,SC	Mch. 7,'65	Apr. 7,'65	Disc. Aug. 4, '65.

Non-Commissioned Staff.

Name and Rank.	Residence.	Date of Enlistment.	Date of Muster in this organization.	Remarks.
Sergeant-Majors.				
Theodore Gray,	Bridgeport,	July 22,'62	Aug.29,'62	Pro. 2d Lt. Co. E, Oct. 3, '62.
George C. Peck,	Greenwich,	Aug.14,'62	Aug.28,'62	Pro. from 1st Sergt. Co. I, Nov. 1, '62; 2d Lt. Co. I, Apr. 18, '63.
H. Whitney Chatfield,	Bridgeport,	Aug.20,'62	Aug.28,'62	Pro. from Priv. Co. G, Apr. 18, '63; Adj. June 4, '63.
C. Frederick Betts,	Norwalk,	July 18,'62	Aug.28,'62	Pro. from Corp. Co. A, June 4, '63; 2d Lt. Co. A, Sep. 1, '63.
John W. Rae,	Greenwich,	Aug. 9,'62	Aug.28,'62	Pro. from Sergt. Co. I, Nov. 1, '63. Died Dec. 9, '63.
Henry McDonough,	Westport,	Aug.13,'62	Aug.28,'62	Pro. from 1st Sergt. Co. E, Dec. 13, '63; 2d Lt. Co. E, Mch. 19, '64.
Frank S. Middlebrook,	Norwalk,	Aug.11,'62	Aug.28,'62	Pro. from Corp. Co. F, Aug. 28, '64; 2d Lt. Co. F, Mch. 30, '65 (not must.). M. o. July 19, '65.
Q.M.-Sergeants.				
John S. Ward,	Bridgeport,	July 22,'62	Aug.29,'62	Pro. Q.M. Oct. 24, '63.
William H. Keeler,	Stratford,	July 22,'62	Aug.28,'62	Pro. from Corp. Co. D, Nov. 4, '63. M. o. July 19, '65.
Com.-Sergeants.				
Josiah L. Day,	Danbury,	July 19,'62	Aug.29,'62	(See Priv. Co. E, 1st C. V.) Disc. dis. Mch. 6, '63.
Edwin D. Hurd,	Fairfield,	Aug. 8,'62	Aug.28,'62	Pro. from Priv. Co. D, Mch. 6, '63. M. o. July 19, '65.

Name and Rank.	Residence.	Date of Enlistment.	Date of Muster in this organization.	Remarks.
Hospital Stewards.				
Jesse S. Nash,	Bridgeport,	Aug.14,'62	Aug.29,'62	Disc. dis. Nov. 26, '62. [Nov. 19, '63.
George H. Spencer,	Newtown,	Aug.14,'62	Aug.28,'62	Pro. from Corp. Co. E, Apr. 4, '63. Redc. to ranks and trans. to Co. E,
Samuel B. Barnum,	Bridgeport,	July 23,'62	Aug.28,'62	Pro. from Priv. Co. D, Nov. 19, '63. M. o. July 19, '65.
Principal Musicians.				
Thomas Hearn,	Norwalk,	Aug.12,'62	Aug.28,'62	Pro. from Musc. Co. F, July 1, '63. M. o. July 19, '65.
John P. Hearn,	Norwalk,	Feb. 20,'63	Feb. 20,'63	Pro. from Musc. Co. F, Nov. 10, '63. Cap'd Feb. 4, '65, Dunn's Lake, Fla. Par. Apr. 21, '65. M. o. July 19, '65.

Company A.

Name and Rank.	Residence.	Date of Enlistment.	Date of Muster in this organization.	Remarks.
Captains.				
Douglas Fowler,	Norwalk,	July 14,'62	Aug.28,'62	Pro. Lt.-Col. May 2, '63.
John McQuhae, Jr.,	Norwalk,	July 14,'62	Aug.28,'62	Must. 1st Lt. Pro. June 2, '63. Dismissed Nov. 9, '63.
James H. Ayres,	New Canaan,	July 21,'62	Aug.28,'62	Pro. from 1st Lt. Co. H, Mch. 5, '64. M. o. July 19, '65.
1st Lieutenants.				[16, '64.
R. Lorenzo Ells,	Norwalk,	July 16,'62	Aug.28,'62	Must. Sergt. Pro. 2d Lt. May 2, '63; 1st Lt. July 1, '63. Disc. dis. May
Henry North,	Bridgeport,	July 23,'62	Aug.28,'62	Pro. from 1st Sergt. Co. D, July 15, '64. M. o. July 19, '65.
2d Lieutenants.				[missed June 17, '63.
John W. Craw,	Norwalk,	July 14,'62	Aug.28,'62	(See Sergt. Co. A, 3d C. V.) Pro. 1st Lt. May 2, '63 (not must.). Dis-
C. Frederick Betts,	Norwalk,	July 18,'62	Aug.28,'62	Must. Corp. Ap. Sergt.-Maj. June 4, '63. Pro. from Sergt.-Maj. Sep. 1, '63; Capt. Co. F, Mch. 5, '64.
1st Sergeants.				
John Jarvis,	Norwalk,	Aug. 7,'62	Aug.28,'62	Cap'd May 2, '63, Chancellorsville, Va. Par. May 14, '63. Redc. to ranks (sick) Dec. —, '63. Trans. to Co. G, 6th Regt. V. R. C. Jan. 6, '64. Pro. Com.-Sergt. Apr. 1, '64. Redc. to ranks and trans. to Co. H, Sep. 5, '64. Disc. June 26, '65.
Albert Holley,	Norwalk,	Aug. 2,'62	Aug.28,'62	Must. Corp. Pro. Sergt. June 4, '63. Wd. and cap'd July 1, '63, Gettysburg, Pa. Par. Aug. 25, '63. Pro. 1st Sergt. Dec. 27, '63; 2d Lt. June 29, '65 (not must.). M. o. July 19, '65.
Sergeants.				
Brady, Stephen A.	Norwalk,	Aug. 7,'62	Aug.28,'62	Must. Priv. Cap'd May 2, '63, Chancellorsville, Va. Par. May 14, '63. Pro. Corp. Nov. 1, '63; Sergt. Jan. 1, '64. M. o. July 19, '65.
Buttery, Rufus	Norwalk,	July 17,'62	Aug.28,'62	(See Corp. Co. A, 3d C. V.) Cap'd May 2, '63, Chancellorsville, Va. Par. May 14, '63. M. o. July 19, '65.
Crowe, John M.	Norwalk,	July 14,'62	Aug.28,'62	(See Priv. Co. A, 3d C. V.) Cap'd Feb. 4, '65, St. Augustine, Fla. Par. Apr. 21, '65. Disc. July 10, '65.
Smith, Edwin R.	Norwalk,	Aug. 5,'62	Aug.28,'62	(See Sergt. Co. A, 3d C. V.) Died Oct. 21, '63.
Weed, Thomas B.	Norwalk,	Aug. 7,'62	Aug.28,'62	Must. Priv. Pro. Corp. June 4, '63; Sergt. Nov. 1, '63; 2d Lt. July 15, '64 (not must.); 1st Lt. July 19, '65 (not must.). M. o. July 19, '65.
Corporals.				
Brown, Thomas D.	Norwalk,	July 17,'62	Aug.28,'62	(See Priv. Co. E, 1st C. V.) Died May 17 '63
Buttery, George M.	Wilton,	Aug. 2,'62	Aug.28,'62	Must. Priv. Pro. Apr. 15, '63. Cap'd July 2, '63, Gettysburg, Pa. Par. Aug. 25, '63. M. o. July 19, '65. [M. o. July 19, '65.
Campbell, George H.	Norwalk,	Aug. 6,'62	Aug.28,'62	Must. Priv. Wd. May 2, '63, Chancellorsville, Va. Pro. Nov. 1, '63.
Gray, William H.	Wilton,	July 21,'62	Aug.28,'62	(See Priv. Co. A, 3d C. V.) Redc. to ranks Apr. 24,'64. M. o. July 19,'65.
Merritt, William O.	Norwalk,	July 19,'62	Aug.28,'62	Must. Priv. Pro. June 4, '63. M. o. July 19, '65. [19, '65.
Olmsted, George F.	New Canaan,	Aug.11,'62	Aug.28,'62	(See Priv. Co. A, 3d C. V.) Must. Priv. Pro. Sep. 1, '64. M. o. July
Painter, Jasper E.	Norwalk,	Aug.11,'62	Aug.28,'62	Must. Priv. Cap'd July 1, '63, Gettysburg, Pa. Par. Aug. 25, '63. Pro. Jan. 1, '64. M. o. July 19, '65.
Paynton, William W.	Wilton,	Aug.11,'62	Aug.28,'62	Must. Priv. Pro. Sep. 1, '64. M. o. July 19, '65.
Van Hoosear, Henry	Norwalk,	Aug. 7,'62	Aug.28,'62	M. o. July 19, '65.
Waterworth, James	Norwalk,	Aug. 6,'62	Aug.28,'62	Died Oct. 15, '63. [July 4, '63.
Westlake, William W.	Norwalk,	Aug. 9,'62	Aug.28,'62	Must. Priv. Pro. June 4, '63. Wd. July 2, '63, Gettysburg, Pa. Died
Whitney, Charles H.	Norwalk,	July 15,'62	Aug.28,'62	Disc. dis. Feb. 6, '63.
Wilcox, Robert M.	Norwalk,	Aug. 4,'62	Aug.28,'62	M. o. July 19, '65.
Musician.				
Fowler, William G.	Norwalk,	July 16,'62	Aug.28,'62	Des. Dec. 24, 62.
Wagoner.				
Lounsbury, Alexander	Norwalk,	July 29,'62	Aug.28,'62	Disc. dis. Feb. 18, '64.
Privates.				
Aiken, Joseph F.	Norwalk,	July 25,'62	Aug.28,'62	(See Priv. Co. A, 3d C. V.) M. o. July 19, '65.
Akin, Henry H.	Norwalk,	Mch.15,'64	Mch.15,'64	Died July 25, '65.
Albin, Charles H.	Norwalk,	Aug. 7,'62	Aug.28,'62	Disc. dis. Jan. 17, '63.
Allen, Albert M.	Wilton,	Aug. 8,'62	Aug.28,'62	Died July 25, '64.

Name and Rank.	Residence.	Date of Enlistment.	Date of Muster in this organization.	Remarks.
Austin, Mortimer S.	Norwalk,	Aug. 6, 62	Aug.28,'62	Trans. to 143d Co. 2d Batt. V. R. C. Jan. 29, '64. Disc. Aug. 3, '65.
Ayres, Almon H.	Norwalk,	July 25,'62	Aug.28,'62	M. o. July 19, '65.
Bates, Waterman	Redding,	Aug. 9,'62	Aug.28,'62	Disc. dis. Dec. 18, '63.
Beers, Samuel	Wilton,	Jan. 1,'64	Jan. 1,'64	M. o. July 19, '65.
Beers, William W.	Norwalk,	Aug.21,'62	Aug.28,'62	(See Priv. Co. A. 3d C. V.) Disc. dis. Mch. 25, '63.
Bell, Thomas D.	Norwalk,	Aug. 8,'62	Aug.28,'62	M. o. July 19, '65.
Benedict, James Jr.	Norwalk,	Aug. 8,'62	Aug.28,'62	Trans. to 49th Co. 2d Batt. V. R. C. Jan. 28, '64. Disc. June 26, '65.
Bishop, Hiram H.	Norwalk,	Aug. 5,'62	Aug.28,'62	(See Priv. Co. A, 3d C. V.) Wd. May 2, '63, Chancellorsville, Va. Trans. to 23d Co. 2d Batt. V. R. C. Aug. 17, '63. Re-en. Vet. Aug.
Booth, Charles L.	Norwalk,	July 16,'62	Aug.28,'62	M. o. July 19, '65. [30, '64. Disc. Nov. 15, '65.
Bouton, Leroy H.	Norwalk,	Aug. 7,'62	Aug.28,'62	Disc. July 19, '65.
Britto, Lafayette F.	Wilton,	Dec. 28,'63	Dec. 28,'63	M. o. July 19, '65.
Brown, Henry W.	Norwalk,	Aug. 7,'62	Aug.28,'62	Disc. dis. Nov. 27, '62. (See Priv. Co. A, 6th C. V.)
Brown, George E.	Norwich,	Jan. 15,'64	Jan. 15,'64	M. o. July 19, '65.
Buckley, Patrick	Norwalk,	Aug. 8,'62	Aug.28,'62	Wd. July 1, '63, Gettysburg, Pa. Disc. July 5, '65.
Buttery, Edgar	Wilton,	Jan. 20,'64	Jan. 20,'64	M. o. July 19, '65.
Buttery, Elias	New Canaan,	July 17,'62	Aug.28,'62	Died Mch. 27, '63.
Buttery, Ira	Norwich,	Jan. 15,'64	Jan. 15,'64	M. o. July 19, '65.
Buttery, John D.	Stamford,	Aug. 2,'62	Aug.28,'62	Wd. and missing in action July 2, '63, Gettysburg, Pa. N. f. r. A. G. O.
Buttery, Samuel	Norwalk,	July 28,'62	Aug.28,'62	M. o. July 19, '65.
Collins, John C. Jr.	Norwalk,	July 14,'62	Aug.28,'62	Disc. dis. Oct. 9, '63.
Comstock, Marcus E.	Wilton,	Jan. 5,'64	Jan. 5,'64	M. o. July 19, '65. [Disc. May 18, '65.
Davis, Charles	Norwalk,	Aug. 6,'62	Aug.28,'62	Wd. and cap'd May 2, '63, Chancellorsville, Va. Par. May 14, '63.
Davis, John L.	Wilton,	Aug. 8,'62	Aug.28,'62	Disc. dis. Mch. 9, '63. [Feb. 6, '64. Disc. July 14, '65.
DeForrest, Samuel C.	Wilton,	Aug. 8,'62	Aug.28,'62	Wd. July 1, '63, Gettysburg, Pa. Trans. to Co. G, 6th Regt. V. R. C.
Donovan, Timothy	Norwalk,	July 28,'62	Aug.28,'62	Cap'd July 1, '63, Gettysburg, Pa. Par. Aug. 25, '63. M. o. July 19, '65.
Dyer, James L.	New Canaan,	July 24,'62	Aug.28,'62	Disc. dis. Jan. 20, '63.
Ells, Julius E.	Norwalk,	Aug. 9,'62	Aug.28,'62	M. o. July 19, '65.
Finney, George L.	Norwalk,	Aug. 4,'62	Aug.28,'62	Trans. to Co. B, 21st Regt. V. R. C. Sep. 16, '63. Pro. 1st Sergt. Dec. 19, '64. Ap. Sergt.-Maj. May 30, '65. Disc. July 5, '65.
Flynn, Robert	Norwalk,	Aug. 7,'62	Aug.28,'62	Wd. May 2, '63, Chancellorsville, Va. Trans. to 46th Co. 2d Batt.
Ford, Patrick	Norwalk,	July 24,'62	Aug.28,'62	M. o. July 19, '65. [V. R. C. Aug. 22, '63. Disc. Aug. 27, '65.
Fox, William H.	Norwalk,	Aug. 1,'62	Aug.28,'62	Cap'd May 3, '63, Chancellorsville, Va. Par. May 15, '63. Trans. to Co. E, 1st Regt. V. R. C. Oct. 7, '63. Pro. Corp. Aug. 30, '64. Disc. Nov. 21, '65.
Gilbert, Isaac W.	Norwalk,	July 14,'62	Aug.28,'62	(See Priv. Co. H, 8th C. V.) Wd. July 2, '63, Gettysburg, Pa. Trans. to 17th Co. 2d Batt. V. R. C. Sep. 15, '63. Disc. June 29, '65.
Goodrich, Milo J.	Meriden,	Jan. 2,'64	Jan. 2,'64	(See 2d Lt. Co. K, 8th C. V.) Trans. to Co. K, 8th C. V. June 24, '64.
Gray, George B.	Wilton,	July 21,'62	Aug.28,'62	Trans. to Co. E, 21st Regt. V. R. C. Sep. 1, '63. Re-trans. Mch. 24, '64. M. o. July 19, '65.
Gregory, Hyatt	Wilton,	July 30,'62	Aug.28,'62	Disc. dis. July 18, '63. (See Priv. 3d C. V. Light Batty.) [Dec. 14, '63.
Grindrod, Edward	Norwalk,	Aug. 8,'62	Aug.28,'62	Cap'd May 2, '63, Chancellorsville, Va. Par. May 14, '63. Disc. dis.
Guthrie, St. Clair	Norwalk,	July 24,'62	Aug.28,'62	Wd. May 2, '63, Chancellorsville, Va. M. o. July 19, '65.
Guthrie, Alexander	Norwalk,	Aug.21,'62	Aug.28,'62	M. o. July 19, '65.
Hagar, Abijah	Wilton,	Aug. 9,'62	Aug.28,'62	Wd. July 2, '63, Gettysburg, Pa. M. o. July 19, '65.
Hendricks, George B.	Norwalk,	Aug. 8,'62	Aug.28,'62	Died Oct. 30, '63.
Hoyt, Warren	Wilton,	Aug. 9,'62	Aug.28,'62	Wd. May 2, '63, Chancellorsville, Va. M. o. July 19, '65.
Humphrey, Henry E.	Norwalk,	July 25,'62	Aug.28,'62	Cap'd July 2, '63, Gettysburg, Pa. Par. Aug. 25, '63. M. o. July 19, '65.
Hurlbutt, James B.	Norwalk,	Aug. 4,'62	Aug.28,'62	M. o. July 19, '65.
Hyatt, Isaac B.	Norwich,	Jan. 15,'64	Jan. 15,'64	M. o. July 19, '65.
Jackson, John W.	Norwalk,	Aug.12,'62	Aug.28,'62	Died Oct. 8, '62.
Kellogg, Normas S.	Bridgeport,	Jan. 5,'64	Jan. 5,'64	M. o. July 19, '65.
Knapp, James F.	Norwalk,	Mch.15,'64	Mch.15,'64	M. o. July 19, '65.
Lester, Samuel A.	Norwalk,	Aug.11,'62	Aug.28,'62	Trans. to 166th Co. 2d Batt. V. R. C. Apr. 24, '64. Disc. June 27, '65.
Lockwood, John S.	Wilton,	Aug. 5,'62	Aug.28,'62	M. o. July 19, '65.
Lounsbury, Chas. W.	Norwalk,	Aug.11,'62	Aug.28,'62	Trans. to 96th Co. 2d Batt. V. R. C. Nov. 25, '63. Disc. Aug. 28, '65.
Maloney, Edward	Norwalk,	July 16,'62	Aug.28,'62	M. o. July 19, '65.
Moore, George	Norwalk,	Aug. 8,'62	Aug.28,'62	Cap'd July 1, '63, Gettysburg, Pa. Par. Aug. 25, '63. Des. Dec. 18, '63.
Morrison, Samuel C.	Norwalk,	Aug. 8,'62	Aug.28,'62	M. o. July 19, '65.
Newcomb, William B.	Norwalk,	Aug. 8,'62	Aug.28,'62	M. o. July 19, '65. [A. G. O.
Nobles, Calvin	Norwalk,	Aug. 5,'62	Aug.28,'62	Missing in action July 2, '63, Gettysburg, Pa.; supposed killed. N. f. r.
Northrup, Seth A.	Norwalk,	Aug.11,'62	Aug.28,'62	Wd. July 1, '63, Gettysburg, Pa. Cap'd Feb. 4, '65, St. Augustine, Fla. Par. Apr. 21, '65. Disc. July 10, '65. [M. o. July 19, '65.
Palmer, William H.	Norwalk,	July 31,'62	Aug.28,'62	Wd. and cap'd May 2, '63, Chancellorsville, Va. Par. May 14, '63.
Pelham, Augustus	Wilton,	July 17,'62	Aug.28,'62	Disc. dis. Dec. 8, '62. [Disc. dis. Sep. 28, '63.
Pendleton, Charles M.	Norwalk,	July 31,'62	Aug.28,'62	Wd. and cap'd May 2, '63, Chancellorsville, Va. Par. May 14, '63.
Platt, Chauncey C.	Norwalk,	Aug. 8,'62	Aug.28,'62	M. o. July 19, '65.
Roonain, Mathew	Norwalk,	Aug. 6,'62	Aug.28,'62	Cap'd May 2, '63, Chancellorsville, Va. Par. May 14, '63. Des. Dec. 18, '63.
Saunders, George P.	Norwalk,	July 19,'62	Aug.28,'62	Cap'd July 2, '63, Gettysburg, Pa. Par. Aug. 25, '63. M. o. July 19, '65.
Seymour, Richard G.	Wilton,	Aug. 6,'62	Aug.28,'62	Cap'd July 1, '63, Gettysburg, Pa. Par. Aug. 25, '63. M. o. July 19, '65.
Smith, Alfred M.	Norwalk,	Aug. 8,'62	Aug.28,'62	M. o. July 19, '65.
Smith, Charles J.	Norwalk,	Aug. 5,'62	Aug.28,'62	M. o. July 19, '65.
Smith, Geo. W. 1st	Norwalk,	Aug. 8,'62	Aug.28,'62	(See Priv. Co. A, 3d C. V.) M. o. July 19, '65.
Smith, Geo. W. 2d	Norwalk,	July 18,'62	Aug.28,'62	Cap'd July 1, '63, Gettysburg, Pa. Par. Aug. 25, '63. M. o. July 19, '65.
Smith, Henry T.	Norwalk,	Aug. 6,'62	Aug.28,'62	Trans. to 159th Co. 2d Batt. V. R. C. Sep. 14, '64. Disc. June 22, '65.
Smith, Samuel T.	Norwalk,	Aug. 7,'62	Aug.28,'62	Cap'd July 2, '63, Gettysburg, Pa. Par. Aug. 25, '63. M. o. July 19,'65.
Smith, Stephen I.	Norwalk,	July 23,'62	Aug.28,'62	M. o. July 19, '65.
Smith, William H.	Norwalk,	Aug. 6,'62	Aug.28,'62	M. o. July 19, '65.
St. John, Charles C.	Norwalk,	Aug. 7,'62	Aug.28,'62	M. o. July 19, '65. [Oct. 14, '63. Disc. June 29, '65.
Swords, Alfred	Norwalk,	Aug. 9,'62	Aug.28,'62	Wd. July 1, '63, Gettysburg, Pa. Trans. to 75th Co. 2d Batt. V. R. C.
Titus, William A.	Norwalk,	Aug. 7,'62	Aug.28,'62	Cap'd May 2, '63, Chancellorsville, Va. Par. May 15, '63. Trans. to Co. H, 19th Regt. V. R. C. Oct. 14, '63. Disc. dis. Feb. 12, '64.

NAME AND RANK.	Residence.	Date of Enlistment.	Date of Muster in this organization.	Remarks.
Tuttle, George O.	Norwalk,	July 28,'62	Aug.28,'62	Missing in action May 2, '63, Chancellorsville, Va.; supposed killed. [N. f. r. A. G. O.
Waterbury, John W.	Norwalk,	July 21,'62	Aug.28,'62	Disc. dis. Dec. 18, '63.
Weed, Fitzgerald S.	Norwalk,	Mch.19,'64	Mch.19,'64	Disc. dis. July 4, '65.
Wheeler, John B.	Norwalk,	Aug. 7,'62	Aug.28,'62	M. o. July 19, '65.
Whitney, David B.	Wilton,	Aug. 9,'62	Aug.28,'62	M. o. July 19, '65.
Williams, Henry H.	Norwalk,	Aug. 2,'62	Aug.28,'62	M. o. July 19, '65.
Wyman, Samuel	Norwalk,	Aug. 9,'62	Aug.28,'62	M. o. July 19, '65.

Company B.

NAME AND RANK.	Residence.	Date of Enlistment.	Date of Muster in this organization.	Remarks.
Captains.				
Allen G. Brady,	Torrington,	July 18,'62	Aug.28,'62	Pro. Maj. Aug. 29, '62.
Charles A. Hobbie,	Darien,	July 18,'62	Aug.29,'62	(See 1st Sergt. Rifle Co. F, 3d C. V.) Must. 1st Lt. Pro. Aug. 29, '62. Wd. May 2, '63, Chancellorsville, Va. Cap'd May 19, '64, Welaka, Fla. Par. Nov. 18, '64. M. o. July 19, '65.
1st Lieutenants.				
Marcus Waterbury,	Stamford,	July 21,'62	Aug.28,'62	(See Sergt. Co. F, 3d C. V.) Must. 2d Lt. Pro. Aug. 29, '62. Cap'd May 2, '63, Chancellorsville, Va. Released June 8, '63. Pro. Capt. Co. I, Sep. 1, '63.
John Harvey,	Stamford,	July 25,'62	Aug.28,'62	(See Priv. Rifle Co. F, 3d C. V.) Must. Sergt. Pro. 1st Sergt. Sep. 3, '62; 1st Lt. Oct. 8, '63; Capt. June 29, '65 (not must.). M. o. July 19, '65.
2d Lieutenants.				
Edgar Hoyt,	Stamford,	Aug. 6,'62	Aug.29,'62	Must. 1st Sergt. Pro. Aug. 29, '62. Resgd. May 14, '63.
Charles E. Doty,	Norwalk,	Sep. 20,'64	Oct. 29,'64	(See 2d Lt. Co. F.) Must. 2d Lt. Pro. 1st Lt. Co. I, Mch. 30, '65.
1st Sergeant.				
George A. Scofield,	Stamford,	July 24,'62	Aug.28,'62	(See Priv. Rifle Co. F, 3d C. V.) Must. Sergt. Pro. Sep. 19, '63. Cap'd May 19, '64, Welaka, Fla. Par. Nov. 18, '64. M. o. July 19, '65.
Sergeants.				
Harrison, Edwin O.	Stamford,	July 11,'62	Aug.28,'62	Cap'd May 2, '63, Chancellorsville, Va. Par. May 14, '63. M. o. July 19, ['65.
Hobbie, Selah R.	Stamford,	July 28,'62	Aug.28,'62	Must. Priv. Pro. Corp. Oct. 12, '62. Wd. July 1, '63, Gettysburg, Pa. Pro. Sergt. Nov. 1, '63. Cap'd May 19, '64, Welaka, Fla. Par. Nov. 18, '64. M. o. July 19, '65.
Jones, William	Bridgeport,	Feb. 10,'65	Feb. 10,'65	Must. Priv. Pro. Sergt. Mch. 13, '65. M. o. July 19, '65.
Macrea, Murray H.	Stamford,	July 22,'62	Aug.28,'62	Must. Corp. Pro. Sep. 3, '62. Cap'd May 3, '63, Chancellorsville, Va. Par. May 14, '63. Cap'd May 19, '64, Welaka, Fla. Died Jan. 1, '65, Florence, S. C.
Morehouse, Joseph E.	Darien,	July 18,'62	Aug.28,'62	Pro. 2d Lt. Co. F, Oct. 26, '63.
Scofield, Lewis W.	Stamford,	July 28,'62	Aug.28,'62	Must. Corp. Pro. Nov. 1, '63. Cap'd May 19, '64, Welaka, Fla. Par. Nov. 18, '64. Disc. June 10, '65.
Corporals.				
Beardsley, Edson C.	Litchfield,	July 24,'62	Aug.28,'62	Redc. to ranks Oct. 12, '62. Cap'd Dec. 19, '62, Dumfries, Va. Par. Jan. 6, '63. Cap'd May 19, '64, Welaka, Fla. Trans. from Andersonville Prison to Col. O'Neil, a rebel recruiting officer. N. f. r. [A. G. O.
Burns, Henry	Norwalk,	July 21,'62	Aug.28,'62	Killed July 1, '63, Gettysburg, Pa.
Cash, Martin	Darien,	July 23,'62	Aug.28,'62	Redc. to ranks at own request Feb. 15, '63. Cap'd May 19, '64, Welaka, Fla. Par. Nov. 18, '64. M. o. July 19, '65.
Cox, Walter H.	Greenwich,	July 23,'62	Aug.28,'62	Must. Priv. Pro. Feb. 1, '64. Cap'd May 19, '64, Welaka, Fla. Par. Nov. 18, '64. Died May 15, '65.
Dayton, John S.	Darien,	July 24,'62	Aug.28,'62	Wd. July 1–4, '63, Gettysburg, Pa. M. o. July 19, '65.
Jessop, Edwin B.	Stamford,	July 21,'62	Aug.28,'62	Died Mch. 2, '63.
Scofield, Andrew	New Canaan,	July 30,'62	Aug.28,'62	Wd. July 2, '63, Gettysburg, Pa. Must. Priv. Pro. Feb. 1, '64. Cap'd May 19, '64, Welaka, Fla. Par. Nov. 18, '64. Disc. June 8, '65.
Scofield, Alfred V.	Stamford,	Aug.11,'62	Aug.28,'62	Must. Priv. Pro. Sep. 19, '62. Cap'd May 19, '64, Welaka, Fla. Par. Nov. 18, '64. Disc. June 10, '65.
Scofield, James T.	Stamford,	July 24,'62	Aug.28,'62	(See Priv. Rifle Co. F, 3d C. V.) Must. Priv. Pro. Sep. 3, '62. M. o. [July 19, '65.
Seeley, Albert O.	Darien,	Aug. 9,'62	Aug.28,'62	(See Priv. Rifle Co. F, 3d C. V.) Must. Priv. Pro. Sep. 15, '62. Cap'd July 1, '63, Gettysburg, Va. Par. Aug. 21, '63. Cap'd May 19, '64, Welaka, Fla. Par. Dec. 16, '64. Died Jan. 9, '65.
Searles, Mortimer	Stamford,	Aug. 6,'62	Aug.28,'62	Must. Priv. Wd. July 1–4, '63, Gettysburg, Pa. Pro. Jan. 1, '64. Cap'd May 19, '64, Welaka, Fla. Par. Nov. 18, '64. Disc. dis. May 27, '65.
Stottler, Christopher	Greenwich,	July 21,'62	Aug.28,'62	Redc. to ranks. Pro. Feb. 1, '64. Cap'd May 19, '64, Welaka, Fla. Par. Dec. 16, '64. M. o. July 19, '65.
Whitney, George A.	Darien,	July 26,'62	Aug.28,'62	Must. Priv. Pro. Feb. 29, '65. M. o. July 19, '65.
Musicians.				
Dunham, William H.	Stamford,	July 25,'62	Aug.28,'62	Trans. to 65th Co. 2d Batt. V. R. C. Sep. 12, '63. Disc. dis. Jan. 7, '65.
Lounsbury, Henry T.	Stamford,	July 18,'62	Aug.28,'62	(See Priv. Rifle Co. F, 3d C. V.) Disc. dis. Feb. 7, '63.
Wagoner.				
Chadwick, John H.	Stamford,	July 18,'62	Aug.28,'62	M. o. July 19, '65.

Name and Rank.	Residence.	Date of Enlistment.	Date of Muster in this organization.	Remarks.
Privates.				
Aldrich, William H.	Norwalk,	Aug.31,'64	Aug.31,'64	(See Musc. Co. G, 28th C. V.) M. o. July 19, '65.
Ayres, Elbert	Stamford,	July 18,'62	Aug.28,'62	Wd. and cap'd May 2, '63, Chancellorsville, Va. Par. May 14, '63. Wd. and cap'd May 19, '64, Welaka, Fla. Par. Nov. 18, '64. Disc. June
Barrett, Patrick	Bethel,	Sep. 2,'64	Sep. 2,'64	M. o. July 19, '65. [20, '65.
Bates, George R.	Darien,	Aug. 8,'62	Aug.28,'62	Cap'd May 2, '63, Chancellorsville, Va. Par. May 14, '63. M. o. July 19, '65.
Bates, James H.	Darien,	Aug. 9,'62	Aug.28,'62	Cap'd May 19, '64, Welaka, Fla. Par. Feb. —, '65. Died Mch. 13, '65.
Bates, Lewis E.	Norwalk,	Jan. 2,'64	Jan. 2,'64	(See Priv. Rifle Co. F, 3d C. V.) Disc. dis. Dec. 15, '64.
Bell, John W.	Darien,	Aug.12,'62	Aug.28,'62	Cap'd May 19, '64, Welaka, Fla. Par. Nov. 18, '64. M. o. July 19, '65.
Bishop, John W.	Norwalk,	Aug.31,'64	Aug.31,'64	M. o. July 19, '65.
Burns, Dennis	Stamford,	Aug.11,'62	Aug.28,'62	Disc. dis. Aug. 12, '63.
Buttry, John	Stamford,	Aug. 9,'62	Aug.28,'62	Cap'd May 19, '64, Welaka, Fla. Par. Nov. 18, '64. Died Dec. 22, '64.
Chamberlain, Geo. W.	Stamford,	July 18,'62	Aug.28,'62	Trans. to Co. M, 2d Regt. U. S. Cav. Feb. 3, '63. Disc. Dec. 10, '64.
Cheal, John	Norwalk,	Nov.11,'64	Nov.11,'64	M. o. July 19, '65.
Christison, George B.	Stamford,	Aug.15,'62	Aug.28,'62	Cap'd July 1, '63, Gettysburg, Pa. Par. Aug. 25, '63. M. o. July 19, '65.
Collins, John	Stamford,	July 28,'62	Aug.28,'62	Wd. July 1–4, '63, Gettysburg, Pa. Disc. May 18, '65.
Crabb, Ebenezer S.	Stamford,	July 22,'62	Aug.28,'62	Trans. to Co. D, 20th Regt. V. R. C. Oct. 7, '63. Pro. Corp. Aug. 23, '64.
Dibble, William H.	Darien,	July 21,'62	Aug.28,'62	Disc. dis. June 3, '64. [Disc. July 6, '65.
Dow, Charles E.	Danbury,	Sep. 7,'64	Sep. 7,'64	M. o. July 19, '65.
Dudley, Arthur M.	Norwalk,	Aug.11,'64	Aug.11,'64	M. o. July 19, '65.
Egan, Michael	Stamford,	Aug.12,'62	Aug.28,'62	M. o. July 19, '65.
Farnold, William	Stamford,	Aug. 6,'62	Aug.28,'62	Cap'd May 19, '64, Welaka, Fla. Par. Mch. 14, '65. Died Mch. 20, '65.
Farrell, John	Stamford,	July 19,'62	Aug.28,'62	Cap'd May 2, '63, Chancellorsville, Va. Par. May 14, '63. M. o. July 19, '65. [Fla. Par. Nov. 18, '64. Died Mch. 13, '65.
Feeks, George D.	Stamford,	Aug.11,'62	Aug.28,'62	Disc. dis. Feb. 3, '63. Re-en. Jan. 28, '64. Cap'd May 19, '64, Welaka,
Feeks, Joseph	Stamford,	Aug. 6,'62	Aug.28,'62	Cap'd May 19, '64, Welaka, Fla. Par. Nov. 18, '64. Disc. June 8, '65.
Fitzpatrick, John	Stamford,	July 18,'62	Aug.28,'62	Wd. July 2, '63, Gettysburg, Pa. Trans. to Co. F, 19th Regt. V. R. C. Jan. 15, '64. Disc. July 13, '65. [A. G. O.
Fitzpatrick, Patrick	Stamford,	Aug.11,'62	Aug.28,'62	Reported on M. O. Roll of Co., supposed des. July 15, '63. N. f. r.
Fox, Michael	Stamford,	Aug.22,'62	Aug.28,'62	Killed July 1, '63, Gettysburg, Pa. [Va., Nov. 7, '63. N. f. r. A. G. O.
Gillespie, William	Stamford,	July 31,'62	Aug.28,'62	Cap'd July 1, '63, Gettysburg, Pa. Admitted to Hosp. No. 21, Richmond,
Gray, Abel B.	Danbury,	Aug.24,'64	Aug.24,'64	(See Corp. Co. B, 23d C. V.) M. o. July 19, '65.
Graham, Thomas R.	Stamford,	Aug. 9,'62	Aug.28,'62	Killed May 2, '63, Chancellorsville, Va.
Hall, Samuel T.	Stamford,	Aug. 2,'62	Aug.28,'62	Cap'd May 19, '64, Welaka, Fla. Par. Nov. 18, '64. M. o. July 19, '65.
Hartman, John	Stamford,	July 29,'62	Aug.28,'62	M. o. July 19, '65. ['65.
Heiser, George	Stamford,	Aug. 9,'62	Aug.28,'62	Cap'd May 2, '63, Chancellorsville, Va. Par. May 14, '63. M. o. July 19,
Heiser, Martin	Stamford,	July 15,'62	Aug.28,'62	Cap'd Feb. 5, '65, Bradock Farm, Fla. Released Apr. 18, '65. Disc. June 14, '65.
Hennessy, Patrick	Stamford,	July 18,'62	Aug.28,'62	Wd. May 2, '63, Chancellorsville, Va. Trans. to 173d Co. 2d Batt. V. R. C. Sep. 19, '64. Disc. dis. Nov. 29, '64. [A. G. O.
Hounslow, Eli	Stamford,	July 26,'62	Aug.28,'62	Trans. from draft rendezvous to Co. May 25, '65; failed to report. N. f. r.
Hoyt, Edward S.	Darien,	July 24,'62	Aug.28,'62	Cap'd May 19, '64, Welaka, Fla. Died Aug. 27, '64, Andersonville, Ga.
Hoyt, John D.	Norwalk,	July 22,'62	Aug.28,'62	Dishon. disc. by G. C. M. Oct. 22, '64.
Hoyt, Joseph N.	Stamford,	Aug. 4,'62	Aug.28,'62	M. o. July 19, '65. ['65.
Hoyt, Lorenzo L.	Darien,	July 25,'62	Aug.28,'62	Cap'd May 19, '64, Welaka, Fla. Released Nov. 18, '64. Disc. Aug. 5,
Hull, Henry S.	Danbury,	Sep. 15,'64	Sep. 15,'64	M. o. July 19, '65.
Ives, George W.	Danbury,	Sep. 5,'64	Sep. 5,'64	M. o. July 19, '65.
Jackson, Andrew	Plymouth,	Feb. 9,'64	Feb. 9,'64	Cap'd May 19, '64, Welaka, Fla. Par. Nov. 18, '64. Disc. July 25, '65.
Jackson, William H.	Stamford,	July 25,'62	Aug.28,'62	Wd. July 1, '63, Gettysburg, Pa. Trans. to 57th Co. 2d Batt. V. R. C.
Johnson, Elias	Darien,	Aug.11,'62	Aug.28,'62	Died Oct. 27, '62. [Nov. 13, '63. Disc. Aug. 28, '65.
Jordan, George D.	Darien,	Apr. 2,'64	Apr. 2,'64	Cap'd May 19, '64, Welaka, Fla. Died Oct. 19, '64, Millen, Ga.
June, John L.	Stamford,	Aug.20,'62	Aug.28,'62	Cap'd July 1, '63, Gettysburg, Pa. Par. Aug. 25, '63. Cap'd May 19, '64, Welaka Landing, Fla. Par. Feb. 28, '65. M. o. July 19, '65.
Kelly, John	Stamford,	July 29,'62	Aug.28,'62	Des. May 3, '63.
Kennedy, Daniel	Stamford,	Aug. 6,'62	Aug.28,'62	Disc. dis. Jan. 16, '63.
Kinner, George A.	Danbury,	Sep. 5,'64	Sep. 5,'64	M. o. July 19, '65.
Kreig, Jacob	Stamford,	Aug. 5,'62	Aug.28,'62	Trans. to 173d Co. 2d Batt. V. R. C. Sep. 19, '64. Disc. dis. Nov. 29, '64.
Lincoln, George	Stamford,	July 29,'62	Aug.28,'62	Wd. May 2, '63, Chancellorsville, Va. Trans. to 2d Co. 2d Batt. V. R. C. July 1, '63. Disc. June 28, '65.
Lockwood, Joseph H.	New Canaan,	Aug.12,'62	Aug.28,'62	Cap'd July 1, '63, Gettysburg, Pa. Par. Aug. 25, '63. Cap'd May 19, '64, Welaka Landing, Fla. Par. Nov. 19, '64. M. o. July 19, '65.
Mahan, Hugh	Stamford,	Aug.18,'62	Aug.28,'62	Killed May 2, '63, Chancellorsville, Va.
Marlin, Richard	Stamford,	Aug. 8,'62	Aug.28,'62	Disc. dis. June 30, '63.
Marvin, Charles	Norwalk,	Sep. 16,'64	Sep. 16,'64	M. o. July 19, '65.
McDonald, Lewis	Stamford,	July 11,'62	Aug.28,'62	Disc. dis. Jan. 19, '64. [Nov. 18, '64. M. o. July 19, '65.
Mills, William E.	Darien,	Aug.11,'62	Aug.28,'62	Wd. July 3, '63, Gettysburg, Pa. Cap'd May 19, '64, Welaka, Fla. Par.
Mills, Orrin E.	Wilton,	Aug.31,'64	Aug.31,'64	M. o. July 19, '65.
Morehouse, Alfred	Darien,	July 26,'62	Aug.28,'62	M. o. July 19, '65.
Morehouse, Robert N.	Norwalk,	Aug.11,'64	Aug.11,'64	M. o. July 19, '65.
Morell, Charles E.	Stamford,	Aug. 6,'62	Aug.28,'62	Died Oct. 31, '64.
Murphy, Thomas	Darien,	July 23,'62	Aug.28,'62	Cap'd May 19, '64, Welaka, Fla. Par. Nov. 18, '64. M. o. July 19, '65.
Nichols, John A.	Greenwich,	Jan. 2,'64	Jan. 2,'64	M. o. July 19, '65. [Died Nov. 19, '64, Florence, S. C.
Northrop, William H.	Darien,	July 25,'62	Aug.28,'62	Wd. July 1, '63, Gettysburg, Pa. Cap'd May 19, '64, Welaka, Fla.
Parks, James E.	Norwalk,	Sep. 15,'64	Sep. 15,'64	(See Priv. Co. E, 12th C. V.) M. o. July 19, '65.
Parketon, Lewis	Stamford,	Aug. 1,'62	Aug.28,'62	M. o. July 19, '65.
Perry, Andrew	Norwalk,	Aug.29,'64	Aug.23,'64	M. o. July 19, '65.
Potts, Joseph W.	Stamford,	Aug. 6,'62	Aug.28,'62	Killed May 2, '63, Chancellorsville, Va. ['65.
Quigley, Edward H.	Stamford,	July 24,'62	Aug.28,'62	Cap'd May 19, '64, Welaka, Fla. Par. Nov. 18, '64. Disc. dis. June 30,
Repke, John	Stamford,	Aug.11,'62	Aug.28,'62	Disc. dis. May 21, '63.
Rich, Charles F.	Greenwich,	Aug.11,'62	Aug.28,'62	M. o. July 19, '65.
Rusco, William W.	Greenwich,	Sep. 9,'64	Sep. 9,'64	M. o. July 19, '65.
Scofield, Charles E.	Darien,	Dec. 30,'63	Dec. 30,'63	Cap'd May 19, '64, Welaka, Fla. Par. Nov. 18, '64. M. o. July 19, '65.

NAME AND RANK.	Residence.	Date of Enlistment.	Date of Muster in this organization.	Remarks.
Scofield, Frank	Darien,	July 23,'62	Aug.28,'62	Cap'd May 19, '64, Welaka, Fla. Par. Nov. 18, '64. M. o. July 19, '65.
Scofield, Samuel	Stamford,	July 21,'62	Aug.28,'62	Dishon. disc. by G. C. M., date not shown.
Scofield, William H.	Stamford,	Aug. 7,'62	Aug.28,'62	Disc. dis. Feb. 7, '63.
Searles, John H.	Danbury,	Sep. 5,'64	Sep. 5,'64	M. o. July 19, '65.
*Seymour, George W.	Danbury,	Aug.15,'64	Aug.15,'64	(See Sergt. Co. H, 8th C. V.) Disc. dis. June 25, '65.
Slawson, Silas F.	Darien,	Jan. 1,'63	Jan. 1,'63	Cap'd May 19, '64, Welaka, Fla. Died Oct. 20, '64, Millen, Ga.
Slosson, Harvey	Darien,	Aug.11,'62	Aug.28,'62	M. o. July 19, '65.
Smalart, John	Stamford,	Aug. 7,'62	Aug.28,'62	Des. Sep. 26, '62. ['64. Disc. Oct. 14, '65.
Smith, Edwin L.	Stamford,	July 26,'62	Aug.28,'62	Trans. to Co. A, 9th Regt. V. R. C. June 9, '63. Re-en. Vet. Aug. 30,
Smith, John M.	Norwalk,	Aug.11,'64	Aug.11,'64	M. o. July 19, '65.
Smith, Lewis	Darien,	Dec. 30,'63	Dec. 30,'63	Cap'd May 19, '64, Welaka, Fla. Par. Nov. 18, '64. Disc. June 10, '65.
Steinert, George	Stamford,	Aug. 6,'62	Aug.28,'62	Disc. dis. Mch. 28, '63.
Stevens, Albert	Stamford,	July 29,'62	Aug.28,'62	(See Capt. Rifle Co. F, 3d C. V.) Died June 18, '64.
Stevens, James E.	Darien,	July 23,'62	Aug.28,'62	Disc. dis. Nov. 13, '62.
Stevens, William T.	Stamford,	July 21,'63	Aug.28,'62	Died Feb. 1, '63.
Stottler, Jacob	Stamford,	Aug.18,'62	Aug.28,'62	Trans. to 41st Co. 2d Batt. V. R. C. Aug. 8, '63. Disc. July 17, '65.
Thompson, Charles H.	Bethel,	Sep. 1,'64	Sep. 1,'64	M. o. July 19, '65.
Tuttle, Edwin L.	Durham,	Sep. 3,'64	Sep. 3,'64	M. o. July 19, '65.
Vennervaldt, Emanuel	Stamford,	July 28,'62	Aug.28,'62	Des. Sep. 4, '62. [S. C.
Vincent, Jacob W.	Darien,	Aug. 5,'62	Aug.28,'62	Cap'd May 19, '64, Welaka Landing, Fla. Died Nov. 30, '64, Florence,
Void, Joseph	Darien,	July 22,'62	Aug.28,'62	Wd. May 2, '63, Chancellorsville, Va. Cap'd May 19, '64, Welaka, Fla. Par. Nov. 18, '64. Died Feb. 25, '65. ['65.
Walters, John W.	Stamford,	Aug. 8,'62	Aug.28,'62	Cap'd May 2, '63, Chancellorsville, Va. Par. May 14, '63. M. o. July 19,
Waterbury, John W.	East Haven,	Aug.31,'64	Aug.31,'64	M. o. July 19, '65. [Nov. 18, '64. M. o. July 19, '65.
Weed, George	Stamford,	Aug. 2,'62	Aug.28,'62	(See Priv. Rifle Co. F, 3d C. V.) Cap'd May 19, '64, Welaka, Fla. Par.
Weed, Raymond	Darien,	Aug.11,'62	Aug.28,'62	Died July 7, '63.
Whaley, Edward	Stamford,	Aug.13,'62	Aug.28,'62	Cap'd May 19, '64, Welaka, Fla. Died Nov. 18, '64, Millen, Ga.
Whitney, Henry P.	Darien,	Aug. 8,'62	Aug.28,'62	Cap'd May 19, '64, Welaka, Fla. Par. Nov. 18, '64. M. o. July 19, '65.
Whitney, Morando H.	Darien,	Aug. 9,'62	Aug.28,'62	Wd. July 2, '63, Gettysburg, Pa. Cap'd Feb. 5, '65, Dunn's Lake, Fla.
White, Alexander J.	Norwalk,	Sep. 2,'64	Sep. 2,'64	M. o. July 19, '65. [Released Apr. 21, '65. Disc. June 14, '65.
White, Marcus B.	Cromwell,	Sep. 26,'64	Sep. 26,'64	M. o. July 19, '65.
Wilson, John H.	Stamford,	Aug. 6,'62	Aug.28,'62	Disc. dis. Feb. 24, '63.
Williams, William	Stamford,	July 28,'62	Aug.28,'62	Des. Sep. 4, '62.
Wood, Hezekiah	New Canaan,	Sep. 5,'64	Sep. 5,'64	M. o. July 19, '65.

Company C.

NAME AND RANK.	Residence.	Date of Enlistment.	Date of Muster in this organization.	Remarks.
Captains.				
James E. Moore,	Danbury,	Aug.25,'62	Aug.28,'62	(See Capt. Co. C, 3d C. V.) Killed July 1, '63, Gettysburg, Pa.
Milton H. Daniels,	Danbury,	Aug.25,'62	Aug.28,'62	(See Corp. Co. C, 3d C. V.) Must. 1st Lt. Pro. July 15, '63. Wd. Aug. 19, '63, Fort Wagner, S. C. Resgd. Mch. 6, '64.
Henry Quien,	Danbury,	Aug.25,'62	Aug.28,'62	(See Priv. Co. C, 3d C. V.) Must. 2d Lt. Wd. July 2, '63, Gettysburg, Pa. Pro. 1st Lt. July 15, '63; Capt. Aug. 15, '64. Cap'd Feb. 4, '65, St. Augustine, Fla. Released Apr. 21, '65. Disc. May 15, '65.
1st Lieutenant.				
William L. Daniels,	Danbury,	July 19,'62	Aug.28,'62	Must. Sergt. Cap'd July 1, '63, Gettysburg, Pa. Par. Aug. 25, '63. Pro. 1st Sergt. July 15, '63; 1st Lt. Aug. 22, '64. M. o. July 19, '65.
2d Lieutenant.				
Walter K. Mills,	Bridgeport,	Aug.16,'62	Not must.	Pro. from Sergt. 2d C. V. Light Batty. July 23, '63 (not must.). Commission revoked Sep. 30, '63; no vacancy.
1st Sergeants.				
William O. Dauchy,	Danbury,	Aug. 6,'62	Aug.28,'62	Killed July 1, '63, Gettysburg, Pa.
H. Eugene Williams,	Bethel,	July 26,'62	Aug.28,'62	Must. Corp. Cap'd May 2, '63, Chancellorsville, Va. Par. May 14, '63. Pro. Sergt. July 15, '63; 1st Sergt. Aug. 28, '64; 2d Lt. July 15, '64 (not must.); 1st Lt. June 29, '65 (not must.). M. o. July 19, '65.
Sergeants.				
Barnum, Bethel S.	Bethel,	July 24,'62	Aug.28,'62	Killed July 1, '63, Gettysburg, Pa. [5, '63.
Bronson, Augustus E.	Danbury,	July 22,'62	Aug.28,'62	(See Priv. Co. C, 3d C. V.) Wd. July 1, '63, Gettysburg, Pa. Died July
Dauchy, Robert S.	Bethel,	Aug. 6,'62	Aug.28,'62	(See Priv. Co. C, 3d C. V.) Trans. to 52d Co. 2d Batt. V. R. C. Aug. 24, '63. Pro. 1st Sergt. Sep. 1, '64. Disc. July 7, '65.
Kyle, James	Danbury,	Aug.12,'62	Aug.28,'62	Must. Priv. Pro. Corp. Feb. 26, '63; Sergt. Jan. 10, '65. M. o. July 19, '65.
McCorkell, John	Bethel,	July 24,'62	Aug.28,'62	Must. Priv. Pro. Corp. Aug. 24, '63; Sergt. Jan. 1, '65. M. o. July 19, '65.
Scott, George	Danbury,	July 19,'62	Aug.28,'62	Must. Corp. Pro. July 15, '63. M. o. July 19, '65.
Ward, Lewis A.	Danbury,	Aug.13,'62	Aug.28,'62	Must. Corp. Pro. Aug. 24, '63. M. o. July 19, '65.
Corporals.				
Baldwin, William E.	Danbury,	July 28,'62	Aug.28,'62	Disc. dis. Dec. 22, '62. [July 19, '65.
Barber, George W.	Danbury,	Aug.11,'62	Aug.28,'62	Must. Priv. Wd. July 1-4, '63, Gettysburg, Pa. Pro. Feb. 1, '64. M. o.
Beers, Jarvis F.	Bethel,	Aug. 7,'62	Aug.28,'62	Must. Priv. Pro. Jan. 14, '63. Wd. and cap'd May 2, '63, Chancellorsville, Va. Par. May 14, '63. M. o. July 19, '65
Benedict, John H.	Danbury,	Aug.12,'62	Aug.28,'62	Must. Priv. Pro. Dec. 2, '62. Wd. July 1, '63, Gettysburg, Pa. Trans. to 108th Co. 2d Batt. V. R. C. Oct. 22, '64. Disc. July 29, '65.

*Substitutes and drafted.

Name and Rank.	Residence.	Date of Enlistment.	Date of Muster in this organization.	Remarks.
Brotherton, Charles	Danbury,	Aug.14,'62	Aug.28,'62	Must. Priv. Cap'd July 1, '63, Gettysburg, Pa. Par. Aug. 25, '63. Pro. Jan. 10, '64. M. o. July 19, '65.
Champion, Henry	Canaan,	Mch. 5,'64	Mch. 5,'64	Must. Priv. Pro. Mch. 1, '65. M. o. July 19, '65.
Curtis, Charles G.	Newtown,	July 11,'62	Aug.28,'62	Must. Priv. Pro. Mch. 16, '63. M. o. July 19, '65.
Dickens, George	Danbury,	Aug. 8,'62	Aug.28,'62	Redc. to ranks at own request Dec. 2, '62. Cap'd July 1, '63, Gettysburg, Pa. Released Oct. —, '63. Pro. Mch. 1, '65. M. o. July 19, '65.
Humphries, William	Danbury,	Aug.11,'62	Aug.28,'62	Must. Priv. Pro. Nov. 1, '63. M. o. July 19, '65. [Died Feb. 5, '64.
Lobdell, Eli	Wilton,	Aug. 2,'62	Aug.28,'62	(See Priv. Co. C, 3d C. V.) Redc. to ranks Sep. 24, '62. Pro. Aug. 24, '63.
Lounsbury, Phineas C.	Ridgefield,	Aug.11,'62	Aug.28,'62	Must. Priv. Pro. Sep. 30, '62. Disc. dis. Dec. 22, '62. [July 19, '65.
McHugh, John	Danbury,	July 26,'62	Aug.28,'62	Must. Priv. Wd. July 1-4, '63, Gettysburg, Pa. Pro. Mch. 23, '65. M. o.
Osborn, Lewis P.	Danbury,	Aug.25,'62	Aug.28,'62	(See Priv. Co. C, 3d C. V.) Must. Priv. Pro. Aug. 24,'63. Died Oct. 31, '64.
Sears, George	Danbury,	Aug.16,'62	Aug.28,'62	(See Priv. Co. E, 1st C. V.) Must. Priv. Pro. Jan. 14, '63. Redc. to ranks. Cap'd July 1, '63, Gettysburg, Pa. Par. Aug. 25, '63. Disc. dis. June 16, '65.
Warren, Edward S.	Danbury,	Aug. 8,'62	Aug.28,'62	(See Priv. Co. C, 3d C. V.) Trans. to Co. H, 2d Batt. 12th Regt. U. S. I. Jan. 24, '63, as Priv. Pro. Corp. Nov. 1, '63. Redc. to ranks May 1, '64. Trans. to Co. E, 1st Batt. Aug. 6, '64. Disc. Aug. 7, '65.
White, Benjamin S.	Danbury,	July 24,'62	Aug.28,'62	Disc. dis. Jan. 20, '63.
Musicians.				
Jenkins, Horatio G.	Danbury,	July 19,'62	Aug.28,'62	M. o. July 19, '65.
Keeler, Justin S.	Danbury,	July 19,'62	Aug.28,'62	M. o. July 19, '65.
Wagoner.				
McCorkell, Thomas	Bethel,	Aug. 6,'62	Aug.28,'62	M. o. July 19, '65.
Privates.				
Bailey, James M.	Danbury,	Aug.18,'62	Aug.28,'62	Cap'd July 1, '63, Gettysburg, Pa. Par. Aug. 21, '63. M. o. July 19, '65.
Benedict, Charles H.	Ridgefield,	July 28,'62	Aug.28,'62	Disc. dis. Feb. 27, '63. (See Priv. Co. L, 1st C. V. Cav.)
Benedict, Charles S.	Bethel,	Aug.12,'62	Aug.28,'62	Died June 1, '63.
Benedict, William E.	New Milford,	Aug.14,'62	Aug.28,'62	Died Nov. 17, '63.
Bennett, Alfred	Ridgefield,	July 26,'62	Aug.28,'62	Disc. dis. Jan. 17, '63.
Benson, Frank J.	Brookfield,	Aug.15,'62	Aug.28,'62	Wd. July 2, '63, Gettysburg, Pa. Died July 17, '63.
Blackman, Theodore	Bethel,	Aug. 8,'62	Aug.28,'62	Killed July 2, '63, Gettysburg, Pa.
Booth, Henry	Danbury,	Aug.14,'62	Aug.28,'62	Trans. to 49th Co. 2d Batt. V. R. C. Sep. 16, '63. Disc. June 26, '65.
Bouton, John W.	Danbury,	Aug. 9,'62	Aug.28,'62	Wd. July 1, '63, Gettysburg, Pa. M. o. July 19, '65.
Bradley, George F.	Danbury,	Aug.14,'62	Aug.28,'62	M. o. July 19, '65.
Bradley, David	Danbury,	Aug. 8,'62	Aug.28,'62	Disc. dis. Dec. 21, '63.
Bradley, Lewis	Danbury,	Aug. 9,'62	Aug.28,'62	Cap'd July 1, '63, Gettysburg, Pa. Par. Aug. 25, '63. M. o. July 19, '65.
Bronson, Orrin L.	Danbury,	Aug.15,'62	Aug.28,'62	Cap'd July 1, '63, Gettysburg, Pa. Par. Aug. 25, '63. Disc. July 5, '65.
Bussing, Frederick H.	Danbury,	July 19,'62	Aug.28,'62	Disc. dis. Jan. 5, '63. (See Priv. Co. I, 1st C. V. H. A.)
Clark, Samuel G.	Danbury,	Aug. 6,'62	Aug.28,'62	Disc. dis. Nov. 9, '63.
Clark, William A.	Danbury,	Aug. 1,'62	Aug.28,'62	Trans. to Co. D, 19th Regt. V. R. C. May 17, '64. Disc. Aug. 19, '65.
Clark, William B.	New Fairfield,	Aug. 6,'62	Aug.28,'62	Absent (sick) at Philadelphia, Pa., July 1, '63. N. f. r. A. G. O.
Curtis, William H.	Danbury,	July 30,'62	Aug.28,'62	Disc. dis. Dec. 31, '62.
Curtis, William	Newtown,	Aug. 9,'62	Aug.28,'62	Died Dec. 3, '63.
Daniels, Patrick	Bethel,	Dec. 24,'63	Dec. 24,'63	(See Priv. Co. G, 23d C. V.) M. o. July 19, '65.
Day, Amos C.	Danbury,	July 19,'62	Aug.28,'62	M. o. July 19, '65.
Delavan, Chas. T.	Brookfield,	Aug.11,'62	Not must.	Died Aug. 19, '62, prior to muster in.
Delevan, Smith	Danbury,	Aug. 6,'62	Aug.28,'62	Wd. July 1, '63, Gettysburg, Pa. Died July 15, '63.
Downs, Samuel M.	Danbury,	Aug. 6,'62	Aug.28,'62	M. o. July 19, '65.
Driscolls, Michael	Somers,	Feb. 27,'64	Mch.18,'64	M. o. July 19, '65.
Edwards, Thaddeus	Bethel,	July 26,'62	Aug.28,'62	Wd. July 1, '63, Gettysburg, Pa. Disc. Oct. 31, '64.
Fairchild, Alpheus B.	Newtown,	July 12,'62	Aug.28,'62	M. o. July 19, '65.
Fairchild, Leverett B.	Danbury,	July 28,'62	Aug.28,'62	Cap'd May 2, '63, Chancellorsville, Va. Par. May 14, '63. M. o. July 19, '65.
Farvour, Robert	Ridgefield,	Aug.12,'62	Aug.28,'62	Cap'd May 2, '63, Chancellorsville, Va. Par. May 14, '63. Des. June —, '63.
Feeks, Thaddeus	Danbury,	July 6,'62	Aug.28,'62	Wd. July 3, '63, Gettysburg, Pa. M. o. July 19, '65.
Ferrin, Charles Z.	Danbury,	July 23,'62	Aug.28,'62	Died Jan. 21, '63. [Aug. 30, '64. Disc. July 25, '65.
Ferry, Francis H.	Bethel,	July 23,'62	Aug.28,'62	Wd. July 1, '63, Gettysburg, Pa. Trans. to 159th Co. 2d Batt. V. R. C.
Foote, Joseph I.	Danbury,	July 25,'62	Aug.28,'62	Trans. to 143d Co. 2d Batt. V. R. C. Feb. 20, '64. Disc. Aug. 4, '65.
Fry, Robert W.	Danbury,	Aug. 4,'62	Aug.28,'62	M. o. July 19, '65.
Ganung, John	Danbury,	Aug. 9,'62	Aug.28,'62	M. o. July 19, '65.
Goodale, Frederick W.	Danbury,	July 26,'62	Aug.28,'62	M. o. July 19, '65. [N. f. r. A. G. O.
Grannis, John H.	Ridgefield,	July 24,'62	Aug.28,'62	Trans. to U. S. N. Aug. 30, '64. Name not borne on U. S. N. records.
Griffin, Lewis B.	Danbury,	Aug. 4,'62	Aug.28,'62	Disc. dis. Nov. 25, '63.
Hall, Ezra S.	Ridgefield,	Aug.12,'62	Aug.28,'62	Disc. dis. Jan. 28, '63.
Harmon, James	New Fairfield,	July 21,'62	Aug.28,'62	Cap'd July 1, '63, Gettysburg, Pa. Par. Aug. 25, '63. M. o. July 19, '65.
Hawley, Henry P.	Danbury,	Jan. 11,'64	Jan. 11,'64	M. o. July 19, '65. [ville, Va. Par. May 14, '63. Disc. dis. June 8, '64.
Holmes, John W.	Ridgefield,	July 26,'62	Aug.28,'62	(See Musc. Co. G, 11th C. V.) Wd. and cap'd May 2, '63, Chancellors-
Jennings, Oscar S.	Danbury,	July 22,'62	Aug.28,'62	Trans. to 21st Co. 2d Batt. V. R. C. Aug. 10, '63. Disc. dis. Aug. 20, '64.
Kellogg, Norman	Danbury,	July 31,'62	Aug.28,'62	M. o. July 19, '65.
Knapp, Edgar L.	Danbury,	July 19,'62	Aug.28,'62	M. o. July 19, '65.
Kyle, William	Bethel,	Dec. 26,'63	Dec. 26,'63	M. o. July 19, '65.
Maddock, Joseph	Brookfield,	Aug.13,'62	Aug.28,'62	Disc. Dec. 30, '63.
Morris, Theodore S.	Danbury,	July 31,'62	Aug.28,'62	Cap'd July 1, '63, Gettysburg, Pa. Par. Aug. 29, '63. Cap'd Feb. 4, '65, St. Augustine, Fla. Par. Apr. 28, '65. Disc. July 10, '65.
Northrop, Edward H.	Brookfield,	July 24,'62	Aug.28,'62	Disc. dis. Jan. 13, '63. (See Corp. Co. L, 2d C. V. H. A.)
O'Brien, Thomas	Stratford,	Feb. 9,'64	Feb. 9,'64	M. o. July 19, '65.
Otis, William F.	Danbury,	July 19,'62	Aug.28,'62	Cap'd July 1, '63, Gettysburg, Pa. Par. Aug. 21, '63. M. o. July 19, '65.
Purdy, Daniel H.	Danbury,	Aug.14,'62	Aug.28,'62	Wd. July 1, '63, Gettysburg, Pa. Died July 15, '63.
Purdy, George S.	Danbury,	Aug.12,'62	Aug.28,'62	M. o. July 19, '65.
Raymond, Amos	Ridgefield,	July 19,'62	Aug.28,'62	(See Priv. Co. C, 3d C. V.) Wd. May 2,'63, Chancellorsville, Va. Trans. to 48th Co. 2d Batt. V. R. C. Sep. 11,'63. Re-trans. Sep. 7,'64. M. o. July 19,'65.

Name and Rank.	Residence.	Date of Enlistment.	Date of Muster in this organization.	Remarks.
Rice, Rufus S.	Danbury,	Aug.19,'62	Aug.28,'62	Disc. dis. Jan. 17, '63.
Ryan, Patrick	Danbury,	Aug.11,'62	Aug.28,'62	Trans. to Co. E, 14th Regt. V. R. C. Aug. 5, '63. Disc. June 28, '65
Sherman, Ira	Newtown,	July 22,'62	Aug.28,'62	Disc. dis. Oct. 24, '64.
Shepard, Samuel G.	Bethel,	July 28,'62	Aug.28,'62	M. o. July 19, '65.
Small, Charles S.	Danbury,	Aug.14,'62	Aug.28,'62	Died Oct. 2, '62.
Smith, Frederick S.	Bethel,	Aug.14,'62	Aug.28,'62	Trans. to Co. B, 20th Regt. V. R. C. Sep. 20, '63. Disc. July 3, '65.
Smith, William H.	Bethel,	July 26,'62	Aug.28,'62	Wd. July 3, '63, Gettysburg, Pa. M. o. July 19, '65.
Stilson, David F.	Danbury,	Aug.14,'62	Aug.28,'62	Trans. to 112th Co. 2d Batt. V. R. C. Dec. 10, '63. Disc. Feb. 12, '64.
Taylor, Richard D.	Danbury,	Aug.14,'62	Aug.28,'62	Wd. July 1, '63, Gettysburg, Pa. Died July 2, '63.
Tomlinson, Horace E.	Bethel,	Aug. 6,'62	Aug.28,'62	Disc. dis. Sep. 9, '62.
Walders, John M.	Ridgefield,	July 25,'62	Aug.28,'62	Trans. to Co. B, 9th Regt. V. R. C. Aug. 6, '63. Disc. June 26, '65
Warren, Rufus	Ridgefield,	Aug.11,'62	Aug.28,'62	Wd. July 1, '63, Gettysburg, Pa Died July 17, '63.
Warren, William H.	Danbury,	July 26,'62	Aug.28,'62	Cap'd July 1, '63, Gettysburg, Pa. Par. Aug. 25, '63. M. o. July 19, '65.
Wheeler, Moses W.	Danbury,	Aug. 4,'62	Aug.28,'62	Cap'd July 1, '63, Gettysburg, Pa. Par. Aug. 23, '63. M. o. July 19, '65.
Whitlock, Joseph S.	Ridgefield,	July 25,'62	Aug.28,'62	Wd. July 1, '63, Gettysburg, Pa. Died July 16, '63.
Whitlock, Nephi	Ridgefield,	July 25,'62	Aug.28,'62	Wd. July 1, '63, Gettysburg, Pa. Trans. to 159th Co. 2d Batt. V. R. C.
Williams, Adam C.	Bethel,	Aug. 6,'62	Aug.28,'62	Disc. dis. Jan. 5, '63. [Feb. 17, '64. Disc. July 24, '65.
Wilcox, Arthur B.	Danbury,	Jan. 11,'64	Jan. 11,'64	M. o. July 19, '65.
Wilcox, Charles H.	Danbury,	July 23,'62	Aug.28,'62	Cap'd Feb. 4, '65, St. Augustine, Fla. Par. Apr. 21, '65. Disc. June 8, '65.
Wood, George W.	Danbury,	July 22,'62	Aug.28,'62	M. o. July 19, '65.
Wood, George L.	Danbury,	July 22,'62	Aug.28,'62	Cap'd May 2, '63, Chancellorsville, Va. Par. May 14, '63. M. o. July 19, '65.
Wooster, Charles	Newtown,	July 22,'62	Aug.28,'62	Disc. dis. July 31, '63. (See Priv. Co. A, 11th C. V.)
Woodman, Iraneus P.	Bethel,	July 26,'62	Aug.28,'62	Wd. May 2, '63, Chancellorsville, Va. Died May 19, '63.

Company D.

Name and Rank.	Residence.	Date of Enlistment.	Date of Muster in this organization.	Remarks.
Captains.				
William H. Lacey,	Bridgeport,	Aug. 1,'62	Aug.28,'62	Wd. May 1, '63, Chancellorsville, Va. Resgd. May 9, '63.
William L. Hubbell,	Bridgeport,	July 23,'62	Aug.28,'62	Must. 1st Lt. Ap. Adj. Nov. 15, '62. Pro. from Adj. June 4, '63. Cap'd July 1, '63, Gettysburg, Pa. Par. Aug. 25, '63. M. o. July 19, '65.
1st Lieutenants.				[ville, Va. Par. May 14, '63. Resgd. Nov. 13, '63.
Samuel E. Blinn,	Bridgeport,	July 23,'62	Aug.28,'62	Must. 2d Lt. Pro. Nov. 15, '62. Wd. and cap'd May 2, '63, Chancellors-
Albert W. Peck,	Bridgeport,	July 23,'62	Aug.28,'62	Must. 1st Sergt. Pro. 2d Lt. Nov. 15, '62; 1st Lt. Mch. 5, '64. M o. July 19, '65.
1st Sergeants.				
Henry North,	Bridgeport,	July 23,'62	Aug.28,'62	Must. Sergt. Pro. Nov. 15, '62. Cap'd May 2, '63, Chancellorsville, Va. Par. May 14, '63. Pro. 2d Lt. Feb. 20, '64 (not must.); 1st Lt. Co. A, July 15, '64.
Garrett D. Bowne,	Bridgeport,	July 23,'62	Aug.28,'62	Must. Priv. Cap'd May 2, '63, Chancellorsville, Va. Par. May 14, '63. Pro. Sergt. Jan. 30, '64; 1st Sergt. Aug. 28, '64; 2d Lt. Jan. 26, '65 (not must.); 1st Lt. June 29, '65 (not must.). M. o. July 19, '65.
Sergeants.				
Bachelder, Cyrus T.	Bridgeport,	Aug.12,'62	Aug.28,'62	Cap'd July 1, '63, Gettysburg, Pa. Par. July —, '63. Redc. to ranks Mch. 12, '65. Disc. July 5, '65.
Blakeman, Selah G.	Stratford,	July 29,'62	Aug.28,'62	Must. Priv. Pro Sergt. Jan. 30, '64. M. o. July 19, '65.
Bosworth, James	Fairfield,	Aug. 6,'62	Aug.28,'62	Wd. and cap'd May 2, '63, Chancellorsville, Va. Par. May 15, '63. Trans. to 57th Co. 2d Batt. V. R. C. Sep. 9, '63. Disc. dis. Oct. 13, '64.
Foley, John H.	Bridgeport,	Aug. 7,'62	Aug.28,'62	Must. Corp. Pro. Nov. 15, '62. Wd. July 1, '63, Gettysburg, Pa. Trans. to Co. F, 19th Regt. V. R. C. Oct. 14, '63. Disc. July 13, '65.
Garrett, Daniel S.	Huntington,	Aug.11,'62	Aug.28,'62	Must. Priv. Pro. Sergt. Jan. 30, '64. Pro. 2d Lt. June 29,'65 (not must.).
Hope, Thomas	Bridgeport,	Feb. 10,'65	Feb. 10,'65	Must. Priv. Pro. Sergt. Mch. 13,'65. M. o. July 19,'65. [M. o. July 19,'65.
Keeler, Henry W.	New Haven,	Aug. 7,'62	Aug.28,'62	Wd. July 1, '63, Gettysburg, Pa. Trans. to Co. D, 24th Regt. V. R. C. Jan. 25, '64. Redc. to ranks (sick) July 5, '64. Disc. dis. June 1, '65.
Keyes, Henry F.	Bridgeport,	Feb. 16,'65	Feb. 16,'65	(See Band 9th C. V.) Must. Priv. Pro. Sergt. Mch. 13, '65. M. o. July 19, '65.
Corporals.				
Brinsmade, James R.	Bridgeport,	July 23,'62	Aug.28,'62	Redc. to ranks Jan. 30, '64. Disc. Aug. 31, '64.
Carpenter, Fred'k H.	Bridgeport,	July 23,'62	Aug.28,'62	Must. Priv. Pro. Nov. 15, '62. Wd. July 1, '63, Gettysburg, Pa. Cap'd Feb. 5,'65, Dunn's Lake, Fla. Released Apr. 21,'65. Disc. June 8,'65.
Clark, Frederick R.	Huntington,	Aug.11,'62	Aug.28,'62	Must. Priv. Wd. and cap'd May 2, '63, Chancellorsville, Va. Par. May
Curtis, Wright	Bridgeport,	July 23,'62	Aug.28,'62	Disc. dis. Feb. 23, '63. [14, '63. Pro. Jan. 30, '64. M. o. July 19, '64.
Green, John J.	Bridgeport,	Aug.15,'62	Aug.28,'62	Redc. to ranks at own request Oct. 1, '62. Disc. dis. Apr. 15, '63.
Keeler, William H.	Stratford,	July 22,'62	Aug.28,'62	Ap. Q.M.-Sergt. Nov. 4, '63.
Lewis, Luther W.	Bridgeport,	Aug. 5,'62	Aug.28,'62	(See Priv. Co. H, 1st C. V.) Must. Priv. Cap'd July 1, '63, Gettysburg, Pa. Released Aug. —, '63. Pro. Jan. 30, '64. M. o. July 19, '65.
Lewis, John F.	Bridgeport,	Aug.16,'62	Aug.28,'62	Must. Priv. Cap'd July 1, '63, Gettysburg, Pa. Par. July —, '63. Pro.
Lewis, Charles B.	Bridgeport,	July 23,'62	Aug.28,'62	Died Aug. 6, '63. [Jan. 30, '64. Died Mch. 11, '64.
Middlebrook, James R.	Trumbull,	Aug.12,'62	Aug.28,'62	Must. Priv. Pro. Jan. 30, '64, 2d Lt. June 20, '65 (not must.). M. o. July 19, '65. [Va. Par. May 15, '63. Disc. dis. June 29, '65.
Phillips, George D.	Bridgeport,	July 28,'62	Aug.28,'62	Must. Priv. Pro. Oct. 1, '62. Wd. and cap'd May 2, '63, Chancellorsville,
Quick, Charles E.	Easton,	Aug. 9,'62	Aug.28,'62	Must. Priv. Pro. May 1, '65. M. o. July 19, '65.
Wilcox, Alva E.	Bridgeport,	July 22,'62	Aug.28,'62	Wd. July 3, '63, Gettysburg, Pa. Died July 6, '63.

Name and Rank.	Residence	Date of Enlistment.	Date of Muster in this organization.	Remarks.
Wirtz, William	Bridgeport,	Aug.14,'62	Aug.28,'62	Must. Priv. Cap'd July 1, '63, Gettysburg, Pa. Released Aug. —, '63. Pro. Corp. May 1, '65. M. o. July 19, '65.
Wordin, Gilbert	Fairfield,	Aug. 6,'62	Aug.28,'62	Cap'd July 1, '63, Gettysburg, Pa. Par. July —, '63. M. o. July 19, '65.
Musicians.				[19, '65.
Huss, Henry	Fairfield,	July 23,'62	Aug.28,'62	Cap'd May 3, '63, Chancellorsville, Va. Par. May 14, '63. M. o. July
Wilmott, Frederick M.	Bridgeport,	July 24,'62	Aug.28,'62	Cap'd Feb. 4, '65, St. Augustine, Fla. Par. Apr. 21,'65. Disc. June 8,'65.
Wagoner.				
Taylor, James H.	Monroe,	Aug. 6,'62	Aug.28,'62	Disc. dis. Dec. 23, '62. (See Priv. Co. H, 2d C. V. H. A.)
Privates.				
Adams, William H.	Monroe,	Aug. 8,'62	Aug.28,'62	Disc. dis. Mch. 13, '63.
Banks, Charles	Bridgeport,	Feb. 27,'65	Feb. 27,'65	M. o. July 19, '65.
Barnum, Samuel B.	Bridgeport,	July 23,'62	Aug.28,'62	Ap. Hosp. Stewd. Nov. 19, 63.
Bartlett, John F.	Bridgeport,	Aug.13,'62	Aug.28,'62	Wd. and cap'd May 2, '63, Chancellorsville, Va. Par. May 15, '63. Trans. to 41st Co. 2d Batt. V. R. C. Dec. 2, '63. Disc. Aug. 27, '65.
Barlow, Samuel J.	Bridgeport,	July 23,'62	Aug.28,'62	Disc. dis. Dec. 17, '62.
Bachelder, Melvin C.	Bridgeport,	July 22,'62	Aug.28,'62	M. o. July 19, '65.
Blakeman, J. Henry	Stratford,	July 29,'62	Aug.28,'62	Wd. July 1, '63, Gettysburg, Pa. M o. July 19, '65.
Blakeman, Charles G.	Woodbury,	Aug.13,'62	Aug.28,'62	M. o. July 19, '65.
Booth, John W.	Monroe,	Aug.11,'62	Aug.28,'62	M. o. July 19, '65.
Booth, John R.	Stratford,	Aug. 7,'62	Aug.28,'62	Killed July 1, '63, Gettysburg, Pa.
Bradley, William F.	Monroe,	Aug.11,'62	Aug.28,'62	Killed July 1, '63, Gettysburg, Pa.
Burton, Franklin P.	Trumbull,	Aug. 5,'62	Aug.28,'62	M. o. July 19, '65.
Burditt, Samuel J.	Huntington,	Aug.13,'62	Aug.28,'62	Died Nov. 29, '62.
Carritt, William P.	Bridgeport,	July 24,'62	Aug.28,'62	(See Priv. Co. D, 3d C. V.) Des. Sep. 1, '62.
Clark, Charles H.	Stratford,	July 29,'62	Aug.28,'62	Disc. dis. Apr. 10, '63.
Clark, James W.	Monroe,	Aug. 8,'62	Aug.28,'62	Disc. dis. June 21, '64.
Clark, William S.	Monroe,	Aug. 7,'62	Aug.28,'62	Killed May 2, '63, Chancellorsville, Va.
Crofut, Stephen C.	Stratford,	Aug.11,'62	Aug.28,'62	Killed July 1, '63, Gettysburg, Pa.
Curtis, Frederick W.	Huntington,	Aug. 6,'62	Aug.28,'62	Trans. to Co. F, 13th Regt. V. R. C. July 8, '63. Disc. June 28, '65.
Curtis, John B.	Bridgeport,	Aug.15,'62	Aug.28,'62	M. o. July 19, '65.
Dewhirst, William S.	Bridgeport,	Aug.15,'62	Aug.28,'62	Wd. July 1, '63, Gettysburg, Pa. M. o. July 19, '65.
Dikeman, George	Danbury,	Mch. 1,'65	Mch. 1,'65	(See Priv. Co. D, 10th C. V.) M. o. July 19, '65.
Dunning, Charles F.	Bridgeport,	July 23,'62	Aug.28,'62	M. o. July 19, '65.
Dunning, John W.	Bridgeport,	Aug. 4,'62	Aug.28,'62	Disc. dis. Feb. 23, '63.
Goodhue, Joseph H.	Bridgeport,	Aug.12,'62	Aug.28,'62	Disc. dis. June 3, '64.
Gorgas, George S.	Bridgeport,	July 23,'62	Aug.28,'62	M. o. July 19, '65. [Pa. Par. Aug. 25, '63. M. o. July 19, '65.
Gregory, George H.	Stratford,	Aug. 8,'62	Aug.28,'62	Wd. Dec. 16, '62, Stafford Court House, Va. Cap'd July 1,'63, Gettysburg,
Hall, Frederick B.	Bridgeport,	Aug.11,'62	Aug.28,'62	Disc. dis. Dec. 24, '62.
Hannaford, George W.	Bridgeport,	Aug.13,'62	Aug.28,'62	Wd. July 1, '63, Gettysburg, Pa. M. o. July 19, '65.
Hayes, Charles	Brookfield,	Aug.11,'62	Aug.28,'62	Disc. dis. Dec. 23, '62.
Hayes, George R.	Bridgeport,	Aug.13,'62	Aug.28,'62	Wd. July 1, '63, Gettysburg, Pa. Died Feb. 5, '64.
Howe, Elias Jr.	Fairfield,	Aug.14,'62	Aug.28,'62	M. o. July 19, '65.
Hubbell, Eugene	Monroe,	Aug.11,'62	Aug.28,'62	Disc. dis. Feb. 2, '63.
Hurd, Charles A.	Bridgeport,	Aug. 7,'62	Aug.28,'62	Cap'd July 21,'63, Loudon County, Va. Par. Sep. 23,'63. M. o. July 19,'65.
Hurd, Edwin D.	Fairfield,	Aug. 8,'62	Aug.28,'62	Ap. Com.-Sergt. Mch. 6, '63.
Jennings, Moses B.	Easton,	Aug.12,'62	Aug.28,'62	M. o. July 19, '65.
Keefe, William	Darien,	Jan. 26,'65	Jan. 26,'65	M. o. July 19, '65.
Keeler, George W.	Stratford,	July 23,'62	Aug.28,'62	M. o. July 19, '65.
Kehrer, Ernest	Bridgeport,	Aug. 7,'62	Aug.28,'62	Disc. dis. Dec. 31, '62.
Larkin, James	Fairfield,	Aug. 6,'62	Aug.28,'62	M. o. July 19, '65. [19, '64.
Leavenworth, Andrew	Monroe,	Aug.11,'62	Aug.28,'62	Cap'd May 2, '63, Chancellorsville, Va. Par. May 14, '63. Disc. dis. Feb.
Lewis, Stephen C.	Bridgeport,	Aug. 9,'62	Aug.28,'62	Cap'd Feb. 5, '65, Dunn's Lake, Fla. Par. Apr. 21,'65. Disc. June 23,'65.
Maby, William H.	Bridgeport,	Feb. 23,'65	Feb. 23,'65	M. o. July 19, '65. [Aug. 30, '64. Disc. dis. Aug. 12, '65.
Marsh, Thomas A.	Easton,	Aug. 9,'62	Aug.28,'62	Wd. July 1, '63, Gettysburg, Pa. Trans. to 159th Co. 2d Batt. V. R. C.
Marshall, Barney	Trumbull,	Aug. 6,'62	Aug.28,'62	Wd. July 1, '63, Gettysburg, Pa. M. o. July 19, '65.
Morse, Edward A.	Bridgeport,	Aug.14,'62	Aug.28,'62	M. o. July 19, '65. [14, '65.
Mott, Joseph	Bridgeport,	July 23,'62	Aug.28,'62	Cap'd Feb. 4, '65, St. Augustine, Fla. Par. Apr. 21, '65. Disc. June
Munger, John N.	Stratford,	July 29,'62	Aug.28,'62	Died Feb. 13, '63.
Nichols, Edward	Monroe,	Aug. 7,'62	Aug.28,'62	(See Priv. Rifle Co. F, 3d C. V.) M. o. July 19, '65. [Disc. July 11, '65.
Nichols, Henry B.	Monroe,	Aug. 9,'62	Aug.28,'62	Trans. to Co. E, 21st Regt. V. R. C. Dec. 12, '63. Pro. Corp. Nov. 1, '64.
Norton, Patrick	New Canaan,	Aug.14,'62	Aug.28,'62	Wd. and cap'd July 1,'63, Gettysburg, Pa. Par. July —,'63. Cap'd Feb. 5, '65, Dunn's Lake, Fla. Par. Apr. 21, '65. Disc. June 8, '65.
Northrop, Alonzo	Bridgeport,	Aug.13,'62	Aug.28,'62	M. o. July 19, '65.
Northrop, Ira C.	Huntington,	Aug.15,'62	Aug.28,'62	M. o. July 19, '65.
Parrott, Joseph R.	Bridgeport,	July 23,'62	Aug.28,'62	Disc. dis. Feb. 16, '63.
Peck, Lemuel	Brookfield,	Aug.12,'62	Aug.28,'62	Died Dec. 6, '62.
Penfield, Ira	Monroe,	Aug.11,'62	Aug.28,'62	Cap'd May 2,'63, Chancellorsville, Va. Par. May 14,'63. M. o. July 19,'65.
Pinn, Jacob Jr.	Fairfield,	Aug. 6,'62	Aug.28,'62	M. o. July 19, '65.
Pitcher, Oliver E.	Bridgeport,	Aug.12,'62	Aug.28,'62	Trans. to Co. B, 20th Regt. V. R. C. Sep. 20, '63. Died Nov. 10, '64.
Plumb, Horace	Bridgeport,	July 25,'62	Aug.28,'62	M. o. July 19, '65.
Riley, John	Washington,	Nov.11,'64	Nov.11,'64	M. o. July 19, '65.
Rogers, William A.	Bridgeport,	Aug.13,'62	Aug.28,'62	Killed May 2, '63, Chancellorsville, Va. [Jan. 5, '64. Disc. July 6, '65.
Rounds, Sylvester	Huntington,	Aug.16,'62	Aug.28,'62	Wd. July 1, '63, Gettysburg, Pa. Trans. to 136th Co. 2d Batt. V. R. C.
Sault, James	Norwalk,	Jan. 25,'65	Jan. 25,'65	M. o. July 19, '65. [July 19, '65.
Sclipp, William H.	Bridgeport,	Aug.11,'62	Aug.28,'62	Cap'd July 1, '63, Gettysburg, Pa. Returned to duty Sep. 7, '63. M. o.
Scranton, Alonzo	Bridgeport,	Aug. 2,'62	Aug.28,'62	Wd. July 1, '63, Gettysburg, Pa. Trans. to Co. B, 4th Regt. V. R. C.
Scranton, Leonard D.	Madison,	Aug. 2,'62	Aug.28,'62	M. o. July 19, '65. [Sep. 27, '64. Disc. July 17, '65.
Smith, William R.	Monroe,	Aug. 8,'62	Aug.28,'62	Cap'd July 1, '63, Gettysburg, Pa. Par. Aug. 25, '63. M. o. July 19, '65.
Stratton, Legrand	Bridgeport,	Aug. 4,'62	Aug.28,'62	Trans. to 21st Co. 2d Batt. V. R. C. Aug. 10, '63. Disc. July 19, '65.
Taylor, Milton C.	Newtown,	Aug.12,'62	Aug.28,'62	Cap'd May 2, '63, Chancellorsville, Va. Par. May 14,'63. M. o. July 19,'65.

Name and Rank.	Residence.	Date of Enlistment.	Date of Muster in this organization.	Remarks.
Treadwell, Edmund	Redding,	Aug.12,'62	Aug.28,'62	Cap'd Feb. 5, '65, Dunn's Lake, Fla. Par. Apr. 21, '65. Disc. July 10,'65.
Underhill, George E.	Bridgeport,	Aug.14,'62	Aug.28,'62	M. o. July 19, '65.
Van Amburgh, Marion	Danbury,	Jan. 24,'65	Jan. 24,'65	M. o. July 19, '65.
Wayland, John B.	Monroe,	Aug. 8,'62	Aug.28,'62	Disc. dis. Oct. 8, '63.
Webster, Edgar L.	Huntington,	Aug. 6,'62	Aug.28,'62	Disc. dis. Jan. 27, '63.
Webster, George S.	Huntington,	Aug. 6,'62	Aug.28,'62	Disc. June 2, '65.
Wells, Charles S.	Huntington,	Aug. 9,'62	Aug.28,'62	Wd. July 1–4, '63, Gettysburg, Pa. Disc. dis. Nov. 28, '64.
Whittlesey, Samuel F.	Trumbull,	Aug. 8,'62	Aug.28,'62	Wd. July 1, '63, Gettysburg, Pa. Cap'd Feb. 5, '65, Dunn's Lake, Fla. Par. Apr. 21, '65. Disc. July 10, '65. [Nov. 11, '63.
Wilcoxson, Edgar S.	Fairfield,	Aug.14,'62	Aug.28,'62	Cap'd May 2, '63, Chancellorsville, Va. Par. May 16, '63. Trans. to Co. I,

Company E.

Name and Rank.	Residence.	Date of Enlistment.	Date of Muster in this organization.	Remarks.
Captains.				[28, '64.
Henry P. Burr,	Westport,	Aug. 1,'62	Aug.28,'62	Cap'd May 2, '63, Chancellorsville, Va. Par. May 15, '63. Resgd. May
James E. Hubbell,	Westport,	Aug. 7,'62	Aug.28,'62	Must. 1st Sergt. Pro. 2d Lt. Sep. 1, '63; 1st Lt. Mch. 5, '64; Capt. Aug. 15, '64. M. o. July 19, '65.
1st Lieutenants.				[Light Batty.)
William C. Johnson,	Westport,	Aug. 1,'62	Aug.28,'62	(See Priv. Co. E, 5th C. V.) Resgd. Oct. 3, '62. (See 1st Sergt. 3d C. V.
John F. Clancey,	Bridgeport,	Aug. 1,'62	Aug.28,'62	Must. 2d Lt. Pro. Oct. 3, '62. Dismissed June 20, '63.
Theodore Gray,	Bridgeport,	July 22,'62	Aug.29,'62	Pro. from Sergt.-Maj. to 2d Lt. Oct. 3, '62; 1st Lt. June 20, '63; Capt Co. K, Mch. 5, '65.
Henry McDonough,	Westport,	Aug.13,'62	Aug.28,'62	Must. Sergt. Wd. July 2, '63, Gettysburg, Pa. Pro. 1st Sergt. Sep. 1, '63. Ap. Sergt.-Maj. Dec. 13, '63. Pro. from Sergt.-Maj. to 2d Lt. Mch. 19, '64; 1st Lt. Mch. 5, '65. M. o. July 19, '65.
1st Sergeant.				
George C. Lees,	Westport,	Aug. 7,'62	Aug.28,'62	Must. Sergt. Pro. Jan. 1, '64; 2d Lt. July 15, '64 (not must.); 1st Lt. June 29, '65 (not must.). M. o. July 19, '65.
Sergeants.				
Carrodus, Charles H.	Weston,	Aug. 4,'62	Aug.28,'62	Must. Corp. Pro. Feb. 1, '65. M. o. July 19, '65.
Glover, Martin V. B.	Newtown,	Aug.14,'62	Aug.28,'62	Died May 1, '63.
Gordon, James	Newtown,	Aug.11,'62	Aug.28,'62	Must. Corp. Pro. May 1, '63. Killed July 1, '63, Gettysburg, Pa.
Hale, George	Westport,	Aug. 8,'62	Aug.28,'62	Must. Corp. Wd. July 2, '63, Gettysburg, Pa. Pro. Sergt. Sep. 1, '63;
Murray, Charles	Westport,	Aug. 7,'62	Aug.28,'62	M. o. July 19, '65. [2d Lt. June 29, '65 (not must.). M. o. July 19, '65.
Perry, James A.	Westport,	Aug. 8,'62	Aug.28,'62	Must. Corp. Cap'd July 2, '63, Gettysburg, Pa. Par. Aug. 25, '63. Pro. Sergt. Jan. 1, '64. M. o. July 19, '65.
Corporals.				[6, '64. M. o. July 19, '65.
Baker, Joseph H.	Westport,	Aug.14,'62	Aug.28,'62	Must. Priv. Pro. Jan. 30, '64. Redc. to ranks Feb. 18, '64. Pro. June
Bennett, Aaron	Westport,	Aug.11,'62	Aug.28,'62	Trans. to Co. C, 3d Regt. V. R. C. July 1, '63. Redc. to ranks Nov. 4, '63. Disc. July 12, '65. [Pro. Mch. 7, '65. M. o. July 19, '65.
Chipman, Charles C.	Newtown,	Aug.11,'62	Aug.28,'62	Must. Priv. Cap'd May 2, '63, Chancellorsville, Va. Par. May 14, '63.
Crapo, Beroth B.	Weston,	Aug. 4,'62	Aug.28,'62	Must. Priv. Wd. and cap'd May 2, '63, Chancellorsville, Va. Par. May 14, '63. Pro. Jan. 30, '64. M. o. July 19, '65.
Hayes, Dennis	Newtown,	Aug.13,'62	Aug.28,'62	Must. Priv. Cap'd July 2, '63, Gettysburg, Pa. Par. Aug. 25, '63. Pro.
Lees, Edward M.	Westport,	Aug.18,'62	Aug.28,'62	Pro. 2d Lt. Co. K, Feb. 23, '63. [Jan. 1, '64. M. o. July 19, '65.
McBride, George	Bridgeport,	Aug. 9,'62	Aug.28,'62	Disc. dis. June 9, '63.
Northrop, Alpheus	Newtown,	Aug.12,'62	Aug.28,'62	Must. Priv. Wd. May 2, '63, Chancellorsville, Va. Wd. and cap'd July 2, '63, Gettysburg, Pa. Par. Aug. 25, '63. Pro. Feb. 1, '65. M. o. July 19, '65. [Aug. 25, '63. M. o. July 19, '65.
Perry, Roscoe	Westport,	July 11,'62	Aug.28,'62	Must. Priv. Pro. Apr. 17, '63. Cap'd July 2, '63, Gettysburg, Pa. Par.
Perry, Aaron B.	Westport,	Aug. 7,'62	Aug.28,'62	Disc. dis. Dec. 10, '62.
Spencer, George H.	Newtown,	Aug.14,'62	Aug.28,'62	Must. Priv. Ap. Hosp. Stewd. Apr. 4, '63. Trans. as Priv. from Hosp. Stewd. Nov. 19, '63. Pro. Corp. Jan. 1, '64. Redc. to ranks Mch. 7, '65. M. o. July 19, '65. [19, '65.
Taylor, Orrin	Westport,	Aug. 8,'62	Aug.28,'62	Must. Priv. Pro. Sep. 7, '63. Redc. to ranks Feb. 18, '64. M. o. July
Tilbe, Rufus	Westport,	Aug. 8,'62	Aug.28,'62	Must. Priv. Pro. Apr. 17, '63. Wd. Aug. 20, '63, Morris Island, S. C. Trans. to 128th Co. 2d Batt. V. R. C. Dec. 31, '63. Disc. dis. July
Wakeman, Rufus	Westport,	Aug. 8,'62	Aug.28,'62	Must. Priv. Pro. May 1, '63. M. o. July 19, '65. [2, '64.
Westerfield, Wm. C.	Norwalk,	Aug. 9,'62	Aug.28,'62	Must. Priv. Cap'd July 2, '63, Gettysburg, Pa. Par. Aug. 25, '63. Pro. June 6, '64. M. o. July 19, '65.
Musicians.				
Beck, John	Bridgeport,	Aug. 7,'62	Aug.28,'62	Must. Priv. Detailed Musc. M. o. July 19, '65.
Stratton, Charles S.	Trumbull,	Aug. 4,'62	Aug.28,'62	M. o. July 19, '65.
Turney, George R.	Trumbull,	Aug. 5,'62	Aug.28,'62	Trans. to ranks. Disc. dis. June 7, '64.
Wagoners.				
Bacon, Charles A.	Bridgeport,	Aug.18,'62	Aug.28,'62	Must. Priv. Detailed Wag. M. o. July 19, '65.
Hadley, William	Westport,	Aug.20,'62	Aug.28,'62	Trans. to ranks. Disc. dis. Apr. 1, '63.
Sweeten, David	Weston,	Aug. 7,'62	Aug.28,'62	Must. Priv. Detailed Wag. Oct. 17, '63. Returned to ranks. Disc. dis. Aug. 29, '63.
Privates.				
Ahearn, Patrick	Westport,	Aug. 8,'62	Aug.28,'62	Disc. dis. Apr. 15, '63.
Allen, Elnathan	Westport,	Aug. 7,'62	Aug.28,'62	M. o. July 19, '65.

NAME AND RANK.	Residence.	Date of Enlistment.	Date of Muster in this organization.	Remarks.
Allen, Theodore	Westport,	Aug. 8,'62	Aug.28,'62	Cap'd July 2, '63, Gettysburg, Pa. Par. Aug. 25, '63. M. o. July 19, '65.
Baggs, Edmund	Bridgeport,	July 28,'62	Aug.28,'62	Trans. to 12th Co. 2d Batt. V. R. C. July 28, '63. Disc. Aug. 20, '63.
Banks, Horace O.	Weston,	Dec. 30,'63	Dec. 30,'63	M. o. July 19, '65.
Banks, Wesley O.	Weston,	Jan. 1,'64	Jan. 1,'64	M. o. July 19, '65.
Barnes, James H.	Westport,	Aug. 8,'62	Aug.28,'62	Trans. to Co. D, 9th Regt. V. R. C. Aug. 14, '63. Disc. June 26, '65.
Bigelow, Henry B.	Newtown,	Aug.11,'62	Aug.28,'62	Cap'd July 2, '63, Gettysburg, Pa. Par. Aug. 25, '63. M. o. July 19, '65.
Birmingham, James	Bridgeport,	Aug.14,'62	Aug.28,'62	M. o. July 19, '65.
Bloomer, John H.	Westport,	Aug. 4,'62	Aug.28,'62	Cap'd May 2, '63, Chancellorsville, Va. Par. May 14, '63. M. o. July 19, ['65.
Bothwell, David	Westport,	Aug. 6,'62	Aug.28,'62	Disc. dis. Apr. 15, '63.
Bradley, Thomas	Newtown,	Aug.11,'62	Aug.28,'62	Cap'd Feb. 5, '65, Dunn's Lake Fla. Par. Apr. 28, '65. Disc. July 10, ['65.
Brown, John	Bridgeport,	Aug. 4,'62	Aug.28,'62	M. o. July 19, '65.
Brotherton, Benjamin	Westport,	Aug. 8,'62	Aug.28,'62	Wd. May 2, '63, Chancellorsville, Va. M. o. July 19, '65.
Buckley, Thomas	Westport,	Aug. 9,'62	Aug.28,'62	M. o. July 19, '65.
Burr, John T.	Westport,	Aug. 6,'62	Aug.28,'62	M. o. July 19, '65.
Chase, Dennis O.	Westport,	Aug.12,'62	Aug.28,'62	Cap'd July 2, '63, Gettysburg, Pa. Par. Aug. 25, '63. M. o. July 19, '65.
Clarkson, Charles H.	Weston,	Aug. 9,'62	Aug.28,'62	Cap'd May 2, '63, Chancellorsville, Va. Par. May 15, '63. M. o. July 19, '65.
Colgan, Matthew	Newtown,	Aug.14,'62	Aug.28,'62	Wd. and cap'd July 1, '63, Gettysburg, Pa. Par. Aug. 2, '63. M. o. July [19, '65.
Connelly, John	Bridgeport,	Aug. 4,'62	Aug.28,'62	M. o. July 19, '65.
Darrow, Francis	Westport,	Aug.13,'62	Aug.28,'62	Disc. dis. Dec. 23, '62.
Dixon, Samuel	Weston,	Aug. 4,'62	Aug.28,'62	Disc. dis. Apr. 1, '63.
Doran, Peter	Bridgeport,	Aug.11,'62	Aug.28,'62	Trans. to Co. D, 12th Regt. V. R. C. Aug. 13, '63. Disc June 28, '65.
Downs, Oliver	Newtown,	Aug. 9,'62	Aug.28,'62	Disc. dis. June 23, '65.
Dunn, John	Bridgeport,	Aug.13,'62	Aug.28,'62	M. o. July 19, '65.
Egan, James	Newtown,	Aug. 5,'62	Aug.28,'62	Disc. dis. Jan. 22, '63.
Egan, Michael	Bridgeport,	Aug.13,'62	Aug.28,'62	Disc. dis. Dec. 5, '62.
Ellwell, Herman	Westport,	Aug. 4,'62	Aug.28,'62	M. o. July 19, '65.
Ellwood, Francis H.	Westport,	Aug. 8,'62	Aug.28,'62	Cap'd May 2, '63, Chancellorsville, Va. Par. May 14, '63. M. o. July [19, '65.
Fanton, David W.	Bridgeport,	Aug.11,'62	Aug.28,'62	Disc. dis. Aug. 12, '63.
Flynn, James	Westport,	Aug.15,'62	Aug.28,'62	Wd. July 2, '63, Gettysburg, Pa. Died July 14, '63.
Foot, Francis	Westport,	Aug. 7,'62	Aug.28,'62	Supposed killed July 1, '63, Gettysburg, Pa. N. f. r. A. G. O.
Gordon, William A.	Newtown,	Aug.12,'62	Aug.28,'62	Wd. and cap'd May 2, '63, Chancellorsville, Va. Par. May 15, '63. Trans. to Co. H, 1st Regt. V. R. C. Dec. 8, '63. Disc. July 13, '65.
Guernsey, George H.	Westport,	Aug. 7,'62	Aug.28,'62	Wd. July 1, '63, Gettysburg, Pa. Died Aug. 9, '63.
Hendricks, Lewis B.	Westport,	Aug. 7,'62	Aug.28,'62	Disc. dis. June 23, '65.
Hickey, John	Newtown,	Aug. 9,'62	Aug.28,'62	Died May 9, '63.
Hoyt, Charles G.	Westport,	Aug. 7,'62	Aug.28,'62	M. o. July 19, '65.
Hugh, James	Weston,	Aug. 4,'62	Aug.28,'62	Cap'd July 2, '63, Gettysburg, Pa. Par. Aug. 25, '63. M. o. July 19, '65.
Keyser, William R.	Westport,	Aug. 8,'62	Aug.28,'62	Disc. dis. Jan. 17, '63.
Leahy, Jeremiah	Bridgeport,	July 29,'62	Aug.28,'62	Des. Sep. 10, '62. [Redc. to ranks Oct. 6, '63. Disc. July 6, '65.
Lockwood, Samuel	Westport,	Aug.13,'62	Aug.28,'62	Trans. to Co. F, 3d Regt. V. R. C. July 13, '63. Pro. Corp. July 24, '63.
McMahon, Michael	Newtown,	Aug. 9,'62	Aug.28,'62	Disc. dis. Jan. 17, '63.
Monteith, James	Westport,	Aug. 7,'62	Aug.28,'62	Wd. July 2, '63, Gettysburg, Pa. M. o. July 19, '65.
Morehouse, Calvin	Westport,	Aug. 7,'62	Aug.28,'62	Des. Mch. 22, '63.
Nash, Francis	Westport,	Aug.18,'62	Aug.28,'62	Supposed killed July 1, '63, Gettysburg, Pa. N. f. r. A. G. O.
Nash, Joseph B.	Westport,	Aug.11,'62	Aug.28,'62	M. o. July 19, '65.
Newton, James	Bridgeport,	Aug.12,'62	Aug.28,'62	Wd. July 1, '63, Gettysburg, Pa. Disc. dis. Dec. 31, '63.
Oakley, William	Weston,	Dec. 21,'63	Dec. 21,'63	M. o. July 19, '65.
O'Halloran, Michael T.	Newtown,	July 11,'62	Aug.28,'62	Wd. Dec. —, '62, Chantilly, Va. Disc. dis. Sep. 15, '63.
Olmsted, Charles	Westport,	Aug. 7,'62	Aug.28,'62	Trans. to 173d Co. 2d Batt. V. R. C. Sep. 19, '64. Disc. July 7, '65.
O'Nell, Michael	Bridgeport,	July 29,'62	Aug.28,'62	M. o. July 19, '65.
Peet, Henry A. S.	Newtown,	Aug.14,'62	Aug.28,'62	Des. Mch. 19, '63.
Porter, Frederick M.	Westport,	Aug.12,'62	Aug.28,'62	M. o. July 19, '65.
Roache, James	Westport,	Aug. 7,'62	Aug.28,'62	Died Jan. 6, '65.
Roche, Lewis	Roxbury,	Dec. 30,'63	Dec. 30,'63	Died Jan. 26, '65.
Ryan, Michael	Newtown,	Aug. 9,'62	Aug.28,'62	M. o. Jan. 19, '65.
Schriver, Andrew	Newtown,	Aug.13,'62	Aug.28,'62	M. o. July 19, '65.
Scofield, Orlando F.	Westport,	Aug. 8,'62	Aug.28,'62	Died May 1, '63.
Seery, John	Westport,	Aug. 4,'62	Aug.28,'62	Disc. dis. Dec. 5, '62.
Shaughness, Lawrence	Newtown,	Aug.11,'62	Aug.28,'62	Cap'd July 2, '63, Gettysburg, Pa. Par. Aug. 25, '63. M. o. July 19, '65.
Smith, Nelson	Westport,	Aug. 7,'62	Aug.28,'62	Cap'd July 2, '63, Gettysburg, Pa. Par. Aug. 2, '63. Trans. to Morris Island, S. C., Oct. 6, '63; failed to report. N. f. r. A. G. O.
Smith, Pearl	Newtown,	Aug.11,'62	Aug.28,'62	Disc. dis. Dec. 5, '62.
Stockton, John W.	Stamford,	Mch. 5,'64	Mch. 5,'64	M. o. July 19, '65.
Taylor, Augustus	Westport,	Aug.11,'62	Aug.28,'62	M. o. July 19, '65.
Turney, Rice	Trumbull,	Aug. 6,'62	Aug.28,'62	Disc. dis. Dec. 10, '62.
Wakeman, Frederick	Westport,	Aug. 9,'62	Aug.28,'62	Cap'd May 2, '63, Chancellorsville, Va. Par. May 15, '63. M. o. July [19, '65.
Warren, Eugene	Westport,	Aug.14,'62	Aug.28,'62	Wd. July 1, '63, Gettysburg, Pa. M. o. July 19, '65.
Walsh, John	Newtown,	Aug.12,'62	Aug.28,'62	Missing in action July 2, '63, Gettysburg, Pa.; probably killed. N. f. r. [A. G. O.
Williams, William	Weston,	Aug. 8,'62	Aug.28,'62	Disc. dis. Jan. 1, '63.
Wilbur, Henry U.	Westport,	Aug.11,'62	Aug.28,'62	Trans. to Co. B, 13th Regt. V. R. C. July 6, '63. Disc. dis. Jan. 2, '64.
Wolfe, John W.	Westport,	Aug.15,'62	Aug.28,'62	Des. Feb. 19, '63.
Worden, Amos	Westport,	Aug. 7,'62	Aug.28,'62	Disc. dis. Jan. 22, '63.

Company F.

Name and Rank.	Residence.	Date of Enlistment.	Date of Muster in this organization.	Remarks.
Captains.				
Enoch Wood,	Norwalk,	Aug. 1,'62	Aug.28,'62	Resgd. Mch. 23, '63. [Maj. Mch. 5, '64.
Henry Allen,	Norwalk,	Aug.11,'62	Aug.28,'62	Must. 1st Lt. Pro. Mch. 23, '63. Wd. July 3, '63, Gettysburg, Pa. Pro.
C. Frederick Betts,	Norwalk,	July 18,'62	Aug.28,'62	Pro. from 2d Lt. Co. A, Mch. 5, '64. Cap'd Feb. 5, '65, Dunn's Lake,
				Fla. Par. Apr. 21, '65. Disc. May 17, '65.
1st Lieutenants.				[Dec. 1, '63.
William S. Knapp,	Norwalk,	Aug.11,'62	Aug.28,'62	Must. 1st Sergt. Pro. 2d Lt. Nov. 25, '62; 1st Lt. Apr. 17, '63. Resgd.
Joseph E. Morehouse,	Darien,	July 18,'62	Aug.28,'62	(See Corp. Rifle Co. F, 3d C. V.) Pro. from Sergt. Co. B to 2d Lt. Oct. 26,
				'63; 1st Lt. Mch. 5, '64; Capt. June 29, '65 (not must.). M. o. July 19,
2d Lieutenants.				'65.
William A. Kellogg,	Norwalk,	Aug. 9,'62	Aug.28,'62	Resgd. Nov. 25, '62. [Aug. 4, '63. (See 2d Lt. Co. B.)
Charles E. Doty,	Norwalk,	Aug.11,'62	Aug.28,'62	Must. Sergt. Pro. 1st Sergt. Nov. 25, '62; 2d Lt. Mch. 24, '63. Resgd.
George W. Shaw,	Norwalk,	Aug.13,'62	Aug.28,'62	(See Priv. Co. A, 3d C. V.) Must. Corp. Pro. Sergt. Apr. 24, '63; 2d Lt.
				Apr. 24, '64. M. o. July 19, '65.
1st Sergeants.				[July 27, '64.
N. Raymond Griffith,	Norwalk,	Aug. 9,'62	Aug.28,'62	(See Priv. Co. A, 3d C. V.) Must. Sergt. Pro. Mch. 23, '63. Disc. dis.
Charles F. Loomis,	Norwalk,	Aug.12,'62	Aug.28,'62	Must. Sergt. Pro. July 27, '64. M. o. July 19, '65.
Sergeants.				[Sergt. July 1, '64. M. o. July 19, '65.
Brush, Theodore	Norwalk,	Aug.11,'62	Aug.28,'62	Must. Corp. Cap'd July 1, '63, Gettysburg, Pa. Par. Aug. 25,'63. Pro.
McDonald, Willis	Norwalk,	Aug. 9,'62	Aug.28,'62	Must. Priv. Pro. Sergt. Nov. 25, '63. M. o. July 19, '65.
St. John, Oscar	Norwalk,	Aug.12,'62	Aug.28,'62	(See Priv. Co. A, 3d C. V.) M. o. July 19, '65.
Stevens, James E.	Norwalk,	Aug.20,'62	Aug.28,'62	Must. Priv. Pro. Corp. Nov. 21, '62; Sergt. July 27, '64. M. o. July 19,'65.
Corporals.				
Barbour, James E.	Norwalk,	Aug. 9,'62	Not must.	Pro. Hosp. Stewd. 21st C. V. Aug. 22, '62, prior to muster in.
Brotherton, Theodore	Norwalk,	Aug.18,'62	Aug.28,'62	Must. Priv. Pro. Apr. 24, '63. M. o. July 19, '65.
Campbell, Ensign J.	Norwalk,	Aug.11,'62	Aug.28,'62	Redc. to ranks Nov. 25, '62. Dropped as a deserter Jan. 5, '63.
Comstock, John A.	Norwalk,	Aug.12,'62	Aug.28,'62	Must. Priv. Pro. Nov. 25, '63. Wd. May 2, '63, Chancellorsville, Va.
				Trans. to Co. E, 19th Regt. V. R. C. Oct. 29, '63. Disc. July 13, '65.
Cockfur, Austin	Norwalk,	Aug. 9,'62	Aug.28,'62	Must. Priv. Pro. July 27, '64. M. o. July 19, '65.
Day, Francis W.	Norwalk,	Aug.11,'62	Aug.28,'62	Must. Priv. Pro. Mch. 29, '63. Wd. May 2, '63, Chancellorsville, Va.
				Trans. to 17th Co. 2d Batt. V. R. C. Jan. 25, '65. Disc. dis. Aug. 21,
Holland, John B.	Norwalk,	Aug.11,'62	Aug.28,'62	Disc. dis. Feb. 13, '63. ['65.
Keyser, William R.	Norwalk,	Aug. 9,'62	Aug.28,'62	Must. Priv. Cap'd May 2, '63, Chancellorsville, Va. Par. May 15, '63.
Middlebrook, Frank S.	Norwalk,	Aug.11,'62	Aug.28,'62	Ap. Sergt.-Maj. Aug. 28, '64. [Pro. Mch. 1, '65. M. o. July 19, '65.
Morehouse, Albert Jr.	Norwalk,	Aug. 8,'62	Aug.28,'62	(See Priv. Co. A, 3d C. V.) Redc. to ranks Nov. 25, '62. Pro. Sep. 17, '63.
				M. o. July 19, '65. [July 19, '65.
Perry, Robert N.	Norwalk,	Aug.22,'62	Aug.28,'62	Must. Priv. Wd. July 2, '63, Gettysburg, Pa. Pro. Jan. 1, '65. M. o.
Rockwell, Darius B.	Wilton,	Aug.11,'62	Aug.28,'62	Must. Priv. Pro. Nov. 25, '62. Wd. July 2, '63, Gettysburg, Pa. M. o.
Smith, Oscar	Norwalk,	Aug.13,'62	Aug.28,'62	Must. Priv. Pro. July 27, '64. M. o. July 19, '65. [July 19, '65.
Wilcox, Stephen R.	Norwalk,	Aug. 9,'62	Aug.28,'62	Redc. to ranks Nov. 25, '62. Pro. Sep. 17, '63. M. o. July 19, '65.
Musicians.				
Hearn, Thomas	Norwalk,	Aug.12,'62	Aug.28,'62	Ap. Prin. Musc. July 1, '63.
Hearn, John P.	Norwalk,	Feb. 20,'63	Feb. 20,'63	Ap. Prin. Musc. Nov. 10, '63.
Wagoner.				
Hyatt, George A.	Norwalk,	Aug.11,'62	Aug.28,'62	Trans. to 78th Co. 2d Batt. V. R. C. Oct. 19, '64. Disc. June 28, '65.
Privates.				
Allen, Rufus J.	Norwalk,	Aug. 9,'62	Aug.28,'62	Trans. to 21st Co. 2d Batt. V. R. C. Aug. 10, '63. Disc. dis. Sep. 28, '64.
Armstrong, Joseph H.	Norwalk,	Aug. 9,'62	Aug.28,'62	Died Oct. 21, '63.
Arnold, Lewis	Norwalk,	Aug.13,'62	Aug.28,'62	Killed May 2, '63, Chancellorsville, Va.
Barnes, Edwin	Norwalk,	Aug.13,'62	Aug.28,'62	M. o. July 19, '65.
Bates, Bradley	Wilton,	Aug.13,'62	Aug.28,'62	Died Oct. 5, '64.
Batteson, John H.	Norwalk,	Aug.11,'62	Aug.28,'62	Cap'd July —, '63, Gettysburg, Pa. Par. Aug. 25,'63. M. o. July 19, '65.
Beach, Nelson	Norwalk,	Aug.11,'62	Aug.28,'62	Died July 20, '63.*
Benedict, William F.	Norwalk,	Aug.22,'62	Aug.28,'62	M. o. July 19, '65.
Britto, Henry	Norwalk,	Dec. 30,'63	Dec. 30,'63	(See Corp. Co. G, 28th C. V.) M. o. July 19, '65.
Britto, Sylvester	Wilton,	Aug.11,'62	Aug.28,'62	Wd. July 1, '63, Gettysburg, Pa. Died July 4, '64.
Brown, James	Wilton,	Aug.15,'62	Aug.28,'62	Des. Dec. 12, '62.
Brown, John R.	Wilton,	Aug.18,'62	Aug.28,'62	Disc. dis. Nov. 25, '62.
Brophy, James	Norwalk,	Aug.20,'62	Aug.28,'62	Cap'd July 1, '63, Gettysburg, Pa. Par. Aug. 21, '63. Wd. Nov. 18, '63,
				James Island, S. C. Trans. to 173d Co. 2d Batt. V. R. C. Sep. 19, '64.
Brophy, Martin	Norwalk,	Aug.20,'62	Aug.28,'62	Des. Jan. 5, '65. [Disc. dis. Jan. 31, '65.
Brotherton, Ira M.	Norwalk,	Aug.31,'64	Aug.31,'64	Trans. from Co. G, Nov. 21, '64. Cap'd Feb. 5, '65, Dunn's Lake, Fla.
				Par. Apr. 21, '65. Disc. June 8, '65.
Bulger, John	Norwalk,	Aug. 9,'62	Aug.28,'62	Wd. July —, '63, Gettysburg, Pa. Cap'd Feb. 5, '65, St. Augustine, Fla.
Bundy, Alexander	Norwalk,	Aug.12,'62	Aug.28,'62	Des. Mch. 29, '63. [Par. Apr. 21, '65. Disc. June 1, '65.
Cahill, Edmund	Norwalk,	Aug. 8,'62	Aug.28,'62	M. o. July 19, '65.
Cahill, John	Norwalk,	Aug.13,'62	Aug.28,'62	Cap'd July 1, '63, Gettysburg, Pa. Par. Aug. 21, '63. M. o. July 19, '65.
Cargill, Charles	Norwalk,	Mch. 9,'64	Mch. 9,'64	Cap'd Feb. 5, '65, Dunn's Lake, Fla. Par. Apr. 21, '65. Disc. June 14, '65.
Camp, Isaac	Norwalk,	Aug.14,'62	Aug.28,'62	Disc. dis. Jan. 15, '63.
Castle, Charles H.	Norwalk,	Aug.11,'62	Aug.28,'62	Trans. to 58th Co. 2d Batt. V. R. C. Dec. 20, '63. Disc. Aug. 28, '65.

Name and Rank.	Residence.	Date of Enlistment.	Date of Muster in this organization.	Remarks.
Comstock, Le Grand	Norwalk,	Aug.12,'62	Aug.28,'62	Disc. dis. Dec. 7, '63.
Cudmore, Daniel	Norwalk,	Aug.13,'62	Aug.28,'62	M. o. July 19, '65.
Cutler, Alfred W.	Norwalk,	Aug.21,'62	Aug.28,'62	Cap'd July 1, '63, Gettysburg, Pa. Par. July —, '63. M. o. July 19, '65.
DeGroot, Benjamin	Westport,	Dec. 11,'63	Dec. 11,'63	M. o. July 19, '65.
Dougherty, Michael	Norwalk,	Aug.12,'62	Aug.28,'62	Disc. dis. Mch. 19, '63.
Dowd, Russell F.	Norwalk,	Aug.14,'62	Aug.28,'62	M. o. July 19, '65.
Downs, William H.	Norwalk,	Aug.11,'62	Aug.28,'62	Cap'd July 1, '63, Gettysburg, Pa. Par. Aug. 25, '63. M. o. July 19, '65.
Downes, Chauncey B.	Bridgeport,	Mch.24,'63	Mch.24,'63	M. o. July 19, '65.
Duggan, John	Norwalk,	Aug.11,'62	Aug.28,'62	M. o. July 19, '65.
Fairweather, John	Norwalk,	Aug. 9,'62	Aug.28,'62	M. o. July 19, '65.
Farrell, Thomas	Norwalk,	Dec. 30,'63	Dec. 30,'63	M. o. July 19, '65.
Fields, David	Norwalk,	Aug.12,'62	Aug.28,'62	Wd. Aug. 16, '63, Morris Island, S. C. M. o. July 19, '65.
Fields, William	Norwalk,	Aug.12,'62	Aug.28,'62	M. o. July 19, '65.
Gilbert, William W.	Norwalk,	Aug.13,'62	Aug.28,'62	Cap'd, date and place not shown; date of parole not shown. M. o. July 19, '65.
Godfrey, Alfred	Norwalk,	Aug. 9,'62	Aug.28,'62	Trans. to U. S. Sig. Corp. Dec 5, '63. Pro. 1st Class Priv. Aug. 1, '64. Disc. June 24, '65
Godfrey, William O.	Norwalk,	Aug.18,'62	Aug.28,'62	M. o. July 19, '65.
Grace, William	Norwalk,	Aug.19,'62	Aug.28,'62	Trans. to Co. K, Sep. 23, '62.
Gray, Henry H.	Norwalk,	Aug.11,'62	Aug.28,'62	Disc. dis. Oct. 26, '64.
Green, Byron	Norwalk,	Dec. 19,'63	Dec. 19,'63	M. o. July 19, '65.
Hannagan, William	Norwalk,	Aug.15,'62	Aug.28,'62	Trans. to 102d Regt. N. Y. Vols. Apr. —, '63, a deserter therefrom.
Hayes, John L.	Norwalk,	Aug.13,'62	Aug.28,'62	Wd. July 2, '63, Gettysburg, Pa. Trans. to Co. C, 16th Regt. V. R. C. Jan. 23, '65. Disc. July 6, '65.
Hoyt, George	Norwalk,	Aug.22,'62	Aug.28,'62	Cap'd May 3, '63, Chancellorsville, Va. Par. May 14, '63. Des. May —, '63.
Hoyt, James C.	Wilton,	Aug.22,'62	Aug.28,'62	Trans. to 159th Co. 2d Batt. V. R. C. Sep. 14, '64 Des. June 5, '65.
Jackson, Henry J.	Newtown,	Dec. 31,'63	Dec. 31,'63	M. o. July 19, '65.
Keeler, Sylvester	Norwalk,	Aug.11,'62	Aug.28,'62	M. o. July 19, '65.
Kellogg, Jarvis	Norwalk,	Aug.12,'62	Aug.28,'62	Trans. to 22d Co. 2d Batt. V. R. C. Dec. 7, '63. Disc. Aug. 28, '65
Keyser, Milton S.	Wilton,	Jan. 19,'64	Jan. 19,'64	M. o. July 19, '65.
Knapp, Charles H.	Wilton,	Aug.13,'62	Aug.28,'62	Des. Dec. 12, '62.
Lake, George	Roxbury,	Dec. 30,'63	Dec. 30,'63	Cap'd Feb. 5, '65, Dunn's Lake, Fla. Par. Apr. 21, '65. Disc. July 10, '65.
Lake, Hiram	Monroe,	Dec. 23,'63	Dec. 23,'63	(See Priv. Co. A, 8th C. V.) M. o. July 19, '65.
Lounsberry, James H.	Norwalk,	Aug.13,'62	Aug.28,'62	Cap'd Feb. 5, '65, Dunn's Lake, Fla. Par. Apr. 21, '65. Disc. June 19, '65.
Lounsberry, Joshua	Norwalk,	Aug.22,'62	Aug.28,'62	Cap'd Feb. 5, '65, Dunn's Lake, Fla. Par. Apr. 21, '65. Died June 23, '65.
Lyon, James	Norwalk,	Aug.18,'62	Aug.28,'62	M. o. July 19, '65.
McCormick, William	Norwalk,	Aug. 8,'62	Aug.28,'62	M. o. July 19, '65.
McCauley, John	Norwalk,	Aug.12,'62	Aug.28,'62	Disc. Sep. 29, '62, by civil authorities (minor).
McLaughlin, Thomas	Norwalk,	Aug. 8,'62	Aug.28,'62	Wd. May 2, '63, Chancellorsville, Va. Died May 22, '63.
Metcalf, John W.	Norwalk,	Aug.12,'62	Aug.28,'62	Killed July 2, '63, Gettysburg, Pa.
Mills, Aaron	Westport,	Dec. 9,'63	Dec. 9,'63	M. o. July 19, '65.
Morgan, Charles F.	Wilton,	Aug. 9,'62	Aug.28,'62	Disc. dis. Oct. 5, '63.
Morgan, Wilber B.	Wilton,	Aug.12,'62	Aug.28,'62	Wd. July 1, '63, Gettysburg, Pa. Died July 9, '63.
Mulligan, Martin	Norwalk,	Aug. 8,'62	Aug.28,'62	M. o. July 19, '65.
Newell, Samuel	Norwalk,	Aug.12,'62	Aug.28,'62	M. o. July 19, '65.
Partric, George S.	Norwalk,	Aug.14,'62	Aug.28,'62	Cap'd May 2,'63, Chancellorsville, Va. Par. May 15,'63. M. o. July 19,'65.
Peck, Charles	Wilton,	Aug.12,'62	Aug.28,'62	M. o. July 19, '65.
Purdy, Patrick	Norwalk,	Aug. 9,'62	Aug.28,'62	Wd. July 2, '63, Gettysburg, Pa. M. o. July 19, '65.
Raymond, William H.	Norwalk,	Aug.13,'62	Aug.28,'62	Des. Mch. 19, '63.
Reid, William A.	Norwalk,	Aug.19,'62	Aug.28,'62	M. o. July 19, '65.
Reynolds, Warren A.	Norwalk,	Aug.11,'62	Aug.28,'62	M. o. July 19, '65.
Riggs, Charles M.	Wilton,	Aug.13,'62	Aug.28,'62	M. o. July 19, '65.
Riggs, Smith	Fairfield,	Dec. 11,'63	Dec. 11,'63	Disc. dis. June 12, '65.
Rogers, Reuben A.	Norwalk,	Aug.11,'62	Aug.28,'62	Disc. June 13, '65.
Ryan, John	Norwalk,	Aug. 8,'62	Aug.28,'62	M. o. July 19, '65.
Sherwood, Henry	Norwalk,	Aug.14,'62	Aug.28,'62	Disc. dis. Mch. 28, '63.
Smith, Charles L.	Norwalk,	Aug.15,'62	Aug.28,'62	Disc. Dec. 11, '62.
Smith, Isaac A.	Norwalk,	Aug.11,'62	Aug.28,'62	M. o. July 19, '65.
Smith, Lawrence W.	Norwalk,	Aug. 8,'62	Aug.28,'62	Disc. dis. Jan. 30, '63.
Smith, Sydney D.	Norwalk,	Aug.11,'62	Aug.28,'62	Cap'd May 2, '63, Chancellorsville, Va. Par. May 15, '63. M. o. July 19, '65.
Taylor, Abijah F.	Norwalk,	Aug.11,'62	Aug.28,'62	Des. Apr. 30, '63.
Treacy, John	Norwalk,	Aug.21,'62	Aug.28,'62	M. o. July 19, '65.
Walton, George	Wilton,	Aug.15,'62	Aug.28,'62	Disc. June 20, '65.
Webb, Henry I.	Norwalk,	Aug.11,'62	Aug.28,'62	Trans. to 22d Co. 2d Batt. V. R. C. Dec. 7, '63. Disc. June 5, '65.
Weed, Oscar	Norwalk,	Aug. 9,'62	Aug.28,'62	Cap'd Feb. 5, '65, Dunn's Lake, Fla. Par. Apr. 21, '65. Disc. July 10, '65.
Whitney, Charles	Wilton,	Aug.12,'62	Aug.28,'62	Disc. dis. Jan. 15, '63.
Whitney, James	Norwalk,	Aug.20,'62	Aug.28,'62	Trans. to 65th Co. 2d Batt. V. R. C. Oct. 9, '63; trans. to Co. G, 7th Regt. Disc. June 28, '65.
Whitney, Noble L.	Wilton,	Aug.12,'62	Aug.28,'62	Cap'd Feb. 5, '65, Dunn's Lake, Fla. Par. Apr. 21, '65. Disc. June 19, '65.

Company G.

Name and Rank.	Residence.	Date of Enlistment.	Date of Muster in this organization.	Remarks.
Captains.				
James E. Dunham,	Bridgeport,	Aug. 1,'62	Aug.28,'62	Resgd. May 8, '63.
Wilson French,	Stratford,	Aug. 1,'62	Aug.28,'62	Must. 1st Lt. Aug. 28, '62. Pro. May 8, '63. Wd. July 1, '63, Gettysburg, Pa. Cap'd Feb. 5, '65, Dunn's Lake, Fla. Par. Apr. 21, '65. Disc. May 26, '65.
1st Lieutenants.				
Edward Denis,	Bridgeport,	Aug.19,'62	Aug.28,'62	Must. Sergt. Pro. 1st Sergt. Aug. 28, '62; 2d Lt. Nov. 18, '62; 1st Lt. May 8, '63. Resgd. June 27, '64.
Charles Smith, Jr.,	Ridgefield,	Aug.11,'62	Aug.28,'62	Must. Corp. Pro. Sergt. June 4, '63; 1st Sergt. July 1, '63; 1st Lt. Oct. 29, '64. M. o. July 19, '65.
2d Lieutenants.				
Niram Dykeman,	Ridgefield,	Aug. 1,'62	Aug.28,'62	Resgd. Nov. 17, '62.
David S. Bartram,	Redding,	Aug.16,'62	Aug.28,'62	Must. Sergt. Pro. 1st Sergt. Nov. 17, '62; 2d Lt. June 4, '63. Cap'd July 1, '63, Gettysburg, Pa. Par. Aug. 25, '63. Disc. May 15, '65.
1st Sergeants.				
George W. Banks,	Redding,	Aug.20,'62	Aug.28,'62	Redc. to ranks (sick) Aug. 28, '62. Company Rolls for September and October, '62, report him sick at home. N. f. r. A. G. O.
Edwin D. Pickett,	Ridgefield,	Aug. 9,'62	Aug.28,'62	Must. Corp. Pro. Sergt. Nov. 17, '62; 1st Sergt. June 4, '63. Killed July 1, '63, Gettysburg, Pa.
George F. Godfrey,	Ridgefield,	Aug.13,'62	Aug.28,'62	Must. Priv. Pro. Sergt. Sep. 1, '63; 1st Sergt. Nov. 1, '64. M. o. July 19, '65.
Sergeants.				
Brinkerhoff, Benj. F.	Ridgefield,	Aug.13,'62	Aug.28,'62	Must. Priv. Pro. Corp. Mch. 21, '64; Sergt. Sep. 1, '64. M. o. July 19, '65.
Jennings, Charles A.	Ridgefield,	Aug.13,'62	Aug.28,'62	Must. Corp. Pro. Aug. 28, '62. Wd. and cap'd May 2, '63, Chancellorsville, Va. Par. May 15, '63. Trans. as Sergt. to Co. E, 22d Regt. V. R. C. Nov. 18, '63. Disc. July 1, '65.
Lee, Aaron W.	Ridgefield,	Aug.11,'62	Aug.28,'62	Must. Corp. Wd. July 1, '63, Gettysburg, Pa. Pro. Sergt. Sep. 1, '64. M. o. July 19, '65.
Main, James C.	Ridgefield,	Aug.11,'62	Aug.28,'62	Must. Priv. Pro. Corp. Aug. 28, '62; Sergt. Jan. 10, '64; 2d Lt. June 29, '65 (not must.). M. o. July 19, '65.
Parker, Charles W.	Bridgeport,	Aug.11,'62	Aug.28,'62	Redc. to ranks for absence Sep. 1, '64. M. O. Roll reports him absent, sick in hosp. since Apr. 27, '63. N. f. r. A. G. O.
Rich, Alfred	Wallingford,	Feb. 13,'65	Feb. 13,'65	Must. Priv. Pro. Sergt. Mch. 13, '65. M. o. July 19, '65.
White, Edwin P.	Ridgefield,	Aug.11,'62	Aug.28,'62	Redc. to ranks Jan. 10, '64. Trans. to 159th Co. 2d Batt. V. R. C. Feb. 17, '64, as Sergt. Disc. Aug. 10, '65.
Corporals.				
Austin, David	Ridgefield,	Aug.11,'62	Aug.28,'62	Must. Priv. Pro. Nov. 1, '64. Cap'd Feb. 5, '65, Dunn's Lake, Fla. Par. Apr. 21, '65. Disc. July 10, '65.
Austin, Jacob	Ridgefield,	Aug.11,'62	Aug.28,'62	Must. Priv. Wd. and cap'd July 1, '63, Gettysburg, Pa. Par. July 2, '63. Pro. Nov. 1, '64. M. o. July 19, '65.
*Combs, William C.	Meriden,	Aug.24,'64	Aug.24,'64	Must. Priv. Pro. Nov. 1, '64. M. o. July 19, '65.
Couch, Andrew D.	Redding,	Aug.12,'62	Aug.28,'62	Must. Priv. Pro. Aug. 28, '62. Killed May 2, '63, Chancellorsville, Va.
Dove, Daniel G.	Ridgefield,	Aug.13,'62	Aug.28,'62	Must. Priv. Cap'd May 2, '63, Chancellorsville, Va. Par. May 15, '63. Pro. Sep. 1, '64. M. o. July 19, '65.
Finch, Nelson A.	Ridgefield,	Aug.14,'62	Aug.28,'62	Must. Priv. Pro. Mch. 21, '64. M. o. July 19, '65.
Grey, George	Ridgefield,	Aug.15,'62	Aug.28,'62	Redc. to ranks. Disc. dis. Mch. 28, '63.
Judd, Horace Q.	Ridgefield,	Aug.13,'62	Aug.28,'62	Cap'd July 1, '63, Gettysburg, Pa. Escaped July 10, '63. Trans. to 159th Co. 2d Batt. V. R. C. July 4, '64. Disc. Aug. 12, '65.
Lockwood, John	Redding,	Aug.12,'62	Aug.28,'62	Must. Priv. Pro. Sep. 1, '64. M. o. July 19, '65.
Mead, Jeremiah O.	Ridgefield,	Aug.13,'62	Aug.28,'62	M. o. July 19, '65.
Smith, Allen	Ridgefield,	Aug.13,'62	Aug.28,'62	Must. Priv. Pro. Sep. 1, '64. M. o. July 19, '65.
Warner, Henry A.	Bridgeport,	Aug.12,'62	Aug.28,'62	Cap'd July 1, '63, Gettysburg, Pa. Par. July 1, '63. Redc. to ranks Apr. 12, '64. M. o. July 19, '65.
Musicians.				
Jennings, Morris	Redding,	Aug.28,'62	Aug.28,'62	Disc. dis. Mch. 26, '63.
Smith, Sherman H.	Ridgefield,	Aug.11,'62	Aug.28,'62	Cap'd Feb. 4, '65, St. Augustine, Fla. Par. Apr. 20, '65. Disc. July 10, 65.
Whalen, George	Redding,	Dec. 31,'63	Dec. 31,'63	Must. Priv. Detailed Musc. M. o. July 19, '65.
Wagoner.				
Hurd, George W.	Bridgeport,	Aug.14,'62	Aug.28,'62	M. o. July 19, '65.
Privates.				
Aiken, Edgar	Norwalk,	Aug.31,'64	Aug.31,'64	M. o. July 19, '65.
Albin, Sylvester	New Canaan,	Sep. 1,'64	Sep. 1,'64	Cap'd Feb. 5, '65, Dunn's Lake, Fla. Par. Apr. 21, '65. Disc. June 23, '65.
Austin, Hiram	Ridgefield,	Aug.11,'62	Aug.28,'62	Disc. dis. Aug. 19, '63.
Avant, William	Ridgefield,	Aug.15,'62	Aug.28,'62	Died Mch. 30, '63.
Avery, Charles W.	Ridgefield,	Aug.11,'62	Aug.28,'62	Disc. dis. Jan. 19, '63.
Baker, Samuel B.	Westport,	Aug.18,'64	Aug.18,'64	Cap'd Feb. 5, '65, Dunn's Lake, Fla. Par. Apr. 21, '65. Disc. July 7, '65.
Barsley, Elbert J.	Bethel,	Sep. 2,'64	Sep. 2,'64	(See Priv. Co. K, 23d C. V.) M. o. July 19, '65.
Beers, James M.	Redding,	Aug. 7,'62	Aug.28,'62	Disc. dis. Mch. 9, '63.
Bennett, Abner F.	Fairfield,	Aug.19,'62	Aug.28,'62	Wd. July 1, '63, Gettysburg, Pa. Trans. to 122d Co. 2d Batt. V. R. C. Dec. 22, '63; trans. to Co. I, 24th Regt. Apr. 27, '64. Re-en. Vet. Sep. 2, '64. Disc. dis. Sep. 28, '65.
Bennett, Jerome	Bridgeport,	Aug.20,'62	Aug.28,'62	Cap'd July 1, '63, Gettysburg, Pa. Par. Aug. 29, '63. M. o. July 19, '65.
Benedict, Rufus S.	New Canaan,	Sep. 1,'64	Sep. 1,'64	M. o. July 19, '65.
Blake, George	Bridgeport,	Aug.14,'62	Aug.28,'62	Disc. June 14, '65.
Black, John A.	Bridgeport,	Aug.13,'62	Aug.28,'62	Killed July 1, '63, Gettysburg, Pa.
Braunschweiger, Fred.	Darien,	Jan. 5,'64	Jan. 5,'64	M. o. July 19, '65.
Brotherton, Ira M.	Norwalk,	Aug.31,'64	Aug.31,'64	Trans. to Co. F, Nov. 21, '64.
Brown, Franklin	Ridgefield,	Aug.13,'62	Aug.28,'62	Des. Feb. 24, '63.
Brown, Jefferson	Ridgefield,	Aug.12,'62	Aug.28,'62	Des. Oct. 14, '62.

* Substitutes and drafted.

Name and Rank.	Residence.	Date of Enlistment.	Date of Muster in this organ-ization.	Remarks.
Brown, Nehemiah	Ridgefield,	Aug.12,'62	Aug.28,'62	Disc. dis. Dec. 18, '62. (See Priv. Co. E, 1st C. V. H. A.)
Burr, Daniel D.	Ridgefield,	Aug.13,'62	Aug.28,'62	M. o. July 19, '65.
Carney, Lawrence	Ridgefield,	Aug.14,'62	Aug.28,'62	Killed July 1, '63, Gettysburg, Pa.
Chatfield, H. Whitney	Bridgeport,	Aug.20,'62	Aug.28,'62	Ap. Sergt.-Maj. Apr. 18, '63.
Collins, Stephen	Danbury,	Sep. 12,'64	Sep. 12,'64	M. o. July 19, '65. [14, '65.
Costello, Martin	Redding,	Aug. 4,'62	Aug.28,'62	Cap'd Feb. 5, '65, Dunn's Lake, Fla. Par. Apr. 21, '65. Disc. June
Crabbe, Cassius M.	Bridgeport,	Aug. 4,'62	Aug.28,'62	Killed July 1, '63, Gettysburg, Pa.
Creedon, William	Ridgefield,	Aug.13,'62	Aug.28,'62	Wd. May 2, '63, Chancellorsville, Va. M. o. July 19, '65.
Davis, Albert G.	Darien,	Sep. 6,'64	Sep. 6,'64	(See Priv. Co. C, 28th C. V.) M. o. July 19, '65.
DeForrest, Henry W.	Bridgeport,	Sep. 1,'62	Dec. 29,'62	Wd. July 1, '63, Gettysburg, Pa. Trans. to Co. C, 24th Regt. V. R. C.
DeForrest, John W.	Redding,	Aug.15,'62	Aug.28,'62	Disc. dis. Apr. 4, '63. [Jan. 21, '64. Disc. Aug. 11, '65.
Dickens, Charles H.	Ridgefield,	Aug.11,'62	Aug.28,'62	Disc. dis. Jan. 14, '63.
Dunning, Elijah C.	Bridgeport,	Aug.11,'62	Aug.28,'62	(See Corp. Co. D, 3d C. V.) Disc. dis. Mch. 25, '63.
Edmond, Elias H.	Ridgefield,	Aug.11,'62	Aug.28,'62	Disc. dis. Feb. 27, '63.
Egan, James	Newtown,	Sep. 2,'64	Sep. 2,'64	M. o. July 19, '65.
Elwood, Samuel P.	Norwalk,	Sep. 1,'64	Sep. 1,'64	M. o. July 19, '65.
Ferry, George S.	Bethel,	Aug. 6,'64	Aug. 6,'64	Cap'd Feb. 5, '65, Dunn's Lake, Fla. Par. Apr. 21, '65. Disc. June 14, '65.
Finch, Smith H.	Darien,	Sep. 6,'64	Sep. 6,'64	M. o. July 19, '65.
Fry, John G.	Ridgefield,	Aug.13,'62	Aug.28,'62	Died Jan. 18, '63.
Fulford, John	Trumbull,	Aug.20,'62	Aug.28,'62	Disc. dis. Dec. 15, '62.
Gaffney, James	Norwalk,	Aug.19,'64	Aug.19,'64	(See Priv. Co. G, 28th C. V.) M. o. July 19, '65.
Gilbert, Frederick A.	Branford,	Sep. 5,'64	Sep. 5,'64	M. o. July 19, '65.
Gilbert, Smith	Ridgefield,	Aug.15,'62	Aug.28,'62	Disc. dis. Feb. 4, '63.
Godfrey, Edmond	Redding,	Aug. 8,'62	Aug.28,'62	Disc. dis. Mch. 9, '63.
Gorham, Hiram W.	Norwalk,	Sep. 1,'62	Dec. 27,'62	M. o. July 19, '65.
Gregory, David	Ridgefield,	Aug.13,'62	Aug.28,'62	Disc. dis. Dec. 10, '62.
Harrington, John H.	Ridgefield,	Aug.11,'62	Aug.28,'62	Wd. July 1, '63, Gettysburg, Pa. M. o. July 19, '65.
Hauks, William H.	Bridgeport,	Sep. 1,'62	Dec. 27,'62	Died Apr. 26, '63.
Holley, Gould L.	Norwalk,	Aug.27,'64	Aug.27,'64	M. o. July 19, '65.
Hoyt, John W.	Ridgefield,	Aug.12,'62	Aug.28,'62	Died June 28, '63.
Hull, George	Redding,	Aug. 6,'62	Aug.28,'62	M. o. July 19, '65.
Hull, Silas	Ridgefield,	Aug.13,'62	Aug.28,'62	Disc. dis. Mch. 25, '63.
Jarvis, John J.	Ridgefield,	Aug.11,'62	Aug.28,'62	Cap'd July 2, '63, Gettysburg, Pa. Par. Aug. 2, '63. Cap'd Feb. 5, '65, Dunn's Lake, Fla. Par. Apr. 28, '65. Disc. June 14, '65.
Jennings, William H.	Ridgefield,	Aug.13,'62	Aug.28,'62	Disc. dis. Mch. 9, '63.
Keeler, Eli J.	Ridgefield,	Aug.11,'62	Aug.28, 62	M. o. July 19, '65.
Kinney, Richard	Danbury,	Sep. 3,'64	Sep. 3,'64	M. o. July 19, '65. [Mch. 7, '65. Disc. July 6, '65.
Lindhein, Frederick	Bridgeport,	Aug.16,'62	Aug.28,'62	Wd. July 1, '63, Gettysburg, Pa. Trans. to Co. H, 21st Regt. V. R. C.
Lockwood, Andrew	Ridgefield,	Aug.13,'62	Aug.28,'62	Cap'd May 2, '63, Chancellorsville, Va. Par. May 14, '63. M. o. July
Lockwood, Burr	Redding,	Aug.12,'62	Aug.28,'62	M. o. July 19, '65. [19, '65.
Mallett, Abel W.	Bridgeport,	Aug.12,'62	Aug.28,'62	M. o. July 19, '65.
Mead, Rufus N.	Ridgefield,	Aug.11,'62	Aug.28,'62	Disc. dis. Nov. 29, '62.
Mead, Samuel O.	Danbury,	Sep. 3,'64	Sep. 3,'64	M. o. July 19, '65.
McConnell, John	Ridgefield,	Aug.11,'62	Aug.28,'62	Cap'd July 1, '63, Gettysburg, Pa. Par. Aug. 29, '63. M. o. July 19, '65.
Merritt, William M.	Ridgefield,	Sep. 1,'62	Dec. 27,'62	Wd. May 2, '63, Chancellorsville, Va. Cap'd Feb. 5, '65, Dunn's Lake, Fla. Par. Apr. 28, '65. Disc. June 14, '65.
Monroe, Alsop L.	Ridgefield,	Aug.11,'62	Aug.28,'62	(See Priv. Co. C, 3d C. V.) Disc. dis. Dec. 29, '62.
*Monroe, William	Ridgefield,	Aug.19,'64	Aug.19,'64	M. o. July 19, '65.
Morris, John	Weston,	Sep. 7,'64	Sep. 7,'64	M. o. July 19, '65.
Morgan, Russell P.	Bridgeport,	Aug.20,'62	Aug.28,'62	Disc. dis. Mch. 9, '63. [Mch. 15, '64. Disc. July 12, '65.
Morgan, William W.	Bridgeport,	Aug.14,'62	Aug.28,'62	Wd. May 2, '63, Chancellorsville, Va. Trans. to Co. K, 6th Regt. V. R. C.
Murphy, Robert	Bridgeport,	Aug.18,'62	Aug.28,'62	Des. Oct. 9, '62.
Murphy, Walter S.	Bridgeport,	Aug.13,'62	Aug.28,'62	Disc. dis. Dec. 10, '62.
Nickerson, Benj. V.	Ridgefield,	Aug.13,'62	Aug.28,'62	Disc. dis. Apr. 16, '63.
Northrop, David 2d	Ridgefield,	Aug.13,'62	Aug.28,'62	Cap'd July 1, '63, Gettysburg, Pa. Par. Aug. 25, '63. M. o. July 19, '65.
Northrop, Warner H.	Bethel,	Sep. 2,'64	Sep. 2,'64	Cap'd Feb. 5, '65, Dunn's Lake, Fla. Par. Apr. 28, '65. Disc. July 10, '65.
Oakley, Miles	Ridgefield,	Jan. 5,'64	Jan. 5,'64	M. o. July 19, '65.
Oboy, Bryan	Danbury,	Aug.20,'62	Aug.28,'62	Trans. to Co. C, 14th Regt. V. R. C. Feb. 2, '65. Disc. June 28, '65.
Peck, Aaron	Redding,	Aug.13,'62	Aug.28,'62	Wd. July 1, '63, Gettysburg, Pa. M. o. July 19, '65.
Perry, William H.	Bethel,	Sep. 1,'64	Sep. 1,'64	(See Priv. Co. E, 23d C. V.) M. o. July 19, '65.
Pettit, Henry	Bridgeport,	Aug.16,'62	Aug.28,'62	Disc. dis. Nov. 13, '62.
Rasco, Charles B.	Ridgefield,	Aug.11,'62	Aug.28,'62	Disc. dis. Dec. 10, '62. [Par. Nov. 18, '64. Disc. June 10, '65.
Rhan, Charles A.	Ridgefield,	Aug.12,'62	Aug.28,'62	Wd. Aug. —, '63, Morris Island, S. C. Cap'd May 19, '64, Welaka, Fla.
Rich, Jerod	Ridgefield,	Sep. 2,'62	Sep. 2,'62	Disc. Dec. 4, '62.
Roberts, Robert	Norwalk,	Aug.15,'64	Aug.15,'64	M. o. July 19, '65.
Seymour, Francis E.	Ridgefield,	Aug.15,'62	Aug.28,'62	Died Apr. 26, '63.
Sherman, John M.	Redding,	July 31,'62	Aug.28,'62	Disc. dis. Dec. 10, '62.
Sherwood, Joseph B.	Bethel,	Sep. 6,'64	Sep. 6,'64	M. o. July 19, '65.
Smith, Charles H. 2d	Bridgeport,	Sep. 1,'62	Dec. 27,'62	M. o. July 19, '65.
Smith, William H.	Ridgefield,	Aug.15,'62	Aug.28,'62	Disc. dis. Feb. 25, '64.
Squires, Edgar	Bridgeport,	July 22,'62	Aug.28,'62	(See Priv. Co. H, 1st C. V.) Disc. dis. Dec. 10, '62.
Stevens, George W.	Ridgefield,	Aug.14,'62	Aug.28,'62	M. o. July 19, '65.
Tucker, Jesse W.	New Canaan,	Sep. 1,'64	Sep. 1,'64	M. o. July 19, '65.
Vanderhoff, Jacob C.	Greenwich,	Sep. 6,'64	Sep. 6,'64	(See Corp. Rifle Co. F, 3d C. V.) M. o. July 19, '65.
*Waters, Frank	New Milford,	Aug.19,'64	Aug.19,'64	M. o. July 19, '65.
*Welch, Thomas	Goshen,	Aug.19,'64	Aug.19,'64	M. o. July 19, '65.
Wheelock, Henry	Bethel,	Sep. 2,'64	Sep. 2,'64	(See Wagoner Co. G, 23d C. V.) M. o. July 19, '65. [July 19, '65.
Williams, Sylvester	Ridgefield,	Aug.12,'62	Aug.28,'62	Wd. and cap'd May 2, '63, Chancellorsville, Va. Par. May 15, '63. M. o.
Wood, George L.	Ridgefield,	Aug.13,'62	Aug.28,'62	Disc. dis. Feb. 13, '64. [19, '65.
Wurz, Charles	Bridgeport,	Aug.16,'62	Aug.28,'62	Cap'd May 2, '63, Chancellorsville, Va. Par. May 15, '63. M. o. July

* Substitutes and drafted.

42

Company H.

NAME AND RANK.	Residence.	Date of Enlistment.	Date of Muster in this organization.	Remarks.
Captain.				
Enos Kellogg,	New Canaan,	July 11,'62	Aug.28,'62	(See Priv. Rifle Co. F, 3d C. V.) M. o. July 19, '65.
1st Lieutenants.				
J. Irving Benedict,	New Canaan,	July 11,'62	Aug.28,'62	Resgd. Dec. 23, '62.
James H. Ayres,	New Canaan,	July 21,'62	Aug.28,'62	Must. 2d Lt. Pro. Dec. 23, '62; Capt. Co. A, Mch. 5, '64.
Thomas P. Cave,	Darien,	Aug.11,'62	Aug.28,'62	(See Priv. Rifle Co. F, 3d C. V.) Must. Sergt. Pro. 1st Sergt. Mch. 1, '63; 1st Lt. Sep. 22, '64. M. o. July 19, '65.
2d Lieutenant.				
Francis M. Bliss,	New Canaan,	Aug.11,'62	Aug.28,'62	Must. 1st Sergt. Pro. Dec. 23, '62. Resgd. Oct 27, '63.
1st Sergeant.				
Horace Whitney,	Darien,	Aug.12,'62	Aug.28,'62	(See Priv. Rifle Co. F, 3d C. V.) Must. Corp. Pro. Sergt. May 15, '63. Cap'd July 2, '63, Gettysburg, Pa. Par. Aug. 25, '63. Pro. 1st Sergt. Aug. 28, '64; 2d Lt. July 15, '64 (not must.). M. o. July 19, '65.
Sergeants.				
Bossa, Norbert	New Canaan,	Aug. 6,'62	Aug.28,'62	Must. Corp. Cap'd July 1, '63, Gettysburg, Pa. Par. Aug. 25, '63. Pro. Sergt. Sep. 27, '63. M. o. July 19, '65.
Brown, Isaac B.	New Canaan,	July 25,'62	Aug.28,'62	Must. Corp. Pro. Feb. 1, '64. M. o. July 19, '65.
Comstock, Samuel 2d	New Canaan,	July 23,'62	Aug.28,'62	Wd. July 1, '63, Gettysburg, Pa. Died Sep. 27, '63.
Criesey, Isaac N.	New Canaan,	Aug.11,'62	Aug.28,'62	Wd. May 2, '63, Chancellorsville, Va. Trans. to 21st Co. 2d Batt. V. R. C. Aug. 10, '63. Des. Oct. 15, '63. [19, '65.
DeForrest, Samuel E.	New Canaan,	Aug.14,'62	Aug.28,'62	Must. Priv. Pro. Corp. Aug. 28, '62; Sergt. Mch. 1, '63. M. o. July
North, Joseph W.	Bridgeport,	Feb. 10,'65	Feb. 10,'65	(See Band 5th C. V.) Must. Priv. Pro. Sergt. Mch. 13, '65. M. o. July 19, '65.
Palmer, Warren S.	New Canaan,	Aug. 6,'62	Aug.28,'62	Disc. dis. Apr. 23, '63. (See Sergt. Co. E, 1st C. V. H. A.)
Corporals.				
Bauzhof, John G.	New Canaan,	Aug.12,'62	Aug.28,'62	Must. Priv. Pro. July 1, '65. M. o. July 19, '65.
Bennett, Peter	New Canaan,	Aug.11,'62	Aug.28,'62	(See Priv. Rifle Co. F, 3d C. V.) Disc. dis. Feb. 23, '63.
Benedict, Andrew B.	New Canaan,	Aug.22,'62	Aug 28,'62	Must. Priv. Pro. Jan. 10, '63. Trans. to Co. F, 3d Regt. V. R. C July 17, '63. Pro. Sergt. Sep. 10, '64. Disc. July 6, '65.
Comstock, Stephen	New Canaan,	Aug.11,'62	Aug.28,'62	Must. Priv. Pro. Mch. 1, '63. Trans. to Co. F, 3d Regt. V. R. C. July 20, '63. Disc. July 6, '65.
Crabb, Andrus	New Canaan,	Aug. 8,'62	Aug.28,'62	Must. Priv. Pro. July 1, '65. M. o. July 19, '65.
Mather, Wm. H. Jr.	Norwalk,	Aug.23,'62	Aug.28,'62	Must. Priv. Cap'd May 2, '63, Chancellorsville, Va. Par. May 15, '63. Pro. Mch. 1, '65. M. o. July 19, '65.
Raymond, Arza	New Canaan,	Aug. 7,'62	Aug.28,'62	Must. Priv. Pro. Feb. 1, '64. M. o. July 19, '65.
Richards, Edward	New Canaan,	Aug.14,'62	Aug.28,'62	Must. Priv. Pro. Mch. 1, '63. Died May 7, '63.
Remington, Seth	New Canaan,	Aug.11,'62	Aug.28,'62	Must. Priv. Wd. and cap'd July 1, '63, Gettysburg, Pa. Par. Aug. 25, '63. Pro. Sep. 27, '63. Wd. and cap'd Feb. 5, '65, Dunn's Lake, Fla. Released Apr. 21, '65. Disc. June 8, '65.
Rusco, Floyd T.	New Canaan,	July 24,'62	Aug.28,'62	Must. Priv. Cap'd May 2, '63, Chancellorsville, Va. Par. May 15, '63. Pro. Feb. 1, '65. M. o. July 19, '65.
Rusco, DeWitt C.	New Canaan,	Aug.11,'62	Aug.28,'62	Must. Priv. Wd. May 2, '63, Chancellorsville, Va. Cap'd July 1, '63, Gettysburg, Pa. Par. Aug. 25, '63. Pro. July 1, '65. M. o. July
Seeley, Joseph F.	New Canaan,	July 11,'62	Aug.28,'62	Disc. dis. Feb. 7, '63. [19, '65.
Stevens, George J.	New Canaan,	July 31,'62	Aug.28,'62	(See Priv. Rifle Co. F, 3d C. V.) Redc. to ranks at own request. M. o. July 19, '65.
Weed, Levi St. John	New Canaan,	Aug.18,'62	Aug.28,'62	Redc. to ranks at own request Aug. 28, '62. Cap'd July 2, '63, Gettysburg, Pa. Par. Aug. 25, '63. Pro. July 1, '64. M. o. July 19, '65.
Weed, Charles A.	New Canaan,	July 25,'62	Aug.28,'62	Redc. to ranks (sick) Feb. 5, '65. Died Feb. 12, '65.
Weed, George W.	New Canaan,	Aug.22,'62	Aug.28,'62	Must. Priv. Pro. May 15, '63. Cap'd July 2, '63, Gettysburg, Pa. Par. Aug. 25, '63. M. o. July 19, '65.
Musicians.				
Innis, Patrick	New Canaan,	Jan. 7,'64	Jan. 7,'64	Must. Priv. Detailed Musc. M. o. July 19, '65. [Disc. Aug. 28, '65.
Jones, Miles O.	New Canaan,	July 28,'62	Aug.28,'62	Trans. to ranks; trans. to 48th Co. 2d Batt. V. R. C. Dec. 1, '63
Scofield, Franklin H.	Darien,	Aug. 7,'62	Aug.28,'62	Trans. to ranks; trans. to Co. E, 22d Regt. V. R. C. Nov. 8, '63. Detailed Musc. Trans. to ranks. Died Aug. 14, '64.
Wagoner.				
Hodges, James L.	New Canaan,	Aug.12,'62	Aug.28,'62	M. O. Roll reports him absent, sick Dec. 14, '62; supposed deserted. N. f. r. A. G. O.
Privates.				
Acker, John	New Canaan,	Aug. 9,'62	Aug.28,'62	Cap'd July 1, '63, Gettysburg, Pa. Par. Aug. 25, '63. M. o. July 19, '65.
Albin, Henry	Wilton,	Aug.13,'62	Aug.28,'62	Cap'd Feb. 5, '65, Dunn's Lake, Fla. Par. Apr. 21, '65. Disc. June 8, '65.
Avery, David M.	New Canaan,	Aug.20,'62	Aug.28,'62	Wd. May 2, '63, Chancellorsville, Va. M. o. July 19, '65.
Ball, William C.	New Canaan,	July 23,'62	Aug.28,'62	Cap'd July 1, '63, Gettysburg, Pa. Par. Aug. 25, '63. M. o. July 19, '65.
Barr, Ira T.	Wilton,	Aug.13,'62	Aug.28,'62	Disc. dis. Mch. 24, '63. (See Priv. Co. G, 1st C. V. H. A.)
Barton, Charles L.	New Canaan,	Dec. 29,'63	Dec. 29,'63	Cap'd Feb. 5, '65, Dunn's Lake, Fla. Par. Apr. 21, 65. Disc. June 8, '65.
Benedict, Enoch B.	Sharon,	Mch. 1,'64	Mch. 1,'64	Cap'd Feb. 5, '65, Dunn's Lake, Fla. Par. Apr. 21, '65. Disc. June 3, '65.
Benedict, Lewis B.	New Canaan,	Aug.12,'62	Aug.28,'62	Disc. dis. Oct. 12, '63.
Birdsall, John	New Canaan,	Feb. 9,'64	Feb. 9,'64	Died Jan. 2, '65.
Bishop, Robert	New Canaan,	Aug.21,'62	Aug.28,'62	Disc. dis. Nov. 20, '63.
Britto, Frank	New Canaan,	Aug.14,'62	Aug.28,'62	Disc. dis. Nov. 26, '62.
Britto, Loren W.	New Canaan,	Aug. 9,'62	Aug.28,'62	M. o. July 19, '65.

NAME AND RANK.	Residence.	Date of Enlistment.	Date of Muster in this organization.	Remarks.
Brown, William L.	New Canaan,	Aug. 9,'62	Aug.28,'62	Disc. dis. Oct. 12, '63.
Brodhurst, Alfred Z.	Stamford,	July 29,'62	Aug.28,'62	Wd. and cap'd May 2, '63, Chancellorsville, Va. Par. May 15, '63. Cap'd Feb. 5, '65, Dunn's Lake, Fla. Par. Apr. 21, '65. Disc. June 23, '65.
Bryan, Nathaniel	Brooklyn,N.Y.	Sep. 22,'64	Nov.20,'64	En. for the 40th Regt. N. Y. Vols., assigned to Co. H, 17th C. V. by error. Trans. to 40th Regt. N. Y. Vols. June 30, '65.
Burtis, Warren J.	Bridgeport,	Aug.30,'62	Dec. 29,'62	Wd. July 1, '63, Gettysburg, Pa. Cap'd Feb. 5, '65, Dunn's Lake,
Byington, Aaron	Wilton,	July 23,'62	Aug.28,'62	Disc. dis. Jan. 9, '63. [Fla. Released Apr. 21, '65. Disc. June 8, '65.
Byington, John L.	New Canaan,	Aug.19,'62	Aug.28,'62	Cap'd May 3, '63, Chancellorsville, Va. Par. May 15, '63. Trans. to Co. D, 6th Regt. V. R. C. Oct. 21, '63. Disc. July 5, '65.
Comstock, Anthony	Norwalk,	Dec. 30,'63	Dec. 30,'63	M. o. July 19, '65.
Comstock, David C.Jr.	New Canaan,	Aug.12,'62	Aug.28,'62	Ap. Hosp. Stewd. U. S. A. Jan. 27, '64. Disc. dis. Jan. 31, '67.
Crabb, Lynus W.	New Canaan,	Aug.11,'62	Aug.28,'62	M. o. July 19, '65.
Crofoot, Charles	New Canaan,	Jan. 4,'64	Jan. 4,'64	M. o. July 19, '65.
DeForrest, Wm. H.	New Canaan,	Aug.14,'62	Aug.28,'62	Disc. dis. Jan. 12, '63.
DeFisheur, Maximil'n	New Canaan,	Aug.20,'62	Aug.28,'62	Disc. dis. Feb. 27, '63.
Dixon, Levi	New Canaan,	Aug.20,'62	Aug.28,'62	Wd. July 1, '63, Gettysburg, Pa. Disc. dis. Oct. 8, '64.
Driscoll, Thomas	New Canaan,	Aug.12,'62	Aug.28,'62	Disc. dis. Jan. 19, '63. [Disc. dis. Oct. 21, '65.
Faber, Christian	New Canaan,	Aug.12,'62	Aug.28,'62	Wd. and cap'd May 2, '63, Chancellorsville, Va. Released May 15, '63.
Fitch, William S.	New Canaan,	Jan. 20,'64	Jan. 20,'64	M. o. July 19, '65.
Foote, Gaius St. John	Ridgefield,	Aug.16,'62	Aug.28,'62	Died Nov. 17, '63.
Fox, Samuel W.	New Canaan,	Aug.11,'62	Aug.28,'62	M. o. July 19, '65.
Ganning, Augustus	New Canaan,	Aug. 9,'62	Aug.28,'62	Disc. dis. Mch. 27, '63.
Gray, Samuel	New Canaan,	Aug.14,'62	Aug.28,'62	M. o. July 19, '65.
Greenwold, John	New Canaan,	Aug.12,'62	Aug.28,'62	M. o. July 19, '65.
Haas, John T.	New Canaan,	Aug.12,'62	Aug.28,'62	Trans. to Co. B, 24th Regt. V. R. C. Dec. 4, '63. Disc. June 27, '65.
Hall, Charles W.	Warren,	Aug.18,'62	Aug.28,'62	Disc. dis. Jan. 29, '63.
Harrison, Orrin	New Canaan,	July 28,'62	Aug.28,'62	M. o. July 19, '65.
Hartung, William	New Canaan,	Aug.20,'62	Aug.28,'62	Died Mch. 29, '63.
*Jones, David R.	Wilton,	Sep. 20,'64	Sep. 20,'64	Cap'd Feb. 5, '65, Dunn's Lake, Fla. Par. Apr. 21, '65. Disc. June 10,'65.
Jones, Henry	North Canaan,	Aug.25,'62	Aug.28,'62	Des. Sep. 1, '62.
Kaiser, John	New Canaan,	Aug.20,'62	Aug.28,'62	M. o. July 19, '65.
Mallett, Charles S.	Easton,	Sep. 1,'62	Dec. 29,'62	Wd. and cap'd July 1, '63, Gettysburg, Pa. Par. Aug. 2, '63. Trans. to Co. F, 1st Regt. V. R. C. Oct. 28, '63. Re-trans. Oct. 25, '64. Cap'd Feb. 5, '65, Dunn's Lake, Fla. Released Apr. 21, '65. Disc.
Marlton, Charles E.	Monroe,	Aug.15,'62	Aug.28,'62	M. o. July 19, '65. [June 8, '65.
McNally, Francis	Norwalk,	Aug.25,'62	Aug.28,'62	Wd. and cap'd July 1, '63, Gettysburg, Pa. Par. Aug. 25, '63. M. o.
Mead, Eliphalet	New Canaan,	July 28,'62	Aug.28,'62	Killed July 1, '63, Gettysburg, Pa. [July 19, '65.
Monroe, Alanson T.	New Canaan,	July 28,'62	Aug.28,'62	Disc. dis. Dec. 28, '62.
Ogden, Orson C.	New Canaan,	Aug. 6,'62	Aug.28,'62	Disc. dis. Jan. 9, '63.
Olmsted, Chris. S.	New Canaan,	Aug.11,'62	Aug.28,'62	Died Nov. 10, '62.
Osborn, Samuel S.	New Canaan,	Aug.11,'62	Aug.28,'62	Disc. dis. Apr. 30, '63. (See Priv. Co. M. 2d C. V. H. A.) [July 19, '65.
Pattenden, Ebenezer J.	New Canaan,	July 18,'62	Aug.28,'62	Wd. and cap'd July 1, '63, Gettysburg, Pa. Par. Sep. 29, '63. M. o.
Patterson, George	New Canaan,	Aug.11,'62	Aug.28,'62	Wd. May 2, '63, Chancellorsville, Va. Died May 14, '63.
Peatt, Henry	New Canaan,	Aug.11,'62	Aug.28,'62	Disc. dis. Jan. 23, '63.
Potts, George H.	New Canaan,	Aug.20,'62	Aug.28,'62	Disc. dis. Nov. 28, '62. (See Priv. Co. H, 1st C. V. H. A.)
Purdy, George E.	New Canaan,	Aug.11,'62	Aug.28,'62	Trans. to Co. D, 20th Regt. V. R. C. Oct. 7, '63. Disc. June 29, '65.
Randle, Lewis	New Canaan,	Aug.20,'62	Aug.28,'62	Died June 19, '64.
Raymond, Chauncey	New Canaan,	Aug.15,'62	Aug.28,'62	Disc. dis. Dec. 23, '62.
Raymond, Cyrus	New Canaan,	Aug.12,'62	Aug.28,'62	Cap'd July 2, '63, Gettysburg, Pa. Par. Aug. 21, '63. M. o. July 19, '65.
Raymond, Cyrus J.	Stamford,	Feb. 10,'65	Feb. 10,'65	(See Priv. Co. A, 28th C. V.) M. o. July 19, '65
Raymond, C. Edward	New Canaan,	Aug.11,'62	Aug.28,'62	Disc. dis. Jan. 20, '63.
Raymond, John W.	New Canaan,	Aug. 6,'62	Aug.28,'62	Disc. dis. Oct. 26, '62.
Rusco, George	Wilton,	July 23,'62	Aug.28,'62	M. o. July 19, '65.
Rusco, Sands R.	Norwalk,	Dec. 30,'63	Dec. 30,'63	Disc. dis. July 11, '65.
Seeley, Charles E.	New Canaan,	Aug.11,'62	Aug.28,'62	M. o. July 19, '65.
Selleck, Benjamin	Darien,	Aug. 6,'62	Aug.28,'62	Wd. July 1, '63, Gettysburg, Pa. M. o. July 19, '65.
Silliman, Justus M.	New Canaan,	Aug.22,'62	Aug.28,'62	Wd. July 1, '63, Gettysburg, Pa. M. o. July 19, '65.
Smallhorn, James A.	New Canaan,	Sep. 1,'62	Sep. 1,'62	Cap'd Feb. 5, '65, Dunn's Lake, Fla. Par. Apr. 21, '65. Disc. June 8, '65.
Smedley, William	Norwalk,	Aug.27,'62	Aug.28,'62	Cap'd May 2, '63, Chancellorsville, Va. Par. May 15, '63. Died June
Smith, Edwin	Bridgeport,	Aug.19,'62	Aug.28,'62	Wd. Nov. 14, '62, Antioch, Va. Disc. dis. Jan. 26, '63. [20, '65.
Strong, Francis M.	Weston,	Aug.20,'62	Aug.28,'62	Disc. dis. Apr. 30, '63.
Thompson, Albert F.	Norwalk,	Aug.22,'62	Aug.28,'62	Disc. dis. Dec. 10, '62. [Sep. 19, '64. Disc. dis. Jan. 31, '65.
Thompson, Henry	Huntington,	Aug.11,'62	Dec. 29,'62	Wd. July 1, '63, Gettysburg, Pa. Trans. to 173d Co. 2d Batt. V. R. C.
Vittenheimer, Charles	New Canaan,	Feb. 9,'64	Feb. 9,'64	M. o. July 19, '65.
Wassing, Martin	New Canaan,	Aug.12,'62	Aug.28,'62	Disc. dis. Mch. 16, '63.
Waterbury, George E.	New Canaan,	Aug.23,'62	Aug.28,'62	Trans. to 58th Co. 2d Batt. V. R. C. Oct. 9, '63. Disc. July 14, '65.
Waterbury, Squire A.	New Canaan,	Aug.22,'62	Aug.28,'62	Disc. dis. Dec. 23, '62.
Waterbury, Henry	New Canaan,	Aug.20,'62	Aug.28,'62	M. o. July 19, '65. [M. o. July 19, '65.
Weinberg, Francis	New Canaan,	Aug.19,'62	Aug.28,'62	Wd. May 2, '63, Chancellorsville, Va. Wd. July 1, '63, Gettysburg, Pa.
Wilson, William	New Canaan,	July 21,'62	Aug.28,'62	Trans. to 49th Co. 2d Batt. V. R. C. Dec. 30, '63. Disc. June 26, '65.
Wood, George H.	New Canaan,	July 19,'62	Aug.28,'62	Died Oct. 12, '63. ['63. Disc. July 12, '65.
Youngs, George B.	Westport,	July 24,'62	Aug.28,'62	(See Priv. Co. C, 3d C. V.) Trans. to Co. E, 3d Regt. V. R. C. Aug. 17,

* Substitutes and drafted.

Company I.

NAME AND RANK.	Residence.	Date of Enlistment.	Date of Muster in this organization.	Remarks.
Captains.				
D. Olyphant Benson,	Greenwich,	Aug. 1,'62	Aug.28,'62	Died Nov. 9, '62.
Albert H. Wilcoxson,	Norwalk,	July 16,'62	Aug.29,'62	Pro. from Adj. Nov. 15, '62; Lt.-Col. Sep. 1, '63.
Marcus Waterbury,	Stamford,	July 21,'62	Aug.28,'62	(See Sergt. Rifle Co. F.) Pro. from 1st Lt. Co. B, Sep. 1, '63. M. o. July 19, '65.
1st Lieutenants.				
Thomas A. Haight,	Greenwich,	Aug. 1,'62	Aug.28,'62	Resgd. Mch. 28, '63.
David W. Mead,	Greenwich,	Aug. 1,'62	Aug.28,'62	Must. 2d Lt. Pro. Apr. 18, '63. Disc. dis. Dec. 26, '63.
George C. Peck,	Greenwich,	Aug.14,'62	Aug.28,'62	Must. 1st Sergt. Ap. Sergt.-Maj. Nov. 1, '62. Pro. from Sergt.-Maj. to 2d Lt. Apr. 18, '63. Cap'd May 2, '63, Chancellorsville, Va. Par. May 23, '63. Pro. 1st Lt. Mch. 5, '64. Ap. Adj. Mch. 30, '65 (not placed). M. o. July 19, '65.
Charles E. Doty,	Norwalk,	Sep. 20,'64	Oct. 29,'64	Pro. from 2d Lt. Co. B, Mch. 30, '65. M. o. July 19, '65.
2d Lieutenant.				
Edgar S. Wilcoxson,	Fairfield,	Aug.14,'62	Aug.28,'62	Trans. from Priv. Co. D, Nov. 11, '63. Pro. Sergt. Nov. 11, '63; 2d Lt. Apr. 10, '65. M. o. July 19, '65.
1st Sergeants.				
Dennis Eagan,	Greenwich,	Aug. 9,'62	Aug.28,'62	Must. Sergt. Pro. Nov. 1, '62. Wd. July 1, '63, Gettysburg, Pa. Trans. [to unassigned detachment V. R. C. Feb. 3, '65. Disc. July 3, '65.
J. Henry Held, Jr.,	Greenwich,	Aug.14,'62	Aug.28,'62	Must. Sergt. Wd. July 1, '63, Gettysburg, Pa. Pro. 1st Sergt. Feb. 3, '65; 2d Lt. June 29, '65 (not must.). M. o. July 19, '65.
Sergeants.				
Chard, Samuel S.	Greenwich,	Aug. 8,'62	Aug.28,'62	Des. June 3, '63.
Christie, George E.	Bridgeport,	Feb. 10,'65	Feb. 10,'65	Must. Priv. Pro. Sergt. Mch. 13, '65. M. o. July 19, '65.
Ingersoll, Oliver S.	Greenwich,	Aug. 7,'62	Aug.28,'62	Must. Corp. Cap'd May 2, '63, Chancellorsville, Va. Par. May 15, '63. Pro. July 1, '64. Cap'd Feb. 4, '65, St. Augustine, Fla. Par. Apr. 21, '65. Disc. June 8, '65.
Maguire, James E.	Greenwich,	Aug.11,'62	Aug.28,'62	Must. Priv. Pro. Corp. May 17, '64; Sergt. May 1, '65. M. o. July 19, ['65.
Mead, Isaac L.	Greenwich,	Aug. 6,'62	Aug.28,'62	Must. Priv. Pro. Sergt. Nov. 1, '62. Redc. to ranks (sick) Feb. 19, '64. Trans. to Co. C, 6th Regt. V. R. C. Aug. 10, '64. Disc. July 5, '65.
Peck, Henry V.	Greenwich,	Aug.13,'62	Aug.28,'62	Must. Corp. Pro. Nov. 1, '63. M. o. July 19, '65.
Sackett, Whitman	Greenwich,	Aug.11,'62	Aug.28,'62	Must. Priv. Pro. Corp. Sep. 1, '64; Sergt. June 8, '65. M. o. July 19, ['65.
Rae, John W.	Greenwich,	Aug. 9,'62	Aug.28,'62	Ap. Sergt.-Maj. Nov. 1, '63.
Corporals.				
Baker, William A.	Greenwich,	Aug.12,'62	Aug.28,'62	Redc. to ranks June 4, '64. M. o. July 19, '65.
Brundage, Thomas	Greenwich,	Aug. 7,'62	Aug.28,'62	Redc. to ranks Sep. 10, '62. Disc. dis. June 15, '65.
Comings, Harrison H.	Greenwich,	Aug.19,'62	Aug.28,'62	Must. Priv. Pro. Corp. Aug. 28, '62. Disc. dis. Jan. 15, '63.
Dayton, Charles A.	Greenwich,	Aug.11,'62	Aug.28,'62	Redc. to ranks (sick). Des. July 13, '63.
Elliott, B. Frank	Greenwich,	Aug.11,'62	Aug.28,'62	Redc. to ranks at own request Nov. 5, '62. M. o. July 19, '65.
Fisher, Samuel	Greenwich,	Aug.11,'62	Aug.28,'62	Must. Priv. Pro. May 1, '64. M. o. July 19, '65.
Marshall, John	Greenwich,	Aug.12,'62	Aug.28,'62	Must. Priv. Pro. Jan. 10, '63. Redc. to ranks May 17, '64. M. o. July [19, '65.
McElroy, James	Greenwich,	Aug. 7,'62	Aug.28,'62	Must. Priv. Pro. Sep. 1, '64. M. o. July 19, '65.
Peck, Benjamin	Greenwich,	Aug. 8,'62	Aug.28,'62	Must. Priv. Cap'd July 1, '63, Gettysburg, Pa. Par. July 23, '63. Pro. Mch. 1, '65. M. o. July 19, '65.
Platt, Charles P.	Greenwich,	Aug.11,'62	Aug.28,'62	Redc. to ranks (sick) May 17, '64. Disc. dis. Oct. 31, '64.
Purdy, Vincent B.	Greenwich,	Aug.11,'62	Aug.28,'62	Must. Priv. Pro. Jan. 10, '63. M. o. July 19, '65.
Purdy, Charles E.	Greenwich,	Aug. 7,'62	Aug.28,'62	Must. Musc. Trans. to ranks Dec. 27, '62. Pro. Mch. 1, '65. M. o. July [19, '65.
Warren, Daniel W.	Greenwich,	Aug.12,'62	Aug.28,'62	Must. Priv. Pro. Sep. 1, '64. M. o. July 19, '65.
Worden, Abram M.	Greenwich,	Aug. 8,'62	Aug.28,'62	Redc. to ranks Jan. 17, '63. Cap'd May 3, '63, Chancellorsville, Va. Released May 14, '63. Trans. to 21st Co. 2d Batt. V. R. C. Aug. 10, '63. Disc. July 14, '65.
Musicians.				
McKay, William T.	New York,	Aug.13,'62	Dec. 22,'62	Must. Priv. Detailed Musc. M. o. July 19, '65.
Purdy, John Jr.	Greenwich,	Aug. 6,'62	Aug.28,'62	M. o. July 19, '65.
Privates.				
Alexander, Henry	Greenwich,	Aug.11,'62	Aug.28,'62	Trans. to Co. K, 95th Regt. N. Y. Vols. Sep. 30, '62, a deserter therefrom.
Barmore, John B.	Greenwich,	Aug.12,'62	Aug.28,'62	Cap'd May 2, '63, Chancellorsville, Va. Par. May 15, '63. Des. Aug 28, ['63.
Barrett, Patrick	Greenwich,	Aug.11,'62	Aug.28,'62	Disc. dis. Mch. 25, '63. (See Priv. Co. I, 10th C. V.)
Birdsell, James	Greenwich,	Aug. 8,'62	Aug.28,'62	Wd. and cap'd July 1, '63, Gettysburg, Pa. Par. Aug. 25, '63. M. o. [July 19, '65.
Bones, Robert	Norwalk,	Nov.16,'64	Nov.16,'64	M. o. July 19, '65.
Booth, Daniel	Greenwich,	Aug. 6,'62	Aug.28,'62	M. o. July 19, '65.
Booth, R. William	Greenwich,	Aug. 6,'62	Aug.28,'62	Disc. dis. Dec. 10, '62.
Burns, Alfred	Greenwich,	Aug. 7,'62	Aug.28,'62	M. o. July 19, '65.
Burnett, John	Greenwich,	Aug. 8,'62	Aug.28,'62	Wd. and cap'd May 2, '63, Chancellorsville, Va. Par. May 15, '63. M. o. [July 19, '65.
Clark, Charles A.	Norwalk,	Dec. 28,'64	Dec. 28,'64	M. o. July 19, '65.
Clarke, Gustavus	New Hartford,	Nov.19,'64	Nov.19,'64	M. o. July 19, '65.
Clark, Michael	Greenwich,	Aug. 8,'62	Aug.28,'62	Wd. July 1, '63, Gettysburg, Pa. M. o. July 19, '65.
Collins, Thomas C.	Greenwich,	Aug.11,'62	Aug.28,'62	Cap'd May 2, '63, Chancellorsville, Va. Par. May 15, '63. Trans. to 75th Co. 2d Batt. V. R. C. Disc. June 28, '65.
Confroy, Edward	Danbury,	Feb. 28,'65	Feb. 28,'65	(See Priv. Co. A, 11th C. V.) M. o. July 19, '65.
Cooper, William	Plymouth,	Nov.17,'64	Nov.17,'64	M. o. July 19, '65.
Corbin, Robert	Stamford,	Oct. 27,'64	Oct. 27,'64	M. o. July 19, '65.
Cromma, Archibald	Greenwich,	Aug. 8,'62	Aug.28,'62	Died Oct. 25, '62.
Cumisky, John	Greenwich,	Aug. 4,'62	Aug.28,'62	Accidentally killed by discharge of his own gun Jan. 18, '63.
Darrow, Courtland S.	New London,	Mch.28,'64	Mch.28,'64	M. o. July 19, '65.

NAME AND RANK.	Residence.	Date of Enlistment.	Date of Muster in this organization.	Remarks.
Dayton, Clinton	Greenwich,	Aug.11,'62	Aug.28,'62	M. o. July 19, '65.
Dayton, Gilbert W.	Greenwich,	Aug. 7,'62	Aug.28,'62	Des. Feb. 28, '63.
Deblois, William D.	Greenwich,	Aug.13,'62	Aug.28,'62	Des. Jan. 1, '63. [dis. May 27, '65.
Doharty, John	Greenwich,	Aug. 6,'62	Aug.28,'62	Wd. and cap'd May 2, '63, Chancellorsville, Va. Par. May 15, '63. Disc.
Dove, William	Greenwich,	Aug. 7,'62	Aug.28,'62	Disc. dis. Jan. 1, '63.
Drumm, Charles	Greenwich,	Aug.11,'62	Aug.28,'62	M. o. July 19, '65.
Edwards, Thomas	Greenwich,	Aug.11,'62	Aug.28,'62	Trans. to 37th Co. 2d Batt. V. R. C. Oct. 7, '63. Disc. June 28, '65.
Farrell, John	Greenwich,	Aug.11,'62	Aug.28,'62	M. o. July 19, '65.
Fay, John	Greenwich,	Aug. 8,'62	Aug.28,'62	Disc. July 13, '65.
Ferris, John W.	Greenwich,	Aug.11,'62	Aug.28,'62	Disc. dis. Mch. 9, '63.
Finch, Washington I.	Greenwich,	Aug.11,'62	Aug.28,'62	Cap'd July 1, '63, Gettysburg, Pa. Par. Aug. 25, '63. M. o. July 19, '65.
Fitzgerald, Thomas	Greenwich,	Aug. 6,'62	Aug.28,'62	Trans. to 21st Co. 2d Batt. V. R. C. Aug. 10, '63. Re-trans. Sep. 15, '64.
Flood, John R.	Greenwich,	Aug.11,'62	Aug.28,'62	M. o. July 19, '65. [M. o. July 19, '65.
Foster, Thomas H.	Litchfield,	Nov.26,'64	Nov.26,'64	M. o. July 19, '65.
Frary, William	Greenwich,	Aug. 9,'62	Aug.28,'62	Disc. dis. Jan. 1, '63.
Gallahan, James	New Britain,	Feb. 8,'65	Feb. 8,'65	M. o. July 19, '65.
Grady, Thomas	Greenwich,	Aug. 8,'62	Aug.28,'62	Disc. dis. Nov. 11, '62.
Gregory, William S.	Greenwich,	Aug. 8,'62	Aug.28,'62	Killed July 1, '63, Gettysburg, Pa.
Griffin, William	Canton,	Oct. 27,'64	Oct. 27,'64	M. o. July 19, '65.
Hearne, James	Greenwich,	Aug. 9,'62	Aug.28,'62	Died Apr. 21, '63.
Herkenstrine, John	Wilton,	Jan. 5,'65	Jan. 5,'65	M. o. July 19, '65.
Homans, William	Darien,	Dec. 30,'64	Dec. 30,'64	M. o. July 19, '65.
Hull, Andrew C.	Newtown,	Jan. 27,'65	Jan. 27,'65	M. o. July 19, '65.
Husted, Elnathan	Greenwich,	Aug.11,'62	Aug.28,'62	Died Mch. 4, '64.
Jarman, Walter M.	Greenwich,	Aug.11,'62	Aug.28,'62	Killed Aug. 20, '63, Morris Island, S. C.
Johnson, George	Wilton,	Jan. 5,'65	Jan. 5,'65	M. o. July 19, '65.
June, William M.	Greenwich,	Aug. 9,'62	Aug.28,'62	M. o. July 19, '65.
Kinch, Elbert R.	Greenwich,	Aug.11,'62	Aug.28,'62	Cap'd Dec. 27, '62, Dumfries, Va. Par. Jan. 6, '63. Des. Jan. 8, '64.
Light, David	Greenwich,	Aug.11,'62	Aug.28,'62	Wd. July 1, '63, Gettysburg, Pa. M. o. July 19, '65.
Light, James H.	Greenwich,	Aug.15,'62	Aug.28,'62	Died Apr. 2, '63.
Lockwood, Fitch	Greenwich,	Aug.11,'62	Aug.28,'62	Disc. July 1, '63. [Camp Finnegan, Fla. M. o. July 19, '65.
Lowdon, John A.	Greenwich,	Aug.11,'62	Aug.28,'62	Cap'd July 1, '63, Gettysburg, Pa. Par. Aug. 25, '63. Wd. May 15, '65,
Lowdon, Merritt A.	Greenwich,	Jan. 16,'64	Jan. 16,'64	M. o. July 19, '65.
Magill, Bernard	Danbury,	Dec. 21,'64	Dec. 21,'64	M. o. July 19, '65.
Marshall, Enoch Y.	Greenwich,	Aug. 8,'62	Aug.28,'62	Disc. dis. Jan. 29, '63.
Medbury, John	Danbury,	Feb. 3,'65	Feb. 3,'65	M. o. July 19, '65.
Meeker, George H.	Norwalk,	Aug.11,'64	Aug.11,'64	(See Corp. Co. G, 28th C. V.) M. o. July 19, '65.
Moffit, Joseph	Chatham,	Dec. 26,'64	Dec. 26,'64	M. o. July 19, '65.
Moore, James T.	Greenwich,	Aug.12,'62	Aug.28,'62	M. o. July 19, '65.
Morrell, George	Greenwich,	Aug.11,'62	Aug.28,'62	Cap'd July 1, '63, Gettysburg, Pa. Par. Aug. 25, '63. M. o. July 19, '65.
O'Doharty, Philip	Greenwich,	Aug. 6,'62	Aug.28,'62	Wd. July 1, '63, Gettysburg, Pa. Disc. dis. Dec. 11, '63.
Olmsted, Marcus T.	Ridgefield,	Jan. 18,'65	Jan. 18,'65	M. o. July 19, '65.
Palmer, Lewis	Greenwich,	Aug.11,'62	Aug.28,'62	Cap'd July 1, '63, Gettysburg, Pa. Par. Aug. 25, '63. M. o. July 19, '65.
Palmer, Solomon	Greenwich,	Aug. 8,'62	Aug.28,'62	Cap'd July 1, '63, Gettysburg, Pa. Par. Aug. 25, '63. Des. Aug. 28, '63.
Peck, Nathan E.	Greenwich,	Aug.12,'62	Aug.28,'62	Trans. to Co. G, 10th Regt. V. R. C. July 10, '64. Disc. June 28, '65.
Pinkney, Edward A.	Wallingford,	Aug.23,'64	Aug.23,'64	M. o. July 19, '65.
Platt, William J.	Greenwich,	Aug. 9,'62	Aug.28,'62	M. o. July 19, '65.
Provost, William H.	Greenwich,	Aug.11,'62	Aug.28,'62	Reported on M. O. Roll absent sick since July 1, '63. N. f. r. A. G. O.
Purdy, William	Greenwich,	Aug. 6,'62	Aug.28,'62	Disc. dis. May 22, '65.
Reddington, Edward	Greenwich,	Aug. 4,'62	Aug.28,'62	Trans. to 128th Co. 2d Batt. V. R. C. May 15, '64. Disc. June 29, '65.
Reynolds, George W.	Greenwich,	Aug.13,'62	Aug.28,'62	Wd. May 2, '63, Chancellorsville, Va. Died May 28, '63.
*Riley, John	Barkhamsted,	Sep. 26,'64	Sep. 26,'64	M. o. July 19, '65.
Riordan, John	Greenwich,	Aug.13,'62	Aug.28,'62	M. o. July 19, '65.
Sackett, John	Greenwich,	Aug.13,'62	Aug.28,'62	Disc. dis. Mch. 9, '63.
Scofield, John W.	Greenwich,	Aug.11,'62	Aug.28,'62	M. o. July 19, '65.
Sargent, George B.	Greenwich,	Aug. 8,'62	Aug.28,'62	Disc. dis. Jan. 28, '64.
Smith, Henry	Monroe,	Dec. 7,'64	Dec. 7,'64	M. o. July 19, '65.
Smith, Silas	Sharon,	Jan. 18,'65	Jan. 18,'65	M. o. July 19, '65.
Smith, Thomas	Winchester,	Dec. 2,'64	Dec. 2,'64	M. o. July 19, '65.
Sturdevant, Edward	Bridgeport,	Feb. 27,'65	Feb. 27,'65	M. o. July 19, '65.
Van Ness, George S.	Greenwich,	Aug. 9,'62	Aug.28,'62	Disc. dis. Jan. 5, '63.
Van Wert, Samuel	Greenwich,	Aug.11,'62	Aug.28,'62	Trans. to Co. K, 95th Regt. N. Y. Vols. Sep. 30, '62, a deserter therefrom.
Walker, Andrew	Plymouth,	Nov.17,'64	Nov.17,'64	M. o. July 19, '65.
Weed, Edward	Greenwich,	Aug.11,'62	Aug.28,'62	M. o. July 19, '65.
Whitlock, Harmon A.	Monroe,	Aug.20,'62	Aug.28,'62	Disc. dis. Mch. 25, '63.
Whitney, Luthur M.	Bridgeport,	Feb. 27,'65	Feb. 27,'65	M. o. July 19, '65.
Wood, William L.	Greenwich,	Aug.11,'62	Aug.28,'62	Cap'd July 1, '63, Gettysburg, Pa. Par. Aug. 25, '63. M. o. July 19, '65.
Worden, Eliakim F.	Greenwich,	Aug. 8,'62	Aug.28,'62	M. o. July 19, '65. [July 19, '65.
Wright, James	Greenwich,	Aug. 9,'62	Aug.28,'62	Wd. and cap'd May 2, '63, Chancellorsville, Va. Par. May 15, '63. M. o.
Wright, William	New Canaan,	Jan. 12,'64	Jan. 12,'64	M. o. July 19, '65.

* Substitutes and drafted.

Company K.

Name and Rank.	Residence.	Date of Enlistment.	Date of Muster in this organization.	Remarks.
Caotains.				
John J. McCarty,	Fairfield,	Aug.18,'62	Aug.28,'62	(See Priv. Co. H, 1st C. V.) Disc. Dec. 16, '63.
Theodore Gray,	Bridgeport,	July 22,'62	Aug.29,'62	Pro. from 1st Lt. Co. E, Mch. 5, '65. M. o. July 19, '65.
1st Lieutenants.				
John H. Norris,	Fairfield,	Aug.18,'62	Aug.28,'62	(See 1st Lt. Co. H, 11th C. V.) Resgd. May 13, '63.
Edward M. Lees,	Westport,	Aug.18,'62	Aug.28,'62	Pro. from Corp. Co. E, to 2d Lt. Feb. 23, '63. Cap'd May 3, '63, Chancellorsville, Va. Par. May 23, '63. Wd. July 1, '63, Gettysburg, Pa. Pro. 1st Lt. Oct. 3, '63 (not must.). Disc. Oct. 10, '63
George B. Ruggles,	Bridgeport,	Aug.15,'62	Aug.28,'62	Must. Sergt. Pro. 2d Lt. Nov. 1, '63; 1st Lt. Apr. 3, '64. Cap'd Feb. 4, '65, St. Augustine, Fla. Par. Apr. 21, '65. Disc. May 15, '65.
2d Lieutenant.				
John C. Mills,	Fairfield,	Aug.14,'62	Aug.28,'62	Resgd. Jan. 11, '63.
1st Sergeants.				
John H. Porter,	Bridgeport,	Aug.14,'62	Aug.28,'62	(See Sergt. Co. D, 3d C. V.) Redc. to ranks (sick) May 15, '63. Pro. [Sergt. Sep. 1, '63. M. o. July 19, '65.
Morris Jones,	Bridgeport,	Aug.18,'62	Aug.28,'62	Must. Corp. Pro. 1st Sergt. May 15, '63; 2d Lt. July 15, '64 (not must.). M. o. July 19, '65.
Sergeants.				
Neilson, Theodore	Fairfield,	Aug.13,'62	Aug.28,'62	M. o. July 19, '65.
Seich, Joseph Jr.	New Haven,	Aug.11,'62	Aug.28,'62	Redc. to ranks (sick). Trans. to 75th Co. 2d Batt. V. R. C. Feb. 15, '64. [Disc. June 28, '65.
Thorp, Samuel	Bridgeport,	Aug. 8,'62	Aug.28,'62	Wd. July 1, '63, Gettysburg, Pa. Redc. to ranks (sick) Dec. 31, '64. Disc. dis. June 2, '65.
Wade, Patrick	Bridgeport,	Aug.15,'62	Aug.28,'62	Must. Priv. Pro. Corp. May 16, '63; Sergt. Jan. 1, '65. M. o. July 19, '65.
Wilson, Cornelius C.	Bridgeport,	July 15,'62	Aug.28,'62	Must. Corp. Pro. Jan. 10, '64. M. o. July 19, '65.
Corporals.				
Birge, George	Bridgeport,	July 15,'62	Aug.28,'62	Disc. dis. Dec. 10, '62.
Cavanagh, John	Fairfield,	Aug.15,'62	Aug.28,'62	(See Priv. Co I, 5th C. V.) Redc. to ranks May 15, '63. Missing in action July 1, '63, Gettysburg, Pa.; probably killed. N. f. r. A. G. O.
Edwards, Robert	Easton,	Aug.15,'62	Aug.28,'62	Must. Priv. Pro. May 15, '63. Redc. to ranks at own request Apr. 23, '64. M. o. July 19, '65.
Hale, Nathan	Fairfield,	Aug. 1,'62	Aug.28,'62	Must. Priv. Cap'd July 3, '63, Gettysburg, Pa. Par. Aug. 25, '63. Pro. [Nov. 1, '64. M. o. July 19, '65.
Hill, Frank	Fairfield,	Aug.20,'62	Aug.28,'62	Must. Priv. Pro. July 1, '64. M. o. July 19, '65.
Johnson, Wm. O.	Bridgeport,	Aug. 8,'62	Aug.28,'62	Must. Priv. Pro. July 1, '64. M. o. July 19, '65.
Kirk, Warren	Stamford,	Aug.15,'62	Aug.28,'62	Trans. to Co. H, 2d Regt. V. R. C. Aug. 30, '64. Disc. July 3, '65.
Mallird, William	Bridgeport,	Aug.20,'62	Aug.28,'62	Disc. dis. Aug. 7, '63.
McCarty, John J.	Bridgeport,	July 6,'62	Aug.28,'62	Des. Dec. 14, '62.
McKay, Fred. A.	Fairfield,	Aug.19,'62	Aug.28,'62	Must. Priv. Pro. May 15, '63. Wd. July 2, '63, Gettysburg, Pa. Disc. [dis. Jan. 2, '64.
Morris, William	Fairfield,	Aug. 7,'62	Aug.28,'62	Must. Priv. Pro. July 1, '64. M. o. July 19, '65.
Price, William	Fairfield,	July 31,'62	Aug.28,'62	Disc. dis. Apr. 16, '63.
Spencer, Timothy C.	Bethlehem,	Aug.14,'62	Aug.28,'62	Must. Priv. Pro. Jan. 10, '64. M. o. July 19, '65.
Troutt, James A.	Fairfield,	Aug.19,'62	Aug.28,'62	Must. Priv. Pro. Jan. 2, '63. M. o. July 19, '65.
Musicians.				
Ainscow, James	Bridgeport,	July 6,'62	Aug.28,'62	Cap'd Feb. 4, '65, St. Augustine, Fla. Par. Apr. 21, '65 Disc. June 1, '65.
Crane, William B.	Bethlehem,	July 14,'62	Aug.28,'62	Disc. dis. Nov. 28, '62.
Wagoners.				
Batterson, Morris	Fairfield,	July 25,'62	Aug.28,'62	Disc. dis. Jan. 18, '63.
Brodrick, James	Bridgeport,	Aug.20,'62	Aug.28,'62	Must. Priv. Detailed Wag. M. o. July 19, '65.
Privates.				
Allen, George W.	Fairfield,	July 31,'62	Aug.28,'62	Cap'd July 3, '63, Gettysburg, Pa. Par. Aug. 25, '63. M. o. July 19, '65.
Allen, James R.	Fairfield,	Aug. 4,'62	Aug.28,'62	Cap'd May 2, '63, Chancellorsville, Va. Par. May 15, '63. M. o. July 19, '65.
Allen, John	Fairfield,	Aug.16,'62	Aug.28,'62	Trans. to 173d Co. 2d Batt. V. R. C. Sep. 19, '64. Disc. July 7, '65.
Banks, Benjamin	Fairfield,	Aug.15,'62	Aug.28,'62	Trans. to Co. D, 6th Regt. V. R. C. Oct. 21, '63. Died July 5, '65.
Bassett, Hanford M.	Brookfield,	Aug.19,'62	Aug.28,'62	Trans. to 120th Co. 2d Batt. V. R. C. Dec. 15, '63. Disc. June 29, '65.
Birchum, Henry	Easton,	Aug.20,'62	Aug.28,'62	Disc. dis. Oct. 29, '62.
Brennan, Edward	Bridgeport,	Aug. 6,'62	Aug.28,'62	Des. Dec. 14, '62.
Brown, John	Fairfield,	Aug.19,'62	Aug.28,'62	Disc. dis. Dec. 30, '62.
Broadbrook, George	Bridgeport,	Sep. 20,'62	Dec. 27,'62	M. o. July 19, '65.
Cable, James W.	Fairfield,	Aug.19,'62	Aug.28,'62	Missing in action July 1, '63, Gettysburg, Pa.; probably killed. N. f. r. [A. G. O.
Cahill, Michael	Fairfield,	Aug. 9,'62	Aug.28,'62	Disc. dis. Aug. 22, '63.
Canfield, George	Easton,	Aug.15,'62	Aug.28,'62	Disc. dis. Dec. 10, '62.
Carpenter, Edward H.	Fairfield,	Aug.20,'62	Aug.28,'62	Trans. to Co. D, 12th Regt. V. R. C. Aug. 13, '63. Disc. June 6, '65.
Coggswell, Eli	Fairfield,	Aug.20,'62	Aug.28,'62	M. o. July 19, '65.
Cooley, Charles W.	Bridgeport,	Aug.14,'62	Aug.28,'62	Disc. dis. Feb. 7, '63.
Dawson, Wm. T.	Southport,	July 31,'62	Aug.28,'62	Rejected by Surgeon Aug. 28, '62.
Dean, Jerry B.	Bridgeport,	Sep. 1,'62	Dec. 27,'62	Disc. dis. Apr. 16, '63. Re-en. Jan. 18, '64. M. o. July 19, '65.
Demott, Lewis H.	Bridgeport,	Aug.15,'62	Aug.28,'62	M. o. July 19, '65.
Dennis, James	Bridgeport,	Aug.13,'62	Aug.28,'62	Wd. July 3, '63, Gettysburg, Pa. Died Mch. 15, '65.
Dennis, John H.	Westport,	Aug. 6,'62	Aug.28,'62	Wd. July 2, '63, Gettysburg, Pa. Trans. to Co. C, 20th Regt. V. R. C. Oct. 3, '63. Disc. July 10, '65.

NAME AND RANK.	Residence.	Date of Enlistment.	Date of Muster in this organization.	Remarks.
Dougherty, Anthony	Fairfield,	Aug.20,'62	Aug.28,'62	Trans. to 173d Co. 2d Batt. V. R. C. Sep. 19, '64. Disc. July 7, '65.
Garigon, John	Bridgeport,	Aug.14,'62	Aug.28,'62	M. o. July 19, '65.
Goodell, Marvin	Fairfield,	Aug.18,'62	Aug.28,'62	Disc. dis. Jan. 11, '64. [Aug. 19, '63.
Grace, William	Norwalk,	Aug.19,'62	Aug.28,'62	Trans. from Co. F, Sep. 23, '62. Wd. July 2, '63, Gettysburg, Pa. Disc.
Hawley, Abijah R.	Fairfield,	Aug.15,'62	Aug.28,'62	Trans. to Co. D, 22d Regt. V. R. C. Nov. 11, '63. Disc. Nov. 19, '65.
Hawkins, Elihu S.	Fairfield,	Aug.14,'62	Aug.28,'62	Cap'd May 2, '63, Chancellorsville, Va. Par. May 15, '63. M. o. July 19, '65.
Hull, David Jr.	Easton,	Aug. 7,'62	Aug.28,'62	M. o. July 19, '65.
Hull, Levi	Westport,	Aug. 7,'62	Aug.28,'62	Died Nov. 20, '62.
Hunt, Daniel	Bethlehem,	Aug.15,'62	Aug.28,'62	Cap'd July 3, '63, Gettysburg, Pa. Par. Aug. 25, '63. M. o. July 19, '65.
Irving, James H.	Fairfield,	Aug.30,'62	Dec. 27,'62	Cap'd May 2, '63, Chancellorsville, Va. Par. May 15, '63. M. o. July 19, '65.
Kabel, John U.	Bridgeport,	Aug.19,'62	Aug.28,'62	Cap'd July 3, '63, Gettysburg, Pa. Par. Aug. 25, '63. Disc. July 25, '65.
Kasson, Edgar N.	Bethlehem,	Aug.14,'62	Aug.28,'62	Disc. dis. Feb. 6, '63.
Kelley, Jeremiah	Bridgeport,	Aug. 7,'62	Aug.28,'62	Disc. dis. Dec. 3, '62.
Kelly, Enos	Bridgeport,	Aug.13,'62	Aug.28,'62	M. o. July 19, '65.
Kelly, James	Fairfield,	July 31,'62	Aug.28,'62	M. o. July 19, '65.
Kelly, Nathan	Sherman,	Aug.13,'62	Aug.28,'62	Disc. dis. Jan. 3, '63.
Kelly, Orville	Bridgeport,	Aug. 7,'62	Aug.28,'62	Disc. dis. Feb. 20, '63.
Kelly, Simmons	Bridgeport,	Aug.13,'62	Aug.28,'62	M. o. July 19, '65.
Kirk, Demmond	Bridgeport,	Aug.14,'62	Aug.28,'62	Disc. dis. Dec. 5, '62.
Lavey, James	Bridgeport,	Aug.19,'62	Aug.28,'62	Missing in action July 1, '63, Gettysburg, Pa. N. f. r. A. G. O.
Lein, William	Bridgeport,	Aug.19,'62	Aug.28,'62	Wd. Sep. 6, '63, Fort Wagner, S. C. M. o. July 19, '65.
Lennan, John	Bridgeport,	Aug.28,'62	Aug.28,'62	Des. Sep. 5, '62.
Lewis, John M.	Bridgeport,	Aug.14,'62	Aug.28,'62	M. o. July 19, '65.
Looney, Peter	Fairfield,	Aug.19,'62	Aug.28,'62	M. o. July 19, '65.
Lord, James	Easton,	Sep. 1,'62	Dec. 27,'62	Trans. to 21st Co. 2d Batt. V. R. C. Aug. 10, '63. Disc. Aug. 11, '65.
Lupitz, John M	Bridgeport,	Aug.19,'62	Aug.28,'62	Trans. as Saddler to Co. C, 1st C. V. Cav. Dec. 30, '62. Re-trans. Mch. 1,
				'65. M. o. July 19, '65. [Apr. 14, '64.
McElroy, Charles	Bridgeport,	Aug.20,'62	Aug.28,'62	(See Priv. Co. C, 1st C. V.) Wd. July 2, '63, Gettysburg, Pa. Disc. dis.
McGee, Richard Jr.	Bethlehem,	Aug.15,'62	Aug.28,'62	M. o. July 19, '65.
Mills, Francis	Fairfield,	Aug.13,'62	Aug.28,'62	Cap'd May 2, '63, Chancellorsville, Va. Par. May 15, '63. Des. June 20, '63.
O'Connor, Morris	Fairfield,	Aug.20,'62	Aug.28,'62	Trans. to 23d Co. 2d Batt. V. R. C. Aug. 17, '63. Re-trans. Jan. 28, '64.
O'Rourke, Patrick	Bethlehem,	Aug.20,'62	Aug.28,'62	Died Nov. 2, '63. [M. o. July 19, '65.
Picker, Michael	Fairfield,	Aug. 9,'62	Aug.28,'62	Disc. dis. Dec. 23, '62.
Seerey, John	Fairfield,	Aug.13,'62	Aug.28,'62	Wd. July 2, '63, Gettysburg, Pa. Disc. dis. May 14, '64.
Sherwood, Andrew	Fairfield,	Aug.13,'62	Aug.28,'62	Furl'd Apr. 1, '63; failed to return. N. f. r. A. G. O.
Sherwood, Bottsford	Fairfield,	Aug.13,'62	Aug.28,'62	M. o. July 19, '65.
Sherwood, Stephen	Fairfield,	Aug.27,'62	Aug.28,'62	Disc. dis. Mch. 25, '63.
Stewart, Thomas	Fairfield,	Aug.30,'62	Dec. 27,'62	Disc. dis. Jan. 18, '63.
Sturll, Charles	Fairfield,	Aug.20,'62	Aug.28,'62	M. o. July 19, '65.
Tilisson, Jesse	Easton,	Aug. 9,'62	Aug.28,'62	M. o. July 19, '65.
Tyrrell, John M.	Fairfield,	Aug.14,'62	Aug.28,'62	Wd. July 2, '63, Gettysburg, Pa. M. o. July 19, '65.
Wagner, Stephen	Bridgeport,	Aug.19,'62	Aug.28,'62	(See Priv. Co. B, 3d C. V.) Trans. to Co. D, 20th Regt. V. R. C. Oct. 7,
Waite, Henry	Bridgeport,	Aug.15,'62	Aug.28,'62	M. o. July 19, '65. ['63. Died Aug. 19, '64.
Waldron, Philip L.	Bethlehem,	Aug.20,'62	Aug.28,'62	Trans. to 23d Co. 2d Batt. V. R. C. Aug. 17, '63. Disc. July 5, '65.
Wallace, James	Bridgeport,	Aug.30,'62	Dec. 27,'62	Des. May 5, '63. [Disc. July 5, '65.
Wallace, William	Bridgeport,	Aug.14,'62	Aug.28,'62	Wd. July 3, '63, Gettysburg, Pa. Trans. to Co. C, 6th Regt. V. R. C.

Unassigned Recruits.

NAME.	Residence.	Date of Muster.	Remarks.
Brown, Lewis B.	New Haven,	Jan. 24,'65	(See Corp. Co. K, 10th C. V.) Disc. May 10, '65.
Ells, William E.	Fairfield,	Aug. 18,'64	Disc. Oct. 8, '64.
Fitch, William	Norwalk,	Aug. 15,'64	Disc. Sep. 13, '64
Gregory, David	Ridgefield,	Dec. 8,'63	Disc. dis. May 14, '64.
Harris, John	Easton,	Sep. 16,'64	Trans. to Regt. Oct. 20, '64; failed to report. N. f. r.
Johnson, Thomas	Harwinton,	Dec. 7,'64	Trans. to Regt. Jan. 7, '65; failed to report. N. f. r.
Jones, George J.	Bridgeport,	Mch. 22,'65	Disc. May 10, '65.
Kiernan, Patrick	Danbury,	Jan. 10,'65	Trans. to Regt. Mch. 4, '65; failed to report. N. f. r.
McCarty, John	Norfolk,	Nov. 17,'64	Disc. Dec. 9, '64.
McPherson, John	Salisbury,	Jan. 24,'65	Trans. to Regt. Mch. 4, '65; failed to report. N. f. r.
Porter, Thomas	Chatham,	Dec. 6,'64	Trans. to Regt. Mch. 4, '65; failed to report. N. f. r. A. G. O.
Russell, Frank	Middletown,	Sep. 28,'64	Trans. to Regt. Oct. 20, '64; failed to report. N. f. r.
Sayers, Abram	Norwalk,	Feb. 1,'65	Disc. May 10, '65.
Sibert, James	Greenwich,	Jan. 24,'65	Trans. to Regt. Mch. 4, '65; failed to report. N. f. r.
Snider, James	Greenwich,	Jan. 24,'65	Trans. to Regt. Mch. 4, '65; failed to report. N. f. r.
Sullivan, Thomas	Danbury,	Sep. 9,'64	Disc. Oct. 22, '64.
Weston, William	Salisbury,	Jan. 24,'65	Trans. to Regt. Mch. 4, '65; failed to report. N. f. r.

Casualties Seventeenth Connecticut Volunteers.

	Field and Staff.	A.	B.	C.	D.	E.	F.	G.	H.	I.	K.	Unassigned Recr'ts.	
Killed,	3	......	5	4	5	1	2	5	1	2	......	......	28
Missing in action, probably killed,	....	2	......	......	......	3	......	......	......	......	3	......	8
Deaths from accident,	....	......	......	......	......	......	......	......	......	1	......	......	1
Fatally wounded,	1	1	......	8	1	2	3	......	2	1	......	......	19
Wounded,	2	16	15	15	21	13	10	14	18	10	11	......	145
Captured,	4	21	56	21	30	21	20	24	27	18	11	......	253
Died in prison,	1	......	8	......	......	......	......	......	......	......	......	......	9
Died of disease,	1	8	13	8	6	5	3	5	9	5	3	......	66
Discharged for disability,	3	16	16	19	19	24	12	27	30	18	24	1	209
Unaccounted for at muster-out,	....	......	1	1	......	......	......	2	1	1	......	......	6
Total,	15	64	114	76	82	69	50	77	88	56	52	1	744

Appendix C

Major Brady's Official Report on the Battle of Gettysburg, July 4, 1863

Maj. Brady's Field Report Head Quarters
17 Regt Conn Vol. July 4, 1863

GENERAL: In compliance with instructions from headquarters, I have the honor to make the following-report of the part taken by the Seventeenth Regiment Connecticut Volunteers in the engagement of the 1st, 2d, and 3d instant:

The regiment arrived in Gettysburg between 1 and 2 p.m. of the 1st instant, and was marched with the other regiments of the brigade through and to the lower end of the town, and there halted for a moment.

Four companies were immediately ordered out by Brigadier-General Ames, under command of Major Brady, to the right of the bridge at the lower end of the town, with instructions to throw out two companies as skirmishers, the other two to be held as a reserve, and to take and hold the brick house to the left and beyond the bridge. Two companies were thrown out, and deployed as skirmishers as rapidly as possible to the right of the bridge, along the creek. The other two, held as reserve, were advanced in line, loading and firing as rapidly as possible, making at the same time a left wheel, so as to swing our right around the house, the reserve keeping near and conforming to the movements of the skirmishers.

When near the house, the enemy opened upon us with shot, shell, grape, and canister, which retarded our advance for a moment, until Major Brady dismounted, went in front of the line of skirmishers, and led them on until quite near the house. The enemy, anticipating our movements, shelled the house, and set it on fire. We, however, held our ground, and held the enemy's skirmishers in check. Their loss up to this time was at least 5 to 1, most of the men in the four companies being excellent marksmen and having volunteered for this occasion. They consisted of Companies A, B, F, and K, commanded, respectively, by Captains McQuhae, Hobbie, Allen, and McCarty.

We continued skirmishing briskly until Major Brady received orders from Brigadier-General Ames to draw in his skirmishers and return to town as rapidly as possible, and take command of his regiment. The order was obeyed, and we fell back in good order, skirmishing with the enemy, who advanced as we retreated, and tried to cut us off and capture us before we got to the town, but we foiled them in this attempt by making a circuit and entering the town near the upper end, and soon joined the remainder of the regiment, which we found near the lower end of the town.

The loss in the four companies under Major Brady was 3 men killed, 1 captain and 1 lieutenant wounded, 1 sergeant and 3 men taken prisoners.

I would here state that I had great difficulty in drawing in Captain McCarty's company (K), as they were so earnestly engaged and making such sad havoc among the rebels.

The remainder of the regiment (six companies), under Lieutenant-Colonel Fowler, advanced with the other regiments of the brigade to the left and front of the town and directly in rear of the One hundred and seventh Ohio Volunteers, in close column by division; were ordered to the front; advanced and deployed at double-quick, and held their ground–notwithstanding the rush to the rear of troops directly in advance–until ordered by the brigade commander to fall back, which order was obeyed in good order, the men loading and firing as they fell back.

Lieutenant-Colonel Fowler was killed when the regiment advanced and deployed. Captain Moore was killed about this time, and Captain French and Lieutenant Quinn were wounded, and many of the men were killed, wounded, and taken prisoners.

When the regiment reached the town, the four companies under Major Brady were still skirmishing with the enemy, and remained so until Brigadier-General Ames sent an aide with orders for Major Brady to return with his command and assume command of his regiment, he being the only field officer of the regiment present. Upon arriving in the town, Major Brady assumed command of the regiment, and reported immediately to Brigadier-General Ames for instructions. The enemies were at this time advancing rapidly through the town. The regiment was immediately deployed in the streets, and fired several volleys into the ranks of the enemy, which thinned their ranks and retarded their advance. We kept the enemy from advancing through the town until ordered to clear the street of our men for the purpose of planting a battery. The battery not being placed in position as intended, and the regiment being in line on the sidewalk, the enemy took advantage of this, and, with a superior force, rushed though the main street, which compelled us to fall back, which we did reluctantly, but not without contesting the ground inch by inch.

As we retreated, we loaded, halted, and poured destructive volleys into their ranks, which cleared the main street of them several times, but we found the enemy too many for us. They poured in from every street in overwhelming numbers, which broke our ranks. Upon arriving near the battery on Cemetery Hill, the regiment was halted, and formed in line of battle fronting the town.

About this time Major-General Howard, who was in the thickest of the battle, regardless of danger, asked if he had troops brave enough to advance to a stone wall across a lot toward the town, and said he would lead them. We replied, "Yes, the

Seventeenth Connecticut will," and advanced at once to the place indicated, remained a few moments, and again advanced across another lot still nearer the town and behind a rail fence at the upper end of the town, which position we held until late in the evening, exposed to a galling fire from the enemy's sharpshooters, when the whole regiment was ordered out on picket, and performed that duty until 2 o'clock of the 2d instant, when we were relieved, and took a position behind the rail fence and 150 paces farther to the right of the place we occupied before going out on picket.

We remained in this position, exposed to the enemy's batteries and sharpshooters, until 7 p.m., when we were ordered to the extreme right, behind a stone wall on each side of a lane, below the battery opposite the cemetery entrance. Two companies were advanced to the grain field near the woods, through which the enemy were rapidly advancing. We covered the wall on each side of the lane by compelling about 300 stragglers, who had no commander, to fall into our line. We had not more than time to form behind the wall before the enemy were discovered advancing rapidly upon us on our right and a full brigade obliquely toward our left. When within 150 paces of us, we poured a destructive fire upon them, which thinned their ranks and checked their advance. We fired several volleys by battalion, after which they charged upon us. We had a hand-to-hand conflict with them, firmly held our ground, and drove them back.

Soon after, some of the troops on our left giving way, the rebels succeeded in getting in our rear. We again drove them back and held our position. It was during this conflict that Major Brady was wounded by a fragment of shell, which hit him upon the right shoulder. After the enemy had been driven back, the firing ceased, excepting occasional shots from their sharpshooters.

We were relieved by the Fourth Ohio Volunteers, and were ordered to change front to the left behind a wall running at right angles with the one we had just occupied, and fronting the town, and where the enemy entered on our left. We remained at this wall all night and during the whole of the 3d instant, exposed to a cross-fire of the rebel batteries and their sharpshooters. With the latter our best marksmen exchanged shots, and succeeded in dislodging many of them.

When the regiment entered the engagement on the 1st instant, it numbered 17 officers and 369 enlisted men. We report at the present time 9 officers and 120 enlisted men. Capt. Wilson French and Lieutenant Bartram are the only officers known to have been taken prisoners. The former was wounded in the first day's engagement. We are not aware that either of them was paroled.

The regiment behaved gallantly. No troops in the world could behave better. Both officers and men are deserving of great credit for their coolness and bravery throughout the entire three days battle.

There are many deserving of especial mention for bravery on the field, but they are so numerous I will not undertake to give their names. The coolness and bravery displayed by the officers and men of Company D exceeded anything I ever saw.

I am, general, your most obedient servant,
A.G. BRADY, Major, Comdg.

Appendix D

Alternate Maps for the Brickyard Lane Deployment

These maps illustrate possible placements of Ames's division along the Brickyard Lane at East Cemetery Hill on July 2, 1863. They were included as alternate maps in the index of Phil Laino's *Revised and Expanded Edition of the Gettysburg Campaign Atlas* and are included here with his permission.

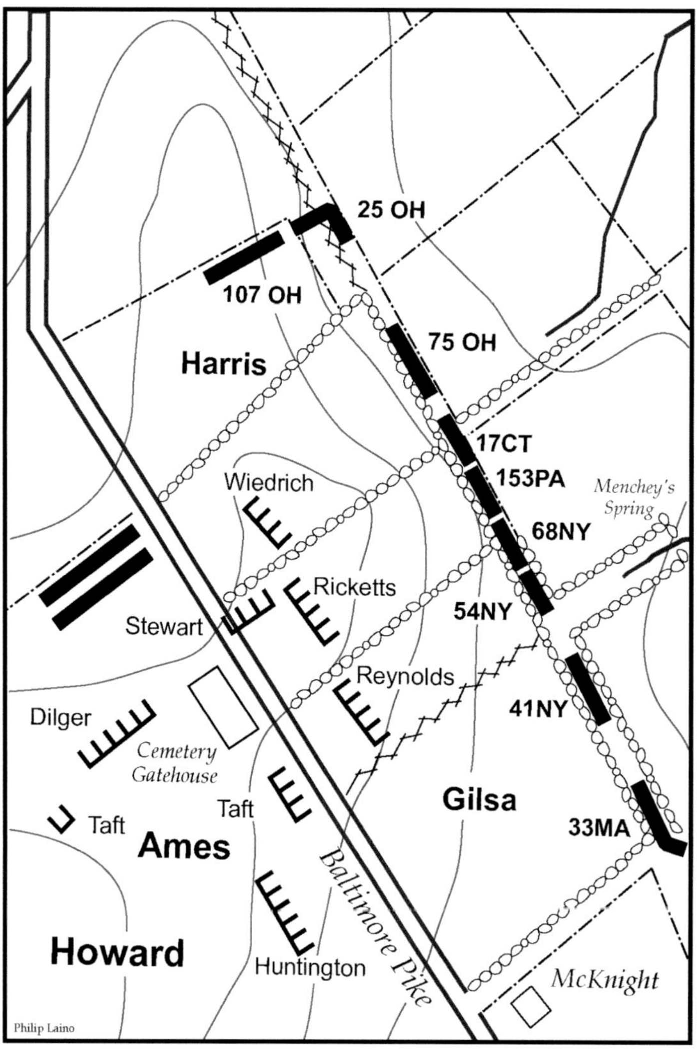

This map places the 153rd Pennsylvania to the right of the 17th Connecticut. It also depicts a gap between the 25th and 75th Ohio that Hays's Louisiana Tigers breached. This placement is derived from the work of Harry W. Pfanz and Gary Lash.

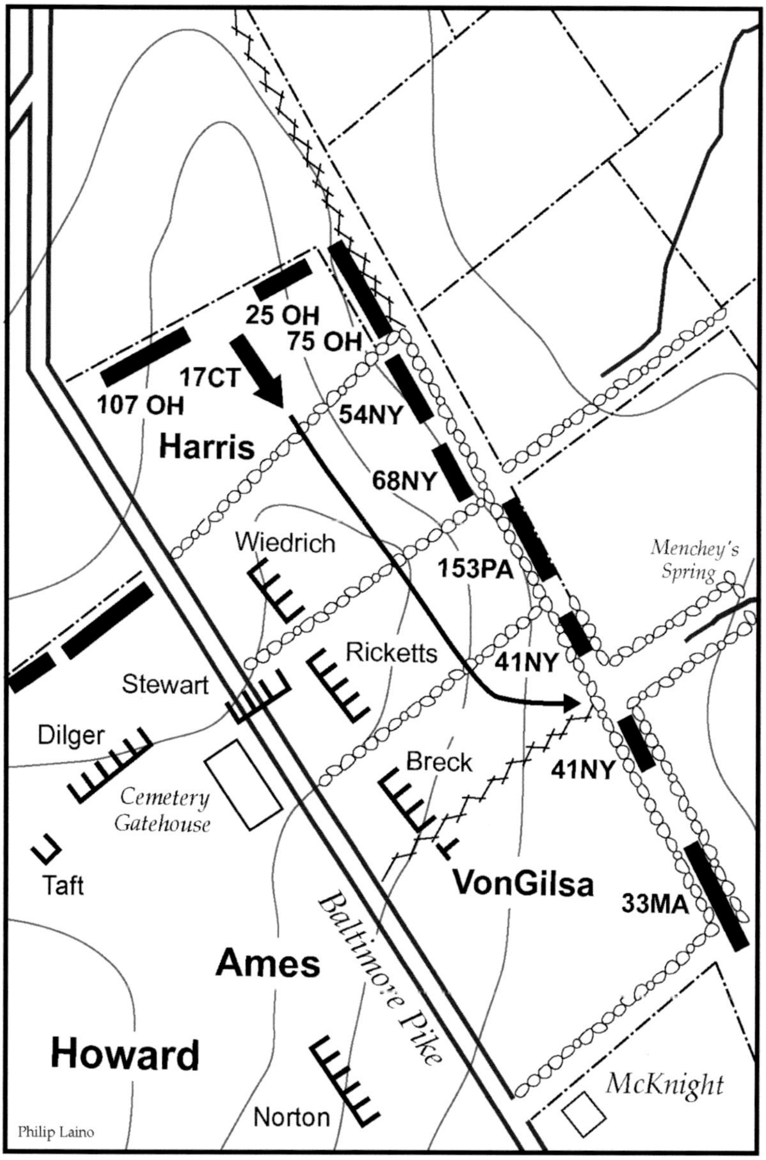

This map shows the 17th Connecticut removed from its original position and placed between the 41st New York. This placement is derived from the work of James Wood in his article "A Revisionist History of the Defense of East Cemetery Hill" in *Gettysburg Magazine,* issue 28.

Appendix E

Who Was William Warren?

William H. Warren was born March 28, 1842. He was listed in the 1860 census as a railroad hand living in Danbury, Connecticut. In August 1862, as the Civil War raged, Warren enlisted in the 17th Connecticut Volunteer Infantry, a three-year regiment, as a private. He enrolled in Company C along with other young men from Danbury. The 17th Connecticut was known as the Fairfield County Regiment, as almost all of its volunteers hailed from towns in that county. William H. Noble, a prominent Bridgeport lawyer and businessman and former P.T. Barnum partner, was appointed colonel. The regiment mustered at Camp Aiken in what is now Seaside Park in Bridgeport and was assigned to the Army of the Potomac's Eleventh Corps, First Division, Second Brigade.

The regiment's first combat was at Chancellorsville, where the Eleventh Corps was routed by Stonewall Jackson's surprise flank attack on May 2, 1863. Companies G and I of the 17th were the first Federal troops to be caught and crushed in Jackson's assault, which rolled up the Union flank and resulted in a costly defeat in the three-day battle. The Gettysburg Campaign then began in early June, and the 17th Connecticut reached the battlefield at the height of the fighting on the first day, July 1, 1863. Overwhelmed by a Confederate onslaught on Barlow's Knoll, the Eleventh Corps collapsed, and the survivors re-formed on East Cemetery Hill where they held that ground for the next two days. Gettysburg would be the 17th's costliest combat; the regiment would suffer its greatest loss of the war on July 1. Many of the regiment were killed, missing, or wounded that day. Many of the men listed as missing were captured, including Private Warren. Warren was marched off with other Federal prisoners to Belle Isle prison camp in Richmond. Most of the POWs of the 17th Connecticut, including Warren, would be exchanged in late August 1863 and would rejoin their regiment in South Carolina. From there the 17th went to Florida, where it was engaged in various actions until the survivors were mustered out at Hilton Head, South Carolina, in July 1865.

For William Warren, like many of the citizen-soldiers of the Civil War, his army service remained a source of intense pride and the defining experience of his life. These men went home to become active in veterans' groups that commemorated their service,

Private William Warren, Company C. (Courtesy of the William H. Warren Family)

honored their comrades who sacrificed their lives, and created monuments throughout the nation. Warren returned home following the war to resume civilian life. In 1866 he married Delia Campbell Keeler and they had seven children. The 1880 census shows the family living in New Haven. Warren listed his profession as a painter.

William Warren's lifelong ambition was to write and publish a regimental history of the 17th Connecticut Volunteer Infantry. He was never successful, but he devoted himself relentlessly to the task until the end of his life. Warren was unceasing in his efforts to compile and collect accounts of the regiment's service and experiences. He corresponded widely with the officers and men of the 17th Connecticut, soliciting their firsthand accounts. He compiled photographs, letters, newspaper clippings, and other sources.

The History Center at the Bridgeport Public Library is the repository of thirteen bound volumes of Warren's collected research. Several of the volumes are typed and devoted to specific events such as Chancellorsville and Gettysburg. Other volumes are handwritten; one is entitled "Gleanings." The most compelling volume contains a handwritten annotated index and almost two hundred photographs of members of the regiment that Warren reproduced from older tintypes, ambrotypes, and cartes de visites (small paper photographs on cardstock that were popular during the Civil War). Several volumes were edited and reworked numerous times by Warren to the point where they have two different sets of handwritten page numbers. The majority of the volumes are labeled as the eighth edition of the work.

The multivolume manuscript is a vast and precious resource for study of the 17th Connecticut. However, these volumes are also a tremendous challenge to the researcher. Many of the accounts are postwar, although they are, for the most part, firsthand, from members of the regiment. Letters that were sent to, or collected by, Warren were written twenty or thirty years after the war and need to be evaluated in the light of years passing and the writers' perhaps faulty memories or reinterpretation of events. Warren used much primary material in compiling the volumes, including his own and several other diaries kept during the war. However, because of the numerous revisions, both handwritten and typed, it is impossible to tell how many edits and rewrites of the original material were made.

Tragically, the material was never published. William Warren's dream of a regimental history never came to pass. There were many reasons for this. The sheer overwhelming volume of material he compiled and collected may have simply paralyzed his efforts to downsize into a viable publication. Warren's failure to come to any publishing agreement with the 17th Connecticut Survivors Association regarding financial arrangements and control of the material probably played a major role in preventing publication. In 1900 when Warren began what he termed his eighth edition he was determined to finish the work. He admitted that none of the volumes were completed and stated, "No sooner has one edition been finished than the addition of more valuable news would render it incomplete. The writer has therefore spent all these years revising and perfecting his work, and now for the eighth and last time, he is making an effort to complete the history." Warren guarded his work possessively and he was unable and unwilling to cut it down to a manageable volume. He knew this about himself, and in the eighth edition preface he included a defiant statement at the bottom of the page: "Comrades, on different occasions have said to the writer, (while talking about the history) that 'you have too much, cut it down.' Such is not his belief. This history as now written, is not designed, by the writer, to go before the public as a public history, but is written to suit his OWN peculiar taste and fancy. All are welcome to read who wish. From one who loves the work. William Henry Warren."

Warren truly loved his work and he researched and wrote almost to the day he died. He simply could not end it or let it go. In many ways Warren's work was ahead of its time. It was a celebration of the American citizen-soldier, whom he deemed as worthy as any general. In an age where history was written to celebrate "great men," Warren offered a different version of the war. "The history of the great war of the Rebellion has been written many times by many of the leading men of the nation," Warren wrote. "We have the lives of all the great soldiers, both Northern and Southern; we have elaborate accounts of every great battle and campaign. Little, however, has been written of the soldier in the ranks, with whose experiences the American people should be more familiar. Many soldiers in the ranks have stories to tell about army life that are as interesting and instructive as the more ambitions histories."

Warren's precious but dilapidated volumes are accompanied at the History Center by four manuscript boxes labeled "Papers of William Warren." The library has no provenance on any of the Warren holdings: when the volumes came to the library, who deposited them and why, and where the original diaries, letters, correspondence, and photographs are (except for material in the four manuscript boxes, much of which is also copied or transcribed) remain mysteries. There are indications in the manuscript, and in Warren's scant existing correspondence, that he borrowed original documents and diaries and returned them to the owners after transcribing and copying them. This is unconfirmed.

Warren worked on the manuscript diligently until the end of his life. He passed away on June 5, 1918, and was interred in Wooster Cemetery in Danbury. His tombstone is inscribed "Father, William H. Warren, Co C 17th Inf. Conn Vols, Died June 5, 1918, AE 76." Warren's lifework was left unfinished, but the service and sacrifices of the men of the 17th Connecticut regiment remain alive in its sprawling volumes.

Three undated cabinet cards, probably from the early 1890s, of William H. Warren. Clockwise from top left: 1) in formal dress; 2) in his GAR uniform. The medals he is wearing are, from left, the Society of the Army of the Potomac, the 17th Connecticut Association, the Civil War Union Prisoners Association, and the Grand Army of the Republic badge; 3) a fascinating and unusual occupational photograph showing Warren practicing his profession as a painter. Courtesy of the Bridgeport History Center, Papers of William Warren (BHC-MSS 0035)

Appendix F

William Warren's Photographic Index of the Regiment

These images are the property of the Bridgeport History Center and are printed in this volume with permission. No part of this photographic index may be reproduced or copied. Images from this album may NOT be used or reproduced without written permission from the author, publisher, and Bridgeport History Center.

As Compiled and Published
By
William H. Warren
December—1916
PREFACE BY WILLIAM H. WARREN

To properly understand the contents of the volume, refer to the index, for each and every picture, as the book contains photos of members of the 17th Connecticut Volunteer Regiment, with other prominent men, besides some important places which are all connected with the regiment.

The photos are copies from the originals. Many of them were taken at enlistment, while others were taken later in the service, and some after the war. Many of the originals were Carte-de-Visite so called, while the others were the old fashion daguerreotypes, which both before and during the war were the up to date portrait of the day. Many of the originals were carried by the soldiers in his pocket or knapsack, or both, during his army life, which is the cause of them being so marred, bent, creased, and faded out. Photography before, and during the war, was in a very crude state, compared with today. So look beyond the imperfections in the portrait to the comrade it represents, and see what he suggests to you of former days, and as we call to mind these familiar faces, let us renew old acquaintances once more.

One hundred and eighteen of the photos were made in 1910 by me which was a work of months. Six years later (1916) I tore the book to pieces, revised it, by taking out the poorest prints, reprinting them over again, and adding many new ones which was a work of months more. The pages numbered on the top are the 1910 edition, while those numbered on the bottom are the 1916 edition. You can learn more about these men by reading the six bound volumes of the eighth edition.

Editor's Note: The following photographic index combines the organization of William Warren's original photographic volume. Warren organized the index, or table of contents, in alphabetical order by each man's surname. He was somewhat challenged in this skill, so several of the photos are not precisely in order. He then organized the photographs themselves by company, with officers at the beginning of each company. All photographs for field and staff appear at the beginning of the album. If a man had two photographs, Warren numbered those as well, or he added ".5" to the number so that it would numerically follow, or precede, the number that had the man's name assigned to it. For group photos, or photos with two or more people, he included all the numbers that matched a man's name.

For the reader's ease of use, the photographs that follow are in Warren's original alphabetical order with his numbers on the top. Any comments Warren wrote about the photograph are above the image. The captions below each photograph contain information about the rank and company of each man, something Warren did not include in his index or listing.

This remarkable volume of faces was created over a number of years. Warren had negatives made of the photographs sent to him by men of the regiment. Using the negative he printed on light-sensitive paper a cyanotype copy of each. Cyanotype is a photographic printing process that produces a cyan-blue print. The process was used well into the twentieth century as a simple and low-cost way to produce copies of drawings, blueprints, and photographs. Cyanotype light-sensitive paper is still sold in craft and art stores and is used in schools and by artists.

Warren then bound the printed images into a book. As Warren stated in his introduction to the volume above, in 1916 he dismantled the book and reprinted the images. He then rebound them; the images that follow are from the 1916 printing. The group image below was awkwardly identified with multiple numbers in Warren's index. It was then printed in alphabetical order under each name and again in the volume under Warren's title, "Group of Five." Here it is printed separately with the names of the comrades who posed for it and a short biographical sketch for each man's service.

Left: Private William Smith, Company C, from Bethel. He was wounded in the right shoulder July 1 at Gettysburg. After more than a year in different hospitals he would muster out with the regiment on Hilton Head in July 1865.

Top right: Private Lewis B. Osborne, Company C, from Danbury. Promoted to corporal on August 24, 1863, he would die of disease October 31, 1864.

Bottom left: Private Charles H. Wilcox, Company C, from Danbury. He was captured February 4, 1865, at St. Augustine, Florida.

Bottom center: Private Henry H. Williams, Company A, from Norwalk.

Bottom right: Private Francis (Frank) Ferry, Company C, from Danbury. He was wounded July 1 at Gettysburg when a ball fractured his right forearm. The ball was extracted. On August 30, 1864, he was transferred to 159th Company Veteran Reserve Corps, 2nd Battalion.

INDEX

159
Ayers James H.
He wrote on the back of his card, "Compliments of Lieut. Jas. H. Ayers Company H 17 Conn Vols. Feb 7, 1864"

Lieutenant James Ayers, Company H, from New Canaan, was promoted to captain of Company A.

21-22
Ayers Almon H.
Taken in Alexandria

Private Almon H. Ayers, Company A, of Norwalk.

Almon H. Ayers, taken after the war.

32
Ayers Elbert

Private Elbert Ayers, Company B, of Stamford. He was wounded and taken prisoner at Chancellorsville and again at Welaka, Florida.

130
Allen Henry

Captain Henry Allen, Company F, of Norwalk. He was wounded at Gettysburg and later promoted to major and then lieutenant colonel.

160
Avery David M.

Private David M. Avery, Company H, from New Canaan. He was wounded at Chancellorsville.

174
Ainscow James

James Ainscow, Company K musician, from Bridgeport. He was taken prisoner at St. Augustine, Florida.

189
Averill Roger
Taken before the war

Roger Averill, lieutenant governor of Connecticut.

47
Bradley Lewis
48
Bronson Augustus E.

Left: Private Lewis Bradley, Danbury, Captured July 1 at Gettysburg
Right: Augustus Bronson, Danbury, died of wounds At Gettysburg on July 5, 1863

199
Badge of the Regiment

162
Boughton John

Private John W. Bouton (or Boughton), Company C, from Danbury, was wounded July 1.

63
Barber George W.
Taken in Philadelphia, Penn while there in the hospital from the effects of a wound received at Gettysburg.

Private George W. Barber, Company C, from Danbury was wounded July 1 at Gettysburg. He was promoted to corporal in February 1864.

190
Bailey Samuel G.
Captain of Company K, 23rd Connecticut Regiment, who came to my home (No. 184) while recruiting the above company, with a squad of men, calling me out into the front yard, and gathering around me, tried their best to influence me to enlist. My mother (No. 187) mistrusting what was going on, also came out, and in strong language informed them that I could not go, so that settled it, and they went away. A few days later I enlisted in another company.

Captain Samuel G. Bailey, Company K, 23rd Connecticut Volunteers.

4-5
Brady Allen G.
He wrote on the back of his card, "William H. Warren, Esq., with compliments of A. G. Brady."

Major Allen G. Brady, from Torrington, commanded the regiment at Chancellorsville and Gettysburg. He was wounded in the shoulder at Gettysburg on July 2. He was transferred to the Field & Staff Veteran Reserve Corps 20th Infantry and served as provost of Point Lookout prison camp in Maryland until the end of the war.

Taken in 1882

Major Allen G. Brady after the war.

127
Burr Henry P.
Taken from a poor, thin, faded out picture.

Captain Henry Burr, Company E, from Westport. He was captured at Chancellorsville May 2, 1863. He resigned May 28, 1864.

150
Bartram David S.
Taken in 1888

Lieutenant David S. Bartram, Company G, from Redding. He was captured July 1 at Gettysburg, Bartram spent twenty months in nine different Confederate prison camps before he was released in 1865.

109
Blakeman J. Henry

Private J. Henry Blakeman, Company D, from Stratford. He was wounded July 1 at Gettysburg.

158
Benedict J. Irving

First Lieutenant J. Irving Benedict, Company H, from New Canaan. He resigned December 23, 1862.

152
Brinkerhoff Benjamin F.
On the back of his card was written, "B. F. Brinkerhoff, Co G, 17th C.V."

Private Benjamin F. Brinkerhoff, Company G, from Ridgefield. He was promoted to corporal March 21, 1865, and to sergeant September 1, 1864.

108
Barnum Samuel B.
He, with Charles F. Marvin (recruit) had their pictures taken at St. Augustine, Florida. Barnum went to Phil, Penn, with the hospital chest and in it were the pictures. Both were lost. This is not one of them.

Private Samuel B. Barnum, Company D, from Bridgeport. He was promoted to hospital steward November 19, 1863. He is pictured here in his steward's uniform.

50
Barnum Bethel S.
Sergeant Bethel S. Barnum, Company C, from Bethel. He was killed July 1 at Gettysburg.

61
Bradley George

Private George F. Bradley, Company C, from Danbury.

102
Blinn Samuel F.

Second Lieutenant Samuel E. Blinn, Company D, from Bridgeport. He was promoted to first lieutenant on November 15, 1862. He was wounded and captured at Chancellorsville on May 2, 1863, and resigned his commission November 13, 1863.

197
Barlows Knoll

Rendering of Barlow's Knoll drawn by Private Justus Silliman of New Canaan.

19
Buttery Rufus

Sergeant Rufus Buttery, Company A, from Norwalk. He was captured at Chancellorsville on May 2, 1863.

107
Bachelder Melvin, C.

Private Melvin Bachelder, Company D, from Bridgeport.

59-60
Bussing Frederick, H.

Taken in Washington DC

Private Frederick Bussing, Company C, from Danbury. He was discharged for disability January 5, 1863, and on February 10, 1864, was mustered into Company I 1st Connecticut Heavy Artillery.

Taken in Danbury

Postwar photograph of Frederick Bussing.

58
Bailey James M.

Taken in 1887

Private James Montgomery Bailey, Company C, from Danbury. He was captured at Gettysburg on July 1.

23½
Bishop Hiram H.

He, with Calvin Nobles, went to Hartford after they had enlisted and had their pictures taken on tintypes, separately. This is one of them. Notice the frame.

Private Hiram H. Bishop, Company A, from Norwalk. He was wounded at Chancellorsville on May 2, 1863. On August 17, 1863, he was transferred into 23rd Company Veterans Reserve Corps, 2nd Battalion.

23
Bishop Hiram H.

Private Hiram H. Bishop, Company A.

153
Chatfield, H. Whitney

Adjutant H. Whitney Chatfield, from Bridgeport. He was killed February 5, 1865, at Dunn's Lake, Florida.

20
Crowe John M.
Taken in 1888

Sergeant John M. Crowe, Company A, from Norwalk. He was captured February 4, 1865, at St. Augustine, Florida.

112
Crofut Stephen C.

Private Stephen C. Crofut, Company D, from Stratford. He was killed July 1 at Gettysburg.

110
Curtis John B.

Private John B. Curtis, Company D, from Stratford.

111
Carpenter Frederick H.

Private Frederick H. Carpenter, Company D, from Bridgeport. He was wounded July 1 at Gettysburg. On February 5, 1865, he was captured at Dunn's Lake, Florida.

193
Carpenter John
Fireman

Warren included in his photographic index pictures of the engineer, conductor, and fireman that ran the train on September 3, 1862, that took the 17th Connecticut from Bridgeport to New York.

24
Campbell George H.
Taken at Hilton Head

Private George H. Campbell, Company A, from Norwalk. He was wounded at Chancellorsville on May 2, 1863.

33
Collins John, Senior

Private John Collins, Company B, from Stamford. He was wounded July 1 at Gettysburg.

126
Curtis Asa

142
Day Francis W.
Taken in 1863

Corporal Francis W. Day, Company F, from Norwalk. He was wounded May 5, 1863, at Chancellorsville and transferred into the 17th Company Veteran Reserve Corps, 2nd Battalion on January 25, 1865.

132
Doty Charles E.

Second Lieutenant Charles E. Doty, Company F, from Norwalk. Doty served as an aide to General Ames during the Battle of Gettysburg. After the battle he was so ill he resigned his commission on August 8, 1863. He returned to the regiment as first lieutenant of Company I on March 30, 1865.

161
Driscoll Thomas

Private Thomas Driscoll, Company H, from New Canaan. He was discharged for disability on January 19, 1863.

154
DeForest Henry W.
Taken in Baltimore

Private Henry W. DeForest, Company G, from Bridgeport. He was wounded at Gettysburg on July 1. On January 21, 1864, he was transferred to Company C, 24th Infantry, Veteran Reserve Corps.

66
Downs Samuel M.
From a card which was taken in Germantown, Penn while there in the hospital as steward.

Private Samuel M. Downs, Company D, from Danbury.

42
Daniels Milton H.
Taken in 1872

Captain Milton H. Daniels, Company C, in a postwar photo.

43
Daniels Milton H.
Taken at enlistment.

Lieutenant Milton H. Daniels, Company C, from Danbury. Immediately following Captain Moore's death at Gettysburg, Daniels was made captain of the company. He was wounded at Fort Wagner, South Carolina, on August 19, 1863, and he resigned March 6, 1864.

45
Dauchy William O.

Sergeant William O. Dauchy, Company C, from Danbury. He was killed July 1 at Gettysburg.

46
Dauchy Robert S.

49
Daniels William, L.
He wrote on the back of his card, "Wm L. Daniels, Co C 17 C.V. St. Augustine, Florida, July 1864."

Sergeant William L. Daniels, Company C, from Danbury. He was taken prisoner July 1 at Gettysburg. He was promoted to first lieutenant August 22, 1864.

53-54
Dickens George
Taken from a tintype. Notice the frame.

Corporal George Dickens, Company D, from Danbury. He was taken prisoner July 1 and nursed the wounded at the German Reformed Church and Spangler Farm hospital sites.

From a tintype as he looked while working in the hat shop.

A postwar image of George Dickens.

25
Donovan Timothy

Private Timothy Donovan, Company A, from Norwalk. He was taken prisoner July 1 at Gettysburg.

185
Danbury Churches

William Warren marked this photograph, from left, Baptist, Methodist, and Congregational Churches in Danbury, Connecticut.

70
Ferry Francis H.
Taken in Phil., Penn while recovering from a wound received at Gettysburg.

Private Francis Ferry, Company C, from Bethel. He was wounded July 1 at Gettysburg. On August 30, 1864, he was transferred into 159th Company Veteran Reserve Corps, 2nd Battalion.

71
Fry Robert

Private Robert W. Fry, Company C, from Danbury.

148-149
French Wilson
Taken the day before the regiment left Bridgeport.

First Lieutenant Wilson French, Company G, from Stratford. French would be promoted to captain after Chancellorsville in May 1863.

Captain Wilson French, Company G, from Stratford. French was wounded and captured at Gettysburg July 1. He would return to the regiment in the fall of 1863. On February 5, 1865, he was captured at Dunn's Lake, Florida. He was sent to Andersonville and would be subpoenaed to Washington, D.C. in the summer of 1865 to testify at the Wirz trial.

65
Foote Joseph
From tintype taken 1888

Photograph Missing From Album

67
Fairchild Leverette B.

Private Leverette B. Fairchild, Company C, from Danbury. He was captured at Chancellorsville on May 5, 1863.

68
Fairchild Alpheus B.
Taken in Florida

Private Alpheus Fairchild, Company C, from Newtown.

104
Foley John

At left is Corporal John H. Foley, Company D, from Bridgeport. He was wounded at Gettysburg on July 1 in the right hip. On October 14, 1863, he was transferred into F Company Veteran Reserve Corps 19th Infantry. Sergeant Henry North, Company D, of Bridgeport is on the right.

69
Feeks Thaddeus

Private Thaddeus Feeks, Company C, from Danbury. He was listed as wounded at Gettysburg.

17
Fowler Douglas

Lieutenant Colonel Douglas Fowler, from Norwalk, was killed July 1 at Gettysburg.

183
Gettysburg Map

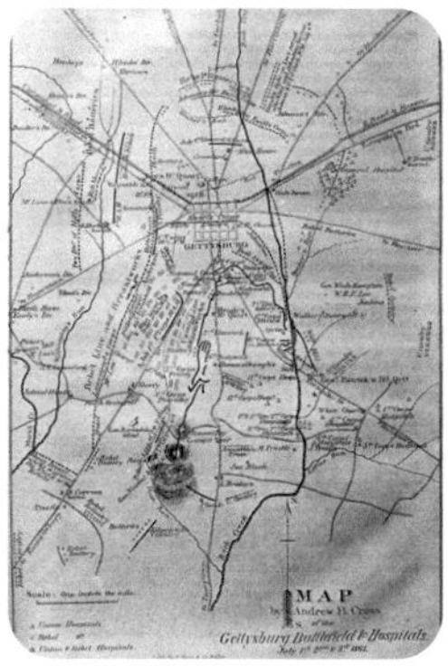

87
Group of Five

Clockwise, from top left: Private William Smith; Private Lewis B. Osborne; Private Frances H. Ferry; Private Henry H. Williams; Private Charles H. Wilcox.

83
Ganung John
From a very poor tintype which was taken in St. Augustine, Florida.

Private John Ganung, Company C, from Danbury (right) and Private Patrick Purdy.

12
Gray Theodore

Lieutenant Theodore Gray, Company E, from Bridgeport. He was promoted to captain, Company K, on March 5, 1865.

133-134
Griffin N. Raymond
Taken in the army

Taken before enlistment

Sergeant N. Raymond Griffin, Company F, from Norwalk. He was promoted to first sergeant March 23, 1863, and discharged for disability on July 27, 1864.

10
Gregory Elijah
Milton H. Daniels wrote on the back of his card, "One of the dear old doctors that saved my life when I was sick at Stafford Court House."

Assistant Surgeon Elijah Gregory.

155
Hull George
Taken about 1867

Private George Hull, Company G, from Redding.

106
Huss Henry

Musician Henry Huss, Company D, from Fairfield. He was captured at Chancellorsville on May 2, 1863.

8
Hayes Hanford N.

First Lieutenant and Quartermaster Hanford Hayes, of Bridgeport. He resigned July 18, 1863.

184
My Home

William Warren's home in Danbury where he lived before his enlistment.

31
Harvey John

First Sergeant John Harvey, Company F, from Stamford. He was promoted to first lieutenant October 8, 1863, and to captain June 29, 1865.

11
Hall William K. Rev.

Chaplain William K. Hall, of New Haven. He resigned November 6, 1863.

72
Holmes John
From a daguerreotype taken long before the war.

Private John W. Holmes, Company C, from Ridgefield. He was wounded and captured at Chancellorsville on May 2, 1863. He was discharged for disability on June 8, 1864.

29
Hobbie Charles A.
Notice the frame.

Captain Charles A. Hobbie, Company B, from Darien. He was wounded and captured at Chancellorsville on May 2, 1863. He was captured again at Welaka, Florida, on May 19, 1864.

39
Hobbie Selah R.

Sergeant Selah Hobbie, Company B, from Stamford. He was wounded on July 1 at Gettysburg in the left hand. On May 19, 1864, he was captured at Welaka, Florida.

98-99
Hubbell William H.

Captain William L. Hubble, Company D, of Bridgeport. He served as an adjutant to General Barlow at Gettysburg, where he was captured July 1.

175
Hunt Daniel
Taken in Annapolis, Maryland in the war

Private Daniel Hunt, Company K, from Bethlehem. He was captured at Gettysburg on July 1.

143
Hearn John P.

Musician John P. Hearn, Company F, from Norwalk. He was captured at Dunn's Lake, Florida, February 5, 1865.

73-74
Humphries William H.
Taken on Folly Island at the Brigade Sutler's Tent

Private William Humphries, Company C, from Danbury. He was promoted to corporal November 1, 1863.

Corporal William Humphries, Company C.

75
Humphries William H.

While the regiment was returning home from the war, and were marching up Chapel Street in New Haven, to the State Capital, on the Public Green, with colors flying, a photographer asked him to come into his gallery and let him take his picture, of which this is a copy. Draped in mourning for President Lincoln.

140-141
Hearn Thomas B.

On the back of his card was written, "To my dear wife H.H. St. Augustine, Fla, 1864."

Principal musician Thomas Hearn, from Norwalk, transferred from Company F to field staff.

Taken after the war

173
Jones Morris

Received in 1888

First Sergeant Morris Jones, Company K, from Bridgeport.

56
Keeler Justin S.

Musician Justin S. Keeler, Company C, from Danbury.

131
Kellogg William A.

Second Lieutenant William A. Kellogg, Company F, of Norwalk, resigned November 25, 1862.

97
Lacey William H.

On the back of his card was written by Milton H. Daniels, "Capt. I remember you well at Baltimore, and at the house of Mr. Krump, the collector of customs and you had the cheek to tell me I did not accord with the rest while singing. Capt. You ought to of said, that the rest did not accord with me."

Captain William H. Lacey, Company D, of Bridgeport. He resigned May 9, 1863.

136
Loomis Charles H.

Sergeant Charles F. Loomis, Company H, from Norwalk.

151
Lee Aaron W.

Corporal Aaron W. Lee, Company G, from Ridgefield. He was wounded at Gettysburg on July 1. He was promoted to sergeant September 1, 1864.

156
Lindhein Frederick

Private Frederick Lindhein, Company G, from Bridgeport. He was wounded July 1 at Gettysburg. On March 7, 1865, he was transferred into H Company Veteran Reserve Corps, 21st Infantry.

176
Lein William
From a tintype taken at Brooks Station at age 19

Photograph Missing From Album

156 ½
Lockwood Andrew
Taken in St. Augustine in 1865

Private Andrew Lockwood, Company G, from Ridgefield. He was captured at Chancellorsville on May 2, 1863.

76-77
Morris Theodore
Taken after enlistment

Taken after the war

Private Theodore Morris, Company C, from Danbury. He was captured at Gettysburg on July 1. On February 5, 1865, he was captured a second time at Dunn's Lake, Florida.

78
McCorkell John

Private John McCorkell, Company C, from Bethel. He was promoted to corporal on August 24, 1863, and sergeant on January 1, 1865.

57
McCorkell Thomas
Taken Christmas Day 1889

Wagoner Thomas McCorkell, Company C, from Bethel.

164
Mead David W.

Lieutenant David W. Mead, Company I, from Greenwich. He was discharged December 26, 1863.

167
Maguire James E.

Private James E. Maguire, Company I, from Greenwich. He was promoted to corporal May 17, 1864, and sergeant May 1, 1865.

168
McKay William

The original card was taken in St. Augustine Fla with James Ainscoe('s) Cap and drum. The tintype was taken in 1876

Musician William McKay, Company I, from New York.

18
McQuhae John

Captain John McQuahe, Company A, from Norwalk. He was dismissed or resigned on November 9, 1863.

113-114
Middlebrook James R.

On the margin of his card was written, "Regimental Flag presented by the Lockwood Guards."

Private James R. Middlebrook, Company D, from Trumbull. He was promoted to corporal January 30, 1864, and to second lieutenant June 6, 1865. (Warren printed this photo twice trying to improve its quality.)

138-139
Middlebrook Frank S.

Corporal Frank S. Middlebrook, Company F, from Norwalk. He was promoted to sergeant major August 28, 1864, and second lieutenant March 30, 1865.

115
Morse Edward A.
Taken at enlistment

Private Edward A. Morse, Company D, from Bridgeport.

116-117
Mott Joseph
Taken at enlistment

Private Joseph Mott, Company D, from Bridgeport. He was taken prisoner February 4, 1865, at St. Augustine, Florida.

Taken about 1888

34
Morell Charles E.

Charles E. Morell, Company B, from Stamford. He died of disease October 31, 1864, at Beaufort, South Carolina.

187
My Mother

William Warren's mother, Susan Matilda Starr Warren Bedient (1806–74).

144
McDonald Willis

Private Willis McDonald, Company F, from Norwalk. He was promoted to sergeant November 25, 1863.

9
McEwen Robert Dr.

Dr. Robert McEwen, assistant surgeon, from Stratford. He resigned September 30, 1863.

41
Moore James E.
Taken at enlistment. Milton H. Daniels wrote on the back of his card, "Dear old Captain, I mourn your loss, you was a friend to all, and the boys loved you. Capt. Moore I hope to meet you again. I must."

Captain James E. Moore, Company C, from Danbury. He was killed July 1 at Gettysburg.

1
Noble William H.
Taken at enlistment. From a photo which showed the full length but as the negative got broke, I was obliged to reduce it to this size.

Colonel William H. Noble, from Bridgeport. He was wounded at Chancellorsville May 2, 1863. On December 24, 1864, he was captured at Saint John's County, Florida, and sent to Andersonville, where he was the highest-ranking Union prisoner. On March 13, 1865, he was promoted to brigadier general by brevet.

172
Neilson Theodore

Sergeant Theodore Neilson, Company K, from Fairfield.

118
Northrop Ira

Private Ira C. Northrop, Company D, from Huntington.

103
North Henry

First Sergeant Henry North, Company D, from Bridgeport. He was captured at Chancellorsville May 2, 1863. He was promoted to first lieutenant in Company A on July 15, 1864.

104
North Henry and Foley John H.

Corporal John H. Foley, Company D, from Bridgeport (left) and Sergeant Henry North, Company D, of Bridgeport.

195
Nash Hiram

Reverend Hiram O. Nash, of Ridgefield, traveled to Gettysburg to bring home the body of his nephew, Private Rufus Warren, who died July 17 at the Eleventh Corps hospital at the George Spangler Farm.

14
Nash Jesse

Hospital Steward Jesse Nash, from Bridgeport. He was discharged for disability November 26, 1862.

191
Nichols Ward

Ward Nichols was the conductor of the New York and New Haven Railroad train that took the 17th Connecticut Regiment from Bridgeport to New York on September 3, 1862.

79
Otis William F.
Taken at Annapolis in 1863

Private William F. Otis, Company C, from Danbury. He was taken prisoner July 1 at Gettysburg.

80
Osborne Lewis B.

Private Lewis B. Osborne, Company C, of Danbury. He was promoted to corporal August 24, 1863. He died of disease October 31, 1864.

165
Peck George C.
On the back of his card was written, "Truly your friend." Geo C. Peck

Second Lieutenant George C. Peck, Company I, of Greenwich. He was captured at Chancellorsville May 2, 1863. He was promoted to first lieutenant March 1, 1864.

119
Peck Lemuel

Private Lemuel Peck, Company D, of Brookfield. He died December 6, 1862.

169
Peck Henry V.
On the back of his card was written, "Compliments of Henry V. Peck, Sergt. Co I C.V."

Corporal Henry V. Peck, Company I, from Greenwich. He was promoted to sergeant on November 1, 1863.

146
Perry Robert N.
With flag

Private Robert N. Perry, Company F, from Norwalk. He was wounded July 2 at Gettysburg, shot through the left shoulder. He was promoted to corporal January 1, 1865.

83 145
Purdy Patrick

Private John Ganung, Company C, from Danbury (right) and Private Patrick Purdy.

Private Patrick Purdy, Company F, from Norwalk. He was wounded July 2 at Gettysburg.

147
Patric George S.

Private George S. Patric, Company F, from Norwalk. He was captured at Chancellorsville May 2, 1863.

120
Plumb Horace

Private Horace Plumb, Company D, from Bridgeport.

81-82
Purdy George S.

Private George S. Purdy, Company C, from Danbury.

162
Potts George

Private George Potts, Company H, from New Canaan. He was discharged for disability January 23, 1863, and on November 28, 1863, he mustered into Company H, 1st Connecticut Heavy Artillery.

166
Purdy John

Musician John Purdy Jr., Company I, from Greenwich.

100-101
Peck Albert W.

Second Lieutenant Albert W. Peck, Company D, of Bridgeport. He was promoted to first lieutenant March 5, 1864.

44
Quien Henry

Taken at enlistment. Milton H. Daniels wrote on the back of his card, "Dear old Quien, a truer braver heart, never lived, always courteous and kind to all. Was wounded via sword and arm at Gettysburg on the first day's fight."

Lieutenant Henry Quien, Company C, from Danbury. He was wounded July 1 at Gettysburg. He was promoted to captain August 15, 1864. On February 5, 1865, he was taken prisoner at Dunn's Lake, Florida.

84
Rice Rufus

Taken soon after he got home.

Private Rufus Rice, Company C, from Danbury. He was discharged for disability on January 17, 1863.

85
Ryan Patrick

From a poor, scratched, tintype that was taken the day before we left b-port.

Private Patrick Ryan, Company C, from Danbury. He was transferred to the Veteran Reserve Corps, Company E, 14th Infantry on August 5, 1863.

196

Route of the regiment

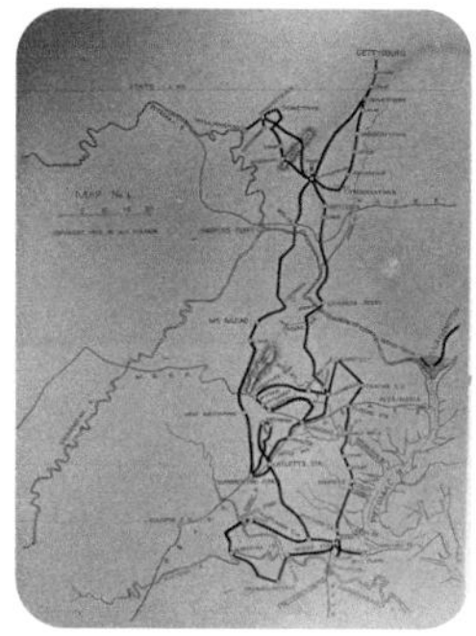

The route of the regiment to and from Gettysburg in 1863.

35
Rich Charles

Private Charles F. Rich, Company B, from Greenwich.

170
Ruggles George B.

Sergeant George B. Ruggles, Company K, from Bridgeport. He was promoted to second lieutenant November 1, 1863, and first lieutenant April 3, 1864. He was captured at Dunn's Lake, Florida, on February 5, 1865.

87
Smith William H.

Private William Smith (top left), Company C, from Bethel. He was wounded in the right shoulder at Gettysburg on July 1.

137
Shaw George W.

Sergeant George W. Shaw, Company F, from Norwalk. He was promoted to second lieutenant April 24, 1864.

135
St. John Oscar

Sergeant Oscar St. John, Company F, from Norwalk.

198
Slave pen

William Warren wrote "Alexandria Virginia slave pen" on this prewar image.

86
Small Charles S.

Private Charles S. Small, Company C, from Danbury. He died October 2, 1862.

93
Small Charles S.

36
Seeley Oscar
(Seeley Albert O)

Warren may have misidentified this image as Lewis Scofield. Strong evidence suggests this is Corporal Albert O. Seeley, Company F, from New Canaan, who was captured July 1 at Gettysburg. Seeley was captured again May 19, 1864, at Welaka, Florida, and sent to Andersonville. He was paroled but died of disease at Annapolis, Maryland, on January 9, 1865.

177-178
Spencer Timothy C.

Private Timothy Spencer, Company K, from Bethlehem. He was promoted to corporal January 10, 1864.

122
Scranton Leonard

Private Leonard Scranton, Company D, from Bridgeport and Madison.

192
Southworth John H.
Engineer

Warren included in his photographic index pictures of the engineer, conductor, and fireman of the train that took the 17th Connecticut Regiment from Bridgeport to New York on September 3, 1862.

15
Stocking Sabin

Dr. Sabin Stocking was commissioned surgeon of the 17th Connecticut on May 31, 1864.

51
Scott George

Corporal George Scott, Company C, from Danbury. He was promoted to sergeant July 15, 1863.

26
Swords Alfred
Taken in summer of 1899

Private Alfred Swords, Company A, from Norwalk. He was wounded July 1 at Gettysburg. On October 14, 1863, he was transferred to 75th Company Veteran Reserve Corps, 2nd Battalion.

27-28
Smith George, 2nd
Taken after enlistment

Private George W. Smith, Company A, from Norwalk.

Taken after the war

36
Scofield Lewis W.

Corporal Lewis W. Scofield, Company B, from Stamford. He was promoted to sergeant on November 1, 1863. He was taken prisoner at Welaka, Florida, on May 19, 1864.
[NOTE: There is a strong possibility that this may be Corporal Albert O. Seeley. This image is marked in other sources with Seeley's name.]

37
Scofield Alfred V.

Corporal Alfred V. Scofield, Company B, from Stamford. He was captured at Welaka, Florida, on May 19, 1864.

171
Thorp Samuel

Sergeant Samuel Thorp, Company K, from Bridgeport. He was shot in the left arm July 1 at Gettysburg. He was discharged for disability June 2, 1865.

123-124
Treadwell Edmund

From a card taken on Folly Island

Private Edmund Treadwell, Company D, from Redding. He was captured at Dunn's Lake on February 5, 1865.

From a tintype taken in 1865 after he got home

179
Wade Patrick

On the back of his card it read, "Yours truly, Corp. P. Wade, Picolata Fla. Dec 19, 1864."

Corporal Patrick Wade, Company K, from Bridgeport. He was promoted to sergeant on January 1, 1865.

89
Warren Rufus

Private Rufus Warren, Company C, from Ridgefield. He was severely wounded at Gettysburg on July 1. His left leg was amputated, and he died of his wounds July 17 at the Eleventh Corps hospital.

94-95
Warren William H.

Private William H Warren, Company C, from Danbury.

Photo taken in April 1863

Private William H. Warren, Company C, from Danbury. He was taken prisoner July 1 at Gettysburg.

96
Warren William H.
Taken after the war

2-3
Walter Charles

Lieutenant Colonel Charles Walter, from Bridgeport. He was killed at Chancellorsville on May 2, 1863.

13
Ward John S.
On the back of his card it read, "Yours truly with the best respect of John S. Ward, Qr. Master Sergt. 17th C.V.

Quartermaster Sergeant John S. Ward, from Bridgeport.

163
Weinberg Francis
Taken in 1873

Private Francis Weinberg, Company H, of New Canaan. He was wounded at Chancellorsville on May 5, 1863, and wounded again at Gettysburg on July 1.

30
Waterbury Marcus
Milton H. Daniels wrote on the back of his card "Waterbury I liked you much."

Lieutenant Marcus Waterbury, Company B, from Stamford. He was promoted to captain in Company I on September 1, 1863.

52
White Benjamin S.
Taken the day before the regiment left B-port.

Corporal Benjamin S. White, Company C, from Danbury. He was discharged for disability January 20, 1863.

87
Wilcox Charles

Private Charles H. Wilcox (bottom left), Company C, from Danbury was captured at Dunn's Lake, Florida, on February 5, 1865.

55
Williams Henry

Private Henry Williams, Company A, from Norwalk.

88
Williams Adam C.
Taken soon after he got home on January 5, 1863

Private Adam C. Williams, Company C, from Bethel. He was discharged for disability January 5, 1863.

105
Wilcox Alva
A daguerreotype was made two or three years before the war. From that was made a Carte de Visite which he carried during his army life and so got creased. This is a copy from the card.

Corporal Alva(h) E. Wilcox, Company D, from Bridgeport and Madison. He was wounded in the chest July 2 at Gettysburg and died from his wounds on July 7 at the Spangler Farm.

188
Wildman Frederick S.
Received in 1890. Taken years before. One of Danbury's rich, prominent, and influential men, who spent much time and money towards recruiting companies, and after their departure for the front, cared for their families with the able assistance of his wife.

Frederick S. Wildman, of Danbury.

6-7
Wilcoxson Albert H.
On the back of his card was written, "Fraternally yours, A. H. Wilcoxson, Capt Co F 17 C.V."

Adjutant Albert H. Wilcoxson, Company I, from Norwalk. He was to promoted lieutenant colonel September 1, 1863. On February 5, 1865, he was wounded and taken prisoner at Dunn's Lake, Florida. He died in captivity March 6, 1865, at Tallahassee, Florida.

128
Wakeman Frederick
Taken in 1862

Private Frederick Wakeman, Company E, of Westport. He was taken prisoner at Chancellorsville on May 5, 1863.

Wayland John B.
Taken at Brooks Station from a very poor tintype

Photograph Missing From Album

Private John B. Wayland, Company D, from Monroe. He was discharged for disability October 8, 1863.

129
Wood Enoch
Milton H. Daniels wrote on the back of his card, "A kind courteous, brave soldier from Norwalk." Taken in 1862

Captain Enoch Wood, Company F, from Norwalk. He resigned March 23, 1863.

90
Woodman Iraneus P.

Private Iraneus P. Woodman, Company C, from Bethel. He was wounded at Chancellorsville on May 2,1863 and died of his wounds May 19.

91
Wood George W. Senior

Private George W. Wood, Company C from Danbury.

92
Wood George Jr.
Taken after the war

George L. Wood, Company G, from Ridgefield. He was discharged for disability on February 13, 1864.

125
Whittlesey Samuel F.
Taken at 40 years of age

Private Samuel F. Whittlesey, Company D, from Trumbull. He was shot in the left side of the neck July 1 at Gettysburg. He was taken prisoner February 5, 1865, at Dunn's Lake, Florida.

191, 192, 193
The three railroad men are the Conductor, (191) Engineer, (192) and Fireman, (193) which run the train on September 3, 1862 that took the 17th Conn Regiment from Bridgeport to New York. All dead.

186
Nobles Calvin

Private Calvin Nobles, Company A, from Norwalk. He was killed at Gettysburg. Listed as missing July 2, his body was never recovered.

194
Unknown

Inside the back cover
Hubbard Robert, MD, the original steel plate cost $125. This is a copy.

Dr. Robert Hubbard, regimental surgeon, from Bridgeport. He resigned December 28, 1863.

Inside the Front cover
Noble William H. The original steel plate cost $125. This is a copy.

Colonel William H. Noble, from Bridgeport. He was wounded at Chancellorsville on May 2, 1863. On December 24, 1864, he was captured at Saint John's County, Florida, and sent to Andersonville, where he was the highest-ranking Union prisoner. On March 13, 1865, he was promoted to brigadier general by brevet.

Notes

CHAPTER 1

1. John Niven, *Connecticut for the Union: The Role of the State in the Civil War* (New Haven, CT: Yale University Press, 1965), 42.
2. Niven, *Connecticut,* 29.
3. Matthew Warshauer, *Connecticut in the Civil War: Slavery, Sacrifice, and Survival* (Middletown, CT: Wesleyan University Press, 2011), 43.
4. W. A. Croffut and John M. Morris, *Military and Civil History of Connecticut during the War of 1861–65* (New York: Ledyard Bill, 1868), 107.
5. Croffut and Morris, *Military and Civil History*, 107–8.
6. Croffut and Morris, *Military and Civil History*, 108.
7. Mary K. Witkowski, "The Civil War Marks City—Unionists Lead Riot," *Bridgeport News*, March 11, 1999.
8. Dean E. Nelson, *Connecticut Arms the Union*, https://connecticuthistory.org/connecticut-arms-the-union/
9. Blaikie Hines, *Civil War Volunteer Sons of Connecticut* (Thomaston, ME: American Patriot Press, 2002), xii.
10. Croffut and Morris, *Military and Civil History*, 223.
11. Niven, *Connecticut*, 78.
12. Niven, *Connecticut*, 81.
13. Warren Picture Index Volume, photo 190, 4.
14. Croffut and Morris, *Military and Civil History*, 228.
15. Croffut and Morris, *Military and Civil History*, 230.
16. Croffut and Morris, *Military and Civil History*, 230.
17. Selah Blakeman, Company D, letter to his brother, Stafford Court House, Virginia, December 24, 1862.
18. Croffut and Morris, *Military and Civil History*, 297.
19. Croffut and Morris, *Military and Civil History*, 230.
20. Croffut and Morris, *Military and Civil History*, 230.
21. Hines, *Volunteer Sons*, 190.
22. Hines, *Volunteer Sons*, 190.
23. Hines, *Volunteer Sons*, 190.
24. Croffut and Morris, *Military and Civil History*, 297.
25. Croffut and Morris, *Military and Civil History*, 358.

CHAPTER 2

1. Chris Mackowski and Kristopher D. White, *That Furious Struggle: Chancellorsville and the High Tide of the Confederacy, May 1–4, 1863* (El Dorado Hills, CA: Savas Beatie, 2014), 12.
2. Stuart Dempsey, "These Men Are No Cowards."
3. Ancestry.com, Find-A-Grave, Civil War Research Database, www.civilwar.org
4. Croffut and Morris, *Military and Civil History*, 373.
5. Warren Manuscript, Bridgeport History Center, Vol. 1.
6. Ancestry.com; Civil War Research database, www.civilwar.org
7. Dempsey, "These Men Are No Cowards."
8. *Voices of the Civil War: Chancellorsville* (Alexandria, VA: Time Life Books, 1996), 85.
9. Mackowski and White, *Furious Struggle*, 13.
10. Mackowski and White, *Furious Struggle*, 13.
11. Hines, *Volunteer Sons*, 190.
12. Selah Blakeman, letter dated May 10, 1863, Stratford Historical Society.
13. Croffut and Morris, *Military and Civil History.*
14. Robert Krick, "Civilians in the Midst of Battle," Part 24 of a series on the 1863 Battle of Chancellorsville, The Free Lance-Star, August 17, 2002.
15. Croffut and Morris, *Military and Civil History*, 361.
16. Mackowski and White, *Furious Struggle*, 77.
17. Numbers of Union and Confederate armies from Fredericksburg and Spotsylvania National Military Park, U.S. National Park Service.
18. Mackowski and White, *Furious Struggle*, 29.
19. *Battles and Leaders of the Civil War*, Vol. III (New York: The Century Company, New York), 159.
20. *Battles and Leaders*, 161.
21. Mackowski and White, *Furious Struggle*, 45-47.
22. *Voices of the Civil War: Chancellorsville* (Alexandria, VA: Time Life Books, 1996), 70.
23. Croffut and Morris, *Military and Civil History*, 362.
24. Croffut and Morris, *Military and Civil History*, 362.
25. *Voices of the Civil War*, 70.
26. Croffut and Morris, *Military and Civil History*, 352.
27. John Niven, *Connecticut for the Union: The Role of the State in the Civil War* (New Haven, CT: Yale University Press, 1965), 229.
28. Wilson French to Martha Bouton French, May 8, 1863, courtesy of Susan Richardson Curry.
29. Croffut and Morris, *Military and Civil History*, 363.
30. *Voices of the Civil War*, 87.
31. Croffut and Morris, *Military and Civil History*, 363.
32. Edward Marcus, ed., *A New Canaan Private in the Civil War: Letters of Justus M. Silliman 17th Connecticut Volunteers* (New Canaan, CT: New Canaan Historical Society, 1984), 33.
33. Selah Blakeman, letter, May 10, 1863, Stratford (CT) Historical Society.
34. *The Connecticut War Record* (New Haven, CT: Peck, White, & Peck Publishers, September 1863, Vol. I, No. 3), 33–34.
35. Hines, *Volunteer Sons*, 193.
36. Hines, *Volunteer Sons*, 193.

CHAPTER 3

1. John Niven, *Connecticut For the Union: The Role of the State in the Civil War* (New Haven, CT: Yale University Press, 1965), 233
2. Edward Marcus, ed., *A New Canaan Private in the Civil War: Letters of Justus M. Silliman, 17th Connecticut Volunteers* (New Canaan, CT: New Canaan Historical Society, 1984).

3. *Voices of the Civil War: Chancellorsville* (Alexandria, VA: Time-Life Books), 141–42.
4. Stuart Dempsey, "These Men are No Cowards."
5. James S. Pula, *Under the Crescent Moon with the XI Corps in the Civil War*, Vol. 1 (El Dorado Hills, CA: Savas Beatie), 17
6. George Curtis Waldo Jr., *History of Bridgeport and Vicinity* (Bridgeport, CT: S. J. Clark, 1917), 608–9.
7. Pula, *Under the Crescent Moon*, 17–18.
8. Pula, *Under the Crescent Moon*, 27.
9. Wilson French to Martha Bouton French, April 1863.
10. American Civil War Research Database, www.civilwardata.com.
11. Selah Blakeman correspondence, Stratford Historical Society; James Middlebrook correspondence, Connecticut Historical Society.
12. Wilson French to Martha Bouton French, April 1863.
13. 1860 census, Ancestry.com.
14. Charles P. Hamblen, *Connecticut Yankees at Gettysburg*, ed. Walter L. Powell (Kent, OH: Kent State University Press, 1993), 20.
15. Dr. Robert Hubbard, 17th Connecticut Surgeon, to his wife, May–June 1863, *The Letters of Robert Hubbard M.D.*, United States Army Heritage and Education Center, Carlisle, PA, 20182960MN000001.pdf.
16. John Banks Civil War Blog, http://john-banks.blogspot.com/2014/05/gettysburg-death-of-17th-connecticut-lt.html.
17. J. P. Rogers, Oliver Cromwell Case blog, https://olivercromwellcase.wordpress.com/2017/03/04/douglass-fowler-what-might-have-been/.
18. William Warren, "No. 13—Looking North Toward Gettysburg," 17thcvi.org: An Online History of the 17th Connecticut Volunteer Infantry During the U.S. Civil War, https://seventeenthcvi.org/blog/history-index/william-warren-history/the-warren-articles-13-17/.
19. Dempsey, "These Men Are No Cowards."
20. Bradley M. Gottfried, *The Brigades of Gettysburg: The Union and Confederate Brigades at the Battle of Gettysburg* (New York: Skyhorse 2002, 2012), 311.
21. Wilson French to Martha Bouton French, June 1863.
22. Diana Halderman Loski, *The Chamberlains of Brewer* (Gettysburg, PA: Thomas Publications, 1998), 15.
23. Pula, *Under the Crescent Moon*, 267.
24. Pula, *Under the Crescent Moon*, 267.
25. Gottfried, *The Brigades of Gettysburg*, 304.
26. Richard F. Welch, *The Boy General: The Life and Careers of Francis Channing Barlow* (Kent State University Press, 2003), 73.
27. Pula, *Under the Crescent Moon*, 130.
28. Gottfried, *The Brigades of Gettysburg*, 304.
29. Welch, *The Boy General*, 75.
30. Welch, *The Boy General*, 78.
31. Welch, *The Boy General*, 78.
32. Warren, "Looking North Toward Gettysburg."
33. Warren, "Looking North Toward Gettysburg."
34. Pula, *Under the Crescent Moon*, Introduction.
35. Pula, *Under the Crescent Moon*, Introduction.
36. Pula, *Under the Crescent Moon*, 247.
37. Warren, "Looking North Toward Gettysburg."
38. Wilson French to Martha Bouton French, June 17, 1863.
39. 1860 Census, Ancestry.com.
40. 17thcvi.org.

41. Welch, *The Boy General*, 75.
42. Pula, *Under the Crescent Moon*, 271–72.
43. Pula, *Under the Crescent Moon*, 272.
44. Pula, *Under the Crescent Moon*, 264.
45. Warren, "Looking North Toward Gettysburg."
46. Betty Ann McNeil, *Charity Afire Civil War Trilogy: Maryland* (Hanover, PA: Sheridan Press, 2011), 9.
47. Warren Manuscript, "Gleanings," 802.
48. John Allen Miller, "Emmitsburg: The Pivotal Crossroad of the Civil War," Emmitsburg Area Historical Society, https://www.emmitsburg.net/archive_list/articles/history/civil_war/short_history_of_civil_way.htm.
49. Miller, "Emmitsburg."
50. Miller, "Emmitsburg."
51. Miller, "Emmitsburg."
52. William Warren, "Article No. 14—Gettysburg," 17thcvi.org: An Online History of the 17th Connecticut Volunteer Infantry During the U.S. Civil War, https://seventeenthcvi.org/blog/history-index/william-warren-history/the-warren-articles-13-17/.
53. Warren Manuscript, letter from T. Bradley, March 5, 1887.
54. St. Joseph's Emmitsburg, Marriage Record, September 25, 1866, p. 38; Reel M2833.
55. James Ainscow, Pension Application #1267650, Certificate #1039684, National Archives.
56. Ancestry.com, death record and burial information.
57. https://www.findagrave.com/.
58. McNeil, *Charity Afire: Maryland*, 8.
59. McNeil, *Charity Afire: Maryland*, 8.
60. Harry W. Pfanz, *Gettysburg: Culp's Hill and Cemetery Hill* (Chapel Hill and London: University of North Carolina Press, 1993), 245.
61. Pfanz, *Gettysburg: Culp's Hill and Cemetery Hill*, 246
62. Pula, *Under the Crescent Moon*, 279.
63. 1860 census, Ancestry.com; Widows Pension application #15102, certificate #15102, Fold3.com.
64. William Warren, "No. 1—The Literature of the Time," 17thcvi.org, An Online History of the 17th Connecticut Volunteer Infantry During the U.S. Civil War, https://seventeenthcvi.org/blog/history-index/william-warren-history/articles-1-4/.
65. *Pictorial and Biographical Memoirs of Indianapolis and Marion County, Indiana; Together with Biographies of Many Prominent Men of Other Portions of the State, Both Living and Dead* (Goodspeed Brothers 1893), 104–5.
66. Betsey J. Daniels, Last Will and Testament, November, 1863, Ancestry.com.
67. Warren Manuscript, Vol. 3: Gettysburg, letter from Milton Daniels, January 14, 1886.

CHAPTER 4

1. James S. Pula, *Under the Crescent Moon with the XI Corps in the Civil War*, Vol 2 (El Dorado Hills, CA: Savas Beatie), 3.
2. Charles P. Hamblen, *Connecticut Yankees at Gettysburg*, ed. Walter L. Powell (Kent, OH: Kent State University Press, 1993), 4.
3. Charles Teague, compiler, *Gettysburg by the Numbers* (Gettysburg, PA: Adams County Historical Society), 6.
4. Warren Manuscript, Vol. 3, "Gettysburg," Bridgeport History Center.
5. Teague, *Gettysburg by the Numbers*, 12.
6. Teague, *Gettysburg by the Numbers*, 14, 15.
7. *Gettysburg Daily*, "Eleventh Corps at Gettysburg Part 1 with Licensed Battlefield Guide Stuart Dempsey," July 11, 2009.
8. Pula, *Under the Crescent Moon* Vol. 2, 3.

9. Warren Manuscript, "Gettysburg," letter from Milton Daniels, January 14, 1886.
10. 1860 census, Ancestry.com.
11. Warren Manuscript, "Gettysburg," letter from T. Bradley, March 5, 1887.
12. Warren Manuscript, Bridgeport History Center, W. W. Paynton, "From Virginia to Gettysburg and Back," Chapter 1.
13. Gettysburg's Stone Sentinels, https://gettysburg.stonesentinels.com/union-monuments/vermont/13th-vermont/.
14. Warren Manuscript, Bridgeport History Center, Volume 3, "Gettysburg," W. W. Paynton, From Virginia to Gettysburg and Back, Chapter 1.
15. Warren Manuscript, "The Battle of Gettysburg as Seen by the Writer," Wednesday, July 1, 1863, William Warren.
16. Warren Manuscript, Vol. 3, "Gettysburg," letter from J. Henry Blakeman, April 30, 1888.
17. Philip Laino, *Gettysburg Campaign Atlas*, 3rd ed. (Trumbull, CT: Gettysburg Publishing, 2014), 76, 77.
18. Laino, *Gettysburg Campaign Atlas*, 122–23.
19. Laino, *Gettysburg Campaign Atlas*, 122, 123.
20. Laino, *Gettysburg Campaign Atlas*, 123.
21. Pula, *Under the Crescent Moon*, 40.
22. Hamblen, *Connecticut Yankees*, 18.
23. Hamblen, *Connecticut Yankees*, 18.
24. Major Brady's Field Report to Head Quarters, 17th Regt, Conn, Vol., July 4, 1863, 17th Regt, Source: Official Records, Series I. Vol. 27. Part I. Reports. Serial No. 43.
25. Warren Manuscript, Bridgeport History Center, Volume 3, "Gettysburg," First Day at Gettysburg, Albert Peck.
26. Warren Manuscript, Bridgeport History Center, Volume 3, "Gettysburg," letter from C. Frederick Betts, July 22, 1884.
27. Laino, *Gettysburg Campaign Atlas*, 123.
28. *Battles and Leaders of the Civil War, The Tide Shifts, Volume III*, Editorial Staff of The Century Magazine (Copyright by Castle, Secaucus, NJ, 1982), p. 281.
29. Laino, *Gettysburg Campaign Atlas*, 124.
30. Richard F. Welch, *The Boy General: The Life and Careers of Francis Channing Barlow* (Kent, OH: Kent State University Press, 2003), 84.
31. Welch, *The Boy General*, 84.
32. Bradley M. Gottfried, *Brigades of Gettysburg* (New York: Skyhorse, 2002, 2012), 313.
33. Gregory A. Coco, *A Vast Sea of Misery* (Gettysburg, PA: Thomas Publications, 1988), 124.
34. Pula, *Under the Crescent Moon*, 49.
35. Warren Manuscript, "Gettysburg."
36. Warren Manuscript, Bridgeport History Center, Vol. 3, "Gettysburg," letter from J. Henry Blakeman, April 30, 1888.
37. Laino, *Gettysburg Campaign Atlas*, 124.
38. Harry W. Pfanz, *Gettysburg: The First Day* (Chapel Hill and London: University of North Carolina Press, 2001), 247.
39. William Augustus Croffut and John Mosses Morris, *The Military and Civil History of Connecticut During the War of 1861–65* (New York: Ledyard Brill, 1868), 733, 734.
40. Hamblen, *Connecticut Yankees*, 24.
41. Warren Manuscript, Bridgeport History Center, handwritten account from *Bridgeport Standard*, July 9, 1863.
42. Scott L. Mingus Sr., *The Louisiana Tigers in the Gettysburg Campaign, June–July, 1863* (Baton Rouge: Louisiana State University Press, 1998), 108–9.
43. Major Brady's Field Report to Head Quarters, 17th Regt, Conn, Vol., July 4, 1863, 17th Regt, Source: Official Records, Series I. Vol. 27. Part I. Reports. Serial No. 43.

44. Laino, *Gettysburg Campaign Atlas*, 124–25.
45. Coco, *Vast Sea of Misery*, 13.
46. Coco, *Vast Sea of Misery*, 13.
47. Coco, *Vast Sea of Misery*, 13.
48. Coco, *Vast Sea of Misery*, 13.
49. Coco, *Vast Sea of Misery*, 13.
50. Major Brady's Field Report to Head Quarters, 17th Regt, Conn, Vol., July 4, 1863, 17th Regt, Source: Official Records, Series I. Vol. 27. Part I. Reports. Serial No. 43.
51. Hamblen, *Connecticut Yankees*, 29.
52. Warren Manuscript, Bridgeport History Center, Vol. 3, "Gettysburg," First Day at Gettysburg by Albert W. Peck, Newtown, Conn, April 2, 1887.
53. Major Brady's Field Report to Head Quarters, 17th Regt, Conn, Vol., July 4, 1863, 17th Regt, Source: Official Records, Series I. Vol. 27. Part I. Reports. Serial No. 43.
54. Warren Manuscript, Bridgeport History Center, Vol. 3, "Gettysburg," First Day at Gettysburg by Albert W. Peck, Newtown, Conn, April 2, 1887.

CHAPTER 5

1. American Civil War Research Database, Fold3, Ancestry.com, Find-A-Grave.
2. Find-A-Grave.
3. Warren Manuscript, Bridgeport History Center, Vol. 3, "Gettysburg," William Warren's account of July 1, 1863.
4. William Warren, "No. 14—Gettysburg," 17thcvi.org, An Online History of the 17th Connecticut Volunteer Infantry During the U.S. Civil War. https://seventeenthcvi.org/blog/history-index/william-warren-history/the-warren-articles-13-17/.
5. *Pictorial and Biographical Memoirs of Indianapolis and Marion County, Indiana; Together with Biographies of Many Prominent Men of Other Portions of the State, Both Living and Dead* (Goodspeed Brothers 1893), 104–5.
6. Fold3, Widow's Pension File for Julia A. Boughton Dauchy and son Frederick Oscar Dauchy.
7. Warren Manuscript, Vol. 3, letter from Milton H. Daniels, January 14, 1886.
8. Jack Saunders, "The Ridgefield Encyclopedia: A compendium of more than 3,300 people, places and things relating to Ridgefield, Connecticut," https://ridgefieldlibrary.org/wp-content/uploads/2020/04/Ridgefield-Encyclopedia-Updated-4-14-2020.pdf.
9. Lee's letter is on the 17th CVI website and is reprinted here with permission. The letter was provided to the 17th CVI website by Eric Johnson of the Ridgefield Historical Society. https://seventeenthcvi.org/blog/the-soldiers-story/corporal-aaron-w-lee-company-g/.
10. Satterlee U.S.A. General Hospital, West Philadelphia, c1864, https://www.flickr.com/photos/library-company-of-philadelphia/4679112953/poor.
11. Satterlee U.S.A. General Hospital, West Philadelphia, c1864, https://www.flickr.com/photos/library-company-of-philadelphia/4679112953/poor.
12. Jack Sanders, "Who Was Who, Grasping the Colors," https://www.facebook.com/groups/oldridgefield, April 16, 2017.
13. W. A. Croffut and John M. Morris, *Military and Civil History of Connecticut during the War of 1861–65* (New York: Ledyard Brill, 1868), 392.
14. Sanders, "Who Was Who."
15. Sanders, "Who Was Who."
16. Warren Manuscript, Vol. 3, *Norwalk Gazette*, July 21, 1863, page 2, http://CTdigitalarchive.org.
17. Ancestry.com, 1860 census, Find-A-Grave.
18. Warren Manuscript, Vol. 3, undated narrative titled "John H. Benedict Wounded."
19. Warren Manuscript, Vol. 3, letter from J. Henry Blakeman, April 30, 1888.

20. Edward Marcus, ed. *A New Canaan Private in the Civil War: Letters of Justus M. Silliman, 17th Connecticut Volunteers* (New Canaan, CT: New Canaan Historical Society, 1984), 48.
21. Ancestry.com, 1860 census.
22. Marcus, *A New Canaan Private*, ix.
23. *Appleton's Cyclopedia of American Biography, 1600–1889, Vol. V: Pickering-Sumter*, 590.
24. Marcus, *A New Canaan Private*, v.
25. Ancestry, 1850 census, 1860 census, Find-A-Grave, American Civil War Research Database.
26. Marcus, *A New Canaan Private*, 43, 48.
27. Amy Sohn, *The Man Who Hated Women: Sex Censorship, and Civil Liberties in the Gilded Age* (New York: Farrar, Straus and Giroux, 2021), 21, 23, 24.
28. Marcus, A New Canaan Private, 41.
29. Warren Manuscript, Vol. 3, letter from Justus M. Silliman, August 2nd 1884.
30. James S. Pula, *Under the Crescent Moon with the XI Corps in the Civil War*, Vol. 1 (El Dorado Hills, CA: Savas Beatie, 2017), 267.
31. Warren Manuscript, Bridgeport History Center, Find-A-Grave, Ancestry.com, Census data.
32. Warren Manuscript, Vol. 3, letter from Charles E. Doty, February 8, 1886.
33. Stuart Dempsey, email to the author, March 11, 2019.
34. *Commemorative Biographical Record of Fairfield County, Connecticut: Containing Biographical Sketches of Prominent and Representative Citizens, and of Many of the Early Settled Families* (Higginson Book Company, 1899), 1021.
35. Albert W. Peck obituary, *Newtown Bee*, April 12, 1918; Albert W. Peck obituary, *Bridgeport Evening Farmer*, April 8, 1918; George Frederick Shrady, Editor, *Medical Record*, A Weekly Journal of Medicine and Surgery, Volume 93, William Wood and Company, 1918, p. 462.
36. American Civil War Research Database, www.civilwardata.com.
37. Warren Manuscript, Vol. 3, letter from Albert W. Peck, April 2, 1887.
38. American Civil War Research Database, civilwardata.com.
39. Warren Manuscript; American Civil War Research Database, civilwardata.com.
40. American Civil War Research Database, civilwardata.com.
41. 1860 Census records, Ancestry.com.
42. Fold3.com, Widow's Pension for Sara L. (Dowd) Wilcox.
43. American Civil War Research Database, www.civilwardata.com.
44. Digital Library Company of Philadelphia, digital.librarycompany.org: description of photographic print of South Street Hospital, 1863.
45. Warren Manuscript, Vol. 3.
46. Warren Manuscript, Vol. 1.
47. Warren Manuscript, handwritten account of William Wurtz, Day 1.
48. Census data, Ancestry.com; Find-A-Grave, American Civil War Research Database, civilwardata.com.
49. William Harrison Taylor, *Taylor's Connecticut Legislative History and Souvenir*, Vol. 5, 1905–1906 (Putnam, 1905), 267. https://www.cga.ct.gov/hco/books/Taylors_Legislative_History_Souvenir_CT_1905_Vol_V.pdf.
50. Find-A-Grave.
51. Warren Manuscript, Vol. 3, undated letter, probably 1885, from DeWitt C. Ruscoe.
52. Find-A-Grave.
53. *Medical and Surgical History of the War of the Rebellion* 1861–65, Vol. 2, Part 3, 228.
54. Find-A-Grave, Ancestry.com census data.
55. Ancestry.com census data; American Civil War Research Database, U.S. Prisoner of War Records.
56. Census data, Ancestry.com; Find-A-Grave.

57. Travis W. Busey and John W. Busey, *Union Casualties at Gettysburg*, Volume 3, McFarland & Company, Inc., Jefferson, North Carolina, and London, 2011, 1293.
58. Warren Manuscript, Vol. 3, letter from Henry Quien, July 13, 1895.
59. Census data, Ancestry.com.
60. American Civil War Research Database, www.civilwar.com.
61. Warren Manuscript, undated account from John Collins.
62. Ronald D. Kirkwood, *Too Much for Human Endurance: The George Spangler Farm Hospitals and the Battle of Gettysburg* (El Dorado Hills, CA: Savas Beatie, 2019), 338.
63. *Hartford Courant*, August 29, 1863; 17th cvi.org, "Lincoln, Gettysburg and 199 Pages," November 18, 2012, www.seventeenthcvi.org/blog/lincoln-getysburg-and-199-pages.
64. J. Henry Blakeman letter, July 4, 1863, Book 40, Lewis Leigh Collection, U.S. Army Heritage Center, USAHEC.
65. Census data, Ancestry.com; Find-A-Grave, American Civil War Research Database, civilwarddata.com.
66. Census data, Ancestry.com; Find-A-Grave, American Civil War Research Database, civilwarddata.com.
67. Warren Manuscript, Vol. 3.
68. 17thCVI.org rosters; American Civil War Research Database, www.civilwardata.com.
69. Warren Manuscript, Vol. 10, handwritten.
70. *Danbury News*, January 14, 1880, printed a candidate bio when Bartram ran for constable in Redding. He severed several terms in that office, Bartram family records courtesy of Sheila Bartram Hislop.
71. Margaret M. Wixted, "Recalling Redding During the Civil War: An Interview with Miss Nellie Bartram in the Late 1940s." *Pilot* (Redding Connecticut), April 11, 1991. Bartram family records courtesy of Sheila Bartram Hislop.
72. Ancestry.com census data.
73. Find-A-Grave; obituary and news article from the *Danbury Times* courtesy of Charlene Henderson.
74. Warren Manuscript, Vol. 3, letter from David S. Bartram, January 26, 1886.
75. Ancestry.com, Census data, Find-A-Grave, www.civilwardata.com.
76. Warren Manuscript, Vol. 10, handwritten, 189.
77. Census data, Ancestry.com; Find-A-Grave, American Civil War Research Database, civilwardata .com.
78. "Reunions," 17thcvi.org, https://seventeenthcvi.org/blog/veterans/.
79. Kirkwood, *Too Much for Human Endurance*, 344.
80. American Civil War Research Database, civilwardata.com.
81. American Civil War Research Database, civilwardata.com; 1860 Census data, Ancestry.com.
82. *Norwalk Gazette*, July 14, 1863; New York Grand Army of the Republic Records, 1866–1931 at Ancestry.com; Find-A-Grave.
83. Pula, *Under the Crescent Moon*, Vol. 2, 37–38.
84. Gerry S. Caughman, *Qui transtulit sustinet: Connecticut Battle Flag Collection* (Wethersfield, CT: Caughman Associates, [2011], 2006), 162, 165.
85. Ancestry.com census data, American Civil War Research Database, www.civilwardata.com
86. Casualty list for 17th Connecticut printed in the *Norwalk Gazette*, Tuesday, July 7, 1863.
87. American Civil War Research Database, civilwardata.com.
88. Ancestry.com census data; American Civil War Research Database, www.civilwardata.com; Find-A-Grave.
89. Ancestry.com census data; American Civil War Research Database, www.civilwardata.com; Find-A-Grave.

90. https://seventeenthcvi.org/blog/the-soldiers-story/stephen-r-wilcox/. This letter was found in the Hawxhurst Collection, Norwalk History Room, Norwalk Public Library and was transcribed by Paul Keroack.
91. French Family Papers.
92. French Family Papers.
93. John Niven, *Connecticut for the Union: The Role of the State in the Civil War* (New Haven, CT: Yale University Press, 1965), 229.
94. https://www.nps.gov/ande/learn/historyculture/wirztestimonies.htm.
95. *Bridgeport Evening Farmer*, July 30, 1912.
96. Warren Manuscript (due to numerous Warren revisions, either page 809 or page 222).
97. Major Brady's Field Report to Head Quarters, 17th Regt, Conn, Vol., July 4, 1863, 17th Regt, Source: Official Records, Series I. Vol. 27. Part I. Reports. Serial No. 43.
98. Kirkwood, *Too Much for Human Endurance*, 342.
99. *Danbury News*, January 14, 1880.
100. Warren Manuscript, Vol. 3.
101. *Bridgeport Evening Standard*, Thursday, July 9, 1863, microfilm, Bridgeport History Center.
102. Warren Manuscript, Vol. 10, handwritten, 187.
103. Letters of Dr. Robert Hubbard, USAHEC.
104. Letters of Dr. Robert Hubbard, USAHEC, Letter 31, Brookes Station, Va., April 16, 1863.
105. Census data; Ancestry.com; American Civil War Research Database; Waite & Bartlett Company illustrated prices lists, 1896 and various years, Open Library. https://openlibrary.org/works/OL15686263W/Illustrated_price_list_of_electro-medical_and_electro-surgical_instruments_for_physicians_and_surgeo?edition=illustratedprice00wait. Directory of Deceased American Physicians 1804–1929.
106. "A Legacy of Caring: The History of Picker International," http://www.trevorwright.com/GEC/Journals/GEC_Review/v10n2/p103.pdf.
107. Find-A-Grave. Illustrated price list of electro-medical and electro-surgical instruments for physicians and surgeons (1896).
108. https://seventeenthcvi.org/blog/rosters/company-a/.
109. Census data, 1910, for Fishkill, New York, and Darien, Connecticut.
110. U.S. Civil War Pension Index: General Index to Pension Files, 1861–1934.
111. *Hartford Courant*, https://www.courant.com/news/connecticut/hc-xpm-2014-07-13-hc-civil-war-fitch-0713-20140712-story.html.
112. Warren Manuscript, author William Paynton's Notebooks.
113. Warren Manuscript, Vol. 3, "From Virginia to Gettysburg and Back Written by W. W. Paynton."
114. Warren Manuscript, Vol. 3, letter from William O. Merritt, August 26, 1896.
115. Jim Slade and John Alexander, *Firestorm at Gettysburg: Civilian Voices, June–November 1863* (Atglen, PA: Schiffer Military/Aviation History, 1998), 58, 88.
116. Bobby Housch, "East Cemetery Hill 1," program for the Adams County Historical Society, January 28, 2021.

CHAPTER 6

1. Silas Casey, *Infantry Tactics, for the Instruction, Exercise, and Manœuvres of the soldier, a company, line of skirmishers, battalion, brigade, or Corps d'Armée* (New York: D. Van Nostrand, 1862).
2. Geraldine Caughman, *Qui transtulit sustinet: Connecticut Battle Flag Collection* (Wethersfield, CT: Caughman Associates, [2011], 2006), 158.
3. Caughman, *Qui transtulit sustinet*, 164.
4. Caughman, *Qui transtulit sustinet*, 165.

5. *Hartford Courant*, Wednesday, September 17, 1879.
6. Caughman, *Qui transtulit sustinet*, 162.
7. Caughman, *Qui transtulit sustinet*, 167.
8. Caughman, *Qui transtulit sustinet*, 167.
9. Michael Dreese, *Never Desert the Old Flag: 50 Stories of Union Battle Flags and Color-Bearers at Gettysburg* (Gettysburg, PA: Thomas Publications, 2002), 43.
10. Dreese, *Never Desert the Old Flag*, 43.
11. Dreese, *Never Desert the Old Flag*, 43.
12. Dreese, *Never Desert the Old Flag*, 43.
13. Warren Manuscript, Bridgeport History Center, Vol. 3, "Gettysburg."
14. Warren Manuscript, Vol. 3, letter from William F. Otis, July 27, 1894.
15. CT Casualty List 189, MD Reg. No. 259, researched and provided to the author courtesy of James Fielden.
16. Warren Manuscript, Vol. 3, letter from J. C. Mayne, June 7, 1884.
17. Warren Manuscript, Vol. 10, handwritten, 28.
18. Warren Manuscript, Vol. 3, letter from James Ainscow, September 3, 1896.
19. Ronald Coddington, "Casualties on Barlow's Knoll—Now 17th Do Your Duty," American Battlefield Trust, https://www.battlefields.org/learn/articles/casualties-barlows-knoll.
20. American Civil War Research Database, civilwardata.com; 1860 Census data, Ancestry.com.
21. Warren Manuscript, Vol. 3, letter from C. Frederick Betts, May 22, 1884.
22. Warren Manuscript, Vol. 3, letter from Albert W. Peck, April 2, 1887.
23. Warren Manuscript, Vol. 3, letter from Albert W. Peck, April 2, 1887.
24. Find-A-Grave, Ancestry.com, American Civil War Research Database www.civilwardata.com.
25. American Civil War Research Database www.civilwardata.com.
26. Warren Manuscript, Vol. 3, Thomas A. Marsh Wounded at Gettysburg.
27. Warren Manuscript, Vol. 3, Thomas A. Marsh Wounded at Gettysburg.
28. Find-A-Grave, Ancestry.com, American Civil War Research Database www.civilwardata.com.
29. Warren Manuscript, Photographic Index, 21.
30. Connecticut Historical Society, Middlebrook, James, Robert (1832–1908), location MS 73139 Box.
31. Warren Manuscript, Photographic Index, 27.
32. Connecticut Historical Society, Middlebrook, James, Robert (8132–1908), location MS 73139 Box.
33. CT Casualty List 189, PA Reg. No. 350, researched and provided to the author courtesy of James Fielden.
34. Find-A-Grave, Ancestry.com, American Civil War Research Database, civilwardata.com.

CHAPTER 7

1. Charles Teague, compiler, *Gettysburg by the Numbers* (Gettysburg, PA: Adams County Historical Society, 2006), 12.
2. Teague, *Gettysburg by the Numbers*, 12.
3. Jay Alfred Bollet, *Civil War Medicine: Challenges and Triumphs* (Tucson, AZ: Galen Press, 2002), 356.
4. Warren Manuscript, Bridgeport History Center, Vol. 3, "Gettysburg," letter from Albert W. Peck, April 2, 1887.
5. Warren Manuscript, Vol. 3, letter from Milton H. Daniels, January 14, 1886.
6. Warren Manuscript, handwritten accounts, William Fields, November 30, 1885.
7. Charles P. Hamblen, *Connecticut Yankees at Gettysburg*, ed. Walter L. Powell (Kent, OH: Kent State University Press, 1993), 30–31.
8. Warren Manuscript, Vol. 3, letter from Milton H. Daniels, January 14, 1886.

9. Major Brady's Field Report to Head Quarters, 17th Regt, Conn, Vol., July 4, 1863, 17th Regt, Source: Official Records, Series I. Vol. 27. Part I. Reports. Serial No. 43.
10. Major Brady's Field Report.
11. Philip Laino, *Gettysburg Campaign Atlas*, 3rd ed. (Trumbull, CT: Gettysburg Publishing, 2014), 294.
12. Warren Manuscript, Vol. 4, undated statement and comments from Peck to Warren.
13. Multiple sources; see specifically Laino, *Gettysburg Campaign Atlas*, 292, 294, 295, 296.
14. Historic American Engineering Record, Creator, Emmor B. Cope, Gettysburg Battlefield Memorial Association, Bureau of Public roads, U.S. Department of War, GNMP Park Tour Roads, Library of Congress, https://www.loc.gov/item/pa.
15. *Gettysburg Daily*, June 21, 2011, https://www.gettysburgdaily.com/section-of-brickyard-lane-revealed-for-what-may-be-a-short-period/.
16. John, M. Archer, *East Cemetery Hill at Gettysburg: The Hour Was One of Horror* (Gettysburg, PA: Thomas Publications, 1997), 81, 85.
17. Warren Manuscript, Vol. 3, letter from J. H. Blakeman, April 30, 1888.
18. James Pula, "'A Promiscuous Fight': Defense of Cemetery Hill," *Gettysburg Magazine* no. 59 (July 2018), 28.
19. James Pula, *Under the Crescent Moon with the XI Corps in the Civil War, Volume 2: From Gettysburg to Victory, 1863–1865* (El Dorado Hills, CA: Savas Beatie, 2018), 144.
20. Pula, "'A Promiscuous Fight,'" 16.
21. Pula, "'A Promiscuous Fight,'" 17.
22. Denise Doyle Killmeyer, *The Vision-Place of Souls: Encounter at Cemetery Hill* (Friends of the National Parks Gettysburg, 2003), 14, 15, 16.
23. Albert W. Peck, *Civil War Reminisces, 1862–1865* (Connecticut Historical Society, 1906), call #86269, 23.
24. Peck, *Civil War Reminisces*, 25.
25. Peck, *Civil War Reminisces*, 25.
26. Laino, Gettysburg Campaign Atlas, 278.
27. Archer, East Cemetery Hill, 24.
28. Laino, Gettysburg Campaign Atlas, 288.
29. Archer, *East Cemetery Hill*, 27.
30. Edward Marcus, ed. *A New Canaan Private in the Civil War: Letters of Justus M. Silliman, 17th Connecticut Volunteers* (New Canaan, CT: New Canaan Historical Society, 1984), 42.
31. Archer, East Cemetery Hill, 28.
32. Archer, East Cemetery Hill, 28.
33. Peck, *Civil War Reminisces*, 25.
34. Pula, *Under the Crescent Moon* Vol. 2, 137.
35. Ronald, D. Kirkwood, *Too Much for Human Endurance: The George Spangler Farm Hospitals and the Battle of Gettysburg* (El Dorado Hills, CA: Savas Beatie, 2019), 154, 155.
36. Archer, *East Cemetery Hill*, 28.
37. Laino, *Gettysburg Campaign Atlas*, 283.
38. Scott Mingus, *The Louisiana Tigers in the Gettysburg Campaign, June–July 1863* (Baton Rouge: Louisiana State University Press, 2009), 144.
39. Archer, *East Cemetery Hill*, 32, 33.
40. Laino, *Gettysburg Campaign Atlas*, 288, 290, 291.
41. Peck, *Civil War Reminisces*, 26.
42. Laino, *Gettysburg Campaign Atlas*, 292, 294.
43. Killmeyer, *The Vision-Place of Souls*, 15.
44. Archer, *East Cemetery Hill*, 41.
45. Major Brady's Field Report.

46. Laino, *Gettysburg Campaign Atlas*, 314.
47. Pula, *Under the Crescent Moon Volume 2*, 149.
48. Laino, *Gettysburg Campaign Atlas*, 295.
49. Killmeyer, *The Vision-Place of Souls*, 16.
50. Archer, *East Cemetery Hill*, 49, 50, 52.
51. Laino, *Gettysburg Campaign Atlas*, 295.
52. Major Brady's Field Report.
53. Warren Manuscript, Vol. 3, W. W. Paynton, Chapter 3rd.
54. Warren Manuscript, Vol. 3, W. W. Paynton, Chapter 3rd.
55. Casualty lists compiled and transcribed by researcher James Fielden from source documents: CT Casualty list 189, PA Reg. No. 554, NJ Reg. No. 54, NJ Reg. No. 54.
56. Warren Manuscript, Vol. 3, W. W. Paynton, Chapter 3rd.
57. Archer, East Cemetery Hill, 53.
58. Warren Manuscript, Vol. 3.
59. Pula, "'A Promiscuous Fight,'" 18.
60. Warren Manuscript, Vol. 3, letter from C. Frederick Betts, July 22, 1884.
61. Pula, "'A Promiscuous Fight,'" 19.
62. Warren Manuscript, Vol. 3, "The Third Day at Gettysburg," Albert W. Peck.
63. Harry W. Pfanz, *Gettysburg: Culp's Hill and Cemetery Hill* (Chapel Hill and London: University of North Carolina Press, 1993), 253.
64. Archer, *East Cemetery Hill*, 66.
65. Mingus, *The Louisiana Tigers*, 156, 157.
66. Archer, *East Cemetery Hill*, 66.
67. Pula, "'A Promiscuous Fight,'" 24.
68. Archer, *East Cemetery Hill*, 65.
69. Archer, *East Cemetery Hill*, 65.
70. Peck, *Civil War Reminisces*, 27.
71. Pula, *Under the Crescent Moon*, Vol. 2, 158.
72. Mingus, *The Louisiana Tigers*, 176.
73. Laino, *Gettysburg Campaign Atlas*, 314.
74. Mingus, *The Louisiana Tigers*, 169.
75. Laino, *Gettysburg Campaign Atlas*, 314.
76. Pfanz, *Gettysburg: Culp's Hill and Cemetery Hill*, 275.
77. Pfanz, *Gettysburg: Culp's Hill and Cemetery Hill*, 181.
78. Major Brady's Field Report.
79. Laino, *Gettysburg Campaign Atlas*, 301.
80. Peck, *Civil War Reminisces*, 26.
81. Archer, *East Cemetery Hill*, 77.
82. *The National Tribune* (Washington, DC), "At Gettysburg Lieut. Peck Tells What Carroll's Brigade Did," Nov. 24 1892, 4.
83. Laino, *Gettysburg Campaign Atlas*, 299.
84. John Bachelder, *Gettysburg: What to See—How to See It*, 7th ed. (Boston: Illustrated Tourist Guide, 1878), 40.

CHAPTER 8

1. Warren Manuscript, Bridgeport History Center, Vol. 3, "Gettysburg," William Warren Diary.
2. Warren Manuscript, Vol. 3, letter from J. Henry Blakeman, April 30, 1888.
3. Gregory A. Coco, *A Vast Sea of Misery: A History and Guide to the Union and Confederate Field Hospitals at Gettysburg, July 1–November 20, 1863* (Gettysburg, PA: Thomas Publications, 1988), 118.

4. Edward Marcus, ed., *A New Canaan Private in the Civil War: Letters of Justus M. Silliman, 17th Connecticut Volunteers* (New Canaan, CT: New Canaan Historical Society, 1984), 41–42.
5. Ancestry, 1850 census, 1860 census, Find-A-Grave, American Civil War Research Database.
6. Warren Manuscript, Vol. 3, William Warren notes on the 17th CV Historical Committee.
7. Warren Manuscript, Vol. 3, letter from Justus Silliman to General Noble, July 28, 1884.
8. Warren Manuscript, Vol. 3, letter from Justus Silliman to General Noble, July 28, 1884.
9. Warren Manuscript, Vol. 3, letter from Milton Daniels, January 14, 1886.
10. Casualty lists compiled and transcribed by researcher James Fielden from source documents: CT Casualty list 189, PA Reg. No. 554, NJ Reg. No. 54.
11. Warren Manuscript, Vol 3, transcribed from W. W. Paynton's account.
12. Bobby Housch, "East Cemetery Hill 1," presentation for the Adams County Historical Society, January 28, 2021.
13. Warren Manuscript, Vol. 3, "Second Day at Gettysburg," Albert W. Peck.
14. Warren Manuscript, Vol. 3.
15. Warren Manuscript, Vol. 3.
16. Warren Manuscript, Vol. 3, letter from Albert Peck, January 2, 1886.
17. Peck, *Civil War Reminisces*, 24.
18. Ancestry.com census data for 1850, 1860, 1870, 1900, 1910; Find-A-Grave.
19. Warren Manuscript, Warren's handwritten account from William T. Fields, December 1885.
20. Ancestry.com census data; American Civil War Research Database, www.civilwardata.com; Find-A-Grave.
21. Pula, *Under the Crescent Moon*, Vol. 2, 218–20.
22. https://seventeenthcvi.org/blog/the-soldiers-story/stephen-r-wilcox/. This letter was found in the Hawxhurst Collection, Norwalk History Room, Norwalk Public Library, transcribed by Paul Keroack.
23. Warren Manuscript, Vol. 3, letter from C. Frederick Betts to Henry Allen, July 22, 1884.

CHAPTER 9

1. Charles Teague, compiler, *Gettysburg by the Numbers* (Gettysburg, PA: Adams County Historical Society, 2006), 12.
2. Major Brady's Field Report to Head Quarters, 17th Regt, Conn, Vol., July 4, 1863, 17th Regt, Source: Official Records, Series I. Vol. 27. Part I. Reports. Serial No. 43.
3. Warren Manuscript, Bridgeport History Center, Vol. 3, "Gettysburg," letter from Milton H. Daniels, January 14, 1886.
4. Albert, W. Peck, *Civil War Reminisces, 1862–1865* (Connecticut Historical Society, 1906), call #86269, 29–30.
5. Cindy L. Small, *Jennie Wade of Gettysburg: The Complete Story of the Only Civilian Killed During the Battle of Gettysburg* (Trumbull, CT: Gettysburg Publishing, 2017), 12, 20, 24.
6. Small, *Jennie Wade*, 25–31.
7. Small, *Jennie Wade*, 32–35, 38–43.
8. Warren Manuscript, Vol. 3, William Warren diary entry, July 3, 1863.
9. Philip Laino, *Gettysburg Campaign Atlas*, 3rd ed. (Trumbull, CT: Gettysburg Publishing, 2014), 322.
10. Warren Manuscript, Vol. 3, letter from Albert Peck, January 2, 1886.
11. Peck, *Civil War Reminisces*, 26–27.
12. Peck, *Civil War Reminisces*, 28.
13. Teague, *Gettysburg by the Numbers*, 12.
14. Warren Manuscript, Vol. 3, "How a Supply of Water was Obtained," W. W. Paynton.
15. American Civil War Research Database, www.civilwardata.com; Ancestry.com; Find-A-Grave.
16. Warren Manuscript, Vol. 3, statement from Frank S. Middlebrook.

17. 1884 Monument Dedication, 17th Connecticut Volunteers at Gettysburg, www.17thcvi.org.
18. American Civil War Research Database, www.civilwardata.com; Ancestry.com; Find-A-Grave.
19. Edward Marcus, ed., *A New Canaan Private in the Civil War: Letters of Justus M. Silliman, 17th Connecticut Volunteers* (New Canaan, CT: New Canaan Historical Society, 1984), 42–43.
20. "Battle 42 Years Ago," *Gettysburg Compiler*, July 5, 1905 (historian Tim Smith located this article).
21. Digital Maryland, https://collections.digitalmaryland.org/digital/collection/cator/id/15/.
22. Warren Manuscript, Vol. 3, letter from Justus Silliman, August 13, 1884.
23. Peck, *Civil War Reminisces*, 27–28; Warren Manuscript, Vol. 3, letter.

CHAPTER 10

1. Gregory A. Coco, *A Vast Sea of Misery: A History and Guide to the Union and Confederate Field Hospitals at Gettysburg, July 1–November 20, 1863* (Gettysburg, PA: Thomas Publications, 1988), 91.
2. Letter from J. Henry Blakeman, July 4, 1863, Lewis Leigh Collection, Book 40, U.S. Army Military History Institute, Carlisle Barracks, PA.
3. Coco, *A Vast Sea of Misery*, 107.
4. Coco, *A Vast Sea of Misery*, 106.
5. Warren Manuscript, Bridgeport History Center, Vol. 3, "Gettysburg," William Warren Diary.
6. Warren Manuscript, Vol. 3, Thomas A. Marsh Wounded at Gettysburg.
7. Warren Manuscript, Vol. 3, Thomas A. Marsh Wounded at Gettysburg.
8. Ronald D. Kirkwood, *Too Much for Human Endurance: The George Spangler Farm Hospitals and the Battle of Gettysburg* (El Dorado Hills, CA: Savas Beatie, 2019), 350.
9. Civil War Research Database, www.civilwardata.org; Find-A-Grave; Ancestry.com.
10. Warren Manuscript, Vol. 3, "From Virginia to Gettysburg and Back," W. W. Paynton, Chapter 4th.
11. Warren Manuscript, Vol. 3, letter from Milton Daniels, Indianapolis, January 14, 1886.
12. Warren Manuscript, Vol. 3, William Warren's handwritten notes from W. T. Fields, December 1885.
13. American Civil War Research Database, www.civilwardata.org.
14. Ancestry.com census data.
15. Warren Manuscript, Vol. 3, F. S. Middlebrook.
16. Ancestry.com, Census records, American Civil War Research Database, www.civilwardata.com.
17. Obituary, December 15, 1899, *Newtown Bee*; Census data and probate records, Ancestry.com.
18. Warren Manuscript, Vol. 3, letter from Patrick Wade, March 1886.
19. Civil War Research Database, www.civilwardata.com.
20. Warren Manuscript, Vol. 3, letter from Albert W. Peck, January 2, 1886.
21. Coco, *A Vast Sea of Misery*, 47.
22. James Gindlesperger, *Bullets & Bandages: The Aid Stations and Field Hospitals at Gettysburg* (Durham, NC: Blair, 2020), 57–58.
23. Peck, *Civil War Reminisces*, 29–30.
24. Peck, *Civil War Reminisces*, 29–30.
25. Warren Manuscript, handwritten account of William Wurtz's experiences.
26. Edward Marcus, ed., *A New Canaan Private in the Civil War: Letters of Justus M. Silliman, 17th Connecticut Volunteers* (New Canaan, CT: New Canaan Historical Society), 1984.
27. Warren Manuscript, Vol. 3, letter from Justus Silliman, August 14, 1884.
28. Marcus, *A New Canaan Private*, 44.
29. Library of Congress, "About The National Tribune (Washington, D.C.) 1877–1917," https://chroniclingamerica.loc.gov/lccn/sn82016187/.

30. Library of Congress, "The National Tribune, October 08, 1896," https://chroniclingamerica.loc.gov/lccn/sn82016187/1896-10-08/ed-1/.

CHAPTER 11

1. James Fielden, researcher and compiler, Hospital Registers from the National Archives; also see casualty list printed July 7, 1863, in the *Norwalk Gazette* and those from *Bridgeport Standard* and *Danbury Times.*
2. Fold3, widow's pension records for 17th Connecticut men with correspondence from company officers.
3. Meg Groeling, *The Aftermath of Battle: the Burial of the Civil War Dead* (El Dorado Hills, CA: Savas Beatie, 2015), 71.
4. Jonathan Letterman, "Official Report of the Battle of Gettysburg," in *The Medical and Surgical History of the War of the Rebellion (1861–65)* Vol 1, Part 1 (Washington: Government Printing Office, 1870–88), 141. https://collections.nlm.nih.gov/bookviewer?PID=nlm:nlmuid-14121350RX1-mvpart#page/942/mode/2up/search/letterman
5. Historic Gettysburg-Adams County and The Hospital & Health System Association of Pennsylvania, Gettysburg Civil War Hospital Tour, July 2001, p. 7
6. Groeling, Meg. The Aftermath of Battle: the Burial of the Civil War Dead. Savas Beatie, 2015, p.46
7. Sheldon, George, When the Smoke Cleared At Gettysburg—The Tragic Aftermath of the Bloodiest Battle of the Civil War, Cumberland House, Nashville, Tennessee, 2003, p.182
8. Letterman, Jonathan, Official Report of the Battle of Gettysburg, The Medical and Surgical History of the War of the Rebellion (1861-65), Washington : G.P.O., 1870-88, Vol 1, Part 1, p. 141 https://collections.nlm.nih.gov/bookviewer?PID=nlm:nlmuid-14121350RX1-mvpart#page/942/mode/2up/search/letterman
9. Historic Gettysburg-Adams County and The Hospital & Health System Association of Pennsylvania, Gettysburg Civil War Hospital Tour, July 2001, p. 7
10. George Sheldon, *When the Smoke Cleared At Gettysburg: The Tragic Aftermath of the Bloodiest Battle of the Civil War* (Nashville: Cumberland House, 2003), 183.
11. Charles Teague, compiler, *Gettysburg by the Numbers* (Gettysburg, PA: Adams County Historical Society, 2006), 38, 39, 40.
12. Sheldon, *When the Smoke Cleared*, 123.
13. Letterman, "Official Report," 141.
14. Gregory A. Coco, *A Vast Sea of Misery: A History and Guide to the Union and Confederate Field Hospitals at Gettysburg, July 1–November 20, 1863* (Gettysburg, PA: Thomas Publications, 1988), 167.
15. Letterman, "Official Report," 142.
16. Coco, *A Vast Sea of Misery*, 167.
17. James Gindlesperger, *Bullets and Bandages: The Aid Stations and Field Hospitals at Gettysburg* (Durham, NC: Blair, 2020), 225–26.
18. Gregory A. Coco, *A Strange and Blighted Land—Gettysburg: The Aftermath of a Battle* (Gettysburg, PA: Thomas Publications, 1995), 167.
19. Barbara Franco, Gettysburg Surgeons Database, provided by email February 29, 2022.
20. Barbara, Franco, Gettysburg Surgeons Database, provided by email February 28, 2022, and March 1, 2022.
21. Warren Manuscript, Bridgeport History Center, undated account from John C. Collins.
22. Gindlesperger, *Bullets and Bandages*, 42.
23. George Curtis Waldo Jr., *History of Bridgeport and Vicinity* (Bridgeport, CT: S. J. Clark, 1917), 5–6, https://seventeenthcvi.org; Obituary Record of Graduates of Yale University, various years, http://mssa.library.yale.edu/obituary_record/.

24. Ancestry.com census data, various years; Civil War Research Database, www.civilwar.com; Find-A-Grave.
25. Blog, Centennial Series, History, Residential Real Estate, 1–2 Franklin Square, Saratoga Springs, December 10, 2015, https://www.roohanrealty.com/blog/franklin-square-part-ii-saratoga-centennial/.
26. Dr. Robert Hubbard Civil War Letters, U.S. Army Heritage and Education Center (USAHEC).
27. Ancestry.com census data, various years, American Civil War Research Database, www.civilwardata.com; Obituary Record of Graduates of Yale University, various years, http://mssa.library.yale.edu/obituary_record/.
28. Elise D. Morey, "Almshouse (Poor House) A House for Employment and Support of the Poor in Adams County," *The Courier*, Cumberland Township Historical Society, Fall 2017.
29. Coco, *A Vast Sea of Misery*, 29.
30. Morey, "Almshouse."
31. Morey, "Almshouse."
32. James Fielden, researcher and compiler, Hospital Registers from the National Archives, CT Casualty list 189, PA Reg. No. 554, PA Reg. No. 217.
33. Warren Manuscript, Bridgeport History Center, Vol. 3, "Gettysburg," letter from Aaron W. Lee, January 31, 1886.
34. "Life and Limb: The Toll of the American Civil War," National Institute of Health, https://www.nlm.nih.gov/exhibition/lifeandlimb/digitaldocuments.html.
35. James Fielden, researcher and compiler, Hospital Registers from the National Archives, CT Casualty list 189, PA Reg. No. 554, PA Reg. No. 568.
36. Warren Manuscript, Vol. 3, letter from John H. Benedict, August 28, 1887.
37. Ancestry.com census data, various years; American Civil War Research Database, www.civilwardata.com.
38. Warren Manuscript, Vol. 3, Gettysburg, letter from John H. Benedict, August 28, 1887.
39. Warren Manuscript, handwritten account of William Wurtz, Day 1.
40. Warren Manuscript, handwritten account of William Wurtz, Day 1.
41. Warren Manuscript, Vol. 3, letter from Justus M. Silliman, August 14, 1884.
42. Coco, *A Vast Sea of Misery*, 123.
43. Coco, *A Vast Sea of Misery*, 123.
44. Major Brady's Field Report to Head Quarters, 17th Regt, Conn, Vol., July 4, 1863, 17th Regt, Source: Official Records, Series I. Vol. 27. Part I. Reports. Serial No. 43.
45. Coco, *A Vast Sea of Misery*, 124.
46. Warren Manuscript, Vol. 3, letter from Justus M. Silliman, August 2, 1884.
47. *Medical and Surgical History*, Volume 2, Part 3, 228.
48. "Janitor Dixon Retires," *The Daily Advocate*, June 25, 1904.
49. "A Trip to Gettysburg," *Stamford Advocate*, May 23, 1884.
50. Gindlesperger, *Bullets and Bandages*, 246, 247, 248.
51. Coco, *A Vast Sea of Misery*, 118–19.
52. Edward Marcus, ed., *A New Canaan Private in the Civil War: Letters of Justus M. Silliman, 17th Connecticut Volunteers* (New Canaan, CT: New Canaan Historical Society, 1984), 41.
53. Marcus, *A New Canaan Private*, 41.
54. Warren Manuscript, Vol. 3, letter from J. Henry Blakeman, April 30, 1888.
55. "Blocher House," Historic American Building Survey/Historic American Engineering Record/Historic American Landscapes Survey, Library of Congress.
56. Gregory A. Coco, *Wasted Valor: The Confederate Dead at Gettysburg* (Gettysburg, PA: Thomas Publications, 1996), 41; Gindlesperger, Bullets and Bandages, 251–52.
57. Gindlesperger, Bullets and Bandages, 107.

58. Michael A. Dreese, *The Hospital on Seminary Ridge at the Battle of Gettysburg* (Jefferson, NC and London: McFarland & Company, 2002), 148, 149.
59. Gindlesperger, *Bullets and Bandages*, 108.
60. Ronald Coddington, "Casualties on Barlow's Knoll—Now 17th Do Your Duty," American Battlefield Trust, https://www.battlefields.org/learn/articles/casualties-barlows-knoll.
61. Fold3, widow's pension for Jane A. Sprague, widow of Private Frank J. Benson, Co. C.
62. Ronald D. Kirkwood, *Too Much for Human Endurance: The George Spangler Farm Hospital and the Battle of Gettysburg* (El Dorado Hills, CA: Savas Beatie, 2019), 336.
63. Kirkwood, *Too Much for Human Endurance*, 369, 370.
64. Jay Alfred Bollet, *Civil War Medicine: Challenges and Triumphs* (Tucson, AZ: 2002), 84.
65. "Barnes, Joseph K.," *Medical and Surgical History*, Vol. 2, Part 1, 6.
66. Fielden, Hospital Registers, CT casualty list 189, PA Reg. No. 554, PA Reg. No. 286.
67. Ancestry.com, American Civil War Research Database, www.civilwardata.com; Find-A-Grave.
68. Coco, *A Vast Sea of Misery*, 13.
69. Coco, *A Vast Sea of Misery*, 13.
70. Coco, *A Vast Sea of Misery*, 13.
71. Warren Manuscript, Vol. 3, from Wilson French.
72. Kirkwood, *Too Much for Human Endurance*, 350.
73. Warren Manuscript, miscellaneous accounts.
74. Warren Manuscript, Vol. 3, undated account.
75. Warren Manuscript, unsigned, handwritten account.
76. Warren Manuscript, handwritten account.
77. Gindlesperger, James, Bullets Bandages, The Aid Stations and Field Hospitals at Gettysburg, Blair, Imprint of Carolina Wren Press, 2020, p. 47
78. Marcus, *A New Canaan Private in the Civil War*, 42.
79. Marcus, *A New Canaan Private in the Civil War*, 42.
80. Warren Manuscript, Vol. 3, Gettysburg, letter from J. Henry Blakeman, April 30, 1888.
81. Warren Manuscript, Vol. 3, Gettysburg, letter from Justus Silliman, July 28, 1884.
82. Coco, *A Vast Sea of Misery*, 28.
83. Gindlesperger, *Bullets and Bandages*, 33, 58.
84. Franco, Gettysburg Surgeons Database, provided by email August 6 and 8, 2020.
85. Ancestry.com census data from various years; Find-A-Grave; Application for Soldier's Pension.
86. Warren Manuscript, Vol. 3, letter from Oscar St. John, August 1890.
87. Warren Manuscript, Vol. 3, letter from Oscar St. John, August 1890.
88. Fred Hawthorne, "140 Places Every Guide Should Know," *Gettysburg Daily*, https://www.gettysburgdaily.com/140-places-every-guide-should-know-part-18-gettysburg-lbg-fred-hawthorne.
89. Dr. Robert Hubbard Civil War Letters, the U.S. Army Heritage and Education Center, USAHEC, letter July 7, 1863.
90. Harry W. Pfanz, *Gettysburg: Culp's Hill & Cemetery Hill* (Chapel Hill and London: University of North Carolina Press, 1993), 371.
91. Gindlesperger, *Bullets and Bandages*, 42.
92. Dr. Robert Hubbard Civil War Letters, the U.S. Army Heritage and Education Center, USAHEC, letter July 7, 1863
93. Dr. Robert Hubbard Civil War Letters, the U.S. Army Heritage and Education Center, USAHEC, letters July 10 and 13, 1863.
94. Brian, A. Kennell, Beyond the Gatehouse: Gettysburg's Evergreen Cemetery (Hanover, PA: Sheridan Press, 2000), 27.
95. Kennell, *Beyond the Gatehouse*, 27–28.
96. Kennell, *Beyond the Gatehouse*, 27–28.

97. Kathryn Porch and Sue Boardman, *Elizabeth Thorn at Gettysburg: The Wartime Caretaker of Evergreen Cemetery* (Trumbull, CT: Gettysburg Publishing, 2013), 16.
98. Kennell, *Beyond the Gatehouse*, 29, 30.
99. Kennell, *Beyond the Gatehouse*, 29, 30.
100. Kennell, *Beyond the Gatehouse*, 31–34.
101. Kennell, *Beyond the Gatehouse*, 45.
102. Deb Novotny, "Tombstones Talk: Evergreen Cemetery Victorian Symbols," walking tour of Evergreen Cemetery, October 9, 2021.
103. Kennell, *Beyond the Gatehouse*, 45.
104. James S. Pula, *Under the Crescent Moon with the XI Corps in the Civil War, Volume 2: From Gettysburg to Victory, 1863–1865* (El Dorado Hills, CA: Savas Beatie, 2018), 134–37.
105. Warren Manuscript, Vol. 3, John C. Collins.
106. *Hartford Courant*, August 29, 1863.
107. Warren Manuscript, Vol. 3, letter from Albert Peck, January 2, 1886.
108. Civil War Rx, http://civilwarrx.blogspot.com/2013/08/closing-chest-wounds.html.
109. The Medical and Surgical History of the War of the Rebellion (1861–65), Barnes, Joseph K., 1817-1883; Washington: G.P.O., 1870-88, https://collections.nlm.nih.gov/catalog/nlm:nlmuid-14121350R-mvset Vol. 2, Part 1, 504.
110. Warren Manuscript, handwritten account of William Wurtz's experiences.
111. Kirkwood, *Too Much for Human Endurance*, 10.
112. Gindlesperger, *Bullets and Bandages*, 191.
113. Teague, *Gettysburg by the Numbers*, 21.
114. Kirkwood, *Too Much for Human Endurance*, 90.
115. Coco, *A Vast Sea of Misery*, 167.
116. Dr. Daniel G. Brinton, *From Chancellorsville to Gettysburg, A Doctor's Diary*, file:///C:/Users/civan/AppData/Local/Temp/42056-Article%20Text-41895-1-10-20121205.pdf.
117. Coco, *A Vast Sea of Misery*, 106.
118. J. Henry Blakeman, letter, Book 40, Lewis Leigh Collection, U.S. Army Military History.
119. Kirkwood, *Too Much for Human Endurance*, 361.
120. Warren Manuscript, Vol. 3, Gettysburg, letter from Justus Silliman, August 14, 1884.
121. Marcus, *A New Canaan Private*, 44.
122. Marcus, *A New Canaan Private*, 45, 46.
123. Kirkwood, *Too Much for Human Endurance*, 361.
124. Kirkwood, *Too Much for Human Endurance*, 361.
125. American Civil War Research Database, www.civilwardata.com.
126. Warren Manuscript, Nephi Whitlock handwritten account.
127. Coco, *A Strange and Blighted Land*, 186, 187
128. Dreese, *The Hospital on Seminary Ridge*, 98.
129. Warren Manuscript, William Wurtz handwritten account.
130. Warren Manuscript, Volume 3.
131. Kirkwood, *Too Much for Human Endurance*, 344.
132. Warren Manuscript, Volume 3.
133. James Fielden, researcher and compiler, Gettysburg Eleventh Corps Casualty Lists, National Archives, CT Casualty list 189, PA Reg. No. 554, MD Reg. No. 14; Civil War Research Database, www.civilwardata.com; Find-A-Grave.
134. Kirkwood, *Too Much for Human Endurance*, 338.
135. Warren Manuscript, Volume 3.
136. Meg Groeling, *The Aftermath of Battle: The Burial of the Civil War Dead* (El Dorado Hills, CA: Savas Beatie, 2015), 71.

137. Coco, *A Vast Sea of Misery*, 159.
138. Coco, *A Vast Sea of Misery*, 160.
139. Coco, *A Vast Sea of Misery*, 160.
140. Kirkwood, *Too Much for Human Endurance*, 354.
141. Warren Manuscript, Volume 3, letter of Pastor J. M. Hinson, July 23, 1863.
142. Gregory A. Coco, *Killed in Action: Eyewitness Accounts of the Last Moments of 100 Union Soldiers Who Died at Gettysburg* (Gettysburg, PA: Thomas Publications, 1992), 23.
143. Coco, *Killed in Action*, 23.
144. Civil War correspondence of Selah G. Blakeman, Company D, Stratford Historical Society.
145. Bollet, *Civil War Medicine*, 265.
146. Letters of James Robert Middlebrook, 17th Connecticut, Company D, Connecticut Historical Society, MS 73139.
147. Gindlesperger, *Bullets and Bandages*, 168.
148. William A. Frassanito, *Early Photography at Gettysburg* (Gettysburg, PA: Thomas Publications, 1995), 140.
149. Coco, *A Vast Sea of Misery*, 56.
150. Warren Manuscript, Volume 3, W. W. Paynton, "Scenes in and Around the Eleventh Corps Hospital."
151. Warren Manuscript, Volume 3, letter from John H. Benedict, August 28, 1887.
152. Kirkwood, *Too Much for Human Endurance*, 351.
153. American Civil War Research Database; Ancestry.com; Find-A-Grave; U.S. Homes for Disabled Volunteer Soldiers, 1866–1938.
154. Kirkwood, *Too Much for Human Endurance*, 335.
155. Warren Manuscript, Volume 3, letter from John H. Benedict, August 28, 1887.
156. Warren Manuscript, Vol. 3, Gettysburg, letter from John H. Benedict, August 28, 1887.
157. Kirkwood, Too Much for Human Endurance, 283–85.
158. Coco, A Vast Sea of Misery, 167.
159. Medical and Surgical History of the War of the Rebellion (1861–65) Volume 2, Part 3, p. 228; James Fielden, researcher and compiler: Hospital Registers from the National Archives, CT PA Reg. No. 554, PA Reg. No. 373.
160. James Fielden, researcher and compiler: Hospital Registers from the National Archives, CT Casualty list 189, PA Reg. No. 554, PA Reg. No. 373, PA Reg. No. 264.
161. James Fielden, researcher and compiler: Hospital Registers from the National Archives, CT Casualty list 189, PA Reg. No. 554, PA Reg. No. 373, PA Reg. No. 264.
162. Marcus, *A New Canaan Private*, 46–48.
163. Marcus, *A New Canaan Private*, 46–48.
164. Marcus, *A New Canaan Private*, 46–48.
165. Civil War Research Database, www.civilwardata.org; Find-A-Grave.
166. Phil Lechak, "Return to Camp Letterman," 763 Leadership Group tour, August 5, 2021.

CHAPTER 12

1. Cornelia Hancock, *Letters of a Civil War Nurse, 1863–1865*, edited by Henrietta Stratton Jaquette, Lincoln and London: University of Nebraska Press, 1998), 4–5.
2. Gregory A. Coco, *A Vast Sea of Misery: a History and Guide to the Union and Confederate Field Hospitals at Gettysburg, July 1–November 20, 1863* (Gettysburg, PA: Thomas Publications, 1988), 91.
3. Edward Marcus, ed., *A New Canaan Private in the Civil War: Letters of Justus M. Silliman, 17th Connecticut Volunteers* (New Canaan, CT: New Canaan Historical Society, 1984), 45, 46.

4. James Gindlesperger, *Bullets and Bandages: The Aid Stations and Field Hospitals at Gettysburg* (Durham, NC: Blair, 2020), 72.
5. Warren Manuscript, Bridgeport History Center, handwritten account of William T. Fields.
6. Albert W. Peck, *Civil War Reminisces, 1862–1865* (Connecticut Historical Society, 1906), 31.
7. Dr. Daniel G. Brinton, *From Chancellorsville to Gettysburg, A Doctor's Diary*, file:///C:/Users/civan/AppData/Local/Temp/42056-Article%20Text-41895-1-10-20121205.pdf.
8. Travis Busey and John W. Busey, *Union Casualties at Gettysburg: A Comprehensive Record, Vols. 1–3* (Jefferson, NC and London: McFarland and Company, 2011), Volume 3, 1261.
9. Lt. Col. William F. Fox, *Regimental Losses in the American Civil War 1861–1865* (Albany, NY: Albany Publishing Company, 1889, repr. eBooksOnDisk.com, 2002), 28.
10. Busey and Busey, *Union Casualties at Gettysburg*, Vol. 3, 1224.
11. Warren Manuscript, Volume 3, "Gettysburg," letter from T. C. Spencer.
12. Busey and Busey, *Union Casualties at Gettysburg*, Vol. 3, 1360.
13. James Montgomery Bailey, *History of Danbury, Conn. 1684–1896* (New York, 1896), 382.
14. Warren Manuscript, Bridgeport History Center, Gettysburg, Volume 3, letter from Milton C. Daniels, January 14, 1886.
15. Warren Manuscript, Volume 3, "From Virginia to Gettysburg and Back," by W. W. Paynton, Chapters 4 and 5.
16. Civil War Research Database, www.civilwardata.org; Ancestry.com census records; Find-A-Grave.
17. Warren Manuscript, Volume 3, letter from C. Frederick Betts, July 22, 1884.
18. Warren Manuscript, Volume 3, letter from C. E. Doty, March 12, 1886.
19. Busey and Busey, *Union Casualties at Gettysburg*, Vol. 3, 1261.
20. Busey and Busey, *Union Casualties at Gettysburg*, Vol. 3, 1360.
21. Busey and Busey, *Union Casualties at Gettysburg*, Vol. 3, 1360.
22. "Recalling Redding During the Civil War," *Redding Pilot*, April 11, 1991, David Bartram Papers, courtesy of Sheila Bartram Hislop.
23. Scrapbook page, Bartram Family Papers, courtesy of Sheila Bartram Hislop.
24. Bartram Family Papers, courtesy of Sheila Bartram Hislop
25. *Hartford Daily Courant*, March 11, 1865.
26. Warren Manuscript, Volume 3, David Bartram's Prison Diary.
27. Warren Manuscript, handwritten notes and handwritten photographic index.
28. https://seventeenthcvi.org/blog/engagements/gettysburg/mantons-account/under-guard-or-sunny-south-in-slices-mantons-pow-account/.
29. Gunn Historical Museum, "A Sabbath in New England"; https://seventeenthcvi.org/blog/wartime-weddings-in-the-17th-connecticut-volunteer-infantry/.
30. Ancestry.com; American Civil War Research Database, www.civilwardata.com; Find-A-Grave.
31. American Civil War Research Database, www.civilwardata.com. Ancestry.com; census data; Find-A-Grave.
32. Warren Manuscript, miscellaneous typed accounts.
33. Warren Manuscript, Volume 3, letter from H. Q. Judd, February 20, 1888.
34. Coco, *A Vast Sea of Misery*, 167.
35. Busey and Busey, *Union Casualties at Gettysburg*, Vol. 3, 1358–59.
36. Coco, *A Vast Sea of Misery*, 167.
37. George Sheldon, *When the Smoke Cleared At Gettysburg: The Tragic Aftermath of the Bloodiest Battle of the Civil War* (Nashville, TN: Cumberland House, 2003), 137.
38. Letter from J. Henry Blakeman, July 19, 1863, Lewis Leigh Collection, the U.S. Army Heritage and Education Center, USAHEC, Carlisle, Pennsylvania
39. Ronald D. Kirkwood, *Too Much for Human Endurance, The George Spangler Farm Hospital and the Battle of Gettysburg* (El Dorado Hills, CA: Savas Beatie, 2019), 341.

40. Civil War Research Database, www.civilwardata.com; PA Reg. No. 286, NARA.
41. James Fielden, researcher and compiler, Hospital Registers from the National Archives: John Boughton, CT Casualty list 189, PA Reg. No. 554, PA Reg. No. 286; William Henry Smith, PA Reg. No. 554, CT Casualty list 189, PA Reg. No 286, MD Reg. No. 194, CT Reg. No 25, 27 and 25.
42. Warren Manuscript, handwritten account from Boughton, Sunday, May 29, 1892.
43. "Dying, Death and Burial on the Gettysburg Battlefield," program by Carolyn Ivanoff.
44. Marcus, *A New Canaan Private*, 46.
45. Marcus, *A New Canaan Private*, 48.
46. Gregory A. Coco, *A Strange and Blighted Land: Gettysburg: The Aftermath of a Battle* (Gettysburg, PA: Thomas Publications, 1995), 128–32.
47. Sheldon, *When the Smoke Cleared At Gettysburg*, 224.
48. Coco, *A Strange and Blighted Land*, 129.
49. Sheldon, *When the Smoke Cleared At Gettysburg*, 225.
50. *Norwalk Gazette*, July 21, 1863.
51. *Soldiers National Cemetery, Gettysburg* (1865; repr., Gettysburg, PA: Thomas Publications, 1988), 150.
52. John T. Miller, "Breaking News From Gettysburg: Battle Reporting in Myth and History," *Gettysburg Magazine*, no. 48 (2013), 7; revised for Academia.edu (2020).
53. *Norwalk Gazette*, July 7, 1863
54. Warren Manuscript, Vol. 10, handwritten, 187.
55. Miller, "Breaking News From Gettysburg," 23, 30–32.
56. Miller, "Breaking News From Gettysburg," 2–6, 23, 30–32.
57. Warren Manuscript, Volume 3, letter from Aaron Lee, January 31, 1886.
58. Charles Pankenier, *Ridgefield Fights the Civil War* (New York: Worthy Shorts, 2011, rev. 2012), 28.
59. Warren Manuscript, Volume 3.
60. Find-A-Grave.
61. Thomas Babington Macaulay, "Lays of Ancient Rome."
62. Warren Manuscript, handwritten notes.
63. Warren Manuscript, Volume 3, letter from Milton C. Daniels, January 14, 1886.
64. Warren Manuscript, Volume 3, letter from David Bartram, January 26, 1886.
65. Warren Manuscript, Volume 3; *Danbury Times*, July 12, 1863.
66. Warren Manuscript Volume 3, letter from Albert Peck, April 2, 1887.
67. Tracy Tomaselli, "Brother vs. Brother (The Six Fowler Brothers)," Fall 2014 insert, Guilford Preservation Alliance, http://guilfordpreservation.org/wp-content/uploads/2014/11/96584-Insert-2nd-version.pdf.
68. Warren Manuscript, Volume 3, W. W. Paynton, "From Virginia to Gettysburg and Back," Chapter 1.
69. Warren Manuscript, Volume 3, letter from John L. Hayes, September 14, 1885.
70. Warren Manuscript, Volume 3, letter from Albert Peck, April 2, 1887.
71. Warren Manuscript, Volume 3, letter from C. Frederick Betts, July 22, 1884.
72. Warren Manuscript, Volume 3, W. W. Paynton, "From Virginia to Gettysburg and Back," Chapter 1.
73. *Norwalk Gazette*, July 14, 1863.
74. *Norwalk Gazette*, July 14, 1863.
75. Warren Manuscript, Volume 3, letter from C. Frederick Betts, July 22, 1884.
76. From Paul Knight, descendant.
77. Ancestry.com; Find-A-Grave.
78. Warren Manuscript, Volume 3, letter from Roscoe Perry, June 8, 1895.
79. Warren Manuscript, Volume 3.

80. *Norwalk Gazette*, July 7, 1863.
81. *Norwalk Gazette*, July 14, 1863.
82. Warren Manuscript, Volume 3, letter from Enoch Wood, June 20, 1896.
83. Letter of Edward Fowler, Veteran of the 14th Connecticut, January 9, 1922, Gettysburg National Military Park, GETT Library File V6-17CT.
84. J. Henry Blakeman August 1, 1863 Letter, Lewis Leigh Collection, the U.S. Army Heritage and Education Center, USAHEC.
85. Warren Manuscript, Volume 3; this account is probably from William Warren's Civil War diary.
86. Kirkwood, *Too Much for Human Endurance*, 361.
87. Kirkwood, *Too Much for Human Endurance*, 366.
88. Kirkwood, *Too Much for Human Endurance*, 366.
89. Warren Manuscript, Volume 3, undated account from Hiram O. Nash.
90. Warren Manuscript, Volume 3.
91. *Medical and Surgical History of the War of the Rebellion* (1861–1865) Volume 2, Part 1, 504.
92. Warren Manuscript, Volume 3, undated account.
93. PA Reg. No. 286, NARA.
94. Busey and Busey, *Union Casualties at Gettysburg*, 1347.
95. Warren Manuscript, Volume 3, from Alonzo Scranton, 1888.
96. Sheldon, *When the Smoke Cleared At Gettysburg*, 226.
97. Busey and Busey, Union Casualties at Gettysburg, 1347.
98. Fold3, Civil War Widow's Pension record for Sarah L. Dowd Wilcox.
99. Ancestry.com; Census data; Find-A-Grave; Fold3, Wilcox, Alvah, E. (WC13622).
100. Coco, *A Strange and Blighted Land*, 109.
101. Sheldon, *When the Smoke Cleared At Gettysburg*, 226.
102. Sheldon, *When the Smoke Cleared At Gettysburg*, 230.
103. Coco, *A Strange and Blighted Land*, 110.
104. Coco, *A Strange and Blighted Land*, 109–12.
105. Coco, *A Strange and Blighted Land*, 117–18.
106. *Soldiers National Cemetery, Gettysburg*, Samuel Weaver's report, 149–50.
107. *Soldiers National Cemetery, Gettysburg*, Samuel Weaver's report, 151.
108. Busey and Busey, *Union Casualties at Gettysburg*, 1301–2.
109. James M. Cole and Roy E. Frampton, *Lincoln and the Human Interest Stories of the Gettysburg National Cemetery* (Hanover, PA: Sheridan Press, 1995), 47.
110. Busey and Busey, *Union Casualties at Gettysburg*, 1302.
111. *Soldiers National Cemetery, Gettysburg*, Samuel Weaver's report, 134.
112. Busey and Busey, *Union Casualties at Gettysburg*, 1302.
113. Coco, *A Strange and Blighted Land*, 124–25.
114. Coco, *A Strange and Blighted Land*, 127–41.
115. National Institute of Health, U.S. National Library of Medicine, *Life and Limb, The Toll of the American Civil War*, https://www.nlm.nih.gov/exhibition/lifeandlimb/horrorsofwar.html.
116. American Civil War Research Database, www.civilwardata.com.
117. Fold3, Civil War Pension Index.
118. National Archives and Records Administration.
119. National Archives and Records Administration.
120. Fold3, Widow's Pension File, George Guernsey, Company E, 17th Connecticut.
121. Busey and Busey, Union Casualties at Gettysburg, 32.
122. American Civil War Research Database, www.civilwardata.com; National Archives and Records Administration, hospital register, 554, 555.
123. Fold3, Widow's Pension File, Smith Delevan, Company C, 17th Connecticut.
124. American Civil War Research Database, www.civilwardata.com; Find-A-Grave.

125. 40th Congress, 1st Session, House of Representatives, Report N. 2878, to accompany bill H.R. 228, June 16, 1888.
126. 40th Congress, 1st Session, House of Representatives, Report N. 2878, to accompany bill H.R. 228, June 16, 1888.

EPILOGUE

1. Middlebrook, James Robert, Letter of July 12, 1865, Connecticut Historical Society, MS73139 Box.
2. Text adapted from 17th Connecticut 1884 Monument Dedication booklet, transcribed at https://seventeenthcvi.org/blog/gettysburg-excursions/1884-monument-dedication/.
3. 17th Connecticut 1884 Monument Dedication booklet.
4. Inscription on the back of the original photograph of the 17th Connecticut monument dedication from the Lewis Leigh Jr. Collection, Col. Noble Papers, Book 43, USAHEC.
5. Copied from the original 17th Connecticut Volunteers 1882 dedication booklet from Lewis Leigh, Jr. Collection, Col. Noble Papers, Book 43, USAHEC.
6. "A Trip to Gettysburg," Stamford Advocate, May 23, 1884.
7. Warren Manuscript, Bridgeport History Center, handwritten notes.
8. Historical information from 17thcvi.org regarding the 1922 Annual Reunion and the *Norwalk Hour* article reporting on the Roton Point reunion of 1922. http://seventeenthcvi.org/blog/david-blocher-and-the-17th-cvi-flagpole/.
9. "Commemoration & Rededication Tribute Book of the 17th Connecticut Flagpole on Barlow's Knoll, July 1, 2018 on the 155th Anniversary of the Battle of Gettysburg Honoring All Who Fought," courtesy of Carolyn Ivanoff.
10. *Bridgeport Times and Evening Farmer*, June 28, 1913.
11. *Bridgeport Times and Evening Farmer*, June 28, 1913.
12. *Bridgeport Times and Evening Farmer*, July 2, 1913.
13. *Bridgeport Times and Evening Farmer*, July 5, 1913.
14. *The Evening Sentinel*, December 19, 1924.
15. *Norwalk Hour*, August 30, 1937, https://seventeenthcvi.org/blog/veterans/1937-reunion-at-roton-point-the-last-reunion/.
16. Letter from Harriet Blakeman to R. D. Hoffsommer, GBPA, October 21, 1964.
17. Letter from R. D. Hoffsommer, GBPA, to Harriet Blakeman, October 24, 1964.

Bibliography

BOOKS

Archer, John, M. *East Cemetery Hill at Gettysburg: The Hour Was One of Horror*. Gettysburg, PA: Thomas Publications, 1997.

Annual Reports of the Gettysburg National Military Park Commission to the Secretary of War—1893–1904. Washington, D.C.: Government Printing Office, 1905.

Bachelder, John B. *Gettysburg: What to See—How to See It*. Seventh edition. Boston: John B. Bachelder, 1878.

Bailey, James Montgomery. *History of Danbury, Conn. 1684–1896*. New York: 1896.

Banks, John, *Hidden History of Connecticut Union Soldiers*. Charleston, SC: History Press, 2015.

Battles and Leaders of the Civil War. The Century Co., 1884.

Busey, Travis W., and John W. Busey. *Union Casualties at Gettysburg: A Comprehensive Record*. Vols. 1–3. North Carolina and London: McFarland and Company, 2011.

Bollet, Alfred Jay. *Civil War Medicine: Challenges and Triumphs*. Tucson: Galen Press, 2002.

Casey, Silas. *Infantry tactics, for the instruction, exercise, and manœuvres of the soldier, a company, line of skirmishers, battalion, brigade, or corp' d'armée*. New York: D. Van Nostrand, 1862.

Caughman, Gerry, S. *Qui transtulit sustinet: Connecticut Battle Flag Collection*. Wethersfield, CT: Caughman Associates, 2011.

The Civil War. Gettysburg: The Confederate High Tide. Revised ed. Alexandria, VA: Time Life Books, 1987.

The Civil War. Rebels Resurgent: Fredericksburg to Chancellorsville. Revised ed. Alexandria, VA: Time Life Books, 1987.

Coco, Gregory, A. *Confederates Killed in Action at Gettysburg*, Gettysburg, PA: Thomas Publications, 2001.

———. *Killed in Action: Eyewitness Accounts of the Last Moments of 100 Union Soldiers Who Died at Gettysburg*. Gettysburg, PA: Thomas Publications, 1992.

———. *A Strange and Blighted Land—Gettysburg: The Aftermath of a Battle*. Gettysburg, PA: Thomas Publications, 1995.

. *A Vast Sea of Misery: A History and Guide to the Union and Confederate Field Hospitals at Gettysburg, July 1–November 20, 1863*. Gettysburg, PA: Thomas Publications, 1988.

———. *Wasted Valor: The Confederate Dead at Gettysburg*. Gettysburg, PA: Thomas Publications, 1996.

Coddington, Edwin, B. *The Gettysburg Campaign: A Study in Command,* Touchstone, NY: 1997.
Cole, James M., and Roy E. Frampton. *Lincoln and the Human Interest Stories of The Gettysburg National Cemetery*. Hanover, PA: Sheridan Press, 1995.
The Complete Gettysburg Guide Audio Driving and Walking Tours: The Battlefield. El Dorado Hills, CA: Savas Beatie, 2010.
Connecticut Volunteer Infantry, in The War of the Rebellion: Reprinted by Permission of the Adjutant-General, from the Record of Connecticut Men in the War of the Rebellion, 1861 to 1865. Press of the Case, Lockwood, Brainard Company, 1889.
The Connecticut War Record. New Haven, CT: Peck, White & Peck Publishers, August 1863–August 1865.
Croffut, William Augustus, and John Moses Morris. *The Military and Civil History of Connecticut During the War of 1861–65*. New York: Ledyard Bill, 1868.
Dreese, Michael A. *The Hospital on Seminary Ridge at the Battle of Gettysburg*. Jefferson, NC and London: McFarland & Company, 2002.
———. *Never Desert the Old Flag! 50 Stories of Union Battle Flags and Color-Bearers at Gettysburg*. Gettysburg, PA: Thomas Publications, 2002.
Faust, Drew Gilpin. *This Republic of Suffering: Death and the American Civil War*. New York: Random House, 2008.
Floyd, Steven A. *Commanders and Casualties at the Battle of Gettysburg*. Trumbull, CT: Gettysburg Publishing, 2014.
Fox, William F. *Regimental Losses in the American Civil War 1861–1865*. 1889. Reprint, Albany, NY: Albany Publishing, 2002.
Frassanito, William A. *Early Photography at Gettysburg*. Gettysburg, PA: Thomas Publications, 1995.
———. *Gettysburg: A Journey in Time*. Gettysburg, PA: Thomas Publications, 1996.
Gindlesperger, James. *Bullets and Bandages: The Aid Stations and Field Hospitals at Gettysburg*. Durham, NC: Blair, 2020.
Gottfried, Bradley, M. *Brigades of Gettysburg*. New York: Skyhorse, 2002, 2012.
———. *The Maps of Gettysburg: An Atlas of the Gettysburg Campaign, June 3–July 13, 1863*. El Dorado Hills, CA: Savas Beatie, 2010.
Groeling, Meg. *The Aftermath of Battle: The Burial of the Civil War Dead*. El Dorado Hills, CA: Savas Beatie, 2015.
Hamblen, Charles P., and Walter L. Powell. *Connecticut Yankees at Gettysburg*. Kent, OH: Kent State University Press, 1993.
Hancock, Cornelia, *Letters of a Civil War Nurse, 1863–1865*. Edited by Henrietta Stratton Jaquette. Lincoln and London: University of Nebraska Press, 1998.
Hines, Blaikie. *Civil War Volunteer Sons of Connecticut*. American Patriot Press, 2002.
Historic Gettysburg-Adams County and The Hospital & Health System Association of Pennsylvania. *Gettysburg Civil War Hospital Tour*. July 2001.
Kennell, Brian, A. *Beyond the Gatehouse: Gettysburg's Evergreen Cemetery*. Hanover, PA: Sheridan Press, 2000.
Killmeyer, Denise Doyle. *The Vision-Place of Souls: Encounter at Cemetery Hill*. Friends of the National Parks at Gettysburg, 2003.
Kirkwood, Ronald, D. *Too Much for Human Endurance: The George Spangler Farm Hospital and the Battle of Gettysburg*. El Dorado Hills, CA: Savas Beatie, 2019.
Laino, Philip. *Gettysburg Campaign Atlas, Revised and Expanded*. 3rd ed. Trumbull, CT: Gettysburg Publishing, 2014.
Lockwood and Merritt. *History of Battle-Flag Day, September 17, 1879*. Hartford, CT: 1879.
Loski, Diana Halderman. *The Chamberlains of Brewer*. Gettysburg, PA: Thomas Publications, 1998.
Mackowski, Chris, and Kristopher D. White. *That Furious Struggle: Chancellorsville and the High Tide of the Confederacy, May 1–4, 1863*. El Dorado Hills, CA: Savas Beatie, 2014.

Marcus, Edward, ed. *A New Canaan Private in the Civil War: Letters of Justus M. Silliman, 17th Connecticut Volunteers*. New Canaan, CT: New Canaan Historical Society, 1984.

McNeil, Betty Ann. *Charity Afire: Daughters of Charity, Civil War Nurses, Civil War Trilogy, Maryland 1862–1865*. Hanover, PA: Sheridan Press, 2011.

Miller, Richard F., ed. *States at War, Volume 1: Reference Guide for Connecticut, Maine, Massachusetts, New Hampshire, Rhode Island and Vermont in the Civil War*. University Press of New England, 2013.

Mingus, Scott L., Sr. *The Louisiana Tigers in the Gettysburg Campaign, June–July, 1863*. Baton Rouge: Louisiana State University Press, 1998.

Morris, John M. *The Military and Civil History of Connecticut*. 1868.

Niven, John, and Allan Nevins. *Connecticut for the Union the Role of the State in the Civil War*. New Haven, CT: Yale University Press, 1965.

Nofi, Albert A. *The Gettysburg Campaign, June–July, 1863*. 3rd ed. Pennsylvania: Combined Publishing, 1997.

Pankenier, Charles. *Ridgefield Fights the Civil War*. New York: Worthy Shorts, 2011, 2012.

Pfanz, Harry W. *Gettysburg: Culp's Hill & Cemetery Hill*. Civil War America, Gary Gallagher, ed. Chapel Hill & London: University of North Carolina Press, 1993.

———. *Gettysburg: The First Day*. Chapel Hill: University of North Carolina Press, 2010.

———. *Gettysburg: The Second Day*. Chapel Hill: University of North Carolina Press, 1998.

Pictorial and Biographical Memoirs of Indianapolis and Marion County, Indiana: Together with Biographies of Many Prominent Men of Other Portions of the State, Both Living and Dead. Indianapolis: Goodspeed Brothers, 1893.

Porch, Kathryn, and Sue Boardman. *Elizabeth Thorn at Gettysburg: The Wartime Caretaker of Evergreen Cemetery*. Trumbull, CT: Gettysburg Publishing, 2013.

Pula, James S. *Under the Crescent Moon with the XI Corps in the Civil War, Volume 1: From the Defenses of Washington to Chancellorsville, 1862–1863*. El Dorado Hills, CA: Savas Beatie, 2017.

———. *Under the Crescent Moon with the XI Corps in the Civil War, Volume 2: From Gettysburg to Victory, 1863–1865*. El Dorado Hills, CA: Savas Beatie, 2018.

Raasch, Chuck. *Imperfect Union: A Father's Search for His Son in the Aftermath of the Battle of Gettysburg*. New York: Stackpole Books, 2016.

Reardon, Carol, and Tom Vossler. *A Field Guide to Gettysburg: Experiencing the Battlefield through Its History, Places, & People*. Chapel Hill: University of North Carolina Press, 2017.

Samito, Christian, G. *Fear Was Not In Him: The Civil War Letters of Major General Francis C. Barlow, U.S.A*. New York: Fordham University Press, 2004.

Sheldon, George. *When the Smoke Cleared At Gettysburg—The Tragic Aftermath of the Bloodiest Battle of the Civil War*. Nashville: Cumberland House, 2003.

Silliman, Justus M., and Edward Marcus. *A New Canaan Private in the Civil War: Letters of Justus M. Silliman, 17th Connecticut Volunteers*. New Canaan, CT: New Canaan Historical Society, 1984.

Slade, Jim, and John Alexander. *Firestorm at Gettysburg: Civilian Voices*. Atglen, PA: Schiffer Military/Aviation History, 1998.

Small, Cindy, L. *Jennie Wade of Gettysburg, The Complete Story of the Only Civilian Killed During the Battle of Gettysburg*. Trumbull, CT: Gettysburg Publishing, 2017.

Sohn, Amy. *The Man Who Hated Women: Sex Censorship, and Civil Liberties in the Gilded Age*. New York: Farrar, Straus and Giroux, 2021.

Taylor, William Harrison. *Taylor's Connecticut Legislative History and Souvenir*, Vol. 5. New York: Putnam, 1905–1906.

Teague, Charles, compiler. *Gettysburg by the Numbers*. Gettysburg, PA: Adams County Historical Society, 2006.

Voices of the Civil War: Chancellorsville. Alexandria, VA: Time Life Books, 1995.

Voices of the Civil War: Gettysburg. Alexandria, VA: Time-Life Books, 1995.

Waldo, George Curtis, Jr. *History of Bridgeport and Vicinity*. Bridgeport, CT: S. J. Clark Publishing, 1917.

Warshauer, Matthew. *Connecticut in the American Civil War: Slavery, Sacrifice, & Survival.* Middletown, CT: Wesleyan University Press, 2011.

Welch, Richard F. *The Boy General: The Life and Careers of Francis Channing Barlow*. Kent, OH: Kent State University Press, 2003.

Whitman, Walt, and James M. McPherson. *Drum Taps: the Complete Civil War Poems*. Cider Mill Press Book Publishers, 2015.

Commemoration & Rededication Tribute Book of the 17th Connecticut Flagpole on Barlow's Knoll, July 1, 2018, on the 155th Anniversary of the Battle of Gettysburg Honoring All Who Fought, courtesy of Carolyn Ivanoff.

Commemorative Biographical Record of Fairfield County, Connecticut: Containing Biographical Sketches of Prominent and Representative Citizens, and of Many of the Early Settled Families. Higginson Book Company, 1899.

Major Brady's Field Report to Head Quarters, 17th Regt, Conn, Vol., July 4, 1863, 17th Regt, Source: Official Records, Series I. Vol. 27. Part I. Reports. Serial No. 43

The Medical and Surgical History of the War of the Rebellion (1861–65), Barnes, Joseph K., 1817–1883; Woodward, Joseph Janvier, 1833–1884; Smart, Charles, 1841–1905; Otis, George A. (George Alexander), 1830–1881; Huntington, D. L. (David Lowe), 1834–1899. Washington, D.C.: Government Printing Office, 1870–88. https://collections.nlm.nih.gov/catalog/nlm:nlmuid-14121350R-mvset.

The Military and Civil History of Connecticut during the War of 1861–65. Comprising a Detailed Account of the Various Regiments and Batteries, through March, Encampment, Bivouac, and Battle; Also Instances of Distinguished Personal Gallantry, and Biographical Sketches of Many Heroic Soldiers: Together with a Record of the Patriotic Action of Citizens at Home, and of the Liberal Support Furnished by the State in Its Executive and Legislative Departments. Ledyard Bill, 1868.

Record of Service of Connecticut Men in the Army and Navy of the United States during the War of the Rebellion, Stephen R Smith; Frederick E Camp; Lucius A Barbour; George M White; Connecticut. Hartford, CT: Adjutant-General's Office, Press of the Case, Lockwood & Brainard Co., 1889.

Soldiers National Cemetery, Gettysburg. 1865. Reprint, Gettysburg, PA: Thomas Publications, 1988.

NEWSPAPERS

Bridgeport Evening Farmer
Bridgeport Evening Standard
Bridgeport Times and Evening Farmer
Connecticut War Record
The Daily Advocate
Danbury Times
Gettysburg Compiler
Hartford Courant
Newtown Bee
New York Times
Norwalk Gazette
Stamford Advocate
Chronicling America, Library of Congress

ARTICLES

Coddington, Ronald. "Casualties on Barlow's Knoll—Now 17th Do Your Duty." American Battlefield Trust, https://www.battlefields.org/learn/articles/casualties-barlows-knoll.

Miller, John T. "Breaking News From Gettysburg: Battle Reporting in Myth and History," *Gettysburg Magazine*, no. 48 (2013), revised for Academia.edu (2020).

Pula, James, S. "'A Most Obstinate Resistance': The Defense of Blocher's Knoll," *Gettysburg Magazine*, no. 57 (July 2017), 15.

Pula, James, S. "Howard at Gettysburg: A Reappraisal," *Gettysburg Magazine,* no. 62 (January 2020), 18.

Pula, James, S. "'A Promiscuous Fight': The Defense of Cemetery Hill," *Gettysburg Magazine*, no. 59 (July 2018), 15

Tomaselli, Tracy. "Brother vs. Brother (The Six Fowler Brothers)," Fall 2014 insert, Guilford Preservation Alliance, http://guilfordpreservation.org/wp-content/uploads/2014/11/96584-Insert-2nd-version.pdf.

Ward, Andy. "Disaster on the Flank: The 17th Connecticut Infantry," *Gettysburg Magazine*, no. 64 (January 2021), 57.

Woods, James A. "The 17th Connecticut and 41st New York: A Revisionist History of the Defense of East Cemetery Hill," *Gettysburg Magazine*, no. 28 (January 2003), 87.

COLLECTIONS

Bartram Family Papers
Buck Zaidel Collection
Connecticut Historical Society Civil War Manuscript Collection
Dale Call Collection
Dr. Robert Hubbard Civil War Letters, the U.S. Army Heritage Center, USAHEC
French Family Papers
Gary Wilkinson Collection
Gettysburg National Military Park
Lewis Leigh Collection, the U.S. Army Heritage Center, USAHEC
Library of Congress Prints and Photographs
Maine State Archives Collection
National Archives Records Administration
National Museum of Civil War Medicine
New Canaan Historical Society and Museum
New York Public Library Digital Collections
Shelton Historical Society
Stratford Historical Society
The Warren Family Collection
U.S. Army Heritage and Education Center
Warren Manuscript, Bridgeport History Center

WEBSITES

17thcvi.org: An Online History of the 17th Connecticut Volunteer Infantry during the U.S. Civil War, https://seventeenthcvi.org

American Civil War Research Database, http://www.civilwardata.com/active/pers_dir.html

Ancestry.com, https://www.ancestry.com/search/

Blog, Centennial Series, History, Residential Real Estate, 1–2 Franklin Square, Saratoga Springs, December 10, 2015, https://www.roohanrealty.com/blog/franklin-square-part-ii-saratoga-centennial/

The Civil War in the East, https://civilwarintheeast.com

Civil War Rx, http://civilwarrx.blogspot.com
Connecticut Digital Archive, https://collections.ctdigitalarchive.org
Digital Maryland, https://collections.digitalmaryland.org
Dr. Daniel G. Brinton, From Chancellorsville to Gettysburg: A Doctor's Diary, file:///C:/Users/civan/AppData/Local/Temp/42056-Article%20Text-41895-1-10-20121205.pdf
Emmitsburg Area Historical Society, https://www.emmitsburg.net/archive_list/articles/history/civil_war/short_history_of_civil_way.htm
Findagrave.com, https://www.findagrave.com/
Fold3, https://www.fold3.com/
Gettysburg Daily, https://www.gettysburgdaily.com
Gettysburg Stone Sentinels, https://gettysburg.stonesentinels.com/union-monuments
Historic American Engineering Record, Creator, Emmor B. Cope, Gettysburg Battlefield Memorial Association, Bureau of Public Roads, U.S. Department of War, GNMP Park Tour Roads, Library of Congress, https://www.loc.gov/item/pa3648/
J. P. Rogers, Oliver Cromwell Case Blog, https://olivercromwellcase.wordpress.com/2017/03/04/douglass-fowler-what-might-have-been/
John Banks Civil War Blog, http://john-banks.blogspot.com/
Life and Limb: The Toll of the American Civil War, National Institute of Health, U.S. National Library of Medicine, https://www.nlm.nih.gov/exhibition/lifeandlimb/exhibition.html
The National Museum of Civil War Medicine, https://www.civilwarmed.org
National Park Service, https://nps.gov
Newspapers.com, https://www.newspapers.com/
Obituary Record of Graduates of Yale University, http://mssa.library.yale.edu/obituary_record/
Signs of History: A Waymarking.com Category, www.waymarking.com/cat/details.aspx?f=1&guid=fd0d1ba6-fcb4-4d43-a9a8-7aa748628c23&wo=True&p=4&wst=9&w=gettysburg&gid=3&sg=ebdeb67c-9371-4e5a-8b85-7bc3dca6ec77&st=2
Witnesses Who Testified at the Trial of Henry Wirz, https://www.nps.gov/ande/learn/historyculture/wirztestimonies.htm

PROGRAMS/PRESENTATIONS/EXHIBITS

Dempsey, Stuart. "These Men Are No Cowards." Field program.
Housch, Bobby. "East Cemetery Hill 1 and 2." Presented at the Adams County Historical Society, Gettysburg, PA, January 28, 2021, and February 4, 2021.
Ivanoff, Carolyn B. "Dying, Death and Burial on the Gettysburg Battlefield." 2019.
Lechak, Phil. "Return to Camp Letterman" Presented at 763 Leadership Group, August 5, 2021.
Morey, Elise, D. "Almshouse (Poor House)" A House for Employment and Support of the Poor in Adams County." Cumberland Township Historical Society, the Courier, Fall 2017.
National Institute of Health, U.S. National Library of Medicine. *Life and Limb: The Toll of the American Civil War*. https://www.nlm.nih.gov/exhibition/lifeandlimb/horrorsofwar.html. Online exhibition catalog.

Index

About the Author

Carolyn Ivanoff is a retired high school administrator and independent historian. She writes and speaks on American history in a variety of formats and venues. *We Fought at Gettysburg* is her first book.